W9-CKL-133

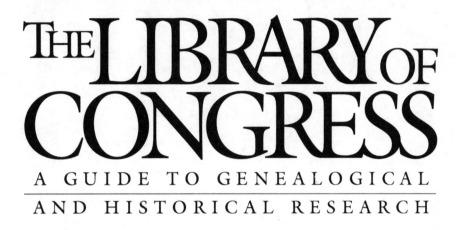

THE LIBRARY OF CONGRESS

A GUIDE TO GENEALOGICAL

AND HISTORICAL RESEARCH

THE LIBRARY OF CONGRESS

A GUIDE TO GENEALOGICAL
AND HISTORICAL RESEARCH

By James C. Neagles
Assisted by Mark C. Neagles

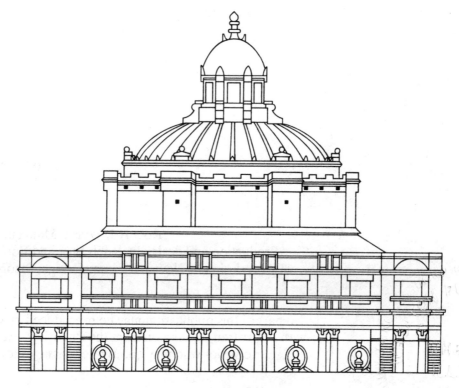

Ancestry
Publishing

P.O. Box 476
Salt Lake City, Utah 84110
801-531-1790

ISBN 0-916489-48-5

Robert J. Welsh, Managing Editor
Production and design by Robb Barr and Bob Passaro
Cover design by Newman Passey Design, Incorporated

First printing 1990
10 9 8 7 6 5 4 3 2 1

Printed in the United States of America

If you read about what people have aspired to,
you are somehow better fortified for your own path

—JAMES H. BILLINGTON
Librarian of Congress

Contents

James H. Billington
Librarian of Congress

Foreword

When I was sworn in as the thirteenth Librarian of Congress, I characterized libraries as "today's living link between the record of yesterday and the possibilities of tomorrow. The Library of Congress is not just all these marvelous books and buildings. It is the anguish, achievements, and the aspirations of our forefathers living on here near the heart of this country." This description seems particularly relevant to all of the Library of Congress's collections that lend themselves to genealogical research. Not only do many researchers find connections with history through their genealogical investigations, but they also contribute both to the library and to future generations by publishing their findings in the form of family or regional histories. The library has become a major repository not only of individual family histories but also, in a larger sense, of the nation's memory as seen through the recounting of histories of local communities and families.

In 1815 Thomas Jefferson sold his personal library to Congress to help rebuild the Library of Congress after the fire of the War of 1812. Among the works Jefferson included were the *Domesday Book;* Sir William Dugdale's *The Baronage of England;* Edward Kimber's *Peerage of England, Peerage of Scotland,* and *Peerage of Ireland; History of the Robinhood Society;* John Winthrop's *Journal of the Transactions and Occurrences in the Settlement of Massachusetts and the other New-England Colonies, from the year 1630 to 1644;*

John Smith's *Generall Historie of Virginia, New-England, and the Summer Isles, with the names of the Adventurers, Planters, and Governours from their first beginning Ano. 1584 to this present 1626;* as well as many more state histories and personal narratives. These were among the first titles of genealogical interest in the library's collection, which has grown over the years to become one of the premier collections of genealogy and United States local history.

I take great pleasure in writing this foreword to a book that introduces genealogists to the collections of the Library of Congress. Because the collections are both extensive and dispersed in various reading rooms within the library, the more knowledge one has about them, the more likely it is that a scholar's research will be fruitful. There are many published guides to individual collections in the Geography and Map Division, the Rare Book and Special Collections Division, the Newspaper and Current Periodical Reading Room, the Manuscript Division, and the Local History and Genealogy Reading Room. This is the first time that those parts of the collections of interest to genealogical researchers have been brought together in one book. This compilation takes what might appear to be an unmanageable body of material and presents it in such a way as to make it useful and accessible. We are indebted to Ancestry, Inc., and James Neagles for providing this guide.

September 1989

James C. Neagles
Waldorf, Maryland

Preface

A comprehensive guide to the genealogical resources at the Library of Congress, reputed to be the largest library in the world, has never been published. Along with the National Archives and the Family History Library at Salt Lake City, the Library of Congress serves as one of the three foremost genealogical research centers in the nation. Typically, family historians visiting the library for the first time briefly discuss their project with one of the reference librarians in the Local History and Genealogy Reading Room and are referred to the published indexes, the card catalog, and, in recent years, the computer catalog. After examining some of the more promising sources cited in those finding aids, they may further discuss their project with a librarian to gain more information and receive suggestions for additional searching. It is believed that both researchers and librarians will profit from a guide that names and describes the library's genealogically important published works and other materials, not only in the Local History and Genealogy Reading Room but also in the other divisions and reading rooms. That is why this book was written.

When the scope of this project was first discussed, it was agreed that an attempt should be made not merely to reproduce the cards in the catalog, but rather to provide a straightforward and informal description of the genealogical sources in the library and how to locate them. Titles and names of authors are listed here as examples of the library's holdings, arranged as they pertain to various categories of research. More than 2,700 titles are cited (not including directories and social registers), each of which includes the Library of Congress call number, thus making it unnecessary for the researcher to look it up in the catalogs. For each category of material, there are simplified instructions showing how to use the card or computer catalog to locate titles other than those cited here.

Part 1 (chapters 1 and 2) describes the general history of the library and how to use its resources, the catalogs, and the published and unpublished material in the specialized reading rooms. Part 2 (chapters 3 through 8) describes the resources available in the library relative to material that might mention an ancestor's name, such as published genealogies, local histories, censuses, directories, maps, newspapers, periodicals, land ownership records, military service records, and lists of immigrants from both English- and non-English-speaking countries. Part 3 (chapters 9 through 15) contains citations of works concerning material relating to specific geographical regions and states of the United States. In addition to the categories listed above, these works include biographies; accounts of early settlers; state, county, and town records; and indexes to periodicals published by state or local genealogical and historical societies. Included in the section for each state is an inventory listing of city, county, and business directories and the years for which they are available in the Library of Congress.

When family historians choose to employ a professional genealogical researcher to find material in the Library of Congress, their search will be more productive and efficient if they study this guide before making specific assignments. If they visit the library personally, they are encouraged to bring this guide with them, or ask a reference librarian in the Local History and

Genealogy Reading Room to lend them one of the copies available at the desk for ready reference.

Any omission of especially important works in the selected lists of titles, and any errors that inevitably creep into a work of this magnitude, are entirely mine. Certainly, those who advised me in this project did their best to help keep such errors at a minimum. The librarians in the Local History and Genealogy Reading Room will be happy to receive your comments, favorable or unfavorable, and will note any corrections that may be needed in future revisions.

When Robert J. Welsh, managing editor of Ancestry, Inc., suggested that I prepare this guide, we realized that the project was too large for one person acting alone; therefore, he made the task manageable by affording the means to use the services of my son, Mark C. Neagles, an accomplished genealogical records searcher, to help compile bibliographical data and perform dozens of other needed chores. Entirely by his own undertaking, Mark also conducted a hands-on inventory of the city, county, and business directories, social registers, and foreign directories available in the library, most of which have never been cataloged. Those lists form an important part of this book.

P. William Filby, well-known historian, genealogist, and bibliographer, graciously agreed to act as my general consultant. His advice, counsel, and encouragement have been very helpful, especially in matters of immigration and naturalization, heraldry, and foreign records, particularly those concerned with his native England. His encyclopedic knowledge of published works and their value to genealogists was freely shared with me, and I am honored that a person of such stature took an active interest in this project.

The reference librarians in the Local History and Genealogy Reading Room were anxious to do everything possible to assure that the contents of this book would be accurate, reliable, and helpful. They quickly perceived that I needed their suggestions and oversight. To that end, they agreed to my requests that they read and review various drafts of chapters and sections according to their expertise in selected specialties. Because of their training in library science and their intimate knowledge of the genealogical sources in the library, they were able to point out many sources of which I was unaware. Throughout the many months during which I collected data for this guide, they included me as a member of their team. Readers of this book may join me in expressing thanks to the following: Judith P. Austin, Sandra M. Lawson, Judith P. Reid, Thomas E. Wilgus, and Virginia S. Wood. Samuel M. Andrusko, now assigned to another division, was also helpful as this project got underway early in 1987.

The advice received by the above named librarians is typical of similar advice received from reference librarians in the other reading rooms including the Manuscript Division Reading Room, the Microform Reading Room, the Newspaper and Current Periodical Reading Room, the Geography and Map Reading Room, and the Prints and Photographs Reading Room, and reading rooms devoted to foreign and ethnic sources.

As this eighteen-month, labor-intensive project draws to a close, I wish, in concluding, to express my appreciation to those who were patient until I could finish it and be free to pursue other adventures. Now it is done—on to other things.

The five librarians of the Local History and Genealogy Reading Room. *Left to right:* Judith P. Reid, Thomas E. Wilgus, Judith P. Austin, Virginia S. Wood, Sandra M. Lawson.

Photo by J. Norman Reid

PART ONE

The Library: Its History, Divisions, and Catalog Systems

The first part of this guide consists of an overall description of the Library of Congress, its three public buildings, and its several specialized reading rooms where genealogical and historical material may be found. Chapter 1 provides a brief historical background, with special emphasis on the types of material gathered by the library from both American and foreign sources. Described are the general categories of works according to availability in the Thomas Jefferson Building (with its Main Reading Room), the John Adams Building, or the James Madison Building. The Library of Congress classification system, its Main Card Catalog, and *The National Union Catalog* are also described, with explanations about finding certain types of information. The modern computer catalog, which supplements and expands the card catalog, is also described in detail, with simplified instructions for using the strategically placed computer terminals.

Chapter 2 describes various types of library material, in addition to published works, and how to obtain it. Included are discussions on manuscripts, microfilm, prints and photographs, maps and charts, newspapers, and genealogical periodicals. The genealogical and historical importance of various specialized reading rooms is discussed, and in each instance the special value to genealogists is cited along with special indexes and finding aids. Particular emphasis is placed on the Local History and Genealogy Reading Room, with its instructions on using the computer terminals and retrieving printed material.

CHAPTER 1

The Library, Its Resources, and How to Use It

Thomas Jefferson Building: First Street S.E. (directly east of the Capitol).

John Adams Building: Second Street S.E. (directly east of the Jefferson Building).

James Madison Building: Independence Avenue S.E. (directly south of the Jefferson Building).

Hours of Operation: Selected Rooms and Divisions

Main Reading Room, Local History and Genealogy Reading Room, Microform Reading Room, Newspaper and Current Periodical Reading Room:

8:30 A.M.–9:30 P.M.: Monday through Friday
8:30 A.M.–5:00 P.M.: Saturday
1:00 P.M.–5:00 P.M.: Sunday

Geography and Map Reading Room:

8:30 A.M.–5:00 P.M.: Monday through Friday
8:30 A.M.–12:30 P.M.: Saturday (closed Sunday)

Manuscript Division Reading Room:

8:30 A.M.–5:00 P.M.: Monday through Saturday (closed Sunday)

Rare Book and Special Collections Reading Room:

8:30 A.M.–5:00 P.M.: Monday through Friday (closed Saturday and Sunday)

The library is open for study and research, without charge or special arrangement, to anyone over high school age. Non-users who wish merely to view the magnificent Main Reading Room in the Thomas Jefferson Building should go to the visitors' gallery, via the elevator or stairway from the Great Hall on the first floor.

Before beginning any actual research at the Library of Congress, it is recommended that time be set aside for a brief orientation to the history and contents of the library, the general functions of its divisions, and how to obtain a book or other resource material. A working understanding of the library's cataloging and indexing system is imperative. It is suggested that this be obtained in three stages. First, read the first two chapters of this guide. Even in the event you do not make a personal visit to the library, the information will facilitate your instructions to a professional researcher should you decide to employ one. Second, if you visit the library personally, locate the Orientation Theatre on the ground floor of the Thomas Jefferson Building, inside the front (or west) entrance near the gift shop. The fifteen minute slide show presented Monday through Friday between 9:00 A.M. and 4:00 P.M. is worthwhile. Following that presentation, join a group tour, free to the public, which assembles outside the theatre. Third, begin the "hands-on" experience of actually using the resources available as suggested below.

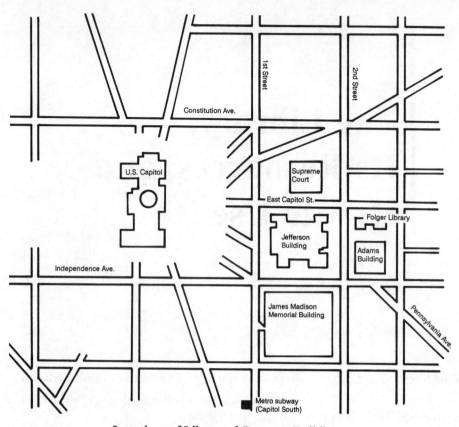

Locations of Library of Congress Buildings.

Walk through the Main Reading Room and the adjacent deck where the Main Card Catalog is located—being aware that at some future time the catalog may be replaced by computers for faster and simpler access to authors, titles, subjects, and call numbers of printed material. Notice the location of the computer terminals. Next, go to the Local History and Genealogy Reading Room. This is where you will probably spend most of your time tracing your family history, with visits to other rooms for supplemental information.

Some Misconceptions

To give some idea of exactly what the Library of Congress is and what materials may be found there, a few popular misconceptions are noted below.

Belief: The Library of Congress receives all of its books from publishers in compliance with the United States copyright laws.

Fact: It is true that large numbers of books in the Library of Congress are received through copyright deposit. A revision of the copyright law in 1864 provided that three copies of each copyrighted publi-

cation be sent to the federal government—one copy to the Department of State, one to the Smithsonian Institution, and one to the Library of Congress. In subsequent legislation, the number of copies required was reduced to two, with the Library of Congress designated the sole recipient.

Publications are also received by the library as gifts or obtained by purchase. Anyone who writes his or her family history and puts it into some type of folder or binder may donate one or two copies to the library. If it is deemed acceptable (and most are), the library will eventually process it, bind it if necessary, catalog it, and place it on the shelves for public use. Large collections of private papers have been donated by noted persons or their heirs, and they are available in the Manuscript Division Reading Room. Certain important collections held in other libraries and repositories have been microfilmed and are available at the Library of Congress. Certain newspapers, foreign books and magazines, non-copyrighted material, and publications for the blind are purchased with government funds. (Some materials for the blind, such as "talking books," are produced directly by the Library of Congress.)

Belief: The Library of Congress has a copy of every book published in the United States.

Fact: Many books published in the United States are not in the Library of Congress. The copyright law provides that "Of the articles deposited in the Copyright Office (of the Library of Congress) . . . , the Librarian of Congress shall determine what books and other articles shall be transferred to the permanent collection of the Library of Congress." Under this authority, some materials are not selected for retention. Some acquisitions once housed in the library are lost or have simply worn out. There are other reasons why the library does not have a copy of every publication: (1) some are not copyrighted and no copy was sent to the library, (2) many were published before the present copyright provisions came into effect, and (3) in some

Jefferson Building, Library of Congress.
Reproduction from the collections of the Library of Congress (date unknown)

instances publishers have not complied with the copyright deposit requirements.

Belief: The Library of Congress is a repository only of printed material such as books, magazines, documents, and newspapers.

Fact: In addition to printed matter, both published and unpublished, the library also has large collections of musical instruments and musical literature, recorded music and other sound recordings, motion pictures, television tapes, computer tapes, maps, prints, and photographs. These are available to the researcher in one of the three primary buildings of the Library of Congress or in another location such as the Performing Arts Library of the John F. Kennedy Center, Washington, D.C. Special arrangements must be made to use this latter material.

Belief: The Library of Congress contains only items produced in the United States.

Fact: In the early days of the Library of Congress, before copyright laws provided free copies of domestic publications, Congress enacted legislation stipulating that "all government material" be sent to the library. Most of it was used for trade in order to obtain material from various foreign countries. This practice was accelerated when funds were appropriated for the purchase of foreign publications. At that point, the library set up foreign branch offices. Agents stationed in various parts of the world bought valuable material, cataloged it on the spot, and shipped it to Washington, D.C., for immediate use. As a result, a large percentage of the library's published material is in languages other than English. Separate reading rooms such as the Asian and Near East Reading Room, the African Reading Room, the Hebraic Reading Room, the European Reading Room, and the Hispanic

Main Reading Room, Jefferson Building.
Reproduction from the collections of the Library of Congress (date unknown)

Reading Room have been established to house such material. The Law Library (a separate department) also has divisions specializing in legal material relating to the countries in Europe, the Far East, the Near East, and Central and South America, as well as the British Isles and the United States.

Belief: The Library of Congress continues to grow because it never throws anything away.

Fact: Each year the library receives approximately 10 million items, but at the same time sends approximately 8.5 million items to its Exchange and Gifts Division for disposition outside the library. Many items go to other libraries or nonprofit organizations. This material is judged to be of limited research value, and it consists of duplicate, obsolete, or deteriorated copies. Much of it, especially that which has seriously deteriorated, is reproduced in microform before its final disposition.

Historical Background

When the first Congress met in Philadelphia it recognized that its members needed a library. Not having one of its own, it arranged to use books at the Library Company of Philadelphia. Later, when Congress met briefly in New York City, it made a similar arrangement with the New York Society Library. In 1789, a farsighted congressional committee recommended that Congress establish its own library and urged an initial appropriation of $1,000 with subsequent annual appropriations. After being roundly denounced by most of the members, the proposal was disapproved. In 1800, when Congress moved to Washington, D.C., where no suitable private library was available, it authorized an appropriation of $5,000 for the purchase of books and for the "fitting up of a suitable apartment for containing them." That apartment was a large room in the upper Capitol. Two years later the position of Librarian of Congress, at a salary of two dollars a day, was authorized.

For many years, use of the library was restricted almost exclusively to members of Congress, but gradually the president and the judiciary branch of government, as well as their staffs, were invited to use it. In 1901 Congress extended use of the library to "duly qualified individuals" outside Washington, D.C. Although historically a "congressional library," it rapidly and inexorably became a "national library" with the broad goal of serving the needs of the entire nation and its citizens engaged in scholarly endeavors. This development was set into motion as early as 1814 when Thomas Jefferson sold a large collection of his own books, gathered during more than fifty

Great Hall, Jefferson Building.
Photo courtesy of the Library of Congress (date unknown)

years of residence and travel in the capitals of France and other European countries. His collection, being general in nature, went beyond the practical needs of Congress in preparing legislation.

During the early days of the War of 1812, American forces conquered the Canadian capital of Toronto and burned the buildings of Parliament, including its library and archives. Two years later, in retaliation, the British invaded Washington, D.C., and burned the Capitol along with all the volumes in its library that had not been removed for safekeeping. Several wagonloads of books and other printed material had been collected by the staff and hidden in the countryside. A contemporary report stated that "Claims and Pensions, and Revolutionary Claims" were not loaded into the wagons and were therefore lost. According to an unnamed

Adams Building, Library of Congress.
Photo courtesy of the Library of Congress (date unknown)

source, these records were not burned as they were stored in a sealed vault, but rather they were thrown out during the ensuing cleanup by someone unaware of their value.

When Thomas Jefferson was aged seventy-one, retired to Monticello, and heavily in debt, he offered to sell his library to the United States. Congress accepted his offer by a ten-vote margin and paid him $23,950, two-thirds of that sum going directly to his creditors. In return, the library received 6,457 volumes all cataloged by Jefferson and all crated and transported in some twenty wagons on a six-day journey to Washington, D.C. It is only fitting that the main library was named the Thomas Jefferson building.

Madison Building, Library of Congress.
Reproduction from the collections of the Library of Congress
(date unknown)

The numbers of volumes in the library increased dramatically in the years following, filling the room provided for the collection, then spilling over onto the floor and down adjacent hallways. In 1851 a fire in the Capitol destroyed 25,000 volumes, along with Gilbert Stuart's paintings of Washington, Adams, and Jefferson. This catastrophe alerted Congress to the ever-present danger of fire, and it began to consider means of improving the library facilities. Without waiting, however, the Librarian of Congress, Ainsworth Spof-

ford, built an ever-growing collection of both domestic and foreign publications, but with no suitable place to put them. They were stacked helter-skelter, with no organization or means to care for them. To provide space, he prevailed upon Congress to approve the construction of a separate library building—the present Thomas Jefferson Building. Spofford brought in architects and artisans from around the world to plan and construct the huge structure. It was built in the eight years between 1889 and 1897. A few months before it opened, President William McKinley replaced Spofford with John R. Young. At Young's request, Spofford graciously stayed on in a subordinate position to assist in making the move and beginning the reorganization of the library.

At the end of two years, both Young and his successor, Herbert Putnam, created specialized divisions within the library, and a meaningful classification system was devised to make the holdings more accessible. Melville Dewey, the famous librarian, cooperated with Putnam and his colleagues to establish the Library of Congress classification system, which replaced the original classification system devised by Thomas Jefferson. It was used in lieu of the Dewey decimal system so popular in other libraries.

During the presidencies of Franklin D. Roosevelt and Harry S. Truman, more divisions were created and the library was charged with the responsibility of more efficiently reshelving books for more speedy retrieval. During the period 1954 to 1974, when librarian L. Quincy Mumford was in charge, the staff was increased from 1,500 to 4,250. Also during this period the first stages of computerization began, the goal being eventual replacement of the card catalog to eliminate the labor-intensive creation and filing of cards. This new system was dubbed "Machine Readable Cataloging" and was given the acronym "MARC." An outgrowth was the "MUMS" and "SCORPIO" computer files, as well as others currently being perfected for future use.

Historical Highlights

1800   Congress established the Library of Congress.

1814   British troops destroyed most of the library's books.

1815   Thomas Jefferson sold his private collection to the library.

1830   Government officials other than members of Congress invited to use the holdings.

1864   Ainsworth Spofford was appointed librarian, serving until 1897.

1867   Purchase of the huge collection owned by Peter Force made the Library of Congress the nation's largest library.

1870   Revisions in the copyright laws gave the library new authority, and it became the recipient of copyrighted materials.

1897   The present Thomas Jefferson Building opened, with John R. Young the newly appointed librarian.

1899   Librarian Herbert Putnam inaugurated an interlibrary loan system and began to sell the library's printed catalog cards to other libraries.

1914   A special Legislative Reference Service was created to serve Congress exclusively; in 1946 it became a separate department.

1930   The Annex, now the John Adams Building, was opened.

1954   L. Quincy Mumford was appointed librarian, serving until 1974.

1966   The Machine Readable Cataloging System (MARC) and the National Program for Acquisitions and Cataloging Systems were inaugurated.

1975   Daniel J. Boorstin was appointed librarian.

1980   The James Madison Building was opened.

1986   Remodeling of the Jefferson and Adams Buildings was begun.

1987   James H. Billington was appointed librarian.

Librarians of Congress

Librarian	Tenure	By Whom Appointed
John J. Beckley	1802–07	Pres. Thomas Jefferson
Patrick Magruder	1807–15	Pres. Jefferson
George Watterston	1815–29	Pres. James Madison
John W. Meehan	1829–61	Pres. Andrew Jackson
John G. Stephenson	1861–64	Pres. Abraham Lincoln
Ainsworth R. Spofford	1864–97	"
John R. Young	1897–99	Pres. William McKinley
Herbert Putnam	1899–1939	"
Archibald MacLeish	1939–44	Pres. Franklin Roosevelt
Luther H. Evans	1945–53	Pres. Harry Truman
L. Quincy Mumford	1954–74	Pres. Dwight Eisenhower
Daniel J. Boorstin	1975–87	Pres. Gerald Ford
James H. Billington	1987–present	Pres. Ronald Reagan

How to Use the Library

Staff Assistance

The Library of Congress is a research library, not a circulating library. Although under certain conditions some publications may be sent out on loan, these do not include published genealogies, local histories, or heraldic materials. No personal research can be undertaken by the staff. Written queries should be addressed to the Library of Congress, Washington, DC 20540. Researchers and scholars are urged to exhaust the facilities of local libraries, genealogical libraries, and state libraries before contacting the Library of Congress. A request for help or advice often will be returned with the suggestion that locally based sources be used. By agreement with many state libraries, many written requests will be forwarded to the state library for response to the inquirer. If warranted, staff at the Library of Congress will make a reasonable effort to assist a researcher who has a specific question or problem. Usually such assistance is provided by specialists stationed in appropriate reading rooms. Most questions concerning genealogy are referred to the librarians in the Local History and Genealogy Reading

Room, and those who visit this room in person may ask for assistance. Other assistance is available at the alcove labeled "Research Guidance Office" located just off the Main Reading Room.

Personal Visits

When visiting the library to engage in personal research, it is helpful to become aware of the facilities available and the rules of procedure as described below.

Most books and other publications are in closed stacks and must be obtained by submitting a call slip, as explained in detail later. Others are in reference collections (on the open shelves) and may be taken to one's table or desk for examination. When they are no longer needed, they should be returned to a designated table or desk for reshelving.

Adjacent to the reading rooms are areas set aside for photocopying machines and money changing machines. Certain materials such as rare books, certain manuscripts, and some documents may not be copied except through the library's Photoduplication Service. That office will determine how materials may be reproduced as well as which materials are protected under the copyright laws. Inquiries concerning fee and delivery schedules should be directed to staff in the reading room where the material is located. Personal typewriters and voice recorders are permitted in some reading rooms but not in the Main Reading Room. Cameras may be used if they are operable with normal light, not flash or strobe lights. Inquiries should be made before any of the above mentioned equipment is used.

Cafeterias and food and drink vending machines are located in all buildings, and staff will direct you to them. Smoking is allowed only in designated areas, not in the reading rooms or hallways. All briefcases, purses, bags, and such personal property are subject to inspection by security guards on departure from the buildings.

Much effort will be saved if one takes the time to learn something about the Library of Congress classification system, how to read the catalog cards and entries on the computer terminals, and how to locate a book in the reference collections. Use of special indexes will save a good deal of time, and some of these located in special reading rooms are described in detail.

The Cataloging System

When it was determined that Thomas Jefferson's classification system was inadequate for the ever-growing collections, use of the Dewey decimal classification scheme was considered, since it would be compatible with the systems generally used in the nation's public and school libraries. However, a committee of eminent librarians, including Mr. Dewey himself, agreed that an entirely new system was needed to classify the great disparity of material in the Library of Congress and to accommodate the projected volume of items expected in the ensuing decades. As a result, the system they devised, which used a large number of subject headings all with their own call numbers, was published in a reference catalog made available in 1898. As of 1986, that catalog is in its tenth edition and consists of two large, red-bound volumes entitled *Library of Congress Subject Headings*. These volumes are visible throughout the library and are helpful in making sure the correct terminology is used when doing a subject search, either in the card catalog or the computer catalog. For example, the subject heading "lawyers" is used instead of "attorneys"; the term "physician" is used instead of "medical doctor." Delving into these two volumes can save the researcher a great deal of time.

In 1901 the Library of Congress began to print catalog cards and sell copies to libraries across the nation to apprise them of the holdings in the Library of Congress. At the same time, it began to publish specialized bibliographies of its holdings for dissemination. Increasingly, large libraries throughout the United States are switching from the Dewey system to the Library of Congress classification system. These libraries may purchase copies of the cards, which include author, subject, title, call number, subject headings, notes, and other information, for use in their own card cabinets. These cards are useful to those who wish to compile bibliographies and specialized lists, such as for family newsletters and family histories. Since fall 1979, the library's response time for catalog card owners has been greatly facilitated by the use of a laser-computer technique. For more information about this service, a librarian may write directly to: Cataloging Distribution Service, Customer Services Section, Room 3014, John Adams Building, Library of Congress, Washington, DC 20540.

The Library of Congress classification scheme is an alphanumeric system using the alphabet plus numbers to signify subject matter and author (or originating organization). A pamphlet entitled *LC Classification Outline*, which gives complete details of the system, may be purchased or examined at the alcove labeled "Information" just off the Main Reading Room. The first letter, or letters, assigned to a publication signifies the general subject of the work; the numbers that follow the first letter signify subdivisions of the subject; the letter that follows a decimal point refers to the initial of the author's surname or originating organization; and subsequent numbers differentiate that particular work or edition from similar works by the same author, or by authors with the same initial. Once the proper classification symbol is determined by the library, it is placed on a tab and affixed to the spine or cover of the publication. Until 1980, for each publication, cards were printed bearing the subject, title, author, and classification number (the call number) and filed in trays in wooden cabinets. Between 1968 and 1980, for English language works, the information was processed on cards as well as entered into the computer databases. Since 1 January 1980 no cards have been filed, and there is now total reliance on computer entries for works cataloged.

For handy reference, the primary letter symbols used for subject matter of special interest to historians and genealogists are listed below:

AN	Newspapers
AP	Periodicals
BX	Religion
CR	Heraldry
CS	Genealogy
CT	Biography
DS	British History
E	History, American
F	United States Local History
G	Geography (including maps)
J	Official Documents (governmental)
UA	Armies
VD	Naval Seamen
VE	Marines
Z	Bibliographies

Such materials as city and county directories, telephone directories, and social registers ("blue books") are not cataloged.

The Library of Congress Catalog Card Number often seen printed opposite the title page of a book is not the Library of Congress call number. Rather, it is merely evidence that the publisher has submitted to the Library of Congress an advance copy of the galley sheets of a forthcoming book, which the library "rush-catalogs" and gives a number for identification. Using that number, a local library or any business office may order catalog cards from the Library of Congress at the same time the book is ordered from the publisher. This eliminates time-consuming and expensive local cataloging and makes the book quickly available to readers.

How to Obtain a Publication

The procedure for obtaining a book or other publication from the shelves of the Library of Congress begins with a determination of its author, title, and call number. This is done either by studying the card catalog or using a computer terminal. For convenience, the books cited in this guide generally include the Library of Congress call number.

The Card Catalog

Before 1 January 1980, each publication received was classified and listed on several catalog cards, with the call number placed at the upper left-hand corner. These cards were then filed alphabetically by author, title, and subject in the Main Reading Room's card catalog. Other reading rooms filed appropriate cards in their specialized card catalogs. Often, more than one subject heading is used for each book, and cards are filed under each subject heading. Following these subject headings is a series of subdivisions that narrow the reader's search. For instance, under the subject heading **United States History—Civil War,** there are dozens of subdivisions, such as addresses and sermons, Afro-American troops, casualties, claims, Indian troops, maps, portraits, prisons and prisoners, regimental histories, registers and lists, registers of dead, and many others.

Another way to locate catalog cards for related publications is by referring to the "tracings" found at the bottom of the card. By using these, one may discover many other avenues for research. See illustrations on the facing page. These "tracings" are related subject headings pertaining to a particular area of knowledge.

The card catalog was frozen in 1980 for English-language works, and between 1978 and 1980 cards were filed only by name of author, not subject or title. All 20 million cards filed before 1980 have been microfilmed and are still available for use, at least until all the data has been correctly entered into a computer. The database used for this purpose, dubbed PREMARC,

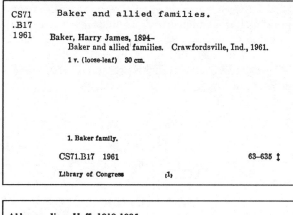

Catalog cards.

contains a large number of errors and omissions and must be corrected to make it fully reliable.

The National Union Catalog

The National Union Catalog, begun in 1901 by Librarian of Congress Herbert Putnam, is a project in which over a thousand libraries throughout North America began cooperating to compile and publish catalog cards of their holdings. The sponsor, publisher, and chief contributor is the Library of Congress. The cards represent approximately 9 million items, including books, serials, pamphlets, maps, atlases, broadsides, and printed musical scores, plus a few manuscripts. Among the more important contributing libraries are those at Harvard, Yale, the University of Chicago, and the New York Public Library. Contributions of the Library of Congress include all the cards in its general collection, plus some kept exclusively in certain divisions. Titles held by the Library of Congress are identified by the symbol DLC; each library has its own symbol, and most of these are listed inside the front and back covers of each volume. Complete listings are found in volumes 200, 560, and 754.

When the cut-off date of 1967 for the receipt of cards was reached, a 754-volume set was published, entitled *The National Union Catalog: Pre-1956 Imprints* (often referred to as the *N.U.C. Pre-56*). It consists of volumes 1 through 685, with the supplement in volumes 686 through 754. Each volume contains a reproduction of the catalog cards held by the contributing libraries, and the entries are arranged alphabetically by name of the author (not the subject). The supplement contains entries for new publications, i.e., those works received from 1967 to 1977. Some of the entries provide corrections and cross-references to those cited in volumes 1 through 685.

The National Union Catalog is available in the Local History and Genealogy Reading Room and at several other locations in the Library of Congress. It is also available on microfiche. There is an ongoing project to collect and publish new titles as they appear, and these are published as five-year cumulations with annual volumes through 1982. Since 1983 these have been available only on microfiche.

The Library of Congress also publishes the *National Union Catalog of Manuscript Collections,* which identifies the location of manuscript collections in the Library of Congress and many other contributing libraries. To locate journals or other periodicals consult the *Union List of Serials* and its supplements. Staff can direct you to these works.

The Computer Catalog

In 1968 the Library of Congress began entering cataloging data into a computer, calling the file MUMS (Multiple-Use-MARC-System); but it continued to add printed cards to its card catalog until 1 January 1980 when all card filing ceased. Therefore, there is an overlap between 1969 and 1980 when publications are found both in the card catalog and the computer catalogs. Use of the computer terminals makes the task of locating bibliographic data and call numbers much simpler than by searching in the card catalog. By typing a few key commands on a terminal, a researcher can instruct the computer to display books on the screen according to subject, author, or even key words in titles. The data that appears on the screen of a terminal can be reproduced by using a connected printer.

Despite the relative ease in operating the computer terminals, many resist using them in the belief they are too complex to master. There are complications, but the library staff has placed simplified directions by each terminal. One need not be a skilled typist to operate a terminal since the one-finger approach will suffice. Personal assistance is available on request at the Computer Catalog Center near the Main Reading Room and in the specialized reading rooms. Free instructional classes are also available.

Before learning the basic commands employed when operating a computer terminal, the following tips should be helpful:

1. Capital letters are unnecessary.

2. Punctuation must be used exactly as shown in the instruction guides provided by each terminal. Spaces between letters or words are used only when so designated.

3. The keys for L and O may not be used for the numbers one and zero.

4. Press the **ENTER** key after each command; a response will then be displayed on the screen.

5. The keys marked with an arrow permit backing up, moving forward, or moving up or down to correct misspelled words or incorrect commands.

6. To erase the entire screen display, press the **ALT** key, and while holding it down, press the **CLEAR** key.

7. When the symbol for "reset" appears at the bottom of the screen (staff will identify this if necessary), press the **RESET** key and then the **TAB FORWARD** key. You are then ready to begin again.

8. A blinking light (cursor) at the upper left-hand corner of the screen indicates that the terminal is ready for a command.

9. Where terminals are connected to printers, you may obtain a paper copy of the data that appears on the screen by pressing the **PRINT** key.

Computer Systems Available

The Library of Congress Information System (LOCIS) is comprised of two files: MUMS and

SCORPIO. A more detailed description of the computer facilities and instruction guides in the Local History and Genealogy Reading Room may be found in chapter 2 of this guide, but a brief description of the MUMS and SCORPIO files is presented here for background purposes.

MUMS (Multiple-Use-MARC-System)

This file was created to reflect, on a current basis, the library's cataloging operations using the alphabetical order of the card catalog. It retrieves and displays records of English language publications cataloged by the Library of Congress since 1968 and foreign publications received since the mid-1970s. Titles of publications ordered or received by the library but not yet processed and placed on the shelves may also be called up and displayed on the screen. Titles may be retrieved by typing the key words from almost every publication that has been entered into the computer. For example, one may request all the titles that have a bearing on a specific subject, such as a family name, from a variety of books and serials in the library's holdings. This system also locates serials cataloged since 1973 and maps cataloged since 1968, regardless of their date of publication. To sign the terminal on to this file, type **zsgn aid = mums**.

SCORPIO (Subject Content Oriented Retriever for Processing Information On-line)

This file was devised primarily for use by members of Congress and their staffs. There is, however, one sub-file within it called "Library of Congress Computerized Catalog" (LCCC) that indexes books cataloged by the Library of Congress from 1968 to the present by author, title, and subject, and displays them on the screen. The user may then use the "browse," "select," or "display" commands to select particular titles for partial or full bibliographic display. To sign the terminal on to this file, type **bgns lccc**.

Use of Databases Outside the Library of Congress

For those who cannot use terminals at the Library of Congress or who have their own computer, a search of the catalog databases (MUMS, LCCC, PREMARC) is available from the Library of Congress on a fee basis. Through this service, a bibliographic listing can be produced by accessing any data found on catalog records. The listing can be produced in printed form or on magnetic tape. Address letters of request or inquiry to Customer Services, Cataloging Distribution Service, Library of Congress, Washington, DC 20541.

Locating a Publication

Once a publication has been located in a catalog or cited in this guide, and its author, title, and call number are ascertained, it may be called for from the stacks. Although most publications are in the closed stacks (barred to the public), many may be found in reference collections (open shelves) in one of the specialized reading rooms. When this is the case, one may take it to a table or desk and examine it at leisure.

If a desired publication is not on an open shelf, it must be requested by using call slips (see example at right), which are color-coded for each building. Place the completed slip in a designated box or give it to a staff member, being sure that your desk number has been included on the slip. The material will be delivered to you at the desk number. This may take twenty minutes to an hour, depending on location of the material, so be prepared to wait. If the publication is not located, the slip will be returned to you, usually with the notation "Not on Shelf" (NOS). Sometimes a microfilm number (MICRO) will be noted on the call slip. In that event, ask a staff member where the film may be located. Some are in the Microform Reading Room and some are in the reading room where you requested it. If the returned call slip has the notation LH&G or RARE BOOK, the material may be found at those locations. Incidentally, the notation OFFICE indicates the Rare Book Room. If you wish to call for the material on the following day, be sure to indicate that desire on the call slip (lower left-hand corner). Arrangements may also be made to have material placed on three-day reserve.

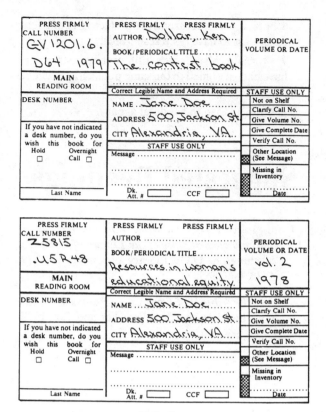

Call slips.

Sometimes a publication cannot be located by a deck attendant, and no helpful notations appear on the call slip. If you are reasonably certain that you have not made an error on the slip, you may ask a Special Searcher to check the Central Charge File to see if the publication is being rebound or for some reason is charged out. If not, you may ask for assistance at the Special Search Section, either in the Main Reading Room or the Social Science Reading Room located in the John Adams Building. According to a pamphlet distributed by the library entitled "Solving the Mystery of 'NOS' Report," the following are the most common reasons for receiving a "Not on Shelf" message:

1. illegible or incomplete call number;

2. unverified call number (may need to be checked against the computer catalog or the card catalog in or near the Main Reading Room);

3. an abbreviation follows the call number (designating that the publication is on the open shelves of a reading room, i.e., LH&G);

4. current periodicals (recent issues require a period of time before being bound and cataloged);

5. size (oversized books must bear the word "folio" on the call slip);

6. book recently returned to the stacks (insufficient time for it to have been reshelved);

7. alternate call numbers (different numbers might have been assigned to the same publication—check the bottom of the catalog card);

8. book on loan to a federal agency.

Suggested Readings

Cole, John Y. *For Congress and the Nation—A Chronological History of the Library of Congress.* Washington, D.C.: Library of Congress, 1979. Z733 .U6C565.

———. *The Library of Congress in Perspective.* New York and London: R.R. Bowker and Co., 1978. Z733 .U6L494.

Goodrum, Charles A., and Helen W. Dalyrimple. *The Library of Congress.* Boulder, Colo.: Westview Press, 1982. Z733 .U6G67.

Library of Congress. "Information for Readers in the Library of Congress." Washington, D.C.: 1985.

A pamphlet free upon request from the Central Services Division, Library of Congress.

Mann, Thomas. *A Guide to Library Research Methods.* New York and Oxford: Oxford University Press, 1987. Z710 .M23.

Mearns, David C. *The Story Up to Now—the Library of Congress, 1800–1946.* Washington, D.C.: 1946. Reprint from the Annual Report of the Librarian of Congress. Z733 .U645.

CHAPTER 2

Specialized Reading Rooms

Although you will probably use extensively the facilities of the Main Reading Room, with its adjacent card catalog, there are also several specialized reading rooms at the Library of Congress of particular value to historians and genealogists. Each of these rooms has unique catalogs, reference collections on open shelves, and a staff of reference librarians to help you. While each of these rooms is described here in a general way, more detailed information can be found in later chapters dealing with particular types of source material.

Local History and Genealogy Reading Room

At the time of the nation's centennial celebration in 1876, Congress passed a joint resolution calling for local communities to ". . . cause to have delivered historical sketches of the various counties or towns. Copies are to be filed both in the county clerk's office and in the Library of Congress." This resolution set the stage for the creation, in August 1935, of a separate "Reading Room for American Local History and Genealogy." Since then this reading room has been in five different locations and will soon move again to quarters now being prepared as part of a major renovation of both the Thomas Jefferson and John Adams buildings.

The new Local History and Genealogy Reading Room will be on the second floor, north side, of the Thomas Jefferson Building. The architects have planned a colonnade consisting of exhibits and book shelves situated forward of the main entrance. Most of the book shelves, tables for readers, and a station for reference librarians will be in the reading room. The specialized card catalogs, now in use in the present reading room, will most likely be transferred to the new quarters where they will continue to be used along with the computer catalogs.

Reference librarians assigned to the Local History and Genealogy Reading Room have been trained in special library services and special aspects of history, genealogy, and heraldry, and they are available for consultation and assistance. These librarians do not conduct complicated or lengthy research in response to inquiries in person, by mail, or by telephone, but they do check catalogs and indexes to the library's collections for specific items. They suggest research methods or approaches, provide information about the library's policies and genealogical collections, and make referrals to other libraries and collections when appropriate.

Although one is encouraged to use the special indexes and catalogs in this room and to personally locate any book on the open shelves (the reference collection), the most helpful resources in time of confusion or special need are the exceedingly knowledgeable reference librarians assigned full time to this room. Not only are they skilled in library science by their academic training and experience, but they have chosen their assignment to this reading room. Some, on their own time, are authors who write scholarly articles and books. They have myriad behind-the-scenes respon-

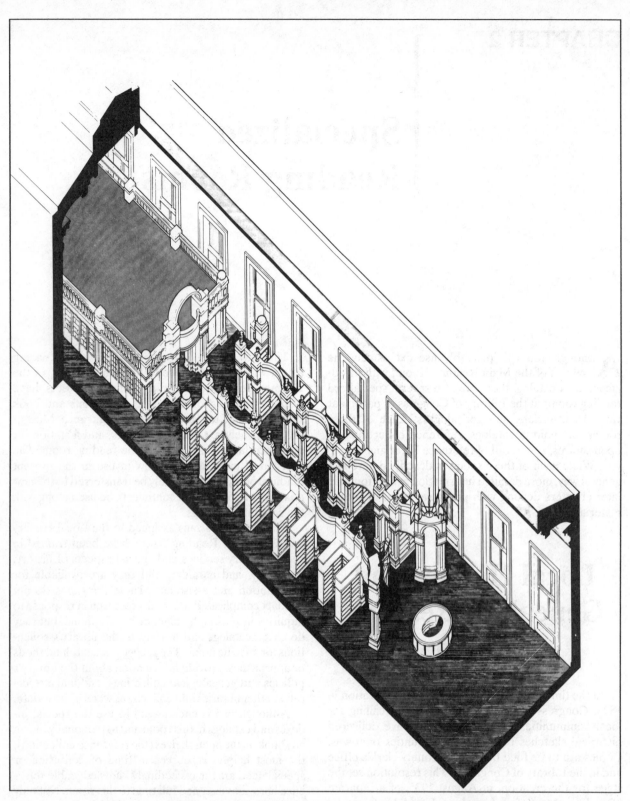

Local History and Genealogy Reading Room after 1988 renovation — architect's drawing.
Courtesy of ACM/A.C.P., 1987

sibilities that include preparing bibliographies, answering inquiries by mail, keeping abreast of current literature in the field, reviewing and selecting incoming books for the reference collection, and so forth.

Each librarian in this reading room has his or her specialty. For instance, one may be particularly versed in genealogical periodicals and ethnic sources, another in heraldry and military records, another in maritime and naval history, while another may be knowledgeable in foreign sources and have a detailed knowledge of the computer catalogs. All of them scour publishers' and out-of-print dealers' catalogs in order to recommend purchases for the library. These dedicated librarians work hard to assist the public.

Specialized Card Catalogs

The specialized card catalogs available in the Local History and Genealogy Reading Room are described below. Generally, these card catalogs cover only publications received before 1980, and the computer catalog contains all received thereafter. Supplementing the card catalogs is a "vertical file" located at the reference desk. This collection contains various miscellaneous, unbound material relative to a broad range of genealogical research. Some folders contain data on families, and cards for these are found in the "family name index" described below.

Family Name Index (white labels)

This catalog index contains a card for each published genealogy received by the Library of Congress prior to 1980. It is alphabetically arranged by family name, then chronologically arranged by date of publication.

Analyzed Surname Index (green labels)

This is an incomplete index primarily of names in biographical sketches included in approximately 350 county histories. The books included in this issue are listed in a drawer labeled "Local Histories Indexed."

United States Biographical Index (pink labels)

This index has a card for each family name extracted from at least one published history for each state, plus a few regional histories. Many of the books are not strictly histories but are collections of biographical sketches. Included on each card are the individual's surname, given name, date of birth, occupation, the book title, volume and page, and call number. The first drawer, labeled "Books Indexed," identifies the histories used to compile this index.

Coat of Arms Index

This index lists references to more than 100,000 illustrations of coats of arms found in various publications in the Library of Congress. Published indexes pertaining to coats of arms and related material are described in chapter 8 of this guide, which includes a section on heraldry.

United States Local History Shelflist

The titles found in this catalog are in the F series of the Library of Congress classification system, denoting United States local history. The arrangement of the index is alphanumeric. Within each state, as a class, are ten numerical subclasses arranged by subject. In one of those subclasses the counties of the state are separately and alphabetically arranged. A description of all the subclasses is provided on a large poster located adjacent to the catalog cabinet. Because there is considerable overlap between subclasses, it is suggested that one peruse every card in the drawer pertaining to a state for potentially useful titles.

Subject Catalog to the Local History and Genealogy Reference Collection

Presently, there is no sign indicating the location of this catalog, but it is contained in twelve labeled drawers to the left of the United States local history shelflist. This catalog is helpful although of limited use since it is fairly new and includes only about 60 percent of the material available in the Local History and Genealogy Reading Room. There are subclasses for each state, plus several headings for other subjects, all alphabetically arranged.

The Computer Catalog

As in the other reading rooms, there are several computer terminals available for public use in the Local History and Genealogy Reading Room. Adjacent to each are instructions. Although either of the files

(MUMS or SCORPIO) may be used, it is recommended that readers use the all-encompassing procedure called LOCIS (Library of Congress Information System), by which one gains access to both MUMS and SCORPIO. LOCIS has been developed as a first step in merging these two files for ease of use. Because changes in methods of computer cataloging and retrieval systems are continual, one is advised to ask the reference librarians for recent improvements.

To use the LOCIS system, sign onto it by typing **bgns locis**.

This "signing on" may have already been done by staff, and if so, need not be repeated. If this is the case, simply request the information desired by using the instructions given below or those posted adjacent to each terminal. The words "ready locis" appearing at the upper left-hand side of the screen indicate that the computer has been "signed on" and is ready for your command. Following are some examples of commands that will be useful to a genealogist or historian:

1. To find a published genealogy or other material concerning a particular family name, type **find "reed family"** (substitute family name desired). The use of quotation marks narrows the number of titles displayed and limits the search primarily to family material.

2. The Library of Congress has grouped the various spellings of a family name in the publications received and has placed them, in some cases, under one selected spelling version. To learn the ways a name has been spelled, type **find smythe;f=su** (substitute the family name desired).

Before using any of the commands shown below, it is helpful to know the letters of the alphabet that identify a specific field to be searched:

t	title
p	personal name (author)
s	subject
c	corporate name (an organization rather than a person)

3. To find a publication such as a local history, census, map, or other material concerning a county or town, type **find s muhlenberg ky** (substitute county and state desired). Usually, one must abbreviate the name of the state or the word "county" (co.), but since this rule is inconsistent, one may have to try again by spelling out the name of the state or the word "county" rather than using an abbreviation to obtain a response.

4. To find a publication when only the title is known, type **find t summer soldiers** (substitute the *key words* of any title desired).

5. To find a publication when only the author's name is known or to learn the titles of all publications by that author, type **find p wood katherine** (substitute name of author desired).

6. If only the subject matter is known, use the headings as found in the *Library of Congress Subject Headings,* and type **find s heraldry great britain** (substitute the subject desired).

7. When the terminal screen indicates that the material requested is too voluminous or too general to search, one may refine the search by typing **find s census macoupin il** (substitute as desired) or **find s genealogy annapolis md** (substitute as desired).

8. To find a regimental history, type **find s louisiana regimental civil war** (substitute as desired). For this category, spell out the name of the state.

In any of the examples shown above, when the terminal screen lists more titles (called "hits") than can be displayed on one screen, it is possible to see the remaining titles by typing one of the following commands:

1. When the *next page* is desired, type **page np**.

2. Because the titles listed are numbered *sequentially,* you may call up a group of titles beginning with the number opposite any of the titles by typing **page s** (plus the number opposite the first title desired), for example, **page s25**.

3. When the full *bibliographic* data for a displayed title is desired, type **page b** (plus the number opposite the title), for example, **page b25**. To return to the display of the titles from which the bibliographic display was obtained, type **page s** (plus the number of the next listed title, as in 2, above).

A file called PREMARC has been produced by a commercial firm in an attempt to enter into the computer all publications received and cataloged before 1968. This file contains brief and unedited records, is incomplete, and rife with errors. It is undergoing correction, however, in the hope that some day it will be fully accurate. Nonetheless, it is useful today as an adjunct to the card catalog. To use this file, type the commands as when using LOCIS, and then add the following: ;f = prem. Examples are **find "reed family" ;f = prem** and **find s heraldry great britain ;f = prem**

This file is used primarily by the librarians. When deemed advisable or necessary because a publication cannot be located in a card catalog, a librarian may assist in using this special file.

Obtaining a Publication

Once the title, author, and call number of a desired publication have been ascertained, it may be obtained by one of three methods: (1) by submitting a call slip and waiting for a deck attendant to bring it to your table, (2) by asking where a microfilm copy can be located (when the catalog card indicates a MICRO number or when the returned call slip has a MICRO number on it), or (3) by finding it in the reference collection (on an open shelf) in the Local History and Genealogy Reading Room. To save time and needless searching, take note of the catalog card to see if the symbol LH&G is under the call number. This and other notations such as MICRO, "Rare Book Coll." or "Office" indicate where the book is located.

Publications of General Genealogical Instruction

The Local History and Genealogy Reading Room has several handbooks and guides useful to beginning or intermediate genealogists. One or more of these should be read before beginning family history research. The following are examples of what is readily available in this reading room. A more complete listing may be obtained by asking at the reference desk for the pamphlet "Guides to Genealogical Research, No. 4." Listed below are a few books pertaining to the United States and Britain.

American Genealogical Research Institute. *How to Trace Your Family Tree: A Complete and Easy to Understand Guide for the Beginner*. Arlington, Va.: the Institute, 1973. CS16 .A48.

Andereck, Paul, and Richard A. Pence. *Computer Genealogy*. Salt Lake City: Ancestry, Inc., 1985. CS14 .A52.

Askin, Jayne. *Search: A Handbook for Adoptees and Birthparents*. New York: Harper and Row, 1982. HV881 .A8.

Bremer, Ronald A. *Compendium of Historical Sources: The How and Where of American Genealogy*. Salt Lake City: Butterfly Publishing, ca. 1982. CS49 .B74.

Cavanaugh, Karen B. *Directory of Family Newsletters for Genealogists: A Computerized List of Known Surname Publications*. Ft. Wayne, Ind.: the author, ca. 1983. CS44 .C38.

Charzempa, Rosemary A. *My Family Tree Handbook: Genealogy For Beginners*. New York: Dover Publications, 1981. CS16 .C47.

Eakle, Arlene, and Johni Cerny, eds. *The Source: A Guidebook of American Genealogy*. Salt Lake City: Ancestry, Inc., 1984. CS49 .S65.

Everton, George B. *The Handy Book for Genealogists*. Logan, Utah: Everton Publishers, ca. 1981. CS47 .E9.

Goerlich, Shirley B. *Genealogy—A Practical Research Guide*. Sidney, N.Y.: RST Publishing, 1984. CS16 .G57.

Greenwood, Val D. *The Researcher's Guide to American Genealogy*. Baltimore: Genealogical Publishing Co., 1973. CS47 .G73.

Helmbold, F. Wilbur. *Tracing Your Ancestry*. Birmingham: Oxmoor House, 1976. CS47 .H44.

Jaussi, Laureen R., and Gloria D. Chaston. *Fundamentals of Genealogical Research*. 3d ed. Salt Lake City: Deseret Book Co., 1977. CS16 J38.

Meyer, Mary K. *Meyer's Directory of Genealogical Societies in the United States and Canada*. 6th ed, Pasadena, Md.: the author, 1986. CS44 .M44.

Rubincam, Milton, ed. *Genealogical Research: Methods and Sources*. Washington, D.C.: The American Society of Genealogists, 1971. Vol. 2, CS16 .A5. Vol. 2, rev., 1983. CS16 .C43.

Schweitzer, George K. *Genealogical Source Handbook*. Knoxville: the author, 1984. CS42.7 .S38.

Publications Relating to Surnames

The Local History and Genealogy Reading Room has several publications on its open shelves that deal with surnames and their origin. Those listed below are only selected examples. For a more complete list, especially of surnames of foreign countries or written in a foreign language, refer to a pamphlet entitled "Surnames: A Selected List of References, No. 8," available at the reference desk.

Bannister, John. *A Glossary of Cornish Names* .... London: Williams and Norgate, ca. 1871. CS2401 .B3.

Bardsley, Charles W.E. *A Dictionary of English and Welsh Surnames* .... London and New York: H. Forwde, 1901. Reprint. Baltimore: Genealogical Publishing Co., 1980. CS2505 .B3.

Black, George F. *The Surnames of Scotland.* New York: New York Public Library, 1946. 4th ed., 1983. CS2435 .B55.

Brown, Samuel L. *Surnames are the Fossils of Speech.* N.p.: the author, 1967. CS2385 .B7.

DeBreffny, Brian. *Irish Family Names.* Dublin: Gell and MacMillan, Ltd., 1982. CS2415 .D43.

Fucilla, Joseph G. *Our Italian Surnames.* Evanston, Ill.: Chandlers, 1949. CS2715 .F8.

Hassall, William O. *History Through Surnames.* Oxford: Pergamon Press, 1967. CS2385 .H3.

Hughes, James P. *Is Thy Name Wart?* London: Phoenix House, 1963. CS2505 .H84.

Kelly, Patrick. *Irish Family Names.* Reprint. Detroit: Gale Research Co., 1976. CS2415 .K4.

MacLysaght, Edward. *The Surnames of Ireland.* Dublin: Irish Academic Press, 1914. 6th ed., 1985. CS2415 .M24.

Morgan, T.J., and Prys Morgan. *Welsh Surnames.* Cardiff: University of Wales Press, 1985. CS2445 .M67.

Sims, Clifford S. *The Origination and Signification of Scottish Surnames.* Baltimore: Genealogical Publishing Co., 1968. Reprint. Rutland, Vt.: Tuttle, 1969. CS2435 .S5.

Smith, Elsdon C. *American Surnames.* Philadelphia: Chilton Book Co., ca. 1969. Reprint. Baltimore: Genealogical Publishing Co., 1965. CS2485 .S63.

———. *New Dictionary of American Family Names.* New York: Harper and Row, ca. 1973. CS2481 .S55.

———. *Personal Names: A Bibliography.* New York: New York Public Library, 1952. Reprint. Detroit: Gale Research Co., 1965. Z6824 .S55.

Woulfe, Patrick. *Irish Names and Surnames.* Baltimore: Genealogical Publishing Co., 1967. CS2411 .W6.

Guides to Genealogical Material in Other Libraries

The Local History and Genealogy Reading Room has catalogs of the holdings of some major historical and genealogical society libraries and public libraries. After checking the Library of Congress catalogs for a reference to a desired family name or a local history, it may prove beneficial to see if a publication of value in another library might be found listed in one of those catalogs.

Bancroft Library, University of California, Berkeley. Catalog of Printed Books. 6 vols., plus 2 supps. Boston: G.K. Hall, 1964. Z881 .C15B19.

Cavanaugh, Karen B. *A Genealogist's Guide to the Fort Wayne, Indiana, Public Library.* 3d ed. Fort Wayne: the author, ca. 1980. Z5305 .U5C38.

Cerny, Johni, and Wendy Elliott, eds. *The Library: A Guide to the LDS Family History Library.* Salt Lake City: Ancestry, Inc., 1988. (Cataloging in publication.)

Daughters of the American Revolution, Library Catalog, Vol. 2. Washington, D.C.: National Society Daughters of the American Revolution, 1982. 2nd rev. ed., 1983. Z5313 .U5D38.

Denver Public Library, Catalog of the Western History Department. 7 vols., plus supp. Boston: G.K. Hall, 1970. Z1251 .W5D43.

National Archives and Records Service. *Guide to Genealogical Research in the National Archives.* Washington, D.C.: National Archives and Records Service, 1982. Rev. ed., 1985. Z5313 .U5.

Newberry Library, Chicago. *The Genealogical Index.* 4 vols. Boston: G.K. Hall, 1960. CS44 .N42.

New York Public Library. *United States Local History Catalog.* 2 vols. Boston: G.K. Hall, 1974. Z881 .N59.

New York Public Library. *Dictionary Catalog of the Local History and Genealogy Division.* 18 vols. Boston: G.K. Hall, 1974. Z881 .N59.

Microfilmed Records

The Local History and Genealogy Reading Room has a limited collection of microfilm and microfiche, and they may be viewed on the available machine readers. City directories for the years prior to 1861 are on microfiche. City directories for the period 1861 to 1935 for some large cities are on microfilm. See chapter 4 and chapters 9 through 15 for descriptive material and listings of the cities, counties, and regions for which directories have been filmed. Some local histories have also been microfilmed, and a call slip for those will be returned with a MICRO number written on it. Librarians will direct you to those filmed works.

Surname Queries

The Local History and Genealogy Reading Room provides a query service for those who wish to participate. You may fill out one of the 4 x 6 inch "Surname Query" cards for each family in which you are interested. The data will be added to a printed list displayed on the table set aside for this purpose. One may locate another researcher who is searching for the same family and then initiate personal correspondence to exchange information.

Published Genealogies and Periodicals

The Local History and Genealogy Reading Room has current indexes to published genealogies and many genealogical periodicals. These sources and their indexes are discussed fully in chapters 3 and 5 of this guide.

Rare Book and Special Collections Division Reading Room

This division, created in 1927 as the "Rare Book Room," moved in 1934 to an elegant colonial-style room in the Thomas Jefferson Building. The interior and furnishings were inspired by Independence Hall in Philadelphia. The room accommodates forty-eight readers with additional space for the staff. Two huge, ornately decorated doors are at the entrance to this room. At this time the reading room is in temporary quarters while the building is undergoing a major renovation.

The practice of keeping certain valuable books separate from the general library collection began early in the library's history. Certain books were marked "Office" because they were kept in the office of the Librarian of Congress. There are now some 500,000 such volumes, pamphlets, and other documents, of which more than 27,000 are broadsides. Many important small collections of rare items acquired by the Library of Congress have been deposited in this reading room (others were deposited in the Manuscript Division Reading Room). Among the more important are the Peter Force Collection, the Joseph Toner Collection, and the Lessing Rosenwald Collection.

Some material in the Rare Book Collection of interest to historians and genealogists includes the *Confederate States Imprints;* almanacs; printed documents of the Colonial Congress and the colonial governments of New England; and the Charles H. Banks material pertaining to early Pilgrim families in Massachusetts. In addition, there are a large number of local histories, published and unpublished genealogies, and pre-1861 city directories. (The latter are also available on microfiche, as explained earlier.)

On the first visit, one must complete a registration form, which is given an identification number and kept on file at the registration desk. On subsequent visits it is only necessary to obtain a request form to request material for examination. A card catalog arranged by author, title, and subject is available for reader use. The call number or shelf location is found on those cards. All needed material may be requested at one time. Additional items will be held at the staff desk. There are no copy machines available in this reading room, but copying arrangements can be made with the Photoduplication Service. Members of the reference staff can supply the library's fee schedule.

Manuscript Division Reading Room

Although the Library of Congress is basically a repository of published works, there is a separate division devoted to manuscripts. This division holds personal papers and records of private organizations, many of which are valuable to historians and genealogists. More than 35 million items, organized into approximately ten thousand separate collections, may be examined in this division's reading room. The collections of personal papers include those of many presidents of the United States, justices of the Supreme Court, members of Congress, various other high ranking government officials and military leaders, and private citizens well known in their professional fields. The papers and correspondence of some of America's prominent families have been turned over to this division. Some of the collections have been microfilmed. In some cases microform editions of collections in other libraries or institutions have been acquired by the Manuscript Division.

The importance and size of the manuscript holdings of the Library of Congress were enhanced in 1882 when Dr. Joseph M. Toner donated his extensive collection. In 1867, Congress authorized the expenditure of $100,000 to purchase the collection of material from Peter Force, who amassed a huge collection of material prior to editing the *American Archives.* Included were 22,530 books, 1,000 bound newspapers, 40,000 pamphlets, 1,000 maps, and 429 volumes of manuscripts.

Force, Peter, comp. *American Archives. Fourth Series, 1774–1776; Fifth Series (unfinished), 1776–1873.* Series 1, 2, and 3 never appeared. 3 vols. Orig. pub 1843–53. Reprint. 9 vols. New York: Johnson Reprint, Corp., 1972. E203 .A5.

During the presidency of Theodore Roosevelt, the Department of State turned over to the Library of Congress all official records and papers of presidents George Washington, James Madison, and James Monroe, as well as those of Alexander Hamilton and Benjamin Franklin. At present, the library has the papers of twenty-three American presidents.

For an initial study of the history and holdings of the Manuscript Division, the following publications are recommended:

Melville, Annette, comp. *Special Collections in the Library of Congress.* Washington, D.C.: Library of Congress, 1980. Z2733 .U58U54.

Manuscripts on Microfilm: A Checklist of the Holdings in the Manuscript Division. Washington, D.C.: Library of Congress, 1973. Z621 .U572.

New acquisitions of manuscript collections are published in annual reports of the *Library of Congress Quarterly Reports.*

For listings of manuscripts in both the Library of Congress and other libraries of North America, ex-

Reference desk at the Manuscript Division Reading Room.
Photo by the author

amination of the *National Union Catalog of Manuscript Collections* is recommended. This multi-volume catalog is available in various reading rooms in the Library of Congress.

Abraham	Frye	Porter
Adam	Gallaudet	Pratt
Alden	Geyer	Putnam
Anderson	Goff	Randolph
Arthur	Gray	Read
Baldwin	Hale	Reasoner
Bancroft	Hall	Reeves
Barlow	Hanks	Remey
Bassett	Hardin	Roberts
Bayard	Harding	Rodgers
Bealmer	Harrison	Scott
Beecher	Hasbrough	Sears
Belknap	Henley	Serine
Blair	Herbett	Shaw
Bowdoin	Herndon	Shelvy
Bowie	Hewitt	Short
Boyce	Hill	Smith
Breck	Hood	Speer
Brown	Ingraham	Stanley
Burbank	Jackson	Stanley-Brown
Cain	Jacob	Steele
Cardoza	Jefferson	Stone
Carroll	Johnston	Symmes
Carter	Jones	Tappan
Castle	Langdon	Taylor
Claiborne	Law	Temple
Clapp	Lawrence	Underwood
Croxall	Lee	Vail
Dandridge	Lewis	Wand
Dearborn	Lincoln	Warren
Denison	Lovering	Washington
Duckett	Mangum	Whiting
Dunlop	Martin	Whitney
Durant	McPherson	Wilkes
Duvall	Mills	Wilmer
Dyar	Moler	Winthrop
Eustice	Morris	Woodbury
Everett	Oliver	Woodruff
Ewing	Olmstead	Woods
Fell	O'Neil	Wyatt
Felt	Perry	
Ford	Piccard	

Surnames listed in the current edition of *Manuscript Division—Reference Index for the Dictionary Catalog of Collections.*

Using the Reading Room

On entering this reading room, researchers must register with a security guard. No briefcases, coats, purses, or notebooks are permitted, but free checking is provided. No personal note paper or cards may be taken into the room, but lined note paper and 4 x 8 inch cards (with holes punched in their corners) are provided near the reference desk. A limited number of notes necessary for research purposes may be brought in only after receiving approval from a staff member at the reference desk.

The manuscript holdings are shelved in closed stack areas adjacent to the reading room and are accessible only to staff members. Generally, the material is stored in acid-free containers and arranged in alphabetical or chronological order. Upon submission of a request slip (available at the reference desk) identifying the material desired, it will be brought to your table. There is a limit to the number of containers that may be brought at any given time. After use they should be returned to the reference desk. Care must be taken to handle the material very carefully and to maintain the alphabetical or chronological order in which it is filed.

Copies of unbound papers may be made in coin-operated photocopy machines available in the reading room. Pages from bound volumes may not be copied on these machines because of the potential for damage to their bindings. However, if copies are needed, arrangements may be made with the Photoduplication Service. Procedures, price lists, and order forms for this service can be obtained from the reference staff. On completion of the order form, the material is flagged and payment of the estimated costs is made at the Public Service Counter of the Photoduplication Service. When the photocopies are ready, they can be mailed or picked up in person.

Microfilmed material may be viewed on film readers available in the reading room; copies may be made on coin-operated micro reader-printers also available in the reading room. Certain microfilmed material is available through local public libraries.

On leaving the reading room, the security guard will inspect all items to be removed, including all sheets of paper and note cards. Purloining material from this room will result in prosecution for theft.

Indexes, Finding Aids, and Guides

Indexes

A dictionary catalog and an index to that catalog are located on a counter separating the reception area and the main reading room. This is the place to begin a search in this room. Start with the bound books entitled *Manuscript Division—Reference Index for the Dictionary Catalog of Collections*. These volumes are an alphabetized listing of persons, places, and subjects included in the manuscript holdings of this division. In some instances the name of the collection containing the desired material is given in this index.

The next step is to find the indexed entry in bound books entitled *Manuscript Division—Dictionary Catalog of Collections*. These volumes are arranged by personal name, family name, organization, or place. Entries include the number of items and a general descriptive statement about each collection. Given also is a reference number and whether there is a detailed finding aid available in the reading room.

The catalog includes subject headings, with subheadings. For example, under the letter "I" one finds the following:

Idaho	Indians
Illinois	Iowa
Immigration	Ireland
Indian wars	Iroquois
Indiana	Italy

To determine if there are papers concerning a particular family name in holdings of the Manuscript Division, look for names appearing under the subject heading "genealogy" in the *Manuscript Division—Reference Index for the Dictionary Catalog of Collections*. The current edition lists the surnames found in the table on the preceding page.

Family names are also found in the *National Union Catalog of Manuscript Collections*. To gain ready access to the names in this resource consult the helpful publication *Index to Personal Names in the National Union Catalog of Manuscript Collections* (Alexandria, Va.: Chadwyck-Healey, 1987. Z6620 .U5153). Ask at the reference desk where you may view a copy of this index.

Finding Aids

Any finding aid referred to in the *Manuscript Division—Dictionary Catalog of Collections* may be examined for a detailed description of a specific collection. Finding aids are typescripts in folders located in steel file cabinets along the wall beyond the reference desk. They may be used at a table in the reading room and returned to a table near the reference desk for refiling by the staff. Each of the finding aids contains one or more pages listing the contents of each container of a specific collection to help decide which containers to request.

A sample container list found in the finding aids is one for Dwight L. Moody (see illustration at left, selected only for ex-

```
                    LIBRARY OF CONGRESS
                    MANUSCRIPT DIVISION


                    The Papers of


                    DWIGHT L. MOODY



                    Container List


Container Nos.           Contents

1                        Diary of D. W. Whittle, 1864 (Civil War diary)
                         Book of notes for sermons
                         Family correspondence
                            Holton, Cyrus, 1892
                            Moody, Ambert, 1867-98 and undated
                            Moody, George, 1854-82
                            General, 1867-97
                         General correspondence
                            Northfield Seminary and Mount Hermon School,
                               1882-99 and undated

2                        Printed matter
                            Bible presented to Irene Moody, 1895
                         Scrapbooks
                            1875-1924
                            1937 (Moody centenary)
```

Manuscript Division finding aid — container list.

ample). This list is typical of a relatively small collection, stored in only two acid-free boxes, but it could be compared with a much larger collection (too large to reproduce here) of the papers of the Montgomery family (George R. Montgomery and Marshall H. Montgomery), spanning the years 1771 to 1974 and requiring 13.2 linear feet of shelf space to store the 12,000 items. A researcher who knows of a particular collection that has a finding aid may request a copy by mail or telephone—for which there is no charge. This facilitates research by helping determine in advance which box or boxes to request for examination either personally or by a professional searcher.

In addition to the above mentioned catalogs and finding aids, there is also a card catalog labeled "Special Indexes." Each card provides information about specific groups of items in certain major collections and gives the nature of the item, the name of the person mentioned, and the data included.

Among the many finding aids listed below are some that may contain material of benefit to historians and genealogists.

American Indian Correspondence (Presbyterian missionaries)

American Home Missionary Society

American Missionary Association Society

Avery, Carrie W., Cemetery Index (Virginia)

Black History Collection (includes a few slave records)

Brotherhood of Sleeping Car Porters

Collins, Stephen and Son (a Revolutionary War Merchant of Philadelphia and records of his trade)

Confederate States of America (on microfilm)

Draper, Lyman C., Manuscripts (the Draper Manuscripts) in the State Historical Society of Wisconsin (on microfilm)

East Florida—Criminal/Civil Court Records, Oaths of Allegiance

Ellis and Allan Co. (business records in Virginia, predominantly of the tobacco trade)

Feinstone, Sol, Collection of the American Revolution

Florida (see East Florida and West Florida)

Foreign Copying Project—Canada. Index of Loyalist Muster Rolls, Southern Theatre

(from the Canadian Archives). See *Loyalists in the Southern Campaign* by Murtie June Clark (C963 .C55)

Foreign Copying Project—Germany. Hamburg Passenger Lists, 1850–73

Foreign Copying Project—Great Britain. Genealogical notes (English sources)

Glassford, John and Co. (trade records, 1753–1844, Maryland and Virginia)

Grand Army of the Republic

Great Britain—Commission on Loyalists (Americans)

Great Britain Navy—logbooks

League of Women Voters of the United States

Lowery, Woodbury, Collection regarding Spanish settlements in the United States

Mexican Archives of New Mexico

Missionary Society of Connecticut

Moravian Mission among Indians in North Carolina

Mormon Manuscripts in the Library of Congress Manuscript Division

National American Women Suffrage Association

National Society of Colonial Dames

National Urban League

New Hampshire Revolutionary Collection

Northern Pacific Land Department Records

Proprietors of Locks and Canals on the Connecticut River

Puerto Rico—Miscellany (free Negroes)

Rodgers Family—Naval Historical Foundation

Shaker Collection Records

Shaker Collection—Western Reserve Historical Society

Smith-Carter Family Papers in the Massachusetts Historical Society

Spanish Archives of New Mexico

Spanish Colonial Government (Mariana Islands—Guam) (land grants, military records, church fees, and foreign visitors)

United States—Continental Navy

United States Senate—Guide to Research Collections of Former United States Senators, 1784–1982

United States Treasury Department—Office of the Third Auditor (Revolutionary War lists)

United States War Department (Revolutionary War and post-Revolutionary War lists and records)

United States Works Projects Administration—Federal Writers' Project—Historical Records Survey. Guide to Unpublished Inventories, Indexes, and Transcripts

United States Works Projects Administration—Federal Writers' Project—Manuscript Holdings in State Depositories

Virginia Militia

West Florida (land and other records)

Woodson, Carter Godwin (Negro papers and documents, slave sales)

Women: Colonial and Pioneer (arranged by state)

Guides

At the reference desk are several publications listing and describing manuscript collections in other repositories as well as the Library of Congress. A researcher who is specializing in a particular time period or subject will find the following guides useful:

Griffin, Grace C. *A Guide to Manuscripts Relating to American History in British Depositories.* Washington, D.C.: Library of Congress, 1946.

Describes material in foreign archives, arranged by country, for which the Manuscript Division holds transcripts or photostatic copies.

Harding, Andrea, ed. *Women's History Sources—A Guide to Archives and Manuscript Collections in the United States.* New York: R.R. Bowker Co., 1979. Z7964 .U49W64.

Collections named in this publication are arranged alphabetically by state and then by personal name, family name, or organization. They are numbered serially from 1 to 18,026. The manuscripts numbered 2,157 through 2,662 are found in the Library of Congress listed under "District of Columbia." Each entry describes the

collection, the years covered, and the source from which the entry was taken (often the *National Union Catalog of Manuscript Collections*).

Members of Congress—A Checklist of Their Papers in the Manuscript Division, Library of Congress. Washington, D.C.: Library of Congress, 1980. Z1236 .U613.

Names of senators and representatives are arranged in alphabetical order, with dates of birth and death, name of state, and size of each collection. It is indexed by personal name, state, and congress.

Naval Historical Foundation Manuscript Collection—A Catalog. Washington, D.C.: Library of Congress, 1974. Z1249 .N3U5.

Lists collections by title, describes the contents of each collection, and gives name of the donor.

Sellers, John R., et al., comps. *Manuscript Sources in the Library of Congress—for Research on the American Revolution.* Washington, D.C.: Library of Congress, 1975. Z1238 .U57.

Lists the collections by name and provides a description of their contents. Library of Congress call numbers are penciled in the margins. This guide has the following major parts: Account books—civilian and military; Journals and diaries; Orderly books—British and American; and Foreign reproductions (by country). This guide has a subject index, wherein the heading "Continental Army" has several subheadings, each referring to specific military units.

Sellers, John R. *Civil War Manuscripts—A Guide to Collections in the Manuscript Division of the Library of Congress.* Washington, D.C.: Library of Congress, 1986. Z1242 .L48.

Refers the researcher to 40,000 items arranged in 10,000 separate collections, most of them personal papers of prominent Americans rather than official government records. This guide is alphabetically arranged, includes a brief description of each collection, and indicates if a finding aid is available. A general index is arranged by name of person, name of places, and subject.

Publications

The following works are readily available in the reference collection (open shelves) and are included here because of their value as research tools.

The Complete Works of John Smith

Writings of Washington. 39 vols. (by Fitzpatrick)

Papers of George Washington. 4 vols.

Diaries of George Washington. 6 vols.

Journals of the Continental Congress

The Papers of the Continental Congress

Records of the Virginia Company

Colonial Soldiers of the South, 1732–1774 (by Clark)

Official Records—War of the Rebellion

Dictionary of American Fighting Ships. 8 vols.

American State Papers, 1780–1837:
    Public Lands. 8 vols. 1789–1837
    Claims. 1739–1823
    Indian Affairs. 2 vols. 1789–1827

Biographical works

Appleton's Cyclopedia of American Biography

Biographical Directory of Governors of the United States

Current Biography—Who's News and Why. 24 vols. 1940–86

Dictionary of American Biography

General Callum's Biographical Register of the Officers and Graduates of the United States Military Academy

Historical Register of Officers of the Continental Army During the War of the Revolution, April 1777 to December 1783

National Cyclopedia of American Biography. 6 vols. 1931–84

Navy Register, 1779–1879

Notable American Women

Scribner's Concise Dictionary of American Biography

Webster's American Biographies

Who's Who in America

The Microform Reading Room

The Library of Congress provides a separate location for material that has been reproduced on microfilm or microfiche. The first major use of microfilm technique in the United States was by University Microfilms of Ann Arbor, Michigan, which has since reproduced thousands of books on microfilm. The rapid spread of this technology during the 1940s led to the preservation of valuable documents, economic savings due to decreased need for storage facilities, and easy retrieval of data when needed. For a comprehensive history of the development of filming techniques and the uses to which they have been put, the following book, available in the Microform Reading Room, is recommended:

Meckler, Alan M. *Micropublishing: A History of Scholarly Micropublishing in America, 1938–1980.* Westport, Conn.: Greenwood Press, 1982. Z286 .M5M4.

The Microfilm Reading Room was established at the Library of Congress in 1953, with the name being changed to Microform Reading Room in 1972. This name change reflected the fact that various methods of reproducing material from paper onto film had been developed. The most notable new method is reproduction on flat sheets of film called microfiche.

The Microform Reading Room acquires its collections through the Photoduplication Service or through microfilmed works produced commercially. This room has custody of the general microform collections but not of filmed collections maintained in the Manuscript Division or the Newspaper and Current Periodical Reading Room, and it does not have custody of some government documents. Also, the Rare Book and Special Collections Reading Room does not service microfilm, and many of its works are available on film only in the Microform Reading Room or in the Manuscript Division Reading Room.

Finding Aids

Card and Computer Catalogs

The Library of Congress Main Card Catalog includes cards filed by author, by title, and sometimes by subject, for every title on microform added to the collection prior to 1982, with the notable exception of material contained in large collections filmed by commercial firms. (These are described in special guidebooks and cited below.) A specialized version of the pre-1982 catalog cards is available in the Microform Reading Room. This catalog has cards for items microfilmed under the library's preservation program and microfilm produced by other libraries or commercial firms. Some of the cards have been supplied by micropublishers. Another card catalog in this reading room is labeled "Microform Serial File," and it contains some titles not included in the Main Card Catalog.

Newspaper and Current Periodical Reading Room.
Photo by the author

Beginning in May 1982, monographs and collections of monographs have been entered into the computer catalog. A researcher may use the Library of Congress Information System (LOCIS) for access to materials available on microform since that date. It is recommended that the MUMS file be used, since a search can be made on the basis of the key words of a title or subject. If the word "microform" is part of the title a search may be "keyed in" using the following commands: **find t microform kentucky** (substitute name of the state or other location) or **find t microform women** (substitute subject desired).

A quote found in a Microform Reading Room pamphlet prepared by a librarian is appropriate: "The experts on microforms can be found in the Microform Reading Room; no computer can help as much as they can."

Guides to Microform Collections

There are large numbers of collections in microform that have been produced by commercial firms and purchased by the Library of Congress. In general, they have also published descriptive guides and other publications, all of them available in the reference collection of the Microform Reading Room. They are an important resource and essential for obtaining the specific microform number.

For a list of these guidebooks, titles, and their numbers, consult the heading **Guides to Microform Holdings** in the card catalog. Another listing is found in the two large black binders at the reference desk labeled "Microform Collections and Related Titles in Microform—in the Microform Reading Room." The third edition, prepared in 1984, contains revisions. A companion set of binders list names of new collections, giving not only the name of the collection but also providing bibliographic data as well as the micronumber. If the information in the binders indicates a particular collection may be useful, request it by submitting a "Microform Request" slip and the librarian will obtain the film for you.

Sales catalogs provided by several micropublishers complement the finding aids described above. They are located in boxes in the reference collection. One of the more helpful is published by UMI Research Collections Information Service, which has filmed a great deal of Library of Congress material including "Phonofiche" (described later).

After locating the micronumber and submitting a "Microform Request" slip, the reference librarian will call in the request, which is usually delivered within fifteen minutes. If necessary, you will be shown how to use the microfilm and microfiche readers. Copies may be made on special coin-operated micro reader-printers. These machines accept only dimes. When you have finished, return all the film to the designated shelf. If time does not permit adequate examination of the material and the library has a master negative, you may borrow it on interlibrary loan through your public library.

Special Collections on Film

Listed and described in one or more of the finding aids listed above (particularly in the two black binders) are the following special collections that are useful for genealogical and historical research. If more help is needed, ask the librarian for assistance.

Banks Genealogical Collection. Guidebook No. 9. M5134.

Contains a large number of genealogical and historical records pertaining to Pilgrims in Massachusetts. These records were found at the home of Charles E. Banks after his death in 1931.

Barbour Collection of Connecticut Vital Records. Guidebook No. 62. N82/15.

Index of names: Micro Guide No. 62. Consists of more than 1 million index cards of Connecticut births, marriages, and deaths to 1850, filmed at the Connecticut State Library.

Boston Transcript. Genealogy Newspaper Clippings, 1896–1941.

Ask a librarian for assistance in locating this collection housed at the Godfrey Memorial Library. It contains queries published in a genealogy column that appeared in the *Boston Transcript,* 1896–1941. All personal names from this query column are included in the *American Genealogical and Biographical Index* found in the Local History and Genealogical Reading Room.

British Biographical Archives. Guidebook No. 168. M86/901.

Challen, W.H. *Parish Registers* (England). Guidebook No. 50. M23963. Index: M2282.

Civil War. Guidebook No. 57. M1022.

Contains 1,700 pamphlets and copies of various original documents, largely concerning the northern states, of the State Historical Society of Wisconsin.

Current and Historical Biographical Dictionary. Gale Research Co., 1981. M82/207.

This is also available in a hard-bound volume in the Local History and Genealogy Reading Room.

Daughters of Founders and Patriots of America. Guidebook No. 9. M5564.

Dooling, John. *Great Personalities as Reported in the New York Times.* Available in the reference collection. CT119 .D66 M2432.

Gavit, Joseph. *American Deaths and Marriages, 1784–1829.* Guidebook No. 170. M85/952.

Hollingsworth, Leon S. *Hollingsworth Card File—Southeast United States.* See the guide, "Hollingsworth Genealogical Card File: An Introduction and Inventory." CS42.7 .H64. M49624.

Irish Genealogy Index. Guidebook No. 97. M1616 and M1617.

Filmed at the National Library of Ireland and covering the time periods from the Middle Ages to the present. Included are pedigrees, wills, visitations, parish registers, family histories, and other types of lists with genealogical information.

Leach Frank W. *Genealogies of the Signers of the Declaration of Independence.* Guidebook No. 9. M4498.

Includes much genealogical data about ancestors and descendants of the signers. Many of the grandchildren of the signers were alive when this research was begun in 1855. The original is at the Filson Club, Louisville, Kentucky.

Slave Narratives. Guidebook No. 53. M974.

Telephone Directories on Microfiche

New York City Telephone Directories, 1878–1907. Guidebook No. 38.

Lists the directories available for Metropolitan New York City (plus many small towns) 1878–1907; Westchester, 1906–14, 1923–53; and Rockland, 1910–54/55.

United States Telephone Directories, 1976–present.

In lieu of a guidebook for this series, consult the books in the reference collection in this reading room entitled *Community Cross Reference Guide to Phonofiche.* There is one volume for each year, beginning in 1976. This is an ongoing project by USM Research Collections Information Service. Approximately 2,600 United States and selected foreign telephone directories, encompassing an estimated 90 percent of the United States population in nearly 50,000 communities, have been filmed. The annual cross-reference indexes list the name of the directory for each city and community. For example, the directory for Drummond, Montana, is included in the directory for Butte, Montana. When requesting these filmed directories the title of the directory and year or years desired must be indicated.

Microform Collections in the Local History and Genealogy Reading Room

As mentioned elsewhere, certain collections placed on microform are available in the Local History and Genealogy Reading Room. Guidebooks are as follows:

City Directories of the United States, 1860–1901. Research Publications, Inc.

Also, pre-1861 city directories, the originals of which are in the Rare Book and Special Collections Division.

County and Regional Histories and Atlases.

At present there are guides for California, Michigan, New York, Pennsylvania, and Wisconsin; and checklists for Indiana and Ohio (with Illinois in process). Includes approximately 2,250 titles.

Erickson, Jack T., ed. *Genealogy and Local History.* Microfilming Corporation of America, 1982. Guidebook No. 46. Z5313 .U5C46.

Indexes in this publication are by author, title, geographic locality, and family name. Ask the reference librarian for other similar guides.

Congressional Records

For the sake of convenience, the Microform Reading Room has duplicates of some Congressional material. For complete holdings go to the Library of Congress Law Library.

Serial Set Index

A twelve-part set of volumes published by the Congressional Information Services, Inc., of Washington, D.C., entitled *CIS United States Serial Set Index, 1789–1969,* is available in the reference collection in the Microform Reading Room. These are subject indexes and finding lists designed to locate United States publications compiled under the direction of Congress since its inception in 1789. They consist primarily of *The Congressional Record,* reports of Congress and its committees, reports of Executive Departments, and some annual reports of organizations such as the Veterans of Foreign Wars, Daughters of the American Revolution, and the Girl Scouts of America. They also include the American State Papers. While these serials are extensive, they do not include everything created or authorized by Congress.

Each of the twelve parts of this set is arranged according to the following categories: subjects and keywords (in alphabetical order); private relief and related actions by Congress (gives names and organizations); numerical lists of reports and documents; and numerical lists of serial volumes. A comprehensive publication describing the United States government publications and how to find them, including how to use the *Serial Sets,* is available on reference in this reading room:

Herman, Edward. *Locating United States Government Information: A Guide to Sources.* Buffalo, N.Y.: William S. Hein & Co., 1983. Z1223 .Z7H46.

Also on reference in this reading room are several volumes entitled *Sessional Indexes to the Annals of the United States Congress* (Washington, D.C.: United States Historical Documents Institute, 1970; a reprint of the original volume published by Gales and Seaton in 1851). These cover the first Congress in 1789 through the Congress of 1919, and these volumes are an index by session to "proceedings and debates" as well as acts passed by Congress. Entries are arranged by subject (including names of people who were the subjects of debate or otherwise mentioned). For material created after 1919 one must go to the Law Library of the Library of Congress and use their indexes before obtaining film in the Microform Reading Room.

Prints and Photographs Division

The pleasure and information gained by reading a family history can be enhanced by illustrations. Often one sees a snapshot with family members identified. Old studio portraits can yield a great deal of information, and it is relatively inexpensive to have such portraits touched up, restored, and duplicated by professionals. Modern photographic techniques make it feasible to reproduce such pictures in offset printing. Another type of illustration that can add much interest to a local history is an official or historical photograph found only in collections of public repositories such as archives and libraries. Among these one may even find an ancestor's likeness. A great many photographs were taken of Civil War military personnel and during the administration of President Franklin D. Roosevelt, especially of the activities of the Farm Security Administration and the Office of War Information. Even though names may not be included, these pictures lend authentic documentation to an era, a public project, an important event, or a geographical place, many of which may be associated with the life of a particular ancestor. In Washington, D.C., there are two principal sources for these photographs: the National Archives and the Library of Congress.

Located on the third floor of the James Madison Building, the Prints and Photographs Division Reading Room has more than 9 million pictures in its collections, which were obtained from private photographers, either acquired by donation, received as gifts, or purchased from individuals, corporations, or collectors. In addition to photographs, this reading room has huge collections of prints, posters, and graphic works relating to architecture and the fine arts. It also has a limited reference collection of biographies relating primarily to artists and photographers.

On entering this reading room for the first time you must fill out a registration form and read the "Guide to the Use and Handling of Visual Documents," but on subsequent visits you need only sign the daily register on arrival. Pencils only are to be used for note-taking, but personal notepaper or cards may be brought in; all other reference material must be inspected and approved. No hats, coats, umbrellas, outdoor apparel, briefcases, satchels, large handbags, or packages are permitted.

With approval of the reference staff, material needed for lengthy inspection may be held overnight or possibly longer. Copying of prints or photographs is permitted subject to copyright and other restrictions.

Researchers must determine the propriety of any use they make of the materials, including reproductions of photographs for publication. Restricted material will not knowingly be furnished for copying. If material in the collection is used in a publication a credit line, "Courtesy of the Library of Congress," should be included.

A coin-operated copy machine is available in the reading room for reproduction of photographs and other material. Before copying, all material must be taken to the reference desk for approval. Certain items, such as photographs from the Civil War collections, may not be reproduced on the copy machines because they would be damaged by the bright light and heat. Coin-operated micro reader-printers are available for copying material from microfilm or microfiche.

Better quality reproductions are made by the Photoduplication Service. Submit an "Order for Photographic Prints" form, available at the reference desk; librarians will assist in preparation if necessary. A price list for both negative and positive prints, according to size, is also available, and payment must be made in advance at the Public Service Counter, Photoduplication Service. Orders may also be submitted by mail addressed to the Library of Congress, Photoduplication Service, Washington, DC 20540. Use of personal cameras in the reading room must be cleared in advance, which can take several days. There are certain restrictions on the type of material that may be photographed as well as on the type of equipment used. These restrictions are set forth in a circular available at the reference desk, entitled "Photocopying with Camera."

Searching for Photographs and Prints

The size and diversity of the collections in this division's reading room can be overwhelming, so the researcher should have in mind the type of material needed. If the proper questions are asked, and if there is a general knowledge of how the collections and their indexes are arranged, the reference librarians can assist with greater facility. Typical questions to have in mind before writing or visiting this reading room or employing a freelance searcher, might be similar to the following:

"My ancestor once was associated with [a United States president] [a Congressman] [other prominent person], and may have been present when he was photographed. May I see photographs of this person taken during the years of [state years]?"

"My ancestor was [a migrant worker in California during the Great Depression] [a farmer in West Virginia during the 1930s] [a laborer on the Tennessee Valley Project] [other]. May I see some background photographs relative to those programs?"

"My ancestor lived most of his life in [name of county] and often visited the old courthouse. Do you have photographs of that courthouse? Also, do you have any other photographs of scenes or buildings in that county?"

"My ancestor was in the [name of military unit] of the Union forces in the Civil War. May I see any photographs of his unit or the places where he was in battle?"

"My ancestor was [a groom at the Pimlico Race Track in Maryland] [a fireman on the Southern Pacific Railroad in Oklahoma] [a mason who worked on the Chrysler Building in New York City] [a ticket taker at the St. Louis World's Fair]. May I see any photographs of those places and events?"

This list of hypothetical questions could be tailored to one's own family history. To gain the most from this reading room and to help the reference librarians assist you, it is important to know what subject matter is involved or what event is pertinent to a family for a particular place and time.

The Collections

Becoming generally acquainted with the collections and how they are cataloged in this reading room may enable one to do some searching personally without staff assistance. After finding a pertinent item in a catalog identified by a "negative number," locate it in one of the collections stored in steel cabinets in the center of this room. If such an item is identified, however, by a "lot number," a call slip must be submitted.

The millions of items housed in this division have been separated by subject, by collector, or by the organization that donated or sold the material to the Library of Congress. They are also separated by type of reproduction—photographic works, graphic illustrations, stereoptic cards, and so forth. Some of the collections have been grouped together and placed in steel cabinets that fill most of the reading room. On top of the cabinets are posters indicating the name of each group. For easy reference, the subheadings within each group are also shown on the poster. One may simply

select one of these groups for browsing. Items in the cabinets are arranged alphabetically, geographically, or chronologically, and the cabinets are labeled as follows:

> Architecture, Design, and Engineering
> Archives of Hispanic Culture
> Biographical File
> Civil War File
> Exhibit Catalogs
> Farm Security Administration/Office of War
>   Administration
> Foreign Geographical File
> Presidential File
> Specific Subjects
> Specific Subjects (graphic)
> Stereoptic File

A more practical approach than browsing in these cabinets is to look through the card catalogs located along the walls of the reading room. The first step is to determine the identity of such a picture or other item. Some of the cards refer to a specific collection housed in a related steel cabinet; others refer to more than one collection, either in steel cabinets or outside the room and filed by lot number. Catalogs and indexes to certain collections or files especially useful to a genealogist are described in the following pages.

Divisional Catalog

This is a general card catalog alphabetically arranged by subject, geographical area, photographer, collector, and so forth. Personal names in this catalog usually refer only to specific collectors, photographers, and artists. For portraits of particular people, the cards headed "portraits," or cards bearing the name of a particular occupation or profession, should be checked. Portraits of military personnel are listed according to the war in which they served. A card naming the person in whom you are interested will describe the photograph and show a negative number, lot number, or other identification number.

If the card shows a negative number and the name of a collection, it may be located in the steel cabinets housing the collection cited. If there is a lot number, it should be placed on a call slip (the title need not be included). A necessary intermediate step that must be taken before completing the call slip for items with lot numbers is to use the card catalog entitled "Shelflist Location." The lot number shown on the catalog card must be found there and the symbol showing the location of the item noted. This symbol is an alphabet letter inside an irregularly shaped circle. Both the lot number and the location symbol must be placed on the call slip.

Example: Lot 3063 is at the "G" location
or Lot 9227 is at the "H" location

Some groups of cards in the divisional catalog refer to special collections, including the following: George C. Bain Collection, National Photo Company Collections, Portrait Index, and Fine Print Collections (Index to Artist's Self-portraits, and the American Library Association Portrait Index, which supplements, in part, the book by the same name published by the Library of Congress).

United States Geographical Index

This card catalog lists various photographs and other items according to state, city, and county, and it includes many items found in more than one collection.

Biographical File Index

Next to the steel cabinets containing the "Biographical File" is the "Biographical Index" along the wall. The cards are arranged alphabetically by surname. Each card identifies the people in a picture, the place and date the photograph was taken, and the activity in which they were engaged. Portraits indexed for this file may be found in any of several collections.

Presidential File Index

The "Presidential Index" contains cards referring to photographs, drawings, cartoons, lithographs, and other graphic material relative to presidents of the United States and first ladies, their homes, and their activities.

Civil War Portraits Index

The card catalog for this collection refers the researcher to photographs in the steel cabinets marked "Civil War File," as well as to other portraits of military personnel found in other collections. The items identified by name and negative numbers may be found in the cabinets. There are thousands of these pictures, some of which identify both subject and military unit. Categories of particular interest to genealogists and historians are camps; officers' portraits (Union or Con-

federate); boats; group pictures (military units); and scenes of Washington, D.C., and Virginia.

The photographs in this collection may not be copied on the coin-operated copy machines because of their age and fragile condition. Copies of photographs, drawings, lithographs, engravings, and other prints of the Civil War period found in the following publications may be purchased by arrangement through the Prints and Photographs Division. Full bibliographic data for the following publications are included in the circular "Civil War Scenes" available at the reference desk.

Paul Angle. *A Pictorial History of the Civil War Years.*

Bruce Catton. *The American Heritage Pictures History of the Civil War.*

David Donald. *Divided We Fought.*

Alexander Gardner. *Photographic Sketch Book of the Civil War.*

James Horan. *Mathew Brady, Historian With a Camera.*

———. *Timothy O'Sullivan, America's Forgotten Photographer.*

James Johnson. *Horsemen, Blue and Grey.*

Roy Meredith. *Mr. Lincoln's Camera Man, Mathew B. Brady.*

Francis Miller. *The Photographic History of the Civil War.*

Library of Congress. *Best Photos of the Civil War.*

National Galley of Art. *The Civil War: A Centennial Exhibition of Eyewitness Drawings.*

Ezra Warner. *Generals in Blue.*

———. *Generals in Gray.*

Bell Wiley. *Embattled Confederates.*

Farm Security Administration/ Office of War Information File

A collection of American photographs taken during the 1930s and 1940s was produced by the United States Farm Security Administration. It was joined with another collection produced by the Office of War Information. In 1944 the Library of Congress obtained this very large collection, which includes 1,600 Kodachrome transparencies and 75,000 black-and-white captioned photographs arranged by geographic region and subject. To make selections from this collection use the card catalogs such as the divisional catalog and the geographical index previously described. The subject matter emphasizes programs such as homesteading, the dust-bowl migration, agricultural activities, land and water control projects, urban renewal, people engaged in events of World War II, and military establishments in the United States. These pictures have been microfilmed and may be purchased in units of one or more reels (see below). For other details about this collection, see circular P&P #52, "Farm Security Administration Collection" at the reference desk.

Researcher studying stereographic pictures.
Photo by the author

Stereographic Photographs

These nearly identical pairs of photographs placed side-by-side and affixed to heavy cardboard are seen through a stereoptic viewer that makes them appear three-dimensional. Called "stereopticans," they were popular entertainment in many homes around the turn of the century. They are available on top of the steel cabinets containing the photographic cards. Copies of the stereographic views may be ordered from the Photoduplication Service, and, in some instances, the coin-operated copy machines may produce a usable copy.

These stereographic photographs are arranged in the cabinets according to subject, then by geographical place within the United States or in foreign countries. Most are scenic views of notable buildings and places of historic significance. Select a state or city and browse through the offerings purely for personal enjoyment or select certain ones associated with a place or event connected with a relative or ancestor.

Washingtoniana

This collection, with its accompanying card catalog, is a rich source of scenes in Washington, D.C., its federal buildings, and their significance. Some categories of interest are the Capitol, cemeteries (arranged by name), commerce (building and establishments), houses, nursing homes, and organizations (fraternal, professional, etc.).

Exhibit catalogs

This is a collection of catalogs, advertisements, and brochures relative to fine arts exhibits as well as exhibits of individual artists and sculptors.

Archives of Hispanic Culture

This is a collection of prints and photographs of art work and persons associated with several Latin American countries. A card catalog accompanies this collection, which is located in the steel cabinets near the catalog.

Photographers Index

This card catalog lists pictures by photographer or the film company that created them.

Washington Press Portraits

This card catalog lists pictures created by staff or the Washington, D.C., press corps.

Genthe Collection Portraits

This is a large collection of photographs by Mr. Genthe, the photographer. This special card catalog contains fifteen drawers of cards listing portraits arranged alphabetically by name.

Other Catalogs

In addition to those cited above, there are other card catalogs concerning the following: cartoons, cabinet of American illustrations, fine prints, popular and applied graphic arts, posters, specific subjects, and specific subjects (graphics).

American Indians

A handy list of twenty-three portraits of well-known American Indians may be obtained at the reference desk by asking for circular P&P #62, "American Indian Portraits." There is also a card catalog of pictures which include Indians in various collections.

County Courthouses

During the years 1974 to 1976, a project sponsored by Joseph E. Seagram & Sons, Inc., photographically recorded over 1,000 county courthouses in the United States. They are available in this reading room. The photographs may be used for reproduction and publication within guidelines set forth in a circular entitled "Seagram County Courthouse Archives Collections" available at the reference desk. These pictures are also available on microfiche kept in two large binders in the reading room. Copies may be made on the coin-operated micro reader-printers. Many of the photographs may be seen and copied directly from the pages of *Courthouses—A Photographic Document,* edited by Richard Pare (New York: Horizon Press, n.d. NA4475 .U6C68). Negative numbers of each photograph have been penciled in the margins for quick retrieval. In addition, there are two drawers of cards marked "County Courthouse Archives" in the card catalog labeled "Architecture, Design, and Engineering Index." All have identifying numbers.

Prints and Photographs on Microfilm

The Photoduplication Service will sell copies of microfilm reels of selected photographs and other material which has been filmed as part of the Library of Congress preservation program. A complete list, with detailed descriptions of the contents, may be obtained by asking for the circular "Prints and Photographs Division Collections on Microfilm: A Selective List." At this writing, the cost of each reel sold in the United States is $23. The following titles may be of value to libraries, schools, historical societies, or other organizations interested in genealogy and related history:

Brady Studio Cartes-de-Visite Portraits (1 reel)

Brady Studio Civil War Views (2 reels)

Construction of the Library of Congress Thomas Jefferson Building, 1880–96 (2 reels)

W.E.B. DuBois Albums (3 reels)

Farm Security Administration/Office of War Information Collection—Written Records (23 reels)

Farm Security Administration/Office of War Information Collection (109 reels)

Benjamin Brown French Collections (construction of the United States Capitol and other government buildings) (1 reel)

Historic American Buildings Survey—America's City Halls (2 reels)

National Child Labor Committee Collections (3 reels)

National Child Labor Committee Collection Captions (gives names, ages, places and dates) (2 reels)

Range Work (cowboy life of the American West) (1 reel)

Civil War Drawings by Edwin Forbes (1 reel)

The Optical Disk Index

It is possible to supplement descriptions of the collections found in the card catalogs by using the optical disk available in the division's photographic holdings.

By typing the proper commands into the computer terminal, according to subject or other heading, one may view on a monitor a copy of a particular photograph, complete with negative number. A paper copy of the picture may be reproduced for ready reference. An instruction sheet describing the use of this equipment is available, but personal instruction probably will be needed for the uninitiated. Library staff will provide such instruction on request.

Publications

The reference collection has several biographical dictionaries and indexes, including many concerned with individuals with careers in photography, art, and printing. Many of these books are found in other reading rooms of the Library of Congress, and some are listed with full bibliographic information in chapter 3 of this guide. The titles listed below are shown without full bibliographic data or call numbers because they are available on the open shelves of this reading room.

Avery, Ann, ed. *American Artists of Renown, 1981–1982.*

Biographical Directory of the American Congress, 1774–1971.

Collins, Jim, and Glenn Opitz. *Women Artists in America.*

Eastman, John. *Who Lived Where—A Biographic Guide to Homes and Museums.*

Falk, Peter H. *Who Was Who in American Art.*

Hughes, Langston. *A Pictorial History of Black-americans* [sic].

Jaques Cattell Press. *Directory of American Biography.* 10 vols.

Johnson, Allen, ed. *Dictionary of American Biography.* 10 vols.

Mallet, David T. *Index of Artists—International—Biographical.*

McHenry, Robert, ed. *Liberty's Women.*

McNeil, Barbara. *Artist Biographies Master Index.*

New York Times Obituary Index, 1858–1978.

Rubinstein, Charlotte. *American Women Artists—From Early Indian Times to the Present.*

Scribner's Concise Dictionary of American Biography.

Who's Who in America.

Who Was Who in America—Historical Volumes, 1607–1896.

Willard, Frances, and May Livermore. *Woman of the Century.*

Wilson, James, and John Fiske, eds. *Appleton's Cyclopedia of American Biography.* 7 vols.

Withey, Henry, and Elsie Withey. *Biographic Dictionary of American Architects.*

Newspaper and Current Periodical Reading Room

This reading room maintains an extensive collection of current periodicals and government publications as well as newspapers published in the United States and abroad. The unbound periodicals are those received in the past eighteen to twenty-four months. After binding, they are transferred to the library's general collection. The government documents are those issued by the federal government and by many state and municipalities, the United Nations, and foreign countries. While current periodicals and government publications may have some value to the genealogist or historian, research here is primarily with the newspaper collections.

The library adds approximately 1,000 copies each month to its collection of currently published newspapers, and they are made available as they are received. Older newspapers are available either in bound volumes or microfilm. In many instances, colonial newspapers date from the late 1600s. Since the bound volumes are stored in an area some distance from the library, delivery time is one or two days. Microfilmed copies of newspapers are usually delivered in less than thirty minutes. Unbound newspapers may be photographed on coin-operated copy machines located in the reading room. Copies from bound volumes, however, must be made by the Photoduplication Service. Librarians in this reading room can provide price lists and help make arrangements for copying. Reproductions from microfilmed newspapers may be made on coin-operated micro reader-printers.

Personal names in some newspapers have been indexed and published and are available in the reference

Researchers using original newspapers and microfilm copies.
Photo by the author

collection. Some indexes include obituaries or death notices; some include marriage notices; and some include names mentioned in general news items. Newspapers for which indexes are available appear in chapter 5 of this guide, which also describes how to determine the names and dates of available newspapers.

Reference librarians in this reading room will respond to written requests of a specific nature, but it is far more advantageous to appear in person or employ a professional researcher to make individual searches. Microfilm copies (but not the actual newspapers) are available through interlibrary loan at your public library.

write the information on a piece of note paper provided for that purpose at the reference desk. Be sure to include any call numbers and location numbers you find listed in the finding aids. A librarian will deliver the maps to one of the large tables in the reading room where they may be examined at leisure. When finished, leave them on the table and advise the librarian that they may be refiled.

Published finding aids which describe various types of maps housed in this division are available at the reference desk. They include maps showing land ownership, railroad lines, urban buildings and neighborhoods, military campaigns and battles, charts showing islands and seashores, and so forth. Maps and atlases are also available for the United States and many foreign countries, especially for England and continental Europe. Finding aids as well as the map collection are described in detail in chapter 4 of this guide.

Copies as large as 11 x 17 inches may be made on coin-operated copy machines available in the reading room. Several shots may be necessary to reproduce a large map. Maps on microfilm may be copied on a special coin-operated printer also available in the reading room. Other methods of reproduction can be arranged through the Photoduplication Service.

Geography and Map Division Reading Room

Material from collections of the Geography and Map Division can provide illustrative material to accompany almost all aspects of a family history or historical endeavor. Reference librarians are available for consultation. After determining which maps are needed for a geographical area or specific place, simply

Reading Rooms for Foreign or Ethnic Group Research

There are several special area divisions with reading rooms and reference collections pertaining to particular geographical areas. Some materials in their collections are English language publications, but most are in foreign languages. These rooms are currently located in the Thomas Jefferson and John Adams Buildings,

Researcher studying maps.
Photo by the author

for their services are available at the public service counter of the Photoduplication Service or in the reading rooms. A special order blank must be completed for copies of photographs. Librarians in the reading rooms will assist researchers in completing the forms and will provide a fee schedule. The photoduplication public service counter is currently located on the ground floor of the John Adams Building and is open from 8:30 A.M. to 4:45 P.M., Monday through Friday. Payments must be made in advance, and checks or money orders should be made payable to the Library of Congress Photoduplication Service. After payment, the material to be copied will be transferred from the reading room for processing. A waiting period of several weeks is the norm. Finished work may be picked up personally at the public service counter or, for a fee, it will be mailed.

Copying is made in accordance with the copyright law and regulations of the Library of Congress. Reproduction is made to approximate original size unless enlargements or reductions are requested. Extra charges are made for special services required for locating or gathering of items to be copied, rush-orders, special camera set-up, oversized items, fold-outs, or items in poor condition. Microfilm will be copied only in complete rolls. Some typical charges effective at this writing are listed below:

Manuscript item (per item) (A $7.00 minimum is imposed for each volume or box handled)	$ .25
Photograph—8 x 10 inch glossy	$7.00
Slides—2 x 2 inch, from a bound volume	$7.00
Positive prints—of a complete roll of microfilm	$33.00

but their locations may change following the renovation now going on at the Library of Congress. The following rooms are available: European Reading Room, Hispanic Reading Room, Asian, Near East Reading Room, African Reading Room, and Hebraic Reading Room.

Each division has its own reference librarians who assist researchers pursuing overseas family connections or those studying particular aspects of a region's culture, religion, and history. The publications, finding aids, indexes, and services in these reading rooms are discussed at greater length in chapter 7.

Photoduplication Service

Some items in the Library of Congress are restricted and cannot be copied, and others cannot be satisfactorily reproduced on coin-operated copy machines. In those latter cases one must apply to the library's Photoduplication Service. Good quality copies can be reproduced for a fee, and order forms and price lists

PART TWO

Categories of Research

The chapters in part 2 are concerned with the variety of resources for historical and genealogical research. They are discussed here in a logical order consistent with efficient searching for one's family history. Beginning genealogists, due to lack of training and experience, are often unproductive and engage in useless and frustrating "browsing." Following a logical procedure can save time and avoid overlapping effort as one works backward in time.

Chapters 3 through 8 describe how to find published genealogies that may mention an ancestor, biographies, and local histories that may name an ancestral family or describe the community in which he or she lived. Pinpointing time and place of residence can often be achieved by using the library's published census indexes or abstracts, city and telephone directories, land records, and maps. A next step might be to search for published church records, abstracts of official county records, military records, and items in old newspapers. Other sources to consider are the articles buried in genealogical and historical periodicals. After tracing one's lineage to the approximate time of immigration, a search of ship passenger lists, naturalization records, and foreign emigration lists might turn up the actual date and port of arrival, as well as nationality and former place of residence. Data might also be found in publications dealing specifically with a particular ethnic group or nationality from both English and non-English-speaking countries. The art and science of heraldry is explained in general terms.

Published works cited in this part generally are concerned with more than one state; sources and published works relating to individual states in nine geographical regions are found in part 3.

CHAPTER 3

Genealogies, Biographies, and Local Histories

An initial step in tracing a family history should be to see what others may have written about your family lines. The beginning genealogist has need to search only a handful of family names. Later, as more branches come to light, genealogies, biographies, and local histories may be helpful.

Some publications that might include one's family, or at least mention some of its members, are the tens of thousands of published genealogies or family histories; biographies; and histories of states, counties, towns, and cities. Many local histories are actually collections of biographies of prominent or successful men of a community. These publications are described in this chapter, and the leading bibliographies and master indexes to such works are cited for quick reference and easy searching.

Genealogies

The results of some genealogical research are collections of pedigree sheets, family group sheets, and brief narrative descriptions of the principal branches. They are usually given to close family members but not to libraries. A good way to find copies of such informal papers is to learn who has a natural interest in the same family lines. Such researchers can sometimes be located by placing queries in genealogical publications, journals, newspaper columns, newsletters of genealogical and historical societies, and by using the query box in the Local History and Genealogy Reading Room at the Library of Congress.

Fortunately, many genealogies have been typed or printed and donated to local historical society libraries or university libraries. Many are in large genealogical research libraries throughout the nation, including the Library of Congress. If you locate a published genealogy your task is far from complete. First, it must be determined whether it describes your family or merely some family sharing the same surname. Helpful indications are the names of collateral lines listed in the index—names of persons who are connected in some way, usually by marriage, to the family. Eventually, you must trace your own unbroken family lines and link them with a definite connection to the family described in the publication.

Chances are that the compiler of a genealogy is a descendant through some branch of the family other than yours—although you may well have an early common ancestor. One should not, however, rush to accept everything as true simply because it is in print. Rather, confirm or correct every statement set down as "fact." Do this by checking any sources cited. If none are provided, seek out primary source documents that verify or refute what has been written and cite them.

In some libraries it is not possible to make a personal search of the published genealogies on their shelves since they have card catalogs that must be used in lieu of browsing. Many such catalogs are good quick references. Some are available at the Library of Congress.

The Library of Congress has more than 40,000 published genealogies, most of them donated by the authors. They are shelved in the closed stack areas of the library and must be obtained by consulting an index or catalog that indicates the author, title, and call number.

Bibliographies, Indexes, and Catalogs of Genealogies

Kaminkow, Marion J. *Genealogies in the Library of Congress*. 2 vols. Baltimore: Magna Carta Books, 1976 and 1987. Z5319 .U53.

This bibliography lists all genealogies, typewritten or printed, obtained by the Library of Congress. It includes American as well as British, Canadian, European, and Asian genealogies. Entries in this published bibliography, through 1980, are also included in the "Family Name Index" (white labels) in the Local History and Genealogy Reading Room. The Library of Congress call number is provided for each entry.

Rider, Fremont A. *American Genealogical-Biographical Index*. 146 vols. Middletown, Conn.: Godfrey Memorial Library, 1958. CS44 .A57.

Commonly referred to as "Rider's Index" and currently being published, it is gradually superseding the earlier forty-eight volume set entitled *American Genealogical Index*. These volumes are a master index to some published sources of family information. Included are the 1790 United States federal population censuses *(Heads of Families)*, Revolutionary War records, a few major sets such as the *Pennsylvania Archives*, certain local histories, the query and answer column in the *Boston Transcript* genealogy columns (1904–41), and a number of published genealogies. Entries are alphabetical by surname, followed by given name, year or approximate year of birth, state of residence, a brief citation for the published source, and volume and page number(s). The author, title, and Library of Congress call number of each book cited are provided on catalog cards kept in a drawer on a long table adjacent to the index.

Library of Congress. *National Union Catalog of Manuscript Collections*. Z6620 .U5N3.

This work represents an ongoing project to catalog manuscript collections in libraries throughout the nation, including the Library of Congress. A complete set of this catalog is available in the Main Reading Room, and reference staff will direct you to it. Manuscripts cited in this catalog include diaries, journals, correspondence, church records, and so forth. Under the subject "genealogy," there are at least 75,000 entries with family names. For each entry there is a brief description of the collection, the number of items, and the repository. A very helpful aid is the *Index to Personal Names in the National Union Catalog of Manuscript Collections,* cited previously.

These are the primary bibliographic sources for genealogies in the Library of Congress. In addition, for a particular family name, you may consult the main card catalog for works cataloged before 1980, and the computer catalog for titles received by the library since 1968. To use the computer catalog, use the following command: **find "reed family"** (substitute family name).

Catalogs and Indexes to Genealogies Outside the Library of Congress

The works cited below are available in the Local History and Genealogy Reading Room. Some concern particular geographical areas of the United States, others are all inclusive. They include genealogies found in major libraries, many of which are also in the Library of Congress. Other publications of this type are found in subsequent chapters of this guide that concern religious and ethnic groups and key state resources.

Denver Public Library, Western History Department. *Catalog of the Western History Department, Denver Public Library*. 7 vols., and 1975 supp. Boston: G.K. Hall, 1970. Z1251 .W5D43.

This set copies 36,075 catalog cards or volumes housed in the Denver Public Library. The emphasis is on the western regions of the United States. Names, places, and local histories are included among the subjects.

Ericson, Jack T. *Genealogy and Local History Titles on Microfiche, Microfiche Sales Catalog No. 1*. Sanford, N.C.: Microfilming Corporation of America, 1983. Z5313 .U5C47.

Glenn, Thomas A. *A List of Some American Genealogies*. Reprint. Baltimore: Genealogical Publishing Co., 1969. Z5313 .U5G5.

Greenlaw, William P., comp. *The Greenlaw Index of the New England Historic Genealogical Society*. 2 vols. Boston: G.K. Hall, 1979. M85/4523.

Available in the Microform Reading Room.

Kaminkow, Marion J. *A Complement to Genealogies in the Library of Congress: A Bibliography*. Baltimore: Magna Carta Book Co., 1981. Z5319 .K35.

This compilation is a bibliography of published genealogies that are *not* in the Library of Congress. However, since a few of those listed are indeed available there, it is wise to consult with a reference librarian in the Local History and Genealogy Reading Room.

Titles of approximately 20,000 genealogies are included, as found in forty-five libraries, selected primarily on the basis of broad geographical representation and cooperative library staffs. Some libraries were omitted because their holdings have been reproduced and are available at the Allen County Public Library, Fort Wayne, Indiana (see list below). The libraries surveyed by Kaminkow are listed below.

Alaska Historical Society

Allen County Public Library, Fort Wayne, Indiana, including works copied from the following:
    Amarillo Public Library, Texas
    Cincinnati Public Library, Ohio
    Dallas Public Library, Texas
    Flint Public Library, Michigan
    Florida Public Library, Orlando
    Fort Worth Public Library, Texas
    Greenwood Public Library, Mississippi
    Houston Public Library, Texas
    Iowa Division of Historical Museum
        and Archives, Des Moines
    Kansas City Public Library
    Kansas Public Library, Wichita
    Maryland Historical Society, Baltimore
    Michigan Public Library, Saginaw
    Missouri Public Library, St. Louis
    Mormon Branch Library, Los Angeles
    National Genealogical Society,
        Washington, D.C.
    New England Historical Genealogy
        Society, Boston
    New York Public Library, Syracuse
    Newberry Library, Chicago
    Ohio Public Library, Toledo
    State Historical Society of Iowa, Iowa City
    State Historical Society of Wisconsin,
        Madison
    Western Reserve Historical Society,
        Cleveland

Boston Atheneum

Cincinnati Historical Society

Denver Public Library

Genealogical Forum of Portland, Oregon

Gloucester County Historical Society, Woodbury, New Jersey

Historical Society of Pennsylvania, Philadelphia

Idaho Historical Genealogical Society, Boise

Kansas State Historical Society, Topeka

Long Island Historical Society, Brooklyn

Los Angeles Public Library

Minnesota Historical Society, St. Paul

New York Public Library

Ohio Historical Society, Columbus

Oregon State Library, Salem

St. Louis Public Library

San Francisco Public Library

Seattle Public Library

State Library of Ohio, Columbus

Sutro Branch of the California State Library, San Francisco

Washington Public Library, Spokane

List of Family Genealogies in the Library of the Connecticut Historical Society. Hartford: the society, 1911. Z5313 .U5C7.

Long Island Historical Society Catalog of American Genealogies in the Library of the Long Island Historical Society. Reprint. Baltimore: Genealogical Publishing Co., 1969. Z5313 .U5L8.

Munsell's Index to American Genealogies. Albany, New York: Joel Munsell's Sons, 1900. Supps 1900–08. Reprint. Detroit: Gale Research Co., 1966; Baltimore: Genealogical Publishing Co., 1979. Z5313 .U5D93.

National Society, Daughters of the American Revolution. *Library Catalog Volume One, Family Histories and Genealogies.* 2d ed. Washington, D.C.: the society, 1983. Z5313 .U5D38.

This catalog, now being revised, contains more than 14,000 entries, many of which are typescripts found only at the DAR Library or in a few other libraries. A special index lists families included in genealogies titled under a different surname.

Newberry Library. *Genealogical Index of the Newberry Library, Chicago.* 4 vols. Boston: G.K. Hall, 1960. CD44 .N42.

New York Public Library. The Research Libraries. *Dictionary Catalog of the Local History and Genealogy Division.* 18 vols. Boston: G.K. Hall, 1974. Z881 .N59.

Wisconsin State Historical Society Library. *Subject Catalog of the Library of the State Historical Society of Wisconsin.* 23 vols. Westport, Conn.: Greenwood Publishing Co., 1972. Z1236 .W57.

This set is an alphabetized reproduction of catalog cards of the library's holdings, numbering nearly 1 million.

Schreiner-Yantis, Netti. *Genealogical and Local History Books in Print.* Springfield, Va.: the author, 1975. Supps. Z5313 .U5G45.

Includes hundreds of published genealogies.

Biographies

Biographical works abound in various forms, but there are primarily two types: those that describe prominent citizens on a national or regional level (often by profession) and those that describe prominent citizens on a local level. The "United States Biographical Index" (pink labels) catalog, located in the Local History and Genealogy Reading Room is an index (by surname and given name) to biographical sketches found in a selected group of state or regional publications. The first drawer of the catalog, labeled "Books Indexed," identifies the sources used. The biographical sketches of locally prominent people are discussed in the next section dealing with local histories. Those in the "who's who" type publications are described by profession, occupation, university affiliation, and leadership role (such as government or military). Still being published today, these are valuable to both researchers and business firms that need ready reference of outstanding citizens.

There are a few excellent bibliographies of biographical works. Especially useful are those that include in their indexes the non-principal names. The following are available in the reference collection (on the open shelves) of the Local History and Genealogy Reading Room:

Biographical Books, 1950–1980. New York: R.R. Bowker Co., 1980. Z5301 .B68.

Dargan, Marion. *Guide to American Biography, 1607–1933.* Albuquerque: University of New Mexico Press, 1949. Z5305 .U5D323.

Herbert, Miranda C., and Barbara McNeil. *Biography and Genealogy Master Index.* 8 vols., 1981–82. Supp. Detroit: Gale Research Co., 1975. Z5305 .U5B57.

This is an eight-volume set that provides more than 3,200,000 citations of names culled from over 350 biographical dictionaries, "who's who" publications, and similar works. It does not include local histories that are principally composed of biographical sketches. The sources used for this index, listed on the inside front cover, are primarily concerned with residents of the United States. Each citation provides a birth or death date, if available, and a symbol identifying the source. This is a second edition of the single volume *Biographical Dictionaries Master Index,* published by Gale Research.

The 1981–82 supplement, consisting of three volumes, adds more than 1 million names from over forty biographical dictionaries.

McNeil, Barbara, and Miranda C. Herbert. *Historical Biographical Dictionaries Master Index.* Detroit: Gale Research Co., 1980. Z5305 .U5H57.

This is a consolidated index to biographical information about people of historical importance. Names are alphabetically arranged with birth and death dates, if known. The forty-two sources are coded by symbols.

Published Biographies and Directories of Students

The biographical compilations listed below are illustrative of the types of publications that may include an ancestor's name. Some of these works are in the Local History and Genealogy Reading Room, Newspaper and Current Periodical Reading Room, Prints and Photographs Reading Room, and the Manuscript Division Reading Room.

General

Concise Dictionary of American Biography. New York: Charles Scribner's Sons, 1980. E176 .D564.

This work provides essential facts from every article in the *Dictionary of American Biography* (see Johnson, Allen, below).

Current Biography—Who's News and Why. 24 vols. New York: H.H. Wilson Co., 1940–86. CT100 .C8.

Dictionary of Distinguished Americans. Raleigh, N.C.: American Biographical Institute, 1982. CT220 .D573.

Harrison, Richard K. *Princetonians—A Biographical Dictionary.* 3 vols. 1769, 1783. Reprint. Princeton: 1980. LD4601 .H37(38).

International Who's Who, 1982. Detroit: Gale Research Co., 1983. CT120 .I5.

Jaques Cattell Press. *Directory of American Scholars.* 4 vols. New York: R.R. Bowker Co., 1942. LA2311 .C32.

Johnson, Allen. *Dictionary of American Biography.* 11 vols., 6 supps., separate index. New York: Charles Schribner's Sons, 1964. E176 .D563.

Johnson, Rossiter, ed. *Twentieth Century Biographical Dictionary of Notable Americans.* 10 vols. Boston: The Biographical Society, 1904. E176 .C993.

Kay, Earnest, ed. *Men of Achievement.* Vol. 6. Cambridge, Mass.: International Biographical Centre, 1979. CT120 .M43.

National Cyclopedia of American Biography. 62 vols. Index. New York: James T. White & Co., 1930–84. E176 .N27.

O'Brien, Sue M. *The Registers of Americans of Prominent Descent.* Signal Mountain, Tenn.: Morten Publishing Co., 1982. CT215 .028.

Personalities of America. Raleigh, N.C.: American Biographical Institute, 1981. CT220 .P47.

Preston, Wheeler. *American Biographies.* Detroit: Gale Research Co., 1977. CT213 .P7.

Cites 5,257 names from colonial times.

Sibley, John. *Biographical Sketches of Graduates of Harvard University.* 17 vols. 1643–1771. Cambridge, Mass.: 1873. L901 .F4.

———. *Biographical Sketches of Those Who Attended Harvard College, 1640–.* Boston: Massachusetts Historical Society, 1873. LD2139 .S5.

United Chapter of Phi Beta Kappa. *Phi Beta Kappa Directory, 1776–1941.* New York: n.p., 1941. LJ105 .P483P48.

Venn, John, and J. A. Venn, comps. *Alumni Cantabrigienses* (Cambridge University). 10 vols. Cambridge, Eng.: University Press, 1927. LF124 .A2.

Who's Who in America. Chicago: Marquis Who's Who, Inc., 1899–. E176 .W642.

Who Was Who in America—Historical Volumes, 1607–1891. Chicago: A.N. Marquis Co., 1963. E176 .W64.

Wilson, James C., and John Fiske, ed. *Appleton's Cyclopedia of American Biography.* 7 vols. Reprint. Detroit: Gale Research Co., 1968. E176 .A666.

Governmental

Lanman, Charles. *Biographical Annals of the Civil Government of the United States During its First Century.* Reprint. Detroit: Gale Research Co., 1976. E176 .L2918.

McMullin, Thomas, and David Walker. *Biographical Directory of American Territorial Governors.* Westport, Conn.: Meckler Publishing Co., 1984. E176 .M17.

Morris, Dan, and Inez Morris. *Who Was Who in American Politics. A Biographical Dictionary . . . From Colonial Days . . . .* New York: Hawthorne Books, 1974. E176 .M873.

Patrick, Rembert W. *Jefferson Davis and his Cabinet.* Baton Rouge: Louisiana State University Press, 1944. E487 .P3.

Raimo, John W. *Biographical Directory of American Colonial and Revolutionary Governors, 1607–1789.* Westport, Conn.: Meckler Books, 1980. E187 .5 .R34.

Smith, William H. *History of the Cabinet of the United States of America, from President Washington to President Coolidge.* Baltimore: Industrial Printing Co., 1925. JK611 .S5.

Sobel, Robert. *Biographical Directory of the United States Executive Branch, 1774–1977.* Westport, Conn.: Greenwood Press, 1977. E176 .B576.

United States Congress. *Biographical Directory of the American Congress, 1774–1971.* Washington, D.C.: Government Printing Office, 1971. JK1010 .A5.

Wakelyn, Jon L. *Biographical Dictionary of the Confederacy.* Westport, Conn.: Greenwood Press, 1977. E467 .W2.

Warner, Ezra J. *Biographical Register of the Confederate Congress.* Baton Rouge: Louisiana University Press, 1975. JK9663 .W3.

Professional and Occupational

Directory of Licensed Practitioners of Funeral Services, Funeral Directors and Embalmers . . . Registered Funeral Homes. RA622 .A7M3.

Fiddlers on Field Recordings in the Archives of Folk Song: A List Available at the American Folklife Center, Library of Congress.

Holloway, Lizabeth H. *Medical Obituaries — American Physicians Biographical Notices in Selected Medical Journals Before 1907.* New York: n.p., 1981. R153 .H64.

Jaques Cattell Press. *Who's Who in American Art.* New York: R.R. Bowker, 1940. N6536 .W5.

Mallett, Daniel T. *Mallett's Index of Artists.* New York: R.R. Bowker, 1940. N40 .M5.

McNeil, Barbara, ed. *Artists' Biographies Master Index.* Detroit: Gale Research Co., 1986. N40 .A78.

Meyer, Mary K., and P. William Filby. *Who's Who in Genealogy and Heraldry.* Detroit: Gale Research Co., 1981. CS5 .M49.

National Directory of Morticians, 1987. RA622 .A7N37.

Opitz, Glenn B., ed. *Mantle Fielding's Dictionary of American Painters, Sculptors, and Engravers.* Poughkeepsie, New York: Apollo Books, 1983. N6536 .F5.

Spear, Frank A. *Early Southern and Western Inventors.* 2 vols. Silver Springs, Md.: the author, 1984. T223.1 .C2S6.

Withey, Henry F., and Elsie R. Withey. *Biographical Dictionary of American Architects.* Los Angeles: New Age Publishing Co., 1956. NA7366 .W5.

Local Histories

The 1876 centennial and the 1976 bicentennial of the United States prompted the publication of a host of local histories. These and the thousands produced in other years are a bonanza of information for genealogists and historians. The works that concentrate on the history of a region, county, or city often include lists of names of government officials, school personnel, religious leaders, and soldiers and sailors who fought in various wars. Fortunately, most books of this nature have indexes, making it easy for a researcher to discern immediately whether it mentions his ancestor.

Regional biographical publications are almost always concerned exclusively with the residents of a given area. Some titles are ambiguous, while others masquerade as histories—even though they contain little or no historical data except the personal sketches of individuals.

These were often commercial endeavors that attempted to include as many people as possible in order to increase sales of the books. With a photograph of each person, they were popular around the turn of this century and are often referred to as "mug books." Most of the sketches were prepared by the subjects themselves, or by a member of the immediate family. It appears, however, that a standard outline or format was provided by an editor, since the sketches seem to be rather uniform in style. They tended to emphasize the stellar qualities and achievements of the subject while ignoring other facets. Most of the subjects were men, and they can provide some valuable data including place of residence, profession or occupation, and major accomplishments. They often specified political leanings and religious preferences, with some history. Overall, they take the place of stories that could have been told by relatives who were never interviewed.

As in all family material supplied by others, the researcher must verify the "facts" offered. These sketches seldom cite sources since the person himself or his close relatives simply related the information from personal recollections or reiterated unverified family stories.

The Library of Congress has tens of thousands of local histories of all kinds, both in bound books and on microfilm. See the earlier chapters that describe how to obtain the microfilms either in the Local History and Genealogy Reading Room or in the Microform Reading Room. Refer to the card catalog "United States Local History Shelflist" (see page 17) for titles of local histories, arranged by region and state. This catalog, or the main card catalog, provides author, title, and call number. Use the computer catalog for local histories that have been cataloged by the Library of Congress since 1868 (see page 11).

Another handy finding aid in the Local History and Genealogy Reading Room is the "Analyzed Surname Index" (green labels) that lists family names mentioned in selected local histories. The last drawer of this catalog, labeled "Local Histories Indexed," identifies by author and title the county histories used in compiling this finding aid.

Bibliographies

Described below are the leading bibliographic works listing local histories, most of which may be seen in the Local History and Genealogy Reading Room or obtained by submitting a call slip. These bibliographies may be used to look up the state and county of interest. If call numbers are not included you must consult the card or computer catalog.

Filby, P. William. *A Bibliography of American County Histories.* Baltimore: Genealogical Publishing Co., 1985. Z1250 .F54.

In preparing this book the author cross-checked county histories listed in two other bibliographies; one prepared by the New York Public Library and the other by Marion J. Kaminkow (see below). He then sent questionnaires to state libraries, archives, and historical societies asking for lists of county histories in their collections. As a result, he was able to compile a list of approximately 5,000 titles, doubling the number cited by the New York Public Library and by Kaminkow.

Publications with such titles as "Biographies of Prominent Men" or "Portrait and Biographical Histories" were eliminated by Filby, inasmuch as these are not purely histories. He did, however, include publications with titles such as "Historical and Biographical," since most of these seem to include genuine historical information.

Titles in this volume are arranged alphabetically by state and then by county. Many, but not all, of the titles may be found in the Library of Congress; some are found in only a few libraries in this country. To determine if a particular work is available at the Library of Congress, consult the card or computer catalog for local histories, by state and county.

Kaminkow, Marion J. *United States Local Histories in the Library of Congress—A Bibliography.* 4 vols., supps., 1976, 1986. Baltimore: Magna Carta Book Co., 1975. Z1250 .U59.

This extremely useful guide is a compilation of all local histories in the Library of Congress in 1972, according to the catalog cards on file at that time. Volume 5, issued as a supplement in 1976, includes an index to all five volumes. The 1986 supplement provides an additional 10,000 titles acquired by the Library of Congress between 1976 and 1986.

Sinko, Peggy Tuck. *Guide to Local and Family History at the Newberry Library.* Salt Lake City: Ancestry, Inc., 1988. (Cataloging in publication.)

Peterson, Clarence S. *Bibliography of Local Histories in Fifty States.* Vol. 1: *Bibliography of Local Histories in the Atlantic States, 1966.* 3 vols. supps.; Vol. 2: *Bibliography of Local Histories of Thirty-five States Beyond the Atlantic States;* and Vol 3: *Consolidated Bibliography of County Histories in Fifty States in 1961.* Baltimore: the author, 1961. Z1250 .P47.

Volume 3 of this series (including 4,000 county histories) is superseded by Filby's *Bibliography of American County Histories* (see above).

Catalogs of Local Histories in Other Libraries

Thousands of state and local libraries in this country have anywhere from a few to hundreds of local histories in their collections. Two of the major libraries having large collections of local histories are represented by catalogs of their holdings, which may be seen in the Library of Congress.

National Society, Daughters of the American Revolution Library Catalog. Vol. 2: *State and Local Histories and Records.* Washington, D.C.: the society, 1986. Z5313 .U5D38.

Lists the society's holdings as of 1985. In addition to local histories it also includes Bible records, cemetery lists, and other genealogical material. Both indexes, one by author and one by subject, are arranged by state and alphabetically by title.

New York Public Library. The Research Libraries. *Dictionary Catalog of the Local History and Genealogy Division.* 18 vols. Boston: G.K. Hall & Co., 1974. Z881 .N59.

The contents of this set of folios (large volumes) is a photo-reproduction of the catalog cards of published local histories, many of which are also available at the Library of Congress. Titles are arranged alphabetically by author and place.

In addition to the above, book catalogs of the local histories and genealogies at the Newberry Library, the Denver Public Library, and the Wisconsin State Historical Society Library (cited earlier) are also available at the Library of Congress.

CHAPTER 4

Records Showing Residence

After determining generally where one's ancestors lived at certain times of their lives and what the names of their family members were, the next step is to ascertain if there is a published history or a biography available on that family. If a family history or biography is found, it is important to verify the facts in it. Simply because someone has printed "conclusions" about a family connection, they are not necessarily accurate. One of the best sources for determining an ancestor's whereabouts at a particular place and time are the federal population census schedules. Supplementing these are city, county, and other directories, as well as land ownership maps and atlases, which usually cite place of residence. One should also ascertain if the ancestor in question owned any real estate by examining grantee and grantor indexes of county deeds or abstracts of deeds. In some cases such information can be supplemented with maps indicating water courses that may have been mentioned in land or tax records. There are numerous published sources at the Library of Congress that may be helpful in such a search.

Census Records

Other than county courthouse records, probably the most frequently used documents for genealogical research are the federal population census schedules, hereafter referred to as the federal census. The United States Constitution provided for decennial censuses beginning in 1790, the purpose being to determine population in various districts of the states in order to allot seats in the House of Representatives. The censuses have also been used to ascertain statistical data such as the number of males who could be called for military service, occupation, place of birth, whether foreign or native born, value of real or personal property, number of slaves, number of veterans receiving a military pension, the number attending school, literacy, and whether residence is rented or owned.

The Bureau of the Census collects such data, not the Library of Congress, so the latter does not have the actual census enumeration sheets or copies. However, it does have a large collection of published abstracts and indexes. To examine microfilm copies of the original census schedules, one needs to visit the National Archives or one of its field branches, or a genealogical or public library that has copies. To save time, make a preliminary check for published abstracts of the censuses or published indexes. This can be done at the Library of Congress. All the extant 1790 census data was published by the Government Printing Office, generally entitled *Heads of Families*. States for which the 1790 census is missing are Connecticut, Delaware, Georgia, Kentucky, New Jersey, Tennessee, and Virginia. Many of the 1800 and 1810 census schedules, as well as some of those for 1820, have also been lost. In some states, only partial census enumerations have survived the vicissitudes of time. In cases where the entire census for a state is lost, substitute lists based primarily on tax records have been compiled. These lists, sometimes entitled "census" rather than "tax lists," are incomplete. In 1850 and 1860 separate enumerations were made of slaves, but they usually gave only names of their owners and the age categories, color, and gender of the slaves.

In 1885, when a need arose for a mid-decennial census to document the rapid growth of western states, the federal government shared expenses with any state that wished to take a census in that year. As a result, there are 1885 population census schedules for Colorado, Florida, Nebraska, and the territories of Dakota and New Mexico (then encompassing what is now Arizona).

In 1880, Indians then living on reservations in the Territory of Dakota, plus those in California and Washington, were enumerated. Prior to that year, only those Indians who lived outside a reservation (thus being taxpayers) were included. At various times between 1885 and 1942, there have been special rolls of Indians compiled by agents of the Bureau of Indian Affairs, Department of the Interior.

In 1810 and 1820, censuses were taken of those engaged in manufacturing; between 1840 and 1910, supplemental censuses were taken of those engaged in agriculture. Such census records compiled in other years were either lost or destroyed by congressional order. Those that survived may be examined at the National Archives, state libraries, or university libraries to which they have been transferred.

While not strictly census enumerations, mortality schedules were prepared by the federal government for the years 1850 through 1880, but they exist only for certain states. Those schedules list persons who died during the twelve-month period ending in June of the census year. They give name, cause of death, age, and sometimes information about family members. For example, beginning in 1870, the place of birth of the deceased's parents is shown. Because there is a paucity of death records for that period, these mortality schedules are a valuable resource. Unfortunately, deaths for the intervening nine years of the decade were not recorded by the Bureau of the Census. These schedules may be seen at the National Archives, state libraries, or genealogical libraries that have microfilm copies. Most of the originals have been turned over to state libraries.

Some of the states took their own censuses to compile data pertaining to schools, development of state and county tax laws, and commerce. A few of those were compiled as early as 1703; others were taken in more recent years. During the American Revolution some states compiled lists of citizens who took loyalty oaths or who were potential members of the local militia. During and after the Civil War, some northern cities took special censuses in order to chart movements of blacks who migrated from the South.

Census Guides and Bibliographies

Most published indexes for the federal censuses of 1790 to 1850 may be found on reference in the Local History and Genealogy Reading Room among books pertaining to the individual states. Most of the published abstracts of censuses for individual counties must be requested by submitting a call slip. The card catalog in the Local History and Genealogy Reading Room labeled "United States Local History Shelflist" has listings of these publications received by the Library of Congress before 1980, arranged by state and county. All of those received since 1968 can be found by using the computer catalog. Type the command **find s census (name of state or county)**.

Most of the following helpful guidebooks to censuses may be found in the Local History and Genealogy Reading Room shelves:

Brewer, Mary M. *Index to Census Schedules in Printed Form, 1969.* Huntsville, Ark.: Century Enterprises, 1969. supp., 1970–71. Z7553 .C3B7.

Note that many indexes for county and state censuses have been published since the compilation of this work.

Eakle, Arlene H. "Census Records." In *The Source: A Guidebook of American Genealogy.* Edited by Arlene H. Eakle and Johni Cerny. Salt Lake City: Ancestry, Inc., 1984. CS49 .S65.

This chapter includes detailed tables of censuses, their contents, whether published or indexed, and where they may be located.

Kirkham, E. Kay. *A Survey of American Census Schedules.* Salt Lake City: Deseret Book Co., 1959. CS549 .K5.

National Archives and Records Service. *Federal Population Censuses, 1790–1890. A Catalog of Microfilm Copies of the Schedules.* Washington, D.C.: 1971. HA37 .U548.

Stemmons, John D., comp. *The United States Census Compendium.* Logan, Utah: Everton Publishers, 1973. Z1250 .S83.

Includes federal, state, and local censuses as well as lists of taxables, petitioners, oath takers, and others. It is arranged by state and county indicating which years are available and location.

United States Bureau of the Census. *A Century of Population Growth, 1790–1900*. Reprint. Johnson Reprints, 1966. HA195 .A5.

Directories

City and County Directories

A city directory lists by name the principal residents of a city (and often the nearby suburbs), their home address, occupation, and place of work. Telephone numbers are not included. A county directory is usually a business or agricultural guide listing those who operate farms or other businesses. In most cases, other residents are also listed. Listings are alphabetical by surname and generally include heads of households (male or female); those employed outside the home; adults living in boarding houses and hotels; and boarders in private homes. In early directories wives were omitted unless they were widows and therefore had become heads of households.

City directories are a good way to track movement of people within a city as they moved from place to place. The first and last year their names appear can indicate an approximate time of arrival and departure. Youths going to work for the first time leave a clue as to their approximate ages and the probable names of their parents, or at least a close relative with whom they may have been living. In early directories a widow was often so designated, thereby providing a clue to her husband's time of death.

Many city and county directories are published annually or biennially, others less frequently. Names are sometimes missing but reappear in later editions, often at the same address. The spelling of a name may vary from year to year. Directories are compiled on the basis of door-to-door canvasses; those absent who failed to complete and return the questionnaire would be omitted in the forthcoming edition. In some cases neighbors might have supplied information and errors can be expected.

The first city directories appeared in November 1785, released a week apart by rival publishers: *MacPherson's Directory for the City and Suburbs of Philadelphia* and the *Philadelphia Directory*. A New York directory was published the following year, and several other cities followed suit. Directories became business aids for traveling salesmen and others who needed to know names of citizens and where they lived or worked. This filled a need now supplemented by

telephone directories; however, many city directories are still being published and may be found in public libraries. They are also used in business offices for compiling mailing lists and for locating debtors, customers, and clients. Capitalizing on the need for such directories during the past century, William H. Boyd published many for eastern and midwestern cities. Eventually the firm of R.L. Polk began to publish nationwide and is today the largest publisher of city directories.

City and County Directories As a Resource

Genealogists can use city and county directories in several ways: they can be used to fill gaps between the decennial federal censuses; they can pinpoint locations by ward in large urban areas so the individual may be found in a census; and they may help locate descendants who still reside in the family's ancestral city or county. Each of these benefits are described below.

Filling in the Census Gaps. A directory provides information about place of residence and occupation of adult members of a household during the ten years between censuses. Because the 1890 census was mostly destroyed by fire, directories are especially useful for the period 1880 to 1900. They are also helpful in locating families who were missed by the census enumerators.

If an individual cannot be found in a particular census year, a search of city directories can help provide a time frame for determining when he or she might have left the area, died, or otherwise disappeared. Directories are an excellent resource to determine place of residence between the most recent census year available to the public, 1910, and the present time. (The 1920 census will not be released until at least sometime in 1992.)

Narrowing the Search in the Census. The task of finding a family or individual in a census schedule is sometimes almost impossible if they resided in a large urban area and the address is unknown. As an example, the 1910 census has indexes for only those states without birth records (or with incomplete birth records). The 1880 census index includes only those families or households with children aged ten or younger. Both these indexes were created by the federal government. Indexes for the 1860 and 1870 census years are currently being privately published and to date are incomplete.

Searching the census of a large city is tedious, but it can be facilitated if one knows the ward in which an individual resided. With a street name and house number obtained from a city directory, one can often pinpoint the location on old city maps that show ward divisions. Ward maps are sometimes included in a directory, and occasionally wards are described by bisecting streets. When maps are unavailable, a ward directory may be used as a substitute. Both of these aids are available for some cities in the Geography and Map Reading Room of the Library of Congress or in the Microfilm Room of the National Archives. One should bear in mind that an address shown in a city directory might not be the place of residence when the census was taken, often during the month of June. For this reason, it is prudent to check city directory addresses for the years during, prior, and subsequent to the census year.

Locating Living Relatives in Current Directories. It can be a boon for the genealogist to find someone also doing research on the same family lines who is willing to share information. Find the city and telephone number for such a person by checking current directories for individuals with the family surname who are living in the city or county where the family resided for many years. Supplement these findings by using current telephone directories. This may result in turning up a "lost cousin."

At this writing, current city directories and telephone directories for the United States are shelved on a deck just off the Main Reading Room. They are separately arranged alphabetically by state and then city or town. A card catalog provides a cross-reference to names of smaller towns and the name of the telephone directories in which those towns are included.

Availability of City and County Directories

Many genealogical libraries have a collection of city and county directories, especially pertaining to their own geographical area. Large collections are found at the American Antiquarian Society, Worcester, Massachusetts, and the Boston Public Library collection at the Roslindale Branch (with a catalog of their holdings). Another large collection that formerly belonged to the New England Historic Genealogical Society was given to the Boston Public Library and is located in its East Boston Branch. A list of those directories is available at the reference desk in the Local History and Genealogy Reading Room. The Library of Congress has perhaps the largest collection of city and county directories, occupying some 5,800 shelves with more volumes arriving daily.

Because of their large number, the library no longer catalogs them, although some early ones may be listed in the card catalogs under the city or county name.

Obtain either a city or telephone directory by submitting a call slip with the name of the city or county and year desired. A limit may be imposed on the number of directories delivered at a given time. If a researcher needs to examine large numbers of directories, it is best to discuss this in advance with a reference librarian.

Until now, except for limited card catalogs and a few incomplete lists, there has been no practical way to learn exactly what original city and county directories are available. Many directories have been reproduced on microfilm or microfiche. Research Publications, Inc., is engaged in an ongoing project to microfilm the directories through 1935 of approximately fifty large cities across the nation. Directories for this project are supplied by the Library of Congress as well as by other libraries as necessary to complete the sets. As each is completed, a copy of the film is made available in the Local History and Genealogy Reading Room. Consult a reference librarian for a current list of the directories filmed.

The microfilming project is being done in segments. The first includes all directories reproduced on microfiche through 1860 (as described below). Segment two covers the period 1861 to 1881, segment three covers the period 1882 to 1901, and segment four covers the period 1902 to 1935. There are some gaps, especially in the years just prior to 1935, because publication of city directories for some large cities has ceased.

Segment one, the earliest directories through 1860 on microfiche, is based on Dorothea N. Spear's *Bibliography of American Directories Through 1860* (cited below). To compile this list, the author used directories at the American Antiquarian Society, the Library of Congress, and other libraries. Each listing is coded to indicate location. A copy is available at the reference desk of the Local History and Genealogy Reading Room. Localities and year are indicated on the headings of each piece of microfiche. All original pre-1861 directories at the Library of Congress have been transferred to the Rare Book and Special Collections Division.

Some years ago, Phillip N. Smith compiled a list of "Directories in the Library of Congress" (cited below). In contrast to Spear's bibliography, only the earliest year was given for each city.

In 1987 Mark C. Neagles conducted a thorough "hands-on" inventory of city and county directories at the Library of Congress. His inventory is included in this guide. It is alphabetically arranged by state and then city or county. The fifty-one separate lists (one for each state, plus Washington, D.C.) are found in chapters 9 through 15, which are concerned with key resources on the state level. These lists now supersede earlier lists and are complete through 1987, making it possible to obtain an original or a microfilm copy without preliminary recourse to a card or computer catalog.

Related Publications

Kirkham, E. Kay. *A Handy Guide to Record Searching in the Larger Cities of the United States.* Logan, Utah: The Everton Publishers, Inc., 1974. Z5305 .U5K57.

Remington, Gordon L. "City Directories and Their Cousins." In *The Source: A Guidebook of American Genealogy,* edited by Arlene H. Eakle and Johni Cerny. Salt Lake City: Ancestry, Inc., 1984. CS49 .S65.

Research Publications, Inc. *City Directories of the United States—Guide to the Microfilm Collection, 1860–1901* [actually through 1935]. Woodbridge, Conn., 1985. Z5771 .C58.

Smith, Phillip N. "Directories in the Library of Congress." *The American Genealogist* (1936): 46–55. F104 .N6A6.

Spear, Dorothea N. *Bibliography of American Directories Through 1860.* Worcester, Mass.: American Antiquarian Society, 1961. Z5771 .S68.

Telephone Directories

Telephone directories in the Library of Congress are available in several locations. Each group is described elsewhere in this guide and are listed here only for reference.

1. *New York City and Environs, 1878–1905; Westchester, 1906–14 and 1923–53; and Rockland, 1910–54/55.* On microfilm in the Microform Reading Room.

2. *United States, 1976–1983.* On microfiche as part of the "Phonofiche" collection, available in the Microform Reading Room.

3. *United States, Miscellaneous Years and Cities.* These are in the closed stacks but are not cataloged. Generally, they cover the past ten or twenty years, but they do not include all years or locations. Whenever possible use the "Phonofiche" instead of this collection.

4. *United States, Current Years.* Shelved with current city directories on a deck just off the Main Reading Room.

5. *Foreign Countries.* These are listed by name in chapter 7 of this guide.

Professional Directories

There is a variety of professional directories useful to researchers. The *Martindale-Hubbell* directory of lawyers is available in the Law Library of the Library of Congress. Many states have published volumes entitled *Bench and Bar,* and some of these are listed in chapters 9 through 15 of this guide. Annual directories of physicians are also published. The following are a sample of the types of directories or listings that may be consulted at the Library of Congress. Others may be found by using the following subject headings in the card or computer catalogs:

lawyers—directories—state
(substitute as needed)

physicians—directories—state
(substitute as needed)

Directory of Woman Attorneys in the United States, 1972. N.p., n.d. KF190 .D57.

Farmer, John. *List of Graduates of All of the New England Colleges.* Concord, N.H.: N.p., 1835. L901 .F3.

Includes Harvard, Yale, Brown, Amherst, and others.

Social Registers (Blue Books)

Social registers, or "blue books" have been published since the turn of this century and are still published in limited quantities. These books (called blue books because they are usually bound in blue covers) were created to serve as invitation lists and directories for the more prominent upper-class citizens. They were especially useful to those giving large house parties or debutante balls, or to those who chaired committees created to conduct charity balls and other social events.

Sometimes the names are arranged by neighborhood or street, usually alphabetically. Following an individual's name are abbreviations for their school, social club affiliations, and summer addresses. The publishers relied on women's clubs or "social register associations" to provide the names. Some registers list the officers of social and business clubs as well as local government officials.

In past years several registers received by the Library were cataloged, but now most are uncataloged. As an aid to researchers, Mark C. Neagles supplemented his inventory of city and county directories with an inventory of the library's social registers. These may be obtained by submitting a call slip based on the information given in this guide.

For the past several years there have been registers covering the entire United States, and first reference for modern years might be made to the following work:

Social Register Association. *Social Register—[year]*; annual editions, 1977–86. New York: the Association, 1976–85.

Annual editions are alphabetical listings by name.

Social Registers in the Library of Congress

Alabama

Blue Book and Social Register. 1929 F325 .A3

Argentina

Libro de Oro 1932–37

California

California Register 1954–66

Social Directory of California 1978

Los Angeles

Los Angeles and Pasadena Blue Book 1903

Los Angeles Blue Book 1894

Los Angeles and Southern California Blue Book 1894

Los Angeles and Pasadena Society Blue Book 1903

Society Blue Book (includes Pasadena and seaside resorts) 1908

Los Angeles Blue Book 1952–86

Orange County

Social Yearbook of Orange County 1955

Frances Kay Social Register of Orange County 1966

The Orange Book 1966–67

Palm Beach

Palm Beach Personages 1962–81

Pasadena (see Los Angeles)

San Francisco

New Society Blue Book (includes Alameda, Berkeley, Oakland, Piedmont, San Mateo, San Rafael, and others) 1913–33

Elite Directory 1879

Social Mauve (includes Oakland) 1884

San Francisco Blue Book 1888, 1890, 1905, 1912–22

Our Society Blue Book 1891–95, 1900

San Francisco and Bay Cities Jewish Blue Book 1916

San Francisco Blue Book and Club Directory 1924–31

Social Register, San Francisco 1906–76

Southern California

Social Register, Southern California (includes Los Angeles and Pasadena) 1914–26

Society and Club Register 1925

Canada

Toronto and Hamilton

Tyrell's Society Blue Book 1902

Dau's Blue Book 1910, 1913, 1920

Montreal and Ottawa

Dau's Montreal and Ottawa Blue Book 1925

Muskoka Lakes, Ontario

Muskoka Lakes Blue Book, Directory and Chart 1915

Colorado

Denver

Denver Social Year Book 1898

Who's Who in Denver Society 1908

Social Record and Club Annual 1934–40

Connecticut

First Families of Connecticut 1899

Greenwich

Greenwich Society Directory 1905

Hartford

Hartford Blue Book 1897

Dau's Blue Book—Hartford and Suburban Towns 1911–26

Social Register 1931

New Haven

New Haven List 1886

Blue Book 1894

Dau's Blue Book (includes suburbs) 1911–17, 1924, 1927

Social Register of New Haven 1927, 1930

Social Directory of New Haven and Vicinity 1951

Connecticut (State of) and **New York** (State of)

Countryside Social List (numerous towns) 1923

Cuba

Havana

El Libro Social de la Habana 1906

Directorio Social de Cuba—Havana 1919

Guia Social 1930

Habana Social 1931

District of Columbia

Washington, D.C.

Washington Society Directory 1886

Washington Elite List 1889–1918

Blue Book of Washington 1923–27, 1944, 1957–65, 1973–86

Preferred List and Society Address Book of Washington, D.C., and Vicinity 1920–21

Social Record 1917

Social List 1932–85

Social Register 1901–76

Florida

Boca Raton

Social Register of Boca Raton 1971, 1974–77

Jacksonville

Social Register 1904, 1909

Blue Book or Social Directory 1914

Miami

Social Register and Blue Book 1930

Society Register of Greater Miami 1931–71

Palm Beach

Palm Beach Social Directory 1923–24, 1929

Palm Beach Social Index and Social Index of Winter Resorts (includes Miami Beach and others) 1925–84

Pompano Beach

Social Register of Pompano Beach 1971–77

Southern Florida, Gulf Coast, Bahamas

Society Directory (includes Bahamas, Boca Raton, Delray Beach, Fort Lauderdale, Gulf Coast, Miami, Palm Beach, and Pompano Beach) 1961

Social List of Fort Lauderdale 1955–77

Social Index—Florida (Palm Beach, Miami, and other Resorts) 1932–36

St. Petersburg

Social Register of St. Petersburg, Clearwater, and Belleair 1926

Tampa

Tampa Blue Book 1913–14

Georgia

Atlanta

Atlanta Society Blue Book 1901

Blue Book—A Social Register 1930

Atlanta, Civic, Social and Cultural Register (includes suburbs) 1955

Savannah

Savannah Social Directory 1902, 1906

Valdosta

Social Register 1908

Iowa

Spirit Lake

Lake Region Blue Book and Club Directory of Spirit Lake and Vicinity 1906

Illinois

Illinois Blue Book 1955

Chicago

Reversed Directory of the Elite of Chicago 1880–83

Elite Directory and Club List of Chicago 1884–95

Ladies' Exclusive Directory and Calling List 1895–96

Chicago Blue Book 1890–1916

Bradley Blue Book 1921

Blue Book of the Chicago Community 1935

Chicago Social Register 1896–1976

Cook County

Blue Book of the Grocers, Bakers, and Flour and Feed Dealers of Cook County, Illinois 1886

Decatur

Society Blue Book 1917

Evanston

Evanston's Official Blue Book 1907

Illinois and Missouri

Directory of American Society, Illinois and Missouri 1929–30

Indiana

Indianapolis

Red Book of Indianapolis 1895

Dau's Blue Book 1910–18, 1925

South Bend

Blue Book, South Bend and Nearby Cities 1909

Kentucky

Louisville

Louisville Blue Book 1923

Louisiana

New Orleans

Society's Ready Reference 1899, 1909

Social Register 1912–27, 1950, 1952, 1954

Social and Hereditary Directory of New Orleans 1976–77

Massachusetts

Beverly

Blue Book of Beverly (includes Manchester and Magnolia) 1893

Boston

A Complete and Comprehensive List of the Residents of West–End, Back Bay, and Brookline 1890

Social Register, Boston 1890–1975

Clark's West–End Blue Book 1872

Boston Blue Book 1878–1937

Red Book and Directory of the Elite of Boston 1879

Elite of West–End and Back Bay 1890

Boston Suburban Blue Book (includes Allston, Brighton, Brookline, Cambridge, Malden, Melrose, and Roxbury) 1895

Brighton

Blue Book of Brighton 1891

Brookline

Blue Book of Brookline 1865, 1887–1932

Cambridge

Blue Book of Cambridge (or *Cambridge Blue Book*) 1887–1928

Suburban Best Blue Book (includes Brookline, Malden, Medford, Newton, and Somerville) 1892

Cape and South Shore

Cape . . . Blue Book and Social Register (includes several towns) 1923–40

Dorchester

Blue Book of Dorchester 1885, 1896–1910

Suburban Blue Book (includes Brookline, Cambridge, Newton) 1894

Holyoke

Holyoke Blue Book 1889

Lynn

Blue Book—Lynn 1897

Malden (see also Boston)

Blue Book of Malden and Vicinity 1892

Blue Book and House Guide 1893

Blue Book 1895, 1900–12

Medford

Blue Book 1899

Nantasket

Nantasket Blue Book 1884

Newton

Newton, Massachusetts Blue Book 1887

Blue Book of Newton 1890–1927

North Shore

Blue Book of North Shore 1896–1916

North Shore Blue Book and Social Register 1917, 1936

Who's Who Along the North Shore 1907–19

Oak Bluffs

Blue Book and Directory of Cottages of Oak Bluffs (includes Martha's Vineyard) 1921

Oak Park and River Forest Social Register 1932

Somerville

Blue Book 1897, 1901, 1906–10

South Shore

Blue Book 1903–17, 1922

Springfield

Blue Book 1889

Springfield and Holyoke Blue Book 1899

Dau's Blue Book (includes suburban towns) 1909–19, 1925

Waltham

Blue Book 1896

Wellesley—Western Massachusetts

Blue Book 1904, 1922, 1924–25

Winchester

Society Blue Book 1895, 1905, 1912–16, 1924, 1926

Worchester

Dau's Blue Book (includes suburban towns) 1899, 1909–26

Maryland

Baltimore

Baltimore Society Directory and Ladies Visiting and Shopping Guide (lists only women) 1878

Jewish Social Directory (includes Washington, D.C. and Norfolk) 1908–19. F189 .BIJ58

Ladies' Society Directory of Baltimore City and Suburbs 1888–89

Society Visiting List 1889–90

Social Register 1892–1976

Baltimore Society Address Book 1900

Jewish Social Directory 1920

Dilatory Domiciles, Baltimore Social Register 1965 (Jan.)

Society Visiting List for the Season of [years] 1890–1983

Guilford

Guilford Blue Book (includes Homeland Northwood) 1938

Roland Park (Baltimore County)

Roland Park Blue Book 1908–36

Blue Book of Roland Park (includes suburbs) 1976, 1979–80

Maine

Who's Who at the Leading Watering Resorts in Maine 1919

Mexico

Blue Book of Mexico 1901

Michigan

Michigan Social Register 1938, 1941, 1946, 1972–75

Detroit

Detroit Blue Book (includes Grand Rapids and suburbs) 1885, 1893–1901, 1909–17

Detroit Social Register 1918–27

Social Register 1920–53

Blue Book of Young Detroit 1935, 1937

Grand Rapids (see also Detroit)

Grand Rapids Society Blue Book 1899, 1900

St. Paul

Dual City Blue Book 1887–1917, 1923

Social Register 1907–27

Social Directory and Who's Who in the Twin Cities 1933

Missouri (see also Illinois)

Kansas City

Kansas City Blue Book 1890, 1912, 1914

Blue Book and Club Directory 1910

Kansas City Social Directory 1924

Social Directory 1927–48, 1962

St. Louis

St. Louis Blue Book 1891–1908, 1913–16

Social Register, St. Louis 1903–76

St. Joseph

Social Register 1903

North Carolina

North Carolina Social Register 1963, 1966

Asheville

Asheville Area Personages 1966

Charlotte

Charlotte Blue Book and Business Directory 1913

Nebraska

Nebraska Blue Book 1958

Omaha

Omaha Blue Book 1895, 1898

New Jersey

Dau's New Jersey Suburban Blue Book 1910, 1912, 1916

New Jersey Social Record 1927, 1931, 1933

New Jersey Social Register 1927

Morristown

Society Directory 1905–12

Morristown Social Lists 1944, 1950–52

Newark

Elite Directory 1886

Blue Book 1908

Ramsey

Who's Who in Ramsey, New Jersey 1958, 1960, 1963

Roxbury

Blue Book of Roxbury, Jamaica Plain, and West Roxbury 1897–1911

Roxbury, Dorchester Blue Book 1913–15

Short Hills

Social List 1951

Somerset Hills

Social List 1948–49

The Oranges

Blue Book of the Oranges, New Jersey 1892

Social Register, the Oranges and Montrose 1892–93

Social Directory, the Oranges and Montrose 1902, 1904

Blue Book (includes Bloomfield, Glenridge, Montclair, Morristown) 1903

Blue Book—the Oranges and Suburban Towns (includes Bernardsville, Chatham, Madison, Short Hills, Summit) 1908

Nevada

Lancaster County

Blue Book 1924–25

New York

Visiting List 1879–86

Society 1886

New York Society List 1886–1912

Dau's New York Blue Book 1907–37

Elite of New York 1915

Dau's New York Suburban Blue Book 1917, 1919

Directory of American Society—New York State and Metropolitan District 1929–30

Albany

Society Directory of Albany, New York 1889

Society Directory (includes Troy) 1890–92

Albany and Troy Blue Book (includes suburbs) 1895

Albany Society Directory 1896

Albany and Troy Society Blue Book (includes suburbs) 1903, 1910–25

Brooklyn

Brooklyn Blue Book (includes Wellesley and Weston) 1896–1929, 1939, 1941–51

Brooklyn Heights

Brooklyn Heights Blue Book 1940

Brooklyn, Long Island

Lain's Brooklyn Elite Directory 1877–95

Lain's and Healy's Elite Directory of Brooklyn 1897–1910

Buffalo

Social Register, Buffalo 1903–76

Buffalo Society Directory 1880

Buffalo Elite Directory 1882

Buffalo Blue Book 1909–26

East Hampton

East Hampton Social Guide 1932

Essex County

Essex County Social Register 1930

Hamptons

Social Directory of the Hamptons 1956–57

Blue Book of the Hamptons 1956–67

Long Island

Long Island Society Register 1926–29

New York—Long Island Social Record 1932

Manhattan

Manhattan Visiting List 1900, 1902

New York City

Elite Directory 1875–81, 1892, 1897–1908

Lain's New York and Brooklyn Elite Directory 1882

Phillip's Elite Directory 1894, 1896

New York Hebrew Select Directory and Visiting List 1896

Society List 1887

Social Register 1888–1981

Official Society Directory of New York, Brooklyn, Jersey City and Newark 1892

Cafe Society Register 1941

Visiting Index of Social Register 1900, 1907–19

Rochester

Dau's Rochester Blue Book and Suburban Towns 1909–18, 1923, 1926

Syracuse

Syracuse Blue Book (includes suburban towns) 1889, 1895, 1910–25

Westchester County

Social List (includes adjacent towns) 1913, 1915, 1930–32

Ohio

Ohio Blue Book 1947

Cincinnati

Society Blue Book and Family Directory 1879

Graphic Blue Book of Cincinnati 1886

Who's Who?, A Social Register 1892

Blue Book of Cincinnati 1894, 1898–1908, 1949–57, 1973–79

Social Register, Cincinnati and Dayton 1910–1976

Cleveland

Cleveland Social Directory 1885

Directory of Civic and Welfare Activities of Cleveland 1923

Cleveland Blue Book 1888–1915, 1922–35, 1942–70

Cleveland Jewish Society Book 1915, 1917, 1926

Columbus

Dau's Columbus Blue Book (includes suburbs) 1908–19

Dayton (see also Cincinnati)

Dayton Society Blue Book 1900

Toledo

Toledo Social and Family Directory 1888

Hubbell's Blue Book 1899

Toledo Social Register 1928

Oregon

Blue Book and Social Register of Oregon 1953

Portland

Blue Book—Society and Club Directory 1893–1915

Blue Book Social Register 1939

Portland Social Register—Seattle Social Register 1914–27

Pennsylvania

Bellevue

Red Book and Business Directory (includes suburbs) 1904

Harrisburg

Dau's Harrisburg and Reading Blue Book 1908

Philadelphia

West-End Visiting Directory 1872

Philadelphia Blue Book 1881–1921

Philadelphia Blue Book, Elite Directory, and Club List 1924, 1926

Philadelphia Club Directory 1893–1902

Philadelphia Red Book 1879–80, 1886–91

Social Register 1892–1976

Pittsburgh

Pittsburgh and Allegheny Blue Book 1887–1907

Pittsburgh Blue Book 1909–70

Prominent Families 1911–12

Pittsburgh Jewish Society Book 1917

Pittsburgh Social Secretaire 1920

Society and Business Directory 1921

Social Directory for Greater Pittsburgh 1904–05

Social Register 1904–76

Reading (see Harrisburg)

Scranton and Wilkes Barre

Scranton and Wilkes Barre Blue Book 1908–12

Scranton Blue Book and Elite Directory 1893

Pennsylvania, New Jersey, and **Delaware**

Directory of American Society, Pennsylvania, New Jersey, Delaware 1929–30

Rhode Island

Newport

Newport Blue Book 1884

Social Register 1887

Newport Social Index 1903, 1909–46

Who's Who in Newport, Watch Hill, Narragansett Pier, and Jamestown 1916

Who's Who in Bar Harbor and Newport 1917

Who's Who in Newport, Watch Hill, and Jamestown 1918–19

Pawtucket

Pawtucket Social Register 1907

Providence

Dau's Blue Book of Providence and Suburban Towns 1909–18, 1923, 1926

Providence Social Register 1907–26

Tennessee

Memphis

Social Register of Memphis 1951

Nashville

Social Directory 1911

Social Register 1953

Texas

Beaumont

Standard Blue Book of Texas—Edition Deluxe of Beaumont 1908

Dallas

Dallas Blue Book 1931, 1940

Dallas Social Register 1941, 1943, 1953, 1968, 1970

Fort Worth

Fort Worth Social Directory 1933, 1957, 1959

Houston and Galveston

Houston Blue Book—Galveston Blue Book 1896

Social Register of Houston 1950, 1965–75

South Texas

Standard Blue Book, USA, South Texas Edition 1929

United States

Directory of American Society (includes several western and southern states)

Directory of American Society (includes several states) 1929

Directory of American Society (includes New England states) 1929–30

List of Society 1954–56

National Social Directory 1957–67, 1979

Social Directory of the United States 1928

Social Register (several large cities) 1890–1987

Social Register Locator (several large cities) 1907–76

Social Register—[year] 1977–86

Southern Social Register (includes cities in southeast United States) 1950, 1952

Southwest Blue Book 1919–86

Utah

Salt Lake City

Salt Lake City Blue Book 1902, 1907

Virginia

Richmond

Richmond Elite Directory 1893

Social Register of Richmond, Etc. (includes Atlanta, Augusta, Charleston, and others) 1909–15

Southern City Social Register (includes Atlanta, Augusta, and Savannah) 1910–14

Vermont

Vermont Register and Farm Almanac 1834

Washington

Seattle (see also Portland, Oregon)

Social Blue Book of Seattle 1926, 1947, 1954, 1958, 1961, 1965

Spokane

Spokane Blue Book 1909

Wisconsin

Blue Book 1897–1913, 1948

Milwaukee

Society Blue Book 1884, 1891, 1894–95

Milwaukee Social Register and Directory 1933

West Virginia

West Virginia Blue Book 1937, 1955, 1957

Wheeling

Wheeling Blue Book 1901

Land Records and Maps

Land Records

Once an ancestor has been located in a federal or state census or in a city or country directory, the next step is to pinpoint his or her actual place of residence. The prime sources for this data are records indicating land ownership. These are documents describing an original grant of land, transfer of property by executing and recording of deeds, lists of those who paid real and personal property taxes, and land ownership maps.

Documents pertaining to land ownership are found in county courthouses, state archives, federal land management offices, and the National Archives. Some have been abstracted, compiled, and published by government agencies or private individuals. The Library of Congress has no original land ownership documents, but it does have publications helpful to researchers attempting to verify ancestors as early landowners. Several pertinent publications are listed in this chapter, and some are listed in chapters 9 through 15, which cite key resources on regional and state levels. Some details are provided here to help the reader locate maps and use materials in the Geography and Map Division Reading Room of the Library of Congress.

Any search for land records in the United States will be more meaningful if the researcher has at least a general idea of how an individual came into possession of a piece of land, any surviving record of transactions, and the logical places to look for those records. With those in mind, the following discussion is offered as background.

Methods of Obtaining Land in the United States

Foreign Grants

In the colonial era, European monarchs, principally in England, France, and Spain, controlled the granting of land in the colonies they claimed. Notwithstanding any dubious claim of ownership by a tribe of Indians, the monarchs handled their largess in various ways. Some authorized their appointed governor to grant tracts to individuals or groups. Some authorized "proprietors" to sell or give land, as in the "Granville Grants" of North Carolina. Other monarchs relinquished control completely in favor of one person, such as William Penn, who made grants to settlers after negotiating with the Indians to assure clear and valid title for new owners. Supplementing grants, some settlers received land by virtue of merely coming to this county and claiming a "headright" that was promised by the mother country to encourage settlement.

Creation of Towns

In New England a group of citizens with a common interest (usually religion) sometimes banded together and petitioned the colony for a particular area in order to establish a town. Certain tracts were set aside for a common meeting place and for other communal purposes, and the remainder was granted or sold to individual residents. Each New England town kept its own land records, similar in nature to the county records in other parts of the country.

Private Land Claims

Most of the land grants granted by England, France, and Spain were authentic grants and properly recorded in colony records, but some were invalid or difficult to prove. When the United States government was established, lands held by colonial settlers based on documents issued by foreign governments had to be analyzed for approval or disapproval. Land claims commissions and special land courts were available for that purpose. This was especially true in the Southwest, as well as Texas, Florida, Missouri, Louisiana, and California. Many claimants took their problems directly to Congress to obtain relief from negative findings by a claims commission. Others went to court to press their claims, and all of these legal actions are matters of record.

Military Bounty

Following a custom of the British during colonial wars, our emerging nation offered bounty land to those who would serve in the Continental Army. Some states having unsettled western territory also gave bounties in those regions to encourage enlistment. These states included Massachusetts, New York, Pennsylvania, Maryland, Virginia, Georgia, and the Carolinas. Of these, Massachusetts gave land in an area that became Maine; Virginia granted land in what was to become Kentucky and Ohio. The federal government created military districts in Ohio where it awarded land for Revolutionary War service. In 1830 "warrants" issued for land in that district could be exchanged for "scrip" (a form of currency), which entitled the bearer to claim land in other areas of Ohio, Indiana, and Illinois where land had not already been granted. Both bounty warrants and scrip could be reassigned to others, and the majority of the western settlers were people who bought warrants from a veteran or a speculator who had bought up large numbers of them for resale.

Although veterans with warrants or scrip who had no intention of claiming land in the West profited from sales of their documents, the practice was a bonanza for many who amassed huge land holdings and then waited for inflation to reap profits. Such speculation was legal and merely a continuation of the practice engaged in by some of this country's earlier founders, including George Washington and Benjamin Franklin. Also, there were speculators who engaged in massive fraud to obtain titles to lands in the public domain. Both they and some government officials conspired to issue and reissue certificates of sale for those bogus titles to unsuspecting purchasers. Probably the most notorious of these schemes was the Yazoo Land Fraud of 1795. The state of Georgia sold 30 million acres to four companies at one and a half cents per acre. After the legislature nullified the sales, the courts were flooded with claims by third parties who had bought the invalid titles and who insisted on retaining ownership. Records of such claims and settlements may be ferreted out from court records by those with patience to pursue them.

After the War of 1812, the federal government created a military district in Illinois for veterans of that war. When all warrants had been granted, two smaller military districts in Missouri and Arkansas were created. Warrants for land in those areas could also be exchanged for scrip entitling the bearer to purchase land wherever there was a General Land Office.

Veterans of the Mexican War of 1846–48 also became eligible for bounty land warrants or scrip, but no separate military district was created for them. The claims could be made at any General Land Office.

Special legislation enacted during the years 1850 to 1855 rewarded veterans of all wars from 1790 to date (including the many Indian wars) who had not yet taken advantage of bounty land offers to which they might be entitled. Grants of 160 acres were made available, and any veteran who had previously received a bounty of less than 160 acres could receive a supplemental grant for the balance due him under the new law. These laws also provided bounties for certain veterans who had not previously qualified, including some classes of militiamen, participants in certain battles, naval personnel, and anyone who had served in the Revolutionary War. The overwhelming number of bounty land grants awarded in this country were the result of this special legislation—the last bounty land legislation to be enacted in this country.

State Grants

Following the American Revolution and the demise of foreign control of land in the United States, each newly created state took on the role of land conveyor. Each of the thirteen original states, plus Maine, Vermont, West Virginia, Kentucky, Tennessee, and later most of Texas and Hawaii, established land offices to regulate the disposition of lands within their borders not subject to federal control. Disputed state borders over which long court battles ensued resulted in land records that may be found in either or both land offices of the states involved. Grants were often made by the state to wealthy or influential citizens who operated their own large plantations or who subdivided the acreage and resold it. Other state grants were made directly to prospective homeowners. Each was based on a personal petition, with a final decision being made by officials of the state land office. These petitions described the tracts using a system of "metes and bounds" (meaning measurement and naming). This system involved starting at a corner of the property identified by a geographical or physical feature (such as a large oak, a pile of stones, a water course, or a corner of a line bordering on a neighbor's land) and then proceeding around the perimeter using compass points and a measuring system expressed in "poles," "rods," or similar terms until the starting point was joined. The result was entered into government records and became the legal description.

Federal Grants

Early in the nineteenth century the federal government began surveying land obtained through negotiation, annexation, or conquest. Such land included the Louisiana Purchase from France in 1803 and the Cession of East Florida by Spain in 1819. Surveying was done by mapping the county into grids (separated by "principal meridian" lines), then by "range lines," and then by townships, each a mile square and containing thirty-six sections of 640 acres each. These township boundaries are often discernible by motorists who notice that rural roads occur exactly one mile distant from each other—separating the townships. Comprising more than a billion acres, these townships were in the public domain, and distribution was made under several legislative acts in order to encourage settlement as soon as new areas were surveyed. A legal description of a tract of land in the public domain states includes a section number, a township, range line, principal meridian, and the number of acres in the tract or parcel. Federal land offices were established to aid the new settlers, and they distributed land operating under various systems as described below.

Direct Sales. Much of the public domain land was sold on credit to individual purchasers at $2 per acre. Beginning in 1820, terms were strictly cash, but the price per acre was reduced to $1.25. Some of the early settlers who "squatted" on land not yet available for purchase were given clear title under the so-called "preemption laws" enacted by Congress for just that purpose.

Grants to States. The federal government was generous in turning over vast lands to individual states that could either grant or sell the land. Such federal donations were usually made in the interest of national expansion and to encourage settlement and commercial interests in opening the West. When arid lands in the desert were not desired, and where the land was unfit for agriculture, the federal government took steps to let the state dispose of it. Ironically, many acres of swamp land reverted to the state more as a result of "smart politicking" than because of the presence of any standing water.

Railroad Grants. In an effort to encourage the railroads to extend their lines across the Mississippi and to connect the principal settlements already established in the Midwest, the federal government often granted a right-of-way through the public domain. Alternate sections for a distance of six miles on both sides of a proposed roadbed were granted to railroad companies that could in turn sell the unneeded sections. Alternate sections not granted were sold by the government at twice the normal price of $1.25 per acre, thus assuring that the government actually lost no money on the overall program. Many ancestral homes are still situated along the routes of those railroads or near the towns that sprang up around them.

Homestead Law of 1862. Another means of encouraging settlement in the public domain came after the passage of the homestead law in 1862. After passage of this law no federal bounty land grants were made to Civil War veterans or, for that matter, veterans of any subsequent war. All unclaimed land that had been surveyed and designated as a separate tract was available to any citizen or any foreigner who filed his "declaration of intention" to become a naturalized citizen. In return, he was required to pay a small fee at the nearest General Land Office and to remain on the land for a period of five years while building a shelter and making other improvements. At the end of five years he could file a "proof" detailing his residence and improvements, pay the final fee, and the land became his.

Transfer of Lands

All of the above described ways of obtaining real property in the areas of the United States never before owned by a white settler were actually first-time deeds. Once a grant or patent was obtained, the land was held "in fee simple" and the owner could dispose of it in any fashion he chose. In the case of intestate estates (no will), the next of kin of the decedent could inherit the property. All such transactions were recorded by the Registrar of Deeds (or other designated official) at the local courthouse. In each instance a deed was made, filed, and recorded. Indexes of names of "grantors" and "grantees" of each transaction are also part of the official records. One other method of transferring property was the "sheriff's sale" at the courthouse door after an owner failed to pay his real estate taxes. The winner at such a sale or auction then paid all back taxes and received clear title.

Location of the Records

Following English custom, an official record was made of all land legally obtained in the colonies and subsequently in the United States. It is theoretically possible to trace all various owners of any piece of land in the nation, and land abstract companies thrive on doing just that—providing proof of valid titles each time a piece of land is transferred to a new owner. For historians and genealogists, the most reliable and consistent family records are documents prepared at the time a piece of land was transferred. The concomitant recordings of these transactions, either in state offices (usually by the Secretary of State) or in a county courthouse or town hall, are valuable to the researcher. It must be remembered, however, that many courthouses have burned and the records have vanished. The administrative process of obtaining a first title to a piece of land involved several steps. First, the prospective landowner filed a petition for a particular tract with the government official in charge of distributing land. If approved, the official issued a warrant to the petitioner that ordered a survey be made of the land. When that was done a survey or plat was drawn up showing the exact location and proving that the land had not previously been surveyed for someone else. When those steps were completed without conflict, a grant or patent was issued, which became the official document proving ownership of that land. Any of these documents, or more probably a record of their issuance, may be located. These documents include name of the petitioner, exact location of the land, and the pertinent dates.

Land obtained in the public domain required the filing of an application and payment of a fee, all recorded at the General Land Office. Staff in those offices recorded each transaction in a chronological journal, an abstract book, and on a plat. In addition, the "final proof" required in homesteaded property was also recorded.

The journals, tract books, and plats have been sent to the federal Land Management Office. If one knows the legal description of a piece of land situated in the public domain or knows approximately where and when it was acquired, staff members may be able to provide the date it was acquired. All states east of the Mississippi, plus those states bordering the west bank of the Mississippi, have transferred their records to the Eastern States Land Management Office, Bureau of Land Management, 350 South Pickett Street, Alexandria, VA 22304. For states west of the Mississippi River write to the Land Management office for the state of interest.

Alaska
555 Cordova Street
Anchorage, AK 99501

Arizona
2400 Valley Bank Center
Phoenix, AZ 85073

California
Federal Building, Room E-2841
2800 Cottage Way
Sacramento, CA 95825

Colorado
Colorado State Bank Building
1600 Broadway
Denver, CO 80202

Idaho
Federal Building, Room 398
550 West Fort Street
P.O. Box 042
Boise, ID 83724

Montana, North Dakota, and South Dakota
222 N. 32nd Street
P.O. Box 30157
Billings, MT 59107

Nevada
Federal Building, Room 3008
300 Booth Street
Reno, NV 89509

New Mexico, Oklahoma, and Texas
U.S. Post Office and Federal Building
P.O. Box 1449
Santa Fe, NM 87501

Oregon and Washington
729 N.E. Oregon Street
P.O. Box 2965
Portland, OR 97208

Utah
University Club Building
136 East South Temple
Salt Lake City, UT 84111

Wyoming, Kansas, and Nebraska
2515 Warren Avenue
P.O. Box 1828
Cheyenne, WY 82001

The land-entry case files of the land offices have been accessioned by the National Archives and deposited at the National Records Center in Suitland, Maryland. The mailing address is National Archives and Records Administration, Washington, DC 20408. The National Archives maintains name indexes of the land-entry papers for the years 1800 to 1908 for the states of Alabama, Alaska, Arizona, Florida, Louisiana, Nevada, and Utah, as well as for all public domain states after 1908.

Records of foreign grants or grants made by states may be found in state archives or other state offices. For a detailed description of where to find land records in all fifty states see William Thorndale, "Land and Tax Records," in *The Source: A Guidebook of American Genealogy,* cited below. That chapter is highly recommended to those about to make a serious search of land records in the United States.

Published Sources

Most research for land records must be undertaken at courthouses and the National Archives (in conjunction with the Land Management Offices). Several publications, however, provide quick access to lists of those who obtained first titles to land by grant from foreign countries, individual states, or through state or federal bounties for military service. The Library of Congress has many of those publications, and some representative ones are listed below. Others that cover only one state are listed in chapters 9 through 15, which provide key resources on a regional and state level. In addition to the publications listed here, the researcher will find many others by consulting the card and computer catalogs in the Library of Congress under the following headings:

Land Grants—[state]
Land Grants—[state—county]
Bounties—Military—[state]

Bowden, J.J. *Private Land Claims in the Southwest.* Houston: N.p., 1976. KF5675 .B6.

Brookes-Smith, Joan. *Master Index, Virginia Survey and Grants, 1776–1791.* Frankfort, Ky.: Kentucky Historical Survey, 1971. F450 .B76.

Burgner, Goldene F. *North Carolina Land Grants in Tennessee, 1778–1791.* Easley, S.C.: Southern Historical Press, 1981. F435 .B77.

Connor, Seymour V. *Kentucky Colonization in Texas.* Baltimore: Genealogical Publishing Co., 1983. F390 .C728.

Deville, Winston. *English Land Grants in West Florida: A Register for the States of Alabama, Mississippi, and Parts of Florida and Louisiana, 1766–1776.* Ville Platte, La.: Deville, 1986. F301 .D4.

Holcomb, Brent. *North Carolina Land Grants in South Carolina.* Columbia, S.C.: the author, 1980. F253 .H64.

Hutchinson, William T. *The Bounty Lands of the American Revolution in Ohio.* New York: Arno Press, 1979. JK5574 .A3.

Latham, Allen. *A Roll of the Officers in the Virginia Line of the Revolutionary Army, Who Have Received Land Bounty in the States of Ohio and Kentucky . . . Chillcothe, Ohio: Latham and Leonard, 1822.* Washington, D.C.: 1942. E263 .V8L3.

McMullin, Phillip W. *Grassroots of America . . . Land Grants and Claims.* Salt Lake City: Gendex Corp., 1972. J33 .M3.

Scott, Florence. *Royal Land Grants North of the Rio Grande, 1777–1821.* Rio Grande City, Tex.: La-Retama Press, 1969. F392 .R5S44.

Smith, Clifford N. *Federal Land Series . . . Land Patents Issued by the United States Government, With Subject, Tract, and Name Indexes (Virginia Military District of Ohio).* 4 vols. Chicago: American Library Association, 1972. KF5675 .A73S6.

Taylor, Virginia H. *Index to Spanish and Mexican Land Grants.* Austin, Tex.: General Land Office, 1976. HD211 .T4T28.

Thorndale, William. "Land and Tax Records." In *The Source: A Guidebook of American Genealogy,* edited by Arlene H. Eakle and Johni Cerny. Salt Lake City; Ancestry, Inc., 1984. CS49 S65.

Todd, Charles S. *Bounty Lands to the Regular and Volunteer Officers of the War of 1812.* Washington, D.C.: n.p., 1850. HD240 .T63.

Maps

Good family history is a study of people and how they lived at certain times and at certain places. The use of maps help to define and illustrate the places. While certain records may describe in words places of residence of an ancestor, a better sense of place is achieved if those words are converted into a drawing of a map. For example, when a town in a foreign country is located on a map, such things as the type of terrain, proximity to a large city, transportation routes, and waterways can be discovered. Similarly, locating a place in the United States on a map will show whether it was on one of the well-documented migration trails, along a railroad or river, in a mining area, in the mountains, or on a plain. References in tax records to water courses or addresses in city directories can be used to locate a specific place on a county map or a city ward map. Reproducing such map sections in a family history greatly enhances the story.

Gazetteers with descriptions of the location and origin of counties and towns are helpful, and many are in various reading rooms in the Library of Congress, including the Geography and Map Reading Room. See chapter 2 for a description of that room and how to use its facilities. Millions of maps and charts are available

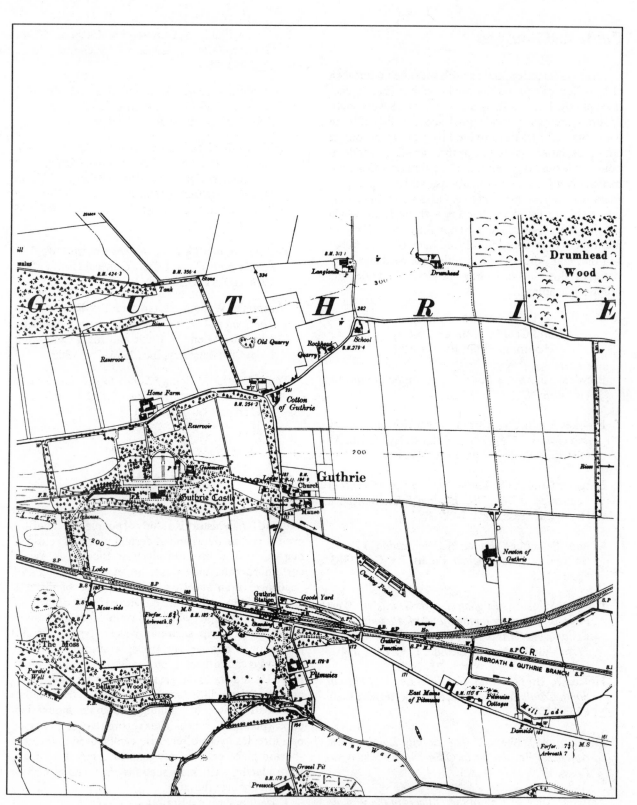

Section of map of Forfarshire, Scotland, showing Guthrie Castle.
Reprinted from Director General, Ordnance Survey Office (Southampton), *Forfarshire, Scotland*
(Washington, D.C.: Library of Congress Map Division, n.d.), sheet 39, N.E.

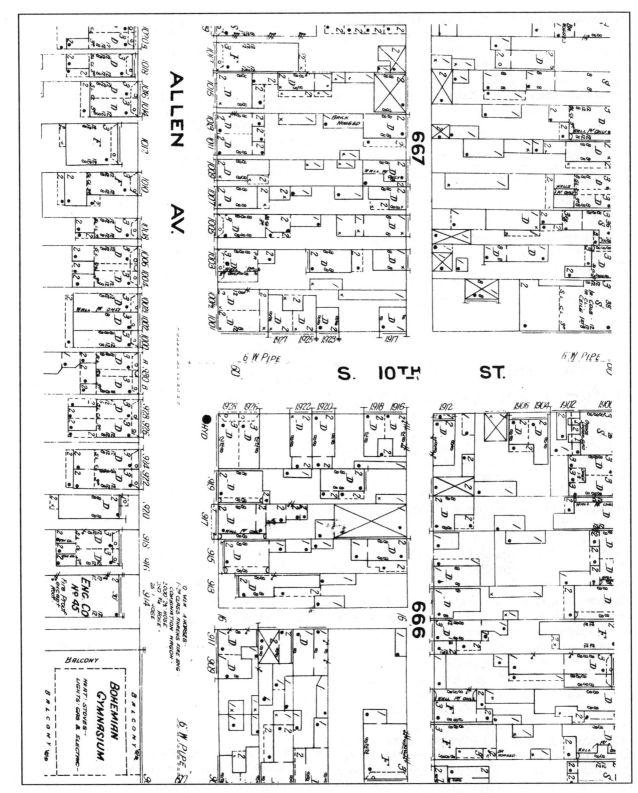

Section of Sanborn Fire Insurance Map—St. Louis, Missouri.

From Sanborn Map Company, *Insurance Maps of St. Louis* (N.p., 1909), vol. 4, sheet 23

for consultation in that room. Chief among its sources are the United States Geological Surveys, maps prepared for fire insurance companies and the United States Department of Agriculture, and military maps. A list of atlases is available in the publication cited below and at the reference desk of the Geography and Map Reading Room:

LeGear, Clara E., comp. Map Division, Library of Congress. *United States Atlases. A Catalog of National, State, County, City, and Regional Atlases in the Library of Congress and Cooperating Libraries.* Washington, D.C.: Library of Congress, 1953.

For maps of a location not specifically mentioned in one of the published finding aids ask the reference librarian for assistance. Since there is a variety of maps for any given area (both old and new), it saves time to discuss specific needs with the librarian.

Geographical Names Information System (GNIS)

On the east wall of the Geography and Map Reading Room there is a series of finding lists labeled GNIS, bound in blue covers, with one volume for each state and territorial possession of the United States. These are helpful in locating towns, villages, churches, schools, cemeteries, lakes, and other topographical features. These lists indicate a map number and the exact location according to the grid coordinates of that particular map. The data obtained from these lists will help the librarian find the map and possibly other maps of the same area. Various maps among their holdings are drawn to different scales and can be viewed as both large areas or small areas, thus more closely pinpointing the exact location of the place of interest.

The first three volumes of this series are labeled PPL, which stands for "populated places," and these are alphabetical lists of towns in the United States. The remaining volumes list not only the populated places but also names of major geographical features (cemeteries, churches, etc.). After locating the place or feature of interest on one of the lists, copy the following data and take them to a librarian: (1) name of the town or geographical feature, (2) identifying number (for the state and county), (3) coordinate numbers, and (4) map number.

If a county map is needed ask the librarian, but know the time span of interest, whether a highway map, topographical map, land ownership map, or other type.

Board of Geographical Names (BGN)

On shelves near the GNIS finding lists is a series of bound books labeled BGN, with each volume indicating the name of a foreign country. From these volumes find the same data as described in the GNIS series, plus the "area number." using that *number,* refer to a key at the front of the book to learn the *name* of the area. Using these area numbers and names will facilitate obtaining maps for those areas in the Library of Congress collections.

Specialized Maps

At the reference desk one can consult several aids that describe specialized maps available in the Geography and Map Reading Room. When a map of interest is found, note its title, number, or other identifying data and ask a librarian to obtain it. Descriptions of maps in some of these finding aids are summarized below.

Land ownership

Stephenson, Richard W. *Land Ownership Maps: A Checklist of Nineteenth Century United States County Maps in the Library of Congress.* Washington, D.C.: Library of Congress, 1967. Z6027 .U5U54.

This checklist describes 1,449 county maps that note names of individuals and the land they owned. These maps cover approximately one-third of the counties in the United States; most of them produced after 1840, but a few (primarily those for Virginia and Pennsylvania) are of an earlier date. Many of these maps are of Texas counties, but all states except Wyoming are represented.

Ward maps

Shelley, Michael H., comp. *Ward Maps of United States Cities. A Selective Checklist of Pre-1900 Maps in the Library of Congress.* Washington, D.C.: Library of Congress, 1975. Z6028 .U572.

This finding aid contains most of the ward maps in the Library of Congress collections and covers the period 1790 to 1899. Since it is difficult to locate a person or family in the census of a major city because of the large population, the street address and ward number is often helpful. Be aware that ward numbers were changed from time to time. Consult a ward map for the approximate time of the census you wish to search. If a city directory does not identify the ward number, consult a ward map at the Library of Congress or the National Archives. Use the ward number to obtain the census enumeration district and save a great deal of time.

The booklet cited above describes the date a map was prepared and the census to which a particular ward map is related. Ward maps are available for the twenty-five most populous cities in 1880, plus ten others, as follows:

Albany, N.Y.
Allegheny, Pa.
Atlanta, Ga.
Baltimore, Md.
Boston, Mass.
Brooklyn, N.Y.
Buffalo, N.Y.
Charleston, S.C
Chicago, Ill.
Cincinnati, Ohio
Cleveland, Ohio
Columbus, Ohio
Denver, Colo.
Detroit, Mich.
Hartford, Conn.
Indianapolis, Ind.
Jersey City, N.J.
Kansas City, Mo.
Louisville, Ky.
Memphis, Tenn.
Milwaukee, Wis.
Minneapolis, Minn.
New Haven, Conn.
New Orleans, La.
New York, N.Y.
Newark, N.J.
Philadelphia, Pa.
Providence, R.I.
Richmond, Va.
Rochester, N.Y.
St. Louis, Mo.
St. Paul, Minn.
San Francisco, Calif.
Washington, D.C.

Urban Building Maps

The Sanborn Map Company, Pelham, New York, produced thousands of maps for fire insurance companies that were used to evaluate risk factors and to set premium rates for individual buildings. These maps date from 1867 to modern times but are no longer being published. They show in great detail the location of commercial, industrial, and residential buildings of 12,000 cities and towns. Useful information such as type of construction, location of windows, fire walls, square feet of space, proximity to fire hydrants or hoses, as well as house and block numbers are shown. Using these maps to learn where an ancestor lived can provide clues regarding changing economic status and the available cultural facilities. In the Library of Congress, see *Fire Insurance Maps in the Library of Congress: Plans of North American Cities and Towns Produced by the Sanborn Map Company: An Alphabetical List*. Washington, D.C.: Library of Congress, 1981. Z663.35 .F57.

The Library of Congress has a collection of 50,000 fire insurance maps, comprising 700,000 individual sheets. Some have been reproduced on microfilm, and others are in bound volumes or stored as unbound sheets. Duplicates of many have been made and furnished to state archival libraries or historical societies, and these may be found locally.

The finding aid cited above lists maps alphabetically by name of state. Indexes by county, city, and town in the United States are provided. There are separate listings in the finding aid for whiskey warehouses, buildings in Canada, sugar warehouses in Cuba, and buildings in Mexico.

If the specific address of a building or house is known, refer directly to the bound index of streets that is available for several cities. These volumes are located on shelves near the BGN series, described above. They are alphabetically arranged by name of city, and for each city the listings are by street and block number. Listed among the buildings are apartments, churches, school, stores, and other buildings. For each entry the volume and shelf number for location of the fire insurance map is given. Cities indexed include:

Alabama
Birmingham
Mobile
Montgomery

Arkansas
    Little Rock
California
    Berkeley
    Fresno
    Glendale
    Long Beach
    Los Angeles
    Oakland
    Pasadena
    San Diego
    San Francisco
    San Jose
Colorado
    Denver
Connecticut
    Bridgeport
    Hartford
    New Haven
Delaware
    Wilmington
District of Columbia
    District of Columbia
    Specials and Federal Offices
    Suburban Maryland (see Maryland, Suburban Washington, D.C.)
Florida
    Jacksonville
    Tampa
Georgia
    Atlanta
    Macon
Hawaii
    Honolulu
Illinois
    Chicago
    Cook County
    Peoria
Indiana
    Evansville

Fort Wayne
    Indianapolis
Iowa
    Des Moines
Kansas
    Kansas City
Kentucky
    Louisville
Louisiana
    Baton Rouge
    New Orleans
    Shreveport
Maryland
    Baltimore
    Suburban Washington, D.C.
Massachusetts
    Boston
    New Bedford
    Springfield
    Worcester
Michigan
    Detroit
    Flint
    Grand Rapids
Minnesota
    Minneapolis
    St. Paul
Missouri
    Kansas City
    St. Louis
Nebraska
    Lincoln
    Omaha
New Jersey
    Camden
    Elizabeth
    Hudson
    Newark
    Paterson
    Trenton

New York
  Brooklyn
  Buffalo
  Nassau County
  New York City
  Borough of the Bronx
  Borough of Manhattan
  Borough of Queens
  Borough of Richmond
  Rochester
  Schnectady
  Staten Island
  Syracuse
North Carolina
  Charlotte
  Winston-Salem
Ohio
  Cincinnati
  Cleveland
  Columbus
  Dayton
  Toledo
  Youngstown
Oklahoma
  Oklahoma City
  Tulsa
Oregon
  Portland
Pennsylvania
  Delaware County
  Erie
  Montgomery County
  Philadelphia
  Scranton
  Specials
  Streets
Rhode Island
  Pawtucket
  Providence
Tennessee
  Chattanooga

Knoxville
Memphis
Nashville
Texas
  Dallas
  Fort Worth
  Houston
  San Antonio
Utah
  Salt Lake City
Virginia
  Norfolk
  Richmond
Washington
  Seattle
  Spokane
  Tacoma
Wisconsin
  Milwaukee

Panoramic Maps of Cities

More interesting than useful are the panoramic maps of cities, or parts of cities, prepared by artists who portrayed a "bird's-eye view" drawn in perspective. The streets and major buildings were drawn as if they were photographed from the air. These are useful to supplement ward maps and fire insurance maps. They show the relationship between a downtown area and its neighboring residential area, and they help one to visualize the relative location of a particular building or physical feature. Such drawings were popular in the period following the Civil War and throughout the nineteenth century. They reflect the rapid growth of cities during that period, primarily in the East and the Midwest. See *Panoramic Maps of Cities in the United States and Canada: A Checklist of Maps in the Collections of the Library of Congress, Geography and Map Division.* 2d ed. Washington, D.C.: Library of Congress, 1984, Z6027 .U5L5, which maps alphabetically by state and city.

Maps of Explorers' Trails

Ladd, Richard S., comp. *Maps Showing Explorers' Routes, Trails, and Early Roads in the United States: An Annotated List.* Washington, D.C.:

Library of Congress, Map Division, 1962. Z6027 .U5U56.

This volume lists 300 maps, arranged according to the authority that prepared them. An index gives the places and other subjects covered, with item numbers. Each map is accompanied by at least a descriptive paragraph. Maps are available for many routes, trails, and roads, such as Chisholm Trail, Pony Express Route, Natchez Trace, Idaho and California State Road, Old Chicago Road, and Vincennes and Indianapolis Road.

Railroad Maps

During the growth of railway systems in the United States many agencies and companies produced maps showing the expansion of rail routes and land areas along those routes. This finding aid, cited below, available at the reference desk, is arranged in three sections: the United States as a whole, the five major regions of the United States, and individual states. There is at least one map for each state. The Library of Congress collections contain 622 maps that show historical growth of the railway systems; each is cited and indexed in this finding aid.

Modelski, Andrew M., comp. *Railroad Maps of the United States: A Selective Annotated Bibliography of Original 19th Century Maps in the Geography and Map Division of the Library of Congress.* Washington, D.C.: Library of Congress, 1975. Z6026 .R3U54.

These railroad maps were prepared by the United States Government and the Pacific Railroad. Some show large land areas, while others are merely strip maps of the rail routes themselves. The United States General Land Office maps show lands granted directly to the railroads and those granted to the states and then given to the railroads. In some cases the maps include the alternating sections of land along a railroad right-of-way (given to the railroad company to dispose of as it saw fit). Those sections not granted to the railroad were held by the government for direct sale to individual settlers at twice the going price for government land at the time. The railroad companies furnished copies of these maps to their European agents for use in recruiting foreign immigrants who might be induced to purchase and settle on "railway land" in the United States. Most companies established their own land offices, and the maps are useful for showing parcels of land sold and those still available.

A study of railroad maps may provide reasons why a city or a town was established, since railroads often influenced location of an agricultural or commercial center. From our limited vantage point, some towns grew up in areas with no discernable reason for their existence; a study of old railroad maps can help in identifying rail routes now long abandoned.

Treasure Maps

Included in this category are maps showing water and land sites where treasure has been or might be found, either in the form of knowledge or valuable objects.

Wise, Donald A., comp. *A Descriptive List of Treasure Maps and Charts in the Library of Congress.* 2d ed. Washington, D.C.: Library of Congress, 1933. Z6026 .T7U62.

Includes the following categories: (1) ship wreck sites, (2) abandoned towns (ghost towns), (3) lost or abandoned mines, and (4) frontier forts.

Civil War Maps

Most maps of the Civil War were prepared by engineers of the federal armed forces or by Northern commercial mapmakers, although some were prepared by Confederate agencies. These maps indicate the location of fortifications, major transportation routes, and often show positions of massed troops and their military campaigns.

Stephenson, Richard W., comp. *Civil War Maps: An Annotated List of Maps and Atlases in Map Collections of the Library of Congress.* Washington, D.C.: Library of Congress, 1961. Z6027 .U5U55.

This volume is arranged by state, county, and city, and it contains hundreds of titles of maps. Because of their great number, the section listing Virginia maps is specific by year, from 1861 to 1865. There is also an alphabetical list of maps arranged according to the battles fought in that state.

Major Jed Hotchkiss was a topographical engineer in the Confederate States of America who, after the war, became a consulting engineer at Staunton, Virginia. He prepared maps of Virginia and West Virginia areas, both during and after the Civil War.

LeGear, Clara E., comp. *The Hotchkiss Map Collection.* Washington, D.C.: Library of Congress, 1951. GA197 .H67U54.

CHAPTER 5

Records Showing Family Activity

After names of ancestors have been found in the censuses and possibly city directories and then located on a specific tract of land, the framework of a family history is established. At this point some feel the work is complete, content with a pedigree sheet, a few family group sheets, or a "family tree" with names and dates. Indeed, this is a laudable accomplishment, but usually the family sheets have missing spaces that beg to be filled. Furthermore, family and relatives will probably be no more than moderately interested if the only result is a chart or list of names and dates. Filling in the blanks requires more digging; not every fact will ever be known, but there are things about those ancestors that will create some interest on the part of even the more detached family members.

Unfortunately, many of the records refer mainly to males, but it is important to find as much as possible about the maternal side of every family. Also, one should learn everything possible about an ancestor's siblings and families—the so-called collateral lines. More importantly, discovery of such things as community events that influenced members of the family, their church affiliations, their occupations, their economic status, and the experiences they had in their local courts bring life to a family history. Write the family history in narrative form, with the pedigree sheets and family group sheets serving as reference guides to the story.

If possible, one should determine the religious affiliations of ancestors and seek any records that relate to them. Civil records in the courthouses could yield records of births, marriages, taxes, deaths, wills, or other probate records. Minute books of local courts are seldom indexed, and searching them can be tedious.

Finding a family Bible with pages listing births, marriages, and deaths is always a boon to the genealogist. Newspaper stories concerning the town or county where ancestors lived might mention their names if they participated in community events; one may find a marriage notice or obituary. Genealogical and historical society periodicals may also include their names.

Much of the above information must be obtained in person. Some data may be obtained through correspondence with county officials. There are many publications in the Library of Congress that can assist in searching for local records: indexes, finding aids, biographies, early newspapers, and periodicals are a few examples. All of these are discussed in this chapter.

Women

Historically, the woman's role has been primarily to produce offspring and take the lead in the family's cultural, religious, and educational pursuits. Unfortunately, activities of men have dominated the written record. Be aware of records that lead to information about the families of a woman. In early population censuses only "heads of household" were listed, which excluded women living with husbands, parents, and so forth. Beginning with the 1850 census, however, names of all individuals in a household were listed, and there may be clues there to a wife's maiden name. For example, her middle name may be her maiden name; one or both of her parents or an unmarried sister or brother may be living with her; families with her maiden name may be living in the same neighborhood; or some of her children may have her maiden name. Naturally, the best source for discerning a maiden name is a marriage record, and these frequently provide names of the bride's parents and their place of residence. Death notices in newspapers or obituaries may include names of parents and surviving relatives.

Once discovered, search for a maiden name in published genealogies of that family, indexes of other published genealogies, city directories, biographies, and local histories. While there are few published vital records in the Library of Congress, it pays to consult the card catalog in the "U.S. Local History Shelflist" for county and town records that may mention the wife's family.

Increasingly, accomplishments of women are included in collected biographies. Such publications usually herald leaders of the women's movement in the United States, and so they are not particularly valuable to the family historian. Those who wish to locate microfilmed reports of studies in such fields as women's rights, politics, history, and literature may obtain a helpful free guide at the Main Reading Room reference desk: "Women's Studies Resources in Microform at the Library of Congress."

There are many collections pertaining to women in the Manuscript Division of the Library of Congress. In particular, see the finding aid entitled "Women: Colonial and Pioneer," alphabetically arranged by state.

Hinding, Andrea, ed. *Women's History Sources: A Guide to Archives and Manuscript Collections in the United States.* 2 vols. New York: R. R. Bowker, 1979. Z7964 .U49W64.

This guide lists publications widely available in libraries, including the Library of Congress. A copy may be consulted at the Manuscript Division Reading Room reference desk. Volume 1 describes some 18,026 collections. Volume 2 is an index by individual family name or organization. Collections are arranged by state and numbered serially. Those collections housed in the Library of Congress are numbered 2,157 through 2,662 and appear under "District of Columbia."

Guides and Bibliographies

Begos, Jane DuPree. *Annotated Bibliography of Published Women's Diaries.* Pound Ridge, New York: Begos, 1977. Z7963 .B6B44.

Fischer, Clare B. *Breaking Through: A Bibliography of Women and Religion.* Berkeley, Calif.: Graduate Theological Union Library, 1980. Z7963 .R45F57.

Harriston, Cynthia E. *Women in American History: A Bibliography.* Santa Barbara, Calif.: American Bibliographic Center, Clio Press, 1979. Z7962 .H37.

Indexes and Lists of Prominent Women

Cameron, Mabel W., and Erma C. Lee, comps. *The Biographical Cyclopedia of American Women.* 2 vols. Reprint. Detroit: Gale Research Co., 1974. CT6360 .B5.

Volume 2 is an index.

Collins, Jimmie L. *Woman Artists in America—Eighteenth Century to the Present.* Chattanooga: n.p., 1973. N43 .C64.

James, Edward, ed. *Notable American Women, 1607–1950.* 4 vols. Cambridge: Harvard University Press, 1971. CT3260 .N57.

McCullough, Joan. *First of All: Significant "Firsts" by American Women.* New York: Holt, Rinehart, and Winston, 1980. HQ1412 .M24.

McHenry, Robert, ed. *Liberty's Women.* Springfield, Mass.: G & C Merriam Co., 1980. HQ1412 .L52.

Munro, Eleanor L. *Originals—American Women Artists.* New York: C.N. Potter, 1975. N6512 .M78.

Neidle, Cecyle S. *America's Immigrant Women.* Boston: Twayne Publishers, 1975. HQ1412 .N44.

Stineman, Esther. *American Political Women: Contemporary and Historical Profiles.* Littleton, Colo.: Libraries Unlimited, 1980. HQ1236 .S74.

Thomas, Dorothy [pseud.], ed. *Women Lawyers in the United States.* New York: Scarecrow Press, 1957. KF299 .W6T46.

Who's Who of American Women. Chicago: A.N. Marquis Co., 1961. E176 .W647.

Williard, Frances L., and Mark K. Livermore. *Woman of the Century.* Buffalo, N.Y.: Charles W. Moulton, 1893. E176 .W691.

Religious Groups and Church Records

Discovering an ancestor's religious affiliation or association presents a golden opportunity to ferret out family records, especially the ceremonial rites concerned with birth, baptism, marriage, death, and burial. In addition, the records may reveal the extent to which he or she participated in affairs of the institution. Transfers of membership and separations, voluntary or involuntary, are often recorded. Family relationships can often be deduced from church registers that provide both names of members as well as of their parents. Since relatives outside the immediate family were often also members of the same religious group, collateral lines may be explored. Even the native country or former residence of an immigrant ancestor can sometimes be found in these records.

Except in the case of the Puritans, who believed that marriage was strictly a civil matter, it was usually the church that sanctioned marriage, conducted the wedding ceremony, and kept the official records. Not until fairly recently has the official responsibility for recording births, marriages, and deaths been assumed by the county in which it took place.

Christenings, confirmations, and baptisms have always been conducted and recorded exclusively by church officials. Other major events kept by the church, such as membership lists, lists of officers, and its activities help in tracing an ancestor. If one's ancestor was a minister, priest, or rabbi, there is an excellent chance that a biographical sketch, obituary, or necrology can be found in a published work or in a church or synagogue archives.

Researchers seldom seek out these treasures because they are so difficult to find. Initially, there are two problems to solve before pursuing them. First, determine (or hypothesize) the ancestor's denominational preference and the names of churches to which he or she may have belonged (or attended). Second, discover where records for the appropriate time frame are located. Each of these problems is discussed below, with suggestions for solving them.

Determining the Denomination and Church

For families long allied with a particular denomination or religion, such as Roman Catholic, Lutheran, or Jewish, it may be simple to presume the religious affiliation of an ancestor. But, there are pitfalls in making such assumptions. For families with a variety of religious affiliations, especially with those more recently established denominations in the United States, the task can be more complex. Tracing one's ancestry to the colonial period narrows the possibilities because of the small number of established churches. Also, some colonies were peopled almost exclusively by persons of one particular faith. Each of the colonies tended to follow the pattern of its mother country and established an official religion for the colony. For example, in New England the Congregational Church was dominant, while in the South it was the Church of England (Protestant Episcopal). (Maryland belonged to this category, although it was known as a haven for Roman Catholics who were persecuted and branded as "Papists" in other colonies.) The early Dutch settlers in New York established the Dutch Reformed Church, still strong in that state and in neighboring New Jersey. In Pennsylvania the Society of Friends (Quakers), as well as various German denominations such as Lutherans, were strong even before William Penn arrived. After the American Revolution, state churches were abolished and the new Constitution provided for today's rigorous separation of church and state.

During the nineteenth century a large number of immigrants entered the United States, bringing with them their religious and ethnic traditions and settling among those with similar backgrounds. Thus Spanish, French, Irish, and Acadians ("Cajuns") continued their alliance with Roman Catholicism, as the Jews from South America, Portugal, and later Germany and Russia held fast to their Judaic heritage and established synagogues. When Scandinavians migrated into the upper Midwest, the Lutheran church became dominant in that area. Germans settling in Pennsylvania and along the Mississippi River established Lutheran, Mennonite, and other German denominations.

The dramatic proliferation of religious denominations in this country during the latter half of the nineteenth century and into the twentieth has made the genealogist's work more complex. Although many ancestors of the past five or six generations may yet cling to their European religious roots, it is very likely that they changed from one denomination to another —sometimes several times. In fact, many left their native homes primarily to make possible the separation from their church and to gain the right to worship in their own way, without interference from the community or members of their own family. Given the Constitutional right of "freedom of religion" in America, there emerged a trend toward affiliation with new churches whose primary message concerned entering the Kingdom of Heaven; adults must be "born again" and re-baptized. Many who adopted these new denominations were called Anabaptists (re-baptized). Such a doctrine gave rise to denominations such as Baptists (with early English backgrounds), Mennonites, Amish, and other groups with German backgrounds. Some Germans split into the German Reformed or German Evangelical Church, while those who migrated south often became Methodists. When the Scotch-Irish (Irish from Northern Ireland) came to America, they established Presbyterian churches.

Understanding the demographics of church membership in the United States can narrow the scope of one's search; at least, it permits searching for records of large denominations in the area where particular ancestors lived. In this regard, consult Edwin S. Gaustad's *Historical Atlas of Religions in America* (New York: Harper and Row, 1976. G1201 .E4G3). Gaustad traces the history and growth of the major denominations and augments the narrative with charts, maps, and graphs depicting the changing religious scene. By using his data, one can concentrate the search for church records on the most predominant religious bodies in a given region or state. The following data, based on Gaustad's work, lists denominations alphabetically:

1650 to 1700

Anglican	Lutheran
Baptist	Presbyterian
Congregational	Quaker
Dutch Reformed	Roman Catholic

1820 to 1850
(Add the following to those listed above)

Episcopal	Unitarian
Methodist	Universalist
German Reformed	

(The most rapid growth during this time
 period was among the Methodists and
Baptists.)

1900
(Add the following to those listed above)
Adventist
Assemblies of God
Church of God (all types)
Church of God in Christ
Evangelical United Brethren
Greek Archdiocese of
            North and South America
Mennonites (all types)
Pentecostal (all types)
Polish National Church
Russian Orthodox
Salvation Army

Not included in these lists are the hundreds of smaller denominations that often had only one church. African slaves or free negroes either joined the white church denominations (predominantly Baptist in the South) or established their own.

The Baptist denomination split into various factions, usually based on different interpretations of the Bible. During the Civil War, Baptists, Methodists, and Presbyterians were divided into northern and southern branches; only today are they beginning to reunite.

Jewish migration to the United States was minimal until the turn of the present century. At the time of the 1790 census, only 1,243 Jews were enumerated. These were principally of Portuguese descent and concentrated in New York, Newport, Philadelphia, Charleston, and Savannah. During the 1800s many others came from Russia, Rumania, Poland, Austria, and other European countries. By the mid-nineteenth century there were an estimated 250,000 Jews in America; in 1900 there were 1 million—mostly from Eastern Europe. By 1950 the estimate was 5 million. There are three branches: Orthodox (almost half of the membership), Reformed, and Conservative.

Location of Church Records

One of the best clues to help identify an ancestor's religious preference is to discover the name of the minister, priest, or rabbi who conducted the wedding ceremony, christening, confirmation, baptism, or bar mitzvah, or who presided at a burial. A gravestone in a church graveyard is another good indication of church membership. Obviously, letters of transfer, letter of admission, notices of dismissal, and certificates of membership are positive proof. Do not overlook personal diaries, journals, and letters, which may contain references to religious affiliation.

Many denominations kept extensive records; others did not. Some transferred their records (or copies) to a central denominational archive, while in other instances the minister or other church officer kept them. Many are in private hands and many were destroyed. A number of state and county historical societies and state archives have obtained copies of church records that are available to the public. There are church-supported colleges that act as repositories for the records of their own denomination. Published local histories often include a discussion of churches, often with lists of members appended. Family papers usually include marriage, baptismal, and death certificates, any of which might identify a minister and name a church. Civil marriage records denote no affiliation, but a church marriage record of siblings or children may provide clues to that family's church affiliation.

Use data from land records to locate an ancestor's place of residence, then study maps to learn what churches are located close at hand. There is a good chance that one's ancestor attended a nearby church if only for the sake of convenience.

Pertaining to a variety of denominations, the Library of Congress has several publications that may be helpful in searching for church records. The following are recommended:

Bowden, Henry W. *Dictionary of American Religious Biography.* Westport, Conn.: Greenwood Press, 1977. BL72 .B68.

Clark, Elmer T. *The Small Sects in America.* Rev. ed. New York: Abingdon-Cokesbury Press, 1949. BR515 .C57.

Dougherty, Richard W. "Church Records in the United States." In *The Source,* edited by Arlene H. Eakle and Johni Cerny. Salt Lake City: Ancestry, Inc., 1984.

Provides examples of church records, where they might be found, and a useful bibliography.

Gaustad, Edwin S. *Historical Atlas of Religions in America.* New York: Harper and Row, 1976. G1201 .E463.

Greenwood, Val. "Church Records." In *Researcher's Guide to American Genealogy.* Baltimore: Genealogical Publishing Co., 1973. CS47 .G73.

Hefner, Loretta L. *W.P.A. Historical Records Survey: A Guide to the Unpublished Inventories, Indexes, and Transcripts.* Chicago: Society of American Archivists, 1980. Z1236 .H437.

Johnson, Douglas W., et al. *Churches and Church Membership in the United States.* Washington, D.C.: Glenmary Research Center, 1974. BR526 .J64.

Kirkham, E. Kay. *Survey of American Church Records.* Logan, Utah: Everton Publishing Co., 1978. CD3065 .K5.

Library of Congress. *National Union Catalog of Manuscript Collections.*

Consult the index under the denomination and thereafter by place.

Mead, Frank. *Handbook of American Denominations.* 5th ed. Nashville: Abingdon Press, 1970. BR516.5 .M38.

Moyer, Elgin W., ed. *Who Was Who in Church History.* Chicago: Moody Press, 1968. BR1700 .M64.

National Council of Churches. *Yearbook of American and Canadian Churches.* Nashville: Abingdon Press, (annual). BR513 .Y4.

Lists church-related colleges by affiliation with a denomination.

Sprague, William B. *Annals of the American Pulpit.* 9 vols. New York: Arno Press and *The New York Times,* 1969. BR569 .S72.

Vol. 1, Tritarian Congregational; Vol. 2, Tritarian Congregational; Vol. 3, Presbyterian; Vol. 4, Presbyterian; Vol. 5, Episcopalian; Vol. 6, Baptist; Vol. 7, Methodist; Vol. 8, Unitarian Congregational; Vol. 9, Lutheran, Reformed Dutch, and others.

These volumes contain biographical sketches of ministers as well as names of those who contributed the information.

Sweet, William W. *Religion on the American Frontier, 1783–1840: A Collection of Source Materials.* 4 vols. New York: Cooper Square Publishers, 1964. BS63235 .S8.

Describes records of missionaries and diaries and journals of leaders in the Baptist, Methodist, Congregationalist, and Presbyterian churches.

Who's Who in Religion. Chicago: A.N. Marquis Co., 1976–77. BL2530 .U6W48.

Williams, Ethel L. *Biographical Directory of Negro Ministers.* Boston: G. K. Hall, 1975. BR563 .N4W5.

Card and Computer Catalogs

Finding publications describing church records in the card or computer catalog is a bit difficult. Over the years the Library of Congress has revised its criteria for catalog classification in minor ways, and the organization of a denomination dictates varying classifications of the publications pertaining to them.

When using the card catalog look first under the name of the denomination. Some typical headings are shown below as examples, but they may not apply in all cases. Experimentation is recommended.

Examples:

Methodists—[state]
Methodist church—history—biographical

Catholics—United States—history
Catholics—United States—biography
Episcopal church—history—biographical
Episcopalians—United States—history

When using the computer catalog various search strategies may be used. In the following examples note that the name of a city in which a church is located is enclosed in parentheses unless the city's name is an integral part of the church's name. In some instances, the city's name comes first, followed by the name of the church; in others the reverse order must be used. Try abbreviating the name of the city or state rather than spelling it out, which may result in a positive response. Note that the word "in" must be used between the name of the denomination and the name of the city or state.

Examples: (the letter "s" stands for "subject")

find s first presbyterian church (houston tex)

find s first presbyterian church of baltimore

find s alexandria va—first presbyterian church

find s st louis christ church cathedral

find s third baptist church (st louis mo)

find s methodists—arkansas

find s baptists in new england

find s catholics in maryland

find s catholics—United States—biography

find s lutherans—minnesota—st paul

find s nashville (tenn)—church history

Publications

Listed below are published works available at the Library of Congress that may provide names, or sources of names, by denomination. In addition, published lists of church members, both professional and lay, are sometimes found in local histories and in separately published copies of county or town records, all of which might be found in a local library or the Library of Congress.

Amish

Cross, Harold E., and Beulah Hostetler. *Index to Amish Genealogies*. Baltimore: Johns Hopkins University School of Medicine, 1970. Z5313 .U5C73.

Gingerich, Hugh F., and Rachel W. Kreider. *Amish and Amish Mennonite Genealogies*. Gordonville, Pa.: Pequea Publishing, 1986. E184 .M45G56.

Lutby, David. *The Amish in America: Settlements That Failed, 1840–1960*. Aylmer, Ontario, and LaGrange, Indiana: Pathway Publishers, 1986. E184 .N45L87.

Lists settlements by state. Gives names of original settlers and history of the settlements from their beginning to their abandonment. Also lists some burials.

Baptist

Cathcart, William. *The Baptist Encyclopedia*. Chester, Pa.: American Baptist Historical Society, 1951. BS6211 .C3.

Directory of Southern Baptist Churches, 1986 Update. Nashville: Sunday School Board of the Southern Baptist Convention, 1986. BX6462 .D57.

Encyclopedia of Southern Baptists, 1958. 4 vols. Nashville: Broadman Press, 1982. BX6211 .E5. Index to vols. 1–4: BX6211 .E5E53.

Graham, Balus J.W. *Baptist Biography*. Atlanta: Index Printing Co., 1917. BX6403 .G8.

Hamby, Robert P. *Brief Baptist Biographies, 1707–1982*. Hendersonville, N.C.: the author, 1982. BX6493 .H33.

Hunter, Mary M. *Southern Baptist Foreign Missionaries*. Nashville: Broadman Press, 1940. BX3700 .H8.

Ramond, John S. *Among Southern Baptists*. Vol. 1, *1936–1937*. Shreveport, La.: the author, 1936. BX6493 .A6.

Contains biographical sketches of pastors, foreign missionaries, and others.

Starr, Edward C. *A Baptist Bibliography: Being a register of Printed Materials By and About Baptists*. 25 vols. Rochester, N.Y.: American Baptist Historical Society, 1947–76 and continuing. Z7845 .B2S8.

Stewart, Walter S. *Early Baptist Missionaries and Pioneers*. Boston: Judson Press, 1925–26. BX6493 .S85.

Huguenot

Huguenots were European Protestants of any denomination. In Holland they followed Peter Waldo and were known variously as Waldenareans or Waldroons. Generally, they followed the teaching of John Calvin, and many later became either Lutherans, Presbyterians, Anglicans, Episcopalians, Quakers, Congregationalists, or Baptists. For 200 years they were branded as heretics and persecuted and killed by order of the Catholic church. In France, King Henry IV issued the famous Edict of Nantes in 1595, which forbade their worship but permitted them freedom of conscience. When the edict was revoked in 1685, large-scale massacres took place, and the Huguenots began fleeing France to other European countries, especially Holland and eventually the United States. There are a number of histories of the Huguenots; some helpful titles in the Library of Congress are listed below.

Bennett, Abram E. *Huguenot Migration.* N.p., 1984. E184 .H9B46.

Gannon, Peter S. *Huguenot Refugees in the Settling of Colonial America.* New York: Huguenot Society of America, 1985. E184 .H9H57.

Gives details of American settlements and lists the names of some early settlers.

Morand, Julia P.M. *Catalogue or Bibliography of the Library of the Huguenot Society of America.* 2d ed. Baltimore; Genealogical Publishing Co., 1971. Z7845 .H8H8.

National Huguenot Society. *Register of Huguenot Ancestors.* Washington, D.C.: the society, 1945. E184 .H9C6.

Lists those persons who qualified as Huguenot ancestors. In addition to the members, three appendixes list others who did not qualify because they were born in the United States, were born after 28 November 1787, or for unspecified reasons.

Jewish

While Jews in the United States could be classified as an ethnic group, they are described here as a religious group. A search for Jewish ancestors in the Library of Congress should begin in the Hebraic Division, where trained staff will direct you to several published sources, some in English and others in Hebrew. A folder with an article by Ellen R. Murphy, "Jewish Genealogical Materials in the Library of Congress; An Introductory Checklist with Annotations," is available on request. Among the published sources are the following:

Kranzler, David. *My Jewish Roots: A Practical Guide to Tracing and Recording Your Genealogy and Family History.* New York: Sepher Hermon Press, 1979. CS21 .K69.

Kurzweil, Arthur. *From Generation to Generation: How to Trace Your Jewish Genealogy and Personal History.* New York: William Morrow and Co., 1980. CS21 K87.

Regenstein, Janice M. *American Jewish Genealogy: An Annotated Bibliography of Books on Jewish Local History, and Other Subjects of Use to Genealogists.* Wichita, Kans.: Family Heritage Institute, Inc., 1981. Z6373 .U5R44.

Lists books on local Jewish history in thirty-nine states and sixty-two cities and towns in the United States, all of which are found in the Library of Congress.

―――. *Jewish Genealogy Worldwide—An Annotated Bibliography of Books on Jewish Local History and Other Subjects of Use to Genealogists.* Wichita, Kans.: Family Heritage Institute, Inc., 1981. Z6366 .R44.

Lists books on local Jewish history in sixty countries and continents, and in 184 cities, towns, and regions around the world.

Rosenstein, Neil. *The Unbroken Chain.* New York: Shengold Publishers, Inc., 1976. CS432 .J4R67.

Rottenberg, Dan. *Finding Our Fathers: A Guidebook to Jewish Genealogy.* New York: Random House, 1971. CS21 .R58.

Sack, Sallyann A. *A Guide to Jewish Genealogical Research in Israel.* Baltimore: Genealogical Publishing Co., 1987. Z6374 .B5S23.

Stern, Malcolm H. *Americans of Jewish Descent: A Compendium of Genealogies.* New York: Ktav Publishing House, 1971. CS59 .S75.

―――. *First American Jewish Families—600 Genealogies, 1654–1977.* Cincinnati: American Jewish Archives; Waltham, Mass.: American Jewish Historical Society, 1978. CS59 .S76.

Wolf, Simon. *The American Jew as Patriot, Soldier, and Citizen.* Philadelphia: The Levytype Co., 1895. E184 .J5W8.

Lutheran

The Lutheran church has its background in Germany and the Scandinavian countries. It is divided into several synods, described below; the church records are centered in the headquarters of those synods.

(1) The American Lutheran Church: an amalgamation of several branches, primarily those with Norwegian and Danish backgrounds.

(2) The Lutheran Church in America: created from a merger of smaller groups, primarily those with Swedish, Finnish, Danish, and German backgrounds.

(3) The Lutheran Church—Missouri Synod: made up primarily of members with German background and based largely in the Midwest.

Determine which synod an ancestor's church belongs to by consulting the *Lutheran Church Directory,* for the United States cited below, and one of two major guides to Lutheran research in the Library of Congress.

Bodensieck, Julius. *The Encyclopedia of the Lutheran Church.* 3 vols. Minneapolis: Augsburg Publishing House, 1965. BX8007 .B6.

Lutheran Church Directory for the United States. New York: National Lutheran Council, 1971. BX8009 .L838.

Mennonite

Dougherty's chapter in *The Source: A Guidebook of American Genealogy* (cited earlier) lists some of the centers that have Mennonite records. A major publication is the following:

The Mennonite Encyclopedia: A Comprehensive Reference Work on The Anabaptist—Mennonite Movement. 4 vols. Hillsboro, Kans.: Mennonite Brethren Publishing House, 1955–59. BX8106 .M37.

Methodist

This denomination, especially strong in the South, has begun a program to preserve local church records. A local pastor may know the location of early church records, and the General Commission on Archives and History of the United Methodist Church publishes a directory that lists the record sources for this denomination. Other helpful publications about Methodists in the Library of Congress are the following:

Harmon, Nolan B., ed. *The Encyclopedia of World Methodism.* Nashville: United Methodist Publishing House, 1974. BX8211 .E5.

Gives the location of the archival holdings of some smaller churches.

Little, Brooks R. *Methodist Union Catalog of History: Biography, Disciplines, and Hymnals.* Lake Junalaska, N.C.: Association of Methodist Historical Societies, 1967. Z7845 .M5M52.

Mormon (Church of Jesus Christ of Latter-day Saints)

Since a tenet of the Mormon church requires the production of a family history, there is a great mass of genealogical material available in the societies, libraries, and archives of this denomination. Their records consist not only of names and facts about members of the Mormon church but also millions of others, regardless of religious affiliation. It is important to members that their parents, grandparents, and all earlier ancestors be traced as extensively as possible, which led to the collecting of genealogical material extremely broad in scope. An index of names of individuals who have filed personal papers in one of the church temples is available, along with countless numbers of family group sheets. These records are available to the public at the Family History Library and at the church archives in Salt Lake City. Genealogists can inspect these personally, ask for a reference librarian's assistance by mail, or arrange for delivery of microfilmed records to any of the hundreds of branch libraries around the world. These branches are listed in telephone directories under "Church of Jesus Christ of Latter-day Saints" (LDS). The Library of Congress has several publications dealing with records of this church, which could profitably be studied in advance of, or in lieu of, a trip to Salt Lake City.

Bitton, Davies. *Guide to Mormon Diaries and Autobiographies.* Provo, Utah: Brigham Young University, 1977. Z7845 .M8B58.

During the days of the Work Projects Administration, the Utah branch of the WPA devised two sets of questionnaires to be completed by pioneers of Utah, including many who traveled to that state pushing handcarts laden with personal belongings and led by Brigham Young. Some 450 people were interviewed and others contributed diaries, journals, and autobiographies. A few town and county histories were also added to the collection gathered by the

WPA workers. The original papers in this collection were donated to the Library of Congress, designated the "Library of Congress Collection of Mormon Diaries, Journals, and Life Sketches." Carbon copies of these papers were placed in various repositories. The Library of Congress microfilmed the entire collection on thirteen reels of film and makes them available for circulation in the Manuscript Division Reading Room, as well as in some other major libraries. Bitton's guide alphabetically lists the name of each person, gives a biographical sketch, and cites source data.

Jenson, Andrew. *Latter-day Saints Biographical Encyclopedia.* 4 vols. Salt Lake City: Andrew Jenson History Co., 1901. BX8693 .J4.

Contains a photograph and lengthy sketches of leading members of the LDS church. They are not in alphabetical order, but there is an index.

Merrill Library, Utah State Library, comp. *Western Text Society Series.* Vol. 1, No. 2, *Name Index to the Library of Congress Collection of Mormon Diaries.* Logan, Utah: Utah State University Press, 1971. BX8693 .M47.

Wiggins, Marvin E., comp. *Mormons and Their Neighbors.* Provo, Utah: Brigham Young University, 1984. Z7845 .M8W54.

This is an index to over 75,000 biographical sketches from 1820 to the present, taken from 194 published volumes that include both Mormons and non-Mormons. Geographically, it covers northern Mexico, New Mexico, Arizona, southern California, Nevada, Utah, Idaho, Wyoming, and southern Canada.

Presbyterian

Presbyterian records are scattered and one's first contact should be a local minister of the church where the ancestor was a member. Three helpful books in the Library of Congress are the following:

Beecher, Willis J. *Index of Presbyterian Ministers (Presbyterian Church of U.S.A., 1706–1881).* Philadelphia: Presbyterian Board of Publications, 1883. BX9220 .B45.

General Assembly, Presbyterian Church. *Ministerial Directory of the Presbyterian Church, United States, 1861–1967.* Doraville, Ga.: Foote & Davis, 1967. BX9220 .D7.

Nevin, Alfred. *Encyclopedia of the Presbyterian Church in the United States of America: Including the Northern and Southern Assemblies.* Philadelphia: Presbyterian Encyclopedia Publishing Co., 1884. BX8909 .N4.

Quaker (Society of Friends)

Although there are relatively few Friends (Quakers) today, millions can trace their ancestry to someone who was a member. The diminished number may be attributed to the practice of dismissing members for violation of church rules or ethics, especially marrying a non-Quaker. Thus, unlike the Roman Catholic Church that tends to gain members when a Catholic marries a non-Catholic, the Quakers lose members when there is a mixed marriage. Even though a researcher may not turn up an ancestor in Quaker records, they should be checked.

Quaker records are superb in detail. The congregations (called meetings) kept detailed records both for worship and for business. Appointments of members to committees or special projects, their reports, as well as the minutes of the meetings, form a major portion of their documents. Detailed discussions about various members of a meeting were recorded at length, and those discussions were often warnings to desist from behavior deemed disrespectful to the church. Failure to comply sometimes resulted in shunning by the other members, the issuance of ultimatums, and outright disownment. When recording marriages they also listed names of those who attended the ceremonies. Many of these records have survived.

Most surviving Quaker records have been microfilmed, and the principal repository is the Friends Historical Library, Swarthmore College, Swarthmore, Pennsylvania. Before searching for Quaker records, consult the Ellen and David Berry book cited below. It provides an excellent description of the records, gives locations of copies, and includes a short bibliography.

Berry, Ellen T., and David A. Berry. *Our Quaker Ancestors—Finding Them in Quaker Records.* Baltimore: Genealogical Publishing Co., 1987. E184 .F89B47.

Hinshaw, William W. *Encyclopedia of American Quaker Genealogy.* 6 vols. Ann Arbor: n.p., 1936. Reprint. Baltimore: Genealogical Publishing Co., 1969.

This monumental work, widely known to genealogists, consists of abstracts of many (but not all) Quaker meetings for the states included. Only a surname index is provided, but it can be profitably used in conjunction with the tables of contents. Included are entries for births, deaths, marriages, removals, disownments, and minutes of church business discussions. There are separate records for each of the two branches that split after 1929—Orthodox and the Hicksites. Hinshaw's six volumes include the following states: Vol. 1, North Carolina, South Carolina, Georgia, Tennessee; Vol. 2, Pennsylvania and New Jersey; Vol. 3, New York City and Long Island; Vols. 4 and 5, Southwestern Pennsylvania, Ohio, and one meeting in Michigan; Vol. 6, Virginia.

Hinshaw had millions of additional notes of over 900 Quaker meetings in several midwestern and western states when he died in 1947. His widow gave them to Swarthmore College where they were indexed on 285,000 cards and filed.

Heiss, Willard. *Abstracts of the Records of the Society of Friends in Indiana*. Indianapolis: Indiana Historical Society, 1962. E184 .F89H5.

These abstracts were published after Hinshaw's death and carried on his work. The first six parts of Heiss's volume cover meetings in certain Indiana counties. The seventh part is an index.

Roman Catholic

Records of the Roman Catholic church are usually held in the parish itself rather than in a central repository. Very few membership lists or other records of Catholic churches have been published, but the following may be helpful:

Delaney, John J., and James E. Tobin. *Dictionary of Catholic Biography*. Garden City, N.Y.: Doubleday, 1961. BX4651.2 .D4.

Official Catholic Directory. New York: P.J. Kenedy & Sons, (annual). BX845 .C5.

Phelan, Thomas P. *Catholics in Colonial Days*. New York: P.J. Kenedy & Sons, 1935. E184 .C3P3.

Vollmar, Edward R. *The Catholic Church in America: An Historical Bibliography*. New Brunswick, N.J.: Scarecrow Press, 1956. Z7778 .U6V6.

Vital Records

State archives, county courthouses, and town clerks' offices in New England are the primary sources for birth, marriage, divorce, death, probate, land, court, and tax records. In many states the recording of vital statistics by county and state officials is a fairly recent practice, starting during the late nineteenth and early twentieth century. An exception is New England where some states have records since the seventeenth century. Probate records, land transactions, and tax collections have been a matter of county business since their inception. An exception is Rhode Island where, in lieu of vital records, family Bibles, insofar as they are accurate, have been an alternate source. Applications for military pensions sometimes include family records such as pages from a family Bible used to substantiate a veteran's marriage and the births of his children. In its Rare Book Room and Special Collections, the Library of Congress has a large number of Bibles, in English as well as in foreign languages, but only some with family records. These have not yet been fully evaluated and are not indexed.

The United States mortality census schedules, 1850 through 1880 for some states, provide details of all deaths that occurred during the decennial year ending 30 June. These, as well as cemetery inscriptions, can be helpful.

Location of the Records

The United States Government publication (PHS 82-1142), *Where to Write for Vital Records* (HA38 .A493), is available in the Local History and Genealogy Reading Room, and it is widely available in other libraries and archives. This booklet notes each state with addresses of agencies that file birth, death, marriage, and divorce records; the cost of copies; and the period for which records are available.

A prime source for microfilmed copies of county courthouse records, especially for the eastern half of this country, is the Family History Library in Salt Lake City. It also has microfilm copies of many Bible records. This film is available both at Salt Lake City and at the Family History Center branch libraries across the nation. Various chapters of the National Society Daughters of the American Revolution have compiled lists of names found in family Bibles and on cemetery gravestones. These holdings, as microfilmed by the Genealogical Society of Utah, are listed in E. Kay Kirkham's *Index to Some of the Bibles and Family Records in the United States* (Logan, Utah: Everton Publishers, 1984. Z5313 .U5K57).

For cemetery records consult John and E. Diane Stemmons. *The Cemetery Record Compendium* (Logan, Utah: Everton Publishers, 1979. CS49 .S75).

The Library of Congress does not have original county courthouse records, state records, or documents or typescript copies of collections of the Daughters of the American Revolution and the Latter-day Saints; it does, however, have some of the published mortality schedules. To discover which published state, county, or town records are available in the Library of Congress, consult the card catalog labeled "U.S. Local History Shelflist" in the Local History and Genealogy Reading Room. There is considerable variance in the quantity of such material; for many counties there is nothing. As an example, the above mentioned card catalog was checked for the first twenty-nine counties of Kentucky (those beginning with the letters A through C). Seventeen of them had no local official records listed; the remaining twelve had the following:

Adair
    births and deaths, 1852–62
    marriages, 1802–40
    marriages, 1852–62
    marriages, 1852–59, 1861–94, 1903–04,
        1906–07
    wills, 1801–51

Allen
    births, deaths, marriages, 1852–1962
    marriages, 1815–63
    wills, 1801–51
    cemeteries

Bath
    marriages, 1811–26
    wills

Bourbon
    marriages, 1786–94
    marriages, 1785–1851

Bracken
    marriages, 1796–1851
    wills, 1796–1851

Breckenridge
    births, other

Caldwell
    marriages, 1809–91

Carter
    marriages
    deaths, 1852–62

Christian
    marriages, 1797–1850

Clark
    marriages, 1792–1851
    marriages, 1793–99
    wills, 1792–1851

Clay
    deeds, 1806–45, 1815, 1832

Cumberland
    wills, 1815–1902
    cemeteries
    deeds

For Pennsylvania there are even fewer. Among the first twenty-one counties (A through C), only six had any published records listed in the catalog, as follows:

Allegheny
    marriages, 1802–44
    wills, 1789–1869

Beaver
    taxes, 1802–40

Berks
    wills, 1752–1850
    cemeteries

Bucks
    wills, 1864–50

Cambria
    births, deaths, marriages, 1850–85

Chester
    wills, 1713–1850

The catalog cards refer only to items received by the Library of Congress before 1980; for items received since 1968 one must use the computer catalog. Commands are similar to those in the following examples: **find s kentucky genealogy** or **find s pennsylvania genealogy**.

For Kentucky, there were 225 items (hits) listed; for Pennsylvania there were 283.

Another example: **find s green ky genealogy** or **find s berks pa genealogy**.

For Green County there were thirteen hits; for Berks county there were twenty-nine, but only one of them concerned courthouse records.

Newspapers

The newspaper publishing business is a service institution. Newspapers exist to tell readers what is happening in the community and who is involved. If you wish to know what happened in the past, read the old papers. Finding newspapers published during the era in which an ancestor lived anywhere in the world can provide a fascinating picture of the life-style, social background, and daily activities. Even though a name may not be mentioned, a newspaper story illuminates events that were undoubtedly discussed with neighbors. Advertisements illustrate some of the things he or she probably purchased and how much was paid. Businesses frequently advertised in some of the papers, and the price quotations for crops and livestock give an indication of economic conditions.

Such finds may be considered primary sources since they were written at or close to the actual time of the event. It is recommended, however, that more than one newspaper account or contemporary source be checked. Be aware that errors creep into news accounts. When two or more other sources do not agree on the facts, a newspaper story might provide more information.

Newspapers published in large cities concentrate on state, national, and international affairs, while those published in small towns are concerned with local events and people. For this reason the perusal of a small weekly or biweekly newspaper from a rural area might be more helpful than the big city dailies. Big city newspapers are a good source of such items as ship arrivals, accounts of battles fought, casualty lists, and survivors or casualties in tragedies such as ship sinkings, large fires, floods, or earthquakes. Generally, they include official death notices and, if the relatives could afford them, obituaries. For information about obituaries, see Betty Jarboe's *Obituaries: A Guide to Sources* (Z5305 .U5J37). Sometimes lists of marriage licenses issued and wedding announcements were published. In an early period there were advertisements of runaway slaves and announcement of slave auctions.

Small town newspapers routinely carry columns written by amateur or volunteer writers from the surrounding areas, and they highlight local gossip along with births, marriages, and deaths. Political races for local offices—school board, hospital board, and county offices—are extensively covered. Meetings of the local civic clubs are regularly reported. These newspapers serve as vehicles for announcing legal matters relative to divorce, settlements of estates, sales of public land, or sheriff's sales of private property. Some newspapers carry a weekly column written by a local genealogist or historian, usually heavily laced with queries. Some genealogy columns have been indexed and published. See Anita C. Milner's *Newspaper Genealogy Columns Directory* (CS44 .M5).

Locating Newspapers

While searching in the Library of Congress, attention should be paid to local histories that describe the newspapers for a given geographic region. Remember, if there is no newspaper for a small town or county, there may be one in a nearby town or a neighboring county that includes news of the town of interest.

An attempt to catalog and put the titles of this country's 800,000 newspapers into a computer database is in process. This is being done through the Online Computer Library Center (OCLC) in Dublin, Ohio. See Loretto Szucs's "Newspapers" in *The Source: A Guidebook of American Genealogy* edited by Arlene H. Eakle and Johni Cerny (Salt Lake City: Ancestry, Inc., 1984), which contains an extensive bibliography of sources for newspapers in the United States and cites, on a state by state basis, some which have been indexed. Many other titles are listed on the pages that follow.

On a shelf near the issue desk of the Newspaper and Current Periodical Reading Room are two Union lists of newspapers for the United States and Canada. Clarence Brigham covers the years 1690 through 1820, and Winifred Gregory covers the years 1821 through 1936. Arranged by state, they list titles of newspapers, the frequency of publication, and location.

Brigham, Clarence S. *History and Bibliography of American Newspapers, 1690–1820.* 2 vols. Worcester, Mass.: American Antiquarian Society, 1947. Z6951 .E86.

Under each state or city, alphabetically arranged, are titles of newspapers, a brief publishing history, and where copies are located. Repositories include public and university libraries, historical societies, privately held collections, and the Library of Congress. Volume 2 has both an index of titles and printers.

Gregory, Winifred, ed. *American Newspapers, 1821–1936. A Union List of Files Available in the United States and Canada.* New York: Bibliographical Society of America, 1937. Z6951 .A498.

This volume lists the titles of newspapers by state and gives frequency of publication (daily, weekly, semi-weekly), the years published, and repository. Included under the symbol DLC are newspapers at the Library of Congress.

Newspapers at the Library of Congress

The two works described above can be considered supplements to the narrower lists of titles in the following publications:

Ingraham, John V., comp. (1912 original edition); Parsons, Henry S., comp. (revised 1936 edition). *A Check List of American Eighteenth Century Newspapers in the Library of Congress.* Washington, D.C.: Government Printing Office, 1936. Z6951 .U47.

Includes 1,520 titles arranged by state, city, and publishing dates. There is an index of printers, publishers, editions, and titles.

A handy, one-page list entitled "18th Century Newspapers on Microfilm in Newspaper Reading Room" is available at the issue desk. It gives city, state, title, publishing dates, and microfilm numbers. The following are listed: Hartford, Connecticut; Annapolis, Maryland; Boston, Massachusetts; New Brunswick, New Jersey; Philadelphia, Pennsylvania; Charleston, South Carolina; Alexandria, Virginia; Fredericksburg, Virginia; Richmond, Virginia; and Williamsburg, Virginia.

Library of Congress. *Newspapers in Microform, United States, 1948–1983.* 2 vols. Washington, D.C.

Newspaper titles are listed by state and city, publishing dates, and code symbol showing the repository. Volume 2 has an index of titles.

Swigart, Paul E. *Chronological Index of Newspapers for the Period 1801–1967 in the Collections of the Library of Congress.* Z663.44 .C45. (micro 4752). Vol. 1, 1801–20; Vol. 2, 1821–30; Vol. 3, 1831–45; Vol. 4, 1846–59; Vol. 5, 1860–75; Vol. 6, 1876–91; Vol. 7, 1892–1908; Vol. 8, 1909–24; Vol. 9, 1925–42; Vol. 10, 1943–57; Vol. 11, 1956–67.

This is the primary finding aid for newspapers held by the Library of Congress. It consists of eleven volumes and a separate index. Titles are arranged by year, thereunder by state, city, and title. The symbol MIC indicates that it is available on microform; the symbol PORT indicates that it is a portfolio, and, for these, readers must submit an "overnight request." It is important to include these symbols on request slips. Abbreviations are as follows:

w	weekly
sw	semi-weekly
3w	three times a week
sun	Sundays

The index is alphabetically arranged by title, using only key works. After locating a newspaper title for the years of interest, submit a request slip to a librarian at the issue desk. If the newspaper is available on microfilm, it will be delivered within a matter of minutes. If not, it will be delivered the next day, since the original papers are stored in another building. Ask for a yellow "reserved" slip to place it on three-day reserve.

Bibliographies by State

In the reference collection of the Newspaper and Current Periodical Reading Room, on two shelves bearing works with the prefix call numbers Z6952, are a number of volumes that list newspapers published in particular states or large cities. To discover the existence of a newspaper in the state where an ancestor lived, consult these works. The newspapers listed may or may not be available in the Library of Congress, but these works may help locate them elsewhere. Generally, these bibliographies give the name of the city or town of publication, title of the newspaper, date established, publication history, and frequency of publication (weekly, semi-weekly, etc.). In most cases the name of the repository where they might be found is also shown. These bibliographies are arranged on the shelves by state in the order listed below.

Missouri (no dates)

Missouri, 1808–1963

Alaska (published 1976)

Alaska, 1814–1942

Alabama (published 1904)

Arizona, 1859–1911

California, 1855

Santa Clara County, California, 1850–1972

Southwestern states, on microfilm (published 1966), includes New Mexico, Texas, Oklahoma, Arkansas, and Louisiana

Wisconsin, on microform in the state library (published 1911)

New York, Buffalo, 1825–45

Massachusetts, Boston, 1704–80

New Hampshire, Concord, 1790–1898

South Carolina, Charleston, 1732–1864

Wisconsin, Iowa County, 1837–1940

Pennsylvania, Philadelphia, holdings in Philadelphia libraries (published 1936 by the WPA)

Utah, Ogden (published 1938)

New York, Long Island (published 1973)

Louisiana, holdings on microform in the state library, 1889–1951

New York, Ossining, Westchester County, 1797–1951

Massachusetts, Salem, 1768–1856

Newspapers on Microform

Most newspapers on microfilm must be requested by using a call slip; a few titles available in steel cabinets in the reading room may be obtained on a self-serve basis. Copies can be made using one of the coin-operated reader-printers available nearby. When finished with the reels, place them on top of a cabinet for refiling by a staff member. Newspapers available in these cabinets are the following: *New York Times,* September, 1951–; *Washington Star (Evening Star),* December 1852–August 1981; *Washington Post,* December 1877–; *London Times,* January 1785–; and *London Sunday Times,* November 1822–.

Indexed Newspapers

Small town and county newspapers should be read in their entirety not only to pick up mention of an ancestor's name, but also to experience the flavor of the community's culture and daily activities. When faced with large metropolitan newspapers, however, this is not practical. In such cases, unless a specific date is known, an index is an essential tool for finding a news story or other item concerning an ancestor. Fortunately, there are some published indexes. These vary from those with personal names only to others with place names and subjects. Some are indexes of obituaries; some index marriages and deaths (births are

seldom mentioned in the early newspapers); only a few are comprehensive.

When the death date of an ancestor is known, search the newspapers for up to a month following for a death notice or obituary. An ancestor who might have been listed among participants in a battle, involved in a public tragedy, or was a principal in some other event might only be found through a published index.

Available in the Newspaper and Current Periodical Reading Room reference collection are some published indexes to United States and foreign newspapers. Although these are arranged on the shelves by catalog number—rather than by state or city—they may be located with little difficulty. Titles of newspaper indexes for foreign countries or cities are listed in chapter 8 of this guide. Those for United States newspapers are listed below.

Alabama

Statewide

marriages—early newspapers

marriages, deaths, legal notices, 1819–93

Barbour County

news stories, marriages, deaths (several newspapers, 1890–1905)

Alaska

Anchorage

obituaries, the *Times,* 1915–80

Fairbanks

early history, 1903–07

Sitka

subjects, the *Alaska,* 1885–1907

Arizona

Flagstaff

names and subjects, *Arizona Champion, Coconno Sun,* 1883–94

Tombstone

Weekly Nugget

Tucson

news stories, *Arizona Daily Star,* 1953–65; 1975–79

Arkansas

Little Rock

Arkansas Gazette, 1819–29; 1874–79; 1976

California

Statewide

news stories, July 1970–June 1971, several newspapers

Fresno

Fresno Bee, 1970–74 (M #969A)

Los Angeles

Los Angeles Times, 1972–79; 1984

San Francisco

vital records, 1851, *Chronicle,* 1976–

Stockton

San Joaquin Genealogical Society Indexes. (Vol. one: vital statistics, 1850–55; Vol. two: deaths, 1856–62)

Colorado

Denver Post, 1963–69; 1979– (microfiche)

Connecticut

Connecticut News Handbook, Short Beach, 1978–80

District of Columbia

articles contributed by Charles Chaille-Long, *Evening Star,* 1905–12

"The Rambler," a series of articles of Washington, D.C., and vicinity, 1912–27

National Intelligencer, 1816–21

USA Today, 1982

United States Daily, 1926–32

Washington Post, 1972–81

Florida

Jacksonville

Florida Times Union, 1895–1925; 1929; 1938–80 (M #1025A)

Georgia

Statewide

death notices, mid-1800s; 1978–81, several newspapers

deaths, Macon, Milledgeville and Athens newspapers, 1842–48

Atlanta

Constitution and *Journal and Constitution,* 1971–82

Columbus

deaths, marriages, *Columbia Enquirer,* 1832–52

Savannah

1763–99, WPA index of several newspapers news stories, *Morning News,* 1850–1937

Hawaii

Honolulu Advertiser and *Honolulu Star Bulletin,* 1929–67

Illinois

Wayne County

1855–75

Whiteside County

births, deaths, marriages, 1856–81

Chicago

Tribune, 1972–82

Daily Democratic Press, 1855

Sun-Times, 1972–82

see also: Chicago Genealogical Society. *Index to Vital Records from Chicago Newspapers, 1833–48.* F548.25 C55

Nashville

obituaries, *Democrat,* 1903–08

Oquawka

marriages, deaths, estate notices, 1848–52

Indiana

Fulton County

Rochester newspapers and *Akron Globe,* 1865–68

Shelbyville

Union Banner and *Volunteer,* 1862–63

Winchester

Journal, 1876–80

Iowa

Des Moines

Register, 1982

Kansas

Emporia

Kanzas [sic] *News,* 1857–59

Winchester

Argus, Herald, and *Star,* 1877–1912

Kentucky

Statewide

obituaries, state of Kentucky, 1787–1854

Green River region

several newspapers, 2 vols., 1879–1900

Ohio County

several newspapers, *Herald* and *Republican,* 1881-89

Lexington

genealogical and historical abstracts, 1787–1800

Louisiana

New Orleans

marriages, obituaries, *New Orleans Christian Advocate,* 1851–60

Times-Picayune, 1979–81

Maine

Portland

death notices, *Jenks' Portland Gazette,* 1798–1806

Topsham

Maine Times, 1968–78

Maryland

Eastern Shore

newspapers, 1790–1829

Caroline County

marriages, births, deaths, newspapers of Denton and Easton, 1850–80

Annapolis

marriages, deaths, *Maryland Gazette,* 1727–1839

Baltimore

marriages, deaths, several Baltimore newspapers, 1796–1816

mortalities, *Sun,* 1876–1915

marriages, *Sun,* 1837–38

marriages, deaths, *Sun,* 1837–50

marriages, *Sun,* 1851–60

Virginia and Maryland genealogy, *Sun,* 1903–08

Hagerstown

Gazette, Herald, 1805–09

Herald, 1797–1804

Washington Spy, 1790–97

Rockville

Montgomery County Sentinel, 1855–56

Silver Spring

National Observer, 1969–70

Massachusetts

Boston

Evening Transfer, January–March 1908

Globe, 1982

Guardian, 1902–04: "Collections of Early Black Newspapers," 1880–1915

Christian Science Monitor, 1945; 1949–78

deaths, *Massachusetts Centinel* and *Columbian Centinel,* 1784–1840

marriages (entire United States), 1785–94

obituaries, various Boston newspapers, 1704–1800

Northampton

Hampshire Gazette, 1786–1937

Springfield

Republican, 1899–1903

Michigan

Statewide

various Michigan newspapers, 1925–26

Detroit

"Michigan in the Civil War: A Guide to Material in Detroit Papers, 1861–1866."

Free Press, 1983– (microfiche)

News, 1976–79

Kalamazoo

Gazette, 1972–

Minnesota

Duluth

News-Tribune and *Herald,* 1978–83

Minneapolis

Tribune and *Star,* 1970–82

St. Paul

Dispatch and *Pioneer Press*, 1967–

Missouri

St. Louis

Argus, Globe-Democrat, and *Post-Dispatch*, 1975–79

St. Louis Magazines and Obituaries (quarterly), *Argus, Commerce, Globe-Democrat,* and *Post-Dispatch*, 1980–81

Post-Dispatch, 1980–

Montana

Billings

Gazette, 1977–

Nebraska

Plattsmouth

Weekly Herald, 1865–72

New Jersey

Hackensack

Bergen Evening Record, 1959–

New Mexico

Albuquerque

Journal, 1979–

New York

Albany

Times-Union, 1984–

Brooklyn

Eagle, 1891–1902

Center Moriches (Shirley)

Bay View and *Bay Tide*, 1955–80

Garden City

Newsday, Suffolk edition, 1977–

Huntington

Long Islander, 1839–81

Middletown

deaths, 1851–65

New York City

various colonial newspapers, 1726–83

antebellum Black newspapers, 1827–41

Post, 1907–16

genealogical material, *New York Post-Boy*, 1743–73

Times, 1851–1912; 1913–

Guide to the Incomparable New York Times Index (Morse)

personal names index to *The New York Times Index, 1976–84*

New York Times Biographical Service, 1969–

New York Times File: A Collection of News Articles.

New York Times Obituary Index, 2 vols., 1858–1978

Tribune, 1875–81; 1883–1902; 1904–06

marriages, *Weekly Tribune*, 1843–49

Wall Street Journal, 1955–

Rhinebeck

marriages, deaths, etc., various Rhinebeck newspapers, 1846–99

North Carolina

Statewide

various newspapers from Edenton, Fayetteville, and Hillsborough, 1785–1800

Asheville

marriages, deaths, various newspapers, 1840–70

Durham

Morning Herald, 1930–69

Herald Sun, 1981–

Raleigh

marriages, deaths, *Minerva* and *Star*, 1796–1826

Minerva, Register, and *Star*, 1799–1829

News and Observer, 1967–73; 1975–77

marriages, deaths, *Register* and *North Carolina State Gazette*, 1799–1825; 1826–45; 1867–87

Salisbury

marriages, deaths, *Western Caroliniana*, 1820–42

North Dakota

Fargo

Forum Index, 1976–80

Grand Forks

Herald, 1980

Ohio

Trumbull County

obituaries, several newspapers, 1812–70

Akron

Beacon Journal, 1929–38

Cincinnati

Enquirer, 1934–38

Cleveland

WPA Annals of Cleveland: Register, Whig, Leader-Herald, and Daily True Democrat, 1818–68; 1872–76

WPA. *Cleveland Foreign Language Digest,* 1891–92; 1937–38

Plain Dealer, 1931

Press and *Plain Dealer,* 1976–83; 1982

WPA. *Annals of Cleveland,* 1933–38

Columbus

marriages, Franklin County, *Daily Dispatch,* 1878–

WPA. *State Journal,* 1934–39

Dayton

WPA. *Journal,* 1934–38

Greenville

deaths, Darke County, several newspapers, 1912–

Painesville

Telegraph, 1822–29

Toledo

Blade, 1936–38

Xenia

marriages, deaths, *Torchlight,* 1844–60

Youngstown

Vindicator, 1933–38

Oklahoma

Oklahoma City

Daily Oklahoman, 1925–36

Oregon

Oregon Spectator, 1846–54

Pennsylvania

Beaver County

marriages, Beaver County newspapers, especially the *Beaver Argus,* 1830–73

Warren County

marriages, deaths, Warren County newspapers, 1848–75

Westmoreland County

marriages, deaths, weekly newspapers, 1818–65

Johnstown

marriages, deaths, *Cambria Tribune,* 1853–58

Philadelphia

genealogical abstracts, *American Weekly Mercury,* 1719–46

genealogical data from the *Pennsylvania Chronicle,* 1767–74

abstracts from *Ben Franklin's Pennsylvania Gazette,* 1728–48

marriages, obituaries, *Saturday Bulletin,* 1857–60

Uniontown

marriages, deaths, *Genius of Liberty* and *Fayette Advertiser,* 1804–54

marriages, deaths, *Genius of Liberty,* 1809–51

York

Dispatch, 1972–

South Carolina

Statewide

State Index, State Company Printers, 1892–1901; 1903–11 (M #1471)

marriages, deaths, newspapers from Laurens, Spartanburg, Newberry, and Lexington, 1843–65

marriages, deaths, Baptist newspapers of South Carolina, 1835–65

Camden

marriages, deaths, Camden newspapers, 1818–65

Charleston

marriages, *Courier,* 1803–08

marriages, *South Carolina Gazette* and *Country Journal,* 1765–75; *Charleston Gazette,* 1778–80

marriages, *South Carolina Gazette,* 1732–1801

marriages, *South Carolina Gazette,* 1776–81

deaths, *South Carolina Gazette,* 1732–75

marriages, deaths, *Southern Patriot,* 1815–30

marriages, deaths, *Times,* 1800–21

Columbia

marriages, deaths, Columbia newspapers, 1792–1839

Georgetown

marriages, deaths, estate notices, Georgetown newspapers, 1791–1861

Greenville

marriages, deaths, Greenville newspapers, 1826–63

Pendleton

marriages, deaths, *Messenger,* 1807–51

York

marriages, deaths, South Carolina newspapers, 1823–63

South Dakota

Sioux Falls

Argus Leader, 1979–

Tennessee

Statewide

obituaries, Tennessee newspapers

marriages, obituaries, early Tennessee newspapers, 1794–1851

Benton County

marriages, *Camden Chronicle,* 1832–1957

Camden

Camden newspapers, 1882–1932

Nashville

marriages, obituaries, *Tennessee Baptist,* 1844–62

Tennessee Gazette and *Metro District Advertiser,* 1800–07

Texas

Cherokee County

obituaries, 1836–1908

Marion County

marriages, deaths, several Texas and three Louisiana newspapers, 1853–1927

Houston

Houston Post, 1979–

Post, 1976–

Marshall

marriages, deaths, *Texas Republican,* 1849–69

Utah

Salt Lake City

Tribune, 1980– (M #1501A)

Vermont

Burlington

WPA. *Free Press,* 1848–70

Virgin Islands

Virgin Island newspapers, 1982–

Virginia

Culpeper

several Culpeper newspapers, 1859–99; 1881–82; 1882–89; 1885–1906; 1897–98

Exponent, 1981–

Germanna Records

deaths, *Virginia Star*

Fredericksburg

deaths, Fredericksburg newspapers, various dates; 1853–1926

Ledger, 1865–74

News, 1853–61

deaths, *Free Lance-Star,* 1981; 1982

deaths, *Virginia Herald,* 1788–1836

Virginia Herald and *Advertiser,* 1788–95; 1799–1800; 1806–10; 1853–60

Lynchburg

marriages, deaths, Lynchburg newspapers, 1794–1836

Norfolk

Journal and *Guide,* 1936–38

Richmond

obituaries, *Enquirer,* 1804–28; *Whig,* 1824–38

Williamsburg

Virginia Gazette, 1736–80

Washington

Wahkiamkum County

Gray's River Building, 1936–44; *Shamokawa Eagle,* 1899–1934

Olympia

Pioneer and *Democrat,* 1854–56 (M #1520)

West Virginia

Statewide

obituaries, newspapers from northern West Virginia, 2 vols.

Kanawha Valley

several newspapers from the Kanawha Valley, 1855–65

Charleston

Gazette and *Daily Mail,* 1973–

Martinsburg

Gazette, 1810–13; 1825–29

Wisconsin

Milwaukee

Journal, 1976

Periodicals

The term "periodical" used here includes material published serially, regardless of whether its title contains the words "journal," "magazine," "serial," "newsletter," and so forth. Some periodicals are bound by the publisher, but the majority have paper covers. Articles in genealogical or historical periodicals may be national or international in scope, but most are restricted to genealogical and historical data pertaining to a county, state, or region. The differences depend on the interest of the publisher. (Many, for example, are published by hereditary societies or family associations.) Periodicals are published quarterly, monthly, bimonthly, or semiannually. Frequently, but not always, annual indexes to the articles are published. In some instances, cumulative indexes are compiled that cover a period of years.

In the United States, hundreds of genealogical or historical periodicals are published. They teem with family data, some of which may open new avenues of inquiry. Finding them can be difficult; persistence is essential, and possible success depends on an optimistic outlook. Articles in these periodicals usually deal with the following types of information:

(1) how to conduct genealogical research and tips on available sources and how they are organized and used

(2) descriptive works of genealogical and historical items to be found in archives, libraries, and new publications

(3) local history and events previously unpublished

(4) old maps of a given locality and migration trails

(5) gravestone inscriptions in local cemeteries

(6) abstracts of family record pages in family Bibles and church records

(7) records of marriages in a minister's private journal

(8) abstracts of legal documents such as marriages, probate records, land records, and so forth

(9) abstracts of personal diaries, journals, and daybooks

(10) old business accounts, journals, and ledgers

(11) muster rolls and related military lists

(12) ship passenger lists and proceedings of naturalizations gleaned from old newspapers

(13) personal recollections or reminiscences

(14) photographs of early settlers and their families or homes

(15) biographical sketches

(16) lists of members of the society that publishes the periodical

(17) indexes of genealogical columns appearing in local newspapers

(18) names and addresses of local genealogical researchers

Locating Periodicals in the Library of Congress

Many genealogists join one or more genealogical or historical societies and are thus eligible to receive the organization's publications. One should read them diligently and from time to time submit to the editor any newly discovered material for publication.

Reading through periodicals issued by one's own group provides a sample of what might be found in other such publications. Unfortunately, family historians do not usually have access to a large variety of such periodicals, nor can they devote sufficient time to browse through more than a handful of them. Furthermore, aimless browsing, except in issues devoted to one's particular interest, is seldom fruitful. Therefore, devise a system to enhance the chances of finding something useful in the sea of periodicals. Periodicals at the Library of Congress are plentiful and provide an opportunity to find such material. One should first learn what serials are available, where they are shelved, and how to obtain them. Especially important is learning about the available finding aids.

A particular periodical may be found cited in a bibliography or a footnote where its title, volume number, and date of publication are given. Some periodicals may be interesting because of the geographical scope, especially if the area is where an ancestor lived, and others because they emphasize a particular event involving one or more ancestors who may qualify one for membership in a patriotic or pioneer society.

For an overview of the types of genealogical literature available, the following is recommended:

Sperry, Kip. *A Survey of American Genealogical Periodicals and Periodical Indexes.* Detroit: Gale Research Co., 1978. Z5313 .U5S65.

Card and Computer Catalogs

To learn which periodicals were received by the Library of Congress prior to 1980, consult the periodical catalog, which is separate from the main card catalog. When searching the cards either look under the name of the state of interest, plus the subheading "genealogy" and "periodicals," or the name of the organization plus the subheading "periodicals." Many of these may also be found in the computer catalog, but the card catalog is more reliable. Use the following headings as examples:

Maryland—history—periodicals
Indiana—genealogy—periodicals
California—genealogy—periodicals
Sons of the American Revolution—periodicals
Irish Americans—genealogy—periodicals

To learn which periodicals have been received since 1978, and possibly earlier, use the computer catalog and the same commands as the card catalog. If the title of a particular periodical is already known, determine the call number by using commands as follows:

find t georgia genealogical magazine;f-serials
find t connecticut nutmegger;f-serials

If all else fails, be sure to consult with a reference librarian.

General Indexes to Periodicals

Fortunately for today's researcher, a few people have seen the need for compiled general indexes to genealogical periodicals in order to make it possible to discover some mention of an ancestor: where he or she lived, or some pertinent subject. Although Joel Munsell's fifth edition of *The American Genealogist* (1900, with a 1980 supplement) cites some periodicals that contain references to specific family histories, the first extensive indexes were published by Donald L. Jacobus in 1932, 1949, and 1953. After his work stopped, Inez B. Waldenmaier indexed some periodicals and books published between 1956 and 1962; this was followed by the *Genealogical Periodical Annual Index (GPAI)*. Except for the period 1970 to 1973, this has been published annually under the leadership of a succession of editors and compilers.

In addition to the above mentioned indexes, there are a few others that should be cited. These include Kip Sperry's index of articles pertaining to genealogical matters (his index lists holdings in certain genealogical libraries such as the Michigan Genealogy Society and the St. Louis Genealogical Society) and periodicals listed in Swem's *Virginia Historical Index*. Each of these is described in the following pages.

Obtaining a Periodical

Once one has selected the title of a genealogical periodical and determined its call number, it may be obtained by submitting a call slip in the Local History and Genealogy Reading Room. Specify exactly the volumes or issues needed. If one is merely browsing, request all the periodicals of a particular organization for a given period of time, possibly five years. Remember that it often takes considerable time for deck attendants to retrieve the material, so ample time must be allowed.

If the desired issues of the periodicals were published within the past two years or so, they may still be unbound and located in the Newspaper and Current Periodical Reading Room. Once bound, they are assigned call numbers, treated as books, and shelved in the closed stacks. Those pertaining to genealogy are in the Thomas Jefferson Building. Sometimes the volumes requested cannot be located easily because they are being held for binding or awaiting transfer to the appropriate reading room. Some issues are missing for various other reasons. In many instances, a genealogical or historical society may furnish some issues to the Library of Congress and then fail to send others. When a request slip is returned marked "not on shelf," ask a reference librarian for assistance.

General Indexes of Periodicals

1870–1953 Issuances

Jacobus, Donald L. *Index to Genealogical Periodicals.* 3 vols. New Haven, Conn.: n.p., 1932–53. Reprinted in one volume. Baltimore: Genealogical Publishing Co., 1978. Z5313 .U5J2.

Jacobus published the first of these volumes in 1932. He selected fifty-one periodicals published between 1870 and 1931 that did not have their own indexes and indexed them by "names and places" (the latter including "subjects"). The names are surnames only. For his 1949 volume, he indexed fifty periodicals published between 1931 and 1946 by "names," "family and Bible records," "Revolutionary War pensions," "place," and "topic." At the end of the third volume he included "my own index," consisting of given names and surnames of early settlers and references to published sources. These volumes are available on a long table near the card catalog in the Local History and Genealogy Reading Room.

1956–62 Issuances

Waldenmaier, Inez B., ed. *Annual Index to Genealogical Periodicals and Family Histories.* 8 vols. Washington, D.C.: the author, 1956–63. CS45 .A65.

After a four year gap following cessation of Jacobus's indexes, Waldenmaier published a volume citing entries in more than 100 books and periodicals that included family histories and related genealogical records. Only the principal surnames are included in the index, and these are found as subheadings.

1962–Present Issuances

Genealogical Periodical Annual Index. Bowie, Md.: Heritage Book, 1972. CS42 .G467.

Several indexes to genealogical periodicals issued since 1962 have been published by Heritage Books under a series of editors: Ellen S. Rogers, 1962–66; George E. Russell, 1967–76; and Laird C. Towle, 1976–present , with the help of compilers Catherine Mayhew and Karen T. Ackerman. Exceptions are the publications for 1970 through 1973 (volumes 9–12) for which no indexes have been prepared.

Volumes 1 to 4 include subjects, titles of articles, principal surnames, authors, and places; volumes 5 to 8 include men's names, places, subjects, and authors; volumes 13 and onward include personal names, places, and subjects. Also indexed in all the volumes are book reviews and certain published local records that are published in genealogical periodicals. The number of periodicals indexed varies from year to year, but generally includes 100 to 150 titles. The variance is due to the stipulation that only those organizations that furnish their publication to the editor are included. These indexes are available in the Local History and Genealogy Reading Room on a table near the card catalog.

Specialized Periodical Indexes

Sperry, Kip. *An Index to Genealogical Periodical Literature, 1960–1977.* Detroit: Gale Research Co., 1979. Z5313 .U5S64.

Realizing the need for an index of periodical articles dealing with subject matter other than names and places, Sperry selected those that discussed research techniques and procedures, genealogical and historical sources and collections, and international genealogical topics. Hence, this is not a name index (although authors and titles are included). Only substantial articles offering important viewpoints were selected. Articles describing published local records are indexed by state, city or county, province, and country.

Quigley, Maud. *Index to Family Names in Genealogical Periodicals.* Grand Rapids, Mich.: Western Michigan Genealogical Society, 1981. Z5313 .U5Q53.

This is a family name index to ninety genealogical quarterlies from thirty states available in the Genealogy Room of the Grand Rapids Public Library. Each citation includes title, volume (or date), and page where the family name appears. Names include those located in family Bibles, family cemeteries, genealogies, biographies, wills, pension records, newspaper articles, and other sources.

Bailey, Geraldine. *Topical Index of Genealogical Quarterlies.* St. Louis: St. Louis Genealogical Society, 1973–. Z5312 .U5B342.

These publications are an index to information extracted from approximately 125 genealogical periodicals of societies that exchange their publications with the St. Louis Genealogical Society. The topics cited are arranged by state and county. Listing of foreign records and sources, immigration and migration records, military and pension records, and other sources are also included. Types of information cited include church records, cemetery inscriptions, vital records, tax lists, newspaper items, and many others.

Swem, Earl G. *Virginia Historical Index*. 2 vols. Roanoke, Va.: Stone Printing and Manufacturing Co., 1934–36. F221 .S93.

These two large volumes are an index of personal names, places, and subjects mentioned in the pre-1931 Virginia publications listed below. Because so many early ancestors lived in Virginia, this index is mentioned here because of its national importance and because Donald Jacobus did not include in his indexes the seven publications indexed by Swem. The following periodicals are available in the Local History and Genealogy Reading Room, as well as in many other genealogical libraries: *Virginia Magazine of History and Biography, Virginia Historical Register, Tyler's Quarterly and Historical Magazine, William and Mary Quarterly* (two series), *Calendar of Virginia State Papers, Hening's Statutes at Large,* and *Lower Norfolk County Virginia Antiquary,* 1895–1906.

Periodicals in the Local History and Genealogy Reading Room

The most important genealogical periodicals available in the reference collection of the Local History and Genealogy Reading Room are listed below. Others are in the closed stacks and must be requested by submitting a call slip. Although the material on reference changes from time to time, the major works remain. It must be remembered that some periodicals are incomplete; the first year of publication is usually shown (on the list below), but there is no way to tell which subsequent volumes, if any, were ever published or were represented by having copies sent to the Library of Congress. If necessary, check with a reference librarian for assistance.

Published cumulative indexes are relatively rare, except for a few major periodicals. Those indexes located that represent the key resources by region and state are cited in chapters 9 through 15.

Acadian Genealogy Exchange. Covington, Ky., 1972–. F380 .A2A27.

AGE. Alabama Genealogical Exchange, 1984–. F325 .A25.

America, History and Life. American Bibliographical Center. 1964–. Z1236 .A48.

Americana. American Historical Company, 1906–43. E171 .A53.

The American Genealogist. D.L. Jacobus, 1922–. F104 .N6A6.

Archives of Maryland. Maryland Historical Society, 1883–1972. F176 .A67.

Arkansas Family Historian. Arkansas Genealogical Society, 1962–. FA410 .A7.

Armorial. Edinburgh, 1959–. CR1 .A7.

Backtracker. Arkansas Genealogical Society. F410 .B3.

Biography Index. H.W. Wilson Co., 1946–59. Z5301 .B5.

Coat of Arms. East Knoyle, Eng.: Heraldry Society. CR1 .C6.

Colorado Genealogist. Colorado Genealogical Society, 1939–. F771 .C4.

Computers in Genealogy. London Society of Genealogists, 1982–. CS14 .C65.

Connecticut Magazine. Hartford, Conn., 1899–1908. F91 .C8.

Connections. Quebec Family History Society, 1978–. CS88 .Q4C64.

Copper State Bulletin. Arizona State Genealogical Society, 1971–. F810 .C64.

The Critic. Richmond, Va., 1887–90. AP2 .C922.

Delaware Historical Society—Papers. 1879–. F161 .D35.

Delaware Historical Society—Historical and Biographical Papers. 1879. F161 .D34.

Detroit Society for Genealogical Research—Magazine. 1937–. F574 .D4D547.

East Texas Genealogical Society—Ancestor Charts. 1979–83. F385 .E23.

The English Genealogist. Augustan Society. CS410 .E54.

Essex Institute Historical Collections. 1859–. F72 .E7E81.

Florida Historical Quarterly. Florida Historical Society, 1937–. F306 .F65.

Genealogical Computing. Data Transfer Associates and Ancestry, Inc., 1981–. CS14 .G465.

The Genealogical Exchange. 1904–11. CS42 .G45.

The Genealogical Helper. Everton Publishers, 1947–. CS1 .G38.

Genealogical Journal. Utah Genealogical Association, 1972–. CS1 .G382.

The Genealogical Magazine of New Jersey. Genealogical Society of New Jersey, 1925–. F131 .G32.

Genealogical Newsletter and Research Aids. Waldenmaeir, 1955–63. CS42 .G464.

The Genealogist. American-Canadian Genealogical Society of New Hampshire, 1975–. E184 .F85G46.

The Genealogist. Association for the Promotion of Scholarship in Genealogy, CS1 .G393.

The Genealogists' Magazine. Society of Genealogists, 1925–. CS410 .S61.

Genealogy. Indiana Historical Society, 1973–. CS1 .G43.

The Georgia Genealogical Magazine. Huxford, 1961– . F281 .G2967.

Georgia Genealogical Society Quarterly. 1964–. CS42 .G75.

The Grafton Magazine of History and Genealogy. 1908–. E171 .G73.

Hawkeye Heritage. Iowa Genealogical Society. 1966– . F620 .H39.

Historical New Hampshire. New Hampshire Historical Society, 1944–. F31 .FHF57.

The Hoosier Genealogist. Indiana Historical Society. F525 .H6. (Micro 1019 GS9).

Huguenot Society of America—Proceedings. 1883–. E184 .H9H8.

Idaho Genealogical Society Quarterly. 1959–. F745 .I273.

Indiana Magazine of History. Indiana University, 1913–. F521 .I152.

Irish-American Genealogist. Augustan Society, 1977–. CS480 .I72.

The Journal of American Genealogy. National Historical Society, 1921–. CS42 .J6.

Journal (Florida) Genealogical Society. 1979–. F310 .J68.

Journal of Illinois State Historical Society. 1908–84. F536 .I18.

Journal of the Afro-American Historical and Genealogical Society. Washington, D.C., 1980–. E185.96 .A46a.

The Kentucky Genealogist. 1959–. F450 .FK43.

Key Finder. Northwest Oklahoma Genealogical Society, 1980–. F693 .K49.

Kinfolks. Southwest Louisiana Genealogical Society, 1977–. F368 .FK56.

The Local Historian. National Council of Social Services, 1952–. DA20 .A44.

The Louisiana Genealogical Register. Louisiana Genealogical and Historical Society, 1966–. F366 .L55.

The Lower Norfolk County Virginia Antiquary. 1895–1906. F232 .N8L9.

The Magazine of History, with Notes and Queries. New York, 1905–22. E171 .M23.

The Maine Historical and Genealogical Recorder. 1884–98. F16 .M182.

Maine Historical Society—Collections. 1831–. F16 .M33.

The Maine Genealogist and Biographer. Maine Genealogical and Biographical Society, 1875–78. F16 .M155.

The Maryland and Delaware Genealogist. 1959–. CS42 .M35.

The Maryland Historical and Genealogical Bulletin. 1930–. F180 .M34.

Maryland Historical Magazine. Maryland Historical Society, 1907–. F176 .M18.

Maryland Magazine of Genealogy. Maryland Historical Society, 1978–. F180 .FM347.

The Mayflower Descendant. Massachusetts Society of Mayflower Descendants, 1899–. F68 .FM16.

Midwest Genealogical Register. Midwest Genealogical Society, 1966–. CS42 .M53.

Midwest Historical and Genealogical Register. 1980–. CS42 .M53.

Minnesota Historical Society—Collections. 1872–. F601 .M66.

Minnesota History. Minnesota Historical Society, 1915–. F601 .M72.

The Mississippi Valley Historical Review. Mississippi Valley Historical Association, 1914–59. E171 .J872.

Missouri Miscellany. Independence, Mo.: Mrs. Howard W. Woodruff, 1976–84. F465 .W66.

Missouri State Genealogical Association Journal. 1981–. F465 .M575.

National Genealogical Society Quarterly. 1912–. CS42 .N4.

Nebraska Ancestree. Nebraska Genealogical Society, 1978–. F6865 .N43.

Nebraska State Historical Society—Publications. 1885–. F661 .N3.

The New England Historical and Genealogical Register. New England Historic Genealogical Society, 1874–. F1 .N56.

The New England Quarterly. Colonial Society of Massachusetts and the New England Quarterly, 1928–. F1 .N62.

New Mexico Genealogist. New Mexico Genealogical Society, 1962–. F795 .N49.

New York Genealogical and Biographical Society—Collections. 1890–1969. F116 .FN63.

North Carolina Genealogical Society Journal. 1975–. F253 .N882.

North Carolina Genealogy. Also *North Carolinian, Journal of North Carolina Genealogy.* 1955–. F253 .N89.

The North Carolina Historical and Genealogical Register. 1900–03. F251 .N89112.

The North Carolina Historical Review. Division of Archives and History, North Carolina, 1924–73. F251 .N892.

Ohio, The Cross Road of Our Nation: Records and Pioneer Families. Ohio Genealogical Society, 1960–. F490 .F039.

Pacific Northwest Quarterly. Washington State Historical Society, 1906–. F886 .W28.

The Palimpsest. Iowa State Historical Department, Division of the State Historical Society, 1920–. F616 .P16.

The Pennsylvania Genealogical Magazine. Genealogical Society of Pennsylvania, 1895–. F146 .G32.

Pennsylvania German Society—Proceedings and Addresses. 1891–1966. F146 .P23.

Pennsylvania-German Society—Publications. 1978–. GR110 .P4A372.

The Pennsylvania Magazine of History and Biography. Historical Society of Pennsylvania, 1877–. F146 .P65.

Rhode Island Genealogical Register. 1978–. F78 .R53.

Seattle Genealogical Society Bulletin. 1952. CS42 .S412.

Society of the War of 1812—Proceedings of Biennial Meeting. E351 .A15.

Son of the American Revolution Magazine. 1930–. E202.3 .A5.

The South Carolina Historical Magazine. South Carolina Historical Society. 1900–. F266 .S55.

The South Carolina Magazine of Ancestral Research. 1973–. CS42 .S64.

South Dakota Historical Collections. State Historical Society, 1902–. F616 .S76.

Southern Indiana Genealogical Society Quarterly. 1980–. F525 .S66.

Southern Genealogical Index. 1984–. Z1251 .S7S65.

The Southwestern Historical Quarterly. Texas State Historical Association. 1897–. F381 .T45.

Stripes. Texas State Genealogical Society, 1961–. CS1 .S74.

Swedish American Genealogist. 1981–. E184 .S23S88.

Tap Roots. Genealogical Society of East Alabama. 1963–. F325 .T36.

Toledot: Journal of Jewish Genealogy. 1977–. CS31 .J64.

Tyler's Quarterly Historical and Genealogical Magazine. Richmond, Va. F221 .T95.

The Virginia Genealogist. 1957–. F221 .V79.

The Virginia Historical Register. Reprint. 1973. F221 .VL812.

The Virginia Magazine of History and Biography. Virginia Historical Society. 1893–. F221 .V91.

West Virginia History. West Virginia State Department of Archives and History, 1939–. F236 .W52.

Western States Jewish Historical Quarterly. Southern California Jewish Historical Society, 1968–. F591 .W469.

The William and Mary Quarterly. 1892–. F221 .W68a.

Wisconsin Magazine of History. State Historical Society of Wisconsin, 1917–. F576 .W7.

Writings on American History. American Historical Association, 1909–. Z1236 .L331.

Your Family Tree. 1948–. F146 .Y6.

CHAPTER 6

Records Showing Military Service and Pioneer History

Military Service

During the course of U.S. history this country has participated in a war or other military action on an average of once each generation. This makes it probable that one's ancestors served in the military forces or were citizens involved with the military establishment. Beginning with the American Revolution, the government has kept good records of the fighting personnel and the battles in which they took part. Prior to that time, colonial wars were conducted by the British, with field reports being sent to England. Since the revolution, both the federal government and most of the states have amassed large volumes of published material pertaining to military service. Private researchers, compilers, and authors have also published informative accounts of heroism and actions of individual military units and the campaigns in which they were involved. These records provide a wide range of material for the ancestor hunter and historian. Although the government records are the primary sources, the secondary sources have usually been based on those government documents, and many of them are reliable.

An ancestor's name will often be found on a muster roll, pay roll, or similar list created by a military unit. A record of the date and place of enlistment and discharge from service is usually found in the folders (jackets) that contain the service record of each individual. Occasionally, the age, place of residence, occupation, and possibly a brief physical description is also included, but seldom more. By contrast with a service record, a pension file may be replete with genealogical data such as date and place of birth, marriage, and death of both the pensioner and sometimes his family members. Information about economic status, personal assets and liabilities, details of military service, places of residence since discharge, and, in many instances, the names of comrades-in-arms are also given.

In addition to records of the so-called "volunteers" who served during periods of conflict, there are records of "regular" or "career" soldiers, sailors, and militiamen who only served within the boundaries of their own state. More specific records might be found for those in the following other categories: students of government military academies; recipients of medals for heroism; those who were injured or died while in service; veterans buried in national cemeteries or prisoner-of-war camps; veterans with military grave markers; residents of soldiers' homes; prisoners-of-war; court-martial participants; petitioners who applied to Congress for a pension; spies and agents; civilians employed at military establishments who made claims for war damage, or who otherwise aided the war effort; and Loyalists during the American Revolution.

Records exist, and many have been published, that provide useful information about the following wars or other military actions:

Pequot War, 1633–37

Colonial wars prior to 1750:
       King Philip's War, 1675–76
       King William's War, 1689–97
       Queen Anne's War, 1702–13
       King George's War, 1744–48

106 on 5/1/43; Changed from AP-106 to LSV-1 on 4/21/44; Commissioned 6/30/44.
Capt. R. W. Chambers in command.
Changed from LSV-1 to MCS-1 on 10/18/56; Struck from the U.S. Naval Vessel Register 7/1/61; Authorized for conversion to MCS, FY 1964; Contract for conversion signed with Boland Machine Mfg., Co., New Orleans, La., 4/28/64; Reinstated on the U.S. Naval Vessel Register 6/1/64; Arrived at yard to begin conversion 6/25/64; Conversion commenced 7/9/64; Conversion completed 9/8/67; Recommissioned 10/6/67.
Capt. E. L. West in command.

MCS-2   OZARK (ex-LSV-2, AP-107, CM-7)
Built at Willamette Iron & Steel Corp., Portland, Ore. Keel laid 7/12/41; Launched 6/15/42; Sponsored by Mrs. B. Byrnholdt; Changed from CM-7 to AP-107 on 5/1/43; Changed from AP-107 to LSV-2 on 4/21/44; Commissioned 9/23/44.
Captain F. P. Williams in command.
Changed from LSV-2 to MCS-2 on 10/18/56; Struck from the U.S. Naval Vessel Register 9/1/61; Authorized for conversion to MCS, FY 1963; Contract for conversion signed with Norfolk SB & DD Co., Norfolk, Va., 6/6/63; Arrived at yard to begin conversion 6/29/63; Conversion started 9/16/63; Reinstated on the U.S. Naval Vessel Register 10/1/63; Conversion completed 6/15/66; Recommissioned 6/24/66.
Capt. C. E. Little in command.

OSAGE Class:
MCS-3 to 5 inclusive
Length Overall 451'4"
Extreme Beam: 60'3"
Full-Load Displacement: 8160 tons (MCS-3, 4), 8790 tons (MCS-5)
Max. Draft: 20'
Designed Accommodations: Off.: 114, Enl.: 450
Armament: (2) 5"/38 cal.; (4) twin 40mm.
Designed Speed: 20.3 k.
Engines: Mfr.: G.E.; Type: Geared Turbine
Designed Shaft Horsepower: 11,000

MCS-3   OSAGE (ex-LSV-3, AP-108, AN-3)[1].
Built at Ingalls SB Corp., Pascagoula, Miss.
Keel laid 6/1/42; Changed from AN-3 to AP-108 on

5/1/43; Launched 6/30/43; Sponsored by Mrs. Joseph A. McHenry; Changed from AP-108 to LSV-3 on 4/21/44; Commissioned 12/30/44.
Capt. H. H. Keith in command.
Changed from LSV-3 to MCS-3 on 10/18/56.

MCS-4   SAUGUS (ex-LSV-4, AP-109, AN-4)[1].
Built at Ingalls SB Corp., Pascagoula, Miss.
Keel laid 7/27/42; Changed from AN-4 to AP-109 on 5/1/43; Launched 9/4/43; Sponsored by Mrs. R. J. Carstarphen; Changed from AP-109 to LSV-4 on 4/21/44; Commissioned 2/22/45.
Capt. R. S. Berschy in command.
Changed from LSV-4 to MCS-4 on 10/18/56.

MCS-5   MONITOR (ex-LSV-5, AP-160, AN-1)[1].
Built at Ingalls SB Corp., Pascagoula, Miss.
Keel laid 10/21/41; Launched 1/29/43; Sponsored by Mrs. J. A. Terhune; Changed from AN-1 to AP-160 on 8/2/43; Commissioned 3/18/44.
Comdr. J. B. McVey in command.
Changed from AP-160 to LSV-5 on 4/21/44; Changed from LSV-5 to MCS-5 on 10/18/56.

ORLEANS PARISH Class:
MCS-6
Length Overall 328'
Extreme Beam: 50'
Full-Load Displacement: 3640 tons
Max. Draft: 14'
Designed Accommodations Off.: 13; Enl.: 106
Armament: (2) twin 40mm.; (2) single 40mm.
Designed Speed: 11.6 k.
Engines: Mfr.: G. M.; Type: Diesel
Designed Shaft Horsepower: 1,700

MCS-6   ORLEANS PARISH (ex-LST-1069)
Built at Bethlehem Steel Co., Hingham, Mass.
Keel laid 2/7/45; Launched 3/7/45; Sponsored by Mrs. J. W. Whitfield; Commissioned 3/31/45.
Lt. L. A. Rockwell, USNR, in command.
Named ORLEANS PARISH 7/1/55; Changed from LST-1069 to MCS-6 on 1/19/59.

EPPING FOREST Class:
MCS-7
Length Overall: 457'8"
Extreme Beam: 72'1"
Full-Load Displacement: 8700 tons
Max. Draft: 18'
Designed Accommodations: Off.: 15, Enl.: 247
Armament: (2) quad 40mm.; (44) mines

---

[1] Although designated as Mine Countermeasures Ships, these ships never underwent conversion to MCS's and remain with a Landing Ship Vehicle configuration.

482

Page from the Office of the Chief of Naval Operation, Navy Department, *Dictionary of American Naval Fighting Ships,* 8 vols. (Washington, D.C.: Government Printing Office, 1959–81).

French and Indian War (Seven Years War), 1754–63

Lord Dunmore's War, 1774

American Revolution, 1775–83

War of 1812, 1812–14

Indian Wars, 1817–58

Mexican War, 1846–48

Civil War, 1861–65

Indian Wars, post-Civil War

Spanish-American War, 1898 (also Philippine Insurrection)

European War (World War I), 1917–18

World War II, 1941–45

Korean Action, 1950–53

Vietnam Action, 1961–73

The Library of Congress has reports of the states' adjutant generals, which include lists of uniformed personnel who participated in various wars. There are also hundreds of regimental histories, diaries, and journals written during or soon after a military action occurred. Local histories of counties or towns usually contain lists of the residents who fought or otherwise served the military, and published government lists of pensioners and claimants are also available. For the Civil War there is a published set of volumes entitled *Official Records of the Union and Confederate Armies in the War of the Rebellion,* with a companion set for the naval forces.

The library does not have military records, but there are several centers where these may be found. Chief among these is the National Archives, which has compiled military service records, pension files, and other documents covering the American Revolution through the Philippine Insurrection. In addition, it has crew lists and photographs of a large number of naval vessels up to and including World War II. Another valuable repository is the United States Navy Department Library at the Washington Navy Yard (Building #57), Washington, D.C. Only a few hours from Washington, D.C., at Carlisle, Pennsylvania, is the United States Army Military History Institute, where a large collection of military publications relative to all American wars and military actions is available to the public free of charge.

Guides and Bibliographies

Source material that contains names of military personnel or descriptions of military units may be found by using both the card catalogs and the computer catalog. First, however, consult the many bibliographies and guides to military publications. For quick reference, the most useful ones in the Local History and Genealogy reference collection are listed below.

General

Cerny, Johni. "Military Records." In *The Source: A Guidebook of American Genealogy,* edited by Arlene H. Eakle and Johni Cerny. Salt Lake City: Ancestry, Inc., 1984. CS49 .S65.

Kirkham, E. Kay. *Some of the Military Records of America Before 1900.* Salt Lake City: Deseret Book Co., 1964. CS49 .K49.

Lists of Logbooks of U.S. Navy Ships, Stations, and Miscellaneous Units, 1801–1947, Special List 44. Washington, D.C.: National Archives and Records Service, 1978. Z6835 .U5U43.

Office of the Chief of Naval Operation, Navy Department. *Dictionary of American Naval Fighting Ships.* 8 vols. Washington, D.C.: Government Printing Office, 1959–81. VA61 .A53.

U.S. Congress. *Medal of Honor Recipients 1863–1968.* 93d Cong., 2d Sess. Washington, D.C.: Government Printing Office, 1968. Rev. ed., 1973. UB433 .U55.

U.S. Congress. House. *Digested Summary and Alphabetical List of Private Claims . . . 1st to the 31st Congress . . . .* 1853. Reprint. Baltimore: Genealogical Publishing Co., 1970. KF4932 .A35.

See also separate publications: 32d to 41st Congress (1851–70), and 42d to 46th Congress (1871–81).

U.S. Department of the Army. Public Information Division. *The Medal of Honor of the United States Army.* Washington, D.C.: Government Printing Office, 1948. UB433 .A52.

Witt, Mary E. S. *An Alphabetical List of Navy, Marine, and Privateer Personnel, and Widows, From Pension Rolls, Casualty Lists, Retirement and Dismission Rolls of the United States Navy, Dated 1847.* Dallas: Mew Publishers, 1986. CS68 .W57.

American Revolution

Deutrich, Mabel E. *Preliminary Inventory of the War Department Collection of Revolutionary War Records. Record Group 93.* Washington, D.C.: National Archives and Records Service, 1970. CD3026 .A32, no. 144.

Eakin, Joyce L. *United States Army Military History Research Collection. Special Bibliography 14—Colonial America and the War for Independence.* Carlisle Barracks, Pa.: United States Army Military History Institute, 1976. Z1238 .U55.

Gephart, Ronald M. *Revolutionary America, 1763–89. A Bibliography.* Washington, D.C.: Library of Congress, 1984. Z1238 .G43.

Hatcher, Patricia L. *Graves of Revolutionary Patriots.* 3 vols. Dallas: Pioneer Heritage Press, 1987. E255 .H39.

Neagles, James C., and Lila L. Neagles. *Locating Your Revolutionary War Ancestor.* Logan, Utah: The Everton Publishers, 1983. Z5313 .U5N42.

Schweitzer, George K. *Revolutionary War Genealogy.* Knoxville, Tenn.: the author, 1982. Z5313 .U5S3.

White, J. Todd, and Charles H. Lesser. *Fighters for Independence: A Guide to Sources of Biographical Information on Soldiers and Sailors of the American Revolution.* Chicago: The University of Chicago Press, 1977. Z1238 .W45.

War of 1812

Fredricksen, John C. *Free Trade and Sailors' Rights: A Bibliography of the War of 1812.* Westport, Conn.: Greenwood Press, 1985. Z1240 .F74.

Scott, Kenneth. *British Aliens in the United States During the War of 1812.* Baltimore: Genealogical Publishing Co., 1979. E184 .B7S37.

Civil War

Beers, Henry P. *Guide to the Archives of the Government of the Confederate States of America.* Washington, D.C.: Government Printing Office, 1968. CD3047 .B4.

Broadfoot, Tom, ed. *Civil War Books, A Priced Checklist.* Wendell, N.C.: Avera Press, 1978. Z1242 .45 .B76.

Cooling, B. Franklin. *Bibliography of the Era of the Civil War, 1820–76.* Carlisle Barracks, Pa.: United States Army Military History Research Collection, 1974. Z1242 .U547.

Dornbusch, Charles E. *Military Bibliography of the Civil War.* 3 vols. New York: New York Public Library, 1971. Z1242 .D612.

Dyer, Frederick. *A Compendium of the War of the Rebellion.* 3 vols. New York: Thomas Y. Yoseloff, 1959. E491 .D99.

Groene, Bertram H. *Tracing Your Civil War Ancestor.* Winston-Salem, N.C.: John F. Blair, Publishers, 1973. CD3047 .G76.

Munden, Kenneth W. *Guide to the Federal Archives Relating to the Civil War.* Washington, D.C.: Government Printing Office, 1962. CD3047 .M8.

Neagles, James C. *Confederate Research Sources.* Salt Lake City: Ancestry, Inc., 1986. Z1242 .N3.

Nevins, Allen, et al. *Civil War Books, A Critical Bibliography.* 2 vols. Baton Rouge: State Press, 1967. Z1242 .N35.

O'Quinliven, Michael. *An Annotated Bibliography of the United States Marines in the Civil War.* Washington, D.C.: Headquarters, United States Marine Corps, 1968. Z1242 .068.

Schweitzer, George K. *Civil War Genealogy.* Knoxville, Tenn.: the author, 1982. Z5313 .U5S35.

Smith, Myron J. *American and Civil War Navies.* Metuchen, N.J.: Scarecrow Press, 1972. Z1242 .S63.

Stephenson, Richard W., comp. *Civil War Maps in the Library of Congress, An Annotated List.* Washington, D.C.: Library of Congress. Z6027 .U5U55.

Tancig, William J., comp. *Confederate Military Land Units.* New York: Thomas Y. Yoseloff, 1967. E546 .T3.

United States War Department, War College Division. *Bibliography of State Participation in the Civil War, 1861–65.* Washington, D.C.: Government Printing Office, 1913. Z1242 .U581.

World War I and World War II

Contravitch, James T., comp. *United States Army Unit Histories: A Reference and Bibliography.* Manhattan, Kans.: Kansas State University, 1983. Z6725 .U5C66.

Refers primarily to units since 1900.

Enser, A.G.S. *A Subject Bibliography of the Second World War.* Boulder, Colo.: Westview Press, 1977. Z6207 .W8E57.

Pappas, George S. *United States Army Unit Histories: A Bibliography.* Carlisle Barracks, Pa.: United States Army Military History Research Collection, 1971. Z6725 .U5U415.

Refers primarily to World War I and World War II.

Smith, Myron J. *World War II at Sea: A Bibliography of Sources in English.* Metuchken, N.J.: Scarecrow Press, 1976. Z6207 .W8S57.

United States National Archives. *Federal Records of World War II.* National Archives and Records Service. Reprint. Detroit: Gale Research Co., 1982. Z6207 .W8U767.

Vietnam Action

Burns, Richard D., and Milton Leitenberg. *The Wars in Vietnam, Cambodia, and Laos, 1945–82.* Santa Barbara, Calif.: ABC-Clio Information Service, 1984. Z3228 .V587.

History and Museums Division. United States Marine Corps. *The Marines in Vietnam, 1954–73.* Washington, D.C.: n.p., 1974. DS557 .A632M37.

Leitenberg, Milton, comp. *The Vietnam Conflict.* Santa Barbara, Calif.: ABC-Clio Information Service, 1984. Z3228 .V5B87.

Smith, Myron J. *Air War, Southeast Asia, 1961–73.* Metuchen, N.J.: Scarecrow Press, 1979. Z3228 .V5S63.

Sugnet, Christopher L. *Vietnam War Bibliography.* Lexington, Mass.: Lexington Books, 1983. Z3226 .S9.

Indexes and Lists of Military Personnel

The Library of Congress has a large number of publications containing indexes of names or lists of persons who served in a military unit or were otherwise involved in a war or military action by the United States. Selected publications, arranged by war, are listed below as deserving special attention. Many of these may be found on the open shelves of the Local History and Genealogy Reading Room. Others may be obtained by submitting call slips. To find other related works, refer to the card or computer catalogs under the subject headings for each war.

The titles listed here refer primarily to publications that deal with regional or national units encompassing more than one state. For a complete search, it is necessary to examine those that contain lists of military personnel from particular states, such as where the soldier enlisted, where he lived after his discharge, and where he might be buried. Several books containing this information are listed in chapters 9 through 15.

General

Cullum, George W. *Biographical Register of the Officers and Graduates of the United States Military Academy, 1802–1867.* 3 vols., plus 1879 supp. New York: n.p., 1879. U410 .M5.

Gardner, Charles. *A Dictionary . . . The Army of the United States, 1789–1853.* New York: State of New York, 1860. U11 .U562.

Hamersley, Thomas H. S. *Complete Army Register of the United States for One Hundred Years, 1779–1879.* Washington, D.C.: the author, 1880. U11 .U5H3.

Heitman, Francis B. *Historical Register and Dictionary of the United States Army, 1789–1903.* 2 vols. Washington, D.C.: Government Printing Office, 1903. U11 .U5H6.

Colonial Wars Prior to 1750

In the card catalog, look under **U.S. History — Colonial Period—[name of war]**

Bodge, George M. *Soldiers in King Philip's War, Being a Critical Account of that War, With a Concise History of the Indian Wars of New England From 1620–1677 . . . .* Reprint. Baltimore: Genealogical Publishing Co., 1867. E83.67 .B662.

Clark, Murtie J. *Colonial Soldiers of the South, 1732–74.* Baltimore: Genealogical Publishing Co., 1983. ZF208 .C58.

Society of Colonial Wars. *Annual Register of Officers and Members of the Society . . . .* New York: the society, 1894. E186.3 .A13.

French and Indian War

In the card catalog, look under **U.S. History—Colonial Period—French and Indian War—Regimental Histories** or **U.S. History —Colonial Period—French and Indian War—Registers, Lists**.

Ford, Worthington, C. *British Officers Serving in America, 1754–74.* Boston: David Clapp & Sons, 1894. E199 .F693.

Rinkenbach, William H. *French and Indian Victims of the Indians.* N.p.: the author, 1957. E199 .R56.

Taylor, Philip F. *A Calendar of the Warrants for Land in Kentucky Granted for Service in the French and Indian War.* Baltimore: Genealogical Publishing Co., 1967. HD184 .K42A45.

Toner, J.M., ed. *Journal of Col. George Washington, 1754.* Albany: Joel Munsell's Sons, 1893. E199 .W31.

Revolutionary War—Patriots

For other titles pertaining to the American Revolution, use the following headings in the card or computer catalogs: **U.S. History—Revolution—American Loyalists** or **U.S. History—Revolution—Prisoners and Prisons** or **U.S. History—Revolution—Regimental Histories** or **U.S. History—Revolution—Registers and Lists**.

Allen, Gardner W. *A Naval History of the American Revolution.* Vol. 11. Boston and New York: Houghton-Mifflin, 1970. E271 .A42.

Barnes, John S. *The Logs of the Serapis, Alliance, Ariel, Under the Command of John Paul Jones, 1779–80.* New York: Naval Historical Society, 1911. E271 .B27.

Callahan, Edward W., ed. *List of Officers of the Navy of the United States and of the Marine Corps From 1775 to 1900 . . . .* New York: L.R. Hamersley & Co., 1901. V11 .U7C2.

Coggins, Jack. *Ships and Seamen of the American Revolution: Crews, Weapons, Gear, Naval Tactics and Actions in the War for Independence.* Harrisburg, Pa.: Stackpole Books, 1969. E271 .C63.

Dandridge, Mrs. Danske. *American Prisoners of the Revolution.* Baltimore: Genealogical Publishing Co., 1967. E281 .D17.

DeMarce, Virginia E. *Canadian Participants in the American Revolution—An Index.* Sparta, Wis.: Lost in Canada, 1980. E255 .D4.

Duncan, Louis C. *Medical Men in the American Revolution, 1775–1783. Army Medical Bulletin No. 25.* Carlisle Barracks, Pa.: Medical Field Service School, 1931. E283 .D8.

Egle, William H. *Old Rights, Property Rights, Virginia Entries and Soldiers Entitled to Donation Lands.* Harrisburg, Va.: C.M. Busch, State Printer, 1896. F146 .P41.

Ellet, Elizabeth F. *Women of the Revolution.* New York: Haskett House, 1969. E206 .E45.

France, Ministère des Affairs Étrangeres. *Les Combattants Français de la Guerre Américaine, 1778–83.* Paris: Ancienne Maison Quantin, 1903. Reprint. Baltimore: Genealogical Publishing Co., 1969. E265 .F82.

Godfrey, Carlos E. *The Commander-in-Chief's Guard: Revolutionary War.* Washington, D.C.: Stevenson-Smith Co., 1904. E260 .G58.

Haiman, Miecislaus. *Poland and the American Revolutionary War.* Chicago: Polish Roman Catholic Union of America, 1932. E184 .P7H13.

Headley, J.T. *The Chaplains and Clergy of the Revolution.* New York: Charles Scribner, 1864. E206 .H33.

Heitman, Francis B. *Historical Register of Officers of the Continental Army During the War of the Revolution, April 1777 to December 1783.* Washington, D.C.: Rare Book Shop Publishing Co., 1914. Reprint. Baltimore: Genealogical Publishing Co., 1969. E255 .H48.

Hoyt, Max, et al. *Index of Revolutionary War Pension Applications.* Washington, D.C.: National Genealogical Society, 1966. CS42 .N43.

Ingmire, Frances, and Carolyn Ericson. *Register of Confederate Soldiers and Sailors Who Died in Federal Prisons and Military Hospitals in the North.* St. Louis, Mo.: Ingmire Publications, 1984. E548 .I55.

Taken from National Archives microfilm.

Kaminkow, Marion, and Jack Kaminkow. *Mariners of the American Revolution.* Baltimore: Magna Carta Book Co., 1967. E203 .K23.

Lasseray, Andre. *Les Français Sous les Treize Étoiles.* 2 vols. Macon: Protat Freres, 1935. E265 .L28.

Neagles, James C. *Summer Soldiers: A Survey and Index of Revolutionary War Courts-Martial.* Salt Lake City; Ancestry, Inc., 1986. E255 .N5.

New York Historical Society. *New York Historical Society Collections.* Vols. 1 and 2 (1914–15). F116 .N62.

Newman, Debra S. *List of Black Servicemen, Compiled from War Department Collections of Revolutionary War Records.* National Archives Special List No. 36. Washington, D.C.: National Archives, 1974. E269 .N3N48.

O'Brien, Michael J. *A Hidden Phase of American History: Ireland's Part in America's Struggle for Liberty.* Reprint. Baltimore: Genealogical Publishing Co., 1973. E269 .I6023.

Peterson, Clarence S. *Known Military Dead During the Revolutionary War.* Reprint. Baltimore: Genealogical Publishing Co., 1967. E255 .P4.

Powell, William H. *List of Officers of the Army of the United States from 1779 to 1900.* New York: L.R. Hamersley & Co., 1909. U11 .V5P.

Ray, Alexander, comp. *Officers of the Continental Army Who Served to the End of the War and Acquired the Right to Commutation Pay and Bounty Land.* N.p.: J & C.S. Gideon, Printers, 1849. E255 .R26.

Smith, Charles R. *Marines in the Revolution: A History of the Continental Marines in the Revolution,*

1775–1783. Washington, D.C.: History and Museums Division, U.S. Marine Corps, 1975. E271 .S65.

Society of Old Brooklynites. *A Christmas Reminder, Being the Names of About 8,000 Persons, a Small Portion of the Number Confined on Board the British Ship During the War of the Revolution.* Brooklyn: Eagle Print, 1888. E281 .S67.

Stewart, Mrs. Frank Ross. *Black Soldiers in the American Revolutionary War.* Centre, Ala.: Stewart University Press, 1978. E269 .S74.

Toner, Joseph M. *The Medical Men of the Revolution.* Philadelphia: Collins Printer, 1876. E206 .T66.

U.S. Bureau of the Census. *A Census of Pensioners for Revolutionary or Military Service; With Their Names, Ages, and Place of Residence—1840.* Washington, D.C., 1841. Reprint. Baltimore: Genealogical Publishing Co., 1974. E255 .U42.

See also: *A General Index to "A Census of Pensioners for Revolutionary or Military Service—1840."* published by the Genealogical Society of the Church of Jesus Christ of Latter-day Saints. E255 .U42.

U.S. Congress. *List of the Names of Such Officers and Soldiers of the Revolutionary Army as have Acquired a Right to Lands From the United States and Who Have Not Yet Applied Therefor.* 20th Cong., 1st sess., 1828. Vol. 132, S. Doc. 42. AC901 .M7, Vol. 132.

For a complete bibliography of reports issued by the United States government that contains names of Revolutionary War soldiers and pensioners, see James C. Neagles and Lila L. Neagles's *Locating Your Revolutionary War Ancestor.*

Waldenmaier, Nellie P. *Some of the Earliest Oaths of Allegiance to the United States.* N.p., 1944. E205 .W3.

Revolutionary War—Loyalists

Clark, Murtie J. *Loyalists in the Southern Campaign of the Revolutionary War.* Baltimore: Genealogical Publishing Co., 1981. CS63 .C55.

Coldham, Peter W. *American Loyalist Claims: Abstracted From the Public Record Office, Audit Office Series 13.* Washington, D.C.: National Genealogical Society, 1980. CS42 .N43, no. 45.

DeMond, Robert O. *Loyalists in North Carolina During the Revolution.* Hamden, Conn.: Archon Books, 1964. E277 .D35.

Egerton, Hugh E. *Mass Violence in America: The Royal Commission on the Losses and Services of American Loyalists, 1783–1785.* New York: Arno Press, 1969. E277 .C6.

Flick, Alexander C. *Loyalism in New York During the American Revolution.* New York: AMS Press, 1970. E277 .F62.

Hancock, Harold B. *The Loyalists of Revolutionary Delaware.* Newark: University of Delaware Press, 1977. E277 .H26.

Hast, Adele. *Loyalism in Revolutionary Virginia: The Norfolk Area and the Eastern Shore.* Ann Arbor, Mich.: UMI Research Press, 1982. E277 .H37.

Hill, Isabell L. *Some Loyalists and Others.* Fredericton, New Brunswick: n.p., 1976. E277 .H54.

Jones, E. Alfred. *The Loyalists of New Jersey.* Boston: Gregg Press, 1972. E277 .J78.

Jones, Edward. *The Loyalists of Massachusetts.* Baltimore: Genealogical Publishing Co., 1969. E277 .J77.

Maas, David E. *Divided Hearts: Massachusetts Loyalists, 1756–1790. A Biographical Directory.* Boston: Society of Colonial Wars in the Commonwealth of Massachusetts and New England Historic Genealogical Society, 1980. E277 .M2.

Palmer, Gregory. *Biographical Sketches of Loyalists of the American Revolution.* Westport, Conn.: Meckler Publishers, 1984. E277 .P24.

Sabine, Lorenzo. *Biographical Sketches of Loyalists of the American Revolution.* 2 vols. Port Washington, N.Y.: Kennikat Press, 1966. E277 .S12.

Siebert, Wilbur H. *The Loyalists of Pennsylvania.* Boston: Gress Press, 1972. E277 .S565.

Stark, James H. *The Loyalists of Massachusetts.* Clifton, N.J.: Augustine M. Kelley, Publisher, 1972. E277 .S79.

Tyler, John W. *Connecticut Loyalists.* New Orleans: Polyanthos, 1977. E277 .T93.

War of 1812

In the card catalog, look under **U.S. History—War of 1812—Prisoners and Prisons** or **U.S. History—War of 1812—Regimental Histories** or **U.S. History—War of 1812—Registers and Lists**.

Carr, Deborah E. *Index to Certified Copy List of American Prisoners of War, 1812–15*. N.p.: United States Daughters of 1812, 1924. E362 .C22.

Clark, Byron N. *A List of Pensioners of the War of 1812*. Burlington and Boston: Research Publications, 1904. E359.4 .C62.

Diefenbach, H.B., comp. *Index to the Brave—Records of Soldiers of the War of 1812*. N.p., 1945. E359.4 .D5.

Hickman, Nathaniel. *The Citizen Soldiers at North Point and Fort McHenry, September 12, 13, 1814*. Baltimore: the author, 1858. E359.5 .M2H6.

Morazan, Ronald R. *Biographical Sketches of the Veterans of the Battalion of Orleans, 1814–15*. Baton Rouge: Legacy Publishing Co., 1979. E356 .N5M6.

Peterson, Clarence S. *Known Military Dead During the War of 1812*. Baltimore: the author, 1955. E359.4 .P48.

Peterson, Clarence J. *The Military Heroes of the War of 1812*. Philadelphia: James B. Smith & Co., 1858. E353 .P5.

Todd, Charles S. *Bounty Lands to the Regular and Volunteer Officers of the War of 1812*. Washington, D.C.: n.p., ca. 1880. HD240 .T63.

Tucker, Glenn. *Poltroons and Patriots*. Indianapolis and New York: Bobbs-Merrill, 1954. E354 .T8.

U.S. Congress. House. *Lands in Illinois to Soldiers of the Late War*. 86th Cong., 1st sess. H. Doc. 262, July 21, 1840. E359.4 .U55.

U.S. General Land Office. *Index to Illinois Military Patent Book, 1853*. E359.4 .U553.

Volkel, Lowell M. *War of 1812, Bounty Lands in Illinois*. Thomson, Ill.: Heritage House, 1977. E359.4 .V55.

Yount, Col. Nennet H. *The Battle of the Thames, With a List of the Officers and Privates Who Won the Victory*. Louisville, Ky.: John P. Morton & Co., 1903. E356 .T3Y6.

Zimmerman, James F. "Impressment of American Seamen." Ph.D. diss., Columbia University, 1925. E354.S .Z62.

Mexican War

In the card catalog, look under **U.S. History—War With Mexico, 1845–48—Regimental Histories** or **U.S. History—War With Mexico, 1845–48 — Registers and Lists**.

Bever, Jack. *Surfboats and Horse Marines: U.S. Naval Operations in the Mexican War, 1846–48*. Annapolis: U.S. Naval Institute, 1969. E410 .B3.

Oberly, James S. "Military Bounty Land Warrants of the Mexican War." *Prologue* (Spring 1982): 25–34.

Peterson, Charles J. *The Military Heroes of the Wars of 1812 and Mexico*. Philadelphia: William A. Leary, 1848. E353 .P48.

Peterson, Clarence S. *Known Military Dead During the Mexican War, 1846–48*. Baltimore: the author, 1957. E409 .P4.

Troxel, Naven H., and Susan M. Warner. *Mexican War Index to Pension Files, 1886–1926*. N.p.: the authors, 1983. E409.4 T76.

Tyler, Daniel. *A Concise History of the Mormon Battalion in the Mexican War, 1846–47*. Glorieta, N.M.: Rio Grande Press, 1969. E409.5 .I7279.

Civil War—Union

In the card catalog, look under **U.S. History—Civil War—Prisoners and Prisons** or **U.S. History—Civil War—Regimental Histories** or **U.S. History—Civil War—Registers and Lists**.

Atwater, Dorence A. *A List of the Union Soldiers Buried at Andersonville*. New York: The Tribune Association, 1890. E612. A5A83.

Long, Everette B. *The Civil War Day by Day—An Almanac, 1861–75*. Garden City, N.Y.: Doubleday & Co., 1971. E468.3 .L6.

Powell, William H. *Officers of the Army and Navy Who Served in the Civil War*. Philadelphia: L.R. Hamersley & Co., 1893. E467 .P88.

U.S. Adjutant General's Office. *Official Army Register of the Volunteer Force of the United States Army for the Years 1861–65*. 8 vols. Washington,

D.C.: Adjutant General's Office, 1865–67. E494 .U538.

United States Christian Commission. *Record of the Federal Dead Buried From Libby, Belle Isle, Danville, and Camp Lawton Prisons, and at City Point, and the Field Before Richmond and Petersburg.* Philadelphia: J.B. Rodgers, 1866. E494 .U59.

U.S. Pension Bureau. *List of Pensioners on the Roll, January 1, 1883.* Baltimore: Genealogical Publishing Co., 1980. E494 .U55.

U.S. War Department. *Official Records of the Union and Confederate Armies in the War of the Rebellion.* 128 vols. Washington, D.C.: Government Printing Office, 1901. Reprint. Gettysburg, Pa.: National Historical Society, 1971. E464 .U6.

The general index to this series is available at the desk of the Local History and Genealogy Room. References are to the volume but not the page that contains the name sought. Each volume has its own page index of names.

U.S. War Department. *Official Records of the Union and Confederate Navies in the War of the Rebellion.* 31 vols. Washington, D.C.: Government Printing Office, 1894–1927. E591 .U58.

The index to this series is a separately bound volume.

Wright, Edward N. *Conscientious Objectors in the Civil War.* New York: A.S. Barnes, 1961. HF5636 .B965.

Civil War–Confederate

Brock, R.A. *The Appomattox Roster. Paroles of the Army of Northern Virginia.* Richmond: the society. Reprint. The Antiquarian Press, 1962. E548 .C66.

Brown, Dee A. *The Galvanized Yankees.* Urbana, Ill.: Urbana Press, 1863. E83.863 .B7.

Carroll, J.M. & Co. *The Confederate Roll of Honor.* Mattituck, N.Y.: J.M. Carroll & Co., 1985. E548 .C658.

Confederate Medical and Surgical Journal, 14 vols. Jan. 1864–Feb. 1865. Reprint. Metuchen, N.J.: Scarecrow Press, 1976. R11 .C62.

Confederate Veteran. 40 vols. Nashville: n.p., 1893–1932. E482 .C74. (Micro 10929).

This magazine is currently being published by the Sons of the Confederacy.

Crute, Joseph H., Jr. *Confederate Staff Officers, 1861–1865.* Powhatan, Va.: Derwent Books, 1892. E548 .C83.

Dickinson, Sally B. *Confederate Leaders.* Staunton, Va.: McClure Co., 1935. E467 .D54.

Donnelly, Ralph M. *Biographical Sketches of the Commissioned Officers of the Confederate States Marine Corps.* Alexandria, Va.: the author, 1973. E467 .D66.

———. *Service Records of Confederate Enlisted Marines.* Washington, D.C.: the author, 1979. E596 .D663.

Dotson, Susan M. *Who's Who in the Confederacy.* San Antonio: The Naylor Co., 1966. E467 .D68.

Estes, Claude, comp. *List of Field Officers, Regiments, and Battalions in the Confederate States Army, 1861–1865.* Washington, D.C.: Government Printing Office, 1899. Reprint. Macon, Ga.: J.W. Burke Co., 1912. E484 .E9.

Evans, Clement E. *Confederate Military History.* 12 vols. Atlanta: Confederate Publishing Co., 1899. E484 .E9.

Krick, Robert K. *Lee's Colonels, a Biographical Roster of the Field Officers of the Army of Northern Virginia.* Dayton, Ohio: Morningside Bookshop, 1979. E548 .K75.

———. *The Gettysburg Death Roster—The Confederate Dead at Gettysburg.* Dayton, Ohio: Morningside Bookshop, 1981. E494 .K74.

Mills, Gary B. *Civil War Claims in the South, an Index of Claims Filed Before the Southern Claims Commission, 1871–1880.* Laguna Hills, Calif.: Aegean Park Press, 1980. E480.5 .M54.

Norton, Herman W. *Rebel Religion: The Story of Confederate Chaplains.* St. Louis: Bethany Press, 1961. E547.7 .N6.

Office of Naval Records and Library. *Register of Officers of the Confederate States Navy, 1861–1865.* Washington, D.C.: Government Printing Office, 1898. Reprint. N.p., 1931. E597 .N585.

Powell, William H., ed. *Officers of the Army and Navy, Regular and Volunteer, Who Served in the Civil War.* Philadelphia: L.R. Hamersley & Co., 1894. E467 .P88.

Robertson, James I., Jr., ed. *An Index Guide to the Southern Historical society Papers, 1876–1959.* 2

vols. Millwood, N.J.: Kraus International Publications, 1876–1959. E483.7 .S762R62.

Southern Claims Commission. *Consolidated Index of Claims Reported by the Commissioners of Claims to the House of Representatives, 1871–1886.* Washington, D.C.: Government Printing Office, 1892. HJ8932 .A5.

Southern Historical Society. *Southern Historical Society Papers.* 52 vols. Richmond: the society, 1876–1959. E483.7 .S76.

United States War Department. *General Officers Appointed . . . Confederate States, 1861–1865.* Washington, D.C.: Government Printing Office, 1908. Reprint. Mattituck, N.J.: Carroll Co., 1983. E548 .U617.

———. *List of Staff Officers of the Confederate Army.* Washington, D.C.: Government Printing Office, 1891. Reprint. Mattituck, N.J.: Carroll Co., 1983. E548 .U76.

———. *Medical and Surgical History of the War of the Rebellion,* Vol. 2, part 3. Washington, D.C.: Government Printing Office, 1883. RD205 .U5.

———. *Official Records of the Union and Confederate Armies in the War of the Rebellion,* 128 vols.

See same title under Civil War—Union, above.

———. *Official Records of the Union and Confederate Navies in the War of the Rebellion,* 31 vols.

See same title under Civil War—Union, above.

Wakelyn, Jon L. *Biographical Dictionary of the Confederacy.* Westport, Conn.: Greenwood Press, 1977. E467 .W20.

Wilson, Beverly E. *General Officers of the Confederacy, 1861–1865.* Typescript. Baytown, Tex.: the author, n.d. E548 .W54.

For the titles of several publications relative to prisoners of war, burials, death lists, and regimental histories, see James C. Neagles's *Confederate Research Sources* (Salt Lake City: Ancestry, Inc., 1986, 250–71).

Spanish American War (War of 1898)

In the card catalog, look under **U.S. History—War of 1898—Regimental Histories** or **U.S. History — War of 1898—Registers and Lists.**

Board of Commissioners, Cook County, Illinois. Lewis, E. Robert, comp. *The Roll of Honor, Containing the Names of Soldiers, Sailors, and Marines of All Wars of Our Country Who are Buried in the Cemeteries of Cook County . . . Together With the Military Record and Place of Burial at Each . . . .* Chicago: Printing Products Corp., 1922. E494 .L67.

Cassard, William G., ed. *Battleship* Indiana *and Her Part in the Spanish-American War.* New York: Everett B. Mero, 1898. E727 .G34.

Dunning, William B. *The USS* Yankee *on the Cuban Blockade, 1898.* New York: Members of the *Yankee's* Crew, 1928. E727 .U65.

Gannon, Joseph C. *The USS* Oregon *and the Battle of Santiago.* New York: Comet Press, 1958. E727 .G3.

Johnson, Edward E. *History of Negro Soldiers in the Spanish-American War.* Raleigh: Capital Printing Co., 1899. E725.B .N3J6.

Peterson, Clarence S. *Known Military Dead During the Spanish-American War and the Philippine Insurrection, 1898–1901.* Baltimore: the author, 1950. E725 .8 .P4.

Sons of the American Revolution. *List of Members of Various State Societies of the Sons of the American Revolution Who Served in the War With Spain.* New York: National Society Sons of the American Revolution, 1900. E202 .A35.

U.S. Adjutant General's Office. *Officers of Volunteer Regiments Organized Under the Act of March 2, 1899.* Washington, D.C.: Government Printing Office, 1899. U11 .U7.

U.S. Congress. House. Commission on War Claims. *Officers and Soldiers . . . War With Spain . . . Held in Service in the Philippine Insurrection.* Washington, D.C.: Government Printing Office, 1937. UC744 .A4.

European War (World War I)

In the card or computer catalog, look under **European War, 1914–18—Prisoners and Prisons (by country)** or **European War, 1914–18—Regimental Histories** or **European War, 1914–18—Registers and Lists** or **European War, 1914–18—Registers of Dead (by country).**

Haulsee, W.M., and F. G. Howe. *Soldiers of the Great War.* 3 vols. Washington, D.C.: Soldiers' Record Publishing Co., 1920. D609 .U656.

The military service records of this war are stored at the National Personnel Records Center, 9700 Page Boulevard, St. Louis, MO 63132; unit histories are at the National Records Center, Suitland, Maryland; and the military draft board records are housed at the National Archives Center, East Point, Georgia.

World War II

Service records for military personnel are at the National Personnel Records Center, 9700 Page Boulevard, St. Louis, MO 63132. They are restricted and available only to living veterans, their next of kin, or those who present written permission from the veteran. Many of these records were destroyed by fire on 12 July 1973. However, there is an extensive program of reconstruction of many records of living veterans. Military draft board records for this war were turned over to the National Archives, and, except for a few samples, all were destroyed.

There are two publications of collections that provide valuable information about army divisions in this war.

Kahn, E.J., Jr., and Henry McLemore. *Fighting Divisions—Histories of Each United States Army Combat Division in World War II.* Washington, D.C.: Zenger Publications, Co., 1945. D769.1 .K3.

United States Department of the Army, Office of Military History. *Combat Chronicle.* Washington, D.C.: n.p., 1948. D769.29 .A52.

Korean Conflict

In the card or computer catalogs, look under **Korean War, 1950–52—Prisoners and Prisons** or **Korean War, 1950–53—Regimental Histories**.

United States Department of the Army. *Unit Citations and Campaign Participation Credit Registers.* Washington, D.C.: n.p., 1961. D797 .U7A426.

United States Department of Defense. Office of Public Relations. *Korean War Dead Returns.* Washington, D.C.: n.p., 1952. DS920.6 .U52.

Vietnam Conflict

The Library of Congress has a reference guide by Barbara Grochowski, "The Vietnamese Conflict," which may be obtained at the Information Alcove in the Main Reading Room. Some unit histories are also available at the National Records Center, Suitland, Maryland.

In the card or computer catalog, look under **Vietnamese Conflict, 1961–75—Regimental Histories**.

Patriotic and Lineage Societies

Those who can trace their lineage to a particular war, to a certain group of founders, or to early pioneers, often discover there is an organization so dedicated. The primary purpose of such patriotic societies is to preserve the memory and honor the traditions of an earlier period. Most of these societies have both a national headquarters and state chapters. They promote social and historical programs, thus providing both recreational and patriotic purposes to the organization. Some have published their membership lists, made their membership applications available for genealogical use, compiled lists of descendants from the eligible ancestors, and engaged in various research projects leading to useful publications. Most applications for membership require proof from primary sources for the line of descent and from eligible ancestor to potential member. These membership applications are usually available at the society's headquarters. The Library of Congress has many published membership lists and lists of eligible ancestors, as well as other publications that may have been prepared by the societies.

A description of many of the patriotic societies, along with their membership requirements, addresses, and some of their publications, is given by Grahame T. Smallwood in "Hereditary and Lineage Society Records" in *The Source: A Guidebook of American Genealogy,* edited by Arlene Eakle and Johni Cerny (Salt Lake City: Ancestry, Inc., 1984). Read Smallwood's chapter before consulting the card and computer catalog of the Library of Congress to search for information about these associations. When using the card catalog, look under the name of the society; however, some publications are listed by author rather than by name of the society. When using the computer catalog, search the name of the society; for example: **find c daughters american revolution**.

Brief descriptions from Smallwood's chapter of a few of the organizations are given below, along with some of their most useful publications that are available at the Library of Congress. These societies are listed here roughly in chronological order of the events that prompted their creation.

The Ancient and Honorable Artillery Company of Massachusetts

This is the oldest military body and chartered organization in America. It has a membership limited to 550 regular members. Other members (not regular) qualify by being a descendant of the original artillery company.

Publication

The Ancient and Honorable Artillery Company of Massachusetts. *Roll of Members of the Military Company of Massachusetts . . . With a Roster of the Commissioned Officers and Preachers.* Boston: Alfred Mudge & Son, 1895. US258 .A43.

National Society Women Descendants of the Ancient and Honorable Company

Members are females who qualify as descendants of the original company.

Publication

National Society Women Descendants of the Ancient and Honorable Company. *History and Lineage Book.* 7 vols. N.p.: the society, 1940, 1950, 1959, 1974, 1978. E186.99 .N423.

The General Society of Colonial Wars

Members qualify for membership by descent from a military ancestor or government official who served after the founding of Jamestown, Virginia, and before the start of the Revolutionary War. In addition to the publication listed here, others pertaining to individual states may be found in the card catalog.

Publication

General Society of Colonial Wars. *An Index of Ancestors and Roll of Members.* 3 vols. New York: the society, 1922; Hartford: 1941; Baltimore: 1977. E186.3 .A15.

National Society Daughters of Colonial Wars

Women members have the same membership requirements as men.

Publication

National Society Daughters of Colonial Wars. *Membership List and Index of Ancestors.* 2 vols. Somerville, Mass.: the society, 1941, 1950. E186.99 .D27A6.

The National Society of the Daughters of Founders and Patriots of America

Members must descend in the male line of either of their parents from an ancestor who settled in the American colonies between 13 May 1607 and 13 May 1687.

Publication

Lineage Book of the National Society of Daughters of Founders and Patriots of America. 45 vols. N.p., n.d. E186.8 .A15.

There is a separate index; see also *Guidebook No. 9* in the Microform Reading Room, which describes the contents of Micro 5667.

The Order of the Founders and Patriots of America

Members must descend through the male line of an ancestor who resided in the American colonies prior to 13 May 1686 and whose intermediate ancestor served in the American Revolution.

Publication

The Order of the Founders and Patriots of America Registers. 4 vols. E186.6 .A15.

The National Society of the Colonial Daughters of the Seventeenth Century

Members are lineal descendants of ancestors who rendered service from 1607 through 1699; membership is by invitation only.

Publication

Lineage Books. Brooklyn: the society, 1979. E186.7 .A2.

The National Society of the Colonial Dames of America

Members are women of lineal descent from a resident of the American colonies prior to 1750 who rendered efficient service to the country before 5 July 1776, including the signers of the Declaration of Independence. Membership is by invitation only.

Publication

Register of Ancestors, the National Society of the Colonial Dames of America in the Commonwealth of Virginia. Richmond: the society, 1979. F225 .N37.

National Society of the Sons and Daughters of the Pilgrims

Members are lineal descendants of any "pilgrims" who settled in the American colonies prior to 1700.

Publications

Lineages of Members of the National Society of Sons and Daughters of the Pilgrims to 1 January 1929. 2 vols. Philadelphia: the society, 1929. E186.99 .S523.

Mayo, Mary E. *Sixteen Hundred Lines to the Pilgrims—Lineages. Book III.* Manchester, Conn.: National Society Sons and Daughters of the Pilgrims, 1982. E186.99 .S5A63.

General Society of Mayflower Descendants

Members are the descendants of the Mayflower passengers who landed at Plymouth, Massachusetts, in December 1620.

Publications

Harding, Ann B., ed. *Mayflower Families Through Five Generations: Family of George Soule.* Plymouth, Mass.: the society, 1980. F63 .M39.

Kellogg, Lucy M., ed. *Mayflower Families Through Five Generations: Families of Francis Easton, Samuel Fuller, and William White.* Plymouth, Mass.: the society, 1975. F63 .M39.

Sherman, Robert E., ed. *Mayflower Families Through Five Generations: Families of James Childton, Richard More, and Thomas Rogers.* Plymouth, Mass.: the society, 1978. E63 .M39.

Terry, Milton E., and Anne B. Harding, comps. *Mayflower Ancestral Index.* Plymouth, Mass.: the society, 1981. CS49 .T47.

The Mayflower Descendant. 34 vols. Plymouth: The Massachusetts Society, 1899–1937. F68 .M47.

Two volume index.

Mayflower Index. 2 vols. Rev. ed. Boston: General Society of Mayflower Descendants, 1960. F68 .S6614.

The Saint Nicholas Society of the City of New York

Members are male descendants of residents of the city or state of New York prior to 1785.

Publication:

The Saint Nicholas Society of the City of New York Genealogical Records. 9 vols. New York: the society, n.d. F128.1 .S19.

The Society of the Cincinnati

At the close of the Revolutionary War, a group of officers formed this society. Any officer of that war and his eldest male descendants (but not more than one at a time) are eligible for membership. There were 2,269 officers who joined and 1,257 who were either killed in battle or did not choose to join. Present-day descendants trace their lineage to one of those officers.

Publication

Metcalf, Bryce. *Original Members and Other Officers Eligible to the Society of the Cincinnati, 1783–1838, With the Constitution, Rules of Admission, and Lists of the Officers of the General and State Societies.* Strasburg, Va.: Shenandoah Publishing House, Inc., 1938. E202.1 .A7M5.

National Society Daughters of the American Revolution

This, the largest patriotic society in America, requires its members to qualify as a descendant of a military person, a recognized patriot, or one who provided aid to the cause of the revolution. It keeps the applications for membership on file, most of which may be viewed by prospective members or other qualified persons who wish to establish a family connection with present or past members of the society. Their rules require strict documentation before an applicant is accepted, and source material cited in the application is reviewed carefully by the society's staff.

Names of persons who have been used as the basis for membership are published in the index cited below. The state societies, as well as the headquarters chapter located in Washington, D.C., have published hundreds of books and pamphlets of local vital records for use not only by prospective members but also by any genealogist. To find the titles of some of those publications that may be found in the Library of Congress, consult the card or computer catalog under Daughters of the American Revolution.

Publications

DAR Patriot Index. E255 .D38.

This index, with three supplements that add to or correct the original volume, lists the names of the members' ancestors. It also includes names of ancestors' spouses, birth and death dates of both where known, military rank, type of service or from which state served, and whether a pension was granted to the veteran, patriot, or widow.

Lineage Books.

These books, consisting of 166 volumes, contain the names and "national numbers" of all who became members of the society between 1890 and 1921. The first 160 volumes are indexed in four separate volumes, indexed by name of both the patriot and the member.

The Seventeenth Report, 1913–14. (Containing Pierce's Register.) E202.5 .A17.

This annual report of the society gives, in alphabetical order, names of Revolutionary War personnel in the Continental Army who were issued pay certificates by John Pierce, Paymaster General, at the close of the war. It includes 93,000 names.

An extensive list of publications by state societies, as well as more details about the National Society Daughters of the American Revolution, may be found in James C. and Lila L. Neagles's *Locating Your Revolutionary War Ancestor* (Logan, Utah: Everton Publishers, 1983, Z5313 .U5N42).

National Society Sons of the American Revolution

Membership is based on the service of an ancestor who was in the military, held a high civil office, or was a patriot in the cause of the American Revolution. The society has state chapters in all fifty states, plus France and England. Lineage papers of members on file at the society's headquarters in Louisville, Kentucky, may be reviewed by prospective members.

Publications

Lineage Books (patterned after the *Lineage Books* of the Daughters of the American Revolution).

Clark, A. Howard. *A National Register of the Society Sons of the American Revolution.* 2 vols. New York: Louis H. Cornish, 1902. (Micro 10918E.)

Several state chapters have also published membership and ancestor lists, directories, and yearbooks, all of which contain material of benefit to genealogists. To locate them, consult the card catalog under **Sons of the American Revolution—[state].** A search may be made using the computer catalog with the same subject heading.

Hereditary Order of Descendants of the Loyalists and Patriots of the American Revolution

Members of this organization must trace their lineage to two ancestors, one a Loyalist and the other a Patriot. Although this society has no known publications, there are several that include names of Loyalists during the American Revolution. See Smallwood's chapter in *The Source,* cited earlier. Another good source is Gregory Palmer's *Bibliography of Loyalist*

Source Material in the United States, Canada, and Great Britain (Westport, Conn.: Mecklar Publishers, 1982, A1238 .B52).

Society of the Descendants of Washington's Army at Valley Forge

This is a relatively new society organized for descendants of those who served at Valley Forge, Pennsylvania, during the American Revolution.

Publication

Worley, Ramona C., comp. *Valley Forge . . . In Search of That Winter Patriot.* Louisville, Ky.: National Society Sons of the American Revolution, 1979. Z1238 .W84.

General Society of the War of 1812

Membership is restricted to direct male descendants (or to one collateral descendant if there was no direct male descendant) of a veteran of the War of 1812.

Publications

Ordway, Frederick I., Jr., ed. *Register of the General Society of the War of 1812.* N.p.: the society, 1972. E351.3 .A17.

————. *Bicentennial Supplement to the 1972 Register.* Ann Arbor: Edward Brothers, Inc., 1976. E351.3 .A45.

General Society of the War of 1812. *The Constitution and Register of Membership of the General Society of the War of 1812.* Washington, D.C.: The Law Reporter Printing Co., 1908. E351.3 .A13.

National Society United States Daughters of 1812

Membership is restricted to female lineal descendants of military veterans who served between the end of the Revolutionary War and the end of the War of 1812 (1783–1815).

Publication

1812 Ancestor Index. Washington, D.C.: the society, 1970. E351.6 .A5G3.

Aztec Club of 1847–The Military Society of the Mexican War, 1846–48

Membership is restricted to lineal descendants of officers who served in the Mexican War.

Publication

The Constitution of the Aztec Club and List of Members, 1893. Washington, D.C.: n.p., 1893. E461.1 .A4.

The Military Order of the Loyal Legion of the United States

Membership is restricted to male lineal descendants of officers who served in the Union Army of the Civil War.

Publications

Roll of Commandaries . . . Register of the Military Order of the Loyal Legion of the United States. Boston: n.p., 1906. E402.2 .A19A7.

Roster of the Military Order of the Loyal Legion of the United States. Philadelphia: n.p., 1975. E402.2 .A164.

Dames of the Loyal Legion of the United States

As with their male counterparts, members are descended from officers (or officer's wives) of the Military Order of the Loyal Legion of the United States (MOLLUS).

Publication

Roster of the Loyal Legion of the United States. E402.25 .P46.

Sons of Confederate Veterans

Membership is composed of descendants of Confederate soldiers. This organization has recently reinstituted the publication of *The Confederate Veteran,* a journal published by the United Confederate Veterans during the period 1893 to 1932 (E482 .C74).

United Daughters of the Confederacy

Members are descendants of Confederate soldiers or those who aided the cause of the Confederacy. The organization performs patriotic and scholarship assistance to qualified persons.

Military Order of Foreign Wars of the United States

Members trace their lineage to officers who served in any of this country's foreign wars, but membership is restricted to direct male descendants of those officers.

Publication

Register of the Military Order of Foreign Wars of the United States, 1896, 1897, 1900. New York: National Commandary, 1896–1900. E181 .M65.

The Daughters of the Republic of Texas

Membership is composed of female lineal descendants of citizens of Texas who resided there prior to the state's annexation on 19 February 1846.

Publication

Morris, Mrs. Harry J., comp. *Daughters of the Republic of Texas: Founders and Patriots of the Republic of Texas—Lineages of Members.* Austin: the author, 1963. F385. D25.

The Society of California Pioneers

Membership is restricted to male lineal descendants of California residents prior to 1850.

Publication

Bancroft, Huber H. *California Pioneer Register and Index, 1742–1850: Including Inhabitants of California 1769–1800, and List of Pioneers.* Reprint. Baltimore: Genealogical Publishing Co., 1864. F856 .S65.

The Sons of California Pioneers

Membership is restricted to male descendants of anyone, male or female, who arrived in California before 1 January 1850.

Publication

Allen, Walter E., ed. *Centennial Roster.* San Francisco: the society, 1948. F856 .S65.

Contains membership lists for several years beginning in 1861 and lists of officers for several other years.

Sons of Utah Pioneers

Membership is composed of male descendants of those who arrived in Utah prior to completion of the railroads on 10 May 1869.

Publication

The Pioneers. 32 vols. F821 .P56.

National Society of the Daughters of Utah Pioneers

Members are female descendants of those who arrived in Utah prior to completion of the railroads on 10 May 1869.

Publication

Daughters of Utah Pioneers, Lesson Committee. Salt Lake City: the society, 1978. F826 .D36.

CHAPTER 7

Immigrant Ancestors

The ultimate goal of American family historians is to trace their lineage as far back as possible—tracing the lineage to the country from which the family came before coming to America and, if possible, learning something about the immigrant ancestor. If successful, one discovers the family's ethnic origins. This, no doubt, explains the deep interest in genealogy among Americans. They are prone to say: "I am part German and part English" or "I am Irish and proud of it."

This chapter discusses sources that can help one discover the country of his or her origin. Highlighted are census schedules relating to foreign-born individuals, passenger manifests, emigration lists compiled in European countries, records of aliens who applied for naturalization, and, in particular, records of national or ethnic groups in this country.

To begin, work backwards from the most recent available federal population census schedules. If an ancestor was living in the United States in 1900 or 1910, try to find him or her in those census years and check the "citizenship" columns. These indicate the year they entered the United States and whether or not they were naturalized citizens. Birthplaces of immigrants and their parents is shown in the 1880, 1900, and 1910 census schedules. The 1870 census indicates if the parents were "foreign-born." In 1850 and 1860, the censuses show the birthplace of every person enumerated but not of their parents. One can draw significant conclusions from a study of the census schedules. For instance, if the parents in a family were born in a foreign country but some or all of their children were born in the United States, the approximate year of the family's arrival here may be deduced by noting the year and place of birth of each child.

Ship Passenger Lists

In 1819 a federal law was enacted that required the master of any incoming ship from a foreign port to file with the district collector of customs at the port of entry a passenger manifest (list), including the names of any who had died or had been born en route. For each passenger, the following information was generally included: name, age, sex, occupation, country of origin (not necessarily the country from which the ship last sailed), and the passenger's destination. These lists included Americans returning home from abroad. Unfortunately, many of these manifests have been lost or destroyed; and only lists for the Port of New Orleans have survived intact for the period 1820 to 1905.

Using the original customs lists, the Department of State prepared transcripts and bound them into volumes. These were later microfilmed and made available at the National Archives. The Library of Congress has no original passenger lists or copies of them. It does have, however, the following two publications published from letters prepared by the Secretary of State. These letters contain some 9,000 names of passengers listed as entries in volume 1 and some entries in the missing volume 2 of the transcripts.

U.S. Department of State. *Letter From the Secretary of State, With a Transcript of the List of Passengers Who Arrived in the United States From the 1st October, 1819 to the 30th September, 1820.* Reprint. Baltimore: Genealogical Publishing Co., 1970. JV6461 .A54.

United States, Department of State. *Letter From the Secretary of State, With a Transcript of the List of Passengers Who Arrived in the United States, September, 1821–December, 1823.* Indexed. Reprint. Baltimore: Magna Carta Book Co., 1969. JV6461 .A54.

The National Archives has passenger lists for arrivals at several Atlantic and Gulf Coast ports after 1820, as well as the following lists for earlier arrivals:

Bath, Louisiana (April 1806); Salem and Beverly, Massachusetts (1798–1800); Perth Amboy, New Jersey (1801–37), with some missing; Philadelphia, Pennsylvania (1800–19).

Note that the names from the Salem and Beverly, Massachusetts, lists were published in the *New England Historical and Genealogical Register* 106 (July 1952): 203–09.

Although manifests for the Port of New York are available for the years following 1820, they are not indexed for the period 1846 to 1897. If one knows the approximate time of arrival, name of the ship, and port of entry during that fifty year period, it is possible to narrow the search by referring to the *Morton Allan Directory of European Passenger Steamship Arrivals* (reprinted by Genealogical Publishing Co., Baltimore, 1987, HE945 .A205). This book lists ships (not passengers) and dates of arrival at New York between 1890 and 1930, and at the ports of Baltimore, Boston, and Philadelphia between 1904 and 1926.

Copies of original passenger lists for the Port of Baltimore (1833–36) are included in Michael H. Tepper's *Passenger Arrivals at the Port of Baltimore, 1820–1834: From Customs Passenger Lists* (Baltimore: Genealogical Publishing Co., 1982, CS68 .T56).

Passenger lists for the Port of San Francisco were destroyed by the fires of 1851 and 1940. Except for the National Archives Center at San Bruno, California, which has a few lists for 1820, and possibly some other National Archives Centers on the West Coast, there are no passenger lists for any Pacific port—except those that might be located in individual customs offices on the coast. Using newspaper lists of arrivals at San Francisco, reconstruction of passenger lists was attempted and published as follows:

Rasmussen, Louis J. *San Francisco Ship Passenger Lists.* 4 vols. Colma, Calif.: the author, 1965–70. Reprint of Vol. 1. Baltimore: Genealogical Publishing Co., 1978. CS68 .R37.

See also the following work:

"San Francisco Ship Passenger Lists, 1849–1875." *San Francisco Genealogical Bulletin* (later *San Francisco Historical Records and Genealogy Bulletin*), 1863–65. 17 vols. N.p., n.d. F869 .S8S263.

Published Passenger Lists

Copies of passenger lists and related immigration records—particularly for the early history of our country—have not survived. However, there are many lists that have been transcribed and published in a variety of journals, magazines, and books, most of which are available at the Library of Congress. It is nearly impossible to seek these out by browsing; therefore, it is well to make use of published indexes and bibliographies. The following published aids are available at the library.

Filby, P. Willam, and Mary K. Meyer. *Passenger and Immigration Lists Index: A Guide to Published Arrival Records of About 500,000 Passengers Who Came to the United States and Canada and the West Indies in the Seventeenth, Eighteenth, and Nineteenth Centuries.* 3 vols. with annual supps., 1982–. Filby and Dorothy M. Lower: supps 1986 and 1987. Detroit: Gale Research Co., 1981–87. CS68 .F363.

Until publication of the above, the only well-known index of early passenger lists was Harold Lancour's *Bibliography of Passenger Lists,* which listed 262 sources. Filby and Meyer's indexes included most of Lancour's citations, plus many others, including those by Michael Tepper. Filby and Meyer prepared the three-volume index with an alphabetized list of names in published passenger lists, naturalization lists, and other related immigration records. These volumes contain 480,000 names from 300 published lists, with each source coded and names cross-referenced to aid in locating passengers who arrived with their family members.

Annual supplements have been published since 1982; supplements for 1982–85 were brought out in a cumulative index that added 650,000 names, bringing the total to 1,150,000. Since 1986 the supplements have each contained 125,000 names. More supplements are expected.

In front of each volume there is a list of the sources from which the passengers' names were taken. Ask a reference librarian for assistance and advice relative to call numbers penciled in the margins of these volumes. Publications named in these indexes that are not available in the Library of Congress must be obtained elsewhere. This creates a problem for the researcher at the Library of Congress if he or she has trouble tracking down a specific work. It is anticipated that eventually all sources listed in these volumes will be published by Gale Research Company.

> Filby, P. William. *Passenger and Immigration Lists Bibliography, 1538–1900.* Detroit: Gale Research Co., 1981. Supp. 1, 1984; Supp. 2, 1988. Z5313 .U5F54.
>
> Filby also prepared a bibliography, with two supplements published so far. Indexes are arranged by subject (such as place of emigration, embarkation and debarkation ports, nationality, names of ships, and so forth). Hundreds of passenger lists not yet included in *Passenger Lists Index* are cited. This work is available in the Local History and Genealogy Reading Room.
>
> Miller, Olga K. *Migration, Emigration, Immigration.* 2 vols. Logan, Utah: Everton Publishers, 1974. Z5313 .U5M62.
>
> Although somewhat out of date, this two-volume work will provide many immigration records sources. They are arranged under headings that include: the colonies, New England, indentured servants, convicts and rebel prisoners, foreigners in American wars, passenger lists, ethnic groups, churches, states of the United States, and countries of Europe. Subheadings are arranged by country, state, or nationality groups.

Certain publications of passenger lists cited in all of the above indexes and bibliographies are more extensive than others. Some of these, insofar as they may be found in the Library of Congress, are cited below:

> Baca, Leo. *Czech Immigration Passenger Lists.* 2 vols. Halletsville, Tex.: Old Homestead Publishing, 1983–85. E184 .B67B32.
>
> Bangerter, Lawrence B., comp. *The Compass: A Concise and Factual Compilation of All Vessels and Sources Listed, With References Made of All of Their Voyages and Some Dates of Registration.* Logan, Utah: Everton Publishers, 1983. Z5313 .U5B36.
>
> Banks, Charles E. *Topographical Dictionary of 2,885 English Emigrants to New England, 1620–50.* Philadelphia: Bertram Press, 1937. Reprint; Baltimore: Genealogical Publishing Co., 1981. F3 .B35.
>
> Boyer, Carl, III, ed. *Ship Passenger Lists.* 4 vols. Vol. 1, *National and New England, 1600–1825;* Vol. 2, *New York and New Jersey, 1600–1825;* Vol. 3, *Pennsylvania and Delaware, 1641–1825;* Vol. 4, *The South, 1538–1825.* Newhall, Calif.: the editor, 1977. CS68 .S53.
>
> These volumes, containing a total of 29,000 names, include lists in print, lists reproduced but not in print, and those in foreign publications.
>
> Cassady, Michael. *New York Passenger Arrivals, 1849–68.* Edited by Sylvia Nimmo. Papillion, Neb.: the author, 1983. CS68 .C35.
>
> Colket, Meredith R.J. *Founders of Early American Families: Emigrants from Europe, 1607–37.* Cleveland: General Court of the Order of Founders and Patriots of America, 1975. Rev. ed., 1985. CS61 .C64.
>
> Glazier, Ira A., and P. William Filby, eds. *Germans to America: Lists of Passengers Arriving at United States Ports, 1850–55.* 10 vols., projected. Wilmington, Del.: Scholarly Research Co., 1988–. E184 .G3638.
>
> At this writing the first two volumes (700,000 names) of the proposed ten volume set are being published. They contain names of passengers taken from ship passengers manifests transferred from the National Archives to the Temple University-Balch Institute for Immigration Research in Philadelphia. Plans are to extend this series to include arrivals through 1897.
>
> Glazier, Ira A., and Michael H. Tepper, eds. *The Famine Immigrants: Lists of Irish Immigrants Arriving at the Port of New York, 1846–51.* 7 vols. Baltimore: Genealogical Publishing Co., 1982–86. E184 .I6F25.
>
> Lists immigrants (650,000 names) for part of the period for which the National Archives has no indexes for the Port of New York. Prepared from lists at the Temple University-Balch Institute for Immigration Research in Philadelphia.
>
> Olsson, Nils W. *Swedish Passenger Arrivals in New York, 1820–50.* Chicago: Swedish Pioneer Historical Society, 1967. E184 .S23043.
>
> ———. *Swedish Passenger Arrivals in United States Ports, 1820–50 (Except New York), With Additions and Corrections to Swedish Passenger Arrivals in New York, 1820–50.* Stockholm: Jungi Bibl., 1979. E184 .S23. (Z674 .S8–No.32).
>
> Prins, Edward. *Dutch and German Ships: Passenger Lists, 1846–56.* Holland, Mich.: the author, 1972. F754 .H6P75.
>
> Contains 12,500 names.

Rieder, Milton P., Jr., and Norma G. Rieder, comps. *New Orleans Ship Lists, 1820–23.* 2 vols. Metairie, La.: the authors, 1966–68. F368 .R5.

Rupp, Israel D. *A Collection of Upwards of Thirty Thousand Names of German, Swiss, Dutch, French and Other Immigrants in Pennsylvania From 1727 to 1776 . . . .* Reprint. Baltimore: Genealogical Publishing Co., 1985. F152 .R9614.

Schlegel, Donald M. *Passengers From Ireland, 1811–1817.* Baltimore: Genealogical Publishing Co., 1980. E184 .I6S34.

Contains 7,300 names.

Swierenga, Robert P., comp. *Dutch Immigrants in United States Passenger Manifests, 1820–1880.* 2 vols. Wilmington, Del.: Scholarly Research Co., 1983. E184 .O9S95.

Contains 53,000 names.

Tepper, Michael H., ed. *Immigrants to the Middle Colonies: A Consolidation of Ship Passenger Lists and Associated Data From the New York Genealogical and Biographical Records.* Baltimore: Genealogical Publishing Co., 1978. F106 .I47.

———. *Passengers to America: A Consolidation of Ship Passenger Lists From the New England Historical and Genealogical Register.* Baltimore: Genealogical Publishing Co., 1977. CS68 .P37.

———. *New World Immigrants: A Consolidation of Ship Passenger Lists and Associated Data From Periodical Literature.* Baltimore: Genealogical Publishing Co., 1979. CS68 .N48.

European Emigration Lists

The library has a large collection of publications concerning those who emigrated from European countries. Those who left their home countries did so for various reasons: some fled from religious or political persecution, carried little or no identification, and left no record of their departure; others applied to leave and were issued formal papers; some who could not afford to pay their own passage were indentured to an emigrant agent and bound to a citizen in America for a period of servitude before gaining their freedom. One class of indentured servant was the "redemptioner" or "free-willer," who offered himself as a servant on ar-

rival in America, selling his services at public auction. Another class of indentured servant was a prisoner (often having been confined as a debtor) who was shipped to America from England in lieu of continuing incarceration in a British jail or prison. This class of servant usually was indentured for a period of seven years before being declared free.

European citizens were required to have some type of official document in order to cross borders between countries, and records were kept of those who emigrated. Some of these documents have been translated and published in English in the United States. However, most of the originals were retained in European archives, where some of them have been abstracted and published. By studying these works one may find some written evidence of an immigrant ancestor as he or she prepared to leave the mother country. It has been estimated that some 30 percent of European emigrants (mostly Polish, Romanian, Hungarian, and Austrian) who came to America left through the Port of Hamburg, Germany.

The Manuscript Division has microfilm copies, with indexes, of Hamburg emigration lists for the years 1850 to 1873. The finding aid is "Foreign Copying Project—Germany, Hamburg Passenger Lists, 1850–73." The sixty-six reels in this series contain names written in old German script that is difficult to read. The arrangement for 1850 to 1854 is an alphabetical list by family within each year; names for 1855 to 1873 are arranged chronologically by date of embarkation, with separate name indexes. The lists in this series are "listen direkt" and "listen indirekt" referring to ships that either sailed directly to America from Hamburg or by way of other ports. The Family History Library at Salt Lake City, Utah, has 361 reels, including indexes, covering the years 1850 to 1934.

Researchers who wish to go directly to the source, may visit or write the Emigration Office in Hamburg, which can provide names and dates of departure. Written requests should be addressed to Historic Emigration Office, Museum fur Hamburgerische Geshichte, Holstenwall 24, 2000 Hamburg 36, West Germany. The fee is $30 per inquiry, with an additional $10 fee for each year searched.

Arlene Eakle's "Tracking Immigrant Origins," in *The Source: A Guidebook of American Genealogy,* edited by Arlene H. Eakle and Johni Cerny (Salt Lake City: Ancestry, Inc., 1984), has a helpful table showing locations of many European emigrant lists. Several of them are available on microfilm and can be obtained from the LDS Family History Library or one of its branch libraries. To ascertain what published lists are available at the Library of Congress, use the computer catalog with commands similar to the following examples (substituting the name of the country or port city as appropriate) **find s sweden emigration or find s germany emigration** or **find s wurttemberg emigration registers** or **find s britain emigration.**

The following is a selected bibliography of publications at the Library of Congress.

Baker, Dessie, ed. *Port of Derry Ship Lists From J. & J. Cooke's Line, 1847–1849.* Apollo, Pa.: Closson Press, 1985. E184 .I6P58.

Brandow, James C. *Omitted Chapters from Hotten's Original Lists of Persons of Quality . . . , 1600–1700.* Baltimore: Genealogical Publishing Co., 1982. CS69 .O45.

Contains 6,500 names. See also Hotten, below.

Cameron, Viola R., comp. *Emigrants From Scotland to America, 1774–1775. Copied From a Loose Bundle of Treasury Papers in the Public Record Office, London, England.* London: the compiler, 1930. Reprint; Baltimore: Genealogical Publishing Co., 1978. E187.5 .C18.

Contains 2,000 names.

Coldham, Peter W. *The Complete Book of Emigrants, 1607–1660.* Baltimore: Genealogical Publishing Co., 1987. E184 .B7C59.

———. *Bonded Passengers to America.* 9 vols. in 3. Baltimore: Genealogical Publishing Co., 1983. CS61 .C62.

Contains 50,000 names.

Dobson, David. *A Directory of Scots Banished to the American Plantations, 1650–1775.* Baltimore: Genealogical Publishing Co., 1984. E184 .S306.

Contains 3,000 names.

Faust, Albert B. *Lists of Swiss Emigrants in the Eighteenth Century to the American Colonies.* 2 vols. Reprint. Baltimore: Genealogical Publishing Co., 1976. E184 .S9F22.

Ghirelli, Michael. *A List of Emigrants From England to America, 1682–1692.* Baltimore: Magna Carta Books, 1968. F187.5 .G47.

Hacker, Werner. *Auswanderunger Aud Baden . . .* Stuttgart: Theiss, 1980. CS627 .B336H32. Reprint. N.p., 1985.

Three volumes in this series name 120,000 persons who emigrated from southwestern Germany.

Hall, Charles H. *The Antwerp Emigration Index.* Logan, Utah: Everton Publishers, 1986. CS403 .H35.

Hargreaves-Mawdsley, R., trans. *Bristol and America: A Record of the First Settlers in the Colonies of North America, 1654–1685, Including the Names with Places of Origin of More than 10,000 Servants to Foreign Plantations, Who Sailed From the Port of Bristol to Virginia, Maryland, and Other Ports of the Atlantic Coast, and Also to the West Indies From 1654 to 1685.* London: R.S. Glover, 1929. Reprint with index. Baltimore: Genealogical Publishing Co., 1978. E187.5 B835.

Hotten, John C., ed. *The Original Lists of Persons of Quality; Emigrants; Religious Exiles; Political Rebels; Serving Men Sold for a Term of Years; Apprentices; Children Stolen; Maidens Pressed; and Others Who Went from Great Britain to the American Plantations, 1600–1700 . . . From Manuscripts Preserved in the State Paper Department of Her Majesty's Public Records Office, England.* Reprint. Baltimore: Genealogical Publishing Co., 1974. E187.5 .H7945.

Kaminkow, Jack, and Marion Kaminkow. *A List of Emigrants From England to America, 1718–1759.* Baltimore: Magna Carta Books, 1981. E187.5 .K3.

Contains 3,000 names.

Mitchell, Brian, comp. *Irish Passenger Lists, 1847–1871: Lists of Passengers Sailing from Londonderry to America on Ships of the J. & J. Cooke Line and the McCorkell Line.* Baltimore: Genealogical Publishing Co., 1988. (Cataloging in publication.)

Schenk, Trudy, and Ruth Froelke. *The Wuerttemberg Emigration Index.* 5 vols. Salt Lake City: Ancestry, Inc., 1986. CS627 .S86S34.

These volumes are based on extractions from handwritten official papers pertaining to persons who filed for permission to depart from Wuerttemberg, Germany, during the 1800s. The names are alphabetized and birth dates and places of origin are given. Approximately ten volumes are anticipated, with an estimated 100,000 names.

Smith, Clifford Neal. *British Deportees to America, 1760–65. British-American Genealogical Research Monograph.* 2 vols. McNeal, Ariz.: Westland Publications, 1974–78. E184 .B7S63.

———. *German-American Genealogical Research Series. Cumulative Surname Index and Summary to Monographs One Through Twelve.* McNeal, Ariz.: Westland Publications, 1983. E184 .G3G2837.

This is an index to his series of monographs based on manuscripts found in the Hamburg and Marburg, Germany, archives, translated into English.

————. *Reconstructed Passenger Lists for 1850, Hamburg, Germany and Central European Emigration Series.* McNeal, Ariz.: Westland Publications, 1980–81. C535 .S64.

Contains 10,000 names.

Swierenga, Robert P., comp. *Dutch Emigrants to the United States, South Africa, South America, Southern Asia, 1835–80.* Wilmington, Del.: Scholarly Resources, 1983. CS827 .A1S89.

Yoder, Don, ed. *Rhineland Emigrants: Lists of German Settlers in Colonial America.* Baltimore: Genealogical Publishing Co., 1981. E184 .G3R44.

Zimmerman, Gary J., and Marion Wolfert, comps. *German Immigrants: Lists of Passengers Bound from Bremen to New York, 1855–1862.* Baltimore: Genealogical Publishing Co., 1986. E184 .G3Z563.

Pictures of Ships

Once the name of the ship on which an ancestor arrived is known, it might be interesting to see an illustration of the vessel. The following two publications may be helpful:

Anuta, Michael J. *Ships of Our Ancestors . . . Mostly Late Nineteenth Century and Early Twentieth Centuries.* Menominee, Mich.: Ships of Our Ancestors, Inc., 1983. VM381 .A58.

Kluda, Arnold. *Great Passenger Ships of the World.* 5 vols. Cambridge: Patrick Stephens, Ltd., 1972–74. VM381 .K5813.

Naturalization

Until 1921, when women won the right to vote, only men became naturalized citizens. The naturalization papers of an immigrant ancestor may be discovered before learning the date of his arrival. Although many of these papers do not show the year or port of debarkation or name of the ship, there are exceptions, especially for documents prepared in fairly recent years. They do, however, show the country of origin and will at least give a clue to the approximate time of arrival in the United States. The ancestor may have filed his or her "first papers" shortly thereafter, then filed the "final papers" after having been a resident for five years or longer.

Immigrants arriving at Philadelphia were marched in procession to a magistrate where they were required to take an oath of allegiance to the Pennsylvania government. Some were disabled, and some eluded the march, thus avoiding the requirement. The names of those who did take the oath on arrival or later, at one of the Philadelphia courts (between 1794 and 1880), were listed by the Work Projects Administration (WPA) in eleven volumes prepared, in typescript with carbon copies, by the Pennsylvania Historical Commission.

Pennsylvania Historical Commission. *Index to Records of Aliens' Declarations and Intentions and/or Oaths of Allegiance, Various Courts of Pennsylvania, 1789–1880.* 11 vols. Typescripts. Harrisburg: n.p., n.d. HE554 .P545.

The volumes are fragile, worn from handling, and available in only a few libraries. The work above was published in a single volume.

United States Work Projects Administration. P. William Filby, ed. *Philadelphia Naturalization Records: Index to Records of Aliens' Declarations of Intention and/or Oaths of Allegiance, 1789–1880, in the United States Circuit Court, United States District Court, Supreme Court of Pennsylvania, Quarter Sessions Court, Court of Common Pleas, Philadelphia.* Detroit: Gale Research Co., 1982. CS68 .P47.

Before deciding whether to search for naturalization papers, consider the possibility that an ancestor became a citizen automatically without going through the naturalization process. English subjects living in the colonies prior to the American Revolution were considered citizens since the colonies were an extension of the mother country. After the English Parliamentary Act of 1740, a non-Englishman could become a citizen in one of the colonies after a seven-year residence, provided an oath of loyalty to Crown and colony was taken (an example would be French Huguenots who fled to America to escape religious persecution). See Montague S. Guiseppi's *Naturalizations of Foreign Protestants in the American and West Indian Colonies—1740* (Baltimore: Genealogical Publishing Co., 1964, E184 .A1G52). Before and immediately after the American Revolution some of the states enacted their own naturalization laws—except for the following: Connecticut, Georgia, New Hampshire, North Carolina, and Pennsylvania. When the colonies declared their independence from England in 1776, any white person of European descent, born in the colonies and loyal to the revolutionary cause, automatically became a citizen of the new United States of America.

The first naturalization law in this country was enacted on 26 March 1790. It provided that any free white person with good moral character could become an American citizen after a one-year residence in a state and a two-year residence in the country, provided he or she took an oath to support the constitution. Indentured servants, but not African slaves, were eligible. In 1802 Congress revised the laws and required a one-year residence in a state and a five-year residence in the country. The applicant was required to file a Declaration of Intention and later a petition for citizenship. The declaration specified that applicants renounce forever "all allegiance and fidelity to any foreign prince, potentate, State or Sovereignty whatever," and particularly allegiance to the head of the country to which they had formerly belonged. After naturalization, their wives and minor children were also then considered citizens.

An immigrant arriving after the establishment of the United States may have become a citizen without becoming naturalized, provided he or she was among the following:

1. Those who resided in the Louisiana Territory when it was purchased from France in 1803;

2. Those who resided in Florida when it was acquired or purchased from Spain, in successive cessions in 1810, 1812, and 1821;

3. Those who resided in the Republic of Texas when it was accepted as a state—but only after Congress granted citizenship to them in 1845;

4. Those who resided in Alaska when it was purchased from Russia in 1867;

5. Those who were free Negroes and slaves when the Fourteenth Amendment to the Constitution was enacted in 1868;

6. Those who resided in Hawaii when it was annexed by the United States in 1898;

7. Those who resided in Puerto Rico in 1917 when it became a United States Territory, and those who resided in the Virgin Islands in 1927;

8. American Indians who served honorably in the American military forces during World War I, and all Indians in 1924;

9. Those who resided in Guam after World War II.

Any alien in the United States who did not fall into one of the above mentioned categories was permitted to apply for citizenship. Although citizenship was not required, many chose to become naturalized in order to vote, hold elective or appointed office, or qualify for land under the Homestead Laws of 1862. Some filed their first citizenship papers so they would be eligible to receive the Homestead Law land grants and then failed to become full-fledged citizens. A search in the homestead files often turns up a Declaration of Intention.

A prospective citizen could apply to be naturalized at any court of record that had decided to accept naturalization cases. The applicant could choose any such court, at any government level. Until 1906, federal courts were not required to handle naturalization, but many chose to do so. The Declaration of Intention, and the Petition for Citizenship, with supporting papers, may still be stored in the court. When a Certificate of Citizenship was issued, a record of the transaction was made by completing a stub showing the pertinent facts. That stub may still be available among the court documents.

After 27 September 1906, all naturalizations in any court had to be recorded in duplicate with the United States Immigration and Naturalization Service. If a naturalized citizen ancestor became a citizen before the above date, locate his records in the court that processed the case or in some central repository where they may have been transferred. Most federal courts have transferred their documents to one of the National Archives centers. The National Archives in Washington, D.C., has an index of naturalizations for only some of the New England states; the photostated files (dexigraphs) are stored at the National Archives center at Waltham, Massachusetts. The Library of Congress does not have any original or copies of naturalization documents.

Locating courts and other repositories with naturalization records may be eased by consulting James C. Neagles and Lila L. Neagles's *Locating Your Immigrant Ancestor: A Guide to Naturalization Records* (Logan, Utah: Everton Publishers, 1975; rev. ed., 1986. CS68 .N42). This book is the result of a nationwide survey to discover the availability of records in courts (county, state, and federal), the National Archives, state historical societies, and state genealogical societies.

For a comprehensive discussion of naturalizations in America, see John J. Newman's *American Naturalization Process and Procedures, 1790–1985* (Indianapolis, Ind.: Indiana Historical Society, 1985, KF4710 .N49), located in the law library of the Library of Congress.

The Library of Congress has several published lists of naturalizations conducted in various courts. Consult P. William Filby's *Passenger and Immigration Lists Bibliography,* as well as Olga Miller's *Migration, Emigration, Immigration* (both cited previously). You may also consult the computer or card catalogs, using the following command **find s naturalization [name of state]**.

If a published list of names cannot be found, then visit or write the courts where ancestors resided shortly after settling in the United States, using *Locating Your Immigrant Ancestor* as a guide.

Ethnic Groups

There are numerous published studies and specialized research reports dealing with the history and genealogy of various ethnic groups or nationalities in the United States, many available at the Library of Congress. Some have names of immigrants, others serve as guides or finding aids for genealogists or historians searching for background material. This section notes groups that immigrated to the United States, with a brief statement about their primary settlements and migrations. For purposes of this discussion, a group of persons is considered an ethnic group if its original language was something other than English—arbitrarily putting Native Americans and blacks in that classification; all others, for present purposes, are considered "non-ethnic."

Whether immigrants came alone or in groups, they frequently settled with others of similar backgrounds. Some such groups eventually moved to another location while maintaining their ethnic character. One's ancestor (and/or friends from the home country) might be mentioned in the records of towns where they settled. Using this as a key, you should consult Olga Miller's *Migration, Emigration, Immigration* (cited earlier); it has a very helpful chart showing European migrations from Europe and within the United States.

When looking for material relating to an ethnic group, ask to see the index folder for the vertical file in the Local History and Genealogy Reading Room. This will lead researchers to folders containing pamphlets and other miscellaneous information concerning foreign sources and methods of tracing ethnic ancestors. The headings include Afro, Australia, Canada, Denmark, France, Germany, Great Britain, Ireland, Poland, Scotland, Sweden, North, and Welsh Americans.

There are special rooms or divisions in the library that may have helpful material. Generally, their publications are strong on cultural, social, and economic history; politics; and business; but they are weak on genealogical sources. They do have foreign language/English dictionaries. Some books in these reading rooms might also be found in the general collections of the Local History and Genealogy Reading Room.

The reading rooms include the African and Middle Eastern Division (African section, Hebraic section,

and Near East section); Asian Division; European Division; and Hispanic Division.

Ask at the reference desks for any leaflet or pamphlet describing the reading room and services offered by its reference staff. Browse the reference collections and make use of any material listed in special indexes or finding aids. At this writing, the hours of operation by these reading rooms are 8:30 A.M. to 5:00 P.M., Monday through Friday.

To learn about publications dealing with ethnic groups, consult P. William Filby's *American and British Genealogy and Heraldry* (3d ed., with supp., Boston: New England Historic Genealogical Society, 1983, Z5311 .F55). Other helpful guidebooks are the following:

Baxter, Angus. *In Search of Your European Roots: A Complete Guide to Tracing Your Ancestor in Every Country in Europe.* Baltimore: Genealogical Publishing Co., 1985. CS403 .B59.

Barnardo, Stephanie. *The Ethnic Almanac.* Carden City, N.Y.: Doubleday, 1981. E184 .A1J157.

Currer-Briggs, Noel. *Worldwide Family History.* Boston: Rutledge and Kegan Paul, 1982. CS9 .C87.

Miller, Wayne C., et al. *A Comprehensive Bibliography for the Study of American Minorities.* 2 vols. New York: New York University Press, 1976. Z1361 .E4M529.

Wynar, Lubomyr R. *Encyclopedic Directory of Ethnic Organizations in the United States.* Littleton, Colo.: Libraries Unlimited, 1975. E184 .A1W94.

Foreign Telephone Directories

Anyone who has received a favorable response from a query in a genealogical journal, newspaper, or magazine is usually thrilled on receiving information from a family "cousin." Although this practice is fairly common among American relatives, attempts to locate "cousins" in the ancestral homeland are rare. Many European families have remained in one area for centuries, which enhances the odds of finding a descendant of a common ancestor. Using telephone directories can be helpful.

The Library of Congress has a large collection of foreign telephone directories. Although few are current, most are fairly recent and can be useful in locating families who share the family name. In trying to estab-

Africa (various countries of the continent)	Colombia	Jamaica	St. Kitts, Nevis, Anguilla
Albania	Congo	Japan	St. Lucia
Algeria	Costa Rica	Kenya	St. Martin
Angola	Cuba	Korea	St. Vincent
Aden Colony	Curacao (Dutch Antilles)	Latvia	Seychelles
Arabia Section (includes Kuwait, Egypt, Qator, Saudi Arabia, United Arab Emirates)	Cyprus	Lebanon	Saudi Arabia
	Czechoslovakia	Libya	Senegal
	Dahomey	Lithuania	Spain
Argentina	Denmark	Luxembourg	Sri Lanka
Aruba	Dominican Republic	Malaysia	Sudan
Australia	Ecuador	Macao	Syrinane (Surinane)
Austria	El Salvador	Maldives	Swaziland
Bahrain	England	Mauritania	Sweden
Bangladesh	Estonia	Malta	Switzerland
Barbados	Ethiopia	Mexico	Syria
Belgium	Fiji	Montserrat	Taiwan
Belize	Finland	Mozambique	Tanganyika
Bermuda	France (and possessions)	Nepal	Tangiers
Bhutan	Germany, West	Netherlands	Tanzania
Bolivia	Germany, East	New Caledonia	Thailand
Botswana	Greece	New Zealand	Trinidad and Tobago
Bonaire	Guatemala	Nicaragua	Tynisienne (Tunisia)
Brazil	Guyana (British)	Nigeria	Turkey
British possessions (New Hebrides, British Guyana, Brunei, Virgin Islands, Grenada, Solomon Islands, Tonga)	Guyana	Norway	Uganda
	Haiti	Oman	Union of South Africa (including Southwest Africa, Transvaal)
	Honduras	Pakistan	
	Hungary	Panama	Upper Volta
Burma	Iceland	Paraguay	Uruguay
Cambodia	India	Peru	USSR
Canada	Indonesia	Philippines	Venezuela
Ceylon	Iran (space empty, no books)	Poland	Vietnam
Chile		Portugal	Virgin Islands
China (mainland)	Ireland	Rhodesia	Yugoslavia
	Israel	Romania	Zambia
	Italy	Rwanda	

The foreign telephone directories in the Library of Congress.

lish a family connection by mail to someone in the foreign town be sure to enclose a self-addressed envelope, since the recipient probably will not understand the postal addressing system of the United States. Do not put a United States postage stamp on the return envelope; rather, send a postage reply coupon, obtainable at a post office. That coupon can be used to purchase postage in the foreign country.

The foreign telephone directories in the library are in the closed stacks, arranged alphabetically by country. Since they are in foreign languages, and the counties and towns may not be arranged alphabetically, and since they have not been cataloged, it will be necessary to consult them personally. Ask a reference librarian how to do this. Listed in the figure above are the foreign telephone directories in the library, arranged by country.

Specific Ethnic Groups

In the following pages, references pertaining to certain ethnic groups are cited. Other references may be found by consulting the computer catalog, using the commands shown below, with modifications as appropriate: **find s germany genealogy** (substitute name of country) or **find s irish genealogy** (substitute ethnic name) or **find s filipino genealogy** (substitute ethnic name).

Titles appearing on the computer screen will include a mixture of publications such as guides and bibliographies, foreign records sources, and genealogies of foreign families. Many are in a foreign language.

African-American

The history of people of African descent in America originates in the colonial period when they entered the country as free persons "of color," indentured servants, or slaves—many of whom arrived by way of the West Indies. Lineages for ancestors who were slaves can be difficult to trace prior to the Civil War and the Emancipation Proclamation because often only their first names were recorded. The task is simpler for free Negroes, usually residing in the northern states, who were listed in the censuses by full name and color ("black," "brown," or "colored"). Often they were land owners or operated a business, thereby leaving some written record for posterity.

In 1807 the Continental Congress enacted legislation forbidding the importation of slaves, to take effect in 1808; all slavery in the Northwest Territory was forbidden. Any additional slaves owned from that time forward were the result of birth, purchase, trade or inheritance. Most owners were white, but some were free Negroes or American Indians. Slaves born to mixed black and white parents created a group referred to as "mulatto."

Except for former slaves who gained their freedom by escaping, by manumission, or by purchasing their freedom, the above described situation continued until Lincoln issued the Emancipation Proclamation. Some slaves then left the plantations, willingly or unwillingly, when drafted into a Union regiment. Some remained with their former owners and began to receive wages for their labors. Beginning as early as the late 1870s, some Negroes began to migrate from the South to northern cities to seek employment. Many never left the South, preferring to stay to work as share-croppers or to hire themselves out as agricultural workers. For many of this group, the records of the Freedmen's Bureau, created in 1865 and lasting a few years, may be helpful.

The African section of the library is a reference section with published works relative to political, historical, economic, linguistic, and cultural aspects of African countries south of the Sahara Desert. Reference staff in this reading room can furnish a copy of

"African Names and Naming Practices," which might be of interest. Among works cited in that bulletin are the following:

Puckett, Newbell N. *Black Names in America: Origins and Usage*. Boston: G.K. Hall, 1975. E185.89 .N3P82.

Sanykia, Becktemba. *Know and Claim Your African Names*. Dayton, Ohio: Rucker Press, 1975. CS2375 .A33S26.

Smith, Elsdon C. *Personal Names: A Bibliography*. New York: New York Public Library, 1952. Reprint. Detroit: Gale Research Co., 1965. Z6824 .S55.

Guides and Bibliographies. At the reference desk of the Main Reading Room, obtain the leaflet "Afro-American Genealogical Research" and the pamphlet "How to Find Afro-American Sources in the General Reading Room Division." A selected list of publications are found below:

Abajian, James. *Blacks in Selected Newspapers, Censuses, and Other Sources: An Index to Names and Subjects*. Boston: G.K. Hall, 1977. Z1361 .N39A28.

Beard, Timothy F., and Denise Demong. *How to Find Your Family Roots*. New York: McGraw-Hill, 1977. CS16 .B35.

Contains a chapter on African-American genealogy.

Blockson, Charles L., and Ron Fry. *Black Genealogy*. Englewood Cliffs, N.J.: Prentice-Hall, 1977. CS21 .B55.

Brignano, Russell C. *Black Americans in Autobiography*. Durham, N.C.: Duke University Press, 1984. Z1361 .N39B67.

Cerny, Johni. "Black Ancestral Research." In *The Source: A Guidebook of American Genealogy*, edited by Arlene H. Eakle and Johni Cerny. Salt Lake City: Ancestry, Inc., 1984. CS49 .S65.

Clarke, Robert L., ed. *Afro-American History: Sources for Research*. Washington, D.C.: Howard University Press, 1981. E184.6 .N37.

Greene, Robert E. *Black Defenders of America, 1775–1973*. Chicago: Johnson Publishing, 1974. E185.63 .G73.

Index to Periodical Articles By and About Blacks. Boston: G.K. Hall. 1950, plus annual supps. A13 .04.

Linder, Bill R. "Black Genealogy: Basic Steps to Research," *History News* 36 (Feb., 1981). E172 .A533.

Logan, Rayford W., and Michael R. Winton, eds. *Dictionary of American Negro Biography.* New York: W.W. Norton, 1982. E185.96 .D53.

Miller, Elizabeth W., comp. *The Negro in America, A Bibliography.* 2d ed. Cambridge: Harvard University Press, 1970. Z1361 .N39M5.

Newman, Debra L. *Black History: A Guide to Civilian Records in the National Archives.* Washington, D.C.: National Archives, 1984. Z1361 .N39N576.

Porter, Dorothy B. *The Negro in the United States: A Bibliography.* Washington, D.C.: Library of Congress, 1970. Z1361 .N39P59.

Rose, James M., and Alice Eichholz. *Black Genesis.* Gale Genealogy and Local History Series, Vol. 1. Detroit: Gale Research Co., 1978. CS21 .R57.

Schatz, Walter. *Directory of Afro-American Resources.* New York: R.R. Bowker Co., 1970. Z1361 .N39R3.

Spradling, Mary M. *In Black and White: Afro-Americans in Print: A Guide to Afro-Americans Who Made Contributions to the United States From 1619 to 1969.* 3d ed. 2 vols., plus 1985 supp. Kalamazoo, Mich.: Kalamazoo Library System, 1980. Z1361 .N39S665.

Streets, David H. *Slave Genealogy: A Research Guide with Case Studies.* Bowie, Md.: Heritage Books, 1986. E185.96 .S817.

Toppin, Edgar A. *A Biographical History of Blacks in America Since 1528.* New York: McKay, 1971. E185.96 .T66.

Walker, James D. *Black Genealogy: How to Begin.* Athens, Ga.: University of Georgia Center for Continuing Education, 1977. E185.96 .W29.

Westin, Jeane E. *Finding Your Roots: How Every American Can Trace His Ancestors, at Home and Abroad.* Los Angeles: J.P. Tarcher, 1977. CS16 .W46.

Contains a section on African-American research.

Young, Tommie M. *African-American Genealogy: Exploring and Documenting the Black Family.* Clarksville, Tenn.: Jostens, 1980. E185–96 .Y66.

In addition to the guides and bibliographies listed above the following publications may be helpful for finding mention of an African-American ancestor. Other titles may be found by consulting the computer catalog: **find s afro-american genealogy**.

Boris, Joseph J., ed. *Who's Who in Colored America.* Supps. New York: Who's Who in Colored America Corp., 1929. E185.96 .W57.

Davis, Lenwood, G., and George Hill, comps. *Blacks in the American Armed Forces, 1776–1983. A Bibliography.* Westport, Conn.: Greenwood Press, 1985. Z1249 .M5D38.

Eichholz, Alice, and James M. Rose. *Free Black Heads of Households in the New York State Federal Census, 1790–1810.* Detroit: Gale Research Co., 1981. E185.93 .N56E37.

Hillyer, Andrew F. *Twentieth Century Union League Directory.* Washington, D.C.: Union League, 1901. E185.93 .D6H54.

Jacobs, Donald M., ed. *Index to the American Slave.* Supp 3. Westport, Conn.: Greenwood Press, 1981. E444 .A45.

Newman, Debra L., comp. *List of Free Black Heads of Families in the First Census of the United States, 1790.* Washington, D.C.: National Archives, 1973. E185.96 .N47.

Quarles, Benjamin. *The Negro in the Making of America.* New York: Collier Books, 1987. E185 .Q2.

———. *The Negro in the American Revolution.* Chapel Hill, N.C.: University of North Carolina Press, 1961. E269 .N3Q3.

———. *The Negro in the Civil War.* Boston: Little, Brown, 1969. E540 .N33.

Richardson, Clement, ed. *The National Cyclopedia of the Colored Race.* Montgomery, Ala.: National Publishing Co., 1919. E185 .N27.

Simmons, William J. *Men of Mark: Eminent, Progressive, and Rising.* New York: Arno Press and New York Times, 1968. E185.96 .S45.

Who's Who Among Black Americans. Northbrook, Ill.: Who's Who Among Black Americans, Inc., 1975–76. E185.96 .W52.

Windley, Lathan W. *Runaway Slave Advertisements, A Documentary History From the 1730's to 1790.* 4 vols. Westport, Conn.: Greenwood Press, 1983. E446 .W73.

Vol. 1, Virginia, North Carolina; Vol. 2, Maryland; Vol. 3, South Carolina; Vol. 4, Georgia.

Woodson, Carter G. *Free Negro Owners of Slaves in the United States in 1830*. Negro Universities Press, 1968. E185 .W8873.

American Indians

Among any sizeable group of Americans engaging in a discussion of family roots, there will surely emerge at least one claiming to possess some Indian heritage. This person will explain that one of his or her ancestors married an Indian—more often than not a Cherokee. Further than that, little else is known since neither details of the union nor any written record to substantiate the family tradition has been found. Should evidence emerge that this ancestor lived west of the Mississippi River, in or near Oklahoma after 1835, in or near the mountainous sections of the Southeast, or in the Arkansas Territory, the chances that the tradition is true are enhanced. If the ancestor lived in the more southerly portions of the Southeast, any such marriage probably would have been with a member of the Choctaw or Creek tribe. If they lived in Florida, the marriage was probably with a Seminole. In any event, the marriage may never have been officially recorded, either in the Indian records or the county courthouse. Indeed, the union might well have taken place without a formal legal ceremony of any kind. Because of occasional intermarriages between Indian tribes, a clear tribal ancestry is often impossible to find.

Although it is nearly impossible to find genealogical records of most Indian tribes, the Five Civilized Tribes (Cherokee, Choctaw, Chickasaw, Creek, and Seminole) are an exception. These tribes were forced by the federal government to occupy much of the Indian Territory (now a part of present day Oklahoma). Later, particularly after the American Civil War, several other tribes (Arapahoe, Apache, Cheyenne, and some smaller tribes) moved to reservations in the western portion of the Oklahoma Territory. In 1889 the area was divided into the Indian Territory and the Oklahoma Territory, with plans for white settlement in a portion not assigned. This settlement, made during the famous "Oklahoma Land Rush" by white settlers who were permitted to claim land in a rectangular district in the center of the area, encompassed present day Tulsa. Any Indians then residing in that strip were paid off and moved out prior to the white man's claims.

Cherokee migrations took place over a long period, beginning in 1782, when those who fought with the British were granted lands in the Spanish Territory, now the southeastern portion of Missouri. In 1811 to 1812 they moved to the Arkansas Territory where other Cherokees from the East sometimes joined them. By treaty with the United States government in 1817, they received titles to their lands, and other Cherokees who remained in the East ceded their lands in exchange for similar titles to land just east of the Mississippi. For those who chose to move voluntarily, the federal government provided certain tools and equipment and paid transportation costs and subsistence. In 1828, another treaty provided for the ceding by the Indians of the Arkansas land in exchange for similar land in the Indian Territory. A final treaty in 1835 precipitated the so-called "Trail of Tears" into the Indian Territory, at which time all Cherokee land east of the Mississippi was ceded to the federal government. Some Cherokees escaped into the hills and evaded the forced march; others provided evidence that they could care for themselves where they were, and they were permitted to stay in the East. These were given their own "reservations" in the shape of a small farm; but they had to relinquish all future ties with their tribe. Those who migrated to the Indian Territory were called the "Old Settlers," and those who remained were called the "Eastern Band," although many of them migrated to the West in later years.

Similar treaties were also made with the Choctaw and the Creeks, and they, along with the Chickasaw and the Seminole, were also more or less forcibly removed to the West. Each treaty or removal provided for certain exceptions, and, as the years went by, many Indians filed claims against the government in accordance with those exceptions or for other reasons involving titles to land or payments of subsistence money.

The treaties and removal actions prompted several enumerations, censuses, annuity payrolls, court of claims records, and various other bookkeeping or statistical records. Some of the more important records that have been abstracted and published are the following:

1. Tribal censuses before removal to the West, 1831, 1832, 1835;

2. Old Settler Roll, 1851;

3. Cherokee Censuses, 1880, 1833, 1886, 1890, 1893;

4. The Starr Roll, 1894 and a follow-up in 1897, showed payments for lands in the "Cherokee Strip";

5. Chickasaw Census and Muster Roll, 1837 and 1839;

6. Census of Choctaws, 1831;

7. Emigration rolls, 1831–57 (reservation claims);

8. Census of Choctaw and Creek;

9. Census of Creeks, 1833;

10. Annual censuses of all tribes, 1885 and thereafter. These contain both Indian and English names.

The above are only a few examples of a very large number of record sources dealing with the federal government and the Five Civilized Tribes. In addition, there are millions of papers related to proceedings in various United States courts, ranging from the Claims Courts, the District Courts, and the Supreme Court.

All the various censuses taken of specific tribes were undertaken to determine payment to Indians for subsistence in accordance with the provisions of the treaties and removal actions. Separate counts were made of those who had moved to the Indian Territory and of those who remained in the East. A comparison of names in two or more censuses gave a clue to which ones moved west in the years following the first big removal of 1835.

In 1893 a general commission (the Dawes Commission) was established to obtain agreements with the Five Civilized Tribes. The intent was to prohibit the possession of land by a tribe as an entity and instead to allot land to individual Indians. As a result, the "final rolls of the Five Civilized Tribes" (with an index) were prepared. This list showed those who were either approved or disapproved for land ownership. It also included other personal information such as degree of Indian blood and indication of those who were Indians by marriage or who were "Freedmen" (former slaves).

The first decennial census of the United States that included the Indian Territory and also the Oklahoma Territory was the one taken in 1900. Indians, along with white persons, were counted in both areas; the census sheets contain a special section referring to Indians, showing birthplace and month and year of birth.

Records Outside the Library of Congress. The *Guide to Genealogical Research in the National Archives* (Washington, D.C.: National Archives Trust Fund Board, 1983) contains a list of Indian schools and agencies, with designation of where their records have been deposited, particularly at the National Archives in Washington, D.C., and the National Archives field branches at Atlanta, Chicago, Denver, Fort Worth, Kansas City, San Francisco, and Seattle. This list of sources is reproduced as an appendix to the very helpful chapter by George J. Nixon, "Records Relating to Native American Research—the Five Civilized Tribes" in *The Source: A Guidebook of American Genealogy,* edited by Arlene H. Eakle and Johni Cerny (Salt Lake City: Ancestry, Inc., 1984, CS49 .S65). That chapter also provides many illustrations of Indian records, contains an extensive bibliography, and describes the very large Indian records collections at the Oklahoma Historical Society, Oklahoma City.

Records in the Library of Congress. Several collections and rolls created by the federal government relating to Indians, primarily the Five Civilized Tribes, have been published as books or articles in historical and genealogical periodicals. Some are in the general collection; some are available in the Local History and Genealogy Reading Room; and others are in the Microform Reading Room, the Manuscript Division, and the Serials and Government Publications Division.

The Microform Reading Room has the following collections pertaining to Indians:

1. North American Indians: Photographs from the National Anthropological Archives, Smithsonian Institution;

2. North American Indians: Dissertation Index (a key to doctoral theses);

3. Early State Records (containing some miscellaneous collections).

The Manuscript Division has two collections that may be of interest:

1. American Missionary Collection;

2. American Indian Correspondence Collection.

These collections include correspondence from Presbyterian missionaries to the Indians (1833–93); originals of these 14,000 letters are at the Presbyterian Historical Society, Philadelphia, Pennsylvania. They are arranged by correspondent and Indian tribe, including Apache, Assinboin, Blackfoot, Chickasaw, Chippewa, Choctaw, Creek, Dakota, Fox, Kickapoo, Missouri, Mohawk, Muskogee, Navajo, Nez Perce, Omaha, Otoe, Ottawa, Potawatomi, Pueblo, Sac, Santee, Seminole, Seneca, Shawnee, Shoshone, Sioux, Teton, Wea, Winnebago, Uintah, Umatilla, and Zuni.

The Prints and Photographs Division Reading Room has two large collections of Indian photographs:

1. Edward S. Curtis Collection (containing more than 1,600 photographs of Indians of the Plains, Central Plains, Northwest, Southwest, and California tribes);

2. Heyn-Matzen Collection (containing 550 photographs, mainly of Sioux, Crow, and other Plains tribes).

The Serials and Government Publications Division has a collection of documents relating to treaties of the United States. Before 1868 almost half of them related to Indian tribes. This collection includes letters, reports, and petitions concerning treaties filed by Indians and whites. The reference aid is "Journal of the Executive Proceedings of the Senate to Papers Ordered to be Printed in Confidence" (no longer confidential, despite the title). By locating the state of residence during a given time period, and the name and tribe of an Indian ancestor, one may be able to find the treaty or fellow tribesmen related to the ancestor.

Publications. For titles of published works relating to Indians, the card and computer catalogs should be consulted. Use the following headings as examples: **Indians of North America—Oklahoma [or other state]** or **Indians of North America—treaties** or **Indians of North America—census** or **Indians of North America—claims**.

Guides and Bibliographies. During the initial phase of research one may find the following publications helpful:

Clark, Dick. *Cherokee Ancestor Research.* Modesto, Calif.: Rich-Nor-Lin Publications, 1979. E99 .C5C657.

Hill, Edward E., comp. *Guide to the Records in the National Archives of the United States Relating to American Indians.* Washington, D.C.: National Archives and Records Service, 1982. Z1209.2 .U5H54.

Kirkham, E. Kay. *Our Native Americans.* Logan, Utah: Everton Publishers, 1980. Vol. 2, 1984. Z1209.2 .N67K57.

Nixon, George J. "Records Relating to Native American Research, The Five Civilized Tribes." In *The Source: A Guidebook of American Genealogy,* edited by Arlene H. Eakle and Johni Cerny. Salt Lake City: Ancestry, Inc., 1984.

Parker, Jimmy B. "American Indian Genealogy Records." *National Genealogical Society Quarterly* 63 (March 1975): 15–21.

Smith, Dwight L. *Indians of the United States and Canada. A Bibliography.* 2 vols. Santa Barbara, Calif.: ABC-Clio, 1974–83. Z1209.2 .N67I52.

Published Records

Bell, George M. *Genealogy of "Old and New Cherokee Indian Families."* Bartlesville, Okla.: the author, 1972. E99 .C5B39.

Bogle, Dixie, and Dorothy Nix. *Cherokee Nation Marriages, 1844.* 1901. Reprint. Owensboro, Ky.: Cook and McDowell, 1980. E99 .C5B62.

Burns, Louis F. *Osage Annuity Rolls of 1878—First Roll.* 3 vols. Fallbrook, Calif.: the author, 1980–81. E99 .O8B87.

Campbell's Abstract of Creek Indian Census Records and Index. Muskogee, Okla.: Phoenix Job Printing Co., 1915. E99 .C9C18.

Fay, George E. *Treaties Between the Tribes of the Great Plains and the United States of America, Cheyenne and Arapaho, 1825–1900.* Greeley, Colo.: Museum of Anthropology, University of Northern Colorado, 1977. KF8228 .CS3H3.

Felldin, Jeane R., and Charlotte M. Tucker. *1832 Census of Creek Indians.* Tomball, Tex.: Genealogical Publications, 1978. E99 .C9P37.

Hill, Charles E. *Leading American Treaties.* New York: AMS Press, 1969. JX1487 .H5.

Hodge, Frederick W. *Handbook of American Indians North of Mexico.* 2 vols. Totowa, N.J.: Rowan and Littlefield, 1979. E77 .H93.

Hoskins, Shirley. *Cherokee Blood—Based on Eastern Cherokee Applications of the United States Court of Claims, 1906–1909.* Chattanooga: the author, 1982. E99 .C5H77.

Jordan, Jerry W. *Cherokee by Blood—Records of Eastern Cherokee Ancestry in the United States Court of Claims, 1906–1910.* Bowie, Md.: Heritage Books, 1987. (Cataloging in publication.)

Kappler, Charles J., ed. *Indian Treaties, 1778–1883.* New York: Interland Publishers, 1972. KF8203 .I972b.

Littlefield, Daniel F., Jr. *The Cherokee Freedmen From Emancipation to American Citizenship.* Westport, Conn.: Greenwood press, 1978. E99 .C5L5.

Pompey, Sherman L. *Genealogical Records on the Confederate Indian Troops.* Albany, Ore.: the author, 1984. E78 .I5P65.

Starr, Emmett. *Old Cherokee Families—with Index.* Norman, Okla.: University of Oklahoma Foundation, 1922. Index by J.J. Hill. E99 .C5S83.

Treaties and Agreements of the Eastern Oklahoma Indians. Washington, D.C.: Institute for the Development of Indian Law, 1973. KF8202.

Tyner, James W., et al. *Our People and Where They Rest.* 12 vols. Norman, Okla.: American Indian Institute; University of Oklahoma: Chi-ga-u, Inc., 1969–85. E99 .C5T97.

Tyner, James W., et al. *Those Who Cried: The 16,000—A Record of the Individual Cherokees*

Listed in the United States Official Census of the Cherokee Nation Conducted in 1835. N.p.: Chi-ga-u, Inc., 1974. E99 .C5T98.

Covers Alabama, Georgia, North Carolina, and Tennessee.

United States Congress. *The Final Rolls of Citizens and Freemen of the Five Civilized Tribes in Indian Territory.* Washington, D.C.: n.p., 1886. E78 .I5027.

German-Americans

In terms of numbers, the largest group of immigrants other than the English to this country were German-speaking people, most of whom were Lutherans. After the American Revolution a large number of Roman Catholics arrived. To understand the problems involved in identifying German ancestors, it is well to learn the political history, the wars, and the many boundary changes that occurred in their part of Europe. A good synopsis is included in Johni Cerny and Wendy Elliot's *The Library: A Guide to the LDS Family History Library.* (Salt Lake City, Utah: Ancestry, Inc., 1988) pages 535 through 540.

Mandatory registration by civil authorities was begun in 1876, and included births, marriages and deaths. Previous to that year portions of Germany including Alsace-Lorraine under Napoleon Bonaparte's rule between 1798 and 1815 also engaged in civil registration of vital records. Records before 1798 must be obtained locally.

The first Germans to arrive in America were a group of thirteen families who founded Germantown, Pennsylvania, in 1683, under the leadership of Francis C. Pastorius. Thousands soon followed, and, according to the 1790 census, Germans made up one-third of the Pennsylvania population. They generally resided in the middle portion of the state, flanked by English and Quakers in the eastern portion and Scotch-Irish in the western portion. From this region, both Germans and the Scots-Irish migrated to the Shenandoah Valley of Virginia, Maryland, and North Carolina before and after the American Revolution. In the early 1800s they pushed westward into Kentucky, Tennessee, and midwestern states.

In 1710, a group of indentured servants from the southwestern Palatine region of Germany arrived at New York, having been sent to help produce naval stores for the British who were at war with Spain. Germans also arrived at New Orleans, from which they traveled up the Mississippi River making settlements at Cincinnati, St. Louis, and several villages in rural areas. Others turned to Texas where a number of German settlements were established. The heaviest influx took place just after the failed German revolution in 1848. By 1860, 31 percent of the foreign-born population in the United States was of German ancestry.

In the European Reading Room of the Library of Congress one should obtain the pamphlet "Germanic People in the United States; A Selective List of Reading Materials," which lists eighty-three publications and their Library of Congress call numbers. Among them are the works listed below. Also, see the references to ship passenger and emigration lists cited earlier in this chapter, as well as titles cited in chapters 9 through 15.

Guides and Bibliographies

Arndt, Karl J.R., and Mary E. Olson. *German-American Newspapers and Periodicals, 1732–1955; History and Bibliography.* Heidelberg: Quelle & Meyers, 1961. Z6953.5 .G3A7.

Baxter, Angus. *In Search of Your German Roots: A Complete Guide to Tracing Your Ancestors in the Germanic Areas of Europe.* Baltimore: Genealogical Publishing Co., 1987. CS614 .B39.

Cerny, Johni. *A Guide to German Parish Registers.* Baltimore: Genealogical Publishing Co., 1987. CS613 .C47.

Volume 1 includes Baden, Bavaria, and Wuerttemberg; Volume 2 includes various other German states.

Eschenbach, Virginia. *Searching for Your German Ancestry; West Germany, East Germany: How, Who, Why, When, Where—A Primer.* Dyer, Ind.: the author, 1983. CS613 .E83.

Faust, Albert B. *The German Element in the United States.* 2 vols. New York: Arno Press, 1969. E184 .G3F3.

Friederichs, Heinze F. *How to Find My German Ancestors and Relatives.* Neustadt, West Germany: Degener, 1969. CS614 .F7.

Illinois University of Urbana—Champaign Library. *Guide to the Heinrich A. Ratterman Collection of German-American Manuscripts.* Urbana: University of Illinois Library, 1979. Z6614 .R334I44.

Jensen, Larry O. *A Genealogical Handbook of German Research.* Pleasant Grove, Utah: the author, 1978. CS614 .J46.

Konrad, J. *German Family Research Made Simple.* Munroe Falls, Ohio: Summit Publications, 1974. CS49 .K66.

Kunz, Virginia B. *The Germans in America.* Minneapolis: Lerner Publications, 1966. E184 .G3K8.

Lind, Marilyn. *Researching and Finding Your German Heritage.* Colquet, Minn.: Linden Tree, 1984. CS614 .L56.

Meynen, Emil. *Bibliography on Colonial German Settlements in North America.* Reprint. Baltimore: Genealogical Publishing Co., 1982. F572 .K2M39.

Smith, Kenneth L. *Writing to Germany: A Guide to Genealogical Correspondence with German Sources.* Columbus, Ohio: the author, 1984. CS614 .S65.

Wellauer, Maralyn A. *Tracing Your German Roots.* Milwaukee; the author, 1979. CS49 .W43.

Published Records

Deiler, John H. *The Settlement of the German Coast of Louisiana and the Creoles of German Descent.* Baltimore: Genealogical Publishing Co., 1975. F380 .C3D29.

Diffenderffer, Frank R. *The German Immigration into Pennsylvania Through the Port of Philadelphia From 1700 to 1775, and the Redemptioners.* Baltimore: Genealogical Publishing Co., 1979. C160 .G3D53.

Hall, Charles M. *The Atlantic Bridge to Germany.* 4 vols. Logan, Utah: The Everton Publishers, 1974–78. (Vol. 4 published by Heritage International.) CS614 .H34.

Knittle, Walter A. *Early Eighteenth Century Palatine Emigration: A British Government Redemptioner Project to Manufacture Naval Stores.* Baltimore: Genealogical Publishing Co., 1970. F130 .P2K6.

Smith, Clifford Neal. *German Revolutionists of 1848: Among Whom are Many Immigrants to America.* McNeal, Ariz.: Westland Publications, 1985. E184 .G3S664.

Strassburger, Ralph B. *Pennsylvania German Pioneers: A Publication of the Original Lists of Arrivals in the Port of Philadelphia From 1727 to 1808.* Norristown, Pa.: Pennsylvania German Society, 1934. Vols. 1 and 3 reprint. Baltimore: Genealogical Publishing Co., 1966. F160 .G3R43.

Contains 29,800 names.

Thode, Ernest. *Atlas for Germanic Genealogy.* Rev. ed. Marietta, Ohio: the author, 1983. G1912.2 .T5.

Located in the Geography and Map Reading Room.

Urlsperger, Samuel. *Detailed Reports on the Salsburger Emigrants Who Settled in America.* Athens, Ga.: University of Georgia Press, 1968. F295 .S1U813.

Wittke, Carl F. *Refugees of Revolution.* Westport, Conn.: Greenwood Press, 1970. E184 .G3W5.

Yoder, Don. *Pennsylvania German Immigrants, 1709–86.* Baltimore: Genealogical Publishing Co., 1980. F160 .G3P43.

Lists consolidated from yearbooks of the German Folklore Society.

——. *Rhineland Emigrants.* Baltimore: Genealogical Publishing Co., 1981. E184 .G3R44.

Zucker, Adolf E. *The Forty-eighters: Political Refugees of the German Revolution of 1848.* New York: Russell & Russell, 1967. E184 .G3Z8.

German-Americans From Russia

In 1763, Catherine II of Russia issued a manifesto designed to encourage settlement in the recently acquired lands of the Volga-Black Sea region. Those who accepted her offer were exempt from taxes for thirty years, exempt from military service, and were given a grant amounting to eighty-one acres per family. Most of the settlers came from Germany where its citizens were suffering hardships imposed by economic depression, religious persecution, and political upheaval. In 1804, Catherine's grandson, Alexander I, issued another manifesto limiting settlement— only 200 well-to-do-rural families per year were admitted. The farms granted were increased to 162 acres and were exempt from taxation for ten years; they were exempt from military service, but the generous bonuses awarded to previous enlistees were greatly curtailed. These changes were thought to be necessary because the area had been over-settled and only the more able farmers who could be expected to operate model and prosperous farms were accepted.

During the last quarter of the 1800s, Alexander II imposed yet another set of regulations on this group and all Russians. Worsening economic conditions, increasing population crowding, and by then obligatory military service, led many to consider leaving. Severe crop failures in 1867 and droughts in 1873 and 1875 only increased dissatisfaction. So, after a century in Russia, many Germans began to immigrate to Canada, the United States, and South America. Those who stayed behind suffered severe privation during the Russian

Revolution of 1917, as well as during World Wars I and II.

Many of those who immigrated to the United States were recruited by agents of railroad magnates who owned vast acreages alongside their railways (courtesy of the United States Government) where few settlers had been induced to settle. On arrival, the German immigrants received free rail transportation to those areas in the Midwest. They were to become some of the world's most productive wheat farmers in Kansas, Colorado, Nebraska, and the Dakotas. Those with ancestral ties to these plains farmers may find the following publications of special interest.

Anuta, Michael J. *East Prussians From Russia.* Menominee, Mich.: the author, 1978. F589 .P77A58.

Essig, Walter, comp. *Index I—Work Paper. Heritage Review, Der Stammbaum, 1971 through 1978.* Bismarck: North Dakota Historical Society of Germans From Russia, 1979. E184 .R85E87.

Fleming, Alice M. *The King of Prussia and a Peanut Butter Sandwich.* New York: Scribners, 1988. E184 .M45F58.

Koch, Fred C. *The Volga Germans in Russia and the Americas, From 1763 to the Present.* University Park: Pennsylvania State University Press, 1977. DK34 .G3K62.

Olson, Marie M. *A Bibliography on the Germans From Russia: Material Found in the New York Public Library . . . .* Lincoln, Neb.: American Historical Society of Germans From Russia, 1976. Z1211 .R87044.

Rath, George. *The Black Sea Germans in the Dakotas.* Freeman, S.D.: Pine Hill Press, 1977. F645 .R85R37.

Sack, Sallyann A. *The Russian Consular Records Index and Catalog.* New York: Garland, 1987. CS856 .J4S23.

Sallet, Richard. *Russian-German Settlements in the United States.* Fargo: North Dakota Institute for Regional Studies, 1974. E184 .R85S313.

Hispanic-Americans

The Spanish who explored America and Mexico in the 1500s were adventurers intent on finding gold or other precious metals rather than establishing permanent settlements. However, by the 1600s, Roman Catholics arrived to establish missions and convert the indigenous populations—bringing with them missionaries and soldiers for protection. The Spanish gained control over what is now Florida, Mexico, New Mexico, and California, as well as parts of the Caribbean, and Central and South America.

In Florida, following its claim to the area in 1513, the Spanish ousted the French Huguenots, who claimed the area somewhat later in that century and built the fort at St. Augustine. They dominated until 1763 when it was ceded to Great Britain in 1781. It, along with West Florida, was later recaptured by Spain.

Mexico declared its independence from Spain and in 1824 became a republic, which included the regions of California, New Mexico (a part of which was Arizona), and Texas. Much of that territory was lost to the United States following the Mexican-American War of 1846-48. The New Mexico Territory officially became part of the United States by the Gadsden Purchase in 1853; at the same time a large tract of land was added that had been ceded by Mexico following the Mexican-American War. Texas declared its independence from Mexico in 1836, becoming a republic after the Mexican-American War.

There are limited published resources concerning Spanish and Mexican genealogy available in this country because most Mexican immigration has taken place only during the more recent years.

Hispanic Division Reading Room. The Hispanic Division is complete with murals and the Christopher Columbus Coat-of-Arms. It has many thousands of published works, particularly those concerning the history and culture of Spain and Portugal. Although there is little that helps directly in tracing lineages, there is a wealth of material useful for background reading. The division has published guides to pertinent manuscript collections at the Library of Congress. Among these are the Harkness Collection, the Kraus Collection of Hispanic American Manuscripts, and the Henry Albert Monday Collections of Mexican Colonial Materials. The Kraus Collection of 162 documents relates to the history of Spain in colonial America.

City Directories. In its collection of city directories, the library has a few for Central and South America. Those available in the stacks are the following:

Chile

Guía General de Chile (business) 1918

Cuba

Havana 1859

Directorio de la Habana y Guía Commercial de Cuba 1899

Cuba, Porto Rico, West Indies 1901

Cuba (general information) 1912, 1918, 1927

El Salvador

Business and Government 1921

Directorio de El Salvador 1924

Mexico

Ciudad de México 1901, 1919–26, 1931

Directorio General de los Estados de la República Mexicano (exclusive of La Ciudad de México and El Distrito Federal) 1908

Trinidad

City and business 1899

Published Sources. The following publications available at the Library of Congress might be helpful in searching for Hispanic ancestors.

Arthur, Stanley C. *Index to the Archives of Spanish West Florida, 1782–1810.* New Orleans: Polyanthos, 1975. Z1251 .W5315.

Brandow, James C. *Genealogies of Barbados Families: From the Caribbeans and the Journal of the Barbados Museum and Historical Society.* Baltimore: Genealogical Publishing Co., 1983. CS261 .B3B7.

Church of Jesus Christ of Latter-day Saints, Genealogical Society. *Major Genealogical Record Sources in Mexico.* Salt Lake City: Genealogical Society of Utah, 1970. CS101 .G45.

De Platt, Lyman. *Genealogical Historical Guide to Latin America.* Detroit: Gale Research Co., 1978. CS95 .D45.

———. *Genealogical Historical Guide to Latin America Spanish.* Ramona, Calif.: Acoma Books, 1978. CS95 .D46.

Douglass, William A. *Basque Americans: A Guide to Information Sources.* Detroit: Gale Research Co., 1981. Z1361 .B3D68.

Hutchinson, Cecil R. *Frontier Settlements in Mexican California—the Hijar-Padres Colony and its Origins, 1769–1835.* New Haven: Yale University, 1969. F864 .H94.

Kent, David L. *Barbados and America.* Arlington, Va.: the author, 1980. CS261 .B3K46.

Maduell, Charles R, Jr., comp. *Index of Spanish Citizens Entering the Port of New Orleans, January,* *1820 through December, 1839.* New Orleans: n.p., 1968. F379 .M5M188.

McCall, Grant. *Bibliography of Materials Relating to Basque-Americans.* Basque Studies Program, University of Nevada System, 1968. Z1361 .B3M3.

Mexico. Archivo General de la Nación. *Dirección de Difusión y Publicaciones del Archive General de la Nación, 1980.* N.p., n.d. CS103 .M49.

Robinson, David J. *Research Inventory of the Mexican Collection of Colonial Parish Registers.* Salt Lake City: University of Utah Press, 1980. CD3678 .A1R62.

Ryskamp, George R. *Tracing Your Hispanic Heritage.* Riverside, Calif.: Hispanic Family History Research, 1984. E184 .S75R97.

Sanders, Joanne M. *Barbados Records: Marriages, 1643–1800.* Houston: Sanders Historical Publications, 1982. CS261 .B3S247.

———. *Barbados Records: Baptisms, 1637–1800.* Baltimore: Genealogical Publishing Co., 1984. CS261 .B3S247.

Polish-Americans

Poland has had a turbulent history of wars, invasions, and repression. It has been partitioned by its captors, and between 1795 and 1916 it was divided between the Russian, Prussian, and Austro-Hungarian empires. It was also overrun by Napoleon's armies until his defeat in 1815. After the failure of the Polish revolutions in 1831 and 1848, Poles immigrated to other countries. After an unsuccessful insurrection in 1863, Russia controlled it with strict regulations and even began to eliminate the Polish language from its schools.

There has been civil registration of births, marriages, and deaths in Poland since Napoleon ordered the practice begun in 1808; prior to that time records of baptism, marriage, and burial were recorded by the Catholic church. The dominant religion in Poland has been Roman Catholic, with records in the church archives—many of which are now available for consultation. Microfilmed copies of some are at the Family History Library at Salt Lake City.

The Poles were early arrivals in the United States, many serving with distinction in the Revolutionary War. After the revolution, they came in even larger numbers, tending to settle in close-knit groups. During the 1800s some went to Pennsylvania where they worked in the coal mines or in heavily populated areas, principally in Chicago, Detroit, and mid-coastal California cities.

Since almost all were Roman Catholics, they sent their children to parochial schools. Social life of the adults centered in their ethnic societies, and a number of Polish language newspapers were available throughout the late nineteenth and early twentieth century. For those searching Polish ancestors in this country, the following are suggested.

Bolek, Francis, ed. *Who's Who in Polish America, 1939–70.* New York: Harbinger House, 1943. E184 .P4W4.

Church of Jesus Christ of Latter-day Saints, Genealogical Department. *Records of Genealogical Value for Poland.* Salt Lake City: n.p., 1983. Z5313 .P57R4.

Gnacinski, Janneyne L. *Polish and Proud: Tracing Your Polish Ancestry.* West Allis, Wis.: Janien Enterprises, 1979. CS49 .G57.

Halmun, Mieceslaus, *Poland and the American Revolutionary War.* Chicago: Polish Roman Catholic Union of America, 1932. E184 .P7H1343.

Hoskins, Janina W. *Polish Genealogy and Heraldry: An Introduction to Research.* Washington, D.C.: Library of Congress, 1987. CS872 .H67.

Konrad, J. *Polish Family Research.* Munroe Falls, Ohio: Summit Publications, 1977. CS49 .K67.

Markowski, Benedict, comp. *An Annotated and Topical List of Aids to Polish Genealogy.* Detroit: Burton Historical Collection, Detroit Public Library, 1984. Z1361 .P6M37.

Obal, Thaddeus J. *A Bibliography for Genealogical Research Involving Polish Ancestry.* Hillsdale, N.J.: the author, 1978. Z1361 .P602 E184 .P70.

Ortell, Gerald A. *Polish Parish Records of the Roman Catholic Church, Their Use and Understanding in Genealogical Research.* Astoria, N.Y.: the author, 1978. CS873 .O77.

Parot, Joseph J. *Polish Catholics in Chicago, 1850–1920: A Religious History.* Dekalb: Northern Illinois University Press, 1981. B1418 .C4P37.

Wellauer, Maralyn R. *Tracing Your Polish Roots.* Milwaukee: the author, 1979. CS49 .W45.

Scandinavian-Americans

Beginning in 1397, Sweden, Norway, and Denmark were joined as the Union of Kalmar, but after more than one hundred years the union began to break up. Sweden became independent in 1523, and Norway became a province of Denmark in 1536. Lutheranism was decreed the official religion of each country, although freedom of worship by the small minority who chose other denominations was always permitted. During the subsequent four centuries, other changes and realignments between these countries took place, often following military engagements, until each eventually became independent of one another.

Historical highlights of each of these countries are noted below, along with general comments of the types of genealogical or historical records that are available. See *The Library: A Guide to the LDS Family History Library* (cited earlier), pages 501 to 533, for a brief history of these Scandinavian countries and their records sources.

Sweden. Sweden conquered much of Finland in 1249, losing it to Russia in 1809. The 1397 Union of Kalmar joined Sweden with Denmark and Norway until Sweden declared its independence in 1523. In 1814 Sweden acquired Norway from Denmark; in 1905 Norway gained her independence.

Among the available records pertaining to Sweden are tax lists for most citizens between the ages of fifteen and sixty-three—soldiers were not included as they were exempt from taxes. The church kept vital records of its parishioners, and, since 1800, they also kept track of those who came and went from the parish or the country. Civil registration of births, marriages, and deaths by county generally dates from 1860.

Denmark. Denmark and Norway were first united in 1380 and, along with Sweden, were part of the Union of Kalmar. During the early 1600s, Denmark lost much of its territory to Sweden after a number of military engagements. When Denmark ceded Norway to Sweden in 1814, it retained its control over Iceland and Greenland, which it had colonized during the 1700s. Several censuses have been taken in Denmark beginning in 1787 and continuing thereafter at roughly five to ten year intervals. The church also kept parish registers of baptisms, marriages, and burials, generally from 1645, and of arrivals and departures from the county since 1814. Civil registration of births, marriages, and deaths began about 1851. Military records are a good genealogical source since all males eligible for service were enumerated between 1789 and 1849; after 1849, they registered when they reached the age of fourteen, and after 1869 at the age of seventeen. Records of actual military service are generally available beginning in 1765.

Norway. Norway, united with Denmark in 1380, became its province in 1536. In 1814 it was ceded to Sweden, and in 1905 it gained its independence. The first national census was taken in 1801, when all persons were listed by name, age, family relationship, marital status, and occupation. The second national census did not take place until 1865, and subsequently it was taken in 1875 and 1900. From about 1700, the church maintained parish registers; civil registration of deaths began at about the same time. Military draft records, principally of the navy and merchant marine, are available for the period since 1803.

Finland. Finland was a possession of Sweden until Russia invaded in 1808 and claimed it. In 1917, its vote for independence was accepted, but after World War II, parts of the country were returned to Russia. The dominant religion of Finland is Evangelical Lutheran, and the church has kept records since about 1860. Civil registration of births, marriages, and deaths has been based on the church records. There are tax lists for 1635 and 1809. Censuses were first taken in 1810 and have continued every fifth year thereafter.

Immigration to America. Although settlers from Scandinavia came to colonial America and founded settlements in New Sweden (now New York) and along the Delaware River, there was relatively little emigration from Sweden, Denmark, and Norway until the mid-nineteenth century. During the period of heaviest immigration, generally between 1860 and 1920, approximately 500,000 Swedes, 350,000 Danes, and 600,000 Norwegians came to America, settling mainly in the upper midwestern states of Wisconsin, Minnesota, the Dakotas, northern Illinois, and, to a lesser extent, northern Iowa, Oregon, and Nebraska. One group of Norwegian Quakers settled in New York about 1825, and a large number of Danes who had been converted to Mormonism went directly to Salt Lake City, Utah. The principal factor for leaving was economic. Land agents and others informed them of farm land available in the United States, and many decided to try homesteading. Although in general they landed at the port of New York, most of them moved quickly to the Midwest where they bought or obtained land under the homestead laws and became successful farmers.

Listed below are some publications in the Library of Congress that may help in your search for Scandinavian ancestors; you may search for others by using the computer catalog, using the following command **find s norway genealogy** (substitute name of country).

Benson, Adolph B., and N. Hedin. *Swedes in America, 1638–1938.* New York: Haskell House, 1969. E184 .S23B33.

Blegen, Theodore C. *Norwegian Migration to America, 1825–1860.* 2 vols. Northfield, Minn.: Norwegian-American Historical Association,

1931–40. Reprint. New York: Arno Press, 1969. E184 .S2B62.

Hokanson, Nels. *Swedish Immigrants in Lincoln's Time.* New York: Arno Press, 1970. E184 .S23H6.

Johansson, Carl E. *Cradled in Sweden.* Logan, Utah: Everton Publishers, 1972. CS922 .J6.

Nielsen, George R. *The Danish Americans.* Boston: Twayne Publishers, 1981. E184 .S19N53.

Norlie, Olaf, M. *History of the Norwegian People in America.* New York: Haskell House, 1973. E184 .S2N6.

Qualey, Carlton G. *Norwegian Settlements in various States in the United States.* Northfield, Minn.: 1938. Reprint. New York: Arno Press, 1970. E184 .S203.

Dutch-Americans

The Republic of the Seven United Netherlands, founded in 1588, was under domination of Spain for most of its early history. The Dutch have always been a sea-faring people who explored new lands. In 1602 the East India Company was created to establish a colony in America, and in 1609, Henry Hudson explored the upper parts of America and Canada. The first Dutch settlement in America was in 1624, when New Amsterdam was founded at what is now New York City.

After eighty years of war, the Netherlands gained its independence from Spain in 1648 but lost it in 1795 to Napoleon Bonaparte. After his defeat in 1815, the Netherlands was once again independent; the "Southern Netherlands," now Belgium, gained its independence in 1831.

Historically, the Dutch have been predominantly Roman Catholic in the south and Dutch Reformed in the north, but there were other denominations including the Anabaptists (Mennonites), Lutherans, and Walloons (French Reformed or Huguenot). The country's first census was taken in 1829. These were "population registers" kept in each province and town. After 1850, a card for each family was filed. When a family moved from one place to another, its card was transferred to the new location. Civil registration of vital statistics began in the northern provinces in 1795 and in the southern provinces in 1811. The data have been indexed by family name each ten years, beginning in 1813.

Although Dutch colonies in America were vanquished by the English in 1664, many Dutch settlers remained in the New York and New Jersey area. In 1846 a group of Dutch "separatists" settled on Lake

Michigan's eastern shore, and the next year another group went to Iowa; others settled in Pennsylvania, Indiana, Illinois, Kansas, Wisconsin, Nebraska, and eventually the West Coast.

In addition to the selected titles listed below, others may be identified by using the computer catalog, using the following command: **find s netherlands genealogy**.

Church of Jesus Christ of Latter-day Saints, Genealogical Society. *Guide to Genealogical Sources in the Netherlands.* Salt Lake City: Genealogical Society of Utah, 1971. CS1 .G383.

Dutch Settlers Society of Albany—Yearbook, Vol. 45. Albany, N.Y.: the society, 1977. F129 .A3D8.

Covers 1974 through 1977.

Franklin, Charles M. *Dutch Genealogical Research.* Indiana: the author, 1982. CS814 .F7.

Gehring, Charles T., ed. *New York Historical Manuscripts (Dutch) Land Papers.* Baltimore: Genealogical Publishing Co., 1980.

New York Historical Manuscripts—Dutch. Kingston Court Records, 1661–1675. 2 vols. Baltimore: Genealogical Publishing Co., 1976. F1289 .K2K53.

Swieringa, Robert P., comp. *Dutch Households in United States Population Censuses, 1850, 1860, 1870: An Alphabetical Listing by Family Heads.* Wilmington, Del.: Scholarly Resources, 1987. E184 .D35348.

Van Hinte, Jacob. *Netherlanders in America.* 2 vols. Grand Rapids, Mich.: Backer Book House, 1985. E184 .D9H613.

Wabeke, Bertus H. *Dutch Emigration to America, 1624–1860. A Short History.* Freeport, N.Y.: Books for the Libraries Press, n.d. E184 .D9W3.

Franco-Americans

Although France has had a stormy political history, a monarchy was supreme until the French Revolution of 1789, and the republic was established in 1792. Napoleon Bonaparte created the French Empire, naming himself emperor in 1804; when he was defeated in 1815, Louise XVIII reestablished the monarchy. In 1848, after a second revolution, a republic was established that lasted until 1852 when Napoleon III created the second French Empire. When France was defeated in the Franco-Russian War in 1871, the third republic was established. France was frequently embroiled in war with Germany over territory along the Rhine and Alsace-Lorraine, and in dispute with England and Spain over attempts to establish colonies.

In 1794 France was divided into nearly one hundred departments, each with its own record-keeping system and archives (separate from the national archives in Paris). These archives are repositories for church registers to 1792, civil registration of vital records to 1877, and notarial records since the late 1800s.

Most of the French who came to the American colonies were fur traders and soldiers. Protestant Huguenots fleeing from religious persecution came by way of several European countries to which they had fled after the revocation of the Edict of Nantes in 1685. (Revocation of the Edict prohibited Protestants from church membership and from practicing their religion.) They were among the pilgrims on the *Mayflower,* and some were in Pennsylvania even before William Penn opened that colony to religious refugees. South Carolina and Virginia also became a home for many Huguenot refugees, and records pertaining to them may be found in the counties where they settled. Catholic Acadians (Cajuns) banished by the British from Nova Scotia settled in lower Louisiana. Some French Quakers came to America during the early part of the 1800s and settled in New England and the midwestern states.

The following publications may be helpful in searching for French ancestors, both Huguenot and Acadian.

Baird, Charles W. *History of the Huguenot Emigration in America.* New York: Dodd Mead, 1985. E29 .H9B16.

Caldwell, Norman W. *The French in the Mississippi Valley, 1740–1750.* Philadelphia: Porcupine Press, 1974. F353 .C33.

Catholic Church, Diocese of Baton Rouge. *Diocese of Baton Rouge—Catholic Church Records.* 7 vols. N.p.: Department of Archives, 1978–1986. F368 .C37.

Covers the years 1707 through 1852.

DeVille, Winston. *Acadian Church Records, 1679–1757. Being a Compilation of Miscellaneous Baptismal, Marriage, and Funeral Records.* Vol. 1. New Orleans: Polyanthos, 1975. CS88 .A25P4.

Doty, Steward, ed. *The First Franco-Americans. New England Life Histories From the Federal Writers Project, 1938–39.* Orono, Maine: University of Maine at Orono Press, 1985. F15 .F85F57.

Hebert, Donald J. *Acadians in Exile.* Cecilia, La.: Hebert Publications, 1980. CS31 .H4.

———. *Researching Acadian Families.* Eunice, La.: the author, 1986. CS83 .H47.

Holbrook, Sabra. *The French Founders of North America and Their Heritage.* New York: Athenium, 1976. E131 .H64.

Rieder, Milton P., Jr., and Norma G. Rieder, comps. *The Acadian Exiles in the American Colonies, 1725–68.* Metarie, La.: the compilers, 1977. E184 .A2R53.

———. *The Acadians in France.* Vol. 3., *Archives of the Port of Saint Servan.* Metarie, La.: the compilers, 1973. F380 .A2R5.

Swiss-Americans

The first Swiss Confederation occurred in 1291 and resulted in the merger of four cantons (states). Others followed, and by 1513 there was a Confederation of Thirteen Cantons. In the late 1700s the French occupied Switzerland and the confederation collapsed, but when Napoleon became emperor he established a Confederation of Nineteen Cantons. After his defeat in 1815, a Confederation of Twenty-one Cantons was organized and recognized by the Great Powers as a neutral country.

In 1845 the Catholic-dominated cantons were organized to form an association called a Sonderbund, which resulted in a civil war within the Confederation. Three years later a democratic federal government was organized that is still in effect today. Although Switzerland has not participated in a war for almost two centuries, it maintains its vigilance with a citizen army in which every eligible male is conscripted for two years of active duty, followed by reserve status until middle age. Although the official language is German, depending upon the region of the country, French, Italian, and "Romanish" are also spoken as the chief language for those regions.

Since 1876 there has been a system of civil registration of vital statistics. Dating from the 1500s and earlier, the church maintained parish registers. During the late 1700s the practice of keeping family registers in each canton and city was established, and these may be available on the local level. A Swiss is considered a citizen of his hometown even though he may have moved elsewhere, unless he undergoes a lengthy and expensive process of changing citizenship. In many cantons and towns, records of such changes are available. Records of one who has moved may be found in the original canton or town if his citizenship remained there.

The first Swiss came to America in the mid-1600s when they were encouraged to help establish vineyards in the Carolinas. From there some went to Pennsylvania and settled around Lancaster and in the Lehigh Valley. These were a German-speaking group that by 1750 numbered about 12,000. The nineteenth-century Swiss immigrants came to purchase or claim homesteads where they could continue farming. Some of these were French speaking and settled in the Midwest and other areas, generally seeking other immigrants from their part of Switzerland so they could communicate without difficulty. Intermarriage with other nationalities resulted in a loss of national identity.

The following publications, some previously listed in this chapter dealing with European emigration lists, could be helpful for those seeking Swiss ancestors:

Faust, Albert B. *List of Swiss Emigrants in the Eighteenth Century to the American Colonies.* 2 vols. Reprint. Baltimore: Genealogical Publishing Co., 1976. E184 .S9F22.

Nielson, Paul A. *Swiss Genealogical Research: An Introductory Guide.* Virginia Beach, Va.: Donning, 1979. E184 .S9N53.

Smith, Clifford Neal. *Immigrants to America From France and Western Switzerland, 1859–1866. French-American Genealogical Research Series, Monograph.* McNeal, Ariz.: Westland Publications, 1983. E184 .F8545.

Suess, Jared H. *Handy Guide to Swiss Genealogical Records.* Logan, Utah: Everton Publishers, 1978. CS983 .S93.

Wellauer, Maralyn A. *Tracing Your Swiss Roots.* Milwaukee: the author, 1979. CS982 .W44.

Italian-Americans

Since the ninth century Italy has been dominated by France, Spain, and Austria. Napoleon Bonaparte, who conquered the country in 1796, was defeated in 1815. The United Kingdom of Italy was established in 1861, to which the city of Rome, becoming the capitol, was added in 1871.

In large measure, Italian immigration to the United States has taken place during the twentieth century. Americans of Italian descent can usually trace several generations back to Italy simply by questioning their own relatives and by using recent records. The Catholic church in Italy has kept parish registers since the 1600s, and earlier in some provinces; civil registration has been mandatory since 1869 (and earlier in some provinces). Of these, most church and civil records remain in the Italian provinces, and transcribed or otherwise reproduced copies have not been made available in the United States.

The following are a few publications that will aid the Italian family historian.

Gordasco, Francesco. *Italian-Americans: A Guide to Information Sources*. Detroit: Gale Research Co., 1978. Z1361 .I8C59.

Glynn, Joseph M. *Manual for Italian Genealogy*. Newton, Mass.: Italian Family History Society, 1981. CS754 .G58.

Konrad, J. *Italian Family Research*. Munroe Falls, Ohio: Summit Publications, 1980. CS49 .K665.

Preece, Floren S. *Handy Guide to Italian Genealogical Records*. Logan, Utah: Everton Publishers, 1978. CS753 .P73.

Stevens, Robert K. *Protestant Records in Italy. Some Registers of St. Paul's Within-the-Walls*. Baton Rouge, La.: Oracle Press, 1985. CS68 .S74.

Stevens, Revalee, and Robert K. Stevens. *The Protestant Cemetery of Rome*. Baton Rouge, La.: Oracle Press, 1981. CS68 .S73.

Miscellaneous Ethnic Groups

Some reference works pertaining to other groups that came to America in lesser numbers are listed below, by nationality.

Czechoslovakians

Blaha, Albert J. *Czech Genealogists' Handbook for Tracing Your Czech Ancestors in the Lone Star State and Czechoslovakia*. Houston: the author, 1984. (Cataloging in publication.)

Miller, Olga K. *Genealogical Research for Czech and Slovak Americans*, Vol. 2. Detroit: Gale Research Co., 1974. CS524 .M54.

Schlyter, Daniel M. *A Handbook of Czechoslovak Genealogical Research*. Buffalo Grove, Ill.: Genun Publishers, 1985. E184 .B67S35.

Sturm, Rudolf. *Czechoslovakia, A Bibliographic Guide*. Washington, D.C.: Library of Congress; New York: Arno Press, 1968. Z2136 .S7.

Chinese-Americans

Church of Jesus Christ of Latter-day Saints. Genealogical Society. *Chinese Local Histories as a Source for the Genealogist*. Salt Lake City: Genealogical Society of Utah, 1974. D5737 .D4886.

Filipino-Americans

Vance, Lee M. *Tracing Your Philippines Ancestors*. Provo, Utah: Stevenson's Genealogical Center, 1980. CS1393 .V36.

Greek-Americans

Broadbent, Molly. *Studies in Greek Genealogy*. Leiden, Netherlands: E.J. Brill, 1968. CS736 .B7.

Hungarian-Americans

Suess, Jared H. *Handy Guide to Hungarian Genealogical Records*. Logan, Utah: Everton Publishers, 1980. CS563 .S93.

Icelandic-Americans

Jonasson, Eric. *Tracing Your Icelandic Family Tree*. Winnipeg, Manitoba: Wheatfield Press, 1975. CS933 .J66.

Japanese-Americans

Church of Jesus Christ of Latter-day Saints, Genealogical Society. *Major Genealogical Record Sources in Japan*. Salt Lake City: Genealogical Society of Utah, 1974. CS1303 .M35.

Yugoslav-Americans

Eterovich, Adam S. *A Guide and Bibliography to Research on Yugoslavs in the United States and Canada*. San Francisco: R. and E. Research Associates, 1975. Z1361 .Y8E83.

CHAPTER 8

English-Speaking Ancestors

Because of the historic aggressiveness of the Library of Congress in acquiring foreign publications, there is a wealth of genealogical and historical information available concerning many nationality and ethnic groups from English speaking countries. Americans with such ancestors are especially fortunate because of the common language. Many family lines in America can be traced to Canada, England, Ireland, Scotland, Wales, and even Australia. Since descent from European nobility is important to many researchers, special attention is paid in this chapter to the art and science of heraldry, especially discussions of how and why an ancestor was granted authority to use specially decorated arms to signify his position in society. Selected works that might aid the discovery of ancestral lines of royalty and nobility are also cited.

This chapter provides titles of biographies, directories, vital statistics, censuses, newspaper indexes, and similar records relating to particular nationality groups. Brief historical background and descriptions of genealogical and historical records for five English-speaking countries are given below.

Australia

The continent of Australia was first discovered by Dutch explorer Abel Tasmain in 1642, then rediscovered by Captain John Cook during his voyages of 1769 to 1777. England, after losing the American colonies, began to send prisoners to Australia in lieu of imposing long prison sentences in England. The first group of eleven ships, with 1,350 prisoners, arrived at New South Wales in 1788. The practice continued until 1868. Among those apprehended and transported were political prisoners from rebellious Ireland.

In addition to prisoners, free settlers also went to Australia, many of them government officials and soldiers who helped in the establishment of new colonies. Both separate colonies and regions divided into provinces were established, and in 1901 they were joined as the Commonwealth of Australia, comprised of six states: New South Wales, Queensland, South Australia, Tasmania, Victoria, and Western Australia. Australia joined the British Commonwealth of Nations in 1831.

Because of the historic independence of the six states, each kept its own records and created its own archives. Among the available records are immigration lists, land records, and probate records. Although there have been regular state censuses since 1841, most have been destroyed. The remaining few fragments have been microfilmed by the Family History Library at Salt Lake City. The present state registration of births, marriages, and deaths, begun between 1896 and 1907, continues to the present time.

Few Australians have immigrated to America, primarily because of the abundance of available land and economic opportunities in their own country. Indeed, they have sometimes encouraged Americans to emigrate there, especially during the years following World War II. In researching family history, however, one may find an English or Irish ancestor who moved first (willingly or unwillingly) to Australia, where his family can be traced.

A recommended publication that will assist in determining what records are available in Australia and its six states is Nick Vine Hall's *Tracing Your Family History in Australia* (see below).

Newspaper Indexes

The Newspaper and Current Periodical Reading Room has the following indexes to early Australian newspapers:

Melbourne

    Argus, 1846–54. A121 .A8A73.

Sydney

    Stockwhip, 1875–77. (Margaret Woodhouse) A121 .S85W6.

    Morning Herald, 1851–75. (Ken C. Laycock) CS2008 .C36L38.

Directories

The following Australian city directories may be requested by submitting a call slip in the Local History and Genealogy Reading Room:

Australia, South

    Directory of South Australia, 1943–65. DU300 .S3.

Australia, Western

    Wise's Western Australia Post Office Directory, 1944–47. DU350 .W5.

Melbourne

    Sand's and McDougall's Melbourne, Suburban, and Country Directory, 1909. DU205 .S3.

    Melbourne and Suburban Directory, 1875. DU228 .S3.

New South Wales

    New South Wales Calendar and General Post Office Directories, 1832, 1834. DU150 .N46.

Victoria

    Directory of Victoria, 1912, 1913, 1918, 1925, 1956, 1961–73. DU205 .S3.

Guides and Bibliographies

Gray, Nancy. *Compiling Your Family History: A Guide to Procedures*. 7th ed. Sydney: Society of Australian Genealogists, 1986. CS2003 .G73.

McClelland, James. *James McClelland's A Tracing Your Family History Guide for Beginners . . . .* Silverdale, New South Wales: Keith Ainsworth Printing, 1980. CS2002 .M33.

Peake, Andrew G. *Sources for South Australian Family History*. N.p.: the author, 1977. CS2008 .S68P4.

Vine Hall, Nick. *Tracing Your Family History in Australia: A Guide to Sources*. Dee Why West, New South Wales: Rigby, 1986. CS2002 .V56.

Published Record Sources

Addington, Charles, comp. *Some Passengers from Nova Scotia and New Brunswick to Australia, 1852: Report From the Saint John, New Brunswick Morning News*. Canada: the author, 1987. CS2008 .A1A33.

Cable, Kenneth J., and Jane C. Marchants, eds. *Australian Biographies and Genealogical Record, Series 2, 1842–1899*. Sydney: A.B.G.R., Society of Australian Genealogists, 1985–87. CT2802 .A94.

Census, 1837—Extracted from Volume 58, Inward Correspondence of the Colonial Secretary's Office of Western Australia by Staff of the Battye Library. Perth: Library Board of Western Australia, 1974. CS2008 .W47C46.

Fidlon, Paul G., and R. J. Ryan, eds. *First Fleeters: A Comprehensive Listing of Convicts, Marines, Seamen, Officers, Wives, Children and Ships*. Sydney: Australian Documents Library, 1981. CS430 .F57.

Hughes, Ian A., comp. *Passengers to Port Phillip From Southern England and Ireland*. Northcote, Vic.: the compiler, 1981. CS2008 .A1H84.

————. *Passengers to Port Phillip From Scotland, 1839–51*. Northcote, Vic.: the compiler, 1980. CS2008 .A1H835.

————. *Passengers to Port Phillip From Commonwealth and Foreign Ports, 1838–51*. Northcote, Vic.: the compiler, 1981. CS2008 .A1H8.

———. *Passengers to Port Phillip From Liverpool, 1839–51*. Northcote, Vic.: the compiler, 1982. CS2008 .A1H83.

Jones, Jean M., comp. *Nepean District Cemetery Records, 1806–1976*. Sydney: the compiler, 1977. CS2008 .N46J66.

McClelland, James. *James McClelland's Convict, Pioneer and Immigrant History of Australia*. Vol. 4. Silverdale, New South Wales: McClelland Research, 1980. CS2003 .J36.

———. *Index to All Readable Names of Convicts and Free Persons Arriving Australia*. Silverdale, New South Wales: McClelland Research, 1983. CS2003 .M334.

———. *Names of Convict and Immigrant Ships Known to Me Arriving Australia, 1788 to 1899*. Silverdale, New South Wales: McClelland Research, 1981. CS2003 .M34.

———. *Family History Searchers' Encyclopedia*. Silverdale, New South Wales: McClelland Research, 1985. CS2003 .M3.

Ryan, R. J., ed. *Second Fleet Convicts: A Comprehensive Listing of Convicts Who Sailed in HMS* **Guardian, Lady Julian, Neptune, Scarborough** *and* **Surprise**. Sydney: n.p., Australian Documents Library, 1982. CS430 .R92.

———. *Third Fleet Convicts: An Alphabetical Listing of Names, Giving Place and Date of Conviction, Length of Sentence, and Ship of Transportation*. Cammeray, New South Wales: Horwitz Graham, 1983. CS430 .R92.

Sainty, Malcolm R., and K.A. Johnson, comps. *Index to Birth, Marriage, Death and Funeral Notices in the Sydney Herald*. 3 vols. Sydney: n.p., 1972. CS2008 .A1S24.

Volume 1 is 100 numbered and signed copies; Volumes 2 and 3 are Genealogical Publications of Australia. ·

Smee, C. J., comp. *The Pioneer Register, Spouse Supplement to Volumes VI–X*. Selkirk Prov., New South Wales: n.p., 1982. CS2009 .A2A15.

———. *The 1788–1820 Association Pioneer Register*. 2d ed. Sydney: Griffin Press, 1981–. CS2009 .A2A15.

Canada

The French established a colony at Nova Scotia in 1608, and the British followed with one in 1623. This set the stage for conflict between the two nations for control of Canada for decades. England established the Hudson Bay Company in 1670 to encourage settlement in that northwestern region. France turned over the area named Acadia to England in 1713. Following the Seven Years War (French and Indian Wars) in 1763, some of the French were deported to France and others were banished to the American colonies, including the Acadians to Louisiana. Under the treaty of 1763, "New France" ceased to exist.

During the American Revolution and shortly thereafter, Loyalists from the American colonies (particularly New York, New Jersey, and Pennsylvania) took refuge in Nova Scotia and Quebec. England encouraged this exodus and was generous in granting land to those who chose to remain on the British side. A claims commission was established to reimburse Loyalists who had suffered financial loss during the conflict.

In 1791, Quebec was divided into two parts, and in 1841 became Ontario and Quebec. The Dominion of Canada was established in 1867, comprised of Ontario, Quebec, New Brunswick, and Nova Scotia; Rupert's Land in the west and the Northwest Territory were added in 1870. When gold was discovered in the western areas in 1858 and 1862, thousands of Californians migrated northward; by 1885, the Canadian railroads could take settlers from the Atlantic to the Pacific, which helped in the settlement of western provinces.

Because of the historic independence of the provinces, most records of genealogical importance have been kept at that level rather than by the federal government. Halifax, Nova Scotia, and Quebec City were the ports of entry for most of the emigrants who came from Europe, and some of their records have survived. Some military records exist, but it must be kept in mind that the Canadian armies before 1871 were British. There are some published regimental histories of Canadian units. In this connection, see Charles F. Dornbusch's *The Canadian Army, 1855–1965: Regimental Histories and a Guide to the Regiments* (Cornwallville, N.Y.: Hope Farm Press, 1966. UA600 .O56).

Federal censuses also exist for at least 1851, 1861, and 1871. In addition to the provincial archives, one might contact or visit the Public Archives of Canada in Ottawa, authorized in 1912 as the official repository of many national documents, maps, and other Canadian records.

Locations of the provincial archives are listed below:

Province	City
Newfoundland	St. John's
Nova Scotia	Halifax
Price Edward Island	Charlottetown
New Brunswick	St. John
Quebec	Quebec City
Ontario	Toronto
Manitoba	Winnipeg
Saskatchewan	Regina
Alberta	Edmonton
British Columbia	Victoria
Yukon	Whitehorse

For a detailed description of the provincial records see *The Library: A Guide to the LDS Family History Library,* edited by Johni Cerny and Wendy Elliott (Salt lake City: Ancestry, Inc., 1988) and the guides listed later in this section.

Newspaper Indexes

The Newspaper and Current Periodical Reading Room has the following indexes of Canadian newspapers:

Toronto Information Access, 1977 and annual supplements. A6954 .C2C22. Includes *Calgary Herald, Halifax Chronicle-Herald, Montreal Star, Toronto Glove and Mail, Toronto Star, Vancouver Sun,* and *Winnipeg Free Press.*

Montreal Star (weekend magazine index), 1951–65. Micro 111A

Ontario Legislative Library, Toronto, 1960–65. A13 .057.

Directories

Locating city and specialized directories of Canada's major cities in the card catalog is difficult, and researchers are urged to use the computer catalog instead. An inventory of the library's city directories is given below. Should you wish to locate other types of directories, use the following command in the computer catalog: **find s ottawa directories; f = prem (substitute name of the city)**

City Directories—Cataloged

To obtain any of the following city directories, submit a call slip indicating the city, call number, and the years of interest.

Fredericton, New Brunswick

> *Fredericton City Directory,* 1940, 1941, 1948, 1951–60. F1044.5 .F857.

Guelph, Ontario

> *Vernon's City of Guelph Directory,* 1953. F1056.5 G9A18.

Hamilton, Ontario

> *City of Hamilton Directory,* 1892. F1059.5 .H2A18.

Kamloops, British Columbia

> *Kamloops Directory,* 1949. F1089.5.

Kingston, Ontario

> *Mitchel & Company's General Directory for the City of Kingston,* 1865. F1059.5 .K5A19.

Montreal

> *Montreal Directory,* 1847, 1847, 1853, 1897. F1054.5 .M8A18.

> *The Montreal Directory,* 1849, 1853, 1897. F1054.5 .M8L83.

Ontario

> *The Province of Ontario Gazetteer and Directory,* 1869. F1056.5 .M14.

> *Northern Ontario Directory,* 1869. F1056.5 .N67.

Toronto

> *Toronto City Directory,* 1951–82. F1059.5 .T68A183.

City Directories—Not Cataloged

In addition to the cataloged directories, the library has some uncataloged city directories in closed stacks. To request them talk with a reference librarian in the Local History and Genealogy Reading Room.

Canada (country), 1951, 1953, 1965, 1971, 1811, 1915–45

Alberta

(province) 1920–28

Calgary, 1953

Edmonton, 1943, 1953, 1960

Medicine Hat (Radcliffe), 1953

British Columbia

(province) 1882, 1885, 1891–93, 1895, 1897, 1904, 1919–23, 1939–42, 1955

Dawson Creek, 1958

Fraser Valley, 1955

Kelowna, 1975

Kamloops, 1954

Penticton, 1954

Prince George, 1954

Vancouver (New Westminster, Victoria), 1908, 1924–33, 1953–54

Victoria (Vancouver Island), 1953–54, 1957–60

Manitoba

Winnipeg, 1904, 1929, 1954, 1961, 1962, 1972, 1981

New Brunswick

Fredericton (Devon, Marysville), 1926

Nova Scotia

(province, and Magdallen Islands), 1907, 1914

Cape Breton, 1928

Halifax (Dartmouth), 1908, 1912, 1923–47

Sydney (Dominion, Glace Bay, N. Sydney, Sydney), 1912, 1925

Ontario

(province) 1871, 1910–13

Belleville, 1953

Brantford, 1953

Cananoque (Kingston, Napanee), 1927

(counties) Carleton, Lanark, Renfrew, 1892, 1904

(counties) Dufferin, Ontario, Peel, York, 1898, 1900

Galt (Preston), 1952

Grey (Waterloo, Wellington), 1895

Guelph, 1928

Hamilton, 1953, 1968

(counties) Greenville, Lanark, Leeds, Renfrew, 1866

Kitchener (Waterloo), 1953

London, 1953

Niagara, 1927, 1953, 1967

Oshawa, 1953

Ottawa (Hull), 1791, 1897, 1899, 1908–57, 1965

Peterborough, 1953, 1967

Port William (Port Arthur), 1953

Russell (Dundas, Glengary, Leeds, Prescott, Stonmont), 1892, 1904

St. Catherine's, 1953

St. Thomas, 1953

Sault Ste. Marie, 1928, 1953

Simcoe (county), 1872

Toronto, 1837, 1856, 1859, 1862, 1866, 1868

Welland (Port Colborne), 1952

Windsor, 1958

Woodstock, 1952

York (county), 1870

Prince Edward Island (province), 1909, 1924, 1929

Quebec

Montreal, 1819, 1895, 1901–19, 1929, 1933, 1937–83 (plus an undated one, ca. 1860–80)

Saskatchewan

Moose Jaw, 1953

Regina, 1953, 1960

Saskatchewan, 1951

Saskatoon, 1953

Publications

Representative samples of some important and useful publications pertaining to the genealogy of Canadian-Americans are listed below.

Guides and Bibliographies

Baker, Eunice R. *Searching For Your Ancestors in Canada.* Ottawa: Heritage House, 1974. CS82 .B34.

Baxter, Angus. *In Search of Your Roots: A Guide For Canadians Seeking Their Ancestors.* Toronto: MacMillan of Canada, 1978. Rev. ed., 1984. CS82 .B39.

Coderre, Anita, and John Coderre. *Searching in French-Canadian Records*. Ottawa: Ontario Genealogical Society, 1977. CS83 .C63.

Coderre, John E. *Searching in the Public Archives*. Ottawa: Ontario Genealogical Society, 1972. CS3626.

Denis, Michael J. *Genealogical Researching in Eastern Canada: An Address Guide to Quebec and the Atlantic Provinces*. Rev. ed. Oakland, Maine: Danbury House, 1983. Z5313 .C22C383.

Denomme, Theophile W. *Our French Canadian Ancestry, 1631–1982*. N.p.: the author, 1982. CS89 .D46.

Genealogy and Local History Research Directory. New England Governors and Eastern Canadian Premiers Conference. Rockport, Maine: the conference, 1982. Z1251 .E1G46.

Gutteridge, Paul. *Canadian Genealogical Resources: A Guide to the Materials Held in Surrey Centennial Library*. Surrey, B.C.: Surrey Public Library, 1983. Z5313 .C2G87.

Jonasson, Eric. *The Canadian Genealogical Handbook: A Comprehensive Guide to Finding Your Ancestors in Canada*. 2d ed. Rev. and enl. Winnipeg: Wheatfield Press, 1978. CS82 .J66.

Kennedy, Patricia. *How to Trace Your Loyalist Ancestors: The Use of the Loyalist Sources in the Public Archives of Canada*. Ottawa: Ontario Genealogical Society, 1971. CD3624 .K46.

Public Archives of Canada. *Tracing Your Ancestors in Canada*. 9th ed. Ottawa: Public Archives of Canada, 1988. CS82 .P8.

Public Archives of Canada—Manuscript Division. *Checklist of Parish Registers, Répertoire des Registras Paroissiaux*. Ottawa: Public Archives of Canada, Manuscript Division, 1969. CD3648 .A1P8.

Varennes, Kathleen M. *Annotated Bibliography of Genealogical Works in the Library of Parliament (with Locations in Other Libraries in Canada)*. Ottawa: Library of Parliament of Canada, 1963. Z5319 .V35.

Waterloo-Wellington Branch, Ontario Genealogical Society. *A Representative List of Holdings for the Use of Genealogical Workers Submitted by the Librarians and Others Searching in the Libraries of Wilfrid Laurier University, et al.* Toronto: Ontario Genealogical Society, 1976. Z5313 .C2R46.

Published Records Sources

Addington, Charles, comp. *Some Passengers From Scotland and England to New Brunswick*. Canada: the author, 1985–86. CS88 .N43A35.

Akins, Thomas B., ed. "A List of the Families of English, Swiss . . . , Which Have Been Settled in Nova Scotia Since the Year 1749, and Who Now Are Settlers in the Places Hereafter Mentioned." *Selections from Public Documents in the Province of Nova Scotia, 1869*. N.p., n.d. F1036 .A78. (Micro 87/7226.)

Canada. Toronto Branch. *The United Empire Loyalist's Association of Canada: Loyalist Lineages of Canada, 1783–1963*. Ontario: Generation Press, 1984. CS83 .L69.

DeMarce, Virginia E. *An Annotated List of 317 Former German Soldiers Who Chose to Remain in Canada After the American Revolution*. Arlington, Va.: the author, 1981. E268 .D45.

———. *Canadian Participants in the American Revolution: An Index*. Arlington, Va.: the author, 1980. E255 .D4.

DeVille, Winston. *The Acadian Families in 1686*. Ville Platte, La.: the author, 1986. CS83 .D43.

Elliot, Noel M., ed. *People of Ontario, 1600–1900: Alphabetical Directory of the People, Places, and Vital Dates*. Toronto: Genealogical Research Library, 1984. CS88 .06P44.

Fraser, Alex W. *1001 Name Index of Descendants of John Cameron, "The Wise," "Fairfield," Summerstown, Ontario, Glengarry County*. Lancaster, Ont.: Highland Heritage: Glengarry Genealogical Society, 1985. CS90 .C15.

Fryer, Mary B. *Rolls of the Provincial (Loyalist) Corps, Canadian Command, American Revolutionary Period*. Toronto: Dundurn Press, 1981. E277 .F95.

Harne, David M., ed. *Dictionary of Canadian Biography—1000 to 1890*. Toronto: University of Toronto Press, 1969. F1005 .D49.

Separate index to volumes 1 through 14 (1000 to 1820).

Index to the 1871 Census of Ontario. Toronto: Ontario Genealogical Society, 1986. CS88 .H36153.

Jonasson, Eric. *Canadian Veterans of the War of 1812*. Winnipeg: Wheatfield Press, 1981. E359.85 .C36.

Labont, Youville, comp. *200 Family Trees, 1590–1979: From France to Canada to U.S.A.* Auburn, Maine: the author, 1979–84. CS69 .L32.

Livingston, Edwin A., comp. *A List of Livingston and Similar Names Extracted from the 1871 Census of Ontario.* Prescott, Ontario: the author, 1974. CS90 .L55.

Rock, Lucille F. *Our French Canadian Forefathers.* Woonsocket, R.I.: Rock Publications, 1982. CT284 .R63.

White, Donald. *A Dictionary of Scottish Emigrants to Canada Before Confederation.* Toronto: Ontario Genealogical Society, 1986. CS83 .W48.

England

Some selected high points in the history of England will serve to guide the historian and genealogist in searching for records. The first known people on the English Isles were the Celts, dating from 1,000 B.C. They were invaded in 57 B.C. by the Romans who stayed until A.D. 410. For the next two centuries and more, the land was populated by the Celts, Angles, Jutes, and Saxons, with the Celts retreating to Wales. In 787 the Danish vikings conquered the inhabitants and remained until 871 when they were overthrown by Alfred the Great. The Saxons, Danes, and Jutes (Anglo-Saxons) then ruled jointly under a succession of kings until the Norman king, William the Conqueror, won the Battle of Hastings in 1066. He replaced the ruling class with his own appointments and instituted a system of serfdom to control the land he parcelled out to his faithful. In 1255 King John was obliged to sign the Magna Carta that overhauled the land system and gave sweeping rights to the common man.

In 1529 King Henry VIII defied the Roman Catholic church and established the Church of England as the official state church, appointing himself as its head. He ordered the church parishes to keep registers of the populace; thus the church became the recorder of vital statistics until 1837 when civil registration was instituted.

Under Elizabeth I, English ships defeated the Spanish Armada in 1588, giving England control of the high seas and opening the way to exploration of the Americas, with the first settlement at Jamestown, Virginia, in 1607. Separatists from the Church of England settled in America in 1620, followed by the Puritans in 1630. In 1649 Lord Cromwell led a successful revolt against the monarchy, and parliamentary government was established; it lasted until 1660 when the monarchy was restored.

The Seven Years War with France resulted in the loss of many French possessions in America, but the American Revolution of 1776 to 1783 resulted in England losing all her American colonies south of Canada. Following the War of 1812, England and the United States agreed on the location of the boundary between Canada and the United States, ratified by treaty in 1842. For a century following the War of 1812, some 9 million English immigrated to the United States and 3 million to Canada. During the mid-1800s, several thousand went to Australia and South Africa.

England's genealogical sources are plentiful but not necessarily centralized. Early records in London were destroyed by fire in 1666, and it is believed that emigration and ship passenger lists fell victim to World War II. Records were kept by the church parishes, however, and civil records of births, marriages, and deaths, as well as church recorded baptisms and probate matters, are extant. By identifying the English county (shire) in which one's ancestors lived, it may be possible to unearth the records of the major events in their lives, even though they may not be recorded in a central repository such as the Public Record Office in London. In the United States, the Family History Library in Salt Lake City is a prime source for English records, and copies of them are available through its branch center libraries.

Although it is extremely unlikely that anyone can trace their English ancestry back 200 years or so and then connect with a name in England's early recorded history—the *Domesday Books*—one should be aware of their existence. They were written by order of William the Conqueror in the eleventh century. After William devastated the English Army and, except for a few northern counties, took over the country, he destroyed the prevailing English aristocracy, installed his own noblemen, and revamped the country's land ownership system by establishing manors, divided into "hundreds," and granted farms to landowners (tenants-in-chief).

Late in 1085, William ordered a county by county survey (except in the northern counties) to determine the value of his royal lands and to record the names of those who lived on them. Not only were the lands and tenants-in-chiefs identified by the royal canvassers, but their crops and animals were counted as well. When the task was completed at the close of the following year, the *Great Domesday Book* and the *Little Domesday Book* were ready. Similar surveys were subsequently undertaken and additional books completed. All were published in 1783 and 1815 in the original Latin. During the 1800s some scholars translated the early clerical Latin into English, but during the 1960s it was decided

Typical page from the *Domesday Books*.

From Thomas Hinde, ed., *The Domesday Book — England's Heritage Then and Now*
(Australia: Phoebe Phillips Editions, 1985), page 15

that new translations were needed. Medieval scholars began work in 1969, and the first volumes were published in 1975. By 1985 the thirty-five-volume set was complete with the original Latin and the English translation on facing pages. These volumes constitute the first complete translation of the 900 year old surveys.

The Library of Congress has more than three dozen works that describe the *Domesday Books;* to obtain their titles and call numbers use the computer catalog with one or both of the following commands: **find s domesday** or **find s domesday; f = prem.**

Highly recommended is Henry Ellis's *A General Introduction to Domesday Books, Accompanied by an Index of Tenants-in-chiefs and Under-tenants . . . .* (Baltimore: Genealogical Publishing Co., 1971, DA190 .D735).

Following the years of the above surveys, records of genealogical importance were created both by churches and governments, the parish registers being the prime sources. There are hundreds of published parish registers that may be identified by consulting the computer catalog, using the following command: **find s registers london; f = prem** (substitute name of city).

Repositories of many English records might be found in London at one of the following establishments: Public Record Office, Society of Genealogists, Somerset House, British Museum, Guildhall Library, Friends' House (Quaker records), and Huguenot Society of London.

Other records outside the Library of Congress may be found in England's county libraries and county records offices—similar to state libraries and state archives in the United States. Two publications that list the location of such repositories and how to use them are Angus Baxter's *In Search of Your British and Irish Roots,* and Janet Foster and Julia Sheppard's *British Archives* (both cited under "Guides and Record Sources" below). Another excellent source of English records repositories and the nature of their records is Johni Cerny and Wendy Elliott's *The Library: A Guide to the LDS Family History Library* (Salt Lake City: Ancestry, Inc., 1988). That work cites the *Boyd's Marriage Index,* containing more than 6 million names culled from parish registers of many English counties, which is available at the Family History Library, Salt Lake City.

Manuscript Division Holdings

The Manuscript Division of the Library of Congress has the following collections that may be helpful to those seeking English ancestors.

Foreign Copying Project: Great Britain—British Reproductions

This collection consists of manuscripts relating to American history found in British repositories. Among others, they include:

British Army in America Headquarters Papers, 1747–83. This consists of twenty-eight reels of microfilm.

Claims, American Loyalists—arranged by states of the United States, it consists of forty-four reels of microfilm of decisions and documents pertaining to claims by Loyalists during the American Revolution.

Public Record Office—Genealogy Notes

This collection contains no records, but it consists, rather, of a selection of leaflets issued by the Public Record Office in London, entitled as follows: "Genealogy from the Public Records," "Births, Marriages, and Deaths," "Census," "Probate," "Change of Name," "Immigrants," "Emigrants," "Shipping and Seamen," "Military," "Admiralty," "Private Conveyances," "Apprenticeship," "Royal Marines," "Royal Irish Constabulary," and "Death Duties."

Newspaper Indexes

The Newspaper and Current Periodical Reading Room has the following indexes to English newspapers:

London

General

Palmer's Index to the Times Newspapers . . . , 1868–. A121 .T5.

Index to the Times. Times Publishing Co., 1914–71. A121 .T46.

The Times Index, 1972–77. A121 .T46.

An Index to the Times and to the Topics and Events of the Year 1862–63. A121 .T6.

Smith's Index to the Leading Articles of "The Times." A121 .T63.

Bailey's Index to "The Times," 1899–1901. A121 .T4.

The Times Diary and Index of the War, 1914 to 1918. D510 .T5.

Obituaries

Index to Obituary Notices, 1880–82. A13 .I4.

Obituaries from the Times, 1971–75. CT120 .O17.

Obituaries from the Times, 1951–60. CT120 .O16.

Obituaries from the Times, 1961–70. CT120 .O165.

Chester

Chester Newspaper Indexes, 1960–64. A13 .C42.

Oxford

Jackson's Oxford Journal (1753–1853) (obituary and bibliographical notices). A121 .J3.

Stafford

Staffordshire Advertiser (index to births, marriages, and deaths, 1795–1820). CS435 .S615.

Directories

The library has a large number of English city directories, "blue books," and professional and trade directories. Most of them have been cataloged and may be obtained by submitting a call slip in the Local History and Genealogy Reading Room. Finding a reference in the card catalog is difficult and researchers are urged to rely instead on the computer catalog. Use the following command to locate a directory for either a shire (county) or a city: **find s lincolnshire directories; f = prem** (substitute name of the shire) or **find s bristol directories; f = prem** (substitute name of the city).

Occasionally, a directory will be designated "Rare Book Room" and may be called for there. The Rare Book Room also has a card catalog and a reference librarian will provide information as to how to find directories listed there.

City Directories—Cataloged

In the city directories listed below, you will notice that many are entitled *Kelly's Post Office Directory of _____*. These are not lists of post offices but city directories issued as reference books for post office employees.

Shires (Counties)

Cumberland Directory (Aspatria, Carlisle, Cockermouth, Keswick, Maryport, Millom, Peurith, Whitehave, Widon, and Workington), 1954. DA670 .C9C8.

History, Gazetteer and Directory of Cumberland (with index of places, subjects, and "gentlemen's seats"), 1847. DA670 .C9M2.

History, Directory and Gazetteer of Cumberland and Westmorland (Cartmel, Furness), 1829. DA670 .C9P35.

The Derby County Borough Directory, 1952. DS670 .D42B28.

Kelly's Directory of Watford (Bushey, Rickmansworth), 1949, 1952, 1969–74. DA670 .H5K45.

Jersey Evening Post Almanac and Trade Directory. (St. Clement, St. Heber, St. John, St. Lawrence, St. Martin, St. Ouen, St. Peter, and St. Savior), 1950, 1954, 1965, 1969, 1980. DS670 .J5E94.

Post Office Directory of Lincolnshire, 1855. DA670 .L7L72.

White's 1856 Lincolnshire, 1856. DA670 .L5W57.

Kelly's Directory of Medway Towns, 1969. DA670 .M4K45.

White's 1845 Norfolk, 1845. DA670 .N6W5.

Shrewsbury Burgess Roll, (mostly 1700s). DS670 .S39S5.

Kelly's Directory of Somersetshire, 1894. DA670 .S49K4.

White's 1844 Suffolk, 1844. DA670 .S9W5.

Kelly's Directory of the Isle of Thank (Broadstars, Margate, and Ramsgate), 1951, 1953, 1955. DA670 .T3K45.

Kelly's Directory of Warwick (Kenelworth, Leamington Spa, Stratford-upon-Avon), 1950, 1953, 1969. DA670 .W3K45.

Directory of Worcestershire, 1840. DA670 .W9B4.

Worcestershire Directory, 1820. DA670 .W9L6.

White's 1853 Leads and the Clothing Districts of Yorkshire, 1853. DA670 .Y6W59.

Cities

Andover

Kelly's Directory of Andover, 1950, 1953, 1956, 1969. DA690 .A53K4.

Aylesbury

Kelly's Directory of Aylsebury, 1954, 1964. DA690 .A98K4.

Banbury

Kelly's Directory of Banbury, 1950. DA690 .B22K4.

Basingstoke

Kelly's Directory of Basingstoke, 1952, 1955. DA690 .B29K4.

Bath

Kelly's Directory of Bath, 1934, 1937, 1950, 1952, 1955. DA690 .B3K4.

Bedford

Kelly's Directory of Bedford, 1949, 1952, 1955, 1957, 1959. DA690 .B4K4.

Bexhill

Kelly's Directory of Bexhill, 1950, 1953, 1956. DA690 .B52K4.

Birmingham

Post Office Directory of Birmingham; With the Principal Towns in the Hardware and Pottery Districts, 1856. DA690 .B6A4.

Kelly's Directory of Birmingham, With its Suburbs, and Smethwick, 1909, 1911, 1934–74. DA690 .B6A4.

The Birmingham Post Year Book and Who's Who, 1951–85. DA690 .B6B5.

Bognor Regis

Kelly's Directory of Bognor Regis, 1950, 1955–56, 1959. DA690 .B646K4.

Bournemouth (and Poole)

Kelly's Directory of Bournemouth and Poole, 1950–75. DA690 .B685.K4.

Bradford

City of Bradford Directory, 1953. DA690 .B7C47.

Post Office Directory of Bradford, 1909. DA690 .B7P6.

Brighton Hove

Kelly's Directory of Brighton, 1949–56, 1970. DA690 .B7KK36.

Bristol

Kelly's Directory of Bristol, 1950, 1953, 1956. DA690 .B8K4.

Bromley

Kelly's Directory of Bromley, 1950, 1953. DA690 .B85K4.

Cambridge

Kelly's Directory of Cambridge, 1951–55, 1972–75. DA690 .C2K37.

Canterbury

Kelly's Directory of Canterbury, 1949–70. DA690 .C3K4.

Carlisle

Carlisle Directory, 1952, 1955. DA690 .C335C3.

Chelmsford

Kelly's Directory of Chelmsford, 1950, 1955. DA690 .C48K4.

Chester

Kelly's Directory of Chester, 1952, 1954. DA690 C5K4.

Chichester

Kelly's Directory of Chichester, 1954, 1964. DA690 .C53K4.

Colchester

Benham's Colchester Directory, 1952. DA690 .C7B42.

Coventry

Local Trades and Streets Directories, 1953. DA690 .C75D5.

Croydon

The Croydon Directory, 1951–52. DA690 .C8C76.

Kent Service Ltd., Croydon Directory, 1900. DA690 .C8K46.

Darlington

> *Kelly's Directory of Darlington,* 1953, 1955. DA690 .D22K4.

Dorking

> *Kelly's Directory of Dorking,* 1950. DA690 .D65K4.

Dover

> *Kelly's Directory of Dover,* 1950–71. DA690 .D7K4.

Ealing (and Hanwell)

> *Kemp's Directory of Ealing and Hanwell,* 1950, 1957, 1972. DA690 .E11K4.

Eastbourne

> *Kelly's Directory of Eastbourne, Nailsham,* 1951, 1953, 1955. DA690 .E137K4.

Enfield

> *Enfield Directory, With Southgate,* 1953. DA690 .E45.

Exeter

> *Besley's Exeter Directory,* 1952, 1955. DA690 .E9B47.

> *Kelly's Directory of Exeter,* 1956, 1969. DA690 .E9K4.

Exmouth (and Littleham and Whithycombe)

> *Street Directory and Gazetteer for Exmouth, Littleham and Whithycombe,* 1948–52. DA690 .E93S7.

Felixstowe

> *Kelly's Directory of Felixstowe,* 1950. DA690 .F284K4.

Folkestone (and Sandgate, Hythe, Saltwood)

> *Kelly's Directory of Folkestone, Sandgate, Hythe, and Saltwood,* 1949, 1953. DA690 .F55K4.

Gloucester

> *Kelly's Directory of Gloucester and District,* 1952, 1955. DA690 .G8K4.

Gravesend

> *Kelly's Directory of Gravesend,* 1956. DA690 .G8K4.

Grimsby (and Cleethorpes)

> *Kelly's Directory of Grimsby and Cleethorpes District,* 1958. DA690 .G85A6.

Guildford (and Godalming)

> *Kelly's Directory of Guildford and Godalming,* 1950, 1953, 1955. DA690 .G95K4.

Halifax

> *The Halifax County Borough Directory,* 1952. DA690 .H17H28.

Hampstead (and Kilburn)

> *Hampstead Directory* (Kilburn), 1951, 1954. DA690 .H198H3.

Harrogate (and Knaresborough and Wetherby)

> *Kelly's Directory of Harrogate, Knaresborough and Wetherby,* 1950–55, 1973. DA690 .H32K4.

Harrow

> *Kemp's Harrow Land Directory,* 1950–1977. DA690 .H327K4.

Hastings (and Battle and St. Leonards)

> *Kelly's Directory of Hastings, Battle and St. Leonards,* 1950, 1953, 1958. DA690 .H35K4.

Hendon

> *Hendon Directory, including Cricklewood, Edgeware, and Golders Green,* 1950, 1952. DA690 .H475H4.

Hitchin

> *Hitchin Directory,* 1952, 1956. DA690 .H715H535.

Huddersfield

> *The Huddersfield County Borough Directory,* 1956. DA690 .H87C6.

Ipswich

> *Kelly's Directory of Ipswich,* 1949, 1952, 1954, 1970, 1972–73. DA690 .I6K45.

Kingston Upon Hill

> *Kingston Upon Hill Directory,* 1954. DA690 .H9C53.

Kensington (and Brompton, Knightsbridge, and Notting Hill)

Kelly's Directory of Kensington, Brompton, Knightsbridge, and Notting Hill, 1950, 1953. DA690 .K413K4.

Kings Lynn

Kelly's Directory of Kings Lynn, 1951, 1954. DA690 .K5K45.

Leeds

City of Leeds Directory, 1955. DA690 .L4C5.

Leicester

Kelly's Directory of Leicester, 1951, 1954, 1970. DA690 .L5K45.

Lincoln

Kelly's Directory of Lincoln, 1949–59. DA690 .L67K4.

Liverpool

Gore's Directory of Liverpool, 1816, 1853. DA690 .L8G7.

Kelly's Directory of Liverpool, 1935–70. DA690 .L8K4.

London

For a finding aid to London directories of all kinds, attention is directed to Charles W. Goss's *The London Directories, 1677–1855: A Bibliography* (London: Dorris Archer, 1932, Z5771 .G67). This work lists only business and trades directories, not residences.

Boyle's Court Guide, 1815, 1821, 1843. DA679 .A117.

London Directory, 1884, 1890, 1897, 1905, 1912. DA679 .A12.

City Directory and Diary, and Livery Companies, 1950–65, 1973, 1977–86. DA679 .A12.

City of London Directory, Guilds Guide, and Who's Who, 1966–72. DA679 .A12.

Kent's Directory of London, 1811. DA679 .A128.

The Little London Directory of 1677, including Merchants and Bankers, 1677. DA679 .A13.

Literary Blue Book, 1830. DA679 .A1285.

The London Directory, 1934–41, 1948–74. DA679, A1315.

Lowndes's London Directory for the Year, 1786 (Rare Book Room), 1786. DA679 .A135.

The London Directory of 1677, including Merchants and Bankers, 1677. DA679 .A132 (Micro 82/5040).

Lowndes's London Directory for the Year 1799 (Rare Book Room), 1799. DA679 .A135.

London Post-Office Directory, 1914. DA679 .A4.

London Post-Office Directory, 1848–58, 1879, 1891–1983. DA679 .A14.

Kelly's Post Office Guide to London, 1862. DA679 .K38.

Watkins London Directory, 1853–55. DA679 .A16.

Lowestoft (and Beccles)

Kelly's Directory to Lowestoft and Beccles, 1948, 1952, 1954. DA690 .L845K4.

Maidenhead (and Cockham and Taplow)

Kelly's Directory to Maidenhead, Cockham, and Taplow, 1952, 1957. DA690 .M18K4.

Maidstone

Kelly's Directory of Maidstone, 1949, 1952, 1954. DA690 .M2K4.

Manchester (and Salford and Stretford)

Kelly's Directory of Manchester, Salford and Stretford, 1934–69. DA690 .M4K4.

Newark

Kelly's Directory of Newark, 1950. DA690 .N53K4.

Newbury

Kelly's Directory of Newbury, 1950. DA690 .N55K4.

Newcastle Upon Tyne

Kelly's Directory of Newcastle Upon Tyne, 1950–59, 1968. DA690 .N6M15.

Newport

Kelly's Directory of Newport, 1950, 1955. DA690 .N66K4.

Newton Abbot (and Bovery and Tracey)

Kelly's Directory of Newton Abbot, including Bovery and Tracey, 1951. DA690 .N677K4.

Northampton

Kelly's Directory of Northampton, 1952, 1954, 1956. DA690 .N8K4.

Norwich

> *Kelly's Directory of Norwich,* 1950, 1952, 1954. DA690 .N88K43.

Nottingham

> *Kelly's Directory of Nottingham, and the Urban District of Bridgford,* 1950, 1956. DA690 .N92K4.

Oxford

> *Kelly's Directory of Oxford,* 1949, 1952, 1954, 1962–76. DA690 .N98K4.

Plymouth

> *Kelly's Directory of Plymouth,* 1951, 1953, 1955. DA690 .P7K45.

Portsmouth

> *Kelly's Directory of Portsmouth,* 1948–56, 1969–75. DA690 .P8K4.

Preston

> *Barrett's Directory of Preston and District,* 1952. DA690 .P93B3.

Reading

> *Kelly's Directory of Reading,* 1949, 1952, 1956, 1969, 1972–76. DA690 .R28K4.

Reigate (and Redhill)

> *Kelly's Directory of Reigate and Redhill,* 1951. DA690 .R36K4.

Rochdale (and Milnrow, Littleborough, and Wardle)

> *Rochdale Directory, including Milnrow, Littleborough, and Wardle,* 1954. DA690 .R55R6.

Rochester (and Chatham and Gillingham)

> *Kelly's Directory of Rochester, Chatham, and Gillingham,* 1951. DA690 .R6K4.

Rugby

> *Rugby Directory,* 1952–53, 1956. DA690 .R85R8.

Ryde

> *Kelly's Directory of Ryde,* 1951. DA690 .R89K4.

St. Alban's (and Harpenden, Hatfield, Radlett)

> *Kelly's Directory of St. Albans, Harpenden, Hatfield, and Radlett,* 1949, 1952, 1956, 1984, 1902. DA690 .S13K4.

Salisbury

> *Kelly's Directory of Salisbury,* 1950, 1972–74. DA690 .S16K4.

Scarborough

> *Kelly's Directory of Scarborough,* 1952, 1954. DA690 .S28K4.

Shanklin (and Sandown and Ventnor)

> *Kelly's Directory of Shanklin Sandown, and Ventnor,* 1951. DA690 .S5K4.

Sheffield

> *Kelly's Directory of Sheffield and Rotterdam,* 1934–74. DA690 .S54A15.

Sheringham

> *Sheringham Guide and Directory,* 1969. DA690 .S5677S5.

Sidmouth (and Sidbury, Sidford)

> *Street Directory and Gazetteer for Sidmouth, Sidbury, Sidford, and District,* 1949, 1951. DA690 .S6S7.

Slough

> *Slough Directory,* 1953. DA690 .S623S57.

Southampton

> *Kelly's Directory of Southampton,* 1951, 1960–75. DA690 .S69K4.

Southend

> *Kelly's Directory of Southend,* 1950, 1953. DA690 .S71SK4.

Southgate

> *Southgate Directory,* 1950. DA690 .S72S6.

Southport (and Banks, Formby, Freshfield)

> *Directory of Southport, including Banks, Formby, and Freshfield,* 1951. DA690 .S75D5.

Surbiton

> *Kelly's Directory of Subiton,* 1964. DA690 .S95K4.

Swindon

> *The Swindon and District Directory and Yearbook,* 1951. DA690 .S98S9.

Taunton

> *Kelly's Directory of Taunton,* 1954, 1964. DA690 .T22K4.

Torquay (and Paignton)

> *Kelly's Directory of Torquay and Paignton,* 1948, 1951, 1953. DA690 .T69K4.

Tunbridge Wells

> *Kelly's Directory of Tunbridge Wells,* 1950, 1953. DA690 T92K4.

Warrington

> *Warrington and District Directory,* 1951. DA690 .W28W3.

Weston—Super—Mare

> *Kelly's Directory of Weston—Super—Mare,* 1949, 1952, 1954. DA690 .W53K4.

Weymouth (and Portland)

> *Kelly's Directory of Weymouth and Portland,* 1955, 1972. DA690 .W54K4.

Wimbledon

> *Wimbledon Directory,* 1951. DA690 .W62W63.

Windsor (and Eton, Detchet)

> *Kelly's Directory of Windsor, Eton, Old Windsor, and Datchet,* 1950, 1953, 1974. DA690 .W76K4.

Worthing (and Lancing, Ferring, Sompting)

> *Kelly's Directory of Worthing, Lancing, Ferring, and Sompting,* 1949, 1951, 1953, 1956. DA690 .W925K4.

Yarmouth, Great (and Gorleston, Southtown)

> *Kelly's Directory of Great Yarmouth, Gorleston, and Southtown,* 1948, 1952, 1955. DA690 .Y2K4.

York

> *Kelly's Directory of York,* 1953, 1955, 1969–75. DA690 .Y6K4.

City Directories—Not Cataloged

There are a few uncataloged directories for English cities in the closed stacks shelved following the uncataloged directories of United States cities. For assistance, consult a reference librarian in the Local History and Genealogy Reading Room.

> Great Britain and Ireland (business), 1920

> Liverpool, 1835

> London and suburbs, 1842, 1887, 1897, 1900, 1907, 1927, 1975

> Uxbridge and district (Cowley, Ickenham, and Hillingdon), 1952

Guides and Record Sources

Listed below are general guides for research in England. Following these is a brief list of guides that pertain to specific counties. For a general bibliography, see P. William Filby's *American and British Genealogy and Heraldry,* 3d ed. (Boston: New England Historic Genealogical Society, 1983; supps. 1982–85, Z5311 .F55).

Baxter, Angus. *In Search of Your British and Irish Roots: A Complete Guide to Tracing Your English, Welsh, Scottish, and Irish Ancestors.* Baltimore: Genealogical Publishing Co., 1982. CS414 .B38.

Bethell, David. *English Ancestry.* Leek, Staffordshire: Melandra, 1981. CS414 .B47.

Boreham, John M. *The Census and How to Use It.* Brentwood, Essex: Essex Society for Family History, 1982. CS415 .B67.

Camp, Anthony J. *Tracing Your Ancestors.* London: Gifford, 1970. Reprint: Baltimore: Genealogical Publishing Co., 1979. CS415 .C3.

Catholic Who's Who and Yearbooks, 1909–1941. London: Burns & Oates. DS28 .C3C33.

Cox, Jane. *Tracing Your Ancestor in the Public Record Office.* London: H.M.S.O., 1981. Z5313 .C7C69.

Currer-Briggs, Noel. *English Wills of Colonial Families.* Cottonport, La.: Polyanthos, 1972. KD1512 .C87.

Foster, Janet, and Julia Sheppard. *British Archives: A Guide to Archive Resources in the United Kingdom.* Detroit: Gale Research Co., 1982. CD1040 .F67.

Guide includes addresses.

Gardner, David E., and Frank Smith. *Genealogical Research in England and Wales.* Salt Lake City: Bookcraft Publishers, 1956. CS414 .G3.

Gibson, Jeremy S.W. *A Simplified Guide to Probate Jurisdictions: Where to Look for Wills in Great Britain and Ireland.* Baltimore: Genealogical Publishing Co., 1986. CS49 .G5.

——. *A Simplified Guide to Bishop's Transcripts and Marriage Licenses: Their Location and Indexes of England, Wales, and Ireland.* 2d ed. Baltimore: Genealogical Publishing Co., 1982. Z5313 .G7E54.

——. *Census Returns, 1841–1881, on Microfilm: A Directory to Local Holdings.* 4th ed. Plymouth, England: Federation of Family History Societies, 1982. Z5313 .G69G52.

Guide to the Contents of the Public Record Office (London). 2 vols. London: Her Majesty's Stationery Office, 1963. CD1043 .A553.

Hamilton-Edwards, Gerald K.S. *In Search of British Ancestry.* Baltimore: Genealogical Publishing Co., 1983. CS414 .H35.

Herwig, Holgar H., and Neil M. Heyman. *Biographical Dictionary of World War I.* 2 vols. Westport, Conn.: Greenwood Press, 1982. D507 .H47.

Iredalo, David. *Discovering Your Family Tree: A Pocket Guide to Tracing Your English Ancestors.* Rev. ed. Aylesbury: Shire Publications, 1973. CS415 .I74.

Johnson, James B. *The Place-names of England and Wales.* London: John Murray, 1915. DS645 .J6.

Peskett, Hugh. *Discover Your Ancestors: A Quest for Your Roots.* New York: Arco Publishing Co., 1978. CS16 .P45.

Smith, Frank. *The Lives and Times of Our English Ancestors.* Logan, Utah: Everton Publishers, 1969. CS415 .S56.

Steel, Donald J. *National Index of Parish Registers.* 13 vols. London: Society of Genealogists, 1966–86. CD1068 .A2S8.

Sydney, Lee, ed. *Dictionary of National Biography.* 63 vols. New York: MacMillan & Co., 1885. DS28 .D42.

Webb, C.C. *A Guide to Genealogical Sources in the Borthwick Institute of Historical Research.* York, England: University of York; the institute, 1984. Z5313 .G7Y678.

Published County Records

Once the county in which an English ancestor lived is known, consult the computer catalog for a list of published sources, including parish registers. Use the following command: **find s lancashire genealogy** (substitute name of county).

Some examples of published country records are listed below.

Billington, Eric R., comp. *Parish Registers and Churches of the West Midlands and Black County, Including District Locations of Churches, Commencement Date of Registers, and Guide to Their Whereabouts.* Birmingham, England: Birmindex, 1980. Z5140 .B543.

Dickinson, Robert and Florence Dickinson. "Index to Wills and Administration Formerly Preserved in the Probate Registry Chester, 1831–1833." In *Record Society of Lancashire and Cheshire, Vol. 118,* edited by Brian E. Harris. N.p., n.d. KD6973 .L35.

Earwaker, J.P., ed. *Lancashire and Cheshire Wills and Inventories, 1572–1696.* Manchester, England: Chetham Society, 1893. DS670 .L19C5.

Gloucestershire Notes & Queries. 10 vols. London: W. Kent & Co., 1881–1914. DS670 .G4G5.

Hardy, W.J. *Hertford County Records—Sessions Rolls, 1581–1894.* 10 vols. N.p.: Clerk of the Peace Office, 1905–57. DS670 .H49A53.

Horrocks, Sidney, ed. *Registers, Parochial, Non-parochial, Monumental Inscriptions, Names, Wills.* Manchester, England: Joint Committee on the Lancashire Bibliography, n.d. CD1068 .L36R43.

——. *Lancashire Family Histories, Pedigrees, Heraldry.* Manchester, England: Joint Committee on the Lancashire Bibliography, 1972. Z5313 .G7L354.

Moore, John S., ed. *Clifton and Westbury Probate Inventories, 1609–1761 (Gloucester).* Briton: Avon Local History Association, 1981. DS690 .C624C57.

Price, William B., ed. *Registers of West Derby Chapel in the Parish of Walton-on-the-Hill: Baptisms, 1688–1837; Marriages, 1698–1837.* Vol. 110. Lancashire: Lancashire Parish Registers Society, 1971. CS435 .L3.

Spencer, Wilfred, ed. *Parochial Chapelry of Coine: Marriages From 1654–1754.* Burley: Coine Register Transcriptions, 1975. CS436 .C72A64.

Ireland

During the mid-1500s England became intent on usurping many landowners in Ireland and replacing them with Englishmen who were permitted to purchase large plantations at extremely low prices, and by 1600 Scottish lowland Protestants were being encouraged to settle on confiscated Irish lands. When Cromwell overthrew the English monarchy, the new government confiscated millions of acres in Ireland and continued the practice of offering it at cheap prices to the English.

In 1703 a system was begun to register land by deed; it was not compulsory, and seldom included Roman Catholics who were forbidden to own land. Other settlers in Ireland included Huguenots who escaped religious persecution in France and a large group of Palatine Germans who went to Ireland to escape war. Both of these groups later immigrated to America.

In 1740 an official list was made of the Protestants in northern Ireland. Following this, at different times, separate records of Catholics and Protestants were made, but few have survived. The first national population censuses were taken in 1821 and 1831, but they were almost entirely destroyed by a fire in 1922; the censuses of 1861 and 1871 were destroyed by government order; only the 1901 and 1911 censuses survive. Civil registrations of births, marriages, and deaths in Ireland began about 1864. Lists have also been made of those who took military oaths of allegiance in 1757, and a survey of householders was taken during the period 1848 to 1864; but only fragments are extant.

The Irish Free State was created by treaty with England in 1921, and the Republic of Ireland became free and separate from England in 1948. However, there still remains considerable tension and violence between England and the northern Ireland counties comprising Ulster. To distinguish between the Protestant Scotch-Irish in northern Ireland and the native Catholic Irish in the balance of the country, the counties comprising northern Ireland are Antrim, Armagh, Belfast, Down, Fermanagh, Londonderry, and Tyrone.

After decades of bloody confrontation between the Irish Catholics and the Protestant Irish in northern Ireland (originally from Scotland), the latter began to immigrate to America during the mid-1770s. They were among those who followed the first contingent that had sailed to Boston in 1718. By 1720, 5,000 had arrived, settling in small towns or rural areas along the New England coast; an estimated 250,000 had arrived before the American Revolution.

The Catholic Irish tended to stay in Ireland until the mid-1800s, when the potato blights of 1845 to 1850 reduced large numbers of the population to starvation. To escape the famine, many went to England before taking a passage to America. By 1860 an estimated 1.5 million Irish had come to the United States, primarily settling in New York, Pennsylvania, Massachusetts, New Jersey, Illinois, and Ohio. They found work on the canals, laid ties and steel tracks for the expanding rail system, were household servants, worked in the coal mines, and became civil servants in the cities.

In the mid-1700s Pennsylvania advertised for settlers and the Protestant Irish were happy to take advantage of the opportunity to immigrate, but some were surprised to learn they were expected to pay for the land they claimed. In the opinion of the established Quakers and other entrenched Pennsylvanians in the Philadelphia area, the newcomers were a troublesome and independent group of people, and arrangements were made for them to settle in western counties of the state where they could serve as a buffer to hostile Indians. Now generally referred to as Scotch-Irish, or Scots-Irish, they fought valiantly against British forces during the American Revolution. After the war, large numbers of them moved southward down the Shenandoah Valley through Virginia and into North Carolina where they settled in the mountainous regions. They had little in common with well-established citizens and political leaders who were entrenched along the Atlantic coast. When economic problems arose during a series of depressions in the early 1800s, the Scots-Irish quickly moved westward into Kentucky and Tennessee, and, as land became available elsewhere, their westward trek continued until they inhabited nearly all parts of the country.

Directories

Titles of city, business, and specialized directories of Irish cities may be found by consulting the computer catalog, using the following command: **find s limerick; f = prem** (substitute name of city). A list of cataloged city directories is found below.

Ireland (country)

Thom's Irish Almanac and Directory, 1854–56, 1862, 1866–69, 1875–1957. DA979.5 .T56.

Belfast

> *Belfast and Ulster Directory,* 1868, 1935–84. DA995 .B5B45.

Dublin

> *Thom's Dublin Directory,* 1960–85. DA990 .D8T5.

Guides and Bibliographies

The following sources may be helpful in researching Irish roots, Protestant or Catholic. Many of the early Irish records that would help genealogists today were destroyed, but several published works concerning those who emigrated are listed below.

Baxter, Angus. *In Search of Your British and Irish Roots: A Complete Guide to Tracing Your English, Welsh, Scottish, and Irish.* Baltimore: Genealogical Publishing Co., 1982. CS414 .B38.

Begley, Donal F. *Handbook on Irish Genealogy: How to Trace Your Ancestry and Relatives in Ireland.* Dublin: Heraldic Artists, Inc., 1984. CS483 .H36.

Black, J. Anderson. *Your Irish Ancestors.* New York: Paddington Press, 1974. CS483 .B55.

Campbell, R.G. *Scotch-Irish Family Research Made Simple.* Munroe Falls, Ohio: Summit Publications, 1973. CS49 .C35.

Collins, E.J. *Irish Family Research Made Simple.* Munroe Falls, Ohio: Summit Publications, 1974. CS49 .C64.

Crone, John S. *A Concise Dictionary of Irish Biography.* Rev. and enl. New York: Longmans Green & Co., 1937. DA916 .C7.

DeBreffny, Brian, ed. *Bibliography of Irish Family History and Genealogy.* Cork, Ireland: Golden Eagle Books, 1974. Z5313 .I7P4.

Dickson, Robert J. *Ulster Emigration to Colonial America, 1718–1775.* London: Rutledge and Kegan Paul, 1966. Reprint. Belfast: Ulster Scot Historical Foundation, 1976. E184 .S4D47.

Falley, Margaret D. *Irish and Scotch–Irish Ancestral Research: A Guide to the Genealogical Records, Methods, and Sources in Ireland.* 2 vols. Evanston, Ill.: the author, 1962. Reprint. Baltimore: Genealogical Publishing Co., 1984. CS483 .F32.

Glynn, Joseph M. *Manual for Irish Genealogy: A Guide to Methods and Sources For Tracing Irish*

Ancestors. 2d ed. Newton, Mass.: Irish Family History Society, 1982. CS483 .G58.

MacLysaght, Edward. *Irish Families—Their Names, Arms, and Origins.* 4th ed. Rev. and enl. Dublin: Irish Academic Press, 1985. C2415 .M235.

MacLysaght, Edward. *Bibliography of Irish Family History.* Dublin: Irish Academic Press, 1981. Z5313 .I7M32.

Magee, Penny, comp. *Bibliography of Genealogical Sources For the Counties of the Republic Ireland.* Santa Anna, Calif.: Magee Publications, 1982. Z5313 .I7M33.

McCay, Betty L. *Seven Lesson Course in Irish Research and Sources.* Indianapolis, n.p., 1972. CS483 .M3.

Mitchell, Brian. *A Guide to Irish Parish Registers.* Baltimore: Genealogical Publishing Co., 1980. (Cataloging in publication.)

Ni Aonghusa, Nora. *How to Trace Your Irish Roots.* Tankdardstown, Killmallock Co., Limerick, Ireland: M. & J. Hennessy, 1986. CS483 .N5.

Ryan, James G. *Irish Records: Sources for Family and Local History.* Salt Lake City: Ancestry Publishing, 1988.

Ward, William R. *A Primer for Irish Genealogical Research.* Salt Lake City: the author, 1976. CS483 .W37.

Published Records Sources

Boylan, Henry. *A Dictionary of Irish Biography.* Dublin: Gill and MacMillan, 1978. CT862 .B69.

Church of Jesus Christ of Latter-day Saints. Genealogical Department. *Irish County Maps Showing the Locations of Churches.* Salt Lake City: Genealogical Society of Utah, CS1 .G3828. No. 54–57.

Clare, Wallace. *A Guide to Copies and Abstracts of Irish Wills.* Baltimore: Genealogical Publishing Co., 1972. CS482 .C4.

Clarke, R. S. J., ed. *Gravestone Inscriptions, County Antrim; County Down.* 3 vols. Belfast: Ulster Historical Foundation, 1977–88. CS497 .A57G7.

D'Alton, James. *King James' Irish Army Lists, 1689.* 2 vols. London: John Russell Smith, 1928. DS916 .C7.

Farrer, Henry. *Irish Marriages: Being an Index to the Marriages in Walker's Hibernian Magazine, 1771 to 1812.* Baltimore: Genealogical Publishing Co., 1972. CS482 .F3.

Ireland. Registry of Deeds. P. Beryl Eustace, ed. *Abstracts of Wills.* Dublin: Stationery Office, 1954–84. CS482 .R44.

MacGiolla, Domhnaigh, P. *Some Ulster Surnames.* Dublin: Clodhanna Teo., 1974. CS2419 .U37M3.

Norman, Joyce C. *Who's Who of Your Irish Ancestors: A Compilation of the Early Families of Erin and Their Titles.* N.p., 1977. CS484 .N67.

Pender, Seamus, ed. *A Census of Ireland, Circa 1659.* Dublin: Stationery Office, 1939. HA1142 .I659.

Phillimore, William P. W., and Gertrude Thrift. *Indexes to Irish Wills.* 5 vols. in 1. Baltimore: Genealogical Publishing Co., 1970. CS482 .P62.

Vicars, Arthur. *Index to Prerogative Wills of Ireland, 1536–1810.* Baltimore: Genealogical Publishing Co., 1967. CS482 .V5.

Scotland

The history of Scotland is largely the story of resistance to raiders from other countries, including England, though they later became friendly members of the British Commonwealth. The Roman Catholic church was abolished in 1560, and the Presbyterian church was formally established in 1851 and made the permanent state church in 1891.

When Oliver Cromwell came to power in England in 1649 he transported several Scots to the British colonies, and King James later sent many of them into Ireland to help put down the rebellions of the native Irish, especially in the northern parts.

The first Scottish population census giving names of the residents was taken in 1841, although some parts are missing. There is no index. Civil registration of vital statistics began in 1855, supplementing the parish registers kept by the churches. A few church records date to the late 1500s, and some are available only from the mid-1700s. To find those that have been transcribed and published, consult the computer catalog using the following command: **find s registers scotland; f = prem.**

Scottish military lists consist primarily of militia muster rolls before 1707, at which time Scotland and England united. The Scots had no regular army or navy before that date, and, since they have been a part of the British armed forces, one must search British records for early units in which they might have served.

Small contingents of Scots came to the American colonies in the late 1600s and early 1700s, primarily from the lowlands. They settled in seaport towns where they became merchants or went south to work in tobacco fields as indentured servants. Scots from the highland regions settled along New York's Hudson River and Lake George; some settled along the Cape Fear region of North Carolina, and others moved on to Georgia. A number of those who first went to Nova Scotia moved to Michigan and other northern midwestern states.

Directories

City directories and other specialized directories for cities in Scotland may be located by consulting the computer catalog using the following command: **find s edinburgh directories; f = prem** (substitute name of city).

The following is a list of cataloged city directories that may be obtained by submitting a call slip in the Local History and Genealogy Reading Room.

Aberdeen

Post Office Directory of Aberdeen, 1956–82. DA890 .A2P6.

Dundee

Dundee Directory, 1950–69. DA890 .D8D8.

Edinburgh (and Leith)

Edinburgh and Leith General Directory and Post Office Directory, 1800, 1827–1912, 1934–75. DA890 .E3E15.

Glasgow

Kelly's Directory of Glasgow, 1934–74. DA890 .G45K4.

Post Office Directory, 1909, 1929, 1940–79. DA890 .G49P7.

Guides and Bibliographies

The following are some published works that may be helpful as background reading for beginning a search for Scottish ancestors.

Bain, Robert. *The Clans and Tartans of Scotland.* London: Collins, 1954. DA880 .H76B3.

Church of Jesus Christ of Latter-day Saints. *Scotland: A Genealogical Research Guide.* Salt Lake City: Genealogical Library, 1987. CS463 .S46.

Grimble, Ian. *Scottish Clans and Tartans.* London: Hamlyn, 1973. DA880 .H6G74.

Hamilton-Edwards, Gerald. *In Search of Scottish Ancestry.* 2d ed. Sussex, England: Phillimore & Co., Ltd., 1980. CS463 .H35.

Innes, Thomas. *The Tartans of the Clans and Families of Scotland.* 5th ed. Edinburgh: W. & A.K. Johnson, 1950. DA880 .H7615.

James, Alwyn. *Scottish Roots: A Step-by-Step Guide for Ancestor Hunters.* Gretna, La.: Pelican Publishers, 1982. CS464 .J255.

Johnson, James B. *Place Names of Scotland.* Yorkshire, England: S.R. Publishers, 1970. DS869 .J72.

Livingstone, Alastair, et al., eds. *Muster Roll of Prince Charles Edward Stuart's Army, 1745–46.* Aberdeen: Aberdeen University Press, 1984. DS814.5 .M87.

Martine, Roderick, comp. *A Guide to the Clans and Major Families of Scotland.* Perth: Holmes Mc-Dougall, 1977. DS880 .H6M4.

McLeod, Dean L., and Norman L. Moyes, comps. *Aids in Scottish Research.* Salt Lake City: the compilers, 1983. CS464 .M35.

McClean, John P. *Settlements of Scotch-Highlanders in America.* Baltimore: Genealogical Publishing Co., 1968. E184 .S3M2.

McClelland Research. *A History of Scotland and Guide to Tracing Convicts and Immigrants Who Came From Scotland.* Silverdale, N.W.W.: n.p., 1981. CS2003 .H57.

Pryor, Estella. *Scotland, a Mini-guide to its History and Genealogical Research.* Hurst, Tex.: the author, 1983. CS463 .P78.

———. *Scottish Resources at the L.D.S. Libraries.* Euless, Tex.: Scottish Genealogical Research, 1986. CS644 .P79.

Stewart, Gilbert M. *Galloway Records.* Ann Arbor, Mich.: University Microfilms International, 1979. CS479 .S75.

Stuart, Margaret. *Scottish Family History: A Guide to Works of Reference on the History and Genealogy of Scottish Families.* Baltimore: Genealogical Publishing Co., 1978. Z5313 .S459.

Whyte, Donald. *Introducing Scottish Genealogical Research.* 2d ed. Rev. and enl. Edinburgh: Scottish Genealogy Society, 1979. CS463 .W45.

Published Record Sources

The following publications may be helpful in finding the name of a Scottish ancestor.

Dobson, David. *Directory of Scottish Settlers in North America.* 6 vols. Baltimore: Genealogical Publishing Co., 1986. E184 .S3D63.

Escott, Anne. *Census Returns and Old Parochial Registers on Microfilm: A Directory of Public Library Holdings in the West of Scotland.* 2d ed. Glasgow: Glasgow District Libraries, Publications Board, 1983. Z5313 .G75S363.

Ferguson, Joan P.S., comp. *Scottish Family Histories.* 2d ed. Edinburgh: National Library of Scotland, 1986. Z5313 .S4F39.

Index to Particular Register of Sasines for Sheriffdoms of Elgin, Forres, and Nairn, Preserved in her Majesty's General Register House. Edinburgh: Her Majesty's Stationery Office, 1974–. DS890 .E6. No. 168.

Reeks, Lindsay W. *Scottish Coalmining [sic] Ancestors.* Baltimore: Gateway Press, 1986. CS476 .C6R44.

Scottish Antiquary: Or Northern Notes & Queries. Edinburgh: W. Green & Sons, 1888–1903. DS750 .S2.

Scottish Genealogy. Journal of the Scottish Genealogy Society. Edinburgh: 1954–. CS460 .S35.

Whyte, Donald. *A Dictionary of Scottish Emigrants to the United States of America.* Baltimore: Magna Carta Books, 1972. 184 .S3W49.

Wales

Most of Wales is a rugged, rocky country suitable more for sheep and goat farming than for other agricultural pursuits, although most of the population lives in farming communities. The early immigrants to America continued those agricultural pursuits. The large influx of Welsh who came to America in the nineteenth century were miners from the southern part of the country. They were attracted to opportunities in mining both coal and iron in America. Many went on to the west coast to mine for gold, often returning to Appalachia to work in the coal mines.

Guides and Bibliographies

First Supplement to Original Parish Registers in Records Offices and Libraries. Matlock, Derbyshire: Cambridge Group for the History of Population and Social Structure; Tawney House, 1976. CD1069 .A2T27. Supp. 1.

Fourth Supplement to Original Parish Registers in Record Offices and Libraries. Supp. 4. Matlock, Derbyshire: Cambridge Group for the History of Population and Social Structure; Tawney House, 1982. CD1068 .A2T27.

Gardner, David E., Derek Harland, and Frank Smith. *A Genealogical Atlas of England and Wales.* Salt Lake City: Deseret Book Co., 1960. G1815 .G3.

Gibson, Jeremy S.W., comp. *A Simplified Guide to Bishop's Transcripts and Marriage Licenses, Their Location and Indexes to England, Wales, and Ireland.* Baltimore: Genealogical Publishing Co., 1982. Z5313 .G7E5.

Hall, Joseph. *The Genealogical Handbook for England and Wales.* Salt Lake City: the author, 1977. CS415 .H34.

Rogers, Colin D. *The Family Tree Detective: A Manual for Analysing and Solving Genealogical Problems in England and Wales, 1538 to the Present Day.* Manchester: Manchester University Press, 1983. CS414 .R63.

Published Record Sources

Bartrum, P.C., ed. *Early Welsh Genealogical Tracts.* Cardiff, Wales: U.P., 1966. CS456 .B37.

———. *Welsh Genealogies, A.D. 300–1400.* 8 vols. Cardiff, Wales: University of Wales Press for the Board of Celtic Studies, 1974. Rev. ed., 1980. CS456 .B38.

———. *Welsh Genealogies, A.D 1400–1500.* 18 vols. Aberystwyth: National Library of Wales, 1984. CS459 .A2B37.

Gibson, Jeremy S.W. *Quarter Sessions Records for Family Historians. A Select List.* 2d ed. Plymouth, England: Federation of Family History Societies, 1983. Z5313 .G69G53.

Tallis, J.W., comp. *Original Parish Registers in Record Offices and Libraries.* Matlock: Cambridge Group for the History of Population and Social Structure, 1974. CD1068 .A2T27.

Heraldry

Since the dawn of civilization, man has used symbols to portray his uniqueness. When any group joined together for religious, political, economic, or social reasons, they identified their association with some symbol as a mark of pride and esprit de corps. Military units traditionally have distinguished themselves by a uniform on which was displayed a distinctive badge or other mark of identity. In modern times these have taken the form of a unit patch on the left arm, a green beret, or a brightly colored scarf worn by members of specialized units such as tank corps, rangers, and paratroopers.

There is some disagreement over when military personnel began using decorated symbols on their shields, but most agree that it was not until after the Norman Conquest of England by William the Conqueror in 1066. The famed Bayeaux Tapestry, depicting all the units that participated in that mighty battle shows the varying types of armor worn, but there is no indication of armorial insignia. True heraldry (the systematic use of hereditary devices centered on the shield) is believed to have begun in 1127 with the coat-of-arms of Geoffery of Anjou. In time, the use of armorial insignia was regulated under general authority of the ruler of each kingdom.

The study of heraldry, called by some the shorthand of history, is complex and frustrating to many genealogists, yet fascinating because of its detail and the correlation with family history. This section provides a brief discussion of heraldry, defines some of the more commonly used terms, and cites a few publications that can assist in understanding the subject. It will be advantageous to examine one or more of the following works before making a detailed study of heraldry.

Boutell, Charles. *Boutell's Heraldry.* 8th ed. Revised by J.P. Brooke-Little. New York: Frederick Warne, 1978. CR21 .B7.

Filby, P. William. *American and British Genealogy and Heraldry.* 3d ed. Supps. 1983, 1985. Z5311 .F52. Bibliography: Z5311 .F55.

Franklyn, Julian. *Shield and Crest: An Account of the Art and Science of Heraldry.* 3d ed. London: McGibbon, 1967. Reprint. Baltimore: Genealogical Publishing Co., 1971. CR21 .F76.

Fox-Davies, A.C. *A Complete Guide to Heraldry.* rev of 1910 ed; annotated by J.P. Brooke-Little. London: Thomas Nelson & Sons, 1969. CR21 .F73.

Grant, Francis J. *The Manual of Heraldry.* Rev. ed. Edinburgh: n.p., 1929. Reprint. Detroit: Gale Research Co., 1978. CR23 .G8.

Holden, Edward S. *A Primer of Heraldry for Americans.* Reprint of 1898 ed. Detroit: Gale Research Co., 1978. CR23 .H7.

Moncreiffe of That Ilk, Sir Rupert I.K. Iain, and Don Pottinger. *Simple Heraldry.* New York: Mayflower Books, 1979. CR492 .M6.

Pine, Leslie G. *Heraldry and Genealogy.* London: Teach Yourself Books, 1974. CR21 .P56.

————. *The Story of Heraldry.* Rutland, Vt.: C.D. Tuttle, 1974. CR21 .P56.

Thompson, J. Charles. "Heraldry." In *How to Trace Your Family Tree.* Garden City, N.Y.: Doubleday, 1975.

Reynolds, Jack A. *Heraldry and You; Modern Heraldic Usage in America.* New York: Nelson, 1966. CR27 .R45.

Zieber, Eugene. *Heraldry in America.* 2d ed., 1908. Reprint. Baltimore: Genealogical Publishing Co., 1984. CR1202 .Z5.

HEREFORD

Armorial device — Hereford.

Armorial Insignia

In addition to the armor of chain mail or metal plates topped by a helmet or crest used by medieval knights, a wooden or metal shield was carried to ward off enemy attack. It was on these shields that the knights began placing their personal markings. Later, a crest made of wood or other material was sometimes placed above the helm for decoration and identification. As mentioned above, the shield markings were regulated, but the crest was often added at the whim of the owner and was not regulated. An outer coat worn over the armor as a protection against bad weather carried the same markings as those painted or etched on the shield, hence the term "coat-of-arms."

The markings (known as devices) on both shield and outer coat were usually referred to as "arms," and that general term is used in this section. The arms conformed to the shape of the shield, and within that shape personal stylized symbols and figures were devised, the details of which became fairly well standardized to the point where they could be described. Eventually, a specialized glossary based on the Anglo-French language of the Middle Ages was created to describe each shield or coat-of-arms without the necessity of an illustration. The page from *Burke's General Armory* illustrated on the following page, contains such terms as "Paly of six ar and az on a bend gu, three round buckles displ. with two heads ar. ducally gorged gu. *Crest*—Out of a naval coronet ar. an anchor erect sa. cable or.

Gunsmiths, Company of (London). Ar. two guns in saltire ppr. in chief the letter G, in base the letter Y sa. each crowned with a regal crown, on the dexter side in fesse a barrel, and on the sinister three balls all of the second.

Gunn (Irstead, co. Norfolk). Gu. three lions ramp. ppr. on an escutcheon of pretence erm. on a bend az. three escallops ar. within a bordure or. *Crest*—A lion ramp. ppr. holding a bezant.

Gunn (Sutherland). Ar. a galley of three masts, her sails furled and oars in action sa. flags gu. within a bordure az. on a chief of the third a bear's head of the first, muzzled of the second betw. two mullets of the field. *Crest*—A dexter hand wielding a sword ppr. *Motto*—Aut pax aut bellum.

Gunn (co. Caithness). Ar. a ship under sail in a sea in base all ppr. on a chief gu. three mullets of the field.

Gunner. Az. a saltire ar. guttée de sang. *Crest*—A lion's head erased or.

Gunning (Eltham, co. Kent, bart., afterwards of Horton, co. Northampton). Gu. on a fesse erminois betw. three doves ppr. as many crosses formée per pale of the first and az. *Crest*—A dove holding in the dexter claw a caduceus ppr. *Motto*—Imperio regit unus æquo. The first bart., as a Knight of the Bath, bore for *Supporters*— Dexter, a stag ppr. collared ppr.; sinister, a fox ppr. collared as the dexter. *Motto*—Imperio regit unus æquo.

Gunning (Castle Coote, co. Roscommon; derived from the GUNNINGS, of Kent; the last male heir in the direct line, General JOHN GUNNING, left an only dau. and heiress to Major JAMES PLUNKETT. General Gunning's sisters were— MARY, *Countess of Coventry*: ELIZABETH, *Baroness Hamilton*, wife successively of the *Dukes of Hamilton and Argyll*; and CATHERINE, m. to ROBERT TRAVIS, Esq.). Gu. on a fesse erm. betw. three doves ar. ducally crowned or, as many crosses pattée of the first.

Gunning (cos. Kent, Somerset, and Gloucester; the Kentish branch, of which was the Right Rev. PETER GUNNING, Bishop of Ely, who d. unm. in 1684; arms on the Bishop's Tomb in his Cathedral). Gu. on a fesse betw. three doves ar. as many crosses pattée of the field.

Gunning (Swainswick, co. Somerset; granted 1765). Gu. on a fesse ar. betw. three doves ppr. a barnacle az. betw. two crosses pattée of the field. *Crest*—An ostrich hold. in the beak a horseshoe all ppr. charged on the breast with a cross pattée, as in the arms.

Gunning (co. Kent). This family originally bore . . . three billets in fesse . . . but on 9 May, 1670, the son of Bishop GUNNING obtained from Walker a grant of the following :— Gu. on a fesse betw. three doves ar. as many crosses pattée of the field. *Crest*—A dove ar. supporting with the dexter paw a crozier.

Gunter (Racton, co. Sussex, of Welsh extraction; FRANCES CATHERINE, only dau. of Sir CHARLES GUNTER NICHOLL, K.B., m. WILLIAM LEGGE, second *Earl of Dartmouth*). Sa. three dexter gauntlets ar. *Crest*—A stag's head couped per pale gu. and sa. the attires counterchanged.

Gunter (co. Brecon). Sa. a chev. betw. three gauntlets, fingers clenched or. *Crest*—A stag's head per pale gu. and sa.

Gunter (Chichester and Emley, co. Sussex). Sa. three gauntlets ar. within a bordure or. *Crest*—A stag's head erased per pale sa. and gu. attired or.

Gunthorpe (THOMAS GUNTHORPE, of Tuxford-in-the-Clay; monument in the church there. Visit. Notts). Gu. a bend and border gobony ar. and az. the former charged with two lions' heads erased of the second betw. three leopards' faces or.

Gunthorpe. Gu. a bordure and bend gobonated ar. and az. on the bend betw. two lions' heads erased of the second three leopards' faces or. *Crest*—A lion's head erased, gorged with a plain collar.

Gunton (co. Northampton). Gu. three round buckles or.

Gunvill. Ar. on a chev. sa. three escallops ar.

Gurdon (Assington Hall, co. Suffolk). Sa. three leopards' faces jessant-de-lis or. *Crest*—A goat climbing a rock, with a sprig issuing from the top ppr. *Motto*—Virtus viget in arduis.

Gurdon (Letton, co. Norfolk). Same *Arms*, &c.

Gurdon. Or, a fleur-de-lis gu. (another, az.).

Gurlin. Ar. on a bend per bend gu. and az. betw. two cotises counterchanged three fleur-de-lis of the first. *Crest*— On a mural coronet gu. an eagle with wings endorsed or, in the beak an acorn, stalked and leaved ppr.

435

Gurlyn (co. Cornwall). Per bend ar. and gu. two bendlets betw. three fleurs-de-lis all counterchanged.

Gournay, or Gurnay (*temp.* William the Conqueror, and Henry III.). Paly of six or and az.

Gurnay. Or, three piles (another, pales) gu.

Gurnay. Sa. a chev. betw. three bulls' heads or.

Gurnay. Paly of six ar. and az. a bend gu.

Gurney (West Barsham, co. Norfolk). Ar. a cross engr. gu. *Crest*—1st: On a chapeau gu. turned up erm. a gurnet fish in pale, with the head downwards; 2nd: A wrestling collar or.

Gurney (Norwich, Keswick, Earlham, North Runcton, &c., co. Norfolk). Same *Arms*, &c., as the last.

Gurney (North Runcton, co. Norfolk). Same *Arms* and *Crest*.

Gurney, or Gurnard (Sir RICHARD GURNEY, Lord Mayor of London, was created a bart. 1641, d. s. p. 1647). Paly of six or and az. per fesse counterchanged. *Crest*—A lion's head erased or, gorged with a palisado coronet, composed of spear heads az.

Gurney, or Gurnard (London; granted 26 July, 1633; Her. Off. London, c. 24). Same *Arms* and *Crest*.

Gurney (Causton and Aylesham, co. Norfolk). Ar. a cross engr. gu. in the dexter quarter a crescent az.

Gurney (Reg. Ulster's Office). Az. on a chev. betw. two cotises ar. three leopards' faces gu. crowned or.

Gurnut. Az. three griffins' heads erased or.

Gurteen (granted to STEPHEN HUMPHREYS GURTEEN, Esq., of Bleane, co. Kent). Per chev. sa. and or, in chief two bulls' heads cabossed, and in base a lion ramp. counterchanged. *Crest*—A demi heraldic antelope sa. armed, hoofed, and crined or, supporting betw. the legs a tilting spear gold.

Gurwood. Az. a chev. ar. *Crests*—1st: A unicorn's head issuant; 2nd: Out of a mural coronet a castle ruined in the centre, and therefrom an arm in armour embowed, holding a scymetar all ppr.

Gushill. Ar. a fesse betw. six martlets sa.

Guson (London). Paly of six ar. and az. on a bend gu. three round buckles or.

Gussand. Az. five lozenges in bend or (another, ar.).

Gusset. Ar. two guttées de poix.

Gussey (Woodland, co. Devon). Ar. a fesse sa. betw. three lions ramp. gu.

Gusthart (ROBERT GUSTHART, Esq., M.D., 1750). Ar. three passion nails pileways in point embrued. *Crest*—An eagle displ. sa. pierced through with an arrow bendwise ar. *Motto*—Avitos novit honores.

Guston. Barry of four az. and ar. on a chief of the second three hurts. *Crest*—A demi wolf gu.

Guthrie (that Ilk, co. Forfar). Quarterly, 1st and 4th, or, a lion ramp. gu.; 2nd and 3rd, az. a garb. or. *Crest*—A dexter hand issuing, holding a drawn sword ppr. *Supporters*—Two chevaliers in full armour, with batons in the dexter hands, the visors of their helmets up ppr. *Motto*— Sto pro veritate.

Guthrie (Carsbank, Scotland). Quarterly, 1st and 4th, ar. a cross sa.; 2nd and 3rd, az. three garbs or, all within a bordure engr. gu. *Motto*—Pietas et frugalitas.

Guthrie (Kingedward, co. Banff, bart.). Quarterly, 1st and 4th, or, a lion ramp. reguard. gu. holding in the dexter paw a cross crosslet fitchée az.; 2nd and 3rd, az. three garbs or. *Crest*—A lion's paw issuant, grasping a twig of a palm branch ppr. *Motto*—Sto pro veritate.

Guthrie (Halkertoun, co. Kincardine). Quarterly, 1st and 4th, or, a lion ramp. reguard. gu.; 2nd and 3rd, az. three garbs or, all within a bordure indented ar. *Crest*—A falcon, wings erected, standing on a dexter hand in fess couped behind the wrist ppr. *Motto*—Ad alta.

Guthrie (Provost of Forfar, 1672). Quarterly, 1st and 4th, or, a lion ramp. reguard. gu.; 2nd and 3rd, az. three garbs or, all within a bordure indented ar. *Crest*—A cross crosslet fitchée az. *Motto*—Ex unitate incrementum.

Guthrie (Lunan, co. Forfar). Quarterly, 1st and 4th, ar. a lion ramp. gu.; 2nd and 3rd, az. three garbs or.

Guthrie (Craigie, co. Forfar). Quarterly, 1st and 4th, ar. a cross sa.; 2nd and 3rd, az. three garbs or, banded gu. all within a bordure waved gu. *Crest*—A demi lion ramp. gu. holding in his dexter paw a cross crosslet fitchée gu. *Mottoes*—Above the crest: Sto pro veritate; below the shield: Nec tumidus nec timidus.

Guthrie (*Baron Oranmore*; arms of GUTHRIE, of the Mount, co. Ayr; borne under the limitations of an entail as his only arms). Quarterly, 1st and 4th, or, a lion ramp. gu. armed and langued az. surmounted of a fess ar. charged with a mount betw. two edock leaves vert; 2nd and 3rd, az. three garbs or. *Crest*—A dexter hand erect holding a sword in

Typical page from Sir John Bernard Burke, Ulster King of Arms, *The General Armory of England, Scotland, Ireland and Wales.*

From reprint of 1884 edition (Baltimore: Genealogical Publishing Co., 1967), page 435

or"; and "Sa three leopards faces *jessand-de-lis or.*" These words and abbreviations have a distinct meaning for serious students of heraldry, enabling them to "read" armorial devices and distinguish each from all others. The motto used is often sufficient for an expert to identify the family to which a coat-of-arms belongs. The primary parts of a shield of arms are listed below.

Achievement: the shield of arms and its accessories, including the helm and crest.

Coronet: a gold circlet denoting a peer of the realm placed above the shield.

Insignia of Knighthood: usually a circle around or below the shield, denoting the order of knighthood to which the bearer belonged.

Lozenge: an alternative shape to a shield, used by women.

Mantling: the piece of material hanging down the back of the helm—used to cover the helm to protect against the sun.

Marks of cadency: modifications in the basic arms to show "differences" in the arms of an armiger (one entitled to bear arms).

Motto: a phrase, often in latin, inscribed on a scroll beneath the arms.

Ordinaries: major charges (bands of color) or rectilinear shape (horizontal, vertical, diagonal, or in the shape of a cross).

Supporters: figures, often animals, placed on both sides of the shield.

Wreath: the twisted cloth placed around the helm to conceal the joint between the helm and crest.

The Role of Heralds

To keep their skills honed when not involved in a war or crusade, knights competed in mock battles or tournaments. The complexity of regulating arms grew from the role played by heralds whose duty it was to announce the knights as they entered the tournament field. With their visors down, it was impossible for the heralds to recognize individual knights before trumpeting their entrance, so they came to rely wholly on the arms for identification. As they became experts the heralds enhanced their importance; later they were employed by the Crown to convey important messages and to confer with representatives of other kingdoms about mutual matters of interest, in a manner similar to present day ambassadors.

At the tournaments one responsibility of the herald was to become aware of duplication of arms that could confuse both him and the assembly. That problem was solved by establishment of the College of Arms. This fifteenth-century institution was charged by the Crown to maintain a catalog of each set of arms used in the realm, by whom and by what authority the arms were used. The college employed the standardized language mentioned earlier to describe the thousands of arms in use. When a person (or organization) was granted a right to use arms, he applied to the college for a suitable design. Actually, he may have created his own design and merely asked for approval, but, officially, arms were created and issued by the college. In this way, it was assured that no two people used the same arms. One attained the right to use arms by a grant from a king, prince, or lord; by taking it from a vanquished foe (very rare); by inheritance from a father; by gaining it through marriage; and by taking the initiative and having it granted by a herald as the representative of the College of Arms.

Certain heralds became officers of the College of Arms in London and were granted jurisdiction over parts of the kingdom, with powers to investigate the authenticity of all arms in use. Their immediate supervisor was a King of Arms, appointed by the Earl of Marshall, who, along with the sovereign, could grant the use of arms to qualified applicants. In England there was one herald for each of the following jurisdictions, which still exist today: Windsor, Chester, Lancaster, Somerset, York, and Richmond. They report to the college, where rolls dating to medieval times are still preserved.

At a level just below the heralds are pursuivants, who act somewhat as junior heralds, but with considerable authority in their own right. By 1622 in England there were three Kings of Arms, six heralds, and four pursuivants. To carry out their duties, the heralds and pursuivants made periodic "visitations" to regions within their jurisdiction to interview citizens who used or claimed arms. Since one method of obtaining authority to use arms was through inheritance, the herald or pursuivant had to make a careful investigation of family lineages and prepare charts; at that point they became professional genealogists. The records they created during these visitations are still useful, and many are described, with names, in a large number of publications available at the Library of Congress.

Visitations in England took place between 1530 and 1688. During that period each region received an average of four visits from the herald who recorded family pedigrees, documented them, and recorded their findings. Heralds in Wales, Ireland, and Scotland had authority similar to those in England, but no visitations were ever made in Scotland. The regulation of arms in Scotland was under Lord Lyon, whose title was created by Parliament in 1672; six heralds and six pursuivants served under his direction. Any use of arms in Scotland not registered with his office was illegal under laws of the country. In Ireland there is an Office of Arms, administered by the Ulster King of Arms, officially connected with the Most Illustrious Order of St. Patrick. Serving under him is one pursuivant. Only a few visitations were ever made in Ireland, and each Irish

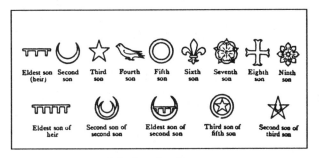

Marks of cadency.

citizen who claims a right to bear arms by heredity must "re-matriculate" at the Office of Arms.

Hereditary Rights

Although the rules for inheriting arms varies between countries, the general rule in English-speaking countries is that no two people may use identical arms at the same time. While the head of the family is alive, his sons may use his arms only by making an alteration known as a "difference." Only upon death may one's arms be passed on to an heir without alteration. Over the centuries symbols of "differencing" as used by successive sons have become fairly standardized. The eldest son adds a "label" to his father's arms and removes it upon his father's death, at which time he becomes the head of the household. Other "cadet sons" alter the father's arms by "differencing" them with "marks of cadency" (see illustration below).

Further complications in the make-up of arms arise when the family status changes by marriage or divorce. For instance, a woman may possess a right to use her own arms as inherited from her father, by her personal position in society, or possibly from a previous marriage. If she is unmarried there is one set of rules to govern how her arms are to be devised, but another set of rules applies when she marries. The most common practice at the time of marriage is the "marshalling" of the two family arms, which may be done by merging or "impaling" the respective symbols side by side. It may also be done by "quartering" in which both family arms are placed in four quarters of the arms. Even though six

to eight, or more, such divisions might be made, they are, nonetheless, referred to as "quarters." If divorced, the woman generally reverts to the use of her former arms if she was the "guilty party," but she retains the marshalled arms (as if she were a widow) if she was the "innocent party."

All the above, greatly simplified, should serve to show there is no such thing as a "family coat-of-arms" or a "family crest"; even in the event that one can trace his or her lineage to a family that was granted such an honor. To use arms one must officially apply for its use only after the correct "differencing" has taken place. There may be an exception when it can be proved that the applicant is a direct male descendant of the original armiger. The mere coincidence of one's surname being the same as a person who was granted arms is no indication of family relationship, nor does it indicate any right to arms. In the United States it is no crime to display arms and related insignia if one wishes. However, it should be understood that such a display is purely decorative.

Americans who trace their lineage to the colonial period may find an ancestor who was granted arms in England, Scotland, Wales, Ireland, or in Europe. The New England Historic Genealogical Society in Boston has a Committee on Heraldry that registers American arms based on the following: (a) those who have been used since time immemorial; (b) those granted or confirmed by a College of Arms or similar heraldic body; and (c) those brought to America by an immigrant or a first settler.

Persons or groups may devise their own arms and place a copy in the society's files, although this alone would not be considered a mandate to use it. The majority of arms registered there are by schools, colleges, and corporations.

In addition to placing a copy of a self-created arms with the society, an application may be made to the American College of Arms, with headquarters at Baltimore, Maryland, and be registered on its rolls. This does not indicate any official government sanction, however. Since 1928, the college has issued six Rolls of Arms. Americans, Canadians, and Australians who claim hereditary rights to arms granted in Europe should correspond directly with the English College of Arms or its Irish or Scottish equivalent.

Some places where arms are used in this country are as follows: Independence Hall, Philadelphia; Old Christ Church, Philadelphia; ancient burial grounds, especially in New England and Virginia; seals of the United States, including its departments and agencies; state, county, and city flags and seals; headquarters offices of religious groups; and letterheads and insignia denoting membership in colonial and other patriotic societies.

Published Sources

Baty, Thomas. *Vital Heraldry*. Edinburgh: The Armorial, 1972. CR23 .B35.

Franklin, Charles A.H. *The Bearing of Coats-armour by Ladies*. Reprint. Baltimore: Genealogical Publishing Co., 1971. CR1613 .F7.

Grosswirth, Marvin. *The Heraldry Book: A Guide to Designing Your Own Coat of Arms*. Garden City, N.Y.: Doubleday, 1981. CR55 .G76.

Lynch-Robinson, Christopher H. *Intelligible Heraldry*. Baltimore: Genealogical Publishing Co., 1967. CR21 .L9.

Murtaugh, Paul. *Your Irish Coat of Arms*. New York: Murtaugh Association, 1964. CR1672 .M8.

Papworth, John W. *Papworth's Ordinary of British Armorials*. Reprint. London: Tabard Publications, Ltd., 1961. CR1619 .P2.

Parker, James. *A Glossary of Terms Used in Heraldry*. Rutland, Vt.: Tuttle, 1970. CR1618 .G6.

Rogers, Hugh C. *The Pageant of Heraldry*. New York: Pitman Publishing, 1957. CR23 .R64.

Wagner, Anthony R. *Heralds of England: A History of the Office and College of Arms*. London: Her Majesty's Stationery Office, 1967. CR185 .G7W27.

Rolls of Arms

After having traced a family to Great Britain or Europe, one may wish to learn if anyone with the same family surname who lived in that locality was granted arms. For instance, in the list of persons named Guthrie who used arms (shown on page 163), three were associated with the town of Forfar, Scotland. Should one trace his ancestry to a Guthrie who lived in the Guthrie Castle at Forfar, there may be some family link to an armiger of that area.

Names may be found in records created by the heralds during their visitations, on rolls pre-dating the visitations, or in publications based on compilations by heraldic scholars, which in turn were based on rolls and other records. The earliest surviving list of grantees of arms is the "Roll of Arms" compiled ca. 1240–45, which includes names of barons and knights during the reign of Henry III. Another manuscript is "The Siege of Carlaverock," a poem that describes the banners used by English peers and knights who fought at Carlaverock Castle in Scotland in February 1301. A third is the "Roll of Arms" consisting of about 1,160 names of persons living between 1308 and 1314, with their county of residence. "The Fourth Roll" names peers and knights of England between 1317 and 1350. The heralds created many lists or rolls based on their visitations, and several of these are cited in the pages that follow.

The most commonly used publications contain-

Typical armorial seals in America.

ing lists of peers and others who bore arms are those by John Burke, an Irishman who founded an organization in 1826 to collect and publish names and related family information. Before he died in 1848 he also compiled *Burke's Peerage and Landed Gentry and Extinct Peerage*. In 1946 his works were revised and jointly published as *Burke's Peerage*, which includes names of those who used arms regardless of whether they had been granted or approved by the College of Arms.

After John Burke's death, his son, Sir John Bernard Burke, carried on his father's work and published several sets of volumes, the best known being *Burke's General Armory*. This is an alphabetical list of some 60,000 families or individuals.

Arthur C. Fox-Davies published a similar set of volumes as a dictionary of families who bore arms, but he included only those approved by the College of Arms; James Fairbairn compiled and published names of persons who used crests. Other lists have been published, some of which are cited below.

Published Sources

Blanche, Pierre. *Dictionnaire et Armorial des Noms de Famille de France.* Fayard, n.d. CR1798 .B55.

Battle Abbey, Roll of. Baltimore: Genealogical Publishing Co., 1978. CS432 .N7B3.

Brault, Gerard J., comp. *Eight Thirteenth-Century Rolls of Arms in French and Anglo-Norman Blazon.* University Park, Pa.: Pennsylvania State University Press, 1973. CR157 .B7.

Bridger, Charles. *An Index to Printed Pedigrees Contained in County and Local Histories, the Heralds' Visitations, and in the More Important Genealogical Collections.* Baltimore: Genealogical Publishing Co., 1969. Z4313. G69B8.

Burke, Sir Bernard. *Dictionary of Peerage and Baronetage, of the British Empire (Burke's Peerage).* 18th to 104th eds. London: Hurst & Blackett, 1856–1967. CS420 .B85.

This series of annual editions was followed by *Debrett's Peerage, Baronetage, and Knightage,* 1920–80, and also by *Whittaker's Peerage, Baronetage, Knightage, and Companionage.*

———. *A Visitation of the Seats and Arms of the Noblemen and Gentlemen of Great Britain.* 2 vols. London: Colburn, 1852. CS419 .B87.

———. *A Genealogical and Heraldic History of the Colonial Genery.* Baltimore: Genealogical Publishing Co., 1979. CS425 .B72.

Burke, Sir John Bernard. *General Armory of England, Scotland, Ireland, and Wales: Comprising a Registry of Armorial Bearings From the Earliest to the Present Time.* 1842–84. Reprint of 1884 edition. Baltimore: Genealogical Publishing Co., 1969. Supp. CR1619 .B73.

This was followed by *Burke's General Armory Two.*

Corder, Joan, ed. *Visitation of Suffolk, 1561.* London: Harleian Society, 1981–84. CS410, H3.

Record of the visitation made by William Hervy.

de Morenas, Henri J. *Grand Armorial de France, Catalogue Général des Armories des Familles Nobles de France.* 1660–1830. Société du Grand Armorial de France. CR1801 .J6.

Fairbairn, James. *Fairbairn's Book of Crests of the Families of Britain and Ireland.* 2 vols. 4th ed. 1904. Reprint. 2 vols. in 1. Baltimore: Genealogical Publishing Co., 1968. CR57 .G7F2.

Fox-Davies, Arthur C. *Armorial Families: A Directory of Gentlemen of Coats-Armour.* 2 vols. Rutland, Vt.: Charles E. Tuttle, 1970. CR1618 .F6.

Friar, Stephen, ed. *A Dictionary of Heraldry.* New York: Harmony Books, 1987. CR13 .D53.

Gayre, Robert, ed. *Armorial Who is Who.* 6th ed., Edinburgh and London: The Armorial, 1961–80. CR1619 .A7.

———. *Roll of Scottish Arms.* 2 vols. Edinburgh and London: The Armorial, 1964. CR1659 .R6.

Howard, Joseph J., and Frederick A. Crisp, eds. *Visitation of England and Wales.* 8 vols. London: the editors, 1896–1919. CS419 .H65.

———. *Visitation of Ireland.* 6 vols. 1897–1918. Reprint. Baltimore: Genealogical Publishing Co., 1973.

Humphrey-Smith, Cecil R., ed. *Alfred Morant's Additions and Corrections to Burke's General Armory.* London: Tabbard Press, 1973. CR1619 .H86.

Murphy and McCarthy. *Irish Heraldry.* New York: Murphy & McCarthy, 1930. CR1679 .I7.

Neubecker, Ottfried. *A Guide to Heraldry.* New York: McGraw-Hill, 1979. CR21 .N482.

New England Historic Genealogical Society. *A Roll of Arms Registered by the Committee on Heraldry of the New England Historic Genealogical Society.* Boston: the society, 1979–80. CR1209 .N45.

Parts 1 to 8 cover 1928 to 1958; parts 8 and 9 cover 1968 to 1971.

Phillipps, Thomas, ed. *Visitation of Gloucestershire, 1568.* Middle Hill, England: Typis Medio-Montanis, 1854. CS437 .G53V57.

————. *Visitation of Hampshire, 1575, 1622 and 1686.* Middle Hill, England: Typis Medio-Montanis, 1854. CS437 .H35V57.

————. *Visitation of Oxfordshire, 1574, 1634 and of Sussex, 1570.* Middle Hill, England: Typis Medio-Montanis, 1844. CS437 .092V54.

Poole, Keith B. *Historic Heraldic Families.* Newton Abbot, England: David & Charles, 1975. CS438 .P66.

Squibb, George D. *Visitation Pedigrees and the Genealogist.* Canterbury, England: Phillimore, 1964. CS419 .S69.

Stevenson, John H., Jr., and Marguerite Wood. *Scottish Heraldic Seals, Royal, Official, Ecclesiastical, Collegiate, Burghal, Personal.* 2 vols. Glasgow: the authors, 1940. CD5899 .S8.

Uden, Grant. *A Dictionary of Chivalry.* London: Longmans Young Books, 1968. CR13 .U3.

Royal Lineages

For those who accurately trace an ancestor to a royal family there should be little difficulty in learning more about the lineage since royal families have been well documented and published. In the Local History and Genealogy Reading Room there is a huge genealogical chart showing George Washington's lineage from English royalty. Those who are interested in royal lineages, even though they find no personal connection to royalty, may enjoy Michael MacLagen and Jiri Louda's *Heraldry of the Royal Families of Europe* (New York: Clarkson N. Potter, 1981. CR1605 .L68). This work has beautiful family charts of the royal houses and color illustrations of their arms. The countries included are listed in the table at right.

A sample of several tables dealing with medieval England include the following: (a) Normans and Early Plantagenets; (b) Plantagenets and the Hundred Years War; (c) Last Plantagenets; and (d) War of the Roses.

Austria (Hapsburg)	Milan
Austria (modern)	Modena
Baden	Monaco
Bavaria, and the Palatinate	Montenegro
Belgium	Norway
Bohemia	Netherlands
Brabant	Oldenburg
Brandenburg	Parma
Brunswick	Poland
Bulgaria	Portugal
Denmark	Prussia
England (medieval)	Rumania
France (medieval)	Russia
France (modern)	Sardinia
Germany	Savoy
Great Britain	Saxony
Greece	Scotland
Hanover	Servie
Hesse	Sicily
Holy Roman Empire	Spain (Hapsburg and Bourbon)
Hungary	
Italy	Spain (medieval)
Liechtenstein	Sweden
Lorraine	Thurinia
Luxembourg	Tuscany
Manua	Wuerttemberg
Mecklenburg	Yugoslavia

Countries listed in *Heraldry of the Royal Families of Europe.*

A similar sample related to Great Britain includes the following: (a) Extirpation of the Plantegenet Blood Under the Tudors; (b) Tudors and Stuarts; (c) House of Hanover; (d) House of Windsor; (e) Ancestors of Elizabeth I and George I; and (f) Ancestors of Queen Victoria, Elizabeth II, and Prince Philip.

Another sample, dealing with Scotland, includes the following: (a) Kings Until the Accession of Robert Bruce; (b) Houses of Bruce and Stuart; and (c) Stuart Kings Until the Accession to the English Throne.

Two other publications concerned with royal lines and lineage charts are below.

Burke, John. *The Royal Families of England, Scotland and Wales, With Their Descendants, Sovereigns and Subjects.* 2 vols. London: E. Churton, 1851. CS418 .B88.

Paget, Gerald. *The Lineage and Ancestry of H.R.H. Prince Charles, Prince of Wales.* 2 vols. Edinburgh and London: Charles Skelton, Ltd., 1977. DA591 .A33P33.

PART THREE

Key Source Material: Regional and State

Discussions and titles cited in previous chapters of this guide were selected because of their national or regional scope. Part 3 is concerned more with local sources, each of which deals with Library of Congress sources pertaining to specific geographic regions and states. Researchers may refer directly to the chapter relating to the area where an ancestor lived and thus focus at once on a more narrow objective.

The sources chosen as they pertain to each state are arranged generally under the following headings: guidebooks; census indexes and abstracts; biographies; land acquisition; early settlers; local records; military records; periodicals ; and directories.

To locate additional sources, consult the card and computer catalogs for titles of works pertaining to local history and genealogy in the states of interest, especially the "U.S. Local History Shelflist" card catalog in the Local History and Genealogy Reading Room. In so doing, references to many sources not listed in the pages that follow will be uncovered. For instance, while a few examples of church records are cited in these chapters, consult the catalogs and indexes to locate many others. The same is true for other categories of records such as those found in county courthouses. These chapters do not list titles of published genealogies and local histories since they may be found in the published indexes described in chapter 3. Except for a few indexes of newspaper items cited in the following chapters, consult chapter 5 to see if there is a list of newspapers published for the area where an ancestor lived. Military service records mentioned in these chapters generally reflect only the residents or units of a state. Regimental histories and lists of personnel from particular counties are not included here, but the catalogs will lead one to them. Chapter 6 contains listings of personnel arranged by war, and these lists pertain to the entire country or a region. Immigration and emigration records, including indexes to published ship passenger lists and naturalization records, are described in chapter 7; therefore, they are seldom mentioned in the chapters that follow. The only periodicals mentioned are those with published indexes; others are listed in chapter 5.

Although seldom cited in this guide, be advised that hundreds of compilations have been prepared by the National Society Daughters of the American Revolution, the National Society Sons of the American Revolution, and other patriotic or lineage societies. Many of these describe Bible, cemetery, and other local records.

The listings of city, county, and business directories housed at the Library of Congress will be especially helpful. Using these directories, listed separately for each state, researchers may discover important facts frequently overlooked because many directories have not been copied on film, indexed, or cataloged.

Along with the titles found in the following chapters, be aware of the following publications that can also serve as guides to further research for local records:

Filby, P. William. *American and British Genealogy and Heraldry.* 3d ed. Boston: New England Historic Genealogical Society, 1983.

Kemp, Thomas J. *Vital Records Handbook.* Baltimore: Genealogical Publishing Co., 1988. (Cataloging in publication.)

MacKenzie, George N. *Colonial Families of the United States of America.* 7 vols. Baltimore: Genealogical Publishing Co., 1966. CS61 .M22.

National Historical Publications and Records Commission. *Directory of Archival and Manuscript Repositories in the United States.* Washington, D.C.: National Archives and Records Service, 1978. Rev. ed. Onyx Publications, 1988. CD3020 .U54.

The arrangement of states used here was devised in an effort to simplify the process of finding a particular state in the chapters that follow. States immediately contiguous to one another are grouped logically together on a geographical basis rather than according to historical origins and development, ethnic backgrounds, or other systems used in various other publications.

New England: Maine, New Hampshire, Vermont, Massachusetts, Rhode Island, Connecticut.

Mid-Atlantic: New York, New Jersey, Pennsylvania, Delaware, Maryland, District of Columbia.

Southeast: Virginia, West Virginia, North Carolina, South Carolina, Georgia, Florida.

South-central: Kentucky, Tennessee, Arkansas, Alabama, Mississippi, Louisiana.

Midwest: Ohio, Indiana, Illinois, Missouri, Michigan, Wisconsin, Minnesota, Iowa.

Northwest: North Dakota, South Dakota, Nebraska, Montana, Wyoming, Idaho, Washington, Oregon, Alaska.

Southwest: Kansas, Oklahoma, Texas, Colorado, New Mexico, Utah, Arizona, Nevada, California, Hawaii.

CHAPTER 9

New England States

Maine • New Hampshire
Vermont • Massachusetts
Rhode Island • Connecticut

The century following the voyages of Christopher Columbus to the West Indies was noteworthy for its many sea-going explorations along America's Atlantic coast. These were underwritten or authorized by several European countries in an attempt to discover natural resources and to investigate the areas with regard to the feasibility of colonization. England, with its mercantile interests and businessmen willing to risk their capital, led the way to the New World.

Historical Highlights

1620   Separatists from the Anglican Church established Plymouth Colony.

English "Puritans" established Massachusetts Bay Colony.

About the turn of the seventeenth century, a few half-hearted attempts at colonization were made in America, notably at Roanoke (North Carolina) and in Maine. The first successful settlement, however, was at Jamestown, Virginia, in 1607, a venture sponsored by the London Company of England. The next successful settlement was at Plymouth, Massachusetts, under the sponsorship of the Plymouth Company, also of England.

Coincident with the English colonization were landings and settlements by the Netherlands under Henry Hudson, who opened up the northern bay that still bears

his name. Settlers from Sweden established New Sweden at present day New York, New Jersey, and along the Delaware River. Far to the south, Spain controlled the Florida region. The French, although not noted for their settlements (except for forts), sent fur traders throughout the more westerly and northerly portions of New France, beyond the English settlements. They traded with the Indians and explored several inland rivers. When the English, in deference to the Indians, drew an imaginary "proclamation line" at their western borders to prohibit white men from settling beyond it, the French wanderers already had been moving with impunity in the region for a hundred years or more.

The genesis of the 1620 landing at Plymouth Rock occurred in 1608 when a group of religious separatists left the Church of England and moved to Amsterdam. Disillusioned by the Dutch way of life, they arranged for a charter to America, departing from Plymouth, England, in 1620. These 120 pilgrims arrived in Massachusetts, far north of where they intended, on 16 December 1620. The day before they landed, they drew up the Mayflower Compact, designed to establish a government for their new home—drawn closely along strict religious concepts and practices. In June 1621 a charter arrived from England establishing them as the Plymouth Colony. After a year of suffering the vicissitudes of a cold and harsh climate, more than half the original settlers died of disease. The following winter a friendly Pemiquid Indian from Maine named Samoset visited the colonists, greeting them in English, having learned something of the language from early traders. He arranged for his locally based friends, Massasoit and Squanto (who acted as an interpreter, having been taken to England and returned by an explorer), to advise and assist the newcomers in survival methods. In return, they agreed to a treaty that protected the Indians from the white men's muskets.

1630   In 1629 England granted a charter to the Massachusetts Bay Colony, and their members bought up the lands granted earlier to the Plymouth Colony pilgrims. This new group was comprised largely of persons who also wished to escape the Anglican Church. These Puritans set sail from England in March 1630, with four ships, followed by seven others the following week. Many more came later. They arrived in Salem in June and July 1630, then moved on to Charlestown in August. During the 1630s and 1640s, boom town settlements rapidly sprang up all along the Massachusetts coastal areas.

1637   Pequot Indian War.

At a site where Englishman John Winthrop had erected a fort at Saybrook (Connecticut), the Pequot Indians, in the spring of 1637, rampaged in retaliation to perceived insults by the white settlers. For the Indians, the result was disastrous; 500 Indian men, women, and children were killed. After this hostility removed the local Indian "menace," the way was open for more expansion.

1643   Confederation of the colonies.

The four colonies that had been established by 1643 banded together into a confederation for mutual assistance and defense against the Indians—and possibly against a threat from the French. This organization, comprised of the Massachusetts Bay Colony, the Plymouth Colony, Connecticut, and the New Haven Colony, lasted forty-one years, during which time settlers continued to arrive from Great Britain. Many new towns and industries were established.

1675   King Philip's Indian War.

Another disastrous Indian war took place in 1675 and 1676 when the Indian chief, King Philip, and his braves began to resist the English westward movement. They burned the new towns and killed the militia. After the settlers lost 600 men, and 600 houses and fifty towns burned, Philip was killed and his head placed on a pole where it rested for many years. His followers were captured and executed or sold as slaves in the West Indies. This ended the Indian threat—at least until the Indians joined with the French later in the century to fight the English settlers.

1684   Dominion of New England established, comprised of Massachusetts, Connecticut, Plymouth, Rhode Island, and New Hampshire.

Edmund Gorges, by charter from England, was given authority over the united colonies. New York and New Jersey also joined this confederation for a brief time. When the Stuart monarchy was overthrown in 1689, the dominion was abolished.

1688–1763 Indian Wars:

(1688–97—King William's War)
(1703–13—Queen Anne's War)
(1744–48—King George's War)
(1755–63—Seven Years War)

The first of the above listed wars was primarily with hostile Indians and fought in the northern parts of New England. King William's War included Indian massacres in Maine, New Hampshire, and Massachusetts. Queen Anne's war was fought in Maine, resulting in much destruction by the Indians. With informal alliances between the Indians and the French, these hostilities took on a more France-versus-England character. King George's War resulted in the taking by the British of the French stronghold at Louisburg, Nova Scotia. The Seven Years War (French and Indian Wars) resulted in domination by the English and control over the Canadian regions. After these wars ceased, settlers began to move freely into the northern regions of Maine and Nova Scotia.

1775–83   American Revolution.

Objection by American colonists over taxation to defray the costs of military protection against the Indians and to vanquish the French, coupled with English restrictions on free trade by New England merchants and ship owners, precipitated the American Revolution. Principal conspirators were Massachusetts leaders, especially Samuel Adams.

Published Record Sources

Guidebooks

Some helpful publications available at the Library of Congress pertaining to genealogical and historical sources for New England are listed below.

Bolton, Ethel S. *Immigrants to New England, 1700–1775.* Baltimore: Genealogical Publishing Co., 1966. F7 .B74.

Crandall, Ralph J., ed. *Genealogical Research in New England.* Baltimore: Genealogical Publishing Co., 1984. F3 .G46.

Cutter, William R., ed. *New England Families, Genealogical and Memorial: A Record of the Achievements of Her People in the Making of a Commonwealth and the Founding of a Nation.* New York: Lewis Historical Publishing, 1913. F3 .C98.

Eliot, John. *A Biographical Dictionary, Containing a Brief Account of the First Settlers . . . in New England.* Boston: Cushing and Appleton, 1809. FE .E42.

Emmerton, James A. *Gleanings From English Records About New England Families.* Essex Institute., Vol. 16, no. 1. Salem, Mass.: Salem Press, 1880. F3 .E54.

Farmer, John. *A Genealogical Register of the First Settlers of New England, Containing an Alphabetical List of the Governours . . .* Reprint. Baltimore: Genealogical Publishing Co., 1969. F3 .F23.

Genealogies of Mayflower Families. Selected From the New England Historical and Genealogical Register. Baltimore: Genealogical Publishing Co., 1985. F3 .G47.

Kull, Andrew. *New England Cemeteries: A Collector's Guide.* Brattleboro, Vt.: Greene Press, 1975. F5 .K84.

LeSeur, William W., comp. *A Selected List of Names of Heads of Prominent Families in the Various Cities and Towns of the New England States.* Boston: the compiler, 1884. F3 .L62.

O'Brien, Robert, and Richard D. Brown, eds. *Encyclopedia of New England.* New York: Facts on File, 1985. F2 .E43.

Savage, James. *Genealogical Dictionary of the First Settlers of New England.* 4 vols. 1860. Reprint. Baltimore: Genealogical Publishing Co., 1975. F7 .S26.

Spear, Burton W. *Search For the Passengers of the Mary and John, 1630.* Rev. ed. Toledo, Ohio: the author, 1985. F3 .S64.

Torrey, Clarence A. *New England Marriages Prior to 1700.* Baltimore: Genealogical Publishing Co., 1985. F3 .T67.

Towle, Laird C., ed. *New England Annals.* Bowie, Md.: Heritage Books, 1980. F1 .N35.

Walker, Marshall W. *Beginnings and Begats: Some Seventeenth Century Emigrants From Britain.* Lynchburg, Va.: the author, 1977. F3 .W25.

Young, David C., and Robert L. Taylor. *Death Notices from Freewill Baptist Publications, 1811–1851.* Bowie, Md.: Heritage Books, 1985. F3 .Y67.

Periodicals

Greenlaw, Lucy H., ed. *The Genealogical Advertiser. A Quarterly Magazine of Family History.* 4 vols. in 1. Reprint. Baltimore: Genealogical Publishing Co., 1974. F1 .G322.

New England Historical and Genealogical Register—Index of Persons, Vols. 1–50. 3 vols. Reprint. Baltimore: Genealogical Publishing Co., 1972. F1 .N56.

New England Historical and Genealogical Register—Index of Subjects and Places, Vols. 1–50. Reprint. Baltimore: Genealogical Publishing Co., 1972. F1 .N56.

Palmer, Waldo, comp. *New England Quarterly—General Index to Vols. 1–10.* Boston: N.p., 1941. F1 .N62.

Covers 1828 to 1937.

Parsons, Margaret W., ed. *New England Historical and Genealogical Register—Index to Vols. 51–112.*

Boston: New England Historic Genealogical Society, n.d. F1 .N56.

Covers 1897 to 1958.

Topical Index to the National Genealogical Society Quarterly, Vols. 1–50. Special Bulletin no. 24. Washington, D.C.: National Genealogical Society, 1964. CS42 .N43.

Covers 1912 to 1962.

Directories

New England area
  pre 1861 (microfiche)
  1915–28, 1933, 1960

Maine

Historical Highlights

1623   First permanent settlement—Saco River area.

1639   An English grant provided the name "Province of Maine."

Since 1630 the area and province of Maine was claimed as part of Massachusetts. Gradually, all divisions of the province agreed to accept Massachusetts's sovereignty. After the Indian wars and the American Revolution, Massachusetts awarded lands in Maine and western Massachusetts to the veterans. Other lands in Maine were awarded by lottery.

1820   Maine declared a separate state.

1842   Border between Maine and Canada settled by treaty with England.

Published Record Sources

Census Indexes and Abstracts

Federal

1790	F18 .U54 (Heads of Families)
1790	F18 .J293
1800	F18 .J29
1810	F18 .J295
1820	F18 .J3
1830	F18 .J32
1840	F18 .J33
1850	F18 .J34

All the above publications except the 1790 census entitled "Heads of Families," are by Ronald V. Jackson, Accelerated Indexing Systems.

State

Gorn, Michael H., ed. *An Index and Guide in the Microfilm Edition of the Massachusetts and Maine Direct Tax Census of 1798.* Boston: New England Historic Genealogical Society, 1979. F63 .M343153.

Jackson, Ronald V. *Early Maine.* Bountiful, Utah: Accelerated Indexing Systems, 1980. F18 .J28.

Biographies

Hatch, Louis C., ed. *Maine: A History.* Vols. 3–5. New York: American Historical Society, 1919. F19 .H36.

Hebert, Richard A. *Modern Maine: Its Historical Background, People, and Resources.* 4 vols. New York: Lewis Historical Publishing Co., 1951. F19 .H4.

Herndon, Richard, comp. *Men of Progress: Biographical Sketches and Portraits of Leaders in Business and Professional Life in and of the State of Maine.* Boston: New England Magazine, 1897. F18 .M54.

Little, George T., comp. *Genealogical and Family History of the State of Maine.* New York: Lewis Historical Publishing Co., 1909. F18 .L77.

Noyes, Sybil, comp. *Genealogical Dictionary of Maine and New Hampshire.* Baltimore: Genealogical Publishing Co., 1972. F18 .N68.

Early Settlers

Banks, Charles E. *History of York, Maine.* Boston: Calkins Press, 1931. F29 .Y6B28.

Mitchell, Harry, et al. *The Saco Register with Old Orchard, 1906.* Brunswick, Maine: H.E. Mitchell Co., 1906. F29 .S1M6.

Pope, Charles H. *The Pioneers of Maine and New Hampshire, 1623 1660 . . .* Baltimore: Genealogical Publishing Co., 1975. F18 .P82.

Ridlon, Gideon T. *Saco Valley Settlements and Families.* 2 vols. Somersworth, N.H.: New England History Press, 1984. Vol. 1; F27 .53R5. Vol. 2; F27 .S15R5114.

Local Records

Attwood, Stanley B. *The Length and Breadth of Maine.* 1946. Reprint. Orono: University of Maine, 1973. F17 .A8.

This is an essential tool for locating Maine towns.

Maine State Archives. Microfilm List: Maine Town Records and Maine Census Records. Augusta: Maine State Archives, 1965. Z1291 .M33.

Patterson, William D., ed. *The Probate Records of Lincoln County, Maine, 1760 to 1800.* Portland: Maine Genealogical Society, 1895. F27 .L7P2.

Military Records

Colonial Wars and American Revolution

In addition to the references below, see also military records under Massachusetts.

Burrage, Henry S. *Maine at Louisburg in 1745.* Augusta: Burleigh & Flint, 1910. E198 .B91.

Fisher, Carleton E., and Sue G. Fisher. *Soldiers, Sailors and Patriots of the Revolutionary War—Maine.* Louisville, Ky.: National Society Sons of the American Revolution, 1982. E262 .M4F54.

Flagg, Charles A. *An Alphabetical Index of Pensioners Living in Maine.* Reprint. Baltimore: Genealogical Publishing Co., 1967. E225 .F57.

House, Charles J., comp. *Names of Soldiers of the American Revolution Who Applied for State Bounty Under Resolves of March 17, 1835, March 24, 1836, and March 20, 1838, As Appears of Record in Land Office.* Reprint. Baltimore: Genealogical Publishing Co., 1967. E263 .M2H8.

Civil War

Dilts, Bryan Lee, comp. *1890 Maine Census. Index of Civil War Veterans or Their Widows.* Salt Lake City: Index Publishing, 1984. E494 .D56.

Maine. Adjutant General. *Annual Reports, 1861 and supp: 1863 and supp.* Augusta: Stevens & Sawyard, State Printers, 1862–67. E511 .M22.

Tobie, Edward P. *History of the First Maine Cavalry, 1861–1865.* Boston: Press of Emery & Hughes, 1887. E511 .6 .1stT.

Periodicals

Down East: A Magazine of Maine. Indexes to Vols. 21–30 (1974–1984). Vol. 31. Orono: University of Maine, 1984. F16 .D64D62.

Maine Historical Society Collections: Index to Vols. 1–9 (1831–1887). Portland, Maine: Brown Thurston Co., 1891. F16 .M33.

Directories

City

Auburn
(Lewiston, Androscoggin Co.) 1926

Augusta
(Farmingdale, Gardiner, Hallowell, Manchester, Randolph, Richwood, W. Gardiner, Winthrop) 1867–1902, 1925–48, 1952–73

Bangor
pre 1861 (microfiche)
(Brewer, Hampden, Old Town, Orono, Veazie) 1864–1903, 1935–45, 1949

Bar Harbor
(Cranberry Isles, Ellsworth, Mt. Desert, Southwest Harbor, Tremont, Trenton) 1928, 1931–35

Bath
(Arrowsic, Brunswick, Georgetown, Phippsburg, Richmond, W. Bath, Woolwich) 1867, 1871–87, 1902, 1905–07, 1912–14, 1919–79

Belfast
  (Camden) 1890, 1894, 1899

Biddeford
  pre 1861 (microfiche)
  (Saco, Old Orchard Beach) 1866, 1870–1923, 1929–72

Boothbay (region) 1931–33

Bridgeton
  (Casco, Harrison, Naples, Raymond) 1927–30

Brunswick
  (Bowdoin, Bowdoinham, Harpswell, Topsham) 1910,
    1917–33, 1942–79

Bucksport
  1973

Calais
  (Eastport, Lubec, Milltown, St. Stephens) 1896, 1901,
    1935

Camden
  (Rockport) 1894, 1899, 1903

Caribou
  (Presque Isle, Fort Fairfield) 1895

Casco Bay 1905–28

Dover
  (Foxcroft) 1940

Eastport

Eliot
  (York) 1921, 1925, 1928

Ellsworth 1886, 1973

Falmouth
  (Chebeauge, Cumberland, Freeport, Gray, N. Yar-
    mouth, Yarmouth) 1902, 1906, 1909, 1912

Gardiner
  (Farmingdale, Randolph, W. Gardiner) 1964–73

Houlton 1895, 1900

Lewiston
  (Auburn) 1860, 1872–96, 1930–83

Norway
  (S. Paris) 1888

Old Town
  (Bradley, Indian Island, Milford, Veazie) 1896, 1953,
    1956

Orono 1973

Paris
  (Norway, S. Paris) 1906, 1932

Portland
  pre 1861 (microfiche)
  1861–1935 (microfilm)
  (suburbs) 1936–79

Rockland
  (Belfast, Camden, Rockport, Thomaston) 1875, 1877,
    1882–92, 1931, 1934–42, 1947–73

Rumford
  (Bethel, Dixiefield, Mexico) 1904–12, 1932, 1944,
    1965

Saco
  pre 1861 (microfiche)

Sanford
  (Springvale) 1893, 1901, 1913–27, 1932–73

Skowhegan 1888

Waterville
  (Fairfield, Oakland, Skowhegan, Winslow) 1885,
    1887, 1892, 1925–73

Webster
  (Litchfield, Monmouth, W. Gardiner) 1909

Westbrook
  (Gorham, Windham) 1894, 1900, 1902–42, 1950–73

County, Business, and Miscellaneous

Androscoggin 1894–1903

Aroostook 1905, 1961–68

Kenebec 1899, 1904–23

Knox 1927, 1929

Maine (region)
  pre 1861 (microfiche)

Maine (state) 1862, 1871–89, 1893–1901

Oxford 1896, 1914–27, 1949

Portland 1898, 1939

Rockland (city) 1868

Sagadahoe 1892

Somerset 1929

New Hampshire

Historical Highlights

1623   First settlements.

1630   "Hampshire Grants" created by division of Maine. Claimed by Massachusetts.

1638   Puritans from Massachusetts settle Exeter and Hampton.

1679   English charter established area as a royal colony. Separated from Massachusetts.

1776   One of the thirteen original states at the time of the American Revolution.

Published Record Sources

Guidebooks

Fogg, Alonzo J., comp. *The Statistics and Gazetteer of New Hampshire.* Concord: D.L. Guernsey, 1874. F32 .F65.

Towle, Laird C., and Ann M. Brown. *New Hampshire Genealogical Research Guide.* Bowie, Md.: Heritage Books, 1983. F33 .T68.

Census Indexes and Abstracts

Federal

1790	F33 .U54 (Heads of Families)
1800	F33 .J47
1810	F33 .J3
1820	F33 .J314
1830	F33 .J318
1840	F33 .J32
1850	F33 .J323

All the above publications, except the 1790 census entitled "Heads of Families," are by Ronald V. Jackson, Accelerated Indexing Systems.

State

Holbrook, Jay M. *New Hampshire Residents, 1633–1699.* Oxford, Mass.: Holbrook Research Institute, 1979. F33 .H638.

———. *New Hampshire 1732 Census.* Oxford, Mass.: Holbrook Research Institute, 1981. F33 .H63.

———. *New Hampshire 1776 Census.* Oxford, Mass.: Holbrook Research Institute, 1976. F33 .H64.

Jackson, Ronald V., and Shirley D. Zachrison. *Early New Hampshire.* Bountiful, Utah: Accelerated Indexing Systems, 1980. F33 .J296.

Wilson, Emily S. *Inhabitants of New Hampshire, 1776.* Lambertville, N.J.: Hunterdon House, 1983. F33 .W72.

Biographies

Carter, Nathan F. *The Native Ministry of New Hampshire.* Concord: Rumford Printing, 1906. BR555 .N4C3.

Herndon, Richard, comp. *Men of Progress: Biographical Sketches and Portraits of Leaders in Business and Professional Life in and of the State of New Hampshire.* Boston: New England Magazine, 1898. F33 .M53.

Metcalfe, Henry H., ed. *One Thousand New Hampshire Notables: Brief Biographical Sketches of New Hampshire Men and Women, Native Residents, Prominent in Public, Professional, Business, Educations, Fraternal or Benevolent Work.* Concord: Rumford Printing, 1919. F33 .M58.

———. *New Hampshire Women: A Collection of Portraits and Biographical Sketches of Daughters and Residents of the Granite State.* Concord: New Hampshire Publishing, 1895. F33 .M57.

Moses, George H., ed. *New Hampshire Men: A Collection of Biographical Sketches, with Portraits, of Sons and Residents of the State Who Have Become Known.* Concord: New Hampshire Publishing Co., 1895. F33 .M9.

New Hampshire Notables: Presenting Biographical Sketches of Men and Women Who Have Helped Shape the Character of New Hampshire and Their Communities. Concord: Concord Press, 1932. F33 .N57.

Noyes, Sybil, comp. *Genealogical Dictionary of Maine and New Hampshire.* Baltimore: Genealogical Publishing Co., 1972. F18 .N68.

Sketches of Successful New Hampshire Men. Manchester, N.H.: J.B. Clark, 1882. F33 .S62.

Early Settlers

Evans, Helen F. *Index of References to American Women in Colonial Newspapers Through 1800.* 2 vols. Bedford, N.H.: the author, 1979. Z5313 .U5E9.

Huse, Hiram. New Hampshire (colony) Governor and Council. *The New Hampshire Grants . . . With an Appendix of Petitions by Proprietors and Settlers and Lists of Subscribers.* Concord: E.N. Pearson, Public Printer, 1895. F31 .N42.

Towle, Glenn C. *New Hampshire Genealogical Digest, 1623–1900.* Bowie, Md.: Heritage Books, 1987. F33 .T67.

Local Records

Bouton, Nathaniel, comp. *New Hampshire Provincial and State Papers.* 7 vols. Concord: State of New Hampshire, 1867. F37 .B78.

———. *Provincial and State Papers . . .* Vol. 10. Concord: E.A. Jenks, State Printer, 1877. F34 .B65.

Dodge, Nancy L. *Northern New Hampshire Graveyards and Cemeteries: Transcriptions and Indexes of Burial Sites in the Towns of Clarksville, Colebrook, Columbia, Dixville, Pittsburg, Stewartstown, and Stratford.* Salem, Mass.: Higginson Books, 1985. F33 .D63.

Goss, Winifred L. National Society Colonial Dames of America. *Colonial Gravestone Inscriptions in the State of New Hampshire.* Reprint. Baltimore: Genealogical Publishing Co., 1974. F33 .G6.

Hammond, Otis G. *Probate Records of the Province of New Hampshire.* 9 vols. Concord: State of New Hampshire, 1938. F31 .N42.

Military Records

General

Potter, Chandler E. *The Military History of the State of New Hampshire, 1623–1861: With Added Indexes . . .* New Hampshire Historical Society.

Reprint. Baltimore: Genealogical Publishing Co., 1972. F34 .P862.

Colonial and American Revolution

Burrage, Henry S. *New Hampshire Men at Louisburg, Cape Breton, 1745.* Concord: Pearson, State Printer, 1896. E198 .N51.

Batchellor, Albert S., ed. *Miscellaneous Revolutionary Documents of New Hampshire. Provincial and State Papers of New Hampshire, Vol. 30.* Manchester: State of New Hampshire, 1910. E263 .N4B22.

Gilmore, George C. "New Hampshire Men at Bunker Hill." In *New Hampshire Secretary of State Manual for the General Court, No. 6.* Manchester: n.p., 1899. JK29 .G1.

Hammond, Isaac W., ed. *Rolls of the Soldiers in the Revolutionary War. Provincial and State Papers of New Hampshire, Vols. 14–17.* Concord and Manchester: 1885–89. Reprint. New York: AMS Press, 1973. E263 .N4.

Hammond, Otis G. *Tories of New Hampshire in the War of the Revolution.* Boston: Gregg Press, 1972. E277 .H22.

Kidder, Frederic. *History of the First New Hampshire Regiment in the War of the Revolution.* Albany, N.Y.: n.p., 1868. Reprint. Hampton: P.E. Randall, 1975. E263 .N4K4.

Civil War

New Hampshire. Adjutant General. *Annual Reports, 1860–.* 2 vols. Concord: State of New Hampshire, 1873. E520.2 .N54.

Periodicals

Index to Granite Monthly. Vols. 1–34 (1877–1902). New Haven: New Haven Public Library, n.d. F31 .G75.

Directories

City

Atkinson
(Kingston, Newton, Pelham, Plaistow, Salem) 1927–34

Barrington
(Epping, Lee, Madbury, Neavington, Northwood, Rollinsford, Salmon Falls) 1927, 1940

Berlin 1903
(Gorham) 1922–72

Canaan
(Enfield) 1914

Claremont
(Newport; Sunapee; Windsor, Vt.) 1901–1907, 1934–72

Concord
pre 1861 (microfiche)
(Hopkintown, Pembroke, Merrimack Co.) 1898–1972

Cornish
(Croyden; Grantham; Meridian; Plainfield; Weathersfield, Vt.) 1915

Dover
pre 1861 (microfiche)
(Great Falls, Rochester, Somersworth, Berwick Co.) 1867–1973

Exeter
(New Market, N.H. coast) 1872, 1907, 1911–29, 1941, 1946–66

Franklin
(Bellingham, Belmont, Boscaven, Canterbury, Norfolk, Northfield, Tilton, Wrentham) 1895, 1899, 1902, 1905, 1909–10, 1913–14, 1919, 1932, 1937–42, 1947–55, 1964–70

Great Falls
pre 1861 (microfiche)

Hanover
(Lyme) 1888, 1916

Hillsborough
(Antrim, Weare) 1922

Keene
pre 1861 (microfiche)
(Chesterfield, Hinsdale, Marlboro, Swanzey, Troy, Winchester) 1874, 1899, 1908, 1913–72

Laconia
(Gilford, Lakeport, Weirs) 1895–1973

Lakes Region 1937, 1939

Lebanon
(Enfield; Hanover; White River Junction; Woodstock; Hartford, Vt.; Windsor, Vt.) 1882, 1915, 1918–41, 1949–54, 1961–72

Manchester
pre 1861 (microfiche)
1861–1935 (microfilm)
(Suborn, Bedford, Candia, Deerfield, Goffstown, Londonderry) 1936–83

Nashua
(suburbs, Amherst, Hollis, Hudson, Merrimack, Milford, Nashville) 1864–1971

New Ipswitch
pre 1861 (microfiche)

Newport
(Claremont, Sunapee) 1896, 1899, 1903, 1907, 1914–31

Newton
(Kingston, Plaistow, Westville) 1916

Peterborough
pre 1861 (microfiche)
(Kittery, Maine) 1867–88, 1891–1967, 1972

Rochester
(Somersworth; Berwick, Maine) 1893–99, 1962–71

Salem
(Atkinson, Canobie Lake Dist., Pelham) 1915

Tilton 1920, 1925

White Mountain (suburbs) 1914, 1917, 1920, 1923, 1926, 1929, 1933, 1943–59

County, Business, and Miscellaneous

Franklin
(Hampshire, Worcester) 1903, 1912

Hillsboro 1891

Manchester
(Concord) 1896

New Hampshire
(region) pre 1861 (microfiche)
1868–69, 1892–1921, 1923, 1946
(state) 1881, 1883

Rockingham (city) 1933, 1935

Southern New Hampshire (state) 1917, 1924, 1929

Suncook Valley 1926

Vermont

Historical Highlights

1724   First settlement—a fort established by Massachusetts.

1761   Claimed by both "Hampshire Grants" and Massachusetts. Also claimed by New York under a grant to the Duke of York.

1764   England decreed that Vermont belonged to New York.

1771   Under leadership of Ethan Allen, the "Green Mountain Boys" refused to pay for or give up their lands.

1777   Republic of Vermont established. Fought alongside the thirteen colonies during the American Revolution.

1791   Settled with New York and admitted to the Union.

Published Record Sources

Guidebooks

Eichholz, Alice. *Collecting Vermont Ancestors.* Montpelier: New Trails, 1986. F48 .E33.

Hemenway, Abby M. *Abby Hemenway's Vermont; Unique Portraits of a State. The Vermont Historical Gazetteer.* Brattleboro: Stephen Greene Press, 1972. F49 .H49.

Swift, Esther M. *Vermont Place Names.* Brattleboro: Stephen Greene Press, 1977. P47 .H8.

Census Indexes and Abstracts

Federal

1790   F48 .U54 (Heads of Families)

1800   F48 .J43

1810   F48 .J3

1820   F48 .J32

1830   F48 .J325

1840   F48 .J33

1850   F48 .J332

All the above publications, except the 1790 census entitled "Heads of Families," are by Ronald V. Jackson, Accelerated Indexing Systems.

State

Holbrook, Jay M. *Vermont 1771 Census.* Oxford, Mass.: Holbrook Research Institute, 1982. F48 .H7.

Jackson, Ronald V. *Early Vermont.* Bountiful, Utah: Accelerated Indexing Systems, 1980. F48 .J29.

Mortality Schedules

1850   F48 .J3325 (Jackson, Ronald V.)
1860   F48 .J333 (Jackson, Ronald V.)

Biographies

Crockett, Walter H., ed. *Vermonters: A Book of Biographies.* Brattleboro: Stephen Daye Press, 1932. F48 .C86.

Herndon, Richard, ed. *Men of Progress . . . Vermont.* Boston: New England Magazine, 1898. F48 .M53.

Jeffrey, William H. *Successful Vermonters: A Modern Gazetteer of Caledonia, Essex, and Orleans Counties . . . and a Series of Biographical Sketches.* East Burke, Vt.: The Historical Publishing Co., 1904. F48 .J46.

———. *Successful Vermonters: A Modern Gazetteer of Lamoille, Franklin and Grand Isle Counties . . . and a Series of Biographical Sketches.* East Burke, Vt.: Historical Publishing Co., 1907. F48 .J463.

Ullery, Jacob G., comp. *Men of Vermont . . . .* Brattleboro: Transcript Publishing Co., 1894. F48 U41.

Land Acquisition

Batchellor, Albert S., ed. New Hampshire (Colony) Governor and Council. *New Hampshire Grants . . . Within the Present Boundaries of the State of Vermont, From 1748 to 1764 . . . Petitions and Lists of Subscribers . . .* Concord: E.N. Pearson, Public Printer, 1895. F37 .N45.

Bogart, Walter T. *The Vermont Lease Lands.* Montpelier: Vermont Historical Society, 1950. KFV455 .B75.

Holbrook, Jay M. *Vermont's First Settlers.* Oxford, Mass.: Holbrook Research Institute, 1976. F48 .H73.

Lists land grants for 1763 to 1803.

Vermont. Secretary of State. *State Papers of Vermont.* Vol. 2. *Charters Granted by the State of Vermont.* Bellows Falls, Vt.: P.H. Bobie Press, 1922. F52 .V47.

Vermont. Secretary of State. Mary G. Nye, ed. *State Papers of Vermont.* Vol. 5. *Petitions for Land, 1778–1811.* Brattleboro: Vermont Printing Co., 1939. F52 .V48.

Vermont. Secretary of State. *Index to the Papers of the Surveyor-General.* Reprint. Montpelier: Editor of State Papers, 1973. F46 .V35.

Early Settlers

Vermont Marriages. Reprint. Baltimore: Genealogical Publishing Co., 1967. F48 .V56.

Volume 1 covers Montpelier and Burlington.

Local Records

Nichols, Joann H. *Index to Known Cemetery Listings in Vermont.* 2d ed. Brattleboro: the author, 1982. Z1343 .N53.

Military Records

American Revolution

Crockett, Walter H. "Soldiers of the Revolutionary War Buried in Vermont, and Anecdotes and Incidents Relating to Some of Them." *Proceedings of the Vermont Historical Society* (1903–04): 93–106, 114–65; (1905–06): 189–203. E255 .C93. (F46 .V55).

Goodrich, John E., comp. The Vermont Legislature. *Rolls of Soldiers in the Revolutionary War, 1775–1783.* Rutland: Tuttle Co., 1904. E263 .V5V5.

War of 1812

Clark, Byron N., ed. *A List of Pensioners of the War of 1812: With an Appendix of Names of Volunteers,*

Officers and Soldiers. Reprint. Baltimore: Genealogical Publishing Co., 1969. E359 .C59.

Civil War

Vermont. Adjutant and Inspector General. *Annual Reports, 1861–1866.* Montpelier: State of Vermont. E533.2 .V52.

Periodicals

Vermont Historical Society—Proceedings (name changed to *Vermont History*). Montpelier: the society, n.d. F46 .V55.

Name and Subject Index to Vols. 1–10 (1930–1942); Vols. 11–20 (1943–1952); Vols. 21–45 (1953–1977).

Directories

City

Barre
(Berlin, E. Montpelier, Middlesex, Montpelier, Williamstown) 1890–1918, 1922–74

Bellows Falls
(Athens; Chester; Springfield; Westminster; Charlestown, N.H.; N. Walpole, N.H.) 1901, 1907–67

Bennington
(Arlington, Hoosick Falls, N. Bennington, Pownal, Shaftsbury, S. Shaftsbury) 1891–94, 1908–73

Brattleboro (suburbs) 1901–73

Burlington
1861–81 (microfilm)
(Essex Junction, S. Burlington, Winooski) 1889–1973

Fairhaven
(Castleton, Hydeville, Poultney) 1902

Hartford
(W. Lebanon, N.H.; White River Junction) 1915

Lamoile Valley 1925

Montpelier
(Barre, suburbs) 1890, 1897, 1898, 1904–21, 1936–41, 1949

Newport
(Banton, Orleans, West Derby) 1916–17

Rutland
(Proctor, West Rutland) 1867, 1872–76, 1889, 1899–1973

Saint Johnsbury
  (Barnet, Concord, Danville, Kirby, Lyndon, Water-
      bury) 1897, 1901–19, 1925–41, 1948–54, 1959,
      1962, 1966–74

South Burlington 1950

Springfield
  (Athens; Chester; Ludlow; Charlestown, N.H.) 1909,
      1912, 1914, 1916

St. Albans
  (Swanton) 1886–91, 1895–1909, 1914–15, 1936, 1938,
      1940, 1947–50, 1953, 1958, 1964, 1967, 1970

West Rutland
  (Proctor) 1919

Woodstock 1916

County, Business, and Miscellaneous

Chittenden 1902–12

Vermont (state)
  pre 1861 (microfiche)
  1854–69, 1870–89, 1890, 1894–1903, 1906–07
  (yearbooks) 1930–33, 1940–41

Windham 1924–84 (1 vol.)

Massachusetts

Historical Highlights

1620   Plymouth Colony founded.

1630   Massachusetts Bay Colony founded. Many
          new towns established, and county govern-
          ment instituted.

1684   Massachusetts Bay Colony charter revoked
          by England. Joined other colonies in the
          Dominion of New England.

1691   Massachusetts declared a royal colony —
          annexed Plymouth Colony.

1776   One of the original states at the time of the
          American Revolution.

1812   Provided militia in war with England but
          restricted it to serve within its own borders.

Published Record Sources

Guidebooks

Flower, Kenneth. *Guide to Massachusetts
  Genealogical Material in the State Library of Massachusetts; With a List of Other Resource Centers
  in Massachusetts Available for Genealogical Research.* Boston: the library, 1978/79. Z1295 .F67.

Hayward, John. *Gazetteer of Massachusetts . . . .*
  Boston: the author, 1846. F62 .H42.

Census Indexes and Abstracts

Federal

1790	F63 .U54 (Heads of Families)
1800	F63 .J27
1810	F63 .J32
1820	F63 .J3
1830	F63 .J32
1840	F63 .J33
1850	F63 .J34

All the above publications, except the 1790 census
entitled "Heads of Families," are by Ronald V. Jackson, Accelerated Indexing Systems.

State

Lainhart, Ann A. *1855 and 1865 Massachusetts State
  Censuses for Names of Towns.* Boston: the author,
  1986. F63 .L35.

Massachusetts. Secretary of State. *Historical Data
  Relating to Counties, Cities and Towns in Massachusetts.* Boston: State of Mass., 1975. F64 .M5.

Shattuck, Lemuel. *Report to the Committee of the
  City Council Appointed to Obtain the Census of
  Boston for the Year 1845; With Index.* Reprint.
  New York: Arno Press, 1976. HA730 .B7S6.

Biographies

Cutter, William R. *Genealogical and Personal
  Memories Relating to the Families of Boston and
  Eastern Massachusetts.* New York: Historical
  Publishing, 1908. F63 .C99.

Eliot, Samuel A. *Biographical History of Massachusetts.* 10 vols. Boston: Massachusetts Biographical Society, 1908. F70 .E42.

Herndon, Richard, ed. *Men of Progress: One Thousand Biographical Sketches and Portraits of Leaders . . . Commonwealth of Massachusetts.* Boston: New England Magazine, 1896. F633 .M533.

Representative Men of Southeast Massachusetts. 3 vols. Chicago: J. H. Beers, 1912. F63 .R4.

Early Settlers

Banks, Charles B. *The Planters of the Commonwealth: A Study of the Emigrants and Emigration in Colonial Times . . . .* Boston: Houghton Mifflin, 1930. F67 .B19.

Banks, Charles E. *The Winthrop Fleet of 1630: An Account of the Vessels, the Voyage, the Passengers, and Their English Homes, From Original Authorities.* Reprint. Baltimore: Genealogical Publishing Co., 1968. F67 .B21.

Flagg, Charles A., comp. *An Index of Pioneers from Massachusetts to the West, Especially the State of Michigan.* Salem: Salem Press, 1915. F63 .F53.

Genealogies of Mayflower Families: From the New England Historical and Genealogical Register. Baltimore: Genealogical Publishing Co., 1985. F63 .G47.

Haxton, Annie A. *Signers of the Mayflower Compact.* Reprint. New York: Mail and Express, 1897. F68 .H291.

Hill, Leon C. *History and Genealogy of the Mayflower Planters and First Comers to Ye Olde Colonies.* Reprint. Baltimore: Genealogical Publishing Co., 1975. F68 .H649.

Holbrook, Jay M. *Boston Beginnings, 1630–1699.* Oxford, Mass.: Holbrook Research Institute, 1980. F73.25 .H64.

Landis, John T. *Mayflower Descendants and Their Marriages For Two Generations After the Landing.* Washington, D.C.: Bureau of Military and Civil Achievement, 1922. F68 .B951.

Massachusetts. Secretary of the Commonwealth. *List of Persons Whose Names Have Been Changed in the Commonwealth, 1780–1892.* Reprint; Baltimore: Genealogical Publishing Co., 1972. F63 .A5.

National Society Colonial Dames of America in the Commonwealth: Register of Ancestors. Boston: Headquarters House, 1975. F63 .B7.

National Society Sons and Daughters of the Pilgrims. Sixteen Hundred Lines to Pilgrims. Lineage Book III. Manchester, Conn.: the society, 1982. E186.99 .S5A63. (Micro 87/5361).

Paige, Lucius R. *List of Freemen of Massachusetts, 1630–1891.* Baltimore: Genealogical Publishing Co., 1978. F63 .P34.

Pope, Charles H. *The Pioneers of Massachusetts: A Descriptive List Drawn From Records of the Colony, Towns, and Churches and Other Contemporaneous Documents.* Boston: the author, 1960. F63 .P82.

Roberts, Gary B. *Mayflower Source Records: Primary Data Concerning Southeastern Massachusetts, Cape Cod, and the Islands of Nantucket, and Martha's Vineyard; From the New England Historical and Genealogical Register.* Baltimore: Genealogical Publishing Co., 1986. F63 .R63.

Stratton, Eugene A. *Plymouth Colony: Its History & People, 1620–1691.* Salt Lake City: Ancestry, Inc., 1986. F68 .S93.

Sawyer, Joseph D. *History of the Pilgrims and Puritans: Their Ancestry and Descendants.* New York: Century History, 1922. F67 .S27.

Whitmore, William H. *Massachusetts: Civil Lists For the Colonial and Provincial Periods, 1630–1774.* Reprint. Baltimore: Genealogical Publishing Co., 1969. .F67 .W61.

Local Records

Bailey, Frederic W. *Early Massachusetts Marriages Prior to 1800.* 3 vols. Reprint. Baltimore: Genealogical Publishing Co., 1968. F63 .B15.

Based on records from the counties of Worcester, Hampshire, Berkshire, Bristol, and the Colony of Plymouth.

Boston, City of. *Boston Births From A.D. 1700 to A.D. 1800.* 2 vols. in 1. Reprint. Baltimore: Genealogical Publishing Co., 1978. F73.25 .B7642.

Boston Records Commissioners (Registry Department). Edward W. McGlenen, ed. *Boston Marriages From 1700 to 1809.* 2 vols. Baltimore: Genealogical Publishing Co., 1977. F73.25 .B7642.

Boston Records Commissioners (Registry Department). *Early History of Boston.* Miscellaneous Papers. Boston: City of Boston, 1904. F73.1 .B74.

Boston Records Commissioners (Registry Department). William S. Appleton, ed. *Boston Births, Baptisms, Marriages, and Deaths, 1630–1699; Boston Births, 1700–1800.* 2 vols. in 1. Reprint. Baltimore: Genealogical Publishing Co., 1978. F73.25 .B7642.

Joslyn, Roger D., ed. *Vital Records of Charlestown, Massachusetts to the Year 1850.* Boston: New England Historic Genealogical Society, 1984. F74 .C4J67.

Kingman, Bradford. *Epitaphs From Burial Hill, Plymouth, Massachusetts From 1657 to 1892 . . . .* Reprint. Baltimore: Genealogical Publishing Co., 1977. F74 .P8K5.

Massachusetts. County of Suffolk. *Records of the Court of Assistants of the Colony of the Massachusetts Bay, 1630–1692.* Boston: County of Suffolk, 1901. F67 .M33.

Pierce, Richard D. *Records in the First Church of Salem, Massachusetts, 1629–1736.* Salem, Mass.: Essex Institute, 1974. F74.51 .S173.

Pugh, Mary, comp. *Leads to Ancestors: Marriage Notices and Death Notices, 1852–1853, From Notices at Boston, Massachusetts.* N.p.: the author, 1976. F73.25 .P84.

Pruitt, Bettye H., ed. *Massachusetts Tax Evaluation List of 1771.* Boston: G.K. Hall, 1978. F63 .P838.

Sherman, Ruth W., and Robert S. Wakefield. *Plymouth Colony Probate Guide: Where to Find Wills and Related Data for 800 People of Plymouth Colony, 1620–1691.* Warwick, R.I.: Plymouth Colony Research Group, 1983. F63 .S53.

Shurtleff, Nathaniel B., ed. *Records of the Governor and Company of the Massachusetts Bay in New England.* 5 vols. (1642–49). Boston: Massachusetts Legislature, 1853. F67 .M32.

————. *Records of the Colony of Plymouth, New England.* 6 vols. New York: AMS Press, 1856. F68 .M55.

Covers 1633 to 1691.

Smith, Leonard H., Jr. *Vital Records of Southeast Massachusetts.* 3 vols. Clearwater, Fla.: the author, 1976. F63 .U57.

Eastham, Orleans, Middleborough, Wareham, Barnstable, Sandwich, Fairhaven.

Worthley, Harold F. *An Inventory of the Records of the Particular (Congregational) Churches of Massachusetts Gathered 1620–1805.* Cambridge: Harvard University Press, 1970. BX714 .M4W65.

Published Vital Records of Massachusetts Towns

In accordance with a state sanctioned program, the vital records of a large number of Massachusetts cities and towns have been published. For each city or town there is a volume (sometimes two) listing the births, marriages, and deaths for the years prior to 1850. The data included were obtained from various sources uncovered by the compilers. No other state has attempted such a monumental series, and reference to these volumes, entitled *Vital Records of* [town] is very important when an ancestor is located in a particular Massachusetts town. To obtain one of these volumes, type the following command on the computer terminal exactly as shown here—but substitute the name of the town: **find s births salem; f = prem** (substitute name of town).

The volume obtained will include not only the births as noted in the command, but also the marriages and deaths.

In more recent years, Jay M. Holbrook, of Holbrook Research Institute, has copied or transcribed a number of previously unpublished vital records of Massachusetts towns, and they are available on microfiche. The Microform Reading Room at the Library of Congress has this collection for some sixty towns, and it plans to add another 300. To obtain them, fill out a request slip in the Microform Reading Room and use the microfiche number M83/100. Reference staff in that room can provide a list of the towns for which they currently have microfiche.

Military Records

General

Council of Minute Men. *Minute Men, 1775–1975.* Southborough, Mass.: Yankee Colour Corp., 1977. E263 .M4M66.

McGhee, Lucy K., comp. *Massachusetts Pension Abstracts of the Revolutionary War, War of 1812, and Indian Wars.* Washington, D.C.: the compiler, 1966. F63 .M44.

Colonial Wars

Bodge, George M. *Soldiers in King Philip's War . . . Indian Wars of New England, 1620–1677.* 3d ed.

Baltimore: Genealogical Publishing Co., 1967. E83.67 .B662.

Doreski, Carole, ed. Society of Colonial Wars in the Commonwealth of Massachusetts. *Massachusetts Officers and Soldiers in the Seventeenth Century Conflicts.* Boston: New England Historic Genealogical Society, 1982. F63 .M35.

Goss, K. David, and David Zarowin, eds. The Society of Colonial Wars in the Commonwealth of Massachusetts. *Massachusetts Officers and Soldiers in the French and Indian War, 1755–56.* Boston: New England Historic Genealogical Society, 1985. E199 .M414.

Voye, Nancy S., ed. *Massachusetts Officers in the French and Indian Wars, 1748–1763.* Boston: Society of Colonial Wars in the Commonwealth of Massachusetts, 1974. E199 .V84.

American Revolution

Allen, Gardner W. *Massachusetts Privateers of the Revolution. Collections of the Massachusetts Historical Society, Vol. 77.* Boston: the society, 1927. F61 .M41.

Hambrick-Stowe, Charles E., and Donna D. Smerlas, eds. *Massachusetts Militia Companies and Officers of the Lexington Alarm.* New England Historical Society, 1976. E241 .L6H35.

Jones, E. Alfred. *Loyalists of Massachusetts; Their Memorials, Petitions, and Claims.* Baltimore: Genealogical Publishing Co., 1969. E277 .J77.

Massachusetts. Secretary of the Commonwealth. *Massachusetts Soldiers and Sailors of the Revolutionary War: A Compilation From the Archives.* 17 vols. Boston: Secretary of the Commonwealth, 1696–1908. E263 .M4M4.

Roberts, Oliver A. *The History of the Ancient and Honorable Artillery Company of Massachusetts, Vol. 2.* Boston: Alred Mudge and Sons, 1897. UA258 .A5R7.

Stark, James H. *Loyalists of Massachusetts and the Other Side of the American Revolution.* Clifton, Mass.: A.M. Kelley, 1972. E277 .S79.

War of 1812

Massachusetts. Adjutant General. John Baker, comp. *Records of Massachusetts Volunteer Militia Called Out, War of 1812.* Boston: State of Mass., 1913. E359.5 .M3M4.

Civil War

Dilts, Bryan L. *1890 Massachusetts Census Index of Civil War Veterans or Their Widows—Microforms.* Salt Lake City: Index Publishers, 1985. E494 .D54.

Massachusetts. Adjutant General. *Annual Reports, 1861–1866.* Boston: Wright and Potter, State Printers, 1862–67. E513.2 .M41.

Massachusetts. Secretary of the Commonwealth. *Massachusetts Soldiers and Sailors in the Civil War.* 8 vols. and Index to Army Records. N.p.: State of Massachusetts, n.d. E513 .M32.

Nason, George W. *History and Complete Roster of the Massachusetts Regiments, Minute Men of '61 Who Responded to the First Call of President Abraham Lincoln, April 15, 1861 . . . .* Boston: Smith and McCance, 1910. E513.4 .N27.

Periodicals

Boston Transcript Genealogy Columns, 1896–1941. (Micro 84/104138).

Codman, Ogden. *Index of Obituaries in the Boston Newspapers, 1704–1795. Deaths Outside Boston.* 2 vols. Boston: G.K. Hall, 1968. F73.23 .C6.

Essex Institute Historical Collections. Subject Index to Vols. 1–67. Salem: the institute, 1932. F72 .E7E81. Covers 1849 to 1931. Index.

Index of Marriages in Massachusetts Centinel and Columbian Centinel, 1784–1840. 4 vols. American Antiquarian Society. Boston: 1941. CS43 .A5.

Index of Deaths in Massachusetts Centinel and Columbian Centinel, 1784–1840. 12 vols. Worcester: American Antiquarian Society, 1952. F69 .A5.

Massachusetts Historical Society Proceedings. Index to Vols. 1–60. 7 vols. Boston: the society, 1941. F61 .M38. Covers 1791 to 1926. Index.

Massachusetts Society of Mayflower Descendants. *The Mayflower Descendant: Index of Persons, Vols. 1–34.* 2 vols. in 1. Boston: the society, 1959. F68 .M46 index.

McAuslan, William A. *Mayflower Index.* 3 vols. Boston: Genealogical Society of Mayflower Descendants, 1960. F68 .S6614.

Nason, Mrs. Frank, ed. *The Mayflower Descendants. Index to Vols. 1–34.* Boston: The Massachusetts Society of Mayflower Descendants, 1959. F68 .M46.

Covers 1620 to 1937.

Publications of the Colonial Society of Massachusetts. Index to Vols. 1–25. Boston: the society, 1932. F61 .C71.

Covers 1892 to 1924.

Directories

City

Abington
(Whitman) 1889

Achushnet
(Dartmouth, Freeport, Westport) 1927–32, 1954–59, 1963

Acton
(Concord, Maynard, Sudbury) 1926, 1947–50

Adams
(Cheshire, Clarksburg, New Ashton, Savoy, Williamstown) 1899, 1902, 1910–25, 1932, 1937, 1953

Amherst
(Belchertown, Hadley, Hatfield, Sunderland, Williamsburg) 1884, 1895–99, 1909–75

Andover
(N. Andover) 1891–93, 1897, 1901–08, 1916–20, 1928–37, 1943–53

Arlington
(Belmont) 1894–1940

Ashburn 1881

Athol
(Erving, New Salem, Orange, Petersham, Phillipston, Royalston, Templeton, Warwick, Wendell, Winchendon) 1893–1978

Attleboro
(N. Attleboro, Plainville, S. Attleboro) 1889–92

Ayer
(Groton, Harvard, Littleton) 1907, 1912, 1916, 1922, 1926, 1929

Barnstable
(Bourne, Falmouth, Sandwich, Mashpee, Yarmouth) 1901, 1926

Belmont
(Cramerton, Mt. Holly, Stanley) 1907–84

Beverly
(suburbs) 1875, 1888, 1895–1979

Boston
pre 1861 (microfiche)
1861–1935 (microfilm)
1936–78

Boston, East
pre 1861 (microfiche)

Boston, South
pre 1861 (microfiche)

Bourne
(Falmouth, Sandwich) 1900, 1908

Boylston 1907

Braintree 1907–43

Bridgewater (suburbs) 1931

Brighton
pre 1861 (microfiche)

Brockton
(suburbs, Arlington, Bridgewater) 1872–1969

Brookline
(Jamaica Plain, W. Roxbury) 1868–1968

Cambridge
pre 1861 (microfiche)
1863–1931, 1937–54, 1961–83

Canton 1911, 1913

Cape Cod 1901, 1929

Carver
(Plymouth, Halifax, Duxbury, Hansen, Pembroke) 1909–

Charlestown
pre 1861 (microfiche)
1862–1974

Chelsea
pre 1861 (microfiche)
1866–1940, 1946

Chicopee
(Chicopee Falls, Fairview, Williamsett) 1950–80

Clinton
pre 1861 (microfiche)
(Lancaster) 1883–1975

Cohasset
(Scituate, Duxbury, Marchfield, Norwell) 1894

Concord 1896–1934

Cottage City 1885

Danvers
(Beverly, Essex, Manchester, Marblehead, Peabody, Topsfield, Wenham) 1879, 1895

Dartmouth
(Acushnet, Westport) 1905, 1909, 1915

Dedham
(Westwood) 1899–1911, 1917–39, 1949

Dighton
(Rehobeth, Seekonk, Somerset, Swanson) 1940, 1951–57

Dorchester
pre 1861 (microfiche)
1861–1935 (microfilm)

Dracut 1900

Duxbury
(Kingston) 1915

Easton 1911

Essex 1931

Everett 1895, 1899, 1904–42

Fall River
pre 1861 (microfiche)
1861–1935 (microfilm)
1936–84

Fitchburg
pre 1861 (microfiche)
(suburbs) 1910, 1926, 1929, 1931, 1938, 1942, 1950–82

Framingham
(Ashland) 1884, 1898, 1906–26, 1930, 1933, 1935, 1939, 1941, 1943, 1946, 1950–70

Gardner 1885, 1888–94, 1899–1980

Gloucester
pre 1861 (microfiche)
(Essex, Rockport) 1869–82, 1886–1980

Grafton 1905

Great Barrington
(Sheffield) 1901, 1904

Greenfield
(Deerfield, Montague, Turners Falls) 1899–1973

Hamilton
(Middleton, Topsfield, Wenham) 1921

Harwich
(Chatham, Dennis) 1901

Haverhill
pre 1861 (microfiche)
(Bradford, Groveland, Merrimac) 1867, 1869, 1872–1974

Hingham
(Cohassett, Hull) 1894, 1898, 1908, 1912, 1915, 1920, 1925, 1928

Holyoke
(S. Hadley Falls) 1869, 1882–1979

Hull
(Nantasket, Pemberton) 1917

Hyde Park
(Canton, Dedham) 1874, 1876, 1897–1915

Ipswich (suburbs) 1891, 1896–97, 1916, 1933, 1944, 1947–58

Lakeville
(Berkeley, Freetown) 1911–31

Lawrence (available at the desk) 1848, 1851, 1853, 1857, 1859, 1864

Lawrence (suburbs)
pre 1861 (microfiche)
1971–77

Lee
(Dalton, Hinsdale, Lanesboro, Otis, Richmond, Stockbridge, Tyringham) 1903, 1911, 1913, 1916, 1919, 1923

Leicester 1905

Leominster 1883–1979

Lexington
(Bedford) 1894–1942

Lowell
pre 1861 (microfiche)
1861–1935 (microfilm)
(suburbs, Billerica, Chelmsford, Dracut, Tewksbury, Tyngsboro, Westford) 1936–82

Lunenburg
pre 1861 (microfiche)

Lynn
pre 1861 (microfiche)
(Lynnfield, Marblehead, Nahant, Saugus, Swampscott) 1851–1982

Malden
  (Everett, Medford, Melrose) 1870–80, 1882–88,
    1898–1983

Mansfield
  (Foxboro, Norton, Raynham, Sharon) 1898–1911,
    1915–21, 1926, 1966–72

Marblehead 1895, 1935

Marborough
  (Berlin, Bolton, Framingham, Hudson, Stow, South-
    boro, Sudbury) 1872, 1885, 1887, 1889, 1900, 1909,
    1911, 1913, 1918–41, 1947, 1951, 1957, 1961

Martha's Vineyard 1907, 1910

Maynard
  (Acton) 1902

Medfield
  (Medway, Millis) 1914

Medford
  pre 1861 (microfiche)
  1896, 1902–30, 1938

Melrose 1893–1941, 1962–68

Methuen 1892, 1901, 1904, 1909–32, 1940, 1946, 1950–
    54

Middleboro
  (Lakeville, Carver) 1897–1921, 1928, 1930

Milford
  pre 1861 (microfiche)
  (Framingham, Holliston, Hopedale, Natick) 1869–89,
    1896, 1900–50, 1964–71

Millbury 1871, 1892, 1905

Monson
  (Brimfield, Wilbraham) 1894, 1897, 1906

Nantucket
  (Chilmark, Cottage City, Edgartown, Tisbury,
    Vineyard Haven, W. Tisbury) 1897, 1909, 1914,
    1919, 1927

Natick 1873, 1882, 1908–23, 1931

Needham
  (Dover, Wellesley) 1888, 1915, 1923, 1928, 1835

New Bedford
  pre 1861 (microfiche)
  (suburbs, Acushnet, Dartmouth, Fairhaven,
    Freetown, Westport) 1865–1955, 1962–71

Newburyport
  (Amesbury, Lake Attitosh, Plum Island, Salisbury)
    1849–60, 1866–82, 1886–1980

Newton 1868–1980

North Adams
  (Cheshire, Clarksburg, Williamstown) 1880, 1894–
    1974

North Andover 1896, 1914

Northbridge
  (Uxbridge) 1906, 1911, 1913, 1936

Northhampton
  (Easthampton, suburbs) 1909, 1912

Norwood
  (Walpole) 1897, 1900–18, 1924, 1928–42

Orange (suburbs) 1936–70, 1978

Palmer
  (Monson, Ware) 1892, 1898–1914, 1948–56, 1961–71,
    1979–85

Peabody
  (Danvers, Marblehead) 1873, 1895, 1921

Pepperell
  (Dunstable, Shirley, Townsend) 1907–17, 1926

Pittsfield
  pre 1861 (microfiche)

Provincetown 1890

Quincy
  (Braintree, Weymouth) 1850, 1873, 1876, 1878–1955,
    1961–67

Randolph
  (Avon, Holbrook) 1908–16, 1921, 1926, 1940, 1947,
    1950

Revere Beach
  (Beachmont, Revere) 1887, 1912–40

Rochester
  (Marion, Mattapoisett, Wareham) 1903

Rockland
  (Abington, Hanover, Norwell) 1888, 1896–1930

Roxbury
  pre 1861 (microfiche)
  1861–64

Salem
(Beverly, Danvers, Hamilton, Manchester, Marblehead, Topsfield) 1842, 1846, 1850–1916, 1921, 1929–80

Scituate
(Marshfield) 1915, 1918, 1926

Shelbourne Falls
(Chesterfield, Hinsdale, S. Vermont) 1907

Somerset
(Dighton, Rehobeth, Seekonk, Swansea) 1904, 1908, 1913, 1917, 1921, 1923, 1930

Somerville
pre 1861 (microfiche)
(Arlington, Belmont) 1869–1933, 1940

South Berkshire
(Alford; Egremont; Great Barrington; Monterey; Mt. Washington; Sheffield; Stockbridge; W. Stockbridge; Falls Village, Ct.) 1957–63, 1969

Southbridge
pre 1861 (microfiche)
(Brimfield, Charlton, Fiskdale, Sturbridge) 1873, 1907, 1912, 1922, 1928–31, 1936, 1949, 1952, 1965–80

Spencer
(Brookefield, Warren) 1884–85, 1928

Springfield
pre 1861 (microfiche)
(Agawam, East Longmeadow, Hampden, Longmeadow, Ludlow, Southwick, Wilbraham) 1897, 1901, 1904, 1908, 1926–41, 1949–78
Springfield (Chicopee, Long Meadow, W. Springfield) 1861–1979, 1985

Stoneham
(Reading, Wakefield) 1869

Swampscott
(Lynnfield, Nahant, Saugus) 1895, 1931

Taunton
pre 1861 (microfiche)
(E. Taunton, Hopewell, Raynham, The Weir, Whittenton) 1850, 1855–85

Tewksbury 1900

Tri-City
(Dighton, Rehobeth, Seekonk, Somerset, Swanson) 1940

Tyngsboro 1900

Upton
(Hopedale, Mendon) 1898

Uxbridge
(Northbridge) 1898

Wakefield
(Lynnfield, North Reading, Reading, Saugus, Stoneham) 1874, 1882–1968

Waltham
(Cochituate; Wayland; Weston; Lincoln, Mass.) 1906–21, 1931

Ware
(Hardwick, Monson, Palmer) 1892, 1879, 1913, 1919, 1922–34, 1941

Wareham
(Marion, Mattapoisett, Rochester) 1907, 1910, 1916, 1919, 1924, 1928

Watertown 1889, 1907, 1909, 1926–35

Webster
(Dudley, Grosvenordale, Mechanicsville, Oxford, Sturbridge, Wilsonville) 1887, 1896, 1899, 1902, 1907, 1922, 1928–35, 1948–53, 1964–71

Wellesley 1907, 1910–39

Westboro
(Northboro) 1905, 1966–68

Westfield 1873, 1895, 1909–77

Westford 1901

Weston
(Lincoln, Wayland) 1929, 1933, 1949

Weymouth 1888, 1891, 1896–1941, 1953

Whitman
(Abington) 1895, 1900–09, 1913–26, 1932

Williamstown 1899, 1903

Winchendon
(Ashburnham) 1885, 1890, 1907, 1910

Winchester 1901, 1905, 1908

Winthrop 1890, 1911, 1913, 1916, 1929, 1931, 1947

Woburn
(Winchester) 1868–77, 1883–1920, 1925, 1932, 1937

Worcester
pre 1861 (microfiche)
1861–1935 (microfilm)

(suburbs) 1936–85
(houses) 1888–1982

County, Business, and Miscellaneous

Attleboro 1900

Barnstable (see Plymouth)

Berkshire 1874–77, 1885, 1903

Berkshire, central 1926–64

Berkshire, southern 1910–31, 1943–58

Boston (city) 1871

Bristol 1867–89, 1903, 1925

Essex 1866–96

Fitchburg (city) 1890

Franklin (see Hampden)

Hampden
  (Franklin, Hampshire) 1872–76, 1885, 1889, 1890,
  1892, 1897

Hampshire (see Hampden)

Hartford 1874

Hyde Park (city) 1888–1901

Massachusetts (see also Providence, R.I.)
  (region) pre 1861 (microfiche)
  (central, west) 1853–56, 1869–95, 1911, 1913

Merrimack River (region) 1872, 1874, 1887–88

Middleboro (region) 1902

Middlesex 1871–90, 1903

New Bedford (city) 1901

Norfolk
  (Plymouth) 1903

North Essex (city) 1907–16

Northampton (city) 186–[*sic*]

Plymouth (see also Norfolk)
  (Barnstable) 1873, 1880, 1889, 1891

Reading (city) 1900

Roxbury (city) 1848

Worcester 1866, 1870–96, 1902

Rhode Island

Historical Highlights

1636	Providence settled by Roger Williams, a Puritan dissenter from Massachusetts. All Christian faiths welcomed.
1642	Royal charter granted to "Rhode Island and Providence."
1686	Joined with other colonies in the Dominion of New England.
1776	One of the thirteen original states at the time of the American Revolution.

Published Record Sources

Guidebooks

Sperry, Kip. *Rhode Island Sources for Family Historians and Genealogists.* Logan, Utah: Everton Publishers, 1986. F78 .S7.

Census Indexes and Abstracts

Federal:

1790	F78 .U54 (Heads of Families)
1800	F78 .J3
1810	F78 .J6
1820	F78 .J32
1830	F78 .J322
1840	F78 .J325
1850	F78 .J327

All the above publications, except for the 1790 census entitled "Heads of Families," are by Ronald V. Jackson, Accelerated Indexing System.

1860	(microfiche 87/2008) (Dilts, Bryan L.)
1870	(microfiche 87/2006) (Dilts, Bryan L.)

State

Rhode Island. General Assembly. *Census of the Inhabitants of the Colony of Rhode Island and Providence Plantations, 1774.* Baltimore: Genealogical Publishing Co., 1969. F78 .A59.

Holbrook, Jay M. *Rhode Island 1782 Census.* Oxford, Mass.: Holbrook Research Institute, 1979. F78 .H47.

Biographies

Austin, John D. *Genealogical Dictionary of Rhode Island, 1887. Reprinted with Additions and Corrections.* Baltimore: Genealogical Publishing Co., 1969. F78 .A935.

Biographical Cyclopedia of Representative Men of Rhode Island. Providence: National Biographical Publishing Co., 1881. F78 .B61.

Carroll, Charles. *Rhode Island: Three Centuries of Democracy.* New York: Lewis Historical Publishing Co., 1932. F79 .C26.

Heren, Richard, ed. *Men of Progress: Biographical Sketches and Portraits of . . . Rhode Island and the Providence Plantations.* Boston: New England Magazine, 1896. F78 .M64.

Representative Men and Old Families of Rhode Island: Genealogical Records and Historical Sketches of Prominent and Representative Citizens and of Many of the Old Families. Chicago: J.H. Beers, 1908. F78 .R42.

Early Settlers

Chace, Henry R. *Owners and Occupants, of the Lots, Houses, and Shops in the Towns of Providence, Rhode Island in 1798.* Providence: the author, 1914. F89 .P9C4.

Ford, Carol L. *Genealogies of Rhode Island Families From Rhode Island Periodicals.* 2 vols. Baltimore: Genealogical Publishing Co., 1983. F78 .G46.

MacGunnigle, Bruce C., comp. *Rhode Island Freemen: A Census of Registered Voters.* Baltimore: Genealogical Publishing Co., 1977. F78 .M33.

Pierce, Ebenezer W. *Pierce's Colonial Lists, Civil, Military, and Professional Lists of Plymouth and Rhode Island Colonies. . . .* Baltimore: Genealogical Publishing Co., 1968. F68 .P37.

Rhode Island Land Evidences, Vol. I (1648–1896). Baltimore: Genealogical Publishing Co., 1970. F82 .R5.

Smith, Joseph J. *Civil and Military Lists of Rhode Island, 1647–1800.* 3 vols. Providence: Preston & Rounds, 1901. F78 .S65; F78 .S67.

Local Records

Arnold, James N. *Vital Records of Rhode Island, 1636–1850.* 21 vols. Providence: Narragansett Historical Society, 1891. F78 .A75.

Ask at the reference desk of the Local History and Genealogy Reading Room for assistance in using this work. A guide in the vertical file shows each town and the volume in which it appears.

Beaman, Alden G. *Rhode Island Vital Records: New Series.* 12 vols. Princeton, Mass.: 1977–86. F78 .B4.

Consult the catalogs for material covered in each volume.

Quintin, Robert J. *Franco-America Burials of Rhode Island.* Providence: the author, 1980. F90 .F85Q56.

Pesaturo, Ubaldo V.M. *Italo-Americans of Rhode Island.* Providence: the author, 1940. F90 I8P47.

Providence, City Registrar. *Alphabetical Index of the Births, Marriages and Deaths Recorded in Providence.* Providence: n.p., 1928. F89 .P9P862.

Volume 1; Births, 1636–1850.

Military Records

Colonial Wars

Chapin, Howard M. *Rhode Island in the Colonial Wars: A List of Rhode Island Soldiers and Sailors in King George's War, 1740–1748.* Providence: Rhode Island Historical Society, 1920. F82 .C48.

———. *Rhode Island Privateers in King George's War, 1739–1748.* Providence: Rhode Island Historical Society, 1926. F82 .C483.

American Revolution

Arnold, James N. *Cowell's "Spirit of '76": An Analytical and Explanatory Index.* Also found in *Arnold's Vital Records of Rhode Island, Vol. 12.* Reprint.

Baltimore: Genealogical Publishing Co., 1973. E263 .R4A

Chamberlain, Mildred M. Rhode Island Genealogical Society. *The Rhode Island 1777 Military Census.* Baltimore: Genealogical Publishing Co., 1985. E263 .R4C48.

Cowell, Benjamin. *Spirit of '76 in Rhode Island . . . .* Boston: n.p., 1850. E263 .R4C83.

Arnold's index is vital to the use of this volume.

Rider, Sidney S. *An Historical Inquiry Concerning the Attempt to Raise a Regiment of Slaves by Rhode Island During the War of the Revolution.* Providence: the author, 1880. F76 .R52.

Smith, Joseph J. *Civil and Military List of Rhode Island, 1647–1800.* 3 vols. Providence: Preston & Rounds, 1901. F78 .S67.

Civil War

Bartlett, John R. *Memoirs of Rhode Island Officers Who Were Engaged in the Service of Their Country During the Great Rebellion of the South.* Providence: S.S. Rider, 1867. F78 .B281.

Directories

City

Apponang
(E. Greenwich, Wickford) 1901–12

Barrington
(Bristol, Warren) 1930, 1942, 1947–54, 1963–78

Bristol
(Arlington, Barrington, E. Providence, Warren) 1876, 1884–88, 1897, 1907–40

Burrillville
(N. Smithfield) 1910

Cranston 1913–84

Cumberland
(Lincoln) 1909–41, 1966–83

East Greenwich
(N. Livingston, Warwick) 1925

East Providence
(Bristol, Warren) 1890–1983

Hopkinton
(Holliston) 1899, 1917, 1922, 1924

Jamestown
(Little Compton, Middleton, New Shoreham, Portsmouth, Tiverton) 1912–30, 1936, 1948–67

Little Compton
(Middleton, Portsmouth, Tiverton)

Newport
pre 1861 (microfiche)
(suburbs, Little Compton, Jamestown, Middletown, Portsmouth, Tivertown) 1970, 1972, 1979

North Providence
(Gloucester, Johnston, Smithfield) 1926, 1937–41

Pawtucket
pre 1861 (microfiche)
(Central Falls, Woonsocket) 1875–76, 1897–1983

Providence
pre 1861 (microfiche)
1861–1935 (microfilm)
1936–83

South Kingstown
(Narragensett) 1910, 1915, 1925

Tiverton
(Little Compton, Middleton, Portsmouth) 1907, 1910, 1913–25, 1937–41

Warren
(Barrington) 1897

Warwick
(E. Greenwich, N. Kingston) 1914, 1920, 1936–42, 1948, 1952, 1959–83

West Warwick 1936–40, 1946–85

Westerly
(Pawtucket) 1895, 1884–1984

Woonsocket 1879, 1890–1983

County, Business, and Miscellaneous

Bristol 1981

Newport (city) 1939

Pawtucket Valley 1892–1927, 1944

Providence (city)
(S. Massachusetts) 1935

Rhode Island (region)
pre 1861 (microfiche)
1872–94

Connecticut

Historical Highlights

1636   Hartford settled by Thomas Hooker, a Puritan dissenter from Massachusetts. Fort erected at Saybrook.

1638   New Haven Colony founded by Puritan merchants.

1662   Connecticut Colony granted royal charter—absorbed New Haven Colony and merged independent towns.

1686   Joined other colonies in the Dominion of New England.

1700   Provided the town of Voluntown for veterans of King Philip's War.

1776   One of the thirteen original states at the time of the American Revolution.

Published Record Sources

Guidebooks

Sperry, Kip. *Connecticut Sources for Family Historians and Genealogists.* Logan, Utah: Everton Publishers, 1980. Z1265 .S67.

Census Indexes and Abstracts

Federal

1790   F93 .U54 (Heads of Families)

1800   F93 .J2

1810   F93 .J22

1820   F93 .J222

1830   F93 .223

1840   F93 .J224

1850   F93 .225

1860   (microfiche 87/2005) (Dilts, Bryan L.)

State

Holbrook, Jay M. *Connecticut 1670 Census.* Oxford, Mass.: Holbrook Research Institute, 1977. F93 .H73.

Mortality Schedules

1860   F93 .J2275

1870   F93 .J2275

All the above publications, except for the 1790 census entitled "Heads of Families," Holbrook and Dilts, are by Ronald V. Jackson, Accelerated Indexing Systems.

Biographies

Cutter, William R., et al., eds. *Genealogical and Family History of the State of Connecticut.* 2 vols. New York: Lewis Historical Publishing Co., 1911. F93 .G99.

Genealogies of Connecticut Families: From the New England Historical and Genealogical Register. Baltimore: Genealogical Publishing Co., 1983. F93 .G46.

Goodwin, Nathaniel. *Genealogical Notes: Or Contributions to the Family History of Some of the First Settlers of Connecticut and Massachusetts.* Baltimore: Genealogical Publishing Co., 1969. F93 .C65.

Herndon, Richard, ed. *Men of Progress: Biographical Sketches and Portraits of Leaders . . . State of Connecticut.* Boston: New England Magazine, 1898. F93 .M53.

Osborn, Norris G. *Men of Mark in Connecticut . . . .* Hartford, Conn.: W.R. Goodspeed, 1906–10. F93 .081.

Perry, Charles E., ed. *Founders and Leaders of Connecticut, 1633–1783.* Freeport, N.Y.: Books For Libraries Press, 1971. F93 .P38.

Representative Men of Connecticut, 1861–1894. Everett, Mass.: Massachusetts Publishing Co., 1894. F93 .R42.

Spalding, J.A., comp. *Illustrated Popular Biography of Connecticut.* Hartford: Press of the Case, Lockwood and Braintree Co., 1891. F93 .S73.

Stevenson, Elias Robert. *Connecticut History Makers, Containing Sketches and Portraits of Men Who Have Contributed to the Progress of the*

State .... Waterbury, Conn.: American-Republican, 1929. F93 .S84.

Early Settlers

Brown, Barbara W., and James M. Rose. *Black Roots in Southeastern Connecticut, 1650–1900.* Detroit: Gale Research, 1980. E185.93 .C7B76.

Buel, Mrs. John L., ed. *Family Records Collected in Commemoration of the 300th Anniversary of the Settlement of Connecticut—New Haven.* Connecticut Chapter, National Society Daughters of Founders and Patriots of America, 1935. F93 .D27.

Carlevale, Joseph W. *Who's Who Among Americans of Italian Descent in Connecticut.* New Haven, Conn.: Carlevale Publishing Co., 1942. F105 .I8C37.

Hinman, Royal R. *A Catalogue of the Names of the First Puritan Settlers of the Colony of Connecticut* .... Baltimore: Genealogical Publishing Co., 1968. F93 .H65.

LeDoux, Albert H. *The Franco-Americans of Connecticut, 1880.* N.p.: the compiler, 1977. F105 .F8L43.

Index compiled from the 1880 federal census.

Ritter, Kathy A. *Apprentices of Connecticut, 1637–1900.* Salt Lake City: Ancestry, Inc., 1986. F93 .R58.

Scott, Kenneth, and Rosanne Conway, comps. *Genealogical Data From Colonial New Haven Newspapers.* Baltimore: Genealogical Publishing Co., 1979. F104 .N653A27.

Local Records

Bailey, Frederic W. *Early Connecticut Marriages as Found in Ancient Church Records Prior to 1800.* Baltimore: Genealogical Publishing Co., 1968. F93 .B16.

Barbour Collection of Connecticut Vital Records to 1850. M82/15.

Ninety-eight reels of film. Use Guide No. 62 (available in the Microform Reading Room and the Local History and Genealogy Reading Room) to determine reel number needed.

Vital Records of Saybrook Colony, 1635–1860 . . . Connecticut. N.p.: Connecticut Valley Shore Research Groups, 1985. F104 .04V57.

Manwaring, Charles W., comp. *A Digest of the Early Connecticut Probate Records—Microforms.* 3 vols. Hartford: R.W. Peck, 1904–06. (Micro 77790).

Military Records

Colonial Wars

Buckingham, Thomas. *Roll and Journal of Connecticut Service in Queen Anne's War, 1710–11.* New Haven: Tuttle, Morehouse and Taylor Press, 1916. E197 .B92.

Rolls of Connecticut Men in the French and Indian Wars, 1755–1762. Hartford: Connecticut Historical Society, No. 3–05, n.d. F91 .C7.

American Revolution

Connecticut. Adjutant General. Henry P. Johnston, ed. *Record of Connecticut Men in the Military and Naval Service During the War of the Revolution, 1775–1783.* Hartford: n.p., 1889. E263 .C5C5.

Connecticut Historical Society. *Rolls and Lists of Connecticut Men in the Revolution, 1775–1783.* Vols. 8 and 12 *Collections of the Connecticut Historical Society.* Hartford: n.p., 1901–09. C263 .C5C55.

Daughters of the American Revolution. *The Twenty-first Report, 1917–18.* Washington, D.C.: National Society Daughters of the American Revolution. E202 5 .A17.

Mather, Frederic G. *The Refugees of 1776 From Long Island to Connecticut.* Albany, N.Y.: J.B. Lyon Co., 1913. Reprint. 1922. E263 .N6M4.

Middlebrook, Louis F. *History of Maritime Connection During the American Revolution, 1774–1783.* 2 vols. Salem, Mass.: Essex Institute, 1925. F99 .M63.

Tyler, John W. *Connecticut Loyalists: An Analysis of Loyalist Land Confiscations in Greenwich, Stamford, and Norwalk.* New Orleans: Polyanthos, 1977. E277 .T93.

White, David O. *Connecticut's Black Soldiers, 1775–1783.* Chester: Pequot Press, 1973. E185.93 .C7W45.

Civil War

> Connecticut. Adjutant General. *Catalogue of Connecticut Volunteer Organization (Infantry, Cavalry, and Artillery)—Civil War.* Hartford: Case, Lockwood & Co., 1864. E499.3 .C77.
>
> Connecticut. Adjutant General. *Connecticut Troops, 1861–63.* N.p.: State of Connecticut, n.d. E944 .C76.
>
> Connecticut. Adjutant General. *Connecticut Troops, 1864.* N.p.: State of Connecticut, n.d. E499.2 .C75.

Directories

City

Ansonia
(Birmingham, Derby, Shelton, Seymour) 1888–1980

Avon
(E. Granby, Simsbury) 1913, 1964–77

Barkhamstead
(New Hartford) 1914

Berlin
(Cromwell, Rocky Hill) 1914, 1922, 1930

Bethany
(Woodbridge) 1927

Bethel 1898

Branford
(N. Branford) 1895–1977

Bridgeport
pre 1861 (microfiche)
(Easton, Fairfield, Southport, Stratford, Trumbell) 1865–1979

Bristol
(Plainville, Terryville) 1882–1977

Danbury
(Bethel, Norwalk) 1885–92, 1897, 1908, 1912–77

Danielson 1913, 1921, 1927, 1948, 1954, 1957

Darien
(New Canaan, Noroton, Noroton Hgts.) 1918, 1921–80, 1986

Derby
(Shelton) 1883–86

Durham
(Hadden, Middlefield) 1868–77, 1887–88, 1897–1984

East Hampton
(Colchester, E. Haddom, Moodus) 1967–75

East Haven 1915, 1926

Enfield
(Hazardsville, Thompsonville) 1901, 1906–27

Essex
(Chester, Deep River, E. Haddam, Haddum, Moodus) 1896

Greenwich
(Byram, Cos Cob, East Port Chester, Harrison, Mamaroneck, Mianus, Old Greenwich, Port Chester, Riverside, Rye, Sound Beach) 1930, 1934–41, 1946–80, 1986

Groton
(Long Point, Mystic, Noank) 1956–77

Guilford
(Clinton, Madison) 1961–78

Hamden
(Cheshire, N. Haven) 1927, 1945, 1950–76

Hartford
pre 1861 (microfiche)
1861–1935 (microfilm)
1936–73, 1986

Manchester 1888–1912, 1923–77

Meriden 1872–80

Middletown
(Cromwell, Portland) 1870, 1880, 1886–1978

Milford
(Amherst, Lyndeboro, Merrimack, Mt. Vernon, Wilton) 1917
(Orange Co.) 1897, 1909, 1913, 1916, 1920–77

Montville
(Gales Ferry, Ledyard, Uncasville) 1966–79

Mystic
(Noank, Stonington) 1912–31

New Britian
(Berlin, Kensington) 1884–1976

New Canaan 1908, 1911, 1913, 1926

New Haven
pre 1861 (microfiche)
(East Haven, West Haven, Woodbridge) 1936–76

New London
(Groton, Niantic, Quaker Hill, Waterford) 1865–80, 1890–1977

New Milford 1884, 1888, 1891, 1897, 1902, 1907, 1910, 1915, 1927, 1950, 1960, 1966–76

Newton
  (Monroe) 1963–78

Norwalk
  (So. Norwalk, Fairfield Co.) 1883, 1886, 1891–1977, 1986

Norwich
  pre 1861 (microfiche)
  (suburbs) 1864–67, 1872, 1875–1978

Old Saybrook
  (Chester, Deep River, Essex, Westbrook) 1964–79

Prospect
  (Beacon Falls, Bethany, Oxford) 1960–78

Putnam
  (Danielson) 1882, 1900, 1907, 1909, 1913–18, 1922, 1928–39, 1947–51, 1964

Ridgefield
  (Georgetown, Redding) 1958–79

Rockville
  (Ellington, Stafford Springs, Tolland, Vernon, Tolland Co.) 1883–1970

South Beach
  (Riverside) 1920, 1922, 1925

Southbury
  (Roxbury, Washington, Woodbury) 1969, 1974, 1976

Southington 1882–89, 1895–1979

Stafford
  (Manson; Palmer; Stafford Springs; Willington; Ware, Maine) 1936, 1939

Stamford
  (Port Chester; Mt. Vernon, N.Y.) 1881–89, 1892, 1895–1980

Stratford 1937–38

Torrington (see also Winstead)
  1883–1927

Vernon
  (Ellington, Rockville, Tolland) 1974–78

Wallingford 1883–1979, 1986

Waterbury
  (Middlebury, Naugatuck, Terryville, Thomaston, Watertown, Wolcott) 1983

Watertown
  (Middlebury, Thomaston) 1956–59

West Hartford
  (Farmington) 1979

Westport
  (Greens Farms, Saugatuck, Weston, Wilton) 1917–76

Willimantic
  (Coventry, Windham) 1884–1980

Winstead
  (Tarrytown) 1883–1926

Wolcott 1963

County, Business, and Miscellaneous

Connecticut (region)
  pre 1861 (microfiche)

Hartford (city) 1897

Northern Connecticut Valley 1951, 1953, 1961–77

Tolland 1887, 1890

CHAPTER 10

MID-ATLANTIC STATES

New York • New Jersey • Pennsylvania
Maryland • Delaware • District of Columbia

New York

Historical Highlights

1603   Northern part of the area explored by Champlain, from France.

1609   Upper Hudson River explored by Henry Hudson, from the Netherlands.

1624   New Netherlands founded; Fort Orange was (Albany) its chief city.

1625   New Amsterdam (Manhattan) founded.

1665   New Netherlands overthrown by the British. New Amsterdam renamed New York.

After the Dutch surrendered to the overwhelming military superiority of the British, many continued to live peacefully alongside the newly arrived Englishmen, especially along the Hudson and Mohawk Rivers. Joining them were French Huguenots and also Spaniards and Portuguese coming by way of the West Indies.

1776   One of the thirteen original states at the time of the American Revolution.

Although heavily Tory in sympathy, the majority of the New Yorkers fought the British after the Declaration of Independence. Many of the Loyalists moved to Nova Scotia to claim lands offered by the British. New York State was a prime battleground during the early years of the war. When the hostilities ended, the western part of the state was opened for settlement by veterans of New York and its neighboring states who were entitled to bounty lands.

1825   Erie Canal opened.

1890   Ellis Island designated as an immigration station.

Until it was closed in 1954, Ellis Island became the funnel through which millions of European immigrants flowed during the nineteenth and early twentieth century. Among the immigrants were those from Germany, Ireland, France, the Scandinavian countries, and many other countries in central and southern Europe, especially Russia, Poland, and Italy. Many of these immigrants settled in New York, while others migrated westward by way of the Erie Canal and the expanding railroad system.

Published Record Sources

Guidebooks

Breton, Arthur J. *A Guide to the Manuscript Collections of the New York Historical Society.* 2 vols. Westport, Conn.: Greenwood Press, 1972. CD3409 .N5B74.

Volume 1, inventories; volume 2, index.

Clint, Florence. *New York Area Key: A Guide to the Genealogical Records of the State of New York.* Elizabeth, Colo.: Keyline Publishers, 1970. F118 .C55.

French, John H. *Gazetteer of the State of New York.* Port Washington, N.Y.: Ira J. Friedman, Inc., 1960. Reissued, 1969. F117 .F75.

New York. Education Department. *Guide to the Records in the New York State Archives.* Albany: State Archives, 1981. CD3406. N.49.

New York. Secretary of State. *Calendar of Historical Manuscripts: Part I—Dutch Manuscripts, 1630–1665.* Reprint; Ridgewood, New Jersey: Gregg Press, 1965. CD3406 .S8A5.

Place, Frank, comp. *Index of Names in J.H. French's Gazetteer of the State of New York.* Cortland, N.Y.: Cortland County Historical Society, 1983. F117 .F753P55.

Schweitzer, George K. *New York Genealogical Research.* Knoxville, Tenn.: the author, 1988. F118 .S33.

Census Indexes and Abstracts

Federal

1790	F118 .U5 (Heads of Families)
1800	F118 .J28

Armstrong, Barbra K. *Index to the 1800 Census of New York:* Baltimore: Genealogical Publishing Co., 1984. F118 .A76.

McMullin, Phillip W. *New York in 1800: An Index to the Federal Census Schedules of the State of New York.* Provo, Utah: Bendex Corp., 1971. F118 .M17.

1810	F118 .J285
1820	F118 .J29
1830	F118 .J293
1840	F118 .J294
1850	F118 .J3 and F128.25 .J33

All the above publications shown without the name of the compiler (except the 1790 census entitled "Heads of Families") are by Ronald V. Jackson, Accelerated Indexing Systems.

State

Jackson, Ronald V. *Early New York.* Bountiful, Utah: Accelerated Indexing Systems, 1980. F118 .J26.

Meyers, Carol M., comp. *Early New York State Census Records, 1663–1772.* Gardena, Calif.: RAM Publishers, 1965. F118 .M6.

Although not available at the Library of Congress, decennial state censuses were taken in New York, beginning in 1825.

Biographies

Fitch, Charles E. *Encyclopedia of Biography of New York.* 8 vols. New York: American Historical Society, 1916. F118. F539.

Hamm, Margerita A. *Famous Families of New York.* 2 vols. New York: G.P. Putnam's Sons, 1902. F118 .H22.

Harrison, Mitchell C., comp. *New York State's Prominent and Progressive Men.* 2 vols. New York: New York Tribune, 1900. F118 .H32.

Matthews, George E. *The Men of New York.* 3 vols. Buffalo: George E. Matthews & Co., 1898. F118 .M53.

Stafford, Hartwell. *Empire State Notables, 1914.* New York: Hartwell Stafford Publishers, 1914. F118 .E55.

Stoddard, Dwight J. *Notable Men of Central New York; 19th and 20th Century.* N.p.: the author, 1903. F118 .N89.

Who's Who in New York City and State. 13 eds. New York: L.R. Hamersly, 1904–60. F118 .W62.

Worden, Jean D. *The New York Genealogical and Biographical Record: Master Index—113 Years (1870–1982).* Franklin, Ohio: the author, 1983. F116 .N28 supp.

Land Acquisition

Bowman, Fred Q. *Landholders of Northeastern New York, 1739–1802.* Baltimore: Genealogical Publishing Co., 1987. HD211 .N7B68.

New York. Secretary of State. *Calendar of New York Colonial Manuscripts—Land Papers, 1643–1803.* Albany: Weed Parsons, 1864. CD3406 .S8.

Rose, Robert S. *The Military Tract of Central New York.* Syracuse: Syracuse Library, 1933. HD243 .N7R67.

Early Settlers

Cutter, William R. *Genealogical and Family History of Central New York.* 3 vols. New York: Lewis Historical Publishing Co., 1912. F118 .C98.

———. *Genealogical and Family History of Northern New York.* New York: Lewis Historical Publishing Co., 1912. F118 .C99. [Micro 85/5663 (F)].

———. *Genealogical and Family History of Western New York.* 2 vols. New York: Lewis Historical Publishing Co., 1912. F118 .C992.

Hoff, Henry B. *Genealogies of Long Island Families: From the New York Genealogical and Biographical Record.* 2 vols. Baltimore: Genealogical Publishing Co., 1987. F127 .L8G45.

———. *Long Island Source Records: From the New York Genealogical and Biographical Record.* Baltimore: Genealogical Publishing Co., 1987. F187 .L8L925.

Jones, Henry Z., Jr. *The Palatine Families of New York: A Study of the German Immigrants Who Arrived in Colonial New York in 1710.* 2 vols. Universal City, Calif.: the author, 1985. F130 .P2J66.

Kelly, Arthur C. *Settlers and Residents.* Vol. 1, *Germantown, 1710–1899;* Vol. 2, *Clermont, 1735–1875;* Vol. 3, *Livingston, 1790–1875.* Rhinebeck, N.Y.: the author, 1973. F129 .G45K44.

O'Callaghan, Edmund B. *Lists of Inhabitants of Colonial New York.* Baltimore: Genealogical Publishing Co., 1979. F118 .O62.

———. *Register of New Netherland, 1626 to 1674.* Albany: J. Munsell, 1865. F122.1 .O42.

Reynolds, Cuyler, comp. *Genealogical and Family History of Southern New York and the Hudson River Valley.* New York: Lewis Historical Publishing Co., 1914. F118 .R45.

———. *Hudson-Mohawk Genealogical and Family Memoirs.* New York: Lewis Historical Publishing Co., 1911. F118 .R46.

Scott, Kenneth, and Roseann Conway. *New York Alien Residents, 1825–1848.* Baltimore: Genealogical Publishing Co., 1978. F118 .S37.

Scott, Kenneth. *Nineteenth Century Apprentices in New York City.* Arlington, Va.: National Genealogical Society, 1986. F128.25 .S382. (CS42 .N43)

Society of the Daughters of Holland Dames. *First Record Book of the Society of the Daughters of Holland Dames.* New York: the society, 1907. F116 .S67; 1913 ed., F116 .S672. 1933 ed., F116 .S673.

Spencer, Alfred, comp. *Spencer's Roster of Native Sons and Daughters.* Savonna, N.Y.: the author, 1941. F118 .S75.

Stillwell, John E. *Historical and Genealogical Miscellany—Data Relating to the Settlement and Settlers of New York and New Jersey.* 5 vols. Reprint. Baltimore: Genealogical Publishing Co., 1970. F118 .S852.

Local Records

Fernow, Berthold, comp. *Calendar of Wills, 1626–1836.* New York: Colonial Dames of New York, 1896. F118 .F36.

Historical Records Survey (WPA). *Guide to Public Vital Statistics Records in New York State.* Vol. 1, *Birth Records;* Vol. 2, *Marriage Records;* Vol. 3, *Death Records.* Albany: Work Projects Administration, 1942. CD3401 .H5.

———. *Guide to Vital Statistics Records of Churches in New York State.* 2 vols. Albany: Work Projects Administration, 1942. CE3401 .H52.

Hoes, Roswell R. *Baptismal and Marriage Records of the Old Dutch Church of Kingston, Ulster Co., New York, 1660–1809.* Reprint. Baltimore: Genealogical Publishing Co., 1980. F129 .K5K5.

Holland Society of New York. *Records of the Reformed Dutch Church of Albany, New York, 1683–1809; Marriages, Baptisms, Members, etc.* Reprint. Baltimore: Genealogical Publishing Co., 1978. F129 .A353A23.

Purple, Samuel S. *Index to the Marriage Records From 1639 to 1801 of the Reformed Dutch Church in New Amsterdam and New York.* New York: the author, 1890. F128.25 .P98.

New York. *Names of Persons for Whom Marriage Licenses were Issued by the Secretary of State of New York. Previous to 1734.* Albany: Weed, Parsons, 1860. F118 .N48.

New York Historical Society. *Abstracts of Wills. Collections of the New York Historical Society.* 14 vols. New York: the society, 1892–1905. F116 .N63.

Sawyer, Ray C., comp. *Abstracts of Wills for New York County, New York.* 13 vols. Typescript. N.p., n.d. F128.25 .S27.

Covers 1801 to 1840.

———. *Index of Wills of New York County, from 1662 to 1850.* 3 vols. Typescript. N.p.: the author, 1930. F128.25 .S277.

Scott, Kenneth, and Kenn Stryker-Rodda. *Denizens, Naturalizations, and Oaths of Allegiance in Colonial New York.* Baltimore: Genealogical Publishing Co., 1975. F118 .S36.

Scott, Kenneth, comp. *Early New York Naturalizations: Abstracts of Naturalization Records From Federal, State, and Local Courts, 1792–1840.* Baltimore: Genealogical Publishing Co., 1981. F118 .S363.

———. *Genealogical Data From Administration Papers From the New York State Court of Appeals in Albany, Middleton, New York.* National Society, Colonial Dames in New York, 1972. F118 .S3635.

———. *Petitions for Name Changes in New York City, 1848, 1899.* Washington, D.C.: National Genealogical Society, 1984. F128.25 .S383.

Vosburgh, Royden W. "Church Records."

On the open shelves of the Local History and Genealogy Reading Room are more than one hundred oversize volumes containing New York church records abstracted by Vosburgh. They contain records of births, baptisms, confirmations, communicants, marriages, deaths, burials, cemetery inscriptions, and registers of members of a great variety of Protestant churches. Selections of volumes to study may be made by personal inspection, according to name of the church. They are cataloged in the F127 section of the room.

Military Records

American Revolution

Beauchamp, William M. *Revolutionary Soldiers Resident in or Dying in Onondaga County, New York, with Supplementary List of Possible Veterans Based on a Pension List of Franklin H. Chase.* N.p.: Syracuse Publications of the Onondaga Historical Association, 1913. Supps. 1914, 1916, 1922. F127.06 .B375.

Fernow, Berthold, ed. *New York State Archives: New York in the Revolution—Documents Relating to the Colonial History of the State of New York, Vol. 15.* Albany, 1887. Reprint. Cottonport, La.: Polyanthos, 1972. E263 .N6N65.

Greene, Nelson, ed. *The History of the Mohawk Valley.* 4 vols. Chicago: S.J. Clarke Publishing Co., 1925. F127 .M55H6.

Heidgard, Ruth P., ed. *Ulster County in the Revolution: A Guide to Those Who Served.* Ulster County Bicentennial Commission, 1977. F127 .U4U38.

New York. Comptroller's Office. *New York in the Revolution as Colony and State.* 2 vols. Albany: J.B. Lyon & Co., 1904. F263 .N6N442.

New York. Secretary of State. *The Balloting Book and Other Documents Relating to Military Bounty Lands in the State of New York.* Albany: State of New York, 1825. E263 .N6N45.

———. *Calendar of Historical Manuscripts Relating to the War of the Revolution in the Office of the Secretary of State.* 2 vols. Albany: State of New York, 1868. E263 .N6N6.

New York Historical Society. *Muster and Pay Rolls of the War of the Revolution, 1775–1781.* Vols. 1–2. New York: the society, 1916. E255 .N56; F116 .N63.

Whittemore, Henry. *Heroes of the American Revolution and Their Descendants (The Battle of Long Island).* New York: Heroes of the Revolution Publishing Co., 1897. E241 .L8W6.

Wright, Albert H. *The Sullivan Expedition of 1779; The Regimental Rosters of Men.* Typescript. N.p.: the author, 1965. E235 .S72.

———. *The Sullivan Expedition of 1779; The Losses. New York Historical Studies.* Typescript. N.p.: the author, 1965. E235 .W719.

War of 1812

New York. Adjutant General. *Index of Awards. On Claims of the Soldiers of the War of 1812.* Albany: Weed, Parsons, 1860. Reprint. Baltimore: Genealogical Publishing Co., 1969. E359.5 .N6N448.

Civil War

Dilts, Bryan L., comp. *1890 New York Census Index of Civil War Veterans or Their Widows.* Salt Lake City: Index Publishers, 1984. E494 .D583.

New York. Adjutant General. *Annual Reports, 1863, 1864, 1865, 1866.* Albany: Comstock & Cassidy, Printers, 1863. E523 .N56.

Phisterer, Frederick, comp. *Annual Report: New York in the War of the Rebellion, 1861–1865.* 5 vols. and index. 3d ed. Albany: Lyon Co., 1912. E523 .P57. (Micro 83/5712).

Townsend, Thomas S. *Heroes of the Empire State in the War of Rebellion.* New York: Lowell & Co., 1889. E523 .T75.

Spanish-American War

Naval and Military Order of the Spanish-American Wars: New York Roster of Members. N.p., 1904. E714.3 .N3.

New York. Adjutant General. *New York in the Spanish-American War, 1896.* 3 vols. N.p., n.d. E726 .N5N5.

Periodicals

Bowman, Fred Q. *10,000 Vital Records of Central New York, 1813–1850.* Baltimore: Genealogical Publishing Co., 1986. F118 .B68.

Taken from early newspapers.

———. *10,000 Vital Records of Eastern New York, 1777–1834.* Baltimore: Genealogical Publishing Co., 1987. F118 .B694.

Taken from early newspapers.

———. *10,000 Vital Records of Western New York, 1809–1850.* Baltimore: Genealogical Publishing Co., 1985. F118 .B696.

Taken from early newspapers.

Maher, James P., comp. *Index to Marriages and Deaths in the New York Herald, 1825–1855.* Bal-timore: Genealogical Publishing Co., 1987. F118 .M27.

Sawyer, Ray C., comp. *Marriages Published in the Christian Intelligencer of the Reformed Dutch Church From 1830–1871—Brooklyn and Long Island....* Typescript. N.p.: the author, 1933. F127 .L8S3.

Scott, Kenneth, comp. *Remington's New York Newspaper Excerpts From a Loyalist Press, 1773–1783.* Binghamton, N.Y.: New York Historical Society, 1973. F128.44 .S36.

Directories

City

Albany
pre 1861 (microfiche)
1861–1935 (microfilm)
(suburbs, Bath, Rensselaer, Schenectady) 1936–80

Albion 1926

Amityville 1951

Amsterdam
(Ft. Hunter, Ft. Johnson, Hagaman, Minneville, Tribe's Hill) 1883–1903, 1913, 1920–59, 1961–74

Auburn
pre 1861 (microfiche)
(Seneca Falls, Waterloo, Cayuga Co.) 1862–82

Baliston
(Corinth, Schuylerville) 1930

Batavia
(E. Pembroke, Genesee Co.) 1888, 1923–74

Bath
(Avoca, Hammondsport, Kanona, Savona) 1931, 1954–70

Beacon
(Fishkill, Glenham, Landing, Matteawan) 1910–16

Binghamton
pre 1861 (microfiche)
(suburbs) 1869–73, 1889–1967

Bridgewater 1951

Brockport 1967

Bronxville
(Tuckahoe) 1929

Brooklyn
 pre 1861 (microfiche)
 1861–1935 (microfilm)

Buffalo
 pre 1861 (microfiche)
 1935–61 (microfilm)
 (suburbs) 1936–84

Cababdaugya 1911, 1930–32, 1941, 1948

Canandaigua
 (Geneva) 1890

Canton 1948, 1967

Carthage
 (Harrisville, Jayville, Natural Bridge, West Carthage)
  1888, 1904, 1923–33, 1943–67

Caskill
 (Athens, Cairo, Coxsackie, Leeds, S. Cairo) 1930,
  1962–70

Chatham
 (Ghent, Paynville, White Halls) 1894–95

Colonie
 (Bethlehem, Guilderland, Schenectady) 1956–80

Cooperstown
 (Oneanta) 1931

Corinth 1915

Corning 1893, 1897, 1973

Cortland
 (Homer, McGraw) 1891, 1902–73

Dansville
 (Wayland) 1939

De Witt
 (Genesee Hills, Lyndon) 1950

Derry
 (Chester) 1904, 1916, 1933, 1966

Dunkirk
 (Fredonia) 1887–92, 1896–1915, 1925, 1930, 1935–72

East Aurora 1962–78

Elmira
 pre 1861 (microfiche)
 (Elmira Hgts., Horseheads) 1871–1974

Endicott 1936

Fishkill Landing
 (Fishkill, Glenham, Matteawan) 1910

Flatbush 1890

Fleming 1904

Floral Park
 (Bellerose, Stewart Manor) 1937–38

Flushing 1889–90

Freeport 1914, 1923, 1926, 1930

Fulton 1903, 1906–42, 1948–72

Garden City 1937

Geneva
 pre 1861 (microfiche)
 1899, 1907–13, 1921–42, 1945–51, 1955–60, 1967–75

Glen Cove 1923

Glen Falls
 (Ft. Edward, Hudson Falls, S. Glen Falls, Sandy Hill)
  1874, 1879, 1886–93, 1899–1972

Gloversville
 (Johnstown) 1888–1972

Goffstown
 (Candia, Hockset, Pittsfield, Suncook, Weare) 1888

Gouverneur 1948, 1967

Granville
 (Fair Haven; Pawlet; Poultney, Vt.; W. Pawlet; Wells)
  1897, 1912–16, 1921, 1925–31

Great Neck 1937

Greenpoint
 pre 1861 (microfiche)

Haddonfield 1950, 1958, 1961

Hamburg 1956–79

Hawthorne 1923, 1926, 1930, 1937

Herkimer
 (Frankfort, Ilion, Mohawk) 1895, 1904, 1910–16, 1925,
  1929, 1936–83

Holley 1926

Hoosick Falls 1898, 1904–19, 1926–37, 1948, 1953

Hornell
 (Almond, Arkport, Canisteo) 1911, 1914, 1937–53,
  1970, 1974

Hornellsville 1875, 1893, 1896–1904

Hudson
 pre 1861 (microfiche)

1862, 1866, 1870, 1876–1984

Huntington
(E. Northport, Huntington Station, Northport) 1929

Ilion (street directory, map) 1916

Irving 1914

Ithaca 1883–1973

Jamaica 1921

Jamestown 1888, 1897, 1899, 1903, 1920–84

Johnstown 1884, 1889, 1895

Kearney
(East Newark, Harrison, N. Arlington) 1960–71

Kingston
pre 1861 (microfiche)
1864–1979

Lackawanna
(Blasdell, Woodlawn) 1960, 1962

Lime Lake 1961, 1969, 1970

Little Falls
(Herkimer, Ilion, Mohawk) 1886, 1888, 1893, 1897, 1899–1918, 1924, 1928, 1936, 1942, 1947–82

Little Neck
(Douglaston) 1933

Liverpool 1924

Long Island 1865–71, 1874, 1888, 1894, 1913–16

Lowville
(Boonville, Craghan, Constaldeville Copenhagen, Forest Port, Glendale, Holland, Patent, Port Leyden, Prospect, Trenton) 1888, 1890

Lynbrook
(E. Rockaway, Malverne) 1923, 1928, 1939

Lyndonville 1926

Lyons
(Clyde) 1886

Malone 1889, 1904, 1906, 1913, 1919–42, 1947–48, 1956, 1960–61, 1968

Mamaroneck
(Harrison, Larchmont, Rye) 1924, 1930

Manhasset
(Plandome) 1938

Massena
(Canton, Potsdam) 1919, 1924, 1930, 1933, 1941, 1947–71

Mastic Beach
(Long Island) 1940

Mechanicville
(Ballston Spa, Stillwater) 1898, 1903, 1911–30, 1936, 1940, 1949, 1952

Medina
(Lyndonville, Middleport) 1926, 1948, 1953–85

Middletown
pre 1861 (microfiche)
(Goshen, Port Jervis, Wallkill) 1886–87, 1890, 1905–79

Milton
(Brookfield; Sanbornville; Wakefield, N.H.; Lebanon, Maine) 1927, 1933

Mineola
(East Williston, Williston Park) 1938, 1940–41

Moravia Village
(Cayuga Co.) 1904

Mt. Vernon
(North Rochele Village, Pelham) 1888–1931, 1937

New Brunswick
pre 1861 (microfiche)

New Providence
(Berkeley Hgts.) 1955–80

New York City
pre 1861 (microfiche)
1861–1935 (microfilm)

Newark 1919, 1931

Newburgh
(Beacon, Cornwall, Fishkill, Glenham, Marlboro, New Windsor) 1860, 1867–75, 1884–1977

Niagara Falls
(Suspension Bridge) 1886–1942, 1946–85

Northville
(Broadalbin, Mayfield) 1896

Norwich
(Oxford, Sherburne) 1930–38

Nyack
(Grandview, Piermont, Sparkill) 1914, 1916, 1924, 1928, 1931

Ogdensburg
  pre 1861 (microfiche)
  1882, 1890, 1894, 1899–1900, 1926–67

Olean
  (Alleghany, Hinsdale, Portville, Westons Mills) 1897–
    1906, 1911, 1916–84

Oneida
  (Durhanville, Gonastata, Oneida Castle, Sherrill,
    Wampsville) 1886–87, 1894, 1896, 1898, 1902,
    1917–72

Oneonta
  (Cooperstown, Sidney, Unadilla) 1889, 1891, 1899–
    1905, 1927–73

Ossining 1912–14, 1924–30

Oswego
  pre 1861 (microfiche)
  1861–1984

Owasco
  (Cayuga Co.) 1904

Owego 1899, 1926, 1930

Oxford 1935

Peekskill 1889, 1892, 1900–19, 1924–42, 1946–79

Penfield
  (Monroe Co.) 1953, 1957

Penn Yan 1913, 1927, 1930, 1941, 1948, 1951, 1961

Plattsburgh 1886–1972

Port Chester
  (East Port Chester; Greenwich; Rye; Byram, Conn.;
    Cos Cob, Conn.) 1908–26, 1928, 1932, 1950, 1956,
    1959, 1967

Port Jervis
  (Matamorast; Monticello; Milford, Pa.) 1886, 1914,
    1930–38

Port Washington
  (Plandome) 1936

Potsdam 1941, 1948, 1950, 1955, 1958, 1972

Poughkeepsie
  pre 1861 (microfiche)
  (Arlington, Fairview) 1862, 1864, 1870–92, 1897–1980

Princeton
  (Princeton Township) 1890, 1909–42, 1947–82

Queens 1898–1912

Raymond
  (Danville; Fremont; Hamstead; Sandown; Wells,
    Maine) 1935

Richmond Hill
  (Woodhaven) 1922

Ridgewood
  (Fairlawn, Glen Rock, Midland Park) 1927–73

Riverhead 1941

Rochester
  pre 1861 (microfiche)
  1861–1935 (microfilm)
  (suburbs) 1936–85

Rockville Centre
  (Rockaway, Oceanside) 1923, 1926, 1937–43

Rome
  pre 1861 (microfiche)
  1861–62, 1877, 1885–1929, 1936–83

Rutherford
  (Carlstadt, East Rutherford, Kingsland, Lyndhurst,
    Union Township, Wallington, Wood Ridge)
    1909–36, 1946, 1957

Salamanca
  (Killbuck, Little Valley) 1896, 1931, 1941

Saratoga Springs
  (Ballston, Ballston Spa, Corinth, Schuylerville, Vic-
    tory) 1882–97, 1904–12, 1934–74

Saugerties 1928

Schenedectady
  pre 1861 (microfiche)
  (Albany suburbs, Grand Boulevard District, Mis-
    kayana, Rotterdam, Scotia) 1860, 1884–67, 1873,
    1875, 1879, 1883–1968

Scipio 1904

Scotch Plains 1960–62, 1972

Seneca Falls
  (Waterloo) 1906, 1927, 1929, 1935, 1942, 1947, 1954,
    1958, 1961, 1968–76

Sheridan
  (Buffalo, Johnson Co., Sheridan Co.) 1907–45, 1950–
    83

Silver Creek
  (Forestville, Irving) 1939, 1963–67

Sing Sing 1889, 1898

Southampton 1935

Syracuse
  pre 1861 (microfiche)
  1861–1935 (microfilm)
  (suburbs) 1936–83

Tarrytown
  (Ardsley, Dobbs Ferry, Hastings, Irvington, N. Tarry-
    town) 1902–19

Ticonderoga
  (Crown Point, Hague, Port Henry, Schroon Lake)
    1929, 1965

Toms River 1963, 1966

Tonawanda
  (N. Tonawanda) 1887, 1895–83

Tri-City
  (Bethlehem, Brunswick, Colonie, E. Greenbush,
    Guilderland, Glenville, Niskayuna, Rotterdam,
    Schaghticoke) 1926

Troy
  pre 1861 (microfiche)
  1861–1935 (microfilm)
  (Cohoes, Green Island, Waterford, Watervliet) 1936–
    84

Tuckahoe
  (Crestwood, Eastchester) 1963

Tupper Lake 1956, 1967, 1970

Utica
  pre 1861 (microfiche)
  1861–1935 (microfilm)
  1936–84

Valley Stream 1923

Waterford 1884

Waterloo
  (Seneca Falls) 1947

Watertown
  pre 1861 (microfiche)
  1877–84

Waverly
  (Athens, Pa.; Sayre, N.Y.) 1908–42, 1948–53, 1958–65

Wellsville
  (Andover, Belmont, Scio) 1930–33, 1940, 1943, 1948,
    1953, 1956

Westfield
  (Mayville) 1963, 1965

White Plains 1903–67

Williamsburg
  pre 1861 (microfiche)

Yonkers 1885–87, 1900–39

County, Business, and Miscellaneous

Albany
  (Rennsalaer) 1884–91, 1900–01, 1916

Allegany 1916–21

Branton 1912

Bronx (see Manhattan)

Broome 1917

Buffalo 1908

Cayuga 1917

Champlain Valley (see Upper Hudson)

Chautauqua 1918

Columbia 1871

Cortland 1917

Duchess 1867, 1870, 1893

Erie 1924, 1931–41

Flatbush 1950

Franklin (northern) 1926

Fulton 1909

Herkimer (see Otsego)

Jefferson
  (Lewis) 1879, 1887, 1918

Livingston (see also Monroe)
  1868

Long Island 1888

Madison 1917

Manhattan
  (Bronx) 1898–1913, 1918, 1926, 1929

Mercer
  (Middlesex) 1914

Middlesex (see Mercer)

Mohawk Valley 1928, 1930

Monroe
  (Livingston) 1864, 1878, 1880, 1917

Montauk (city) 1917

Morrisania
  pre 1861 (microfiche)

Naugatuck & Derby Railroads (handbook) 1872

New York
  (city) 1861–1980
  (region) pre 1861 (microfiche)
  Central & Hudson River Railway 1889, 1892
  New Haven & Hartford Railway 1890, 1892
  Ontario & Western Railway 1886, 1900–14
  West Shore & Buffalo Railway 1883, 1884
  (*Bullingers's* . . . .) 1892–96, 1904, 1908, 1910

Niagara 1895, 1905–14, 1919–42

Onondaga 1917

Oneida 1878, 1884

Ontario (see also Seneca)
  1879, 1884

Orange 1871, 1883, 1885, 1900

Orleans 1887, 1895, 1911, 1915, 1921, 1926

Oswego 1916–17

Otsego 1872, 1875, 1940
  (Herkimer) 1917

Rensselaer (see Albany)

Rochester (city) 1889–90, 1892–96, 1912

Rome (city) 1881

Schoharie 1890–1900

Seneca
  (Ontario) 1888, 1909

St. Lawrence 1885, 1918

Staten Island (borough) 1882–90, 1921, 1933

Sullivan 1872, 1883

Tompkins 1868

Ulster 1871, 1874, 1885

Upper Hudson
  (Champlain Valley) 1889–1901

Washington 1871

Westchester
  pre 1861 (microfiche)
  1868, 1873, 1878, 1884, 1887, 1915, 1922, 1926

New Jersey

Historical Highlights

1609–23 Netherlanders establish settlements, following explorations by Henry Hudson.

1630s New Englanders move into the area and establish towns. Swedes and Finns also arrive.

After Hudson explored the waterways of present-day New Jersey (then called New Netherlands), Dutch traders came to engage in commercial endeavors. Englishmen who had earlier settled in New England began to move into the area, and Swedes and Finns came from their native lands in large numbers, to the point that they dominated the area.

1664 England overthrew the Netherlanders.

In the face of superior military power, the Dutch surrendered to the British, but they remained as settlers. England established a proprietary form of government under John Berkeley and George Carteret. A decade later, the Dutch briefly regained control of the area, but the following year surrendered again to the British.

1676 New Jersey divided into two parts.

1702 The divisions reunited as one colony.

With the influx of Quakers to the area, West Jersey was separated from East Jersey, the Quakers controlling the western portion. New Jersey was then established as a royal colony, the two divisions reunited as one, with the governor of New York placed in charge of the colony. The first governor of New Jersey, Lewis Morris, was appointed in 1739.

1776 One of the thirteen original states at the time of the American Revolution.

New Jersey was a major battleground during the Revolutionary War, with British troops moving across it toward Philadelphia and then back toward the Atlantic coast, always followed by Washington's army.

Published Record Sources

Guidebooks

Historical Records Survey (WPA). *Guide to Vital Statistics Records in New Jersey.* Vol. 1, *Public Archives.* Newark: State Planning Board, 1941. CD3381 .H5.

Hoelle, Edith. *Genealogical Resources in Southern New Jersey.* Woodbury, N.J.: Gloucester County Historical Society, 1979. Z1313 .H63.

New Jersey Historical Society. *Guide to the Manuscript Collections of the New Jersey Historical Society.* Newark: the society, 1979. Z1313 .N6.

Stevens, Henry, comp. *An Analytical Index to the Colonial Documents of New Jersey in the State Papers Offices of England.* Vol 5. New York: D. Appleton, 1858. F131 .N62.

Whitehead, W.A., ed. *General Index to the Documents Relating to the Colonial History of the State of New Jersey.* Newark: Daily Advertiser Printing House, 1888. F137 .W57.

Census Indexes and Abstracts

Federal

1830 F133 .J33

1840 F133 .J335

1850 F133 .J336
Tanco, Barbrae O., comp. *The 1850 Census Together With Index . . . New Jersey, Including the 1840 List of Revolutionary and Military Pensioners.* Fort Worth, Tex.: Millican Press, 1973. F133 .T36.

All the above publications shown without the name of the compiler are by Ronald V. Jackson, Accelerated Indexing Systems.

State

Jackson, Ronald V. *Early New Jersey.* Bountiful, Utah: Accelerated Indexing Systems, 1980. F133 .J3.

Mortality Schedules

1850 George, Shirley J., and Sandra E. Glenn, comps. *New Jersey 1850 Mortality Schedule Index.* Columbus, N.J.: C & G Genealogical Book Co., 1982. F133 .G46.

Biographies

Armstrong, William C. *Pioneer Families of Northwestern New Jersey.* Lambertville, N.J.: Hunterdon House, 1979. F133 .A745.

Bigelow, Samuel F. *The Biographical Cyclopedia of New Jersey.* New York: National American Society, n.d. F133 .B59.

Biographical, Genealogical, and Descriptive History of the First Congressional District of New Jersey. 2 vols. New York: Lewis Publications, 1900. F133 .B63.

Brown, William H., ed. *Biographical, Genealogical, and Descriptive History of the State of New Jersey.* N.p.: New Jersey Historical Publications Co., 1900. F133 .B88.

Carlevale, Joseph W. *Americans of Italian Descent in New Jersey.* Clifton, N.J.: North Jersey Press, 1950. F145 .I8C3.

Chambers, Theodore F. *The Early Germans of New Jersey—Their History, Churches, and Genealogies.* Baltimore: Genealogical Publishing Co., 1969. F145 .G3C4.

Encyclopedia of the United States. *Encyclopedia of New Jersey.* N.p.: Somerset Publications, 1983. F132 .E52.

Huguenot Society of New Jersey. *Huguenot Ancestors Represented in the Membership of the Huguenot Society of New Jersey.* 2d ed. Bloomfield, N.J.: the society, 1956. F145 .H8H8.

Lee, Francis B., ed. *Genealogical and Memorial History of the State of New Jersey.* 4 vols. New York: Lewis Historical Publishing Co., 1910. F133 .L47.

National Society Colonial Dames of America. *New Jersey. Colonial Civil List, 1667–July 4, 1776.* N.p.: the society, 1985. F133 .N428.

Nelson, William, ed. *Nelson's Biographical Cyclopedia of New Jersey.* 2 vols. New York: Eastern Historical Publishing Society, 1913. F133 .N424.

Ogden, Mary D., ed. *Memorial Cyclopedia of New Jersey.* 3 vols. Newark: Memorial Historical Co., 1915. F133 .M53.

Scannell, J. J., ed. *New Jersey's First Citizens: Biography and Portraits of the Notable Living Men and Women of New Jersey.* 5 vols. Paterson, N.J.: J.J. Scannell, 1917. F133 .S38.

Covers 1917 to 1928.

Starr, Dennis J. *The Italians of New Jersey: A Historical Introduction and Bibliography.* Newark: New Jersey Historical Society, 1985. F145 .I8S72.

Stryker-Rodda, Kenn. *Revolutionary Census of New Jersey.* Cottonport, La.: Polyanthos, 1972. F133 .S77.

A list of ratables (taxpayers) among the inhabitants of New Jersey during the period of the American Revolution.

Wiley, Samuel T., ed. *Biographical and Portrait Cyclopedia of the Third Congressional District of New Jersey, Comprising Middlesex, Monmouth, and Somerset Counties.* Philadelphia: Biographical Publishing Co., 1896. F142 .M6W6.

Wilson, Harold F. *The Jersey Shore: a Social and Economic History of the Counties of Atlantic, Cape May, Monmouth, and Ocean.* Vol. 3, *Family and Personal History.* New York: Lewis Historical Publishing Co., 1953. F142 .A13W5.

Who's Who in New Jersey: A Biographical Dictionary of Leading Living Men and Women of the States of New Jersey, Pennsylvania, Delaware, Maryland, and West Virginia. Vol. 1. Chicago: A.N. Marquis Co., 1939. F133 .W57.

Local Records

Dirnberger, Janet D. *New Jersey Catholic Baptismal Records From 1759–1781.* Seabrook, Tex.: Brambles Publishing Co., 1981. F133 .D57.

Nelson, William. *Church Records in New Jersey.* Paterson: Paterson History Club, 1904. F135 .N42.

Contains records of about 150 or the older churches and meetings of the Friends.

———. *New Jersey Historical Society. Documents Relating to the Colonial History of the State of New Jersey.* Vol. 1, *Calendar of New Jersey Wills, 1670–1730.* Paterson: Press Publishing Co., 1901. F133 .N52.

———. *New Jersey Marriage Records, 1665–1800.* Baltimore: Genealogical Publishing Co., 1967. F137 .N437.

———. *Patents and Deeds, and Other Early Records of New Jersey, 1665–1703.* Baltimore: Genealogical Publishing Co., 1976. F133 .P37.

New Jersey. *Index of Wills, Inventories, etc., in the Office of the Secretary of State Prior to 1901.* 3 vols. N.p., ca. 1913. F133 .N54.

New Jersey. Department of State. *New Jersey Index of Wills.* 3 vols. Vol. 1, *Atlantic to Essex Counties;* Vol. 2, *Gloucester to Monmouth Counties;* Vol. 3, *Morris to Warren Counties.* Baltimore: Genealogical Publishing Co., 1969. F133 .A45.

Smeal, Ron, and Ronald V. Jackson, eds. *Index to New Jersey Wills, 1689–1890—The Testators.* Salt Lake City: Accelerated Indexing Systems, 1979. F133 .S63.

Swedish Lutheran Church. *The Records of the Swedish Lutheran Churches at Raccoon and Penn's Neck, 1713–1786.* Reprint. Woodbury, N.J.: Gloucester County Historical Society. 1982. F145 .S23S84.

Whitehead, William A., ed. *New Jersey Archives,* N.p., n.d. F131 .D63.

This multi-volume set of New Jersey records contains the following types of genealogically important records, as listed by volume shown below.

(Newspaper Extracts)

Vol. 11	1704–39
Vol. 12	1740–50
Vol. 19	1751–55
Vol. 20	1756–61
Vol. 24	1762–65
Vol. 25	1766–67
Vol. 26	1768–69
Vol. 28	1772–73
Vol. 29	1773–75
Vol. 31	1775
Vol. 1	1776–77 (Second Series)

(Abstracts of Wills)

Vol. 34	1771–80
Vol. 35	1781–85
Vol. 36	1786–90
Vol. 37	1791–95
Vol. 38	1796–1800
Vol. 39	1801–05
Vol. 40	1806–09
Vol. 41	1810–13
Vol. 42	1814–17

(Marriage Records)

Vol. 22	1665–1800

Military Records

American Revolution

Campbell, James W. W. *Digest and Revision of Stryker's Officers and Men of New Jersey in the Revolutionary War—For the Use of the Society of the Cincinnati in the State of New Jersey.* New York: Williams Printing Co., 1911. E263 .N5C2.

Detwiler, Frederic C. *War in the Countryside—The Battle and Plunder of the Short Hills, New Jersey, June, 1777.* Plainfield: Interstate Printing Corp., 1977.

Hayward, Elizabeth M. *Soldiers and Patriots of the American Revolution: A List Compiled from Baptist Periodicals at the Shirk Library, Franklin College.* Ridgewood, N.J.: n.p., 1947. CS68 .H325.

Historical Records Survey (WPA). *Gloucester County Series, Revolutionary War Documents.* Newark: New Jersey Historical Records Survey Project, 1941. F142 .G5H5.

Jackson, Ronald V. *Index to Military Men of New Jersey, 1775–1815.* Bountiful, Utah: Accelerated Indexing Systems, 1977. E263 .N5N55.

Stryker, William S., comp. *Official Register of the Officers and Men of New Jersey in the Revolutionary War.* Trenton: Nicholson & Co., 1872. E263 .N5N55.

——. *New Jersey Continental Line in the Virginia Campaign of 1781.* Trenton: Murphy, Printer, 1882. E263 .N5S9.

——. *General Maxwell's Brigade of the New Jersey Continental Line in the Expedition Against the Indians in the Year 1779.* Trenton: W.A. Sharp Printing 1885. E235 .S92.

War of 1812

New Jersey. *Records of Officers and Men in New Jersey in Wars 1791–1815.* Trenton: State of New Jersey, 1909. E359.5 .N4N3.

Civil War

New Jersey. Adjutant General. *Officers and Men in the Civil War, 1861–65.* 2 vols. Trenton: State of New Jersey, 1876. E521.3 .N54.

Periodicals

Stryker-Rodda, Kenn. *Index to the Genealogical Magazine of New Jersey.* 4 vols. Cottonport, La.: Polyanthos, 1873. Reprint. Lambertville, N.J.: Hunterdon House, 1982. F131 .G32 supp.

Volumes 1 and 2, index to volumes 1–30; volumes 3 and 4, index to volumes 31–40.

Directories

City

Ashbury Park
   (Avon, Beach, Belmar, Bradley, Ocean Grove, West Park) 1885, 1890–1966

Atlantic
   (Highlands) 1896–1900

Atlantic City
   (suburbs, Longport, Margate City, Ocean City, S. Atlantic, Ventnor) 1885–1979

Audubon
   (Bettlewood, Oaklyn) 1950

Bayonne 1895–1903, 1951

Beachwood 1924

Belleville
   (Nutley) 1909, 1921, 1972

Bloomfield 1945–51, 1955–57

Breton Woods 1954

Burlington (suburbs) 1926, 1929, 1951

Camden
   pre 1861 (microfiche)
   1869, 1879–1931, 1940–47, 1961–84

Clifton 1956–74

Dover 1961

Edison 1964–71

Elizabeth
   (Hillside, Linden, Plainfield, Rahway, Roselle, Roselle Park, Union) 1866, 1868, 1876, 1879–89, 1897–1981

Englewood
   (Leonia, Tenefly) 1921, 1926, 1930, 1939, 1961

Five Mile Beach
(Anglesea, Holly Beach, North Wildwood, Wildwood, Wildwood Crest) 1907

Freehold
(Red Bank, Keyport) 1889, 1937, 1947–81

Garfield 1949, 1961–79

Gloucester
(Camden Co.) 1886, 1951

Hackensack
(Englewood, Hasbrouck Hgts., Maywood, Teaneck, S. Hackensack, Teterboro) 1879, 1894, 1897, 1912–31, 1940, 1947–55

Haddon Heights
(Barrington) 1950

Harrison
(Arlington, E. Newark, Kearney, N. Arlington) 1893–1901, 1907–58

Irvington 1946–67

Jersey City
pre 1861 (microfiche)
1861–1935 (microfilm)
(Hoboken, Union Hill)

Jersey Shore 1887, 1910, 1930

Lake Hiawatha 1949, 1951

Lakewood 1897, 1908

Lodi 1933

Long Branch
(Elberon, N. Long Branch, Oceanport, S. Long Branch) 1909, 1912, 1930, 1937, 1940, 1946–70

Madison
(Chatham, Chatham Township) 1965–71

Metuchen 1961

Millville
(Cumberland Co.) 1921, 1924, 1928, 1937, 1941–79

Montclair
(Belleville, Bloomfield, Caldwell, Essex Falls, Franklin, Glen Ridge, Vernona) 1893–88, 1908–71

Morrisania
(Tremont) 1871

Morristown
(Dover, Madison, Morris, Plains, Rockaway, Wharton, Morris Township) 1887, 1900–81

New Brunswick
pre 1861 (microfiche)
(Highland Park, Metuchen, Milltown) 1886, 1899, 1917–32, 1937, 1940–82

New Rochelle
(Larchmont, Pelham) 1897, 1900–41, 1947–66

Newark
pre 1861 (microfiche)
1861–1935 (microfilm)
1937–43, 1947, 1951, 1955, 1957, 1964

Newton
(Sussex Co.) 1901, 1904, 1928–82

Ocean City 1894, 1921–28, 1937, 1948, 1964, 1967

Orange
(Essex Co.) 1870, 1877–1902

Oranges, the
(Irvington, Livingston, Maplewood, Rosebud) 1904–80

Passaic
(Clifton, Garfield, Wallington) 1886, 1899, 1903–30, 1937, 1946–66

Paterson
pre 1861 (microfiche)
1861–1935 (microfilm)
(suburbs) 1936–68

Perth Amboy
(Fords, Keasby, Roosevelt, Sewaren, Woodbridge) 1905, 1912–67

Philadelphia 1895

Pitman
(Glassboro) 1951

Plainfield
(Dunellen, Fanwood, N. Plainfield, Scotch Plains, Somerville, Westfield) 1888–89, 1895, 1897, 1904, 1909–76

Pleasantville
(Absecon, Linwood, Northchild, Somers Point) 1966–1968

Pompton Lakes 1928–38

Rahway 1889, 1898, 1904, 1916–33, 1940, 1946–79

Ramsey 1959, 1962

Red Bank
(Fair Haven, Little Silver, River Plaza) 1931, 1936, 1945–80

Salem
(Carney's Point, Elmer, Deepwater, Penns Grove, Quinton, Woodstown) 1923, 1930, 1937, 1941, 1948, 1951, 1961, 1963, 1965

Somerville
(Bound Brook, Finderne, Manville, Raritan) 1928, 1930, 1936, 1940–82

South River 1961

Summit
(Millburn, Springfield) 1898, 1905–76

Trenton
pre 1861 (microfiche)
1866–67, 1870–75, 1881, 1894, 1900–71

Twinboro
(Bergenfield, Dumont, Harrington Beach, Haworth) 1923

Union
(Springfield) 1942–76

Union City 1875, 1929

Vineland
(Landis Township, S. Vineland) 1921, 1924, 1929, 1937, 1941–79

Washington 1967

Wayne 1963–74

West Orange
(Livingston, Roseland) 1956–74

Westfield
(Cranford, Garwood, Kenilworth, Mountainside) 1929, 1931, 1936–79

Wildwood 1992–28, 1937, 1946, 1949, 1954–67

Woodbury 1950

County, Business, and Miscellaneous

Bergen 1885

Camden 1913

Cape May 1889, 1912

Cumberland 1881–1904, 1909, 1913
(Salem) 1905

Erie Railroad (from Patterson) 1912, 1914

Essex (see also Newark)
(Hudson, Union) 1859, 1866, 1869–96

Gloucester (see Salem)

Hudson (see North Hudson and Essex)

Hunterdon
(Somerset) 1914

Monmouth 1896–1904, 1914

Morris 1918

New Jersey (see also South Jersey)
(region) pre 1861 (microfiche)
1866, 1872, 1874, 1878, 1882, 1885, 1900, 1952, 1956–58
northern 1950–61

New Jersey & New York Railroad (Hackensack to Spring Valley) 1911

Newark (city)
(Essex) 1879, 1891–92, 1894, 1898–1900, 1910

North Hudson 1896–98, 1905, 1916, 1922

Princeton (city) 1894

Salem (see also Cumberland)
(Gloucester) 1897–1903

South Jersey 1875, 1949

South Jersey Coast 1913

Union (see Essex and Newark)

Pennsylvania

Historical Highlights

1643   New Sweden founded on the banks of the Delaware River.

1655   New Netherlands takes over New Sweden.

1664   England takes over New Netherlands, renaming it New York.

1681   William Penn received a grant from England, naming the area Pennsylvania.

Because of the crown's indebtedness to William Penn's father, William was given the area to be known as Pennsylvania. Penn issued a call to Europeans who wanted to establish a form of government free of religious persecution. Accepting in large numbers were Quakers from the countries of the British Commonwealth. They settled in and around the newly founded city of Philadelphia (the city of "brotherly love").

1701   A local assembly of elected officials, with legislative powers, was established. Immigrants poured in.

During the 1700s, heavy immigration from Germany helped fill the central part of the state; soon to follow were the Scotch-Irish who helped fill the western part of the state. Both groups later moved down the Shenandoah Valley into Virginia and North Carolina. Several boundary disputes with Maryland, Virginia, and Connecticut made some state connections dubious, making it necessary for present-day genealogists to search for family records in neighboring states as well as Pennsylvania.

1776   Under the commonwealth form of government, Pennsylvania was one of the thirteen original states at the time of the American Revolution.

Published Record Sources

Guidebooks

Clint, Florence. *Pennsylvania Area Key.* Kiowa, Colo: the author, 1977. Z1329 .C57.

In addition to the key for the entire state, there is a separate key for each county. All use the same call number—specify the county desired.

Dructor, Robert M. *Guide to Genealogical Sources at the Pennsylvania State Archives.* Harrisburg: Pennsylvania Historical Museum Commission, 1980. Z1329 .P392.

Gordon, Thomas F. *A Gazetteer of the State of Pennsylvania.* New Orleans: Polyanthos, 1975. F147 .G66.

Heisey, John W. *Handbook for Genealogical Research in Pennsylvania.* Indianapolis: Heritage House, 1985. F148 .H45.

Historical Society of Pennsylvania. Historical Records Survey. *Guide to the Manuscript Collections of the Historical Society of Pennsylvania.* 2d ed. Philadelphia: the society, 1949. Z1329 .H68.

Hoenstine, Floyd C. *Guide to Genealogical and Historical Research in Pennsylvania.* Hollidaysburg, Pa.: the author, 1978. Z1329 .H73.

Schweitzer, George K. *Pennsylvania Genealogical Research.* Knoxville, Tenn.: the author, 1986. F148 .S32.

Schenk, Hiram H. and Esther Schenk. *Encyclopedia of Pennsylvania.* Harrisburg: National Historical Association, 1932. F147 .S56.

Census Indexes and Abstracts

Federal

1790   F148 .U54 (Heads of Families)

1800   F148 .J298
Felldin, Jeanne R., and Gloria K. V. Inman. *Index to the 1800 Census of Pennsylvania.* Baltimore: Genealogical Publishing Co., 1984. F148 .F34.
Stemmons, John D., ed. *Pennsylvania in 1800 . . . .* Salt Lake City: the editor, 1972. F158.4 .S8.

1810   F148 .J3
Ohio Family Historian. *Index to 1810 Census of Pennsylvania.* Cleveland: Micro Photo Division, Bell & Howell, 1966. F148 .05.

1820   F148 .J3

1830   F148 .J32

1840   F148 .J323

1850   F148 .J33

All the above publications shown without the name of the compiler, author, or editor, except the 1790 census entitled "Heads of Families," are by Ronald V. Jackson, Accelerated Indexing Systems.

State

Jackson, Ronald V. *Early Pennsylvania.* Bountiful, Utah: Accelerated Indexing Systems, 1980. F148 .J28.

Mortality Schedules

1870   F148 .J29 (Ronald V. Jackson, Accelerated Indexing)

Biographies

Biographical Album of Provincial Pennsylvanians. 2 vols. Philadelphia: American Biographical Publishing Co., 1888. F148 .B59.

Biographical Encyclopedia of Pennsylvanians in the Nineteenth Century. Philadelphia: Galaxy Publishing, 1874. F148 .B61.

Blanchard, Charles, ed. *Progressive Men of the Commonwealth of Pennsylvania.* 2 Vols. Logansport, Ind.: A.W. Bow, 1900. F148 .B63.

Commemorative Biographical Record, Northeastern Pennsylvania. Chicago: J.H. Beers, 1900. F157 .A18C7.

Godcharles, Frederica A., ed. *Encyclopedia of Pennsylvania Biography. Index to vols. 1–20.* New York: Lewis Historical Publishing Co., 1932. F148 .E58.

Jordan, John W. *Encyclopedia of Pennsylvania Biography.* 31 vols. New York: Lewis Historical Publishing Co., 1914. F148 .E58.

Index in each volume.

Nolan, J. Bennett, ed. *Southeastern Pennsylvania.* 3 vols. Philadelphia: Lewis Historical Publishing co., 1943. F157 .A18N6.

Covers the counties of Berks, Bucks, Chester, Delaware, Montgomery, Philadelphia, Schuylkill.

Williamson, Leland M., et al., eds. *Prominent and Progressive Pennsylvanianers of the Nineteenth Century.* 3 vols. Philadelphia: The Record Publishing Co., 1898. F148 .W73.

Land Acquisition

Egle, William H. *Early Pennsylvania Land Records.* Extracted from *Pennsylvania Archives.* 2d ser. Reprint. Baltimore: Genealogical Publishing Co., 1976. F148 .P43.

———. *Provincial Papers—Warranties of Land, 1730–1898.* Vol. 3. Extracted from *Pennsylvania Archives.* 3d ser. Vol. 26. Harrisburg: State of Pennsylvania, 1897. F149 .P41.

Early Settlers

Brecht, Samuel K., ed. *Genealogical Records of the Schwenkfelder Families.* 2 vols. New York: Rand McNally, 1923. F160 .S2B8.

Egle, William H., ed. *Names of Foreigners: Who Took the Oath of Allegiance to the Province and State of Pennsylvania, 1727–1775.* Extracted from *Pennsylvania Archives.* 2d ser. Vol. 17. Reprint. Baltimore: Genealogical Publishing Co., 1967. F148 .E3.

———. *Pennsylvania Genealogies, Chiefly Scot-Irish and German, 1886 and 1896.* Reprint. Baltimore: Genealogical Publishing Co., 1969. F148 .E32.

———. *Pennsylvania Women in the American Revolution.* Cottonport, La.: Polyanthos, 1972. F148 .E325.

Everyname Index to Egle's Notes and Queries. 1st and 2d ser. 2 vols. Decatur, Ill.: Decatur Genealogical Society, 1982. F146 .N92.

Genealogies of Pennsylvania Families: From the Pennsylvania Genealogical Magazine. 3 vols. Baltimore: Genealogical Publishing Co., 1982. F148 .C457.

Genealogies of Pennsylvania Families: From the Pennsylvania Magazine of History and Biography. Baltimore: Genealogical Publishing Co., 1981. F148 .G46.

Glenn, Thomas A. *Welsh Founders of Pennsylvania.* 2 vols. in 1. Baltimore: Genealogical Publishing Co., 1970. F160 .W4G5.

Harriss, Helen L., comp. *Two Lists of Early Residents in Southwestern Pennsylvania.* List No. 1, *Those Holding Virginia Grants, 1779–1785;* List No. 2, *Signers of a Petition to Form a New State.* Pittsburg: the compiler, 1984. F148 .H37.

Hastings, Charles C., Sr. *Pioneer Settlers of Western Pennsylvania.* San Fernando, Calif.: the author, 1976. F157 .A4H35.

Jordan, John W. *Colonial Revolutionary Families of Pennsylvania.* Multiple vols. Reprint. Baltimore: Genealogical Publishing Co., 1978. F148 .C72.

Krebs, Freidrich, and Milton Rubincam. *Emigrants From the Palatinate to the American Colonies in the Eighteenth Century.* Norristown: Pennsylvania German Society, 1953. F160 .P2K5.

Myers, Albert C. *Immigration of the Irish Quakers into Pennsylvania, 1682–1750.* Reprint. Baltimore: Genealogical Publishing Co., 1969. F152 .M98.

McCracken, George E. *The Welcome Claimants Proved, Disproved, and Doubtful.* Philadelphia: Welcome Society of Pennsylvania. Reprint. Baltimore: Genealogical Publishing Co., 1970. F148 .W43.

Pennsylvania-German Immigrants, 1709–1786. From Yearbooks of the Pennsylvania German Folklore Society. Baltimore: Genealogical Publishing Co., 1980. F160 .G3P43.

South Central Pennsylvania Genealogical Society. Ancestral Charts. 2 vols. York, Pa.: the society, 1977. F148 .A63. Index, 1977. CS47 .S66.

Local Records

Crumrine, Boyd. *Virginia Court Records in Southwestern Pennsylvania, 1775–1780.* Baltimore: Genealogical Publishing Co., 1974. KFV2915 .A72.

Duer, Clara E., comp. *Pittsburgh Gazette Abstracts, 1797–1803.* Apollo, Pa.: Closson Press, 1986. F159 .P653A22.

Egle, William, H., ed. *Returns of Taxables For the Counties of Alleheny, Bedford, Fayette, Huntington, Washington, Westmoreland; and census of Bedford (1784); Westmoreland (1783); Harrisburg (1897).* Extracted from *Pennsylvania Archives—Provincial Papers.* 3d ser. N.p.: State of Pennsylvania, n.d. F153 .E373.

Goshenhoppen Registers (Berks Co.), 1741–1819. Records of the Catholic Historical Society Philadelphia. Reprint; Baltimore: Genealogical Publishing Co., 1984. F159 .B16G67.

Hazard, Samuel, ed. *General Index to the Colonial Records (16 vols.) and Pennsylvania Archives (12 vols.).* Philadelphia: State of Pennsylvania, 1860. Reprint. New York: AMS Press, 1976. F146 .C622G96.

Hocker, Edward W. *Genealogical Data Relating to German Settlers of Pennsylvania and Adjacent Territory.* Baltimore: Genealogical Publishing Co., 1980. F160 .G3H6.

Extracted from newspaper items.

Irish, Donna R., comp. *Pennsylvania German Marriages.* Baltimore: Genealogical Publishing Co., 1982. F160 G3174.

Pennsylvania Chapter. Palatines to America. *Pennsylvania German Tombstone Inscriptions.* 2 vols. Harrisburg: Oscar H. Stroh, 1980. F160 .G3S87.

Pennsylvania German Church Records: From the Pennsylvania-German Society Proceedings and Addresses. 3 vols. Baltimore: Genealogical Publishing Co., 1983. F160 .G3P427.

Pennsylvania Marriages Prior to 1790. Extracted from *Pennsylvania Archives.* 2d ser. Vol. 2. Reprint. Baltimore: Genealogical Publishing Co., 1968. F148 .P45.

Philadelphia Mayor. *Record of Indentures, 1771–1773. Excerpted From Pennsylvania-German Society Proceedings and Addresses, 1905.* Reprint. Baltimore: Genealogical Publishing Co., 1973. F148 .P55.

Pennsylvania Vital Records: From the Pennsylvania Genealogical Magazine and the Pennsylvania Magazine of History and Biography. 3 vols. Baltimore: Genealogical Publishing Co., 1983. F148 .P48.

Scott, Kenneth. *Abstracts From Ben Franklin's Pennsylvania Gazette, 1728–1748.* Baltimore: Genealogical Publishing Co., 1975. F148 .S36.

Scott, Kenneth, comp. *Abstracts (Mainly Deaths) From the Pennsylvania Gazette, 1775–1783.* Baltimore: Genealogical Publishing Co., 1976. F148 .A27.

Scott, Kenneth, and Janet R. Clarke. *Abstracts From the Pennsylvania Gazette, 1775–1783.* Baltimore: Genealogical Publishing Co., 1977. F152 .S36.

Scott, Kenneth, and Kenn Stryker-Rodda. *Buried Genealogical Data (undelivered letters), 1748–1780.* Baltimore: Genealogical Publishing Co., 1977. F148 .S37.

Stover, Johann C. *Early Lutheran Baptisms and Marriages in Southeastern Pennsylvania, 1730–1779.* Baltimore: Genealogical Publishing Co., 1982. F148 .S87.

Westcott, Thomason. *Names of Persons Who Took the Oath of Allegiance to Pennsylvania, 1777–1789.* Philadelphia: John Campbell, 1915. F153 .W52.

Pennsylvania Archives

This monumental work consists of one series of colonial records, and nine series of state records published under different editors between 1852 and 1914. A complete set is available on microfiche (MP5263). Ask a reference librarian where it may be obtained. Most, or all, of the 138 bound volumes are located on an open shelf or may be obtained by submitting a call slip. It is often difficult to find a particular list of persons in these volumes because of the complex indexing system it employs. For a complete description of this work see the pamphlet named below, available at the Library of Congress:

Western Pennsylvania Genealogical Society—Special Publication No. 1. Use of the Published Pennsylvania Archives in Genealogical Research. Pittsburgh: the society, 1978. Z1329 .M67.

A helpful pamphlet describing this work, published by the State Library of Pennsylvania, may also be purchased at a nominal cost by writing to the Pennsylvania Bureau of Publication, Harrisburg, Pennsylvania. Ask for *Guide to the Published Archives of Pennsylvania.*

For ready reference, the following guide to the indexes is presented below.

Colonial Records
See the "General Index" to the Colonial Records and Pennsylvania Archives.
First series
(Same as above—beginning at p. 437.)
Second series
Vols. 1–7: Indexes at end of each volume.
Vols. 8–11: No index (use table of contents).
Vol. 12: Index at end of the volume.
Third series
Vol. 27 has a general index. Each of the other volumes has its own index.
Fourth series
Vol. 12 of this series, beginning at p. 643.
Fifth series
Vol. 15 of the sixth series—indexes the fifth series.
Sixth series
All five volumes of the seventh series—indexes the sixth series.
Seventh series
Composed entirely of the index to the sixth series.
Eighth series
No index. However, the Pennsylvania State Library has a manuscript index.
Ninth series
No index. However, the Pennsylvania Division, State Archives has a card index.

Military Records

General

Montgomery, Thomas L., ed. *Military Abstracts From Executive Minutes, Vol. 1–9, 1790–1817.* Ex-

tracted from *Pennsylvania Archives,* 6th ser. Vol. 4. Harrisburg: State of Pennsylvania, 1907. F153 .M62.

———. *Militia Rolls, 1783–1790.* Extracted from *Pennsylvania Archives.* 6th ser. vol. 3. Harrisburg: 1907. F153 .M84.

———. *Muster and Pay Rolls—Pennsylvania Militia, 1790–1800.* Extracted from *Pennsylvania Archives.* 8th ser. Vol. 2. Harrisburg: State of Pennsylvania, 1907. F153 .M98.

Trussel, John B., Jr., ed. *United States Army Military History Research Collection. Special Bibliographic Series, No. 10. Pennsylvania Military History, 1975.* Carlisle Barracks, U.S. Army. Z1329 .T78.

American Revolution

Closson, Bob. *A Census of Pensioners for Revolutionary or Military Services.* Apollo, Pa.: the author, 1978. E263 .P4C58.

The cover title of this volume is *1840 Census of Pennsylvania Pensioners for Revolutionary or Military Service.*

Egle, Wiliam H., ed. *State of the Accounts of the County Lieutenants During the War of the Revolution, 1777–1789.* 3 vols. Extracted from *Pennsylvania Archives,* 3rd ser. vol. 2. Harrisburg: State of Pennsylvania, 1896. F153 .P407.

"Pennsylvania Archives." (see above for complete description).

Records of muster rolls, pay rolls, accounts, militia lists, pensions, land warrants, land donations, and depreciation pay will be found in series two, three, five, and six.

War of 1812

Muster Rolls of the Pennsylvania Volunteers in the War of 1812–14. Extracted from *Pennsylvania Archives.* 2d ser. Vol. 12. Baltimore: Genealogical Publishing Co., 1967. E3595 .P3M8.

Civil War

Bates, Samuel P. *History of the Pennsylvania Volunteers, 1861–1863.* 5 vols. Harrisburg: State of Pennsylvania. Vols. 3–5, E527 .B32. Vols. 1 and 2, M21489.

Pennsylvania Adjutant General. *Annual Reports, 1863, 1864, 1865, 1866.* 4 vols. Harrisburg: State of Pennsylvania, 1863–67. E527.2 .P42.

Pennsylvania. Executive Office, Military Department. *Roster of Commissions Issued to Officers of Pennsylvania Volunteers, 1864–65.* Harrisburg: State of Pennsylvania, 1866. E527.2 .P45.

Spanish-American War

Hoenstine, Floyd G. *Military Services and Genealogical Records of Soldiers of Blair County, Pennsylvania.* Hollidaysburg, Pa.: n.p., 1940. F157 .B5H6.

Periodicals

Fryer, Judith E. *Twenty-five Year Index to Pennsylvania Folklore including The Pennsylvania Dutchman and The Dutchman.* 25 vols. Collegeville, Pa.: the society, 1980. F146 .P2227 supplement.

These bound volumes are available in the Archive of Folklife (LJ .G152) and cover the years 1949 to 1975.

See above under "Early Settlers" for other abstracts and indexes to various Pennsylvania periodicals and old newspapers.

Directories

City

Albion 1916

Allentown
(suburbs, Lehigh Co.) 1886, 1889–93, 1899, 1904, 1930–84

Altoona
(Allegheny Township, Blair, Duncansville, E. Altoona, Eldorado, Ft. Fetter, Frankstown, Greenwood, Harrisburg, Hollidaysburg, Juniata, Lakemont, Logan Township, Sylvan Hill) 1930, 1937–41, 1970–80

Ambridge
(Aliquippa, Avalon, Baden, Bellevue, Ben Avon, Edgeworth, Fair Oaks, Glen Osborne, Glenfield, Haysville, Leetsdale, Sewickley, Woodlawn) 1925

Athens
(Sayre; Waverly, N.Y.) 1897, 1903, 1905

Bangor
(Pen Argyl, Roseto) 1947

Beaver Valley
(Beaver Falls, Freedom, Monaca, Rochester, W. Bridgewater) 1910–16, 1922–39, 1947, 1964–66

Bethlehem (suburbs) 1928, 1929, 1934–84

Bellefonte
(State College) 1943, 1947

Boyertown
(Engelsville, Gabelsville, Gilbertsville, Greshville, Marysville, New Berlinville) 1933, 1940

Braddock
(N. Braddock, Rankin) 1896–1906, 1911–13, 1922, 1926

Bradford 1879, 1885–99, 1913–15, 1948

Bristol (suburbs) 1929–51

Brookville 1917–28

Butler 1892, 1896, 1903–18, 1925–84

Canonsburg
(Houston, Strabane) 1938, 1947, 1961, 1964

Carbondale 1895–1984

Carlisle 1924–42, 1946–85

Carnegie (suburbs) 1907–38

Chambersburg
(Franklin Co.) 1918, 1936, 1947, 1949, 1985

Charleroi 1900, 1943

Chester
pre 1861 (microfiche)
(suburbs) 1904, 1917–59

Clarion
(New Bethlehem) 1963

Clearfield 1915–38, 1953–81

Coatesville 1908, 1923, 1930, 1942, 1947, 1961, 1967, 1971

Columbia 1899, 1926, 1930, 1943, 1960, 1965

Connellsville
(S. Connellsville, Scottdale, Uniontown) 1912–80

Conshohocken 1964

Corry
(Union City) 1910–16, 1961–80

Cumberland Valley
(Carlisle; Chambersburg; Hagerstown, Md.) 1882, 1887, 1890

Doylestown 1908, 1969

Dubois
(Falls Creek, Reynoldsville) 1900–81

Easton
(Bethlehem, Phillipsburg, S. Easton) 1883, 1884, 1887, 1889, 1893, 1894, 1906–82

Ellwood
(Ellport, Frisco) 1937, 1971, 1975

Erie
pre 1861 (microfiche)
1861–1935 (microfilm)
1936–81

Franklin
(Oil City) 1925, 1930–81

Freeland 1928

Gettysburg 1960

Greensburg
(suburbs, Irwin, Jeanette, Latrobe) 1899, 1905–23, 1927–33, 1938–80

Greenville 1899, 1912, 1922–81

Grove City 1905, 1924, 1928, 1931, 1935, 1939–81

Hanover
(McSherreystown, Midway) 1923–83

Harrisburg
pre 1861 (microfiche)
1861–1935 (microfilm)
1936–84

Hazleton
(Freeland, Hazleton Hgts., W. Hazleton) 1886, 1895–1901, 1914–29, 1935, 1937, 1942, 1948–82

Hollidaysburg 1908–21, 1925–41, 1945

Homestead 1908–21, 1925–41, 1945

Honesdale
(Hawley, White Mills) 1931, 1941

Huntingdon
(Mt. Union, Smithfield) 1888, 1891, 1911, 1931, 1948, 1963, 1965, 1968

Indiana 1930–42, 1947, 1963, 1967

Jeanette (suburbs) 1928, 1940, 1948

Jenkintown District
(Ashbourne, Elkins Park, Glenside, Melrose Park, Ogonta, Wyncote) 1907, 1911

Johnstown (suburbs) 1887–1932, 1937–81

Kane 1912–24, 1928, 1940, 1948

Kittanning
(Ford City) 1904–26, 1931, 1935, 1939, 1947–52, 1961–82

Lancaster
pre 1861 (microfiche)
1857, 1888, 1894–1981

Lansdale
(Hatfield, N. Wales) 1967

Latrobe 1923, 1940, 1947, 1949, 1961, 1968–73

Lebanan City (suburbs) 1889, 1891, 1895, 1899, 1905–83

Lewiston
(Burnham, Yeagertown) 1929, 1934–39

Lock Haven
(Bellefonte, Castanea, Dunnstown, Flemington, Mill Hall, Woolrich) 1874, 1931, 1941–42, 1948, 1960, 1967, 1970, 1975

Mahoney 1899

McKee's Rock 1915

McKeesport
(Dravosburg; Duquesne; Versailles; areas of Md., Pa., and W.V.) 1893–1929, 1935, 1939, 1941, 1944–70

Meadville
(Fredericksburg, Kerrtown) 1891, 1905, 1907, 1912–15, 1928, 1936–37, 1949–80

Media 1915

Millcreek Township
(Eire Co.) 1957–76

Milton
(New Columbia, West Milton, Watsontown) 1913, 1930, 1933, 1967

Monessen
(Belle Vernon, Charleroi, Donora) 1924

Monongahela 1911, 1914, 1920, 1923, 1926, 1929, 1938, 1943

Monongahela Valley
pre 1861 (microfiche)

Nanticoke 1910, 1919, 1923

Nazareth 1927, 1946

New Kensington
(Appolo, Arnold, Brackenridge, Cheswick, Creighton, Freeport, Glassmere, Kinloch, Leechburg, Logan's Ferry, Natrona, Oakmount, Parnassus, Springdale, Tarentum, Vandergrift, Vernon) 1911, 1915, 1927, 1940, 1946–65

Norristown
pre 1861 (microfiche)
(Bridgeport, Jeffersonville, Pottstown) 1874, 1884, 1888–1978

Oil City
(Emlenton, Franklin, Reno, Rouseville, Titusville, Venango Co.) 1887, 1900, 1906, 1914, 1916, 1925–30, 1936–80

Philadelphia
pre 1861 (microfiche)
1861–1935 (microfilm)

Phoenixville
(Royersford, Spring City) 1924, 1960–86

Pittsburgh
pre 1861 (microfiche)
1861–1935 (microfilm)
(Allegheny) 1936–73

Pittstown
(Carbondale, W. Pittstown) 1887–96, 1905–27, 1948

Plymouth
(Nanticoke) 1887, 1889, 1891, 1902, 1911

Pottstown
(Kenilworth, Saratoga, South Pottstown, Stowe) 1930, 1934–43, 1948–84

Pottsville
(Mechanicsville, Mt. Carbon, Palo Alto, Schuylkill Co.) 1886, 1871, 1873, 1877, 1887–1941, 1944–85

Punxsutawney 1910, 1915–18, 1924, 1942, 1947, 1951, 1967, 1977

Quakertown
(Milford Square, Richlandtown, Spinnertown, Trumbauersville) 1968, 1975

Reading
pre 1861 (microfiche)
1861–1935 (microfilm)
(Mt. Penn, Pennside, West Reading) 1936–85

Reynoldton 1889

Ridgeway 1911–31, 1948, 1958

Sayre
(Athens; Waverly, N.Y.; S. Waverly) 1967–70

Scranton
pre 1861 (microfiche)
1861–1901 (microfilm)
(Dunmore, suburbs) 1902–84

Shenandoah 1931

Shippensburg 1947, 1986

Somerset 1964, 1966–67, 1971–72, 1975, 1977

Souderton 1967

St. Mary's 1920, 1923, 1927

State College
(Bellefonte) 1943, 1947, 1950, 1969, 1971, 1976

Stroudsburg
(E. Stroudsburg) 1929, 1931, 1933, 1941

Sunbury 1909

Swarthmore 1924–25, 1936

Tarentum
(Brackenridge, Natrona) 1930

Titusville
(Hydetown, Pleasantville) 1866, 1889, 1906–16, 1941, 1961–81

Towanda 1980

Tyrone
(Bellwood, Tipton) 1911, 1932, 1947, 1961, 1966

Uniontown
(Brownsville, Connellsville, Fairchance, Hopwood, Masontown, Smithfield) 1903–11, 1923–81

Vandergrift
(Appolo, Leechburg) 1930, 1940, 1947–52

Warren (suburbs) 1901, 1903, 1926–84

Washington
(Canonsburg, Shannopin, Shousetown) 1886, 1889, 1897, 1903–80

Waynesboro 1912, 1922, 1926–30, 1938, 1947, 1951, 1958–66

Wellsboro 1942

West Chester
pre 1861 (microfiche)
1857, 1879, 1923–42, 1968

West Shore
(Camp Hill, Enola, Harrisburg suburbs, Lemoyne, New Cumberland, Shiremanstown, West Fairview, Wormleysburg) 1934, 1954–84

Wilkensburg
  (Edgewood, Swissvale) 1922, 1926, 1939

Wilkes-Barre 1871–83

Williamsport
  (Duboistown, Montoursville, S. Williamsport) 1869,
    1871, 1873–1982

York
  (suburbs, York Co.) 1883, 1887, 1894, 1898–1919,
    1923–84

County, Business, and Miscellaneous

Adams 1915

Allegheny Valley (region) 1918

Altoona
  (Blair, Clearfield) 1873, 1978

Bath (city) 1950

Berks 1908–18, 1953, 1957

Blair (see Altoona)

Bucks 1884, 1910, 1914, 1936, 1952, 1983

Butler 1916

Chester 1884–90, 1896–1903

Clarion 1892

Clearfield (see Altoona)

Crawford 1871, 1874

Cumberland 1914

Dauphine 1915–62

Delaware
  1897, 1899, 1914
  (Lackawana & Western R.R.) 1912

Erie (see also Northeast Erie)
  pre 1861 (microfiche)
  1907–18

Genessee
  (Orlean, Wyoming) 1893

Lackawanna
  (Luzerne) 1899, 1912, 1914

Lancaster 1859, 1869, 1884, 1909, 1912, 1914, 1916, 1921

Lawrence 1914

Lebanon (includes census) 1880

Lehigh 1914, 1953

Luzerne (see Lackawanna)

Main Line Directory (Penn R.R.)
  (Overbrook to Paoli) 1901

Mercer 1898, 1914, 1962–68

Montgomery 1900, 1913–14, 1949

Northampton 1914

Northeast
  (Erie) 1916

Orleans (see Genesee)

Pennsylvania (state)
  pre 1861 (microfiche)
  1868, 1873, 1887, 1890–92, 1901, 1903–04

Philadelphia (city) 1838, 1844–1952

Pittsburgh (city) 1888, 1892, 1895–96

Reading (city) 1900, 1902

Shenango Valley (see Mahoning, Oh.)

Tioga 1899

Warren 1904–18, 1924

Washington 1901

Wyoming (see Genessee)

York 1915

Maryland

Historical Highlights

1631   Kent Island settled—causing a dispute over
        its ownership between Maryland and Vir-
        ginia.

1634   St. Mary's City established on the Potomac
        River; Cecil Calvert, recipient of a royal
        grant from England, acted as the proprietor.

1689   Established as a royal colony; presided over
        by a royal governor.

1794   Capital moved from St. Mary's City to An-
        napolis.

1714   Royal grant revoked and proprietary government reinstated under Charles Calvert.

Maryland, although known for its policy of religious freedom, was beset with numerous struggles between Protestant and Catholic faiths. In 1689, coincidental with the state becoming a royal colony, the Protestants overthrew the Catholic leaders. A few years later, the heavily Catholic St. Mary's City lost out to Protestant dominated Annapolis as the site for the state's capitol. When Charles Calvert, a Catholic, converted to Protestantism, he was given the proprietorship of the state.

Protestants who settled in the state were Quakers, Methodists, Lutherans, Presbyterians, Baptists, and Dutch Reformed. It has also been settled by Germans and Scotch-Irish who first came to Pennsylvania. Until the mountainous western part was developed, the state was largely agricultural with extensive slave holdings.

1769   The Mason Dixon line established the location of the border between Maryland and Pennsylvania.

1776   One of the thirteen original states at the time of the American Revolution.

1863   Although strongly sympathetic with the Confederacy, remained in the Union during the Civil War.

Published Record Sources

Guidebooks

Cox, Richard J., and Larry E. Sullivan, eds. *Guide to the Research Collections of the Maryland Historical Society.* Baltimore: Genealogical Publishing Co., 1981. Z1213 .M4.

Enoch Pratt Free Library. Susan R. Woodcock, ed. *The Eastern Shore of Maryland: An Annotated Bibliography.* Queenstown, Md.: Queen Anne Press, 1980. Z1294 .E18W66.

Kaminkow, Marion J. *Maryland A to Z: A Topographical Dictionary.* Baltimore: Magna Carta Books, 1985. F179 .K36.

Kenny, Hamill. *Place Names of Maryland, Their Origins and Meaning.* Baltimore: Maryland Historical Society, 1984. F179 .K46.

Maryland Hall of Records Commission. *Catalog of Archival Material, Hall of Records.* Annapolis: State of Md., 1942. CD5280 .A16.

Maryland Hall of Records Commission. *A Guide to the Maryland Hall of Records: Local, Judicial, and Administrative Records on Microfilm.* Annapolis: State of Md., 1978. CD3284 .P36.

Maryland Hall of Records Commission. *An Inventory of Maryland State Papers.* Vol. 1, *The Era of the American Revolution, 1775–1789.* Annapolis: State of Md., 1977. CD3284 .I58.

Maryland Hall of Records Commission. *Maryland State Papers.* No. 1, *The Black Book.* Annapolis: State of Md., 1943. CD3280 .A16.

McCay, Betty L., comp. *Sources for Genealogical Searching in Maryland.* Indianapolis: the compiler, 1972. CD3281 .M3.

Meyer, Mary K. *Genealogical Research in Maryland: A Guide.* 3d ed. Baltimore: Maryland Historical Society, 1983. Z1293 .M485.

Passano, Eleanor P. *An Index of the Source Records of Maryland, Genealogical, Biographical, and Historical.* Baltimore: Genealogical Publishing Co., 1967. Z1392 .P3.

Census Indexes and Abstracts

Federal

1790   F180 .U54 (Heads of Families)

1800   F180 .J32
        Volkel, Charlotte A., and Timothy Q. Wilson, comps. *An Index to the 1800 Federal Census of Allegheny, Anne Arundel, Calvert Counties, and the City of Baltimore, State of Maryland.* Danville, Ill.: the compilers, 1968. F180 .V62.
        ———. *An Index to the 1800 Federal Census of Caroline, Cecil, Charles, Frederick and Kent Counties, State of Maryland.* Danville, Ill.: the compilers, 1968. F180 .V63.
        ———. *An Index to the 1800 Federal Census of Dorchester, Harford, Montgomery, Prince Georges, and Queen Anne Counties, State of Maryland.* Danville, Ill.: the compilers, 1968. F180 .V64.

————. *An Index to the 1800 Federal Census of Saint Mary's, Somerset, Washington, and Worchester Counties, State of Maryland.* Danville, Ill.: the compilers, 1968. F180 .V66.

1810   F180 .J32

1820   F180 .J325
        Parks, Gary W., comp. *Index to the 1820 Census of Maryland and Washington, D.C.* Baltimore: Genealogical Publishing Co., 1986. F182 .P37.

1830   F180 .J327

1840   F180 .J33

1850   F180 .J333

All the above publications shown without the name of the compiler except the 1790 census entitled "Heads of Families" are by Ronald V. Jackson, Accelerated Indexing Systems.

State

Carothers, Bettie S., comp. *1776 Census of Maryland.* Lutherville, Md.: the author, 1977. F180 .C355.

Jackson, Ronald V., ed. *Early Maryland.* Bountiful, Utah: Accelerated Indexing Systems, 1980. F180 .J3.

Biographies

Andrusko, Samuel M., comp. *Maryland Biographical Sketch Index.* Vol. 1, *An Index to Over 10,500 Biographical Sketches Contained in Thirty-three Maryland Local Histories.* New York: the compiler, 1983. Z1293 .A65.

Distinguished Men of Baltimore and Maryland. Baltimore: Baltimore American Publishers, 1914. F189 .B18202.

Luckett, Margie H., ed. *Maryland Women.* Baltimore: the author, 1931. F180 .L93.

Steiner, Bernard C. *Men of Mark in Maryland.* 3 vols. Washington, D.C.: Johnson-Wynne Co., 1907. F180 .M53.

Who's Who in Maryland, 1939. Chicago: A.N. Marquis, 1939. F180 .W56.

Land Acquisition

Burns, Annie W. *Maryland Early Settlers: Land Records, etc.* 14 vols. Annapolis: the author, 1936. F180 .B46.

Carothers, Bettie S., comp. *Maryland Soldiers Entitled to Lands West of Fort Cumberland.* Lutherville, Md.: the author, 1973. E263 .M3C37.

Early Settlers

Carothers, Bettie S., comp. *Maryland Slave Owners and Superintendents, 1798.* Lutherville, Md.: the author, 1974–75. F180 .C367.

————. *Maryland Oaths of Fidelity.* 2 vols. Lutherville, Md.: the author, 1980. F180 .C36.

Clark, Raymond F., Jr., and Donald O. Pinder, comps. *Maryland Genealogies.* St. Michael's, Md.: the compilers, 1984. Z1293 .V57.

Leonard, R. Bernice. *Bound to Serve: The Indentured Children in Talbot County, Maryland, 1794–1820.* St. Michael's, Md.: n.p., 1983. F187 .T2L46.

Maryland Genealogies: A Consolidation of Articles from the Maryland Historical Magazine. 2 vols. Baltimore: Genealogical Publishing Co., 1980. F180 .M335.

O'Rourke, Timothy J., comp. *Catholic Families of Southern Maryland: Records of Catholic Residents of St. Mary's County in the Eighteenth Century.* Baltimore: Genealogical Publishing Co., 1985. F187 .S2075.

Parran, Alice M. *Register of Maryland's Heraldic Families.* Baltimore: H.G. Roebuch & Sons, 1935. F180 .P36.

Local Records

Arps, Walter E. *Maryland Mortalities, 1876–1915: From the Baltimore Sun Almanac.* Silver Spring, Md.: Family Line Publications, 1983. F180 .A77.

Baldwin, Jane, comp. *The Maryland Calendar of Wills. 1635–1743.* 8 vols. Baltimore: Dulany Co., 1901. F180 .C853.

Volume 1, 1635–85; volume 2, 1685–1702; volume 3, 1705–1713; volume 4, 1713–1720; volume 5, 1720–1726; volume 7, 1732–1738; volume 8, 1738–1743.

Barnes, Robert W., comp. *Gleanings From Maryland Newspapers, 1727–1775.* Lutherville, Md.: Bettie Carothers, 1976. F180 .B36.

———. *Maryland Marriages, 1634–1777.* Baltimore: Genealogical Publishing Co., 1975. F180 .B38.

———. *Maryland Marriages, 1778–1800.* Baltimore: Genealogical Publishing Co., 1978. F180 .B383.

———. *Marriages and Deaths From the Maryland Gazette, 1727–1839.* Baltimore: Genealogical Publishing Co., 1973. F180 .B37.

Bell, Annie W. Burns. *Maryland Colonial Statistics and Indices, Maryland Record of Deaths, 1718–1777, Part One.* Annapolis: the author, 1936. F180 .B485.

———. *Maryland Colonial Statistics and Indices, Maryland Rent Rolls.* 2 vols. Annapolis: the author, 1939. A180 .B483.

———. *Maryland Colonial Statistics and Indices, Maryland Will Book, 1686–1744.* Vols. 24–38. Annapolis: the author, 1938. F180 .B485.

Burns, Annie W. *Maryland Colonial Statistics and Indices, Maryland Indices to Testamentary Proceedings, Probate of Wills, and Administration of Estates.* 26 vols. Annapolis: the author, 1938. F180 .B455.

———. *Maryland Colonial Statistics and Indices, Maryland Marriage Records.* 39 vols. Annapolis: the author, 1938. F180 .B47.

———. *Maryland Index to Inventories, 1745 to 1762.* Annapolis: the author, n.d. F180 .B465.

Brown, Helen W. *Index of Marriage Licenses, Prince Georges County, Maryland, 1777–1886.* N.p., 1971. F180 .B87.

Brumbaugh, Gaius M. *Maryland Records: Colonial, Revolutionary, County, and Church: From Original Sources.* 3 vols. Baltimore: Williams & Wilking, 1915. F180 .B89.

Magruder, James M., Jr. *Magruder's Maryland Colonial Abstracts—Wills, Accounts and Inventories.* 5 vols. Annapolis: the author, 1934. F180 .M26.

———. *Index of Maryland Colonial Wills, Annapolis: 1634–1777.* 3 vols. Annapolis: the author, 1933. F180 .M23.

Maryland Hall of Records Commission. *Publication No. 14. Quaker Records in Maryland.* Annapolis: State of Md.: 1966. CD3280 .A16.

Maryland Historical Society. *Proceedings of the Court of Chancery of Maryland, 1669–1679.* Vol. 50. Baltimore: the society, 1934. F276 .A67.

———. *Maryland State Papers, No. 2, The Bankstock Papers.* Annapolis: Hall of Records Commission, State of Maryland, 1947. CD3280 .A16.

———. *Maryland State Papers, No. 3, The Brown Book.* Annapolis: Hall of Records Commission, State of Maryland, 1948. CD3280 .A16.

———. *Maryland State Papers, No. 4, The Red Book* (in two parts). Annapolis: Hall of Records Commission, State of Maryland, 1955. CD3280 .A16.

———. *Calendar of Maryland State Papers, No. 5, Executive Miscellaneous.* Annapolis: Hall of Records Commission, State of Maryland, 1958. CD3280 .A16.

———. *The County Courthouses and Records of Maryland, Publication No. 12. Part One: The Courthouses; Part Two: the Records.* Annapolis: Hall of Records Commission, State of Maryland, 1963. CD3280 .A16.

Maryland Surname Index: Computer Indexes to Marriage Records. North Salt Lake, Utah: Hunting for Bears, 1984. F180 .M37.

Wyand, Jeffry A., and Florence L. Wyand. *Colonial Maryland Naturalizations.* Baltimore: Genealogical Publishing Co., 1973. F180 .W9.

Weiser, Frederick S., ed. *Records of Christ Reformed Church, Middletown, Frederick Co., Maryland, 1778–1848.* Manchester, Md.: Noodle-Doosey Press, 1986. F190 .G3W38.

———. *Maryland German Church Records.* 3 vols. Manchester, Md.: Noodle-Doosey Press, 1986. F190 .G3W38.

Wright, F. Edward. *Maryland Eastern Shore Newspaper Extracts, 1726–1834.* 6 vols. Silver Springs, Md.: Family Line Publications, 1981. F187 .E2W67.

Military Records

Colonial Wars

McGhee, Lucy K. (See below under "American Revolution.")

American Revolution

Brumbaugh, Gaius M. *Maryland Records, Colonial, Revolutionary, County and Church, From Original Sources.* Vol. 2. Lancaster, Pa.: Lancaster Press, 1928. F180 .B89.

————. *Revolutionary Records of Maryland.* Washington, D.C.: Rufus H. Darby Printing Co., 1924. F185 .B89.

Maryland Treasurer's Office. *Report of the Treasurer of the Western Shore, on the Pension List.* Annapolis: December Session, 1824. E263 .M3M3.

Maryland Historical Society. *Muster Rolls and Other Records of Service of Maryland Troops in the American Revolution, 1775–1783.* Vol. 18, *Archives of Maryland.* Baltimore: the society, 1900. E263 .M3M4; F176 .A67.

McGhee, Lucy K. *Maryland Revolutionary War Pensions, Revolutionary, 1812, and Indian Wars.* Typescript. Washington, D.C.: the compiler, 1952. F185 .M15.

Newman, Harry W. *Maryland Revolutionary Records: Data Obtained From 3,050 Pension Claims and Bounty Land Applications, Including 1,000 Marriages of Maryland Soldiers and a List of 1,200 Proved Services of Soldiers and Patriots of Other States.* Washington, D.C.: 1938. Reprint. Baltimore: Genealogical Publishing Co., 1967. F185 .N48.

Scharf, John T. "List of Officers and Men Entitled to Lots Westward of Fort Cumberland." In *History of Western Maryland.* Vol. 1. Baltimore: Regional Publishing Co., 1968. F187 .A15S3.

Steuart, Reiman. *A History of the Maryland Line in the Revolutionary War, 1775–1783.* Towson, Md.: Society of the Cincinnati of Maryland, 1969. E263 .M383.

War of 1812

Marine, Louis H. *British Invasion of Maryland, 1812–18.* Reprint. Baltimore: Genealogical Publishing Co., 1977. E359.5 .M2M3.

Appendix has a Maryland roster of 11,000 names.

Wright, F. Edward. *Maryland Militia, War of 1812.* 5 vols. Silver Spring, Md.: Family Line Publications, 1970. E359.5 .M2W8.

Volume 1, Eastern Shore; volume 2, Baltimore.

Civil War

Booth, George W., comp. *Maryland Line Confederate Soldiers' Home.* Pikesville, Md.: n.p., 1894. E566.4 .B72.

Dilts, Bryan L., comp. *1890 Maryland Census: Index of Civil War Veterans or Their Widows —Microforms.* Salt Lake City: Index Publications, 1985. (Micro M87/2010).

Goldsborough, William W. *The Maryland Line in the Confederate Army, 1861–1865.* Port Washington, N.Y.: Kennikat Press, 1972. E566.4 .G6.

Hartzler, Daniel D. *Marylanders in the Confederacy.* Silver Springs, Md.: Family Line Publications, 1986. E566.3 .H37.

Pompey, Sherman L. *Muster Lists of the American Rifles of Maryland. . . .* Typescript. N.p.: the author, 1965. E566.3 .P65.

Directories

City

Aberdeen
(Havre de Grace) 1857, 1962–76

Annapolis 1910, 1924–29, 1939

Baltimore
pre 1861 (microfiche)
1861–1935 (microfilm)
(suburbs) 1936–63

Bel Air 1957–75

College Park
(Hyattsville, Mt. Ranier, Riverdale) 1963–71

Cumberland
(LaVale; Ridgely, W.V.) 1876, 1884, 1890, 1895–1983

Easton 1948, 1957, 1959, 1970, 1973

Elkton
(N.E. Md.) 1961, 1974, 1977

Frederick
pre 1861 (microfiche)
(Frederick Co.) 1887, 1909, 1923, 1928–84

Frostburg 1962–82

Glen Burnie
(Linthicum Hgts.) 1955–64

Hagerstown
  (Boonesboro, Clear Spring, Funkstown, Hancock,
    Keeysville, Sharpsburg, Smithsburg, Wil-
    liamsport, Bergen Co.)   1884, 1898, 1903–10,
    1922, 1929, 1935–83

LaPlata
  (Waldorf) 1966

Laurel 1933, 1957–78

Lexington Park
  (Leonardtown) 1966, 1972, 1974

Rockville 1958–76

Salisbury
  (Fruitland) 1942, 1948, 1953–74

Silver Spring
  (Bethesda, Chevy Chase, Kensington, Takoma Park,
    Wheaton) 1958–75

Suitland
  (Capitol Heights, District Heights, Forest Heights,
    Morningside) 1971

Towson 1965

Westminster 1957–81

County, Business, and Miscellaneous

Baltimore 1899

Maryland (see also Delaware)
  1878, 1880, 1899, 1902, 1909, 1912–15
  (Va., N.C., D.C.) 1914
  (D.C.) 1891, 1896, 1906, 1912–15, 1954

Montgomery 1911, 1956 (includes 1953–55)

Delaware

Historical Highlights

1609   Henry Hudson, from the Netherlands, ex-
        plored the Delaware River.

1638   New Sweden established a fort at the site of
        present-day Wilmington.

1655   New Netherlands took control of New
        Sweden.

1664   England overthrew New Netherlands.
        Delaware considered part of the newly
        named New York.

1682   Area claimed by Pennsylvania.

1684   Southern and western parts claimed by
        Maryland.

        The first settlers were chiefly Swedes, Finns,
        and Dutch from the Netherlands. After
        1664, many Englishmen who had formerly
        resided in New England moved to
        Delaware. Searching in neighboring states is
        necessary because of several border dis-
        putes.

        During the 1700s, Delaware became a haven
        for worshippers who sought religious
        freedom. These included both Scotch-Irish
        Presbyterians, and Roman Catholics.
        Toward the close of that century, a growing
        slave trade brought many black persons into
        the state.

1776   No longer considered a part of Pennsylvania
        or Maryland, Delaware was one of the thir-
        teen original states at the time of the
        American Revolution.

1863   Although sympathetic with the Con-
        federacy, remained in the Union during the
        Civil War.

Published Record Sources

Guidebooks

United States Geodetic Survey. *The National Gazetteer of the United States of America—Delaware,
  1983.* Washington, D.C.: Government Printing
  Office, 1984. F162 .N37.

Census Indexes and Abstracts

Federal

1800   F163 .J3
        Maddux, Gerald, and Doris G. Maddux,
          comps. *1800 Census.* Baltimore:
          Genealogical Publishing Co., 1964.
          F163 .M32.

1810   F163 .J3751

1820   F163 .J33 1974

1830   F163 .J34

1840   F163 .J1327

1850   F163 .J33
Olmstead, Virginia L., comp. *Index to the 1850 Census of Delaware.* Baltimore: Genealogical Publishing Co., 1977. F163 .045.

1860   Dilts, Bryan L., comp. *1860 Delaware Census Index.* Salt Lake City: Index Publishing, 1984. F163 .D54.

1870   ———. *1870 Delaware Census Index. Microforms.* Salt Lake City: Index Publishing, 1985. M87/2002.

State

Hancock, Harold B., ed. *Reconstructed Delaware State Census of 1782.* Wilmington: Delaware Genealogical Society, 1983. F163 .H36.

Jackson, Ronald V. *Early Delaware Census Records, 1665–1697.* Bountiful, Utah: Accelerated Indexing Systems, n.d. F163 .J285.

———. *Early Delaware.* Bountiful, Utah: Accelerated Indexing Systems, n.d. F163 .J36.

Mortality Schedules

1850   F163 .J333

1860   F163 .J35

1870   F163 .J352

1880   F163 .J353

All the above publications shown without the name of the compiler are by Ronald V. Jackson, Accelerated Indexing Systems.

Biographies

Barrett, Norris S., ed. *Year Book, 1805: The Sons of Delaware at Philadelphia, Pennsylvania.* N.p., n.d. F161 .S69.

Harmond, Seth, ed. *Who's Who in Delaware.* Philadelphia: National Biographical Society, 1932. F163 .W67.

Who's Who in Delaware. 2 vols. Chicago: A.N. Marquis Co., 1939. F163 .W68.

Land Acquisition

Wharton, Walter. *Walter Wharton's Land Survey Register, 1675–1679.* Wilmington: Historical Society of Delaware, 1955. F167 .W48.

Early Settlers

Fernow, Berthold. *Documents Relating to the History of the Dutch and Swedish Settlements on the Delaware River.* Albany, N.Y.: Argus Co., 1877. F122 .D66.

Sellers, Edwin J. *Allied Families of Delaware (Davis, Draper, Kipshaven, Fenwick, Stidham, Stretcher).* Philadelphia: Lippincott, 1901. F163 .S43.

Virdin, Donald O., and Raymond B. Clark, Jr., eds. *Delaware Family Histories and Genealogies.* St. Michael's, Md.: the editors, 1984. Z1267 .V57.

Wilson, W. Emerson. *Forgotten Heroes of Delaware.* Cambridge, Mass.: Delton Publishing Co., 1969. D163 .W53.

Local Records

Clark, Raymond B., comp. *Delaware Church Records.* St. Michael's, Md.: the compiler, 1986. F163 .C54.

———. *Sussex County, Delaware Wills and Administrations, 1680–1800: An Index.* St. Michael's, Md.: the author, 1985. F172 .S8C58.

Delaware. Public Archives Commission. *Calendar of Kent County, Delaware Probate Records, 1680–1800.* Dover: State of Delaware, 1944. F172 .K3A53.

———. *Calendar of Sussex County, Delaware Probate Records, 1680–1800.* Dover: State of Delaware, 1964. F172 .S8D4.

———. *Duke of York Record, 1646–1679.* Wilmington: Sunday Star Print, 1955. F167 .D31.

Delaware. *Records of the Court of New Castle on Delaware, 1676–1681.* Lancaster, Pa.: Colonial Society of Pennsylvania, 1904. F174 .N5N5.

Frazier, Margaret M. *Delaware Advertiser, 1827–1831.* Genealogical Extracts. Newhall, Calif.: Carl Boyer, 1987. F163 .F73.

National Society Colonial Dames of Delaware. *A Calendar of Delaware Wills, New Castle County,*

1682–1800. New York: Frederick H. Hitchcock, 1911. F172 .N5N2.

Turner, C. H. B., comp. *Rodney's Diary and Other Delaware Records*. Philadelphia: Allen Lane & Scott, 1911. F165 .T94.

Military Records

American Revolution

Delaware. Public Archives Commission. *Delaware Archives, Vols. 1–3*. Wilmington: n.p., 1911–19. Reprint. New York: AMS Press, 1974. F161 .D294.

Scharf, John T. *The History of Delaware, 1609–1888*. Vol. 1. New York: Kennikat Press, 1972. F164 .S3.

———. *Index to History of Delaware, 1609–1888*. 3 vols. Wilmington: Historical Society of Delaware, 1976. F164 .S33.

Whiteley, William G. *The Revolutionary Soldiers of Delaware*. Wilmington: James and Walls, 1875. E263 .D3W5.

War of 1812

Delaware. Public Archives Commission. *Delaware Archives, Vols. 4–5*. Reprint. New York: AMS Press, 1974. F161 .D294.

Directories

City

Dover 1948, 1959–81

Milford 1959–77

Rehoboth Beach 1944

Seaford
 (Bridgeville, Laurel) 1966–79

Wilmington
 pre 1861 (microfiche)
 1861–1935 (microfilm)
 (block directory) 1894, 1936–80

County, Business, and Miscellaneous

Delaware
 pre 1861 (microfiche)
 1872–75, 1882, 1884, 1891, 1899, 1908
 (state, Md., and W. Va.) 1905, 1909, 1911, 1964, 1975–80

New Castle 1911, 1914

South, The
 (Del., Md., N.C., Va., and D.C.) 1851

Sussex
 1913

District of Columbia

Historical Highlights

1608   Potomac River explored by Capt. John Smith.

1640   Georgetown, Maryland, established.

1749   Alexandria, Virginia, established.

1789   Georgetown incorporated.

1790   District of Columbia established.

 A ten square mile area, comprised of land belonging to both Maryland and Virginia, was designated as the capital of the United States. Within the boundaries of the district was the City of Washington.

1800   After a brief tenure at New York City, the nation's capital moved from Philadelphia to the District of Columbia.

1846   The Virginia portion (west of the Potomac) was returned to that state.

 Because of their location on the Potomac and with access to the Chesapeake Bay, both Georgetown and Alexandria became thriving ports, especially in the tobacco trade. Early settlers were English, Scotch, and Irish. After the District of Columbia was created as the nation's capital, it grew rapidly, attracting government officials and employees, European diplomats, and merchants. Many of the early records were lost when the British burned the Capitol during the War of 1812. Abraham Lincoln directed the Union forces from Washington during the Civil War.

Published Record Sources

Census Indexes and Abstracts

Federal

1800	F193 .J33
1820	F193 .J333
	Parks, Gary W., comp. *Index to the 1820 Census of Maryland and Washington, D.C.* Baltimore: Genealogical Publishing Co., 1986. F182 .P37.
1830	F193 .J334
1840	F193 .J335
1850	F193 .J336
	Dilts, Bryan L., comp. *1860 District of Columbia Census Index.* Salt Lake City: Index Publishing, 1983. F193 .D54.
1870	Dilts, Bryan L., comp. *1860 District of Columbia Census Index—Microforms.* Salt Lake City: Index Publishing Co., 1985. (Micro M87/2004).

Mortality Schedules

1850	F193 .J3364
1860	F193 .J338
1870	F193 .J339
1880	F193 .J34

All the above publications shown without the name of the compiler are by Ronald V. Jackson, Accelerated Indexing Systems.

Biographies

Eminent and Representative Men of Virginia and the District of Columbia of the Nineteenth Century. Madison, Va.: Brant & Fuller, 1893. F193 .E53.

Johnson, Lorenzo D. *The Churches and Pastors of Washington, D.C.: 1855 and 1856.* New York: M.W. Dodd, 1857. F202.2 .A1J6.

Who's Who in the Nation's Capital, 1921–1922. Washington, D.C.: Consolidated Publishing, 1971. F193 .W6.

Other editions through 1983 are available.

District of Columbia. *Concise Biographies of the Prominent and Representative Citizens and Valu-* *able Statistical Data, 1908–19.* Washington, D.C.: American Biographical Directory, 1908. F193 .D61.

Local Records

Sluby, Paul E. *Columbia Harmony Cemetery Records, 1831–1899.* Washington, D.C.: the society, 1975. F193 .S58.

——. *The Transcribed Ledger of the eastern Methodist Cemetery (also called Old Ebenezer), 1823–1893.* Washington, D.C.: Columbia Harmony Society, 1981. F193 .S584.

——. *Old Methodist Burial Ground, Georgetown, Washington, D.C.* Washington, D.C.: the author, 1975. F193 .S583.

——. *Woodlawn Cemetery, Brief History and Inscriptions.* Washington, D.C.: Columbia Historical Society, 1984. F193 .S585.

Sluby, Paul E., and Stanton L. Wormley. *Holmead's Cemetery (Western Burial Ground).* Washington, D.C.: Columbia Harmony Society, 1985. F193 .S582.

——. *Mt. Zion Cemetery, Brief History and Interments.* Washington, D.C.: Columbia Harmony Society, 1984. F193. S.5827.

Walker, Homer A. *Historical Court Records of Washington; Death Records of Washington, D.C., 1801–1878.* Washington, D.C.: the author, 1951. F193 .W26.

Washington, D.C. Christ Church. *Marriages, Baptisms, Burials, and Communicants, 1795–1921.* Washington, D.C.: Livingston Manor Chapter, D.A.R., 1942. F193 .W3.

Periodicals

Analytical Index to the Records of the Columbia Historical Society. Vols. 31–32 (1957–59). Washington, D.C.: the society, 1978. F191 .C72.

Deane, Roxanna, and Grace L. Smiley, comps. *Analytical Index to the Records of the Columbia Historical Society, Vols. 31–32 (1957–59).* Washington, D.C.: the society, 1978. F191 .C72.

Morris, Maud B., and Lawrence F. Schmeckbier. *Index to Volumes 1 to 48/49, Records of the Columbia Historical Society.* Washington, D.C.: the society, 1950. F191 .C72.

Sciosco, Louis D., ed. *Analytical Index to the Records of the Columbia Historical Society.* Washington, D.C.: the society, 1955, 1956. F191 .C72.

Volumes 1–10, 1897–1907; volumes 11–20, 1909–17.

Directories

City

Washington
  pre 1861 (microfiche)

1861–1935 (microfilm)
(Georgetown; Md.; Va.; suburbs) 1936–43, 1949, 1954, 1956, 1960–73

County, Business, and Miscellaneous

District of Columbia (see Md.)

Washington (see also Alexandria, Va.) 1899

CHAPTER 11

Southeastern States

Virginia • West Virginia
North Carolina • South Corolina
Georgia • Florida

The Library of Congress has a separate grouping of publications in its local history collections that refer specifically to the South. Selected titles from this group are listed below.

Avant, David A., Jr. *Some Southern Colonial Families.* 2 vols. Tallahassee: L'Avant Studios, 1983. F208 .A92.

Clark, Murtie J. *Colonial Soldiers of the South, 1732–74.* Baltimore: Genealogical Publishing Co., 1983. ZF208 .C58.

———. *Loyalists in the Southern Campaign of the Revolutionary War.* Baltimore: Genealogical Publishing Co., 1981. CS63 .C55.

Collier, Mrs. Bryan W. *Representative Women of the South, 1861–1920.* 5 vols. N.p.: the author, 1923–29. F208 .C69.

Holcomb, Brent. *Marriage and Death Notices: From the Southern Christian Advocate.* Easley, S.C.: Southern Historical Press, 1979. F208 .H6.

Volume 1, 1837–60; volume 2, 1861–67.

Ivison, Hazle R., comp. *These Sacred Places.* N.p.: the author, 1965. F208 .I9.

Lester, Memory A. *Old Southern Bible Records: Transcripts of Births, Deaths, and Marriages From Family Bibles, Chiefly of the Eighteenth and Nineteenth Centuries.* Baltimore: Genealogical Publishing Co., 1974. F208 .L47.

Mid-south Bible Records. 2 vols. Memphis: Fort Assumption Chapter, Daughters of the American Revolution, 1973. F208 .M45.

O'Brien, Robert. *The Encyclopedia of the South.* New York: Facts on File Publishing Co., 1985. F207.7 .O27.

Overby, Mary M., comp. *Obituaries Published by the Christian Index, 1880–99.* Macon, Ga.: Georgia Baptist Historical Society, 1982. F208 .O93.

Potter, Dorothy W. *Passports of Southeastern Pioneers, 1770–1823: Indian, Spanish and Other Land Passports for Tennessee, Kentucky, Georgia, Mississippi, Virginia, North Carolina, South Carolina.* Baltimore: Gateway Press, 1982. F208 .P65.

Representative Men of the South. Philadelphia: Charles Robson & Co., 1880. F208 .R42.

The Southerner: Biographical Encyclopedia of Southern People. New Orleans: Southern Editors Association, 1944. F208 .S6.

Who's Who in the South, 1927. Washington, D.C.: Mayflower Publishing Co., 1927. F208 .W62.

Virginia

Historical Highlights

1607 England's first permanent settlement in America established at Jamestown.

1619 First African slaves imported.

1621 House of Burgesses established.

1625 Named a royal colony.

After more than a century of exploration in America and several unsuccessful settlements, the English succeeded, under great hardships, in settling Jamestown on a permanent basis. This opened the area to other Englishmen, causing Virginia to become the heaviest populated area of the New World. During the eighteenth century Virginia was ruled by an English governor, by Cromwell's men, and, after his overthrow, by another royal governor.

1716 Shenandoah Valley explored by Governor Spotswood.

The area situated between the mountain ranges of the Alleghenies attracted migrants, mainly Scotch-Irish and Germans, who travelled down the valley from Pennsylvania. The English on the East Coast migrated inland along the rivers, establishing plantations and small farms as they went. This movement was slowed initially by Indian attacks but increased after they were controlled.

1776 One of the thirteen original colonies at the time of the American Revolution.

1784 Land claimed by Virginia located northwest of the Ohio River ceded to the United States.

1792 Kentucky separated from Virginia.

1861 Seceded from the Union; Richmond became the capitol of the Confederate States of America.

1863 West Virginia, heavily Union in sympathy, seceded from Virginia and was accepted as a separate state of the United States.

Published Record Sources

Guidebooks

Hart, Lyndon H., III. *A Guide to Genealogical Notes and Charts in the Archives Branch, Virginia State Library.* Richmond: Virginia State Library, 1983. Z1345 .H37.

Heisey, John W. *Virginia Genealogy Guide.* York, Pa.: the author, 1906. F225 .H45.

Hodge, Robert A., comp. *An Index to the Germanna Record—Number One.* Fredericksburg: the compiler, 1981. F235 .G3G4 supp.

Johnson, Elmer D., ed. *A Bibliography of Southwestern Virginia History.* Radford, Va.: Radford College, Department of History, 1970. Z1345 .R32.

Long, Charles M. *Virginia County Names.* New York: Neale Publishing Co., 1908. F227 .L84.

Salmon, John J., comp. *A Guide to State Records in the Archives Branch, Virginia State Library.* Richmond: Virginia State Library, 1985. CD3564 .S35.

Schweitzer, George K. *Virginia Genealogical Research.* Knoxville, Tenn.: the author, 1982. Z1345 .S38.

Virginia Genealogy: A Guide to Resources at the University of Virginia Library. Charlottesville: University Press, 1985. Z1345 .V57.

Virginia Historical Society. *Guide to the Manuscript Collection of the Virginia Historical Society.* Richmond: the society, 1985. Z1345 .V564.

Virginia Local History: A Bibliography. Richmond: Virginia State Library, 1971. Z1345 .A56.

Weaks, Mabel C. *The Preston and Virginia Papers of the Draper Collection of Manuscripts.* Vol. 1 of *Calendar Series.* Madison, Wis.: State Historical Society of Wisconsin, 1915. Z1345 .W42.

Census Indexes and Abstracts

Federal

1790

Workman, Velma B. *First Federal Census, 1782–83. Virginia Territatory [sic].* Canton, Mich.: the author, 1985. F225 .W66.

Heads of Families . . . Records of the State Enumerations, 1782–85. Baltimore: Genealogical Publishing Co., 1970. F230 .U5. Bountiful, Utah: Accelerated Indexing Systems, 1978. F225 .U6.

1810   F225 .J3 (substitute)

Bentley, Elizabeth P., comp. *Index to the 1810 Census of Virginia.* Baltimore: Genealogical Publishing Co., 1980. F225 .B45.

Crickard, Madeline W., comp. *Index to the 1810 Virginia Census: Twenty Counties, Town of Petersburg and Borough of Norfolk, From the Original Census Records.* Beverly, W.V.: the author, 1971. F230 .C76.

Yantis, Netti Schreiner, ed. *A Supplement to the 1810 Census of Virginia Tax Lists of the Counties For Which the Census is Missing.* Springfield, Va.: the author, 1971. F230 .Y35.

1820   F225 .J32

Felldin, Jeanne R., comp. *Index to the 1820 Census of Virginia.* Baltimore: Genealogical Publishing Co., 1976. F225 .F4.

1830   F225 .J33

1840   F225 .J3755

1850   F225 .J333

All above publications shown without the name of the compiler or editor are by Ronald V. Jackson, Accelerated Indexing Systems.

1860   Bishop, Brenda C. *1860 Census, Virginia.* Tallahassee: the author, 1983. F225 .B57.

1870   Bishop, Brenda C. *1870 Census, Virginia.* Elizabethown, Tenn.: the author, 1983. F225 .B58.

State

Yantis, Netti Schreiner, and Florene S. Love, comps. *The 1787 Census of Virginia: An Accounting of the Name of Every White Male Titheable Over 21 Years.* Springfield, Va.: Genealogical Books in Print, 1987. F225 .Y36.

Biographies

History of Virginia. Vols. 4, 5, 6, *Biography;* Vol. 7, *Virginia Biography.* New York: American Historical Society, 1924. F226 .H67.

Morton, Richard L., ed. *Virginia Lives, the Old Dominion Who's Who.* Hopkinsville, Ky.: Historical Record Association, 1984. F225 .V88.

Taylor, George B. *Virginia Baptist Ministers.* Lynchburg, Va.: J.P. Bell Co., 1912. BX6248 .V5T3.

Tyler, Lyon G., ed. *Encyclopedia of Virginia Biography.* 5 vols. New York: Lewis Historical Publishing Co., 1915. F225 .T97.

———. *Men of Mark in Virginia.* 5 vols. Washington, D.C.: Men of Mark Publishing Co., 1906. F225 .M53.

Who's Who in Virginia, Vol. 1. Chicago: A.N. Marquis Co., 1939. F240 .W57.

Land Acquisition

Chiarito, Marian D. *Entry Record Book, 1737–70.* Nathalie, Va.: the author, 1984. F225 .C48.

Contains entries for the present counties of Franklin, Halifax, Henry, Patrick, and Pittsylvania.

Duvall, Lindsay O., comp. *Virginia Colonial Abstracts—Series 2.* 6 vols. Easley, S.C.: Southern Historical Press, 1978–79. F225 .D88.

Gentry, Daphne S. *Virginia Land Office Inventory.* Rev. and enl. by John J. Salmon. Richmond: Virginia State Library, Archival Records Division, 1981. CD3566 .L36V57.

Joyner, Peggy S. *Abstracts of Virginia's Northern Neck Warrants and Surveys.* 4 vols. Portsmouth, Va.: the author, 1985. F225 .J76.

Covers the years 1697–1784.

Lawrence-Dow, Elizabeth, ed. *Virginia Rent Rolls, 1704.* New York: the editor, 1979. F225 .L39.

Nugent, Nell M. *Cavaliers and Pioneers: Abstracts of Virginia Land Patents and Grants, 1623–66.* 5 vols.

Baltimore: Genealogical Publishing Co., 1979. F225 .N842.

Parks, Gary. *Virginia Land Records: From the Virginia Magazine of History and Biography, the William and Mary Quarterly, and Tyler's Quarterly.* Baltimore: Genealogical Publishing Co., 1982. F225 .V875.

Virginia State Library. Archives and Records Division. *Virginia Land Office Inventory.* Richmond: Virginia State Library, 1981. CD3566 .L36V57.

Early Settlers

Boddie, John B. *Southside Virginia Families.* 2 vols. Baltimore: Genealogical Publishing Co., 1966. CS69 .B6.

——. *Virginia Historical Genealogies.* Baltimore: Genealogical Publishing Co., 1965. CS69 .B62.

Brock, Robert A., ed. *Huguenot Emigration to Virginia.* Richmond: Virginia Historical Society, 1886. F226 .B76.

——. *Virginia and Virginians, 1606–1888.* Richmond: H.H. Hardesty, 1888. F226 .B76.

Brown, Stuart E., Jr. *Virginia Genealogies,* Vol 2. Berryville, Va.: Virginia Book Co., 1980. Z4313 .U6V76.

Chalkley, Lyman. *Chronicles of the Scotch-Irish Settlement in Virginia: Extracted From the Original Court Records of Augusta County, Virginia, 1745–1800.* 3 vols. Baltimore: Genealogical Publishing Co., 1965. F232 .A9A9.

DuBellet, Louise P. *Some Prominent Virginia Families.* Lynchburg, Va.: J.P. Bell Co., 1907. F225 .P36.

Fazel, Rena B., comp. *Index to Hayden's Virginia Genealogies.* Richmond: Virginia Genealogical Society, 1977. F225 .H283F39.

Fleet, Beverley. *Virginia Colonial Abstracts.* 3 vols. Baltimore: Genealogical Publishing Co., 1988. F225 .F58.

Foley, Louise P. H. *Early Virginia Families Along the James River; Their Deep Roots and Tangled Branches.* 2 vols. Richmond: the author, 1974, 1978. F225 .F596.

Volume 1, Henrico Co. and Goochland Co.; volume 2, Charles Co. South and Prince George Co.

Genealogies of Virginia Families: From the Virginia Magazine of History and Biography. 5 vols. Baltimore: Genealogical Publishing Co., 1981. F225 .G468.

Germanna Record. *Memorial Foundation of the Germanna Colonies in Virginia. Number Six, June 1965.* Culpeper, Va.: The Germanna Foundation, 1965. F235 .G3G4.

Greer, George C. *Early Virginia Emigrants, 1623–66.* Baltimore: Genealogical Publishing Co., 1960. F225 .G81.

Hamlin, Charles H., comp. *Virginia: Ancestors and Adventurers.* Vol. 1. Richmond: the author, 1967. F225 .H225.

——. *They Went Thataway.* 3 vols. Richmond: the author, 1964. F225 .H222.

Handy, Henry B. *The Social Register of Virginia.* Richmond: The Social Register of Virginia, 1928. F225 .H23.

Hayden, Horace E. *Virginia Genealogies.* Reprint. Washington, D.C.: The Rare Book Shop, 1931. F225 .H41.

Houston, William R. M., and Jan M. Mihalyka. *Colonial Residents of Virginia: Order of First Families of Virginia, 1964.* N.p., n.d. F229 .J4.

Jester, Annie L., comp. *Adventures of Purse and Person, 1607–25.* Virginia: Order of First Families of Virginia, 1964. F229 .J4.

Kegley, Frederick B. *Kegley's Virginia Frontier, The Beginning of the Southwest: The Roanoke of Colonial Days, 1740–83.* Roanoke: Southwest Virginia Historical Society, 1938. F229 .K26.

McWhorter, Lucullus V. *The Border Settlers of Northwestern Virginia From 1768 to 1895.* Hamilton, Ohio: Republican Publishing Co., 1915. Reprint. Baltimore: Genealogical Publishing Co., 1975. F241 .M17.

Meade, Bishop W. *Old Churches, Ministers, and Families of Virginia.* 2 vols. Baltimore: Genealogical Publishing Co., 1966. F225 .M4913.

National Society of the Colonial Dames of America in the Commonwealth of Virginia. *Register of Ancestors.* Richmond: the society, 1979. F225 .N37.

Nugent, Nell M. *Cavaliers and Pioneers—Supplement. Northern Neck Grants, No. 1—1690–92.* Richmond: Virginia State Library, 1980. F225 .N842.

Oliver, Lloyd F. *Index to DuBellet's Some Prominent Virginia Families.* Tomball, Tex.: Genealogical Publications, 1979. F225 .O43.

Stanard, William C., and Mary N. Stanard. *The Colonial Virginia Register.* Albany, N.Y.: Joel Munsell's Sons, n.d. F229 .S8.

Stanard, William C. *Some Emigrants to Virginia.* Reprint of the 2d ed., enl. Baltimore: Genealogical Publishing Co., 1964. F225 .S82.

Summers, Lewis P. *Annals of Southwest Virginia, 1769–1800.* Abingdon, Va.: the author, 1929. F226 .S82.

Torrence, Clayton, ed. *The Edward Pleasant Valentine Papers.* 4 vols. Baltimore: Genealogical Publishing Co., 1979. F225 .V17.

Contains genealogies of several Virginia families.

Wardell, Patrick G., comp. *Virginians and West Virginians, 1607–1870.* Bowie, Md.: Heritage Books, 1986. F226 .H673W37.

Abstracted from *History of Virginia,* published by American History Society, 1924.

Local Records

Bell, James P. *Our Quaker Friends of Ye Olden Time: Transcript of Minute Books of Cedar Creek Meeting, Hanover County and South River Meeting, Campbell Co., Va.* Lynchburg, Va.: J.P. Bell Co., 1905. F232 .H3B44.

Bell, Landon G. *Cumberland Parish, Lunenburg Co., Va., 1746–1815; Vestry Book, 1746–1816.* Baltimore: Genealogical Publishing Co., 1974. F225 .B42.

Bentley, Elizabeth P. *Virginia Marriage Records: From Virginia Magazine of History and Biography.* Baltimore: Genealogical Publishing Co., 1982. F225 .V883.

Burns, Annie W. *Virginia Genealogies and County Records.* 2 vols. Washington, D.C.: the author, 1941. F225 .B37.

Clark, Jewell T., and Elizabeth T. Long. *A Guide to Church Records in the Archives Branch, Virginia State Library.* Richmond: Virginia State Library, Archives Branch, 1981. CD3568.5 .V57.

Cocke, Charles F. *Parish Lines, Diocese of Virginia.* Richmond: Virginia State Library, 1967. BX5918 .V8C6.

———. *Parish Lines, Diocese of Southern Virginia.* Richmond: Virginia State Library, 1964. BX5918 .S92206.

———. *Parish Lines, Diocese of Southwestern Virginia.* Richmond: Virginia State Library, 1960. BX5918 .S9212C6.

Crowson, E.T. *Life as Revealed Through Early American Court Records.* Easley, S.C.: Southern Historical Press, 1981. F229 .C93.

Crozier, William A. *Early Virginia Marriages.* Baltimore: Southern Book Co., 1953 .F225 .C9.

Currer-Briggs, Noel. *English Adventurers and Virginia Settlers. 1484–1798.* 3 vols. London: Phillimore Publishing Co., 1969. F225 .C96.

Volumes 1 and 2, Abstracts of Wills; volume 3, Legal Proceedings and Index.

Hart, Lyndon H. III, comp. *A Guide to Bible Records in the Archives Branch, Virginia State Library.* Richmond: Virginia State Library, 1985. Z1345 .V57.

Historical Records Survey (WPA). *Inventory of Church Archives of Virginia.* 2 vols. Typescript. Richmond, Va.: n.p., n.d. F225 .H5.

———. *Index to Marriage Notices in the Southern Churchman, 1835–1941.* 2 vols. Typescript. Richmond: n.p., 1942. F225 .H48.

Hogg, Anne M., and Dennis A. Tosh, eds. *Virginia Genealogist: A Guide to Resources.* Charlottesville: University Press, 1986. F225 .V837.

Hopkins, William L. *Some Wills From the Burned Counties of Virginia, and Other Wills Not Listed in Virginia Wills and Administration, 1632–1800.* Richmond: the author, 1987. F225 .H67.

McDonald, Cecil D. *Some Virginia Marriages, 1700–1799.* Unpublished manuscript. Seattle, 1972. F225 .M38.

McGhan, Judith. *Virginia Vital Records: From Virginia Magazine of History and Biography.* Baltimore: Genealogical Publishing Co., 1982. F225 .V93.

———. *Virginia Will Records: From Virginia Magazine of History and Biography.* Baltimore: Genealogical Publishing Co., 1982. F225 .V94.

McIlvaine, H.N., ed. *Minutes of the Council and General Court of Colonial Virginia.* Richmond: Virginia State Library, 1979. F229 .V523.

Parks, Gary W. *Virginia Tax Records: From Virginia Magazine of History and Biography.* Baltimore: Genealogical Publishing Co., 1983. F225 .V887.

Torrence, Clayton. *Virginia Wills and Administration, 1632–1800.* Richmond: National Society Colonial Dames of America, 1965. F225 .T85.

Virginia Genealogical Society. *Some Marriages in the Burned Record Counties of Virginia.* Richmond: the society, 1972. F225 .V85.

Virginia Marriages in Rev. John Cameron's Register and Bath Parish Register. Richmond: Virginia Genealogical Society, 1963. F225 .V86.

Vogt, John, and T. William Kethley, Jr. *Marriage Records in the Virginia State Library: A Researcher's Guide.* Athens, Ga.: Iberian Publishing Co., 1984. Z1345 .V63.

———. *Wills and Estate Records in the Virginia State Library: A Researcher's Guide.* Athens, Ga.: Iberian Publishing Co., 1987. Z1345 .V64.

Waldenmaier, Inez. *Virginia Marriage Records Before 1853. Part One: A Finding List of the Official County Court Records of Marriage in Virginia Before 1853.* Washington, D.C.: the author, 1956. Z1345 .W3.

Wardell, Patrick G. *Timesaving Aid to Virginia and West Virginia Ancestors.* Athens, Ga.: Iberian Publishing Co., 1985. F225 .W33.

Weddell, Monty T. O., comp. *Virginia Parish Register.* Dallas, Tex.: the compiler, 1980. CD3568.5 .W42.

Wise, Jennings C., comp. *Wise's Digested Index and Genealogical Guide to Bishop Meade's Old Churches, Ministers, and Families of Virginia.* Richmond: the author, 1910. F225 .M494.

Wulfeck, Dorothy F. *Marriages of Some Virginia Residents, 1607–1800.* 2 vols. Reprint. Baltimore: Genealogical Publishing Co., 1986. F225 .W8.

Military Records

General

Bentley, Elizabeth P. *Virginia Military Records: From Virginia Magazine of History and Biography.* Bal-

timore: Genealogical Publishing Co., 1983. F225 .V884.

Colonial Wars

Bockstruck, Lloyd D. *Virginia Colonial Soldiers.* Baltimore: Genealogical Publishing Co., 1988. (Cataloging in publication.)

Crozier, William A., ed. *Virginia Colonial Militia, 1651–1776.* Baltimore: Genealogical Publishing Co., 1965. F229 .C94.

Eckenrode, H.J. *List of Colonial Soldiers of Virginia.* Reprint; Baltimore: Genealogical Publishing Co., 1961. F229 .V94.

McGhee, Lucy K. *Virginia Pension Abstracts of Revolutionary War, War of 1812, and Indian Wars.* 35 vols. Typescript. Washington, D.C.: the author, 1956–66. F225 .M13.

American Revolution

Bland, Schuyler O. *Yorktown Sesquicentennial.* Washington, D.C.: Government Printing Office, 1931. E241 .Y3U65.

Brumbaugh, Gaius M. *Revolutionary War Records: Virginia Army and Navy Forces With Bounty Land Warrants for Virginia Military District of Ohio and Virginia Scrip; From Federal and State Archives.* Washington, D.C.: n.p., 1936. Reprint. Baltimore: Genealogical Publishing Co., 1967. F255 .B85.

Burgess, Louis A., comp. *Virginia Soldiers of 1776. Compiled From Documents on File in the Virginia Land Office; Together With Material Found in the Archives Department of the Virginia State Library and Other Reliable Sources.* 3 vols. Richmond: Richmond Press, 1927–29. Reprint. Spartanburg, S.C.: Reprint Co., 1973. F225 .B9.

Burns, Annie W. *Virginia Invalid Pension List of the Revolutionary War.* Typescript. Washington, D.C.: N.p., 1960s. F225 .B95.

Dorman, John F. *Virginia Revolutionary Pension Applications, Abstracted.* 32 vols. Typescript. Washington, D.C.: n.p., 1936. E206 .D85.

Gwathmey, John H. *Historical Register of Virginians in the Revolution: Soldiers, Sailors, Marines, 1775–1783.* Richmond: Dietz Press, 1938. Reprint. Baltimore: Genealogical Publishing Co., 1973. E263 .V8G9.

Latham, Allen, and B.G. Leonard. *A Roll of Officers in the Virginia Line of the Revolutionary Army Who*

Have Received Land Bounty in the State of Ohio and Kentucky. Chillicothe, Ohio: Latham and Leonard, 1922. E263 .V813.

McAllister, Joseph T. *Virginia Militia in the Revolutionary War: McAllister's Data.* Hot Springs, Va.: McAllister Publishing Co., 1913. E263 .V8M13.

McGhee, Lucy K. *Virginia Pension Abstracts of Revolutionary War, War of 1812, and Indian Wars.* 35 vols. Typescript. Washington, D.C.: the author, 1956–66. F225 .M13.

Palmer, William P., ed. *Calendar of Virginia State Papers and Other Manuscripts . . . Preserved in the Capitol.* 3 vols. Richmond: n.p., 1875–83. Reprint. New York: Kraus Reprint Co., 1968. F221 .V5.

Stewart, Robert A. *The History of Virginia's Navy of the Revolution.* Richmond: Mitchell and Hotchkiss, 1934. F230 .S84.

Summers, Lewis P. *Annals of Southwest Virginia, 1769–1800.* Abingdon, Va.: the author, 1929. F226 .S82.

Tazewell, Littleton W. *A List of Claims for Bounty Land For Revolutionary Services Acted Upon by the Governor Since April, 1884.* Richmond: Virginia State Library, 1835. E265 .V8A5.

Virginia State Library. Department of Archives and History. J. J. Eckenrode, comp. *List of Revolutionary Soldiers of Virginia.* Richmond: D. Bottom, 1911–13. E263 .V8V79.

Wilson, Samuel M. *Virginia Revolutionary Land Bounty Warrants.* Baltimore: Southern Book Co., 1953. E263 .V8W5.

————. *Catalog of Revolutionary Soldiers and Sailors of the Commonwealth of Virginia to Whom Land Bounty Warrants Were Granted to Virginia for Military Services in the War for Independence.* Baltimore: Genealogical Publishing Co., 1967. E202.4 .W37.

Worrell, Anne L. *Revolutionary Records Gathered From County Court Records in Southwest Virginia.* Typescript. Roanoke: n.p., 1936. F232 .B6W6.

War of 1812

McGhee, Lucy K. (See above under American Revolution.)

Virginia. Auditor of Public Accounts. *Pay Rolls of Militia: Muster Rolls of the Virginia Militia in the War of 1812.* N.p., n.d. E3595 .V8V82.

Civil War

For titles of numerous Virginia regimental histories, see James C. Neagles's *Confederate Research Sources* (Salt Lake City: Ancestry, Inc., 1986, Z1242 .N3.), pages 268–71.

Periodicals

Beadles, George A., comp. *Index of Names in the Religious Herald, 1939–75.* N.p.: the author, 1980. F225 .B35.

Casey, Joseph J. *Personal Names in Henings' Statutes at Large of Virginia and Shepherd's Continuation.* Bridgewater, Va.: The Green Bookman, 1933. F225 .V8133.

Headley, Robert K., Jr. *Genealogical Abstracts From 18th Century Virginia Newspapers.* Baltimore: Genealogical Publishing Co., 1987. F225 .H43.

Directories

City

Abingdon 1959–84

Alexandria
(suburbs, Annandale, Fredericksburg, Springfield) 1974–82

Altavista 1963–80

Arlington
(Arlington Co.) 1955–76

Ashland 1961–80

Bassett
(Fieldale) 1866–70

Bedford 1961–80

Berryville 1964

Blacksburg 1961–82

Blackstone 1963–78

Bristol 1901–83

Charlottesville 1888, 1904–84

Chase City
(Clarksville) 1963, 1965, 1975, 1979

Christiansburg 1966–81

238 *The Library of Congress*

Clifton Forge
  (Salem) 1914, 1959–79

Covington 1954–83

Culpeper 1963–81

Danville 1881, 1888–92, 1902, 1917, 1921, 1927–82

Emporia 1958–80

Fairfax City 1863–67, 1973

Falls Church
  (McLean) 1957–75

Farmville 1960–82

Fredericksburg 1944–84

Front Royal 1957–84

Galax
  (Fries, Independence, Hillsville) 1976

Hampton 1959–83

Harrisonburg 1937, 1952–84

Hopewell 1916–17, 1955–84

Lawrenceville 1959, 1964

Leesburg
  (Middleburg, Purcellville) 1962–82

Lexington
  (Buena Vista, Natural Bridge) 1962, 1974–83

Luray
  (Stanley) 1963–81

Lynchburg 1875–82, 1887, 1896–97, 1907–81

Manassas 1960–80

Marion 1954, 1961, 1969–81

Martinsville
  (Axton, Bassett, Collinsville, Fieldale, Ridgeway, Spencertown, Stanley, Henry Co.) 1937, 1947–51, 1956–74

McLean 1964

Newport News
  (Hampton, Old Point, Phoebus, Warwick) 1896–1983

Norfolk
  pre 1861 (microfiche)
  1861–1935 (microfilm)
  (Berkley, Chesapeake, Portsmouth, Eastern N.C.) 1936–84

Norton
  (Wise, Wise Co.) 1967, 1975–84

Orange 1960–78

Pearlsburg Narrows 1967

Petersburg
  pre 1861 (microfiche)
  (Colonial Hgts.) 1866, 1872, 1879, 1888, 1897–1985

Portsmouth 1937–38, 1956–84

Pulaski 1941, 1950, 1958, 1961, 1966–82

Quantico
  (Dumfries, Occoquan, Triangle, Woodbridge) 1963–78

Radford 1942, 1948, 1956, 1959, 1967, 1969, 1971, 1974

Richlands 1964–81

Richmond
  pre 1861 (microfiche)
  1861–1935 (microfilm)
  (suburbs, Manchester) 1936–85

Roanoke
  (Salem, Vinton) 1888, 1889, 1898, 1904, 1909–84

Rocky Mount 1958–81

Salem 1925

Smithfield 1974, 1977, 1980, 1982

South Boston 1957, 1961–85

South Hill 1959–66, 1971–85

Staunton
  (Augusta Co.) 1891–1985

Strasburg
  (Woodstock) 1965–81

Suffolk 1912, 1920, 1935, 1951–85

Tazewell
  (N. Tazewell) 1965–85

Vienna 1966–74

Virginia Beach 1962–84

Warrenton 1863–80

Waynesboro 1935, 1937, 1943, 1954–84

Williamsburg 1957–84

Winchester 1921, 1927, 1940, 1944, 1947, 1951–72

Wytheville 1949, 1958, 1961, 1970, 1974, 1977

County, Business, and Miscellaneous

Alexandria (city)
  (Georgetown; Washington, D.C.) 1872

Arlington 1955–76

Chesterfield (see Henrico)

Fairfax 1906

Henrico
  (Chesterfield) 1935

Henry 1958

Loudon 1955

Virginia (see also Delaware and Maryland)
  pre 1861 (microfiche)
  1873, 1880–93, 1906, 1911, 1917, 1978

Waynesboro 1935

Wythe
  pre 1861 (microfiche)

York (southern) 1970–83

West Virginia

Historical Highlights

Pre-1863   Part of Virginia.

1863   Seceded from Virginia; admitted to the Union.

During the early months of the Civil War, the northwestern counties of Virginia strongly disagreed with the state's decision to secede from the Union. Differences in philosophy grew out of the differing economies of the mountainous northwest and the tidewater east, thus causing disagreements over the slavery question. After declaring its freedom from Virginia, West Virginia was later admitted into the Union, with the Supreme Court approving the move in 1871.

Early migration into the area was slowed because of the presence of Indians. Later, settlers came from Pennsylvania, Maryland, and other eastern states; foreign immigrants from Ireland, Germany and other north-European countries joined them.

Published Record Sources

Guidebooks

Janssen, Quinith, and William Fernbach. *West Virginia Place Names.* Shepherdstown, W.Va.: the authors, 1984. F239 .J36.

Kenny, Hamill T. *West Virginia Place Names: Their Origin and Meaning, Including the Nomenclature of the Streams and Mountains.* Piedmont, W.Va.: The Place Names Press, 1945. F239 .K4.

Stinson, Helen S. *A Handbook for Genealogical Research in West Virginia.* Dallas, Tex.: the author, 1981. F240 .S74.

Census Indexes and Abstracts

Federal

1880   Marsh, William W., comp. *1880 Census of West Virginia.* 7 vols. Parson, W.Va.: McClain Printing Co., 1979. Vols. 2–7. Baltimore: Gateway Press, 1987. F240 .M37.

Mortality Schedules

1880   Jackson, Ronald V. *West Virginia 1880 Mortality Schedule.* Bountiful, Utah: Accelerated Indexing Systems, 1980. F240 .J33.

Biographies

Men of West Virginia. 2 vols. Chicago: Biographies Publishing Co., 1903. F240 .M53.

West Virginia Heritage Encyclopedia. Supplemental Series. 9 vols. Richwood, W.Va.: Jim Comstock, 1974. F241 W64.

Vol. 1—Early West Virginia: Counties of Monroe, Putnam, and Tyler; Vol. 2—Doddridge, Marion, Upshur, Wetzel; Vol. 3—Calhoun, Pocahontas, Braxton, Berkeley; Vol. 4—Jackson, Kanawha, Barbour; Vol. 5—Mason, Pleasants, Lewis, Roane; Vol. 6—Harrison, Cabell, Wirt, Greenbrier; Vol. 7—Gilmer, Ritchie, Lincoln,

Wayne; Vol. 8—Wood, Jefferson; Vol. 9—*Soldiery of West Virginia*—all Wars to World War I (actually also contains casualties from World War II and the Vietnam Conflict).

West Virginia Heritage Encyclopedia. Vol. 25, *Supplemental Series. West Virginia Women.* Richwood, W.Va.: Jim Comstock, 1974. F241 .W64.

Who's Who in West Virginia, 1939. Chicago: A.N. Marquis Co., 1939. F240 .W57.

Early Settlers

Reddy, Anne W., comp. *West Virginia Revolutionary Ancestors: Whose Services Were Non-military and Whose Names, Therefore, Do Not Appear in Revolutionary Indexes of Soldiers and Sailors.* Richmond: the compiler, 1930. F240 .R31.

Local Records

Historical Records Survey (WPA). *Cemetery Readings in West Virginia. Fairmont and Grant Magisterial Districts, Marion County.* Charleston: West Virginia Historical Society, 1941. F240 .H57.

———. *Cemetery Readings in West Virginia: Gideon Magisterial District, Cabell County.* Vol. 2. Charleston: West Virginia Historical Society, 1940. F240 .H57.

———. *Cemetery Readings in West Virginia: Lincoln and Paw Paw Magisterial District, Marion County.* Vol. 1. Charleston: West Virginia Historical Society, 1939. F240 .H57.

———. *Calendar of Wills in West Virginia, No. 49. Upshur County; Buckhannon.* Charleston: West Virginia Historical Society, 1941. F240 .H55.

Johnston, Ross B., comp. *West Virginia Estate Settlements: Index to Wills, Inventories and Appraisements, Land Grants and Surveys to 1850.* Baltimore: Genealogical Publishing co., 1977. F240 .J63.

Military Records

General

Felldin, Jeanne R., and Charlotte H. Tucker, comps. *Index to the Soldiers of West Virginia.* Tomball,

Tex.: Genealogy Publications, 1976. F241 .L6852F44.

Lewis, Virgil A. *The Soldiery of West Virginia in the French and Indian Wars, Lord Dunmore's War, the Revolution . . . War With Mexico.* Reprint; Baltimore: Genealogical Publishing Co., 1972. F241 .L685.

American Revolution

Johnston, Ross B. *West Virginians in the American Revolution.* Baltimore: Genealogical Publishing Co., 1977. E263 .V8J67.

Civil War

Calhoun, Harrison M. *Twixt North and South.* Franklin, W.Va.: McCoy Publishing Co., 1974. F247 .P3C34.

Dilts, Bryan L., comp. *1890 West Virginia Census Index of Civil War Veterans or Their Widows—Microforms.* Salt Lake City: Index Publishing Co., 1987. (Micro 87/2014).

Periodicals

Tetrick, W. Guy, comp. *Obituaries From Newspapers of Northern West Virginia.* 2d series. 2 vols. Clarksburg, W.Va.: the compiler, 1933. F240 .T27.

Directories

City

Beckley
(Mabscott) 1929–84

Bluefield
(Bluefield, Va.) 1910, 1921

Buckhannon 1863–82

Charles Town
(Bolivar, Harper's Ferry, Ransom, Shepardstown) 1965–78

Charleston
(Dunbar, S. Charleston, St. Albans) 1882, 1889, 1967–83

Clarksburg
(Bridgeport, Industrial, O'Neil, Salem, Shinnston, Wilsonsburg) 1905–84

Elkins 1921–84

Fairmont
(suburbs, Farmington, Mannington, Monongah) 1904–18, 1921–84

Follansbee
(Wellsburg) 1975–82

Huntington 1907–84

Keyser 1961–83

Lewisburg
(Ronceverte, White Sulphur Springs) 1974–81

Logan
(Chapmanville, Man) 1923, 1977

Martinsburg 1913–84

Morgantown
(Evansdale, Mona, Riverside, Sabraton, Star City, Westover) 1914–84

Moundsville
(Glendale) 1924, 1929, 1935, 1941, 1947–55, 1960, 1967–84

New Martinsville
(Paden City, Sisterville) 1960, 1965–84

Oak Hill
(Fayetteville, Mt. Hope) 1970–84

Parkersburg
(Belpre, Olie, Wood Co.) 1897, 1900, 1905, 1907, 1912–84

Point Pleasant 1970–80

Princeton
(Bluefield, Va.) 1938, 1940, 1942, 1956–84

Ravenswood
(Ripley) 1975–79

Spencer 1924

Welch 1930, 1975–79

Wellsburg 1908, 1957, 1960, 1967

Weston
(Lewis Co.) 1912, 1922–41, 1947–82

Wheeling
pre 1861 (microfiche)
1867, 1882–1985

Williamson 1930, 1952, 1968, 1971, 1973

County, Business, and Miscellaneous

West Virginia (state) (see also Delaware) 1877, 1882, 1895–1923

North Carolina

Historical Highlights

1585	First English colony failed.
1587	Second English colony (at Roanoke) failed.
1629	England gives charter to Robert Heath. Proprietary government established. Area embraced present day North Carolina and South Carolina.
1691	A governor selected by the proprietors to rule the Carolinas.
	England granted several proprietorships, and counties were organized to distinguish between the boundaries of the granted lands. These were Berkeley, Craven, Colleton, and Granville.
1712	Separate governors selected for North Carolina and South Carolina.
1729	Proprietary rule revoked by England. North Carolina and South Carolina declared separate royal colonies.
	Beginning in the early 1700s, Virginians began to populate the eastern parts of the Carolinas. Others arriving were Scotsmen and Quakers who moved from northern states. Scotch-Irish and Germans from Pennsylvania began to populate the western parts of the state.
1775	Residents of Mecklenburg County signed a "Declaration of Independence" from England.
1776	One of the thirteen original colonies at the time of the American Revolution.

1784   Western areas, to become the state of Tennessee, ceded by North Carolina to the United States.

1861   Seceded from the Union and joined the Confederate States of America.

Published Record Sources

Guidebooks

Corbitt, Davis L. *The Formation of the North Carolina Counties, 1663–1943*. Raleigh: State Department of Archives and History, 1950. 2d printing. 1969. F262 .A15N63.

Duke University, Durham. North Carolina Trinity College Historical Society. Prepared by Nannie N. Tilly and Noma L. Woodwin. *Guide to the Manuscript Collections in the Duke University Library*. New York: AMS Press, 1947. F251 .D832.

Ingmire, Frances T., comp. *Marriage Records, North Carolina*. 46 vols. St. Louis: the compiler, 1984. F253 .I54.

Covers Burke to Warren counties.

King, Henry. *Who Said There Ain't No Such Place?* Wilmington, Del.: the author, 1986. F252 .K56.

North Carolina Historical Commission. *The County Records*. 3 vols. Raleigh: the Commission, 1936. CD3420 .H5.

Covers Alamace to Yancey counties.

North Carolina Historical Commission. *Calendars of Manuscript Collections*. Vol. 1. Raleigh: the commission, 1926. F253 .N73.

North Carolina. Division of Archives and History. *Guide to Research Materials in the North Carolina State Archives; Section B—County Records*. Raleigh: State of North Carolina, 1978. CD3424 .N67.

Schweitzer, George K. *North Carolina Genealogical Research*. Knoxville, Tenn.: the author, 1984. Z1319 .S39.

Williford, Jo Ann, and Elizabeth Buford, eds. *A Directory of North Carolina Historical Organizations*. Raleigh: Federation of North Carolina Historical Societies, 1979. F251 .D57.

Census Indexes and Abstracts

Federal

1790   F258 .U9. Bureau of the Census (Heads of Families).
F258 .U53 Accelerated Indexing Systems (Heads of Families)

1800   F253 .J22
Bentley, Elizabeth P., comp. *Index to the 1800 Census of North Carolina*. Baltimore: Genealogical Publishing Co., 1977. F253 .B46.
Johnson, William P., and Dorothy W. Potter, eds. *1800 North Carolina Census*. Tullahoma, Tenn.: the editors, 1975. F253 .U54.

1810   F253 .J22
Bentley, Elizabeth P., comp. *Index to the 1810 Census of North Carolina*. Baltimore: Genealogical Publishing Co., 1978.

1820   F253 .J233
Potter, Dorothy W., comp. *Index to the 1820 North Carolina Census*. Baltimore: Genealogical Publishing Co., 1978. F253 .P67.

1830   F253 .J234

1840   F253 .J235
Bishop, Brenda C. *1840 Census, North Carolina*. Tallahassee: B.D. Bishop, 1984. F253 .B35.
Petty, Gerald M., comp. *Index of the 1840 Federal Census of North Carolina*. Columbus, Ohio: the compiler, 1974. F253 .P47.

1850   F253 .J236
Bishop, Brenda C. *1850 Census, North Carolina*. Tallahassee: the compiler, 1984. F253 .B36.
Genealogical Society of the Church of Jesus Christ of Latter-day Saints. *Index of Individuals Born Outside the United States—As Enumerated in the 1850 Census of North Carolina*. Salt Lake City: the society, 1972. F253 .I52.

1860   Bishop, Brenda C., ed. *1860 Census, North Carolina*. Tallahassee: the editor, 1982. F253 .B57.

1870   ———. *1870 Census, North Carolina*. Tallahassee: the editor, 1983. F253 .B57.

All the above publications shown without the name of the compiler or editor are by Ronald V. Jackson, Accelerated Indexing Systems.

State

Jackson, Ronald V. *Early North Carolina.* Bountiful, Utah; Accelerated Indexing Systems, 1981. F253 .J2.

North Carolina. State Department of Archives and History. *State Census for North Carolina, 1784–1787.* Baltimore: Genealogical Publishing Co., 1971. 2d ed. Norfolk, Va.: n.p., 1971. F258 .N92.

Biographies

Ashe, Samuel A. *Biographical History of North Carolina.* 8 vols. Greensboro, N.C.: Charles L. Van Noppen, 1905. F253 .A82.

———. *Biographical History of North Carolina. General Index,* Vols. 1–7. Greensboro, N.C.: Charles L. Van Noppen, 1912. F253 .A82

Index.

Peale, W.J., comp. *Lives of Distinguished North Carolinians.* Baltimore: Lord Baltimore Press, 1897. F253 .P37.

Powell, William S., ed. *Dictionary of North Carolina Biography.* 2 vols. Chapel Hill: University of North Carolina, 1979, 1986. CT252 .D5.

———. *North Carolina Lives: The Tar Heel Who's Who.* Hopkinsville, Ky.: Historical Records Association, 1962. F253 .N88.

Land Acquisition

Hofmann, Margaret M. *Colony of North Carolina, 1735–1764. Abstracts of Land Patents.* Vol. 1. Weldon, N.C.: Roanoke News Co., 1982. F253 .H627.

———. *The Granville District of North Carolina, 1748–1763.* Vol. 1 of *Abstracts of Land Grants.* Weldon, N.D.: the author, 1979. F253 .H63.

———. *Province of North Carolina, 1663–1729. Abstracts of Land Patents.* Weldon, N.C.: the author, 1979. F253 .H63.

Holcomb, Brent. *North Carolina Land Grants in South Carolina.* Vol. 1, *Tryon County, 1768–1773.* Clinton, S.C.: the author, 1975. F253 .H64.

Early Settlers

Browder, Nathaniel C. *The Cherokee Indians and Those Who Came Later.* Hyattsville, N.C.: 1973. 2d printing. 1980. F262 .C43B76.

Cunningham, Caroline, comp. *Migrations: Actual and Implied.* Raleigh: the author, 1968. F253 .C8.

Dobson, David. *Directory of Scots in the Carolinas, 1680–1830.* Baltimore: Genealogical Publishing Co., 1986. F265 .S3D63.

Ray, Worth S. *The Lost Tribes of North Carolina.* Part 1, *Index and Digest to Hathaway;* part 2, *Colonial Granville Co.;* part 3, *The Mecklenburg Signers;* part 4, *Old Albemarle and Its Descendants.* Austin, Tex.: the author, 1947. F253 .R38.

———. *Mecklenburg Signers and Their Neighbors.* Austin, Tex.: the author, 1946. F262 .M4R3.

Smallwood, Marilu B., comp. *Some Colonial and Revolutionary Families of North Carolina.* 2 vols. Washington, D.C.: the compiler, 1964. F253 .S6.

Local Records

Bennett, William D., ed. *Orange County Records,* Vol. Q, *Granville Proprietary Land Office Abstracts and Loose Papers.* Raleigh: the author, 1987. F253 .B28.

Burns, Annie W., comp. *North Carolina Genealogical Records.* Washington, D.C.: the author, 1943. F253 .B4.

Clemens, William M., comp. *North and South Carolina Marriage Records From the Earliest Colonial Days to the Civil War.* New York: E.P. Dutton & Co., 1927. F253 .C62.

Fries, Adelaide L. *Records of the Moravians of North Carolina, 1752–.* 11 vols. Raleigh: State of North Carolina. F265 .M7F75.

Mitchell, Thornton W. *North Carolina Wills: A Testator Index, 1665–1900.* 2 vols. Raleigh: the author, 1987. F253 .M57.

Murray, Nicholas R., and Dorothy L. Murray. *Computer Index to North Carolina Marriage Bonds.* Hammond, La.: Hunting for Bears, 1982. F253 .C73.

North Carolina. Secretary of State. Bryan J. Grimes, ed. *Abstracts of North Carolina Wills.* Raleigh: State of North Carolina, 1910. F253 .N86.

————. *North Carolina Wills and Inventories*. Raleigh: State of North Carolina, 1967. F253 .N86115.

Olds, Fred A. *An Abstract of North Carolina Wills, ca. 1760–1800*. Reprint. Baltimore: Genealogical Publishing Co., 1965. F253 .O4.

Pompey, Sherman L. *Some Early North Carolina Records*. Pasadena, Calif.: the author, 1986. F253 .P65.

Radcliffe, Lois A. *North Carolina Taxpayers*. Baltimore: Genealogical Publishing Co., 1984. F253 .R37.

Volume 1, 1701–86; volume 2, 1679–1709.

Saunders, William, ed. *Colonial Records of North Carolina*, Vol. 1, *1662–1712*. Vols. 1–10. Raleigh: State of North Carolina, 1886. F251 .N6.

Spence, Wilma C., and Edna M. Shannonhouse, comps. *North Carolina Bible Records (from early 18th century to the present)*. Logan, Utah: the compilers, 1973. F253 .S63.

Spence, Wilma C., comp. *Tombstones and Epitaphs of Northeast North Carolina: Consisting of Beaufort, Camden, Chowan, Currituck, Gates, Hyde, Pasquotank, Perquimans, and Washington Counties*. Baltimore: Gateway Press, 1973. F253 .S64.

Weeks, Stephen B. *Historical Review of the Colonial and State Records of North Carolina*. Raleigh: E.M. Uzzell & Co., 1914. F251 .N63.

————. *Index to the Colonial and State Records of North Carolina*. Vols. 1–25 in 4 vols. Goldsboro, N.C.: State of North Carolina, 1909. F251 .N61.

Military Records

Colonial Wars

Burns, Annie W. *Abstracts of Pension Papers of North Carolina Soldiers of the Revolution, 1812, and Indian Wars*. 15 vols. Typescript. Washington, D.C.: n.p., 1960–66. F253 .B38.

American Revolution

Battey, George M. *The Tennessee "Bee-Hive;" or Early (1778–1791) North Carolina Land Grants in the Volunteer State, Being an Index With Some 3,100 Names of Revolutionary Soldiers and Settlers Who Participated in the Distribution of More than 5,000,000 Acres of Land*. Typescript. Washington, D.C.: n.p., 1949. E255 .B27.

Burns, Annie W. *Abstracts of Pension Papers of North Carolina Soldiers of the Revolution, 1812, and Indian Wars*. 15 vols. Typescript. Washington, D.C.: n.p., 1960–66. F253 .B38.

Cartwright, Betty G., and Lillian J. Gardiner. *North Carolina Land Grants in Tennessee, 1778–1791*. Memphis: Division of Archives, 1958. E255 .C33.

Section 2 and Appendix A lists military warrants for service in the Revolutionary War.

Clark, Walter E., ed. *State Records of North Carolina*. Vols. 11–26. New York: AMS Press, 1968–78. F251 .N62.

Davis, Charles L. *A Brief History of the North Carolina Troops of the Continental Establishment in the War of the Revolution, With a Register of Officers of the Same*. Philadelphia: n.p., 1896. E263 .N8F25.

Lazenby, Mary E., comp. *Catawba Frontiers, 1775–1781: Memories of Pensioners*. Washington, D.C.: the compiler, 1950. E263 .N8L3.

Rouse, J. K. *Another Revolutionary War Soldier Dies*. N.p., 1978. E206 .R88.

Contains obituaries of Revolutionary War soldiers from North Carolina abstracted from newspapers.

Schenck, David. *North Carolina, 1780–81: Being a History of the Invasion of the Carolinas by the British Army Under Lord Cornwallis in 1780–81*. Raleigh: Edwards & Boughton, 1889. F521 .N87.

War of 1812

Burns, Annie W. *Abstracts of Pension Papers of North Carolina Soldiers of the Revolution, 1812, and Indian Wars*. 15 vols. Typescript. Washington, D.C.: n.p., 1960–66. F253 .B38.

Civil War

Birdsong, James C. *Brief Sketches of the North Carolina State Troops*. Raleigh: Josephus Daniels, 1894. E573.4 .B61.

Clark, Walter. *Histories of the Several Regiments and Battalions From North Carolina in the Great War, 1861–1865*. 5 vols. Raleigh: State of North Carolina, 1901. E573.4 .C59; E573.4 .H57.

Manarin, Louis H., comp. *North Carolina Troops, 1861–1865. A Roster*. 6 vols. Raleigh: State Department of Archives and History, 1966. E573.3 .M3.

Manarin, Louis H., and Weymouth Jordan. *North Carolina Troops, 1861–1865. A Roster.* 9 vols. Raleigh: State Department of Archives and History, 1981–83. E573.3 .M3.

North Carolina. John W. Moore, ed. *Roster of North Carolina Troops in the War Between the States.* 4 vols. Raleigh: Ashe and Gattling, 1882. E573.3 .N87.

Index: Micro 5995 (E).

Pamlico Chapter, Daughters of the Confederacy. *The Confederate Reveille, Memorial Edition.* Raleigh: Edwards and Boughton, n.d. E573 .P18.

Periodicals

Broughton, Carrie L., comp. *Marriage and Death Notices From the Raleigh Register and North Carolina Gazette, 1799–1825.* Baltimore: Genealogical Publishing Co., 1966. F253 .N8616.

Cotten, Elizabeth H. *Marriage and Death Notices From the Raleigh, North Carolina Newspapers, 1796–1826.* Easley, S.C.: Southern Historical Press, 1977. F253 .C79.

Fouts, Raymond P. *Abstracts From the North Carolina Gazette of New Bern, North Carolina.* Cocoa, Fla.: the author, 1983. F253 .F67.

Volume 1, 1751–59 and 1768–90; volume 2, 1790–92.

———. *Abstracts From the State Gazette of North Carolina.* Cocoa, Fla.: the author, 1982. F253 .F68.

Volume 1, 1787–91; volume 2, 1792–95; volume 3, 1796–99.

Hambrick, David O. *Index to the North Carolina Historical and Genealogical Register (Hathaway's Register).* 3 vols. Bradenton, Fla.: n.p., 1963. F251 .N89112 Supp.

Fuller, Marian C. *Obituaries and Marriage Notices From the Carolina Watchman, 1832–1890. An Index.* Greenville, S.C.: A Press, 1981. F253 .F84.

Neal, Lois S., comp. *Abstracts of Vital Records From Raleigh, North Carolina Newspapers.* Spartanburg, S.C.: The Reprint Co., 1979. F264 .R1N34.

Volume 1, 1799–1819; volume 2, 1820–29.

North Carolina Genealogical Society. *Index of North Carolina Newspapers.* 2 vols. Raleigh: the society, 1931. F253 .I53.

Ray, Worth S. *Ray's Index and Digest to Hathaway's North Carolina Historical and Genealogical Register.* Baltimore: Genealogical Publishing Co., 1955. F251 .N8912.

Topkins, Robert M., comp. *Marriage and Death Notices From the Western Carolinian, 1820–1842. An Index.* Raleigh: n.p., 1975. F261 .T66.

Directories

City

Ahoskie 1959–63, 1970–77

Albemarle
(Badin, rural routes) 1951–84

Asheboro
(Liberty, Ramseur, Randleman) 1967–69, 1941, 1947, 1964–67, 1969–74

Asheville 1896–1984

Boone 1968, 1971

Brevard 1962

Burlington
(Graham) 1920, 1927, 1935–83

Canton 1956, 1972

Chapel Hill
(Carrboro) 1957–85

Charlotte (suburbs) 1889–92, 1897–1916, 1927–85

Cherryville 1962–83

Clinton 1960–83

Concord 1913, 1916, 1938, 1949–84

Dunn
(Erwin) 1957–85

Durham 1887, 1888, 1897–1984

Eden (formerly Leaksville) 1967, 1970–82

Edenton 1959, 1962, 1972, 1976, 1980

Fayetteville 1906, 1909, 1913, 1919, 1924, 1937–85

Forrest City
(Rutherfordstown, Spindale) 1958–84

Fuquay Springs
(Varina) 1959–65

Gastonia 1921, 1927, 1934–42, 1945–85

Goldsboro 1906, 1914, 1920, 1928, 1930, 1934, 1938, 1945–83

Greensboro (suburbs) 1899, 1903–84

Greenville 1944–73, 1985

Hendersonville 1935–41, 1947, 1957–85

Hickory
(Granite Falls, Hildebran) 1941–75

High Point 1939–84

Jacksonville 1957–83

Kannapolis 1950–84

Kernersville 1960–67

Kings Mountain
(Bessemer City, Grover) 1969, 1972

Kinston 1908–28, 1949–84

Laurinburg 1959–84

Leaksville
(Draper, Spray) 1958–66

Lenoir
(Granite Falls, Hudson, Patterson, Whitwell) 1948, 1955, 1959, 1961, 1967–76

Lexington 1947–72

Lincolnton 1957–84

Louisburg
(Franklinton) 1966

Lumberton 1938, 1968–75

Madison
(Mayodan) 1959–83

Marion 1952, 1956, 1968

Monroe 1922, 1955, 1960

Morehead City
(Beaufort) 1958–84

Mooresville
(Cornelius, Davidson, Lake Norman, Mt. Mourne) 1939, 1954, 1959, 1961, 1968–76

Morganton
(Drexel, Valdese) 1941, 1950, 1960, 1968, 1971, 1973, 1976

Mt. Airy
(Dobson, Pilot Mountain) 1949, 1954–60, 1969, 1971–77

Mt. Olive 1972–82

New Bern 1904–20, 1926, 1937, 1947, 1951, 1954, 1959, 1961–84

Newton
(Catawba, Claremont, Conover, Maiden) 1955–59, 1968–75, 1985

North Wilkesboro
(Wilkesboro Co.) 1939, 1948, 1953, 1956, 1959, 1967, 1975

Oxford 1959–65, 1972–83

Plymouth 1960–78

Raeford 1959

Raleigh (suburbs) 1899–1983

Reidsville 1932, 1935, 1954–84

Roanoke Rapids
(Weldon) 1948–56, 1960, 1964, 1969–76

Rockingham
(suburbs, Hamlet) 1957–84

Rocky Mount
(Englewood, Swelton Hgts., West Haven) 1908–20, 1928–84

Roxboro 1957, 1959, 1967, 1970, 1973

Salisbury
(Spencer) 1907, 1913, 1935, 1968, 1970, 1973

Sanford
(Jonesboro Hgts.) 1950–83

Scotland Neck 1900–62

Shelby 1937, 1945–53, 1959, 1965–76

Siler 1959, 1971

Smithfield
(Four Oaks, Pine Level, Princeton, Selma, Wilson Mills) 1928, 1957–85

Southern Pines
(Aberdeen) 1958–84

Springlake 1963, 1965, 1967

Statesville 1916, 1932, 1944, 1950–60, 1968–74

Tarboro 1956–85

Thomasville 1886, 1922, 1933, 1935, 1947–60, 1968–76

Valdese 1960

Wadesboro 1958–83

Waynesville
   (Hazelwood, Lake Junalaska) 1954–59, 1971

Wendell
   (Zebulon) 1965, 1967

Whiteville 1959–82

Williamston 1959–80

Wilmington 1860, 1879, 1881, 1889, 1897, 1900–26, 1930–85

Willsboro 1958

Wilson 1908–84

Windsor 1960, 1962

Winston-Salem (suburbs) 1889, 1892, 1900

York 1958–81

County, Business, and Miscellaneous

Guilford 1922–25, 1932

Mecklenburg 1914

North Carolina (state) (see also Maryland; Delaware; south Delaware; and Norfolk, Va.) 1867–96, 1910, 1915

Phelps 1909

Randolph 1894

South Carolina

Historical Highlights

1629   Charter given by England to Robert Heath. Proprietary government established. Area embraced present-day North Carolina and South Carolina.

1633   Charter given by England to the Earl of Clarendon, a proprietor.

1691   A governor selected by the proprietors to rule the Carolinas.

   England granted several proprietorships, and counties were organized to distinguish between the boundaries of the granted lands.

1712   Separate governors selected for North Carolina and South Carolina.

1729   Proprietary rule revoked by England. North Carolina and South Carolina declared separate royal colonies.

   The Low Country, in and around Charleston, was settled primarily by the English and a few from Barbados. The Up Country, in the more northerly and westerly regions, was settled primarily by those from Pennsylvania and other northern states, coming down the Shenandoah Valley, plus those who migrated from the Low Country. Despite the use of counties, all land transactions were registered at Charleston until 1785 when judicial districts were established. From that time the land records were filed in those districts, and copies were sent to Charleston. The districts were eventually eliminated and merged into counties— making research in land records in this state a challenge.

1776   One of the thirteen original colonies at the time of the American Revolution.

1860   First to secede from the Union and join the Confederate States of America.

Published Record Sources

Guidebooks

Hicks, Theresa M. *South Carolina. A Guide for Genealogists.* Columbia: Peppercorn Publishing, 1985. F268 .H56.

Schweitzer, George K. *South Carolina Genealogical Research.* Knoxville, Tenn.: the author, 1984. Z1313 .S39

Census Indexes and Abstracts

Federal

1790   United States Bureau of the Census. *Heads of Families at the First Census of the United States Taken in the Year 1790. South Carolina.* Reprint. Bountiful, Utah: Accelerated Indexing Systems, 1978. F268 .U54.

1800   F268 .J33
        Holcomb, Brent. *Index to the 1800 Census of South Carolina*. Baltimore: Genealogical Publishing Co., 1980. F268 .H635.

1810   F268 .J332

1820   F268 .J334

1830   F268 .J335

1840   F268 .J337

1850   F268 .J34
        Bronson, Patricia P. *An Index, United States Census, 1850. (Orangeburg District; Pickens District)*. Wye Mills, Md.: the author, 1973. F273 .B76.

1860   Arnold, Jonnie P. *Index to the 1860 Federal Census of South Carolina*. Clarkesville, Ga.: the author, 1982. F268 .A76.
        Dilts, Bryan L. *1860 South Carolina Index—Microform*. Salt Lake City: Index Publishing Co., 1984. M87/2007.

All the above publications shown without the name of the compiler or author are by Ronald V. Jackson, Accelerated Indexing Systems.

State

Jackson, Ronald V. *Early South Carolina*. Bountiful, Utah: Accelerated Indexing System, 1980. F268 .J26.

Mortality Schedules

Arnold, Jonnie P. *Index to 1860 Mortality Schedule of South Carolina*. Clarkesville, Ga.: the author, 1982. F268 .A763.

Biographies

Cote, Richard N., ed. *Dictionary of South Carolina Biographies*. Easley, S.C.: Southern Historical Press, 1985. CT259 .C67.

Crawford, Geddings H. *Who's Who is South Carolina*. Columbia: McGaw, 1921. F268 .W62.

Garlington, J.C. *Men of the Time: Sketches of Living Notables—A Biographical Encyclopedia of Central South Carolina Leaders*. Spartanburg: Garlington Publishing Co., 1902. F268 .G37.

Grier, Ralph E., ed. *South Carolina and Her Builders*. Columbia: Carolina Biographical Associates, 1930. F268 .G84.

Hemphill, J.C., ed. *Men of Mark in South Carolina*. 4 vols. Washington, D.C.: Men of Mark Publishing Co., 1907. F268 .H49.

O'Neall, John B. *Biographical Sketches of the Bench and Bar of South Carolina*. 2 vols. Charleston: Courtenay & Co., 1859. F268 .O58.

Early Settlers

Bethea, Mary B. *Ancestral Key to the Pee Dee*. Columbia: R.L. Bryan Co., 1978. CT259 .B47.

Elzas, Barnett A. *The Jews of South Carolina*. Philadelphia: Lippincott, 1905. F280 .J5E52.

Medlin, William F. *Quaker Families of South Carolina and Georgia*. Columbia: the author, 1982. F280 .F89M43.

Milling, Chapman J. *Exile Without an End*. Columbia: Bostich & Thornley, 1943. F280 .F7M5.

Examines Acadians in South Carolina.

South Carolina Genealogical Society Chapters. Lineage Charts. 6 vols. Greenville, S.C.: A Press, 1986. F268 .L56.

Stephenson, Jean. *Scotch-Irish Migration to South Carolina, 1772*. Reprint. Strasburg, Va.: Shenandoah Publishing House, 1971. F280 .S4S8.

Rev. William Martin and his five shiploads of settlers.

Warren, Mary B. *Citizens and Immigrants—South Carolina, 1768*. Danielsville, Ga.: Heritage Papers, 1980. F268 .W36.

Young, Willie P. *A Collection of Upper South Carolina Genealogy and Family Records*. Easley, S.C.: Southern Historical Press, 1979. F268 .Y59.

Local Records

Clemson, William M., comp. *North and South Carolina Marriage Records From the Earliest Colonial Days to the Civil War*. New York: Dutton & Co., 1927. F253 .C62.

Houston, Martha Lou, comp. *Indexes to the County Wills of South Carolina*. Reprint. Baltimore: Genealogical Publishing Co., 1970. F268 .S66.

Moore, Caroline T., comp. *Abstracts of the Wills of the State of South Carolina, 1760–1784*. Columbia: the compiler, 1969. F268 .M67.

——. *Abstracts of Wills of Charleston District, South Carolina, and Other Will Records in the District, 1783–1800.* Columbia: the author, 1974. F279 .C453A225.

Reville, Janie, comp. *A Compilation of Original Lists of Protestant Immigrants to South Carolina, 1763–1773.* Baltimore: Genealogical Publishing Co., 1968. F272 .R49.

——. *Some South Carolina Genealogical Records.* Easley, S.C.: Southern Historical Press, 1986. F268 .R47.

Salley, A. S., Jr., ed. *Register of St. Philip's Parish, Charles Town, South Carolina, 1720–1758.* Columbia: University of South Carolina Press, 1971. Vol. 1 (1720–58). F279 .C453A23; Vol. 2 (1754–1810). F279 .C453A24.

South Carolina. Department of Archives and History. Lee C. Hendrix and Morn M. Lindsay, comps. *The Jury Lists of South Carolina, 1778–1779.* Greenville, S.C.: the compilers, 1975. F268 .S64.

Warren, Mary B. *South Carolina Wills, 1670–1853 or Later.* Danielsville, Ga.: Heritage Papers, 1981. F268 .W37.

Military Records

American Revolution

Bailey, James C. *Some Heroes of the American Revolution.* Spartanburg, S.C.: Band & White, 1924. E206 .B3.

Boddie, William W. *Marion's Men: A List of Twenty-five Hundred.* Charleston: Heiser Printing Co., 1938. C263 .S7B6.

Burns, Annie W. *Abstracts of Pension Papers of Revolutionary Soldiers, 1812, and Indian Wars, Who Lived in South Carolina.* 8 vols. Typescript. Washington, D.C.: n.p., n.d. E263 .S7.

Cox, William E. *Battle of King's Mountain Participants, October 7, 1780.* Typescript. N.p., n.d. E241 .K5C6.

DeSaussure, Wilmot G. "The Names . . . of the Officers Who Served in the South Carolina Regiments on the Continental Establishment: Of the Officers Who Served in the Militia: of What Troops Were Upon the Continent Establishment and Of What Militia Organizations Served."

Charleston, South Carolina Yearbook (1893): 205–37. D263.67 .D36 (also F279 .C4C4.)

Ervin, Sara A., ed. *South Carolinians in the Revolution: With Service Records and Miscellaneous Data . . . 1775–1855.* Ypsilanti, Mich.: n.p., 1949. Reprint. Baltimore: Genealogical Publishing Co., 1971. E263 .S7E78.

Moss, Bobby G. *South Carolina Patriots in the American Revolution.* Baltimore: Genealogical Publishing Co., 1982. E263 .S7M67.

Pruitt, Jayne, C. G. *Revolutionary War Pension Applicants Who Served From South Carolina.* Fairfax Co., Va.: n.p., 1946. E263 .S7P78.

Reville, Janie. *Revolutionary Claims Filed in South Carolina.* Baltimore: Genealogical Publishing Co., 1969. E263 .S7A53.

Salley, Alexander S., ed. *Documents Relating to the History of South Carolina During the Revolutionary War.* Columbia: Historical Commission of South Carolina, 1908. E263 .S7S6.

——. *Records of the Regiments of the South Carolina Line.* Baltimore: Genealogical Publishing Co., 1977. E263 .S7R42.

——. *Accounts Audited of Revolutionary Claims Against South Carolina.* 3 vols. Columbia: Historical Commission of South Carolina, 1935–42. E263 .S7S66.

South Carolina. Department of Archives and History. *Stub-Entries to Indent Issued in Payment of Claims Against South Carolina Growing Out of the Revolution.* 12 vols. N.p., 1919–57. E263 .S7S7.

White, Katherine K. *The King's Mountain Men: the Story of the Battle: With Sketches of the American Soldiers Who Took Part.* Dayton, Va.: J.K. Ruebush Co., 1924. Reprint. Baltimore: Genealogical Publishing Co., 1970. E241 .K5W5.

War of 1812

Burns, Annie W. *Abstracts of Pension Papers of Revolutionary Soldiers, 1812, and Indian Wars, Who Lived in South Carolina.* 8 vols. Typescript. Washington, D.C.: n.p., n.d. E263 .S7.

Civil War

Hagood, Johnson. *Memoirs of the War of Secession. From the Original Manuscripts . . . .* Columbia: The State Company, 1910. E577.4 .H14.

Salley, Alexander S., Jr. *South Carolina Troops in Confederate Service.* 3 vols. Columbia: South Carolina Historical Commission, 1913. E577.3 .S72.

South Carolina. Commissioner of Confederate Rolls. *Report of M.P. Trible, South Carolina Commissioner of Confederate Rolls to the General Assembly, 1903.* Columbia: The State Company, 1904. E577 .S82.

United Daughters of the Confederacy, South Carolina Division. *South Carolina Women in the Confederacy.* Columbia: The State Company, 1903. E628 .U58.

Periodicals

Moran, Alton T., comp. *Genealogical Abstracts From the South Carolina Gazette, 1732–1735.* Bowie, Md.: Heritage Books, 1987. F268 .M677.

Simpson, Robert T. and Mrs. Charles A. Barnham, Jr., comps. *Some South Carolina Marriages and Obituaries and Miscellaneous Information, 1826–1854. Abstracted From Early Newspapers.* Memphis: the compilers, 1970. F268 .S6.

South Carolina Genealogies. *Articles From the South Carolina Historical and Genealogical Magazine.* 5 vols. and index. Spartanburg: The Reprint Co., 1983. F268 .S68.

South Carolina Historical Magazine. Index to Vols. 1–40 (1900–1939); Vols. 41–71 (1940–1970). Columbia: South Carolina Historical Society, 1977. F266 .S55.

Index.

Directories

City

Abbeville 1868–70

Aiken 1952–71

Anderson 1905–10, 1915–85

Barnwell 1861

Batesville
(Leesville) 1961, 1972–82

Beaufort 1961–85

Belton
(Honea Path, Williamston) 1960–73

Bennettsville 1960–78, 1984

Bishopville 1960, 1972, 1973–80

Blacksburg
(Cherokee Co.) 1971

Camden
pre 1861 (microfiche)

Cayce
(Lexington, W. Columbia) 1966–84

Charleston
pre 1861 (microfiche)
1861–1935 (microfilm)
(suburbs, Kanawa Valley) 1936–85

Chester 1958–82

Clinton 1970

Columbia
pre 1861 (microfiche)
1903–84

Conway 1959–85

Darlington 1958, 1961, 1969, 1977

Dillon 1960, 1962, 1973

Easley
(Liberty, Pickens) 1957–85

Florence 1913, 1969, 1972, 1977

Fort Mill 1958–66

Gafney
(Blacksburg) 1961, 1967–84

Georgetown 1960–83

Greenville (suburbs) 1905–12, 1917, 1931–85

Greenwood
(Hodges, Ninety-six, Ware Shoals) 1912, 1916, 1919, 1968–75

Greer 1955–59, 1965, 1967, 1761–85

Hamlet 1961–65

Hartsville 1959, 1961, 1976

Honea Path 1961–63

Kingstree 1969

Lake City 1971, 1975–76

Lancaster 1954–84

Laurens
  (Clinton) 1912, 1961–84

Manning 1960, 1970

Marion (suburbs) 1959–72, 1977–83

Monck's Corner 1974–84

Mullins 1959–79, 1984

Myrtle Beach
  (North Myrtle Beach, Surfside Beach) 1959–84

Newberry 1921, 1971–81

Orangeburg 1907, 1909, 1953–83

Pickens
  (Liberty) 1957, 1959, 1962

Rock Hill
  (Ebenezer, Ford Mill) 1946–85

Seneca
  (Walhalla, Westminster, West Union) 1971–75

Spartanburg 1900, 1908, 1911, 1913, 1916, 1926–84

Sumter 1901, 1905, 1907, 1954–60, 1969, 1972, 1986

Tri-City
  (Senaca, Walhalla, Westminster) 1962

Union 1920, 1961–84

Walterboro 1970, 1985

Waupun 1986

Westminster
  (Oconee Co.) 1955

Winnsboro 1961

Wooddruff 1962

County, Business, and Miscellaneous

South Carolina (state) 1880, 1898

Georgia

Historical Highlights

1732   Charter given by England to James Oglethorpe.

1749   First African slaves imported.

English prisoners were transported to Georgia, which also served as a haven for persecuted Protestants from several northern and central European countries. A plantation economy developing along the Atlantic Coast prompted the beginnings of slave labor. Spanish settlers from Florida made several incursions into Georgia, the Carolinas, and Virginia—convincing them to join together for retaliatory military invasions into Florida.

1753   Declared an English royal province.

1776   One of the thirteen original colonies at the time of the American Revolution.

After Georgia became a royal province, settlements were established, peopled by former settlers in Virginia, the Carolinas, and a few from New England. The presence of hostile Indians slowed white settlement there, however. During the American Revolution a majority of Georgia's inhabitants were sympathetic to the Loyalist cause, many of them fleeing to Florida to escape threats from the rebels. Most of the state remained under British control during the war.

1802   Western land (now part of Alabama and Mississippi) ceded to the United States.

1805   First land lottery conducted to dispose of newly acquired Indian lands.

1813   Creek Indian War

1828   Cherokee Indian disturbances

After the Creeks ceded some of their lands to Georgia, the first land lottery was conducted in 1805. This was followed by similar lotteries (some of them giving preference to veterans) in 1806, 1820, 1821, 1827, and 1832—all after additional Indian lands became available. The Creeks were forced from most of their Georgia land in 1813 and 1814. Under a federal resettlement program in 1832, the Cherokees in northwestern Georgia began to be moved into Indian Territory (Arkansas and Oklahoma).

1861   Seceded from the Union and joined the Confederate States of America.

Published Record Sources

Guidebooks

Dorsey, James C., comp. *Georgia Genealogy and Local History: A Bibliography.* Spartanburg, S.C.: The Reprint Co., 1983. Z1273 .D67.

Georgia. Department of Archives and History. Robert S. Davis, Jr., comp. *Research in Georgia.* Easley, S.C.: Southern Historical Press, 1981. CD3184 .D78.

Goff, John H. *Place Names of Georgia, 1975.* Athens: University of Georgia Press, 1975. F284 .G63.

Hemperley, Marion R., comp. *Cities, Towns and Communities of Georgia Between 1847–1962: 8,500 Places and the County in Which Located.* Easley, S.C.: Southern Historical Press, 1980. F284 .H45.

Jones, Charles C., Jr. *The Dead Towns of Georgia: From Collections of the Georgia Historical Society, Vol. 4.* Savannah: Morning News Steam Printing House, 1878. F289 .J6.

Krakow, Kenneth K. *Georgia Place-Names.* Macon: Winship Press, 1975. F284 .K72.

Schweitzer, George K. *Georgia Genealogical Research.* Knoxville, Tenn.: the author, 1987. F285 .S38.

Census Indexes and Abstracts

Federal

1790   (substitute)
        DeLamar, Marie, and Elisabeth Rothstein. *The Reconstructed 1790 Census of Georgia: Substitutes For Georgia's Lost 1790 Census.* Baltimore: Genealogical Publishing Co., 1985. F285 .D4.

1820   F285 .J28
        Georgia Historical Society. *Index to United States Census of Georgia for 1820.* 2d ed. Baltimore: Genealogical Publishing Co., 1969. F285 .G38.

1830   F285 .J29
        Register, Alvaretta K. *Index to the 1830 Census of Georgia.* Baltimore:

Genealogical Publishing Co., 1974. F285 .R39.

1840   F285 J3
        Sheffield, Eileen, and Barbara Woods. *1840 Index to Georgia Census.* Baytown, Tex.: the authors, 1971. F285 .S5.

1850   F285 .J32
        Otto, Rhea C. *1850 Census of Georgia (Free Citizens).* Savannah: the author, 1970. F285 .086.

1860   Acord, Arlis, and Martha W. W. Anderson, et al. *An Index For the 1860 Federal Census of Georgia.* LaGrange, Ga.: Family Tree, 1986. F285 .A69.

All the above publications shown without the name of the compiler or author are by Ronald V. Jackson, Accelerated Indexing Systems.

State

Jackson, Ronald V. *Early Georgia, 1733–1819.* Bountiful, Utah: Accelerated Indexing Systems, 1980. F285 .J26.

Townsend, Brigid S. *Indexes to Seven State Census Reports For Counties in Georgia, 1838–1845.* 7 vols. Atlanta: R. J. Taylor, Jr., Foundation, 1975. F285 .T68.

Biographies

Butts, Sarah H., comp. *The Mothers of Some Distinguished Georgians of the Last Half of the Century.* New York: J.J. Little & Co., 1902. F285 .B98.

Coleman, Kenneth, and Charles S. Gorn. *District of Georgia Biography.* 2 vols. Athens: University of Georgia Press, 1983. CT230 .D53.

Gilmer, George R. *Sketches of Some of the First Settlers of Upper Georgia—Indexed Edition.* Reprint. Baltimore: Genealogical Publishing Co., 1970. F285 .G5.

Ham, H. W. J. *Representative Georgians: Biographical Sketches of Men Now in Public Life.* Savannah: Morning News Printers, 1887. F285 .H19.

Nevin, James B., ed. *Prominent Women of Georgia.* Atlanta: National Biographical Publishers, 1929. F285 .N49.

Northern, William J., ed. *Men of Mark in Georgia.* 6 vols. Atlanta: A.B. Caldwell, 1907. F285 .N87.

Reeves, Emma B. *Georgia Genealogical Gleanings: Abstracts From Memoirs of Georgia—Historical and Biographical.* N.p., 1984. F285 .R37.

Turbeville, Robert P., ed. *Eminent Georgians.* Vol. 1. Atlanta: Southern Society for Research and History, 1937. F285 .E64.

Land Acquisition

Beckemeyer, Frances H., comp. *Abstracts of Georgia Colonial Conveyance Book C-1, 1950–1761.* Atlanta: R.J. Taylor, Jr., Foundation, 1975. F285 .B42.

Bryant, Pat, comp. *Entry of Claims for Georgia Landholders, 1733–1755.* Atlanta: State Printing Office, 1975. F285 .G35.

Davis, Robert S., Jr., and Silas Lucas, Jr., comps. *The Georgia Land Lottery Papers, 1805–1914.* Easley, S.C.: Southern Historical Press, 1979. F285 .D25.

Hemperley, Marion R. *Military Certificates of Georgia, 1776–1800 On File in the Surveyor General's Department.* Atlanta: State Printing Office, 1983. F285 .H45.

Houston, Martha Lou. *Reprint of Official Register of Land Lottery of Georgia, 1827.* Reprint. Baltimore: Genealogical Publishing Co., 1967. F290 .R42.

Lucas, Silas E. *Index to the Headright and Bounty Grants of Georgia, 1756–1909.* Vidalia, Ga.: Georgia Genealogical Reprints, 1970. F285 .L814.

———. *The Third or 1820 Land Lottery of Georgia.* Easley, S.C.: Southern Historical Press, 1986. F285 .L83.

———. *The Third and Fourth or 1820 and 1821 Land Lotteries of Georgia.* Easley, S.C.: Georgia Genealogical Reprints. Southern Historical Press, 1973. F285 .T48.

———. *The 1832 Gold Lottery of Georgia: Containing a List of the Fortunate Drawers in Said Lottery.* Easley, S.C.: Southern Historical Press, 1976. F285 .L8.

Richardson, Maran M., and Jessie J. Mize, comps. *1832 Cherokee Land Lottery: Index to Revolutionary Soldiers, Their Widows and Orphans Who Were Fortunate Drawers.* Danielsville, Ga.: Heritage Papers, 1969. F285 .R5.

Taken from *Cherokee Land Lottery* by James F. Smith.

Smith, James F. *The Cherokee Land Lottery.* Baltimore: Genealogical Publishing Co., 1969. F285 .S64.

Warren, Mary B. *Alphabetical Index to Georgia's 1832 Gold Lottery.* Danielsville, Ga.: Heritage Papers, 1981. F285 .W28.

Wood, Virginia S., and Ralph V. Wood. *1805 Georgia Land Lottery.* Cambridge, Mass.: The Greenewood Press, 1964. F285 .W6.

Early Settlers

Austin, Jeannette H. *The Georgians: Genealogies of Pioneer Settlers.* Baltimore: Genealogical Publishing Co., 1984. F285 .A89.

Coulter, Ellis M., and Albert B. Saye, eds. *A List of the Early Settlers of Georgia.* Athens: University of Georgia Press, 1949. F285 .C78.

Gnann, Pearl R., ed. *Georgia Salzburger and Allied Families.* Savannah: the author, 1956. F295 .S1G56.

History of the Baptist Denomination in Georgia. Atlanta: James P. Harrison & Co., 1881. F285 .H67.

Huxford, Folks, comp. *Pioneers of Wiregrass Georgia.* 7 vols. Adel, Ga.: Patten Publishing Co., 1951. F285 .H8.

Jones, George F. *The Germans of Colonial Georgia, 1733–1783.* Baltimore: Genealogical Publishing Co., 1986. F295 .G4J66.

Montgomery, Horace. *Georgians in Profile.* Athens: University of Georgia Press, 1958. F285 .M73.

National Society Colonial Dames of America, Georgia. *Some Early Epitaphs in Georgia.* N.p.: the society, 1925. F285 .N27.

Potter, Jane P. *Surname Index to History of the Baptist Denominations in Georgia.* Harlington, Tex.: Tip-O-Texas Genealogical Society, 1982. F285 .H673P68.

Rigsby, Lewis W., comp. *Historic Georgia Families.* Baltimore: Genealogical Publishing Co., 1969. F285 .R53.

Local Records

Austin, Jeannette H. *Georgia Bible Records.* Baltimore: Genealogical Publishing Co., 1985. F285 .A889.

———. *Georgia Intestate Records*. Baltimore: Genealogical Publishing Co., 1986. F285 .A8895.

———. *Index to Georgia Wills*. Baltimore: Genealogical Publishing Co., 1985. F285 .A9.

Baker, Pearl R. *'Neath Georgia Sod—Cemetery Inscriptions*. Albany, Ga.: Georgia Pioneers Association, 1980. F285 .B34.

Brooke, Ted O., comp. *In the Name of God, Amen: Georgia Wills, 1733–1860: An Index*. Atlanta: Pilgrim Press, 1876. F285 .B76.

Davis, Robert S. *The Georgia Black Book: Morbid, Macabre, and Sometimes Disgusting Records of Genealogical Value*. Easley, S.C.: Southern Historical Press, 1982. F285 .D24.

Index to Probate Records of Colonial Georgia, 1733–1778. Atlanta: R. J. Taylor, Jr., Foundation, 1983. F285 .I53.

Index to Georgia Tax Records, 1789–1817. 5 vols. Spartanburg, S.C.: The Reprint Co., 1986. F285 .I52.

Ingmire, Frances F. *Colonial Georgia Marriage Records From 1760's to 1810*. St. Louis: the author, 1985. F285 .I55.

Lucas, Silas E., Jr., comp. *Some Georgia County Records*. 3 vols. Easley, S.C.: Southern Historical Press, 1977. F285 .L82.

National Society Colonial Dames of America, Georgia. *Abstracts of Colonial Wills of the State of Georgia, 1733–1777*. Atlanta: the society, 1962. F285 .N3.

Payne, Dorothy E., comp. *Georgia Pensioners*. 2 vols. McLean, Va.: Sunbelt Publishing Co., 1986. F285 .P39.

Rice, Earldine, et al., comps. *Some Early Tax Digests of Georgia, 1790–1818*. Indianapolis: the compilers, 1971. F285 .R48.

Slave Bills of Sales Project. Vol. 1. Atlanta: African-American Family History Association, 1986. F285 .S57.

Military Records

American Revolution

Candler, Allen D. *Revolutionary Records of Georgia*. 3 vols. Atlanta: Franklin-Turner So., 1908. E263 .G3C35.

Georgia. Department of Archives and History. *Revolutionary Soldiers' Receipts For Georgia Bounty Grants*. Atlanta: Foote & Davies, 1928. F290 .G35.

Georgia. Secretary of State. *Authentic List of All Land Lottery Grants Made to Veterans of the Revolutionary War by the State of Georgia. Taken From Official State Records in the Surveyor-General Department; Housed in the Georgia Department of Archives and History*. Atlanta: State of Georgia, 1955. F290 .G38.

Houston, Martha Lou, comp. *600 Revolutionary Soldiers Living in Georgia in 1827–28*. Washington, D.C.: the compiler, 1932. E255 .H65.

Knight, Lucian L. *Georgia's Roster of the Revolution: Containing a List of the State's Defenders; Officers and Men; Soldiers and Sailors; Partisans and Regulars; Whether Enlisted from Georgia or Settled in Georgia After the Close of Hostilities; Compiled From Various Sources Including Official Documents, Both State and Federal, Certificates of Service, Land Grants, Pension Rolls and Other Records*. Atlanta: Index Printing Co., 1920. Reprint. Baltimore: Genealogical Publishing Co., 1967. E263.3 .G3.

Smith, George G. *The Story of Georgia and the Georgia People, 1732 to 1860*. Macon: George C. Smith Publisher, 1900. F286 .S66.

Contains lists of Revolutionary War soldiers.

Wilson, Caroline P. *Annals of Georgia*. Vol. 1. *Liberty County Records and a State Revolutionary Payroll*. New York: Grafton Press, n.d. F281 .W73.

War of 1812

Kratovil, Judy S. *Index to War of 1812 Service Records For Volunteer Soldiers From Georgia*. Atlanta: the author, 1986. E359.5 .G4K73.

Civil War

Georgia. State Division of Confederate Pensions and Records. Lillian Henderson, ed. *Roster of the Confederate Soldiers of Georgia, 1861–1865*. Hapeville, Ga.: Longino and Porter, 1959. E559 .A5.

Herbert, Sidney. *A Complete Roster of the Volunteer Military Organizations of the State of Georgia*. Atlanta: J.P. Harrison, 1878. VA152 .H53.

Lake Blackshear Regional Library. *Index to Roster of the Confederate Soldiers of Georgia, 1861–1865.* Spartanburg, S.C.: Joel Munsell, 1867. E559.7 .CHA J65.

Stegman, John F. *These Men She Gave.* Athens: University of Georgia Press, 1964. F294 .A7S8.

Periodicals

Master Index to the Georgia Genealogical Magazine, Numbers 1–14 (1961–1972). Easley, S.C.: Georgia Genealogical Magazine, 1973. F281 .G2967.

Thomas, Kenneth H. J. *Ken Thomas on Genealogy: A Collection of the First Two Years of a Genealogy Column From the Atlanta Journal Constitution.* Roswell, Ga.: W. H. Wolfe Association, 1981. F285 .T49.

Walker, Alice O., comp. *Personal Name Index to the Augusta Chronicle, Vol. L (1786–1799).* Atlanta: Augusta-Richmond County Publishing Library, 1987. F285 .W5.

Warren, Mary B., and Sarah F. White. *Marriages and Deaths, 1820 to 1830. Abstracted From Extant Georgia Newspapers.* Danielsville, Ga.: Heritage Papers, 1972. F285 .W3.

Directories

City

Adel
(Nashville, Sparks, Cook Co.) 1903–80

Albany 1912, 1922–25, 1946–82

Alma 1969

Americus
(Andersonville, De Soto, Leslie, Plains, Sumter) 1916, 1921–23, 1959, 1968–72

Ashburn 1970

Athens
(Bogart, Crawford, Hull, Lexington, Watkinsville, Winterville) 1899, 1937, 1968–75

Atlanta
pre 1861 (microfiche)
1861–1935 (microfilm)
(suburbs) 1936–84

Augusta
pre 1861 (microfiche)
(Hamburg, N. Augusta) 1865–67, 1882, 1888, 1895–98, 1904–42
City Directory of Augusta 1899. Maloney Directory Co., 1899. F294 .A9A18.

Austell
(Mableton) 1965–81

Bainbridge 1956–84

Barnesville 1962–66, 1974

Baxley 1962

Blakely 1963–78

Bremen
(Tallapoosa, Buchanan) 1964, 1970–83

Brunswick
(Arco, St. Simon's Island, Sea Island, Golden Isles) 1914–25, 1935–83

Buford
(Duluth, Lawrenceville, Norcross, Sugar Hill, Suwanee) 1962–83

Cairo
(Grady Co.) 1959–84

Calhoun
(Gordon Co.) 1960–84

Camilla
(Pelham, Mitchell Co.) 1971

Canton
(Ballground, Woodstock) 1974

Carrollton 1956–84

Cartersville
(Emerson) 1956–73

Cedar Town 1956–83

Columbus
pre 1861 (microfiche)
(suburbs; Phenix City, Ala.) 1886, 1889, 1894, 1898, 1906, 1910–84

Commerce
(Jefferson, Maysville, Nicholson) 1970, 1974

Conyers
(Lithonia) 1971

Cordelle
(Crisp Co.) 1956–74

Cornelia
(Clarksville) 1950, 1969, 1973–75

Covington 1861–83

Dallas 1974

Dalton
(Chatsworth) 1913, 1951–84

Dawson 1863–81

Decatur
(Avondale Estates, Emory University, Scottdale)
1928

Douglas
(Coffee Co.) 1959–86

Douglasville 1967–80

Dublin 1952–75

Eastman
(Dodge Co.) 1964–79

Elberton 1963, 1968, 1970, 1973

Fairburn
(Palmetto, Union City) 1963–84

Fitzgerald 1920, 1950, 1958, 1968, 1973

Forsyth 1974

Fort Valley
(Byron, Peach Co.) 1960, 1968, 1972, 1975

Gainesville 1928, 1939, 1952–83

Glenville 1962

Griffin 1913, 1917, 1921, 1927, 1953, 1955, 1966–73

Hartwell 1962, 1970

Hazlehurst 1964–81

Jackson 1963, 1972

Jesup 1958, 1968, 1971

Lafayette 1962–83

LaGrange 1912, 1921, 1946–82

Louisville
(Wadley, Wrens) 1970

Macon 1897–1984

Manchester 1962

Marietta
(Smyrna) 1958–75

McDonough
(Hampton, Strockbridge) 1963–67, 1974, 1976, 1982

McRae
(Helena) 1963

Milledgeville 1960, 1970, 1972, 1985

Monroe 1962–81

Moultrie 1922, 1949, 1954–75

Nashville
(Berrien Co.) 1963, 1967, 1971

Newman 1917, 1921, 1956–84

Ocilla 1967

Perry 1962–66, 1971–84

Rockmart
(Polk Co.) 1972–83

Rome
(Chatillon Village, Lindale, Shannon, Tubize) 1947–85

Royston
(Lavonia) 1962

Sandersville
(Tannille) 1964–82

Savannah
pre 1861 (microfiche)
1861–1935 (microfilm)
1950–81
Maddock's Savannah, Georgia Directory and General Advertiser. T.M. Maddock, comp. Savannah: J.H. Estel, 1971. F294 .S2A18.
Rogers' City Directory of Savannah, July 1877. Savannah: George Rogers, 1977. F294 .S2A18.
Savannah City Directory, 1867. Savannah: N.J. Darrell & Co., 1986. F294 .S2A18.

Statesboro 1959–84

Swainsboro 1960–80

Sylvester 1963, 1970

Thomaston 1964–84

Thomasville 1944–84

Thomson 1962, 1970, 1974

Tifton 1949–78

Toccoa 1956, 1959, 1961, 1968, 1971, 1973

Tucker
(Stone Mountain) 1966, 1970–74

Valdosta
(Remerton) 1908, 1913, 1921–25, 1937, 1947–84

Vidalia
  (Lyons) 1960–84

Warner Robins 1962–83

Washington 1962

Waycross 1908, 1912–25, 1939, 1945–84

Waynesboro 1964, 1966, 1971–82

West Point
  (Fairfax, Lanett, Langdale, Riverview, Shawmut)
  1962

Winder 1961, 1965–76, 1980, 1982

County, Business, and Miscellaneous

Georgia (state)
  pre 1861 (microfiche)
  1876, 1881, 1898

Glenn 1913

Gwinnett 1972

Henry 1971

Hollywood (city) 1924, 1941

Houston 1972

Tift 1973

Florida

Historical Highlights

1513   Discovered and claimed for Spain by Ponce DeLeon.

1561   Claimed by French Huguenots.

1565   Huguenots driven out by Spain; Spanish fort erected at St. Augustine to protect against threats from France.

1686   Fort erected at Pensacola to protect against threats to Louisiana from France.

Although Spain militarily controlled the Florida area, it did not colonize it. Slaves who escaped from the English colonies to the north found refuge in Florida, causing dissension and then military forays from the colonies in an effort to retake their human property.

1763   Ceded by Spain to England. Divided into East Florida and West Florida.

1776   Continued as an English province during the time of the American Revolution.

1781   West Florida retaken by Spain.

1783   East Florida ceded by England to Spain.

During the English sovereignty, the area along the northern coast of the Gulf of Mexico was designated West Florida. Settlement was attempted but it remained sparsely settled. During the American Revolution, the area served as a safe place for Loyalists to hide during the fighting in the North. Using the British-American war as an opportunity, Spain re-took West Florida, and, after the Revolution ended, Spain accepted England's cession of the entire Florida area.

1810   Independence from Spain declared.

1812   West Florida annexed by the United States.

1818   East Florida invaded by General Andrew Jackson in an attempt to conquer the Seminole Indians.

1819   All parts of Florida ceded by Spain to the United States.

1836   Second series of United States wars against the Seminoles.

1845   Admitted to the Union.

Beginning in 1810, a series of events led inevitably to Florida becoming a part of the United States. It began with a declared independence from Spain, followed by United States actions to drive out or control the Seminole Indians, and finally by annexation; leading ultimately to admission to the Union.

1861   Seceded from the Union and joined the Confederate States of America.

Only sixteen years after becoming part of the United States, Florida joined the other southern states in the Confederacy. Using its recently established plantation system (making use of African slave labor) it served as an agricultural reservoir for the southern armies.

Published Record Sources

Guidebooks

Marth, Del, and Martha J. Marth. *The Florida Almanac, 1983–1984.* Gretna, La.: Pelican Publishing Co., 1983. F311 .F65.

Census Indexes and Abstracts

1820   Sanders, Mary E. *An Index to the 1820 Census of Louisiana's Florida Parishes and the 1812 St. Tammany Parish Tax List.* F337 .F6526.

1830   F310 .J3
Shaw, Aurora C. *1830 Florida United States Census.* Jacksonville: Southern Genealogist's Exchange Quarterly, 1900. F310 .S53.

1840   F310 .J32
Mallon, Lucille S. *1840 Index to Florida Census.* B.M. Taylor, 1970s. F310 .M245.
Pompey, Sherman L. *Index to the 1840 Census Records of Alachua, Calhoun, Dade, Escambia, Franklin, Hamilton, Hillsborough, Monroe, Mosquito (Orange), Nassau, Walton, and Washington Counties, Florida Territory.* Charleston, Oreg.: Pacific Specialties, 1974. F310 .P65.

1850   F310 .J322
Southern Genealogist's Exchange Society. *Index to the 1850 Florida Census.* Jacksonville: the society, 1976. F310 .S68.

1860   Dilts, Bryan L. *1860 Florida Census Index.* Salt Lake City; Index Publishing Co., 1984. F310 .D54.

1870   Dilts, Bryan L. *1870 Florida Census Index.* Salt Lake City: Index Publishing Co., 1984. F310 .D55.

All the above publications shown without the name of the compiler or author are by Ronald V. Jackson, Accelerated Indexing Systems.

Biographies

Blackman, Lucy W. *The Women of Florida.* Vol. 2, *The Biographies.* N.p.: Southern Historical Publishing, 1940. F310 .B58.

Cozens, Eloise N. *Florida Women of Distinction.* N.p.: College Publishing Co., 1956. F310 .C6.

Florida Historical Society. *Makers of America. Florida Edition: A Historical and Biographical Work.* 2 vols. Atlanta: A.B. Caldwell, 1909. F310 .M23.

Marks, Henry S. *Who Was Who in Florida.* Huntsville, Ala.: Strode Publishing, 1973. F310 .M26.

Trinker, Charles L. *Florida Lives—The Sunshine State Who's Who.* Hopkinsville, Ky.: Historical Records Association, 1986. F310 .T7.

Land Acquisition

Historical Records Survey (WPA). *Spanish Land Grants in Florida.* 5 vols. Tallahassee: State Library Board, 1940. F314 .H7.

United States Commissioners. *Land Claims in Florida.* Washington, D.C.: Gales and Seaton, 1825. F315 .U56.

Early Settlers

Avant, David A. *Florida Pioneers and Their Alabama, Georgia, Carolina, Maryland, and Virginia Ancestors.* Tallahassee: L'Avant Studios, 1977. F310 .A9.

Roselli, Bruno. *The Italians in Colonial Florida: A Repertory of Italian Families Who Settled in Florida Under the Spanish (1513–1762; 1784–1821); and the British (1762–1784) Regimes.* Jacksonville: Drew Press, 1946. F320 .I8R67.

Tampa Tribune. *Pioneer Florida Personnel and Family Records.* 3 vols. Tampa: Southern Publishing Co., 1959. F311 .T3.

Local Records

Index to the Archives of Spanish West Florida, 1782–1810. New Orleans: Polyanthos, 1975. Z1251 .W5315.

Phillips, Ulrich B., ed. *Florida Plantation Records: From the Papers of George Noble Jones.* St. Louis: Missouri Historical Society, 1927. F315 .J77.

Stirk, Kathryn L., comp. *Tombstone Registry of Central Florida.* N.p. the author, 1984. F310 .S75.

Military Records

General

Florida Board of State Institutions. *Soldiers of Florida in the Seminole Indian, Civil, and Spanish American Wars.* Live Oak, Fla.: Democrat Book & Job Print, 1903. E558.3 .F68.

American Revolution

Florida State Historical Society. *Loyalists in East Florida, 1774–1785.* Vol. 2, *Records of the Claims for Losses of Property in the Province.* Deland, Fla.: Florida State Historical Society, 1929. F314 .S58.

Fritot, Jesse R. *Pension Records of Soldiers of the Revolution Who Removed to Florida, With Record of Service.* N.p.: Daughters of the American Revolution, Jacksonville Chapter, 1946. E255 .F7.

Civil War

Dickinson, John. *Military History of Florida.* Vol. 11. Atlanta: Confederate Publishing Co., 1899. E545 .E92.

Pompey, Sherman L. *Civil War Veteran Burials from Florida.* Fresno, Calif.: the author, 1968. E558.3 .P65.

Periodicals

Florida Historical Society Quarterly. *Periodical Cumulative Indexes. Vols. 1–35 (1908–1957); Vols. 36–53 (1957–1975).* N.p.: the society. F306 .F65.

Directories

City

Apalachicola
(Port St. Joe) 1974

Apopka 1970–80

Arcadia 1915–21, 1926, 1956–83

Auburndale 1958–82

Bartow
(rural routes, Polk Co.) 1955–83

Belle Glade
(suburbs, Pahokee) 1957–84

Boca Raton 1956–84

Bradenton
(Anna Maria Island, Palmetto) 1921, 1927–83

Brooksville 1926, 1957–84

Cape Coral
(Lehigh Acres, Pine Island) 1964–82

Clearwater
(Dunedin, Largo, Tarpon Springs, Pinellas Co.) 1920–26, 1931, 1937–84

Clermont
(Groveland) 1864–83

Clewiston
(Moore Haven) 1959, 1972–85

Cocoa
(Cape Canaveral, Cocoa Beach, Merritt Island) 1956–83

Coral Gables 1949–52

Crestview 1957–82

Crystal River
(Homosassa, Homosassa Springs) 1971–81

Dade City
(Pasco Co.) 1926, 1956–83

Daytona 1915–83

DeFuniak Springs 1959–64, 1975–81

Deland 1924, 1926, 1936–83

Delray Beach 1948–79

Eustis
(Mount Dora, Tavares, Umatilla) 1924, 1926, 1955–81

Fernandina Beach 1958–84

Fort Lauderdale (suburbs) 1936, 1942–85

Fort Meade
(Frostproof) 1962–81

Fort Myers
(Arcadia, Lee Co.) 1915, 1921–28, 1935, 1939, 1941, 1945–81

Fort Pierce
(Port St. Lucie, St. Lucie Co.) 1916–22, 1931, 1940, 1945–84

Fort Walton Beach 1956, 1961–85

Gainesville 1915–21, 1925, 1927, 1942–84

Haines City 1971–84

Hollywood
(Dania, Hallandale) 1942, 1946–82

Homestead 1927, 1955, 1957, 1960, 1964, 1970–83

Inverness
(Citrus Co.) 1971–83

Jacksonville 1870, 1971, 1976–1984

Jacksonville Beaches
(DuVal Co.) 1941, 1945, 1947–85

Jupiter
(Tequesta) 1967–85

Kissimmee
(St. Cloud) 1921, 1959–83

Lake City 1926, 1958–85

Lake Wales
(Polk Co.) 1946, 1956–84

Lake Worth
(Boynton Beach, Lantana) 1955–83

Lakeland
(Polk Co.) 1915–83

Leesburg 1924, 1955–83

Live Oak
(Suwanee Co.) 1923, 1926, 1958–83

Madison 1964, 1966, 1973–85

Marathon 1960–80

Marianna (suburbs) 1956–86

Melbourne
(Eau Gallie) 1953–82

Miami
(Miami Beach) 1904, 1908–75

Miami Beach (suburbs) 1937, 1955–75

Milton 1958–83

Mulberry 1965

Naples 1955–83

New Port Richey 1957–85

New Smyrna Beach 1947–84

Niceville
(Valparaiso) 1966–83

Ocala
(Marion Co.) 1908, 1911, 1914, 1919, 1923–30, 1937–79

Okeechobee 1960–85

Orange Park
(Green Cove Springs) 1974–85

Orlando
(suburbs, Maitland, Winter Park, Orange Co.) 1915, 1921–22, 1925, 1932–82

Palatka
(Crescent City, E. Palatka, Putnam Co.) 1915, 1922, 1928, 1936, 1948–84

Panama City 1935, 1948–85

Pensacola 1885, 1890, 1898, 1907–84

Perry (suburbs) 1956–80

Peru
(Bloomfield, Oakdale, S. Peru, Miami Co.) 1898–99, 1919, 1947, 1950, 1957–85

Pinellas Park 1955

Plant City 1956–83

Pompano Beach
(Deerfield Beach) 1955–82

Port Charlotte 1965

Port St. Joe 1984

Punta Gorda
(Port Charlotte, Port Charlotte Co.) 1927, 1958–83

Quincy
(Gadsden Co.) 1927, 1957–83

Sanford
(Seminole Co.) 1909–11, 1917–26, 1947, 1952–83

Sarasota
  (Sarasota Co.) 1926, 1936–40, 1945–83

Sebring
  (Avon Park, Lake Placid) 1926, 1956–85

St. Augustine
  (St. Johns Co.) 1911–40, 1945–83

St. Cloud 1971–85

St. Petersburg
  (Clearwater, Gulf Beaches, Gulfport, Holiday Isles, Pass a Grille, Pinellas Park, Tarpon Springs) 1914–84

Starke 1956, 1964, 1970–85

Stuart
  (Jensen Beach) 1956–85

Tallahassee 1904, 1914, 1919, 1925–86

Tampa (suburbs) 1899, 1905–85

Tarpon Springs
  (Crystal Beach, Palm Harbor) 1956–68, 1971–84

Titusville
  (Cocoa, Eau Gallie, Melbourne, Rockledge, Brevard Co.) 1926, 1957–83

Venice
  (Englewood) 1958–85

Vero Beach 1927, 1953–86

Wauchula
  (Hardy Co.) 1926, 1956–83

West Palm Beach
  (Lakeworth, Riviera, West Gate, West Palm Beach Co.) 1931–84

Winter Garden 1959–85

Winter Haven
  (Polk Co.) 1925–37, 1946, 1951, 1955–85

Zephrhills
  (Pasco Co.) 1972–83

County, Business, and Miscellaneous

Florida (state) 1883–86, 1895, 1907, 1911, 1918, 1925

Highlands 1928

Lake 1938

Polk 1941, 1956

CHAPTER 12

South-Central States

Kentucky • Tennessee • Arkansas
Alabama • Mississippi • Louisiana

Kentucky

Historical Highlights

1750   Dr. Thomas Walker and other frontiersmen explored the lands west of the Cumberland Gap which were claimed as part of Virginia's Augusta County.

1763   Ohio River designated as the boundary between Indian lands and areas set aside for white settlement.

1774   Harrodsburg founded.

1775   Boonesborough founded.

The lands west of the Blue Ridge Mountains were heavily populated by hostile Indians, making settlement difficult. The Transylvania Company, a land speculation firm headed by Richard Henderson from North Carolina, purchased millions of acres of land from the Indians and sent Harrod and Daniel Boone to erect forts and survey the country for eventual sale to future settlers. Other tiny settlements were founded that often vanished after Indian attacks.

1776   Kentucky County, Virginia, created out of Fincastle County.

1778   George Rogers Clark led a military expedition from Kentucky into Illinois to secure Virginia's claim to that area, despite the presence of the British.

1780   Kentucky County divided into Fayette, Jefferson, and Lincoln counties.

The widening of the Wilderness Road down the Shenandoah Valley facilitated migration by settlers moving southward from Pennsylvania, Maryland, Virginia, and North Carolina. Following the American Revolution, Virginia granted many bounty lands to the southern portions of the territory—adding to those who had come earlier and settled in the northern and central portions. Migration was accelerated after Indian troubles lessened and the Louisiana Purchase (1803) opened the Louisiana ports to Kentuckians who could sell their agricultural products down the Mississippi River.

1790   After separation from Virginia, entered the Union.

1861   Officially remained in the Union during the Civil War.

Although wishing to remain neutral, the state legislature voted to remain in the Union. Sympathies were split between loyalty to the Union and to the Confederacy; many residents enlisted on both sides. Primarily, the eastern portion favored the

Union, the western portion favored the Confederacy, and the central portion split.

Published Record Sources

Guidebooks

Elliott, Wendy L. *Guide to Kentucky Genealogical Research.* Bountiful, Utah: American Genealogical Lending Library, 1987. F450 .E44.

Hathaway, Beverly W. *Inventory of County Records of Kentucky.* West Jordan, Utah: Allstates Research Co., 1974. CD3257 .A1K37.

Historical Records Survey (WPA). *Guide to Public Vital Statistics Records in Kentucky.* Louisville: Kentucky Historical Records Survey, 1942. CD3251 .H5.

Kentucky. Department of Libraries and Archives. *The Guide to Kentucky Archival and Manuscript Repositories.* Frankfort: Kentucky Guide Project, 1987. (Cataloging in publication.)

National Society Colonial Dames of America, Kentucky. Elizabeth H. Garr, ed. *The History of Kentucky Courthouses.* N.p., n.d. F542 .G26.

Powell, Robert A. *This is Kentucky.* Frankfort: Kentucky Images, 1975. F452 .P78.

Rennick, Robert M. *Kentucky Place Names.* Lexington: University of Kentucky, 1985. F449 .R46.

Schweitzer, George K. *Kentucky Genealogical Research.* Knoxville, Tenn.: the author, 1981. F450 .S33.

Census Indexes and Abstracts

General

Lawson, Rowena. *Kentucky County Census, 1810–1840.* Bowie, Md.: Heritage Books, 1984–86. F450 .L38.

Federal

1810   F450 .J3
Volkel, Lowell M. *An Index to the 1810 Federal Census of Kentucky.* Springfield, Ill.: the author, 1971–72. F450 .V6.
Wagstaff, Ann T., comp. *Index to the 1810 Census of Kentucky.* Baltimore:

Genealogical Publishing Co., 1980. F450 .W32.

1820   F450 .J314
Felldin, Jeanne R., comp. *Index to the 1820 Census of Kentucky.* Baltimore: Genealogical Publishing Co., 1981. F450 F44.

1830   F450 .J316
Simmons, Don. *1830 Census of the Jackson Purchase.* Murray, Ky.: the author, 1974. F450 .S55.

1840   F450 .J32

1850   F450 .J322
Lawson, Rowena. *Kentucky County Censuses, 1850.* Bowie, Md.: Heritage Books, 1983–84. F450 .L39.
McDowell, Samuel, comp. *A Surname Index to the 1850 Federal Population Census of Kentucky.* Hartford, Ky.: the compiler, 1974. F450 .M16.
Parrish, H.T., Mrs., comp. *1850 Census Index of Eastern Kentucky.* Stamping Ground, Ky.: n.p., 1973. F450 .P37.

All the above publications shown without the name of the compiler or author are by Ronald V. Jackson, Accelerated Indexing Systems.

State

Jackson, Ronald V. *Early Kentucky.* Bountiful, Utah: Accelerated Indexing Systems, n.d. F450 .J27.

Mortality

Smith, Randolph N. *Federal Mortality Census Schedules, 1860, 1870, 1880.* Burkesville, Ky.: the compiler, 1975. F450 .S57.

Index for Adair, Clinton, Cumberland, Metcalfe, and Monroe counties.

Biographies

Biographical Cyclopedia of the Commonwealth of Kentucky. Chicago: John M. Gresham, 1980. CT236 .B56.

Johnson, William W. *Prominent Negro Men and Women of Kentucky.* Lexington: the author, 1897. E185.93 .K3J63.

LaBree, Ben, ed. *Notable Men of Kentucky at the Beginning of the 20th Century, 1900–09.* Louisville: George C. Fetter, 1902. F450 .L118.

———. *Press Reference Book of Prominent Kentuckians.* Louisville: Standard Printing Co., 1916. F450 .L12.

Memorial Record of Western Kentucky. 2 vols. New York: Lewis Publishing Co., 1904. Reprint. Hartford, Ky.: McDowell Publications, 1979. CT236 .M45.

Overstreet, Lillian P. *Kentuckians of Yore and Kinsmen Galore.* Louisville: the author, 1986. F450 .O94.

Perrin, William H. *Kentucky Genealogy and Biography.* 6 vols. Owensboro, Ky.: Genealogical Reference Co., 1970. F450 .P46.

Specify county desired.

Tapp, Hambleton. *Kentucky Lives: The Blue Grass State Who's Who, 1966.* Hopkinsville: Historical Record Association, 1966. F450 .T3.

Land Acquisition

Jillson, Willard R. *The Kentucky Land Grants: A Systematic Index to All of the Land Grants Recorded in the State Land Office at Frankfort, Kentucky, 1782–1924.* Louisville: Filson Club, 1925. F446 .F48 (#33). (HD243 .K4J5).

———. *Old Kentucky Entries and Deeds.* Louisville: Filson Club, 1926. F446 .F48 (#34). (HD243 .K456).

Kentucky Historical Society. Joan E. Brooke-Smith, comp. *Master Index. Virginia Surveys and Grants, 1774–1791.* Frankfort: the society, 1976.

Kentucky Historical Society. *The Great Settlement Area, A map to supplement land grants cited in Kentucky Settlement and Statehood, 1750–1800.* Frankfort: the society, 1975. F450 .B76.

Kentucky Land Office. *A Calendar of Warrants for Land in Kentucky, Granted for Service in the French and Indian War.* Baltimore: Genealogical Publishing Co., 1967. HD184 .K42A45.

Sutherland, James F., comp. *Early Kentucky Landholders, 1787–1811.* Baltimore: Genealogical Publishing Co., 1986. F450 .S973.

Early Settlers

Fowler, Ila E., comp. *Kentucky Pioneers and Their Descendants.* Frankfort: Daughters of Colonial Wars, Kentucky Society, 1941–50. Reprint. Bal-

timore: Genealogical Publishing Co., 1967. F450 .D3.

Genealogies of Kentucky Families: From the Filson Club Quarterly. Baltimore: Genealogical Publishing Co., 1981. F450 .G52.

Genealogies of Kentucky Families: From the Register of the Kentucky Historical Society. 2 vols. N.p., n.d. F450 .G53.

Kirkwood, Alberta C. *They Came to Kentucky: Chiefly Pertaining to Boone, Pulaski, Lincoln, Gallatin, and Casey Counties....* Baltimore: Gateway Press, 1976. F450 .K57.

Kozee, William C. *Early Families of Eastern and Southeastern Kentucky and Their Descendants.* Strasburg, Va.: Shenandoah Publishing House, 1961. Reprint. Baltimore: Genealogical Publishing Co., 1973. F450 .K59. Reprint, F450 .K6.

McDowell, Sam, comp. *Society of Kentucky Pioneers Yearbook, 1983.* Utica, Ky.: the society, 1985. F450 .M155.

Neel, Eurie P. W. *The Statistical Handbook of Trigg County, Kentucky: The Gateway to the Jackson Purchase in Kentucky and Tennessee.* Nashville, Tenn.: Rich Printing Co., 1961. F450 .N4.

Sprague, Stuart S. *Kentuckians in Illinois.* Baltimore: Genealogical Publishing Co., 1987. F450 .S66.

———. *Kentuckians in Ohio.* Baltimore: Genealogical Publishing Co., 1986. F450 .S67.

Thompson, Gerald. *Kentucky Catholic Pioneers.* Vol. 1, *The Rolling Fork Settlement.* Utica, Ky.: McDowell Publishing Co., 1983. F450 .T48.

Van Meter, Benjamin F. *Genealogies and Sketches of Some Old Families.* Louisville: John P. Morton & Co., 1901. F450 .V26.

Includes Virginia and Kentucky.

Winton, Wilma. *Pioneer Ghosts of Kentucky. Rest in Peace John Jay Dickey: A Comprehensive Name Index to the Dickey Diary.* 4 vols. Modesto, Calif.: P. Bullock, 1890–1957. CT275 .D452A3.

Local Records

Antonial, Eleanor, indexer. *Kentucky Marriage Records: From the Register of the Kentucky Historical Society.* Index. Baltimore: Genealogical Publishing Co., 1983. F450 .K455.

Ardery, Julia H. *Kentucky Court and Other Records.* 2 vols. Lexington: the author, 1932. F450 .A67.

Bell, Annie W. *Records of Deaths For the Period of Years 1852–1862.* Washington, D.C.: the author, 1934. F450 .B36.

Volume 1, Clay, Estill, Floyd, Green, Knox, Perry, Laurel; volume 2, Ballard, Bourbon, Breathitt, Jackson, Lawrence, Owsely, Pike; volume 3, Harlan, Letcher, Woodford.

————. *Records of Early Kentucky Marriages, 1785–1851.* Washington, D.C.: the author, n.d. F450 .B352.

Blair, Juan H. *A Window to the Past: Cemetery Records: A Selection of Cemeteries From Rowan and Surrounding Counties.* Morehead, Ky.: the author, 1981. F450 .B47.

Cawthorn, C.P., and N.L. Warnell. *Pioneer Baptist Church Records of South-Central Kentucky—Upper Cumberland of Tennessee, 1799–1899.* N.p., 1985. BS6248 .K4C38.

Clift, G. Glenn, comp. *Kentucky Marriages, 1797–1865.* Reprint. Baltimore: Genealogical Publishing Co., 1966. F450 .C554.

Cook, Michael L., and Bertie A. Cook. *Kentucky Court of Appeals Deed Book.* 4 vols. Evansville, Ind.: Cook Publications, 1985. F450 C57.

Ford, Carol L., indexer. *Early Kentucky Tax Records: From the Kentucky Historical Society.* Baltimore: Genealogical Publishing Co., 1984. F450 .E16.

Fulton Genealogical Society. *Bible Records of Western Kentucky and Tennessee.* Fulton, Ky.: the society, 1975. F450 F84.

Jackson, Evelyn, and William Talley. *Eastern Kentucky References.* Owensboro, Ky.: Cook and McDowell Publications, 1980. F450 .J26.

Jackson, Ronald V. *Index to Kentucky Wills to 1851: The Testators.* Salt Lake City: Accelerated Indexing Systems, 1977. F450 .J28.

Johnson, Robert F. *Wilderness Road Cemeteries in Kentucky, Tennessee, and Virginia.* Owensboro, Ky.: McDowell Publications, 1981. F450 .J63.

McAdams, Ednah. *Kentucky Pioneers and Court Records.* Lexington: the author, 1929. F450 .M13.

National Society Daughters of the American Revolution, Kentucky Chapter. *Kentucky Bible Records.* 6 vols. Lexington: the society, 1962. F450 .D25.

————. *Kentucky Cemetery Records.* 5 vols. Lexington: the society, 1960–72. F450 .D28.

Pease, Janet K. *Kentucky County Court Records.* Vol. 1, *Grant Co. Orders, 1846–1863; Harrison Co. Orders, 1828–1856; Pendleton Co. Orders, 1799–1871.* Vol. 2, *Grant Co. Probates, 1820–1845; Harrison Co. Wills, 1795–1857; Pendleton Co. Orders, 1799–1814.* Vol. 3, *Grant Co. Probates, 1845–1866; Grant Co. Orders, 1820–1845; Harrison Co. Records, 1794–1828; Pendleton Co. Orders, 1815–1823.* Williamstown, Ky.: Grant County Historical Society, 1986. F450 .P43.

Talley, William M. *Talley's Kentucky Papers.* Fort Worth, Tex.: Arrow Printing Co., 1966. F450 .T28.

Military Records

Colonial Wars

Burns, Annie W. (See below under American Revolution.)

American Revolution

Burns, Annie W., comp. *Abstracts of Pensions. Soldiers of the Revolutionary War, 1812, and Indian Wars Who Settled on the Kentucky Side of the Ohio River.* 3 vols. in 1. Washington, D.C.: the author, 1954. F450 .B87.

————. *Revolutionary War Pension Abstracts of Kentucky Counties.* N.p., n.d. F457. [county].

Abstracts of pension files housed at the National Archives. Specify county desired.

Jillson, Willard. *Old Kentucky Entries and Deeds.* Louisville: Filson Club, 1926. F446 .F48 (#34). (HD 243. K456).

Lindsay, Kenneth G. *Kentucky's Revolutionary War Pensioners Under the Acts of 1816, 1832.* Evansville, Ind.: Kenma Publishing Co., 1977. E263 .K4L56.

War of 1812

Burns, Annie W. (See above under American Revolution.)

Kentucky. Adjutant General. *Soldiers of War of 1812. With an Added Index.* Frankfort, 1891. Reprint. Baltimore: Genealogical Publishing Co., 1969. E359.5 .K5A45.

Quisenberry, Anderson C. *Kentucky in the War of 1812. With an Added Index.* Baltimore: Genealogical Publishing Co., 1969. E359.5 .K5Q8.

Civil War

Dilts, Bryan L. *1890 Kentucky Census Index of Civil War Veterans or Their Widows.* Salt Lake City: Index Publishing, 1984. E494 .D55.

Kentucky. Adjutant General. *Kentucky Confederate Volunteers, 1861–1865.* 2 vols. Reprint. Hartford, Ky.: Cook and McDowell Publications, 1979. E564.3 .K37.

Kentucky. Department of Archives and Library. Alicia Simpson, comp. *Index of Confederate Pension Applications, Commonwealth of Kentucky.* Frankfort: State of Kentucky, 1981. E564.3 .K38.

Mosgrove, George D. *Kentucky Cavaliers in Dixie.* Jackson, Tenn.: McCowat-Mercer Press, 1957. E605 .M88.

Periodicals

Trapp, Glenda K., and Michael L. Cook. *Kentucky Genealogical Index.* Vol. 1, *An Everyname Index to Kentucky Ancestors, Kentucky Genealogist, Kentucky Pioneer Genealogy Records, The East Kentuckian. All Issues Through 1980.* Evansville, Ind.: Cook Publications, 1985. Z1287 .T72.

Directories

City

Ashland
(Bellefonte, Cattlesburg, Fairview, Flatwoods, Kenwood, Kendall Acres, Mill Seat, Russell, W. Fairview, W. Russell, Westwood) 1897, 1912–23, 1933–56, 1960–84

Bardstown 1972–82

Bowling Green 1930, 1947–61, 1967–71

Campbellsville 1909, 1973

Corbin 1949, 1963–85

Covington
(suburbs, Newport) 1866–1985

Cynthiana 1969, 1972

Danville 1931, 1942–83

Florence 1974–84

Frankfort 1910–28, 1942–83

Fulton
(S. Fulton) 1936, 1961

Georgetown 1960, 1972–80

Glasgow
(Barren Co.) 1959–84

Harlan 1974

Harrodsburg 1969, 1974

Hazard 1952, 1974, 1978

Henderson 1889, 1915, 1936, 1953

Hopkinsville 1897, 1910–31, 1935, 1942, 1946–60, 1968, 1975

Lexington
pre 1861 (microfiche)
1861–81 (microfilm)
1898, 1904–84

London 1963, 1972–84

Louisville
pre 1861 (microfiche)
1861–1935 (microfilm)
(suburbs) 1886–1942, 1946–85

Madisonville 1936, 1940, 1951, 1958, 1969, 1973–74

Mayfield 1949, 1954, 1958, 1960, 1968

Maysville 1913, 1916, 1922–27, 1932, 1956, 1958, 1968–74

Middlesboro 1912, 1926, 1934, 1950, 1968

Morehead 1972–83

Mt. Sterling 1970

Murray 1958

Newport
(Bellevue, Cold Spring, Dayton, Fort Thomas, Southgate, Woodlawn) 1938–85

Nicholsville 1972–84

Owensboro
(Daviess Co.) 1847, 1889, 1891, 1893, 1899, 1901, 1907, 1914, 1922–84

Paducah
(McCracken Co.) 1888, 1895, 1900, 1906–41, 1947–84

Paris
  (Millersburg, N. Middleton) 1947, 1950, 1957–82

Pikesville 1952, 1967

Princeton 1960–68

Richmond 1912, 1958, 1968, 1971

Russell 1923

Somerset
  (Ferguson, W. Somerset) 1947, 1951, 1954–78, 1983–
  85

Winchester
  (Clark Co.) 1914, 1947, 1958, 1969, 1971, 1974

County, Business, and Miscellaneous

Kentucky (see also Eastern, Western, and Southern—in
  Indiana)
  (region) pre 1861 (microfiche)
  (state) 1859, 1879, 1887–91, 1896

Louisville 1867, 1888

Tennessee

Historical Highlights

1541   Claimed for Spain by explorer DeSoto.

1682   Claimed for France by LaSalle.

1748   Explored by settlers from eastern colonies
        coming through the Cumberland Gap.

1763   Ceded by France to England.

        Until it came under England's jurisdiction,
        Tennessee was populated almost exclusively
        by Indians with only occasional probes by
        explorers who dared to make expeditions to
        hunt game and explore.

1771   Watauga Association established the first
        settlement.

1776   Washington County (comprising all of Ten-
        nessee) became part of North Carolina.

1784   State of Franklin organized.

1790   Ceded by North Carolina to the United
        States.

        After the English took control, settlers
        began to move in, and counties were sub-
        divided as the population increased. Most
        migrants, Scotch-Irish, Germans and a few
        Huguenots, came down the Shenandoah
        Valley from Pennsylvania, Maryland, Vir-
        ginia, and western North Carolina. Quakers
        from the Carolinas stopped briefly on their
        way to Ohio and Indiana.

        Border disputes resulted in some settlers
        not knowing if they lived in Tennessee or
        Kentucky. Early records might be found in
        either of the two states. Although a surveyed
        line was established in 1779 and 1780, final
        agreement was not reached until 1820. Fol-
        lowing the American Revolution, North
        Carolina granted many lands in middle Ten-
        nessee and sold land at five cents per acre.

        John Sevier and others of the Watauga set-
        tlement conspired to establish an inde-
        pendent state, to be called Franklin. After a
        few years the project failed, and it reverted
        to Tennessee.

1796   Entered the Union.

1807   Natchez Trace provided a route for
        migrants heading southwest from Kentucky
        into Mississippi—by way of Tennessee.

1817   Indians began the first of several agreements
        to cede or sell their lands to the United
        States.

        After becoming a sovereign state, estab-
        lishment of migration trails, and eventual
        elimination of the Indian menace, settlers
        began pouring in to take advantage of
        bounty lands and inexpensive farm land.
        The state's area was enlarged by annexation
        of Indian lands in the western and south-
        western portions.

1861   Seceded from the Union.

        Although many Tennesseans, especially
        those in the eastern portion, objected to
        secession, the state elected to join the Con-
        federacy. Acting as a buffer between its
        southern neighbors and the invading sol-
        diers from the North, its residents fought for
        both sides. After the close of the war,
        veterans from both sides were welcomed

back, and the state was the first to rejoin the Union in 1865.

Published Record Sources

Guidebooks

Fulcher, Richard C. *Guide to County Records and Genealogical Resources in Tennessee.* Baltimore: Genealogical Publishing Co., 1987. Z1337 .F85.

Hathaway, Beverly W. *Genealogical Research Sources in Tennessee.* West Jordan, Utah: Allstates Research Co., 1972. F435 .H3.

Mitchell, John L. *Tennessee State Gazetteer and Business Directory for 1860–71.* Nashville: the author, 1860. F434 .M68.

Morris, Eastin. *Eastin Morris' Tennessee Gazetteer, 1834.* Nashville: Gazetteer Press, 1971. F434 .M87.

Schweitzer, George K. *Tennessee Genealogical Research.* Knoxville: the author, 1981. F435 .S37.

Silar, Tom. *Tennessee Towns From Adams to Yorkville.* Knoxville: East Tennessee Historical Society, 1985. F436 .S58.

Sistler, Byron, and Barbara Sistler. *The Yellow Pages. Sources and Suggestions for Searching in Tennessee.* Evanston, Ill.: the authors, 1978. F435 .S59.

Springer, Patricia. "Bibliography of Historical Material of Tennessee in Nashville Libraries." Master's Thesis, George Peabody College for Teachers, 1930. Z1337 .S6.

State Historical Society of Wisconsin. *Calendar of the Tennessee and Kings Mountain Papers of the Draper Collection of Manuscripts, Calendar Series.* Vol. 3. Madison, Wis.: the society, 1929. Z1137 .S7. (F576 .W82).

Tennessee. State Library and Archives. *Writings on Tennessee Counties Available on Interlibrary Loan From the Tennessee State Library and Archives, State Library Division.* Nashville: State of Tennessee, 1967. Z1138 .A15T4.

Census Indexes and Abstracts

Federal

1820 F435 .J3
Bentley, Elizabeth P., comp. *Index to the 1820 Census of Tennessee.* Baltimore: Genealogical Publishing Co., 1981. F435 .B46.

1830 F435 .J32
Sistler, Byron. *1830 Census, East Tennessee.* Nashville: Sistler & Associates, 1983. F442.1 .S57.
——. *1830 Census, Middle Tennessee.* Evanston, Ill.: Sistler & Associates, 1971. F442.2 .S57.
——. *1830 Census, West Tennessee.* Evanston, Ill.: Sistler & Associates, 1971. F442.3 .S67.

1840 F435 .J3768

1850 F435 .J333
Carpenter, Mrs. V.K. *Seventh Census of the United States, 1850 . . . Tennessee: Free Population Schedules.* Fort Smith, Ark.: Century Enterprises of Fort Smith, 1970. F435 .U55.
Sistler, Byron. *1850 Census, Tennessee.* Evanston, Ill.: Sistler & Associates, 1974–76. F435 .S35.

1860 Bishop, Brenda C. *1860 Census, Tennessee.* Elizabethton, Tenn.: the author, 1985. F435 .B565.
Carpenter, Mrs. V. K. *Eighth Census of the United States, 1860 . . . Tennessee: Free Population Schedules.* Fort Smith, Ark.: Century Enterprises of Fort Smith, 1975. F435 .U55.
Sistler, Byron. *1860 Census, Tennessee.* Nashville, Tenn.: Sistler & Associates, 1981. F435 .S56.

1870 Bishop, Brenda C. *1870 Census, Tennessee.* Elizabethton, Tenn.: the compiler, 1983. F435 .B57.

1880 Sister, Byron. *1880 Census, Tennessee.* Evanston, Ill.: Sistler & Associates, 1981. F435 .S564.

All the above publications shown without the name of the compiler or author are by Ronald V. Jackson, Accelerated Indexing Systems.

State

Fulcher, Richard C. *1770–1790 Census of the Cumberland Settlements . . . In What is Now Tennessee.* Baltimore: Genealogical Publishing Co., 1987. F442.2 .F85.

Jackson, Ronald V. *Early Tennessee.* Bountiful, Utah: Accelerated Indexing Systems, 1980. F435 .J27.

Mortality Schedules

Marsh, Helen C., and Timothy R. Marsh. *1850 Mortality Schedule of Tennessee.* Shelbyville, Tenn.: Marsh Historical Publications, 1982. F435 .M39.

Biographies

Burnett, J.J. *Sketches of Tennessee's Pioneer Baptist Preachers.* Nashville: Press of Marshall & Brice, 1919. Reprint. Johnson City, Tenn.: Overmountain Press, 1985. BX6493 .B8.

Crutchfield, James A. *Timeless Tennesseans.* Huntsville: Strode Publishers, 1984. CT261 .C785.

Gillum, James L. *Prominent Tennesseans, 1796–1938.* Lewisburg, Tenn.: Who's Who Publishing Co., 1940. F435 .G55.

Memorial and Biographical Records . . . Cumberland Region of Tennessee . . . . Chicago: George A. Ogle Co., 1898. Reprint. Easley, S.C.: Southern Historical Press, 1980. CT267 .M45.

Mooney, C.J., ed. *The Mid-South and Its Builders: Arkansas, Mississippi, Tennessee.* Memphis: Mid-South Biographical and Historical Association, 1920. F396 .M8.

Moore, John T., and Colleen M. Elliott. *Biographical Questionnaires of 150 Prominent Tennesseans.* Easley, S.C.: Southern Historical Press, 1982. F435 .B56.

Presley, Mrs. Leister E. *Geographical Index to the History of Eastern Tennesseans (Goodspeed's).* Searcy, Ark.: the author, 1970. F436 .H682P69.

Land Acquisition

Burgner, Goldene F., comp. *North Carolina Land Grants in Tennessee, 1778–1791.* Easley, S.C.: Southern Historical Press, 1981. F435 .B77.

Cherokee Property Valuations in Tennessee, 1836. N.p.: Shirley C. Hoskins, 1984. F435 .C48.

McGhee, Lucy K. *Partial Census of 1787 to 1791 of Tennessee As Taken From the North Carolina Land Grants.* 2 parts. Washington, D.C.: the author, 1950. F435 .M45.

Early Settlers

Alderman, Pat. *The Overmountain Men. Early Tennessee History, 1760–1795.* Johnson City, Tenn.: Overmountain Press, 1970. F436 .A37.

Goodspeed's General History of Tennessee. N.p., 1887. Reprint. Nashville: Charles and Randy Elder Booksellers, 1973. F436 .H68.

McDowell, Sam. *East Tennessee History. Reorganized and Indexed.* 4 vols. in 1. Reprint from *Goodspeed's History of Tennessee.* Hartford, Ky.: McDowell Publications, 1978. E442.1 .E145.

Ray, Worth S. *Tennessee Cousins. A History of Tennessee People.* Austin, Tex.: the author, 1950. F435 .R3.

Local Records

Acklen, Jeannette T., comp. *Tennessee Records.* 2 vols. Vol. 1, *Tombstone Inscriptions and Manuscripts, Historical and Biographical.* Vol. 2, *Bible Records and Marriage Bonds.* Nashville: Cullom and Ghertner, 1933. F435 .A345.

Baker, Russell B., comp. *Obituaries and Marriage Notices From the Tennessee Baptist, 1844–1862.* Easley, S.C.: Southern Historical Press, 1979. F435 .B34.

Creekmore, Pollyanna, ed. *Tennessee Marriage Records.* Knoxville: Clinchdale Press, 1965. F436 .T55.

Crutchfield, James A. *The Tennessee Almanac and Book of Facts.* Nashville: Rutledge Hill Press, 1986. F436 .C97.

Curtis, Mary B. *Early East Tennessee Tax Lists.* Ft. Worth, Tex.: Arrow Printing Co., 1964. F442.1 .C8.

Fischer, Marjorie M., comp. *Tennessee Tidbits, 1778–1914.* Vol. 1, *A Collection of Items Showing Birth, Death, Marriage, Divorce, Naturalization, Adoption, etc. . . . .* Easley, S.C.: Southern Historical Press, 1986. F435 .F57.

Garrett, Jill L., comp. *Obituaries From Tennessee Newspapers.* Easley, S.C.: Southern Historical Press, 1980. F435 .G37.

Lucas, Silas E., and Ella L. Sheffield, eds. *35,000 Tennessee Marriage Records and Bonds, 1783–1870.* 3 vols. Easley, S.C.: Southern Historical Press, 1981. F435 .L83.

Lucas, Silas E. *Marriages From Early Tennessee Newspapers, 1794–1851.* Easley, S.C.: Southern Historical Press, 1978. F435 .T37.

———. *Obituaries From Early Tennessee Newspapers, 1794–1851.* Easley, S.C.: Southern Historical Press, 1978. F435 .T37.

Murray, Nicholas R. *Tennessee Surname Index. Computer Indexed Marriage Records.* Hammond, La.: Hunting For Bears, Inc., 1984. F435 .T38.

Sistler, Byron, and Barbara Sistler. *Index to Early Tennessee Tax Lists.* Evanston, Ill.: Byron Sistler and Associates, 1977. F435 .S57.

———. *Vital Statistics From 19th Century Tennessee. Church Records.* 2 vols. Nashville: Byron Sistler and Associates, 1979. F435 .S58.

Soderbert, Gertrude L. *Tennessee Marriage Records, Greene County, 1783–1818.* Knoxville: Clinchdale Press, 1965. F436 .T55.

Whitley, Edythe D. *Tennessee Genealogical Records. Records of Early Settlers From State and County Archives.* Baltimore: Genealogical Publishing Co., 1980. F435 .W46.

Military Records

American Revolution

Allen, Penelope J. *Tennessee Soldiers in the Revolution.* Baltimore: Genealogical Publishing Co., 1975. E263 .N8A37.

Armstrong, Zella, comp. *Some Tennessee Heroes of the Revolution Compiled From Pension Statements.* Chattanooga: Lookout Publishing Co., 1933. Reprint. Baltimore: Genealogical Publishing Co., 1975. F435 .A38.

———. *Twenty-four Hundred Tennessee Pensioners of the Revolution, War of 1812.* Chattanooga: Lookout Publishing Co., 1937. E259 .A76.

Haywood, John. "List of North Carolina Revolutionary Soldiers Given Land in Tennessee, by the Acts of 1782–83." In *The History of Tennessee.*

Knoxville: Keiskell & Brown, 1843. Reprint. New York: Arno Press, 1971. F436 .H4.

McGhee, Lucy K. *Tennessee Revolutionary War Pensioners and Other Patriotic Records.* Typescript. Washington, D.C.: n.p., 1954. E255 .M3.

War of 1812

Armstrong, Zella (See above under American Revolution.)

Civil War

Dyer, Gustavus W., and John T. Moore, comps. *The Tennessee Civil War Veterans Questionnaires.* 5 vols. Easley, S.C.: Southern Historical Press, 1985. E494 .T46.

Elliott, Colleen, and Louise Armstrong, eds. *Tennessee Civil War Questionnaires.* 5 vols. Nashville: Tennessee State Library, 1985. E494 .T46.

Lindsley, John B. *Military Annals of Tennessee Confederates.* Nashville: J.J. Lindsley & Co., 1886. E579.4 .L75.

Sistler, Byron, and Barbara Sistler. *1890 Civil War Veterans Census, Tennessee.* Evanston, Ill.: Byron Sistler & Associates, 1978. E494 .S59.

Tennessee. Civil War Centennial Commission. *Tennesseans in the Civil War.: A Military History of Confederate and Union Units With Available Rosters of Persons.* 2 vols. Nashville: Tennessee Historical Commission, 1904. E579.4 .A53.

United Confederate Veterans. N.B. Forrest Camp, Chattanooga. *Roster of Our Dead Buried in the Confederate Cemetery at Chattanooga.* Chattanooga: n.p., 1894. E475.81 .U53.

United Daughters of the Confederacy. Tennessee Division. *Confederate Patriot Index, 1894–1924; 1924–78.* 2 vols. Columbia, Tenn.: P-Vine Press, 1978.

Mexican-American War

Brock, Reid Sr., et al. *Volunteers. Tennesseans in the War With Mexico.* 2 vols. N.p.: Kitchen Table Press, 1986. E409.5 .T4B76.

Directories

City

Athens 1935, 1941–42, 1953–60, 1968–75

Bristol 1901–83

Chattanooga
  1861–81 (microfilm)
  1884, 1887, 1899–1912, 1919–30, 1938–41

Clarksville
  pre 1861 (microfiche)
  1911, 1922, 1929, 1935, 1942–58, 1971, 1974

Cleveland 1938, 1949–74

Clinton 1952, 1955, 1960, 1970, 1974

Columbia 1925, 1948–74

Cookeville
  (Algood) 1958, 1959, 1967

Crossville
  (Crab Orchard, Homestead, Pleasant Hill) 1971

Dayton
  (Spring City) 1974

Dickson 1972–75

Dyersburg 1936, 1947, 1952, 1958–83

Etowah 1968

Fayetteville 1950, 1970, 1974

Franklin 1957–83

Greenville 1948, 1950, 1958, 1961, 1967–72

Harriman
  (Kinston, Rockwood) 1950, 1954, 1958, 1960, 1974

Henderson 1975

Humboldt 1922, 1973

Jackson 1908, 1913, 1937, 1942, 1947–75

Johnson City 1913–21, 1932, 1935, 1958–61, 1970–75,
  1985

Kingsport
  (Blountville; Church Hill; Gate City; Mt. Carmel;
    Weber City, Va.) 1969, 1971, 1974–75

Knoxville 1880–1942

LaFollette
  (Coryville, Jacksboro) 1955, 1959, 1969, 1973

Lawrenceburg 1958–64, 1970, 1972

Lebanon 1927, 1948, 1959, 1964–83

Lewisburg 1972

Lexington 1968, 1973

Manchester 1971, 1974

McMinnville 1952, 1958–84

Memphis
  pre 1861 (microfiche)
  1861–1935 (microfilm)
  (suburbs) 1936–83

Morristown 1926, 1942, 1949–61, 1969, 1971

Murfreesboro 1950, 1958–85

Nashville
  pre 1861 (microfiche)
  1861–1935 (microfilm)
  (suburbs) 1937–85

Newport 1957–73, 1984

Oak Ridge 1958–60, 1970, 1974

Paris 1936, 1986

Pulaski 1957, 1972, 1976

Rogersville 1975

Savannah 1973

Shelbyville 1936, 1952, 1967, 1970–75, 1986

Smyrna 1975

South Pittsburg
  (Jasper) 1975

Sparta 1975

Springfield 1935, 1947, 1959, 1961, 1969, 1983

Sweetwater
  (Madisonville, Tellico Plains, Vonore) 1974, 1979

Tullahoma 1952, 1959, 1971, 1974

Union City 1936, 1965, 1970, 1973

County, Business, and Miscellaneous

Memphis (city) 1972, 1978

Tennessee
  (state) pre 1861 (microfiche)
  1871–1887, 1891, 1906
  (principal cities; also northern Alabama) 1900
    *Tennessee State Gazetteer and Business Directory For
      1860–1861.* John L. Mitchell, ed. Nashville: the
      editor, 1960. F434 .M68.

Weakley 1923

Arkansas

Historical Highlights

1686   Arkansas Post established by France.

1763   Ceded by France to Spain.

1800   Returned to France.

1803   Part of the Louisiana Purchase from France.

Although three countries claimed the area that encompasses present day Arkansas, it was populated almost entirely by Native Americans: the Cherokee, Choctaw, Quapaw, and Osage. It was not until the nineteenth century that the white man began to assume control.

1806   District of Arkansas established.

1812   Cherokee Territory established in the northern part of present day Arkansas. Arkansas District became part of the Missouri Territory.

1815   Lands given to veterans of the War of 1812.

1817   Indian tribes began ceding their land to the United States or trading them in exchange for other land further west.

1819   Became part of the Oklahoma Territory.

1836   Entered the Union.

In addition to the Indians who settled in Arkansas, Cherokees accepted reservation lands under treaty in exchange for ceding their lands in Georgia and North Carolina. Similarly, in the year preceding 1825, the Choctaw also arrived.

Bounty land given prior to 1855 to veterans of the War of 1812, and also the Mexican War, spurred an influx of white persons; immigrants from Europe also came late in the century. At the start of the present century, many of these settlers moved on to Oklahoma (Indian Territory).

1861   Seceded from the Union and joined the confederate States of America.

Although a part of the Confederacy, many inhabitants were pro-Union. Some of them moved north to escape harassment. Some of the pro-Confederacy inhabitants moved into Texas for the same reason.

Published Record Sources

Guidebooks

Dean, Ernie. *Arkansas Place Names.* Branson, Mo.: Ozark Mountaineer, 1986. F409. D43.

Dillard, Tom W., and Valerie Thwing. *Researching Arkansas History: A Beginner's Guide.* Little Rock: Rose Publishing Co., 1979. F406 .D54.

Census Indexes and Abstracts

Federal

1840   F410 .J177

1850   F410 .J18
        Presley, Mrs. Leister E. *Arkansas Census, 1850: Surname Index.* Searcy, Ark.: the author, 1974. F410 .P73.
        Waldenmaier, Inez, comp. *Arkansas Travelers.* Washington, D.C.: the compiler, 1957. F410 .W34.

1860   Bonner, Kathryn R. *Arkansas 1860 United States Index.* Marianna, Ark.: the author, 1984. F410 .B66.

1870   Dhonau, Robert W. *Federal Census, 1870, Arkansas County, Arkansas.* Little Rock: the author, 1978. F417 .A65D49.

All the above publications shown without the name of the compiler or author are by Ronald V. Jackson, Accelerated Indexing Systems.

Mortality Schedules

1850   McLane, Bobbie S., and Capitola H. Glazner, eds. *1850 Mortality Schedule of Arkansas.* N.p.: the editors, n.d. F410 .M17.

1860   Glazner, Capitola H., ed. *1860 Mortality Schedules of Arkansas.* Hot Springs National Park: the editor, n.d. F410 .A16.

1870   ——. *1870 Mortality Schedules of Arkansas.* N.p.: the editor, n.d. F410 .G45.

1880   ——. *1880 Mortality Schedules of Arkansas.* Hot Springs National Park: the editor, n.d. F410 .A17.

Biographies

Allard, Chester C., comp. *Who is Who in Arkansas.* 2 vols. Little Rock: Allard House Publishing Co., 1959. F410 .W47.

American Historical Society. Thomas D. Yancey, ed. *Arkansas and Its People.* 4 vols. New York: the society, 1930. F411 .T43.

Arkansas Historical Commission. *Arkansas Biographical Sketch Index.* Little Rock: State of Arkansas, 1915. F410 .A1A5.

Biographical and Historical Memoirs of Eastern Arkansas. Chicago: Goodspeed Publishing Co., 1890. Reprint. Easley, S.C.: Southern Historical Press, 1984. F411 .B6.

Biographical and Historical Memoirs of Central Arkansas. Reprint. Easley, S.C.: Southern Historical Press, 1978. F411 .B63.

Biographical and Historical Memoirs of Northeastern Arkansas. Reprint. Easley, S.C.: Southern Historical Press, 1976. F411 .B62.

Biographical and Historical Memoirs of Western Arkansas. Chicago: Southern Publishing Co., 1891. Reprint. Easley, S.C.: Southern Historical Press, 1978. F411 .B67.

Ferguson, John L. *Arkansas Lives: The Opportunity Land Who's Who, 1965.* Hopkinsville, Ky.: Historical Records Association, 1965. F410 .F4.

Goodspeed Biographical and Historical Memoirs of Northwestern Arkansas. Reprint. Easley, S.C.: Southern Historical Press, 1978. F411 .H69.

Hallum, John. *Biographical and Pictorial History of Arkansas.* Albany, N.Y.: Wee, Parsons, 1887. F411 .H19.

Presley, Mrs. Leister E. *Biographical Index to Biographical and Historical Memoirs of Central Arkansas.* Searcy, Ark.: the author, 1973. F411 B63 supplement.

——. *Biographical Index to Biographical and Historical Memoirs of Western Arkansas and Conway County.* Searcy, Ark.: the author, 1973. F411 .B67 supplement.

——. *Biographical Index to Biographical and Historical Memoirs of Southern Arkansas.* Searcy, Ark.: the author, 1973. F411 .B65 supplement.

——. *Biographical Index to Biographical and Historical Memoirs of Northeastern Arkansas.* Searcy, Ark.: the author, 1973. F411 .B62 supplement.

——. *Biographical Index to Biographical and Historical Memoirs of Northwestern Arkansas.* Searcy, Ark.: the author, 1973. F411 .H68.

Shinn, Josiah H. *Pioneers and Makers of Arkansas.* Baltimore: Genealogical Publishing Co., 1967. F410 .S55.

Early Settlers

Arkansas Family Histories: Ancestor Charts. 18 vols. Little Rock: Arkansas Genealogical Society, 1980. F410 .A72.

Published quarterly: February 1976 through March 1980.

Arkansas Family Histories: Family Group Sheets. Little Rock: Arkansas Genealogical Society, 1980. F410 .A722.

Published monthly: September 1978 through March 1980.

Arkansas Folklore: Field Recordings in the Archive of Folk Song. Washington, D.C.: Library of Congress, 1980.

A leaflet available at the Archive of Folk Life, Library of Congress.

Clark, Mrs. Larry P., comp. *Arkansas Pioneers and Allied Families.* 2 vols. Little Rock: the author, 1976. F410 .A83.

Herndon, Dallas T., ed. *Annals of Arkansas.* 4 vols. Hopkinsville, Ky.: Historical Records Association, 1947. F411 .H576.

Local Records

Cemetery Records of Arkansas County, Arkansas. DeWitt, Ark.: Arkansas County Extension Homemakers Council, 1984. F417 .A65C46.

Core, Dorothy J., comp. *Abstracts of Catholic Registers of Arkansas, 1764–1858.* DeWitt, Ark.:

Grand Prairie Historical Society, 1976. F410 .C67.

Frazier, John P., comp. *Cemetery Inscriptions in Southwestern Arkansas.* Vol. 1. Pittsburg, Tex.: the author, 1987. F410 .F13.

Morgan, James L., comp. *Genealogical Records of Arkansas.* Vol. 1, *1804–1830.* Newport, Ark.: Arkansas Records Association, 1973. F410 .M66.

National Society Daughters of the American Revolution. Hall Chapter. *Index to Sources for Arkansas Cemetery Inscriptions.* North Little Rock: the society, 1976. F410 .P75.

Military Records

General

Payne, Dorothy E., comp. *Arkansas Pensioners, 1818–1900.* Easley, S.C.: Southern Historical Press, 1958. F410 .P38.

Civil War

Arkansas. Adjutant General. *Report of the Adjutant General of Arkansas, For the Period of the Late Rebellion and to November 1, 1865.* Washington, D.C.: Government Printing Office, 1867. UA43 .A8.

McLane, Bobbie J., and Capitola Glazner, eds. *Arkansas 1911 Census of Confederate Veterans.* Hot Springs National Park: the editors, 1977–81. E548 .M43.

Pompey, Sherman L. *Civil War Veteran Burials From Arkansas. Regiments, C.S.A.* Independence, Cal.: Historical and Genealogical Publishing Co., 1972. E553.4 .P65.

Wright, Marcus J. *Arkansas in the War, 1861–1865.* Batesville, Ark.: Independence Historical Society, 1963. E553 .W7.

Directories

City

Arkadelphia 1949–54

Benton 1981

Bentonville
(Benton Co.) 1964–66

Blytheville 1956–60

Conway
(Faulkner Co.) 1958–82

Crosett (suburbs) 1966–70

De Queen 1977

Dumas 1977

El Dorado 1927–30, 1935–82

Fayetteville 1904, 1929, 1932, 1939, 1947, 1951–85

Forest City 1958–84

Fort Smith 1897, 1898, 1907–11, 1930, 1936–42, 1948–84

Helena
(W. Helena) 1909, 1911, 1917, 1929, 1936

Hope 1985

Hot Springs National Park 1897, 1903–30, 1935–82

Jonesboro
(Fayetteville area) 1936, 1939, 1947–82

Little Rock
pre 1861 (microfiche)
(Cammack Village, Mabelville, N. Little Rock) 1897, 1903–84

Magnolia 1948–53, 1958, 1985

Malverne 1947, 1953

Marianna 1965, 1974

Monticello 1958

Morrilton
(Conway Co.) 1964, 1970–76

Newport 1950, 1959

Osceola 1976

Paragould
(Greene Co.) 1917, 1965, 1973, 1982

Pine Bluff 1909–13, 1927–31, 1936, 1946–83

Rogers
(Bentonville, Springdale, Benton Co.) 1939

Siloam Springs
(Benton Co.) 1964, 1972, 1975

Stuttgart 1956

Texarkana
(Nash; Wake Village, Tex.) 1898, 1908–84

West Memphis 1958–83

Wynne 1976

County, Business and Miscellaneous

Arkansas (state) 1892, 1906, 1912

Pulaski 1952

Alabama

Historical Highlights

1702   Mobile founded.

1763   Ceded by France to England.

The first settlers to the Alabama area were French and Spanish; control varied between the two countries from time to time and from region to region. After the Treaty of Paris, Great Britain attained control from France.

1776   Still under control of England at the time of the American Revolution.

Loyalists fled from Georgia into Alabama to escape hostilities during the war. Following the war, settlers began to pour in from Georgia, the Carolinas, and Virginia, developing a plantation economy heavily reliant upon imported slaves for labor.

1790   Spain extended its control along the Gulf Coast (West Florida).

1795   Northern part of Alabama ceded by Spain to the United States.

Border disputes abounded, not only between France and Spain but also between Alabama and Georgia. Final settlement of the boundary between the two territories did not come until 1840.

1798   Assigned as part of the Mississippi Territory.

1804   Land that had been ceded by Georgia two years earlier also assigned to the Mississippi Territory.

1805   Indian tribes of Chickasaw, Cherokee, and Choctaw ceded part of their lands to Alabama.

1817   Alabama Territory established.

1819   Entered the Union.

1861   Seceded from the Union and joined the Confederate States of America. Montgomery became the first Confederate capital until it was moved to Richmond, Virginia.

Published Record Sources

Census Indexes and Abstracts

Federal

1820/30   Department of Archives and History. Marie B. Owen, ed. *Alabama Census Returns, 1820 and An Abstract of Federal Census of Alabama, 1830*. Baltimore: Genealogical Publishing Co., 1967. F325 .A28.

1830   F325 .J3
Gangrud, Pauline M., comp. *Alabama: An Index to the 1830 United States Census*. Hot Springs National Park, Ark.: Jones McLane, 1973. F326 .G3.

1840   F325 .J32
Posey, Betty Sue D. *Alabama 1840 Census Index*. Hattiesburg, Miss.: n.p., 1973. F325 .P67.

1850   F325 .J323

Mortality Schedules

1850   Barefield, Marilyn D., comp. *Alabama Mortality Schedule, 1850 . . . .* Easley, S.C.: Southern Historical Press, 1983. F325 .B355.

All the above publications shown without the name of the compiler or author are by Ronald V. Jackson, Accelerated Indexing Systems.

Biographies

DuBose, Joel C. *Notable Men of Alabama.* 2 vols. Spartanburg, S.C.: The Reprint Co., 1976. CT221 .N67.

Garrett, William. *Reminiscences of Public Men in Alabama.* Spartanburg, S.C.: The Reprint Co., 1975. F325 .G24.

Marks, Henry S., and Marsha K. Marks. *Alabama's Past Leaders.* Huntsville: Strode Publishers, 1982. CT221 .M37.

Marks, Henry S. *Who Was Who in Alabama.* Huntsville: Strode Publishers, 1972. F325 .M3.

Matlock, Guy A., comp. *Who's Who in Alabama.* Birmingham: DuBose Publishing Co., 1940. F325 .W57.

Volume 1, 1939–40.

Owen, Marie B. *The Story of Alabama.* New York: Lewis Historical Publishing Co., 1949. F326 .088.

Volume 2, Personal and Family History.

Who's Who in Alabama. Birmingham: Sayers Enterprises, 1969. F325 .W57.

Volume 2, 1969.

Land Acquisition

Barefield, Marilyn D. *Old Huntsville Land Office Records and Military Warrants, 1810–1854.* Easley, S.C. Southern Historical Press, 1983. F325 .B358.

————. *Old Tuscaloosa Land Office Records, 1821–1855.* Easley, S.C.: Southern Historical Press, 1985. F325 .B38.

Cowart, Margaret M. *Old Land Records of Jackson County, Alabama.* Huntsville: the author, 1986. F332 .J2C68.

Hahn, Marilyn D. *Old Sparta and Elba Land Office Records, 1768–1888.* Easley, S.C.: Southern Historical Press, 1983. F325 .B36.

Early Settlers

Alabama Early Settlers—1816: Alabama Counties, Mississippi Territory. Hanceville, Ala.: Briarwood Press, 1984. F325 .A34.

Oliver, Lloyd F. *Index to Col. J. E. Saunder's Early Settlers of Alabama.* Tomball, Tex.: Genealogical Publications, 1978. F325 .S282038.

Saunders, James E. *Early Settlers of Alabama, With Notes and Genealogies.* Reprint. Baltimore: Genealogical Publishing Co., 1969. F325 .S28.

Local Records

Gangrud, Pauline J., comp. *Marriage, Death and Legal Notes From Early Alabama Newspapers, 1819–1893.* Easley, S.C.: Southern Historical Press, 1981. F325 .M33.

Murray, Nicholas R. *Alabama Surname Index: Computer Indexed Marriage Records.* Hammond, La.: Hunting For Bears, Inc., 1985. F325 .A365.

Military Records

General

Gangrud, Pauline J., comp. *Alabama Soldiers: Revolutionary, War of 1812, and Indian Wars.* 5 vols. Hot Springs National Park, Ark.: the compiler, 1979. F325 .G22.

American Revolution

Alabama. Department of Archives and History. *Revolutionary Soldiers in Alabama, Being a List of Names Compiled From Authentic Sources, of Soldiers of the American Revolution, Who Resided in Alabama.* Montgomery: Brown Printing, 1911. Reprint. Baltimore: Genealogical Publishing Co., 1967. E255 .A31.

Indian Wars

Alabama Volunteers. *Cherokee Disturbances and Removals, 1836–1839.* Cullman, Ala.: Gregath Co., 1982. .F325 .A37.

Civil War

Brewer, Willie. "Brief Historical Sketches of Military Organizations Raised in Alabama During the Civil War." In *Alabama: Her History . . . From 1540 to 1872.* N.p.: Alabama Civil War Centennial Commission, 1962. F326 .B84.

Hoole, William S. *Alabama Tories: The First Alabama Cavalry, U.S.A., 1862–1865.* Tuscaloosa: Confederate Publishing Co., 1960. E495.6 1st H6.

Directories

City

Albany
(Decatur) 1922, 1926

Albertville
(Beaz) 1957–83

Alexander 1957, 1961–85

Andalusia 1955–84

Anniston
(Blue Mountain City, Edmonston Hgts., Hobson City, Oxford, Sunset Hgts., W. Anniston) 1898, 1908, 1913, 1922–84

Arab 1969–74

Athens 1954–61, 1967–72

Atmore 1961–84

Bessemer
(Brighton) 1913–26, 1932–40, 1946–63

Birmingham (suburbs) 1888, 1893, 1897–1984

Centerville
(Brent) 1978

Clanton 1957, 1966, 1972–84

Cullman 1958–84

Decatur 1913, 1942, 1949–61, 1969, 1971

Demopolis 1959–84

Dothan 1928, 1951–83

Eufaula 1958–82

Fairbanks
(College, North Pole) 1946–47, 1951, 1953, 1959–84

Fairhope
(Daphne) 1965, 1967, 1972–84

Flomaton
(Century, Fla.; Jay, Fla.; S. Flomaton, Fla.) 1905–80

Florence
(Sheffield, Muscle Shoals, Tuscumbia) 1913, 1926, 1959–85

Fort Payne 1958, 1969, 1973

Gadsden
(Alabama City, Attalla) 1912–17, 1927, 1931, 1935–36, 1947–83

Greenville 1953, 1960, 1969, 1973

Guntersville 1957, 1969, 1972, 1974

Haleysville 1979

Hamilton 1979

Hartselle 1969, 1973

Huntsville 1913, 1931, 1936, 1955–84

Jackson
(Leroy) 1968, 1978

Jasper 1955, 1961, 1970, 1974

Luverne 1974

Marion 1978

Minette 1963–80

Mobile
pre 1861 (microfiche)
1861–1935 (microfilm)
(suburbs) 1936–85

Monroe
(Frisco City) 1965–81

Montgomery 1880, 1897–84

Opelika
(Auburn) 1923, 1960–83

Ozark 1960–84

Phenix City 1971–84

Prattville 1962–82

Prichard
(Chickasaw, Saraland, Satsuma) 1946, 1956–81

Roanoke 1967, 1974

Russellville 1970, 1974, 1979

Saraland 1966

Scottsboro 1960, 1965–75

Selma 1880, 1898, 1904, 1919–39, 1942–85

Sheffield
(Florence, Tuscumbia) 1920

Sylacauga 1952, 1956, 1960, 1971, 1974

Talladega 1957–85

Tallassee 1975

Troy 1956, 1970, 1974

Tuscaloosa
(Alberta City, Highland, Holt, Kaulton, Lee Addition, Northport, Rosedale) 1913, 1916, 1922, 1924, 1932, 1950–84

Tuskegee 1963–84

Valley, The
(Fairfax; Langdale; Lanett; Shawmutt; River View; West Point, Ga.) 1965, 1967, 1971, 1977, 1980, 1984

Wetumpka 1975–82

Winslow
(Holbrook, Joseph City) 1960, 1965, 1970

County, Business, and Miscellaneous

Alabama (state) 1881, 1905
northern (see Tennessee)

Green
pre 1861 (microfiche)

Jefferson 1893

Mississippi

Historical Highlights

1591   Control assumed by Spain.

1688   French colonists arrived to found Biloxi.
With the appearance of French settlers, communities were established along the Gulf Coast and the Mississippi River. Other settlements were the result of French land grants.

1762   Territory east of the Mississippi River ceded by France to Spain.

1763   Balance of the territory ceded by France to England.
Colonists from various southern states began to migrate into the area.

1776   Mississippi still under British control at the time of the American Revolution. Loyalists came to escape the fighting.

1779   Control over the Natchez District attained by Spain.

1798   Natchez District claimed by the United States. Mississippi Territory created.
After the American Revolution the newly created United States began to expand with military force into the Natchez District, claiming all the area including present day Alabama and assigning it to the Mississippi Territory.

1803   Louisiana Purchase from France.
The Northwest Territory, obtained by the United States, opened the Mississippi River to New Orleans and the Gulf Coast, encouraging settlement in the Mississippi Territory. Georgia ceded all its western lands as far as the Mississippi River.

1861   Seceded from the Union and joined the Confederate States of America. Remained under military control for five years after the close of the war.

Published Record Sources

Guidebooks

Brieger, James V., comp. *Hometown, Mississippi.* N.p.: the compiler, 1980. F339 .B74.

Department of Archives and History. Thomas W. Henderson and Ronald E. Tomlin, eds. *Guide to Official Records in the Mississippi Department of Archives and History.* Jackson: State of Mississippi, 1975. CD3324 .M57.

Census Indexes and Abstracts

Federal

1820   F340 .J328

1830   F340 .J33

1850   F340 .J34
Gillis, Irene S. *Mississippi 1850 Census: Surname Index.* Shreveport, La.: the author, 1972. F340 .G473.

1860   F340 .J342

Bonner, Kathryn R. *Mississippi 1860 United States Census Index* .... Marianna, Ark.: 1983. F340 .B66.

All the above publications shown without the name of the compiler or author are by Ronald V. Jackson, Accelerated Indexing Systems.

State

Jackson, Ronald V. *Early Mississippi Census.* Bountiful, Utah: Accelerated Indexing Systems, 1980. F340 .J324.

Mortality Schedules

1850   Gillis, Irene S., comp. *Mississippi 1850 Mortality Schedules.* Shreveport, La.: Gillis Publications, 1973. F340 .G47.

1860   Jackson, Ronald V. *Mississippi 1860 Mortality Schedule.* Bountiful, Utah: Accelerated Indexing Systems, 1981. F340 .J342.

Biographies

Biographical and Historical Memoirs of the Mississippi. 2 vols. Chicago: Goodspeed Publishing Co., 1896. Reprint. Spartanburg, S.C.: The Reprint Co., 1978. F341 .B6.

Gillis, Norman E., comp. *Index to Biographical and Historical Memoirs of Mississippi.* Baton Rouge: the compiler, 1961. F341 .B6.

Lynch, James D. *The Bench and Bar of Mississippi.* New York: E. J. Hale & Sons, 1881. F340 .L98.

Rand, Clayton. *Men of Spine in Mississippi.* Gulfport: Dixie Press, 1940. F340 .R32.

Rowland, Dunbar. *History of Mississippi, Vols. 3 and 4—Biographical.* Spartanburg, S.C.: The Reprint Co., 1978. F341 .R86.

Land Acquisition

Lowrie, Walter. *Early Settlers of Mississippi as Taken From Land Claims in the Mississippi Territory.* Easley, S.C. Southern Historical Press, 1986. F340 .E27.

From *The American State Papers*.

Early Settlers

Lackey, Richard S., comp. *Frontier Claims in the Lower South: Records of Claims Filed by Citizens of the Alabama and Tomigbee River Settlements in the Mississippi Territory for Depredations by the Creek Indians During the War of 1812.* New Orleans: Polyanthos, 1977. F340 .F76.

Johnson, Charles D., ed. *Register—Order of the First Families of Mississippi, 1699, 1817.* Ann Arbor, Mich.: the society, 1981. F340 .O73.

Thomas, Betty W., and J. David Baker, eds. *Mississippi Lineage Charts.* 2 vols. N.p.: the editors, 1980. F340 .M54.

Local Records

Historical Records Survey (WPA). *Guide to Vital Statistics Records in Mississippi.* Vol. 1, *Public Archives;* Vol. 2, *Church Archives.* Jackson: Mississippi Historical Records Survey, 1942. CD3321 .H5.

————. *Inventory of the Church and Synagogue Archives of Mississippi—Jewish Congregations and Organizations.* Jackson: Mississippi State Conference, B'Nai B'rith, 1940. CD3320 .H48J4.

King, J. Estelle, comp. *Mississippi Court Records, 1799–1835.* Reprint. Baltimore: Genealogical Publishing Co., 1970.

McBee, May W., comp. *Mississippi County Court Records.* Greenwood, Miss.: the compiler, 1958. Reprint. Baltimore: Genealogical Publishing Co., 1967. F347 .A15M3.

Mississippi Genealogical Society. *Mississippi Cemetery and Bible Records.* Jackson: the society, 1963–83. F340 .M48.

Murray, Nicholas R. *Mississippi Surname Index: Marriage Records.* Hammond, La.: Hunting For Bears, Inc., 1984. F340 .M546.

Specify county desired.

Strickland, Ben, and Jean Strickland, comps. *Records of Choctaw Trading Post, St. Stephens, Mississippi Territory, 1803–15.* Moss Points, Miss.: the compiler, 1984. F332 .W4S77.

Wiltshire, Betty C., comp. *Marriages and Deaths From Mississippi Newspapers.* Vol. 1, *1837–1863.* Bowie, Md.: Heritage Books, 1987. F340 .W55.

Military Records

General

Rowland, Dumbar. *Military History of Mississippi, 1803–1898.* Spartanburg, S.C.: The Reprint Co., 1978. F341 .M58.

Civil War

Bearss, Edwin C. *Decision in Mississippi.* Jackson: Mississippi Commission on the War Between the States, 1962. E568 .B4.

Dilts, Bryan L., comp. *1890 Mississippi Census Index of Civil War Veterans Or Their Widows—Microforms.* Salt Lake City: Index Publishing Co., 1984. (Micro 87/2015).

Pompey, Sherman L. *Register of the Civil War Dead, Mississippi.* Clovis, Calif.: the author, 1970. E548 .P635.

Directories

City

Aberdeen
(Brown Co.) 1887–1909

Amory 1964–78

Armorel 1980–84

Batesville
(Sardis) 1974–80

Bay St. Louis
(Waveland) 1964–80

Biloxi
(Edgewater Park, Gulfport, Long Beach, Pass Christian) 1913, 1922–27, 1931–36, 1949–58, 1964, 1972–83

Booneville 1976

Brookhaven 1914, 1947, 1960–83

Cleveland 1955, 1959, 1972, 1975

Columbus 1912–75

Corinth 1913, 1936, 1950–59, 1973

Crystal Springs 1965–81

Forest
(Morton, Scott Co.) 1975–81

Greenville
(Leland) 1913, 1916, 1927–31, 1936–40, 1946, 1950–84

Greenwood 1931, 1936, 1947–59, 1964, 1972, 1974, 1985

Grenada 1954, 1960, 1966–84

Gulfport 1912, 1922, 1925, 1931, 1936, 1939, 1947, 1949, 1953, 1958, 1960, 1968, 1971–83

Hattiesburg
(Petal) 1906, 1912, 1914, 1918, 1923, 1927–84

Hernando 1975

Indianola 1966–85

Jackson
pre 1861 (microfiche)
(suburbs) 1899, 1901, 1932, 1937–47, 1954–83

Kosciusko 1965–80

Laurel 1912, 1938, 1941, 1945, 1947, 1955–85

Leland 1964–83

Louisville 1974–82

Magee
(Mendenhall) 1966

McComb
(Fernwood, Magnolia, Summit) 1936, 1947, 1950, 1955–83

Meridian 1888, 1899, 1901, 1908–84

Natchez 1899, 1922–28, 1935, 1939, 1941, 1946–84

New Albany 1975

Newton 1975

Oxford 1960, 1971, 1975

Pascagoula
(Moss Point) 1957–84

Philadelphia 1967–83

Picayune 1954, 1961, 1965–82

Senatobia 1975, 1979

Starkville 1961, 1964, 1971, 1973, 1975

Tupelo
(Bissell, E. Tupelo, Plantersville, Russell, Skyline, Verona) 1957, 1960, 1971, 1974

Vicksburg
pre 1861 (microfiche)
(Waltersville) 1911, 1914, 1921–85

Waynesboro 1978

West Point 1967, 1971, 1974, 1978, 1980

Winona
 (Duck Hill, Kilmichael) 1976

Yazoo 1913, 1916, 1928, 1936, 1959, 1971, 1974

County, Business, and Miscellaneous

Kosciusko 1948

Meridian 1873

Mississippi (state, see Louisiana)

Mississippi Valley
 pre 1861 (microfiche) (includes Cincinnati, Louisville, Memphis, New Orleans, Pittsburgh, Wheeling) 1915

Louisiana

Historical Highlights

1682   Discovered by LaSalle, from France.

The region including present day Louisiana has long been claimed, in parts, by the French, Spanish, and English, with French control being dominant most of the time prior to 1803.

1776   Under French rule at the time of the American Revolution.

1803   The Louisiana Purchase from France.

1811   Part of Spanish West Florida annexed by the United States.

During the American Revolution, British Loyalists fled to Louisiana to escape the fighting. After the revolution, migrants from the older southern states came to present day northern Louisiana, and Frenchmen (Acadians) from Canada came to the Gulf Coast area after England gained control over Canada. After the United States purchased the area from France, it divided it into two parts; the District of Louisiana, comprised of Missouri, Arkansas, and the Northwest Territory; and the Territory of

Orleans, comprised of the southern portions. The District of Louisiana was organized into counties, while the Territory of Orleans was divided into parishes, reflecting the heavy concentration of French and Spanish Catholics.

1812   Entered the Union.

State boundaries remained in dispute for more than a decade. The large area south of the Sabine River was declared "neutral ground," having no governmental organization. Disputes between Louisiana, Texas, and Arkansas continued well after tentative agreements were reached by treaties between Spain and the United States.

1861   Seceded from the Union and joined the Confederate States of America.

Published Record Sources

Guidebooks

Historical Records Survey (WPA). *Line Inventory of the Parish Archives of Louisiana.* New Orleans: Historical Records Survey, 1939. CD3260 .H6.

Holmes, Jack D. L. *A Guide to Spanish Louisiana, 1762–1806.* New Orleans: A.F. LaBorde, 1970. F372 .H64.

Leeper, Clare. *Louisiana Places: A Collection of the Columns From the Baton Rouge Sunday Advocate, 1960–1974.* Baton Rouge: Legacy Publishing Co., 1976. F367 .L43.

Census Indexes and Abstracts

Federal

1810   F368 .J28

1810/20 (by county)
         Ardoin, Robert B. L. *Louisiana Census Records.* 3 vols. Baltimore: Genealogical Publishing Co., 1970–77. Vol. 3, New Orleans: Polyanthos. F374 .A8.

1820   F368 .J29
         Felldin, Jeanne R., and Charlotte M. Tucker, comps. *The United States Census Index: The Louisiana Parishes of*

Avoyelles, Catahoula, Concordia, Feliciana, Iberville, Natchitoches, and West Baton Rouge. N.p., n.d. F368 .F44.

1830   F368 .J3

1830/40   (by county)
Childs, Marietta. *North Louisiana Census Reports (Catahoula, Concordia, Ouachita, Caldwell, Carroll, Madison, Union.)* New Orleans: Polyanthos, 1975. F368 .C47.

1840   F368 .J32

1850   F368 .J33

All the above publications shown without the name of the compiler or author are by Ronald V. Jackson, Accelerated Indexing Systems.

State

Maduell, Charles R., Jr., comp. *The Census Tables For the French Colony of Louisiana From 1688 Through 1732.* Baltimore: Genealogical Publishing Co., 1972. F368 .M3.

Robichaux, Albert J., comp. *Louisiana Census and Militia Lists, 1770–1789.* 2 vols. Harvey, La.: the compiler, 1973. F368 .R62.

Voorhies, Jacqueline K., comp. *Some Late Eighteenth Century Louisianans; Census Records, 1758–96.* Lafayette, La.: University of Southwestern Louisiana, 1973. F368 .V6613.

DeVille, Winston. *Opelousas Post: The Census of 1771.* Ville Platte, La.: the author, 1986. F379 .063D47.

Biographies

Biographical and Historical Memoirs of Northwest Louisiana: Index to Biographical Sketches. Natchitoches, La.: Northwest State College of Louisiana, 1964. F369 .B6 supp.

Moore, Daniel D., ed. *Louisianans and Their State. A Historical and Biographical Text Book of Louisiana.* New Orleans: Louisiana Historical and Biographical Associations, 1919. F369 .L885.

Land Acquisition

DeVille, Winston. *Louisiana and Mississippi Lands: A Guide to Spanish Land Grants at the University of Michigan.* Ville Platt, La.: Evangeline

Genealogical and Historical Society, 1985. F368 .D39.

Properties of Ascension, Attakapas, and Baton Rouge.

Maduell, Charles J., Jr. *Federal Land Grants in the Territory of Orleans: The Delta Parishes.* New Orleans: Polyanthos, 1975. F368 .M32.

Early Settlers

Ericson, Carolyn, and Frances Ingmire. *First Settlers of the Louisiana Territory. Orleans Territory Grants From the American State Papers.* St. Louis: the authors, 1983. F368 .F55.

Gianelloni, Elizabeth B. *Love, Honor and Betrayal: The Notorial Acts of Estevan DeQuinones, 1778–1784.* East Baton Rouge: Louisiana Ancestry Series, 1964. F368 .L62.

Louisiana Ahnentafels. Ancestor Charts and Family Group Sheets. Natchitoches, La.: Natchitoches Genealogical and Historical Association, 1982. F379 .N2S26.

Morrison, Phoebe C. *Generations . . . Past to Present.* 2 vols. Thibedaux, La.: Audrey B. Westerman, 1984. F368 .M67.

Robichaux, Albert. *Colonial Settlers Along Bayou Fourches, 1770–1798.* Vol. 2. Harvey, La.: the author, 1974. F368 .R62.

Villere, Sidney L. *The Canary Islands Migration in Louisiana, 1778–1783.* New Orleans: Genealogical Research Society of New Orleans, 1971. F368 .V54.

Local Records

Adams, Donna B., comp. *Post Office Records, 1732–1800.* 6 vols. Baton Rouge: the author, 1986. F368 .A64.

Volume 1, St. Bernard's, Charles, James, John the Baptist, Martin, Mary, Terrebonne; volume 2, Caddo, Bossier, Webster, Claiborne, Bienville; volume 3, East and West Feliciana, East and West Baton Rouge, Iberville, Ascension, Assumption; volume 4, Caldwell, Franklin, Tensas, Catahoula, Concordia; volume 5, Calasieu, Jefferson Davis, Acadia, Lafayette, Ameron, Vermillion, Iberia; volume 6, Vernon, Rapides, Avoyelles, Beauregard, Allen Evangeline, St. Landry, Pointe Coupee.

Catholic Church. Diocese of Baton Rouge. *Catholic Church Records*. 6 vols. Baton Rouge: the diocese, 1978. F368 .C37.

> Volume 1, 1707, 1769; volume 2, 1770–1802; volume 3, 1804–19; volume 4, 1820–29; volume 5, 1830–39; volume 6, 1840–47.

Civil War Tax in Louisiana. Based on Direct Tax Assessments of Louisiana. Title on binding: *List of Names of Citizens of Louisiana From When the United States Direct Tax Was Collected in 1865.* New Orleans: Polyanthos, 1975. F368 .L57.

Conrad, Glenn, and Carl A. Brasceaux. *Gone But Not Forgotten: Records From South Louisiana Cemeteries.* Vol. 1, *St. Peter's Cemetery.* New Iberia; Lafayette, La.: University of Southeast Louisiana, 1983. F368 .C67.

Forsyth, Alice D., and Earlene L. Zeringue. *German "Pest Ships," 1720–21.* New Orleans: German Research Society of New Orleans, 1969. F368 .F6.

———. *Louisiana Marriages.* Vol. 1, *A Collection of Marriage Records From the St. Louis Cathedral in New Orleans During the Spanish Regime and the Early American Period, 1784–1806.* New Orleans: Polyanthos, 1977. F368 .F64.

———. *Louisiana Marriage Contracts: A Compilation of Abstracts From Records of the Superior Court of Louisiana During the French Regime, 1725–1758.* New Orleans: Polyanthos, 1980. F368 .F63.

Frazier, John P. *Tombstone Inscriptions of Northwest Louisiana Cemeteries.* Pittsburg, Tex.: the author, 1986. F368 .F73.

Hebert, Donald J. *Southwest Louisiana Records: Church and Civil Records of Settlers.* 33 vols. Eunice, La.: the author, 1974. F368 .H42.

> Covers 1756 to 1900. Specify year desired.

Historical Records Survey (WPA). *Transcription of Parish Records of Louisiana.* New Orleans: Historical Records Survey, 1941. F366 .H57.

> Specify parish desired.

Meyers, Brenda L., and Gloria I. Kerns. *Death Notices From Louisiana Newspapers.* 4 vols. Baker, La.: Folk Finders, Inc., 1985. F368 .M39.

> Specify parish desired.

Murray, Nicholas R., comp. *Louisiana Surname Index. Computer Indexed Marriage Records.* 5 vols. Hammond, La.: Hunting For Bears, Inc., 1984. F368 .M86.

> Specify parish desired.

National Society Daughters of the American Revolution. Louisiana. *Louisiana Tombstone Inscriptions.* 10 vols. Shreveport, La.: the society, 1954–57. F368 .D3.

> Specify parish desired.

Military Records

General

Holmes, Jack D. L. *Honor and Fidelity: The Louisiana Infantry Regiment and the Louisiana Militia Company, 1766–1821.* Birmingham: Louisiana Collection Series of Books and Documents on Colonial Louisiana, 1965. F336 .L53.

Colonial Wars

DeVille, Winston. *Louisiana Colonials: Soldiers and Vagabonds.* Mobile, Ala.: the author, 1963. F368 .D4.

———. *Louisiana Troops, 1720–1770.* Baltimore: Genealogical Publishing Co., 1965. F372 .D3.

War of 1812

Pierson, Marion J.B. *Louisiana Soldiers in the War of 1812.* Baton Rouge: Louisiana Genealogical and Historical Society, 1963. F359.5 .L8P5.

Civil War

Bartlett, Napier. *Military Records of Louisiana, Including Biographical and Historical Papers Relating to the Military Organizations of the State.* Baton Rouge: Louisiana State University Press, 1964. E565.4 .B293.

Louisiana. Commission of Military Records. Andrew B. Booth, comp. *Records of Louisiana Confederate Soldiers and Louisiana Confederate Commands.* New Orleans: State of Louisiana, 1920. Reprint. Spartanburg, S.C.: Reprint Co., 1984. E565.3 .B66.

Marchand, Sidney A. *Forgotten Fighters, 1861–1865.* Donaldsonville, La.: the author, 1966. F377 .A7M282.

Periodicals

Broders, Nell H. *Cumulative Subject Index to the Louisiana Genealogical Register, 1958–1975.* Baton Rouge: the author, 1976. F336 .B76.

Cruise, Boyd, comp. *Index to the Louisiana Historical Quarterly.* New Orleans: Plantation Book Shop, 1956. F366 .L792.

Directories

City

Abbeville 1962–81

Alexandria
(Pineville) 1912–19, 1921–29

Algona 1950, 1977, 1981

Baker
(Zachary) 1964

Bastrop 1955, 1958, 1972

Baton Rouge
(suburbs, Baker, Broadmoor, Capital Hgts., College Town, Denham Sprgs., Greenwell Sprgs., Goodwood Place, Istrodana, N. Highlands, Port Allen, Prosperity, Southdown Univ., S. Baton Rouge, Schorten Pl., Sunset Hgts., University Gardens, University View, Zachary) 1890, 1913–18, 1924–34, 1936–59, 1971–84

Bogalusa 1940, 1951–82

Bunkie 1966–78

Covington 1964–82

De Ridder 1967–77

Donaldsonville 1966–80

Eunice 1960–85

Ferriday 1976

Franklin 1955, 1965–74

Gonzales 1966, 1968

Hammond
(Ponchatoula) 1960

Houma 1938, 1941, 1960–84

Jeanerette 1967, 1971, 1973

Jennings 1908, 1947, 1954–82

Kaplan 1965

Lafayette 1928, 1939–85

Lake Charles 1913–83

Lake Providence
(E. Carrol, Oak Grove, Parrish, W. Carrol) 1966, 1977

Leesville 1965–77

Marksville 1966–77

Minden 1957, 1960, 1972, 1975

Monroe
(West Monroe) 1912–13, 1921, 1929, 1930, 1954–85

Morgan City
(Berwick, Patterson) 1960–83

Natchitoches 1960–79

New Iberia 1940, 1954, 1957, 1960, 1969–75

New Orleans
pre 1861 (microfiche)
1861–1935 (microfilm)
(suburbs) 1955–83

Opelousas 1956–84

Plaquemine
(White Castle) 1967–80

Raceland
(Cut-off, Galiano, Golden, Larose, Lockport, Meadow) 1970

Rayne 1973–81

Ruston 1956, 1960

Shreveport 1888, 1917–84

Slidell
(Pearl River) 1963–84

Springhill
(Cullen, Webster) 1964–78

Tallulah
(Madison Parrish) 1966, 1976

Thibodaux
(Schriever) 1954, 1960–85

Ville Platte 1977

Winnfield 1966, 1978

Winnsboro 1975

County, Business, and Miscellaneous

Louisiana (state) 1838, 1898
  (Mississippi) (state) 1870

New Orleans (city) 1884–98, 1896–1911

Red River 1893

Terrebone (no year stated)

CHAPTER 13

Mid-Western States

Ohio • Indiana • Illinois • Missouri
Michigan • Wisconsin
Minnesota • Iowa

Ohio

Historical Highlights

1667   Mississippi and Ohio River valleys explored by LaSalle, from France.

1747   Claimed by Virginia's Ohio Land Company.

1763   Control assumed by England after victories in the "French-Indian Wars."

Before Virginians began to move into the Ohio area, French fur trappers and traders were there, making few settlements except to establish forts for protection against unfriendly Indians. After heavy losses by the French and their Indian allies, Englishmen from Virginia and other colonies purchased land and established permanent settlements.

1776   Part of Virginia at the time of the American Revolution.

1784   Ohio Military District established by Virginia.

1786   Western Reserve established by Connecticut.

1796   Federal land offices established.

During the course of the Revolutionary War, George Rogers Clark led a military expedition from Kentucky into the Illinois and Ohio areas to rebut French claims in the area. After the war, Virginia set aside vast areas of bounty land for its veterans. A decade later, Virginia ceded the Ohio area to the United States, and federal land offices were set up to dispense land to all revolutionary war veterans as well as to private purchasers.

In addition to bounty lands granted both by Virginia and the United States, various other tracts of land were settled. Among these were lands for religious groups such as the Moravians, Quakers, Presbyterians, Shakers, Lutherans, and Mormons. Connecticut residents who had suffered losses from fires during the Revolutionary War were given acreage in the "firelands" of Ohio, on lands originally granted to Connecticut. Some lands still held by France were given to French settlers who had been swindled in earlier land schemes. Englishmen sympathetic with the revolutionary cause who had fled to Canada were awarded relocation land in the Ohio area. These groups were joined by others who purchased large tracts for resale. In summary, the area came to be settled by veterans or those to whom the veterans sold their land warrants, by religious groups, and by those from France, England, and eastern states—predominantly Virginia and Connecticut. The pioneer history of Ohio, therefore, is largely a study of land acquisition.

1799   Ohio Territory created.

1803   Admitted to the Union.

Migrants continued to enter the area, promoting the building of roads to facilitate overland travel. With the coming of the railroads, the English and Irish moved in to help lay the rails.

1861   Remained in the Union during the Civil War.

Published Record Sources

Guidebooks

Bell, Carol W. *Ohio Genealogical Guide.* Youngstown, Ohio: the author, 1984. F490 .B45.

Douthit, Ruth L. *Ohio Resources for Genealogists.* Detroit: Detroit Society for Genealogical Research, 1972. F490 .D68.

Flavell, Carol W. *Ohio Genealogical Guide.* Youngstown: the author, 1978. F490 .F57.

Kilbourne, John. *The 1833 Ohio Gazetteer.* Columbus: Scott & Wright. Reprint. Knightstown, Ind.: The Bookmark, 1978. F489 .K54.

Overman, William D. *Ohio Town Names.* Akron: Atlantic Press, 1959. F489 .08.

Phillips, W. Louis. *Jurisdictional Histories for Ohio's Eighty-eight Counties, 1788–1985.* Bowie, Md.: Heritage Books, 1986. F497 .B7P45.

Western Reserve Historical Society. *A Guide to Manuscripts and Archives of the Western Reserve Historical Society Library.* Cleveland: the society, 1972. CD3449 .C55W47.

Census Indexes and Abstracts

Federal

1820	F490 .J32
1830	F490 .J325
1840	F490 .J33

Wilkens, Cleo G. *Index to the 1840 Federal Population Census of Ohio.* Ft. Wayne, Ind.: 1969. F490 .W67.

1850   Ohio Family Historians Organizations. *Index to the 1850 Federal Population Census of Ohio.* Mineral Ridge, Ohio: L. F. Harshman, 1972. F495 .035.

1860   Harshman, Lida F. *Index to the 1860 Federal Population Census of Ohio.* Mineral Ridge, Ohio: the author, 1979. F490 .H37.

All the above publications shown without the name of the compiler or author are by Ronald V. Jackson, Accelerated Indexing Systems.

State

Jackson, Ronald V. *Early Ohio.* Bountiful, Utah: Accelerated Indexing Systems, 1980. F490 .J26.

———. *Early Ohio Census Records.* Bountiful, Utah: Accelerated Indexing Systems, 1974. F490 .J27.

Biographies

Biographical Cyclopedia and Portrait Gallery, With an Historical Sketch of the State of Ohio. 6 vols. Cincinnati: Western Biographical Publishing Co., 1883. F490. B61.

Brennan, J. Fletcher, ed. *A Biographical Cyclopedia and Portrait Gallery.* Cincinnati: John C. Yorston & Co., 1879. F490 .B83.

Men of Northwestern Ohio: A Collection of Portraits and Biographies. Bowling Green and Toledo: C.S. Van Tassel Publishing Co., 1898. CT254 .V36.

Mercer, James M. *Representative Men of Ohio, 1904–1908.* Columbus: Fred J. Heer, 1908. F490 .M55.

Ohio's Progressive Sons: A History of the State. Cincinnati: Queen City Publishing Co., 1905. F491 .04.

Reed, George I., ed. *Bench and Bar of Ohio.* 2 vols. Chicago: Century Publishing and Engraving, 1897. F490 .R32.

Scobee, F. E., and B. K. McElroy. *The Biographical Annals of Ohio, 1902–05.* 2 vols. State of Ohio, 1893. F490 .B59.

Summers, Ewing, ed. *Genealogical and Family History of Eastern Ohio.* New York: Lewis Historical Publishing Co., 1903. F490 .S55.

Van Tassel, C. S., comp. *The Ohio Blue Book or Who's Who in the Buckeye State.* Toledo: n.p., 1917. F490 .O36.

Who's Who in Ohio. Cleveland: Biographical Publishing Co., 1930. F490 .W62.

Land Acquisition

Berry, Ellen T., and David A. Berry, comps. *Early Ohio Settlers: Purchasers or Land in Southeast Ohio, 1800–1840.* Baltimore: Genealogical Publishing Co., 1984. F490 .B47.

———. *Early Ohio Settlers: Purchasers of Land in Southwest Ohio, 1800–1840.* Baltimore: Genealogical Publishing Co., 1986. F490 .B48.

Clark, Marie T. *Ohio Lands. Chillicothe Land Office, 1800–1829.* Chillicothe: the author, 1984. F478 .C53.

———. *Ohio Lands South of the Indiana Boundary Line.* Chillicothe: the author, 1984. F490 .C55.

Dyer, Albion M. *First Ownership of Ohio Lands.* Baltimore: Genealogical Publishing Co., 1969. F483 .D9.

Ohio. Auditor. *A Short History of Ohio Land Grants.* Columbus: State of Ohio, 1967. HD211 .O3A5. (F495 .O28).

Peters, William E. *Ohio Lands and Their History.* New York: Arno Press, 1979. HD243 .O3P4.

Riegel, Mayburt S., comp. *Early Ohioans' Residences: From the Land Grant Records.* Mansfield: Ohio Genealogical Society, 1976. F490 .R53.

Smith, Clifford N. *Federal Land Series . . . Land Patents Issued by the United States Government . . .* 4 vols. Chicago: American Library Association, 1986. KF5675 .A73S6.

Early Settlers

Brien, Lindsay M. *A Genealogical Index of Pioneers in the Miami Valley, Ohio.* Dayton: Dayton Circle, Colonial Dames of America, 1970. F497 .M64B68.

First Families of Ohio: Official Roster, Vol. 1. Mansfield: Ohio Genealogical Society, 1982. F490 .F49.

Hanna, Charles A. *Ohio Valley Genealogist.* Baltimore: Genealogical Publishing Co., 1968. F516 .H24.

Gardner, Frank W., comp. *Central Ohio Genealogical Notes and Queries in the Columbus Sunday Dispatch, 1933–1934.* N.p.: the compiler, n.d. F490 .G37.

News clippings with notes.

Western Reserve Historical Society, Genealogical Committee. *Index to the Microfilm Edition of Genealogical Data Relating to Women in the Western Reserve Before 1840 (1850).* Cleveland: the society, 1976. Z1324 .W45W45.

Local Records

Jackson, Ronald V., and Garry R. Teeples, eds. *Index to Ohio Tax Lists, 1800–1810.* Bountiful, Utah: Accelerated Indexing Systems, 1977. F490 .J3.

Lee, Susan D., comp. *Ohio Records and Pioneer Families. Subject Index by County: Surname Index A and B, Vols. 1–25 (1960–1984).* Vol. 27, no. 1. Mansfield: the compiler, 1986. F490 .O39.

Ohio Cemetery Records: Extracted From the Old Northwest Genealogical Quarterly (indexed). Baltimore: Genealogical Publishing Co., 1984. F490 .O362.

Ohio Historical Society. Karen L. Matusoff, comp. *Central Ohio Local Government Records of the Ohio Historical Society.* Columbus: the society, 1978. Z1324 .O45.

Ohio Source Records: From the Ohio Genealogical Quarterly. Baltimore: Genealogical Publishing Co., 1986. F490 .O385.

Petty, Gerald M. *Ohio 1810 Tax Duplicate.* Columbus: the author, 1976. F490 .P44.

———. *Index of the Ohio 1825 Tax Duplicate.* Columbus: Petty's Press, 1981. F490 .P43.

Powell, Esther W., comp. *Early Ohio Tax Records.* Akron: the author, 1971. F490 .P68. Index, F490 .P6 supplement.

Smith, Maxine H. *Ohio Cemeteries.* Mansfield: Ohio Genealogical Society, 1978. F490 .O3618.

Yon, Paul D. *Guide to Ohio County and Municipal Government Records for Urban Research.* Columbus: Ohio Historical Society, 1973. CD3447 .A1Y66.

Military Records

General

Petty, Gerald M., comp. *Index of the Ohio Squirrel Hunters' Roster.* Columbus: the compiler, 1984. E525.3 .P47.

American Revolution

Hutchinson, William T. *The Bounty Lands of the American Revolution in Ohio.* New York: Arno Press, 1979. F495 .H95.

Ohio. Adjutant General. *The Official Roster of the Soldiers of the American Revolution Buried in the State of Ohio.* Columbus: F. J. Heer, 1929–59. E255 .O38. (Micro 46367E).

Joint project with the National Society Daughters of the American Revolution.

War of 1812

Ohio. Adjutant General. *Roster of Soldiers in the War of 1812.* Baltimore: Genealogical Publishing Co., 1968. E359.5 .O203.

Civil War

Murdock, Eugene C. *Ohio's Bounty System in the Civil War.* Columbus: Ohio State University Press, 1963. E525 .O337.

Ohio. Adjutant General. *Official Roster of the Soldiers of the State of Ohio in the War of the Rebellion, 1861–1866.* 10 vols. Akron and Cincinnati: State of Ohio, 1887. E525.3 .O38.

Phillips, W. Louis. *Index to Ohio Pensioners of 1883.* Bowie, Md.: Heritage Books, 1987. F490 .P49.

Periodicals

United States Work Projects Administration—Ohio. *Annals of Cleveland. Foreign Language News Digests.* 5 vols. Cleveland: Work Projects Administration, 1939. F499 .C6U6.

Contains news items in foreign languages, translated into English.

Directories

City

Akron
  pre 1861 (microfiche)
  (Barberton, Cuyahoga Falls)   1889–1943, 1962–63, 1981

Alliance
  (Beloit, Sebring) 1944–74

Archbold 1974

Ashland
  (Ashland Co.) 1917–21, 1928–85

Ashtabula
  (Conneaut, Geneva, Jefferson, Kingsville, N. Kingsville) 1921, 1926–84

Athens
  (Mechanicsburg) 1940, 1946–48, 1957, 1960, 1968–70

Avon Lake 1970–87

Barberton 1909

Bedford
  (Bedford Township, Maple Hgts., Oakwood, Walton Hills) 1929, 1931, 1939, 1945–63

Bellaire
  (Bridgeport, Martins Ferry, Shadyside, Belmont Co.) 1913, 1920, 1924, 1956, 1963

Bellefontaine
  (Logan Co.) 1910, 1941–84

Bellevue 1946–59, 1967–73, 1979

Belpre 1964–83

Berea (suburbs) 1948–52 1957–63

Brookville
  (Germantown) 1958

Bryan 1923–34, 1939–52

Buckeye Lake 1932

Bucyrus 1909–18, 1929–85

Canton
  (E. Canton, Louisville, W. Canton) 1888–1952

Celina 1953, 1968, 1970

Chardon 1960–83

Cillicothe
  pre 1861 (microfiche)

1888, 1897, 1904–23, 1930–76

Cincinnati
  pre 1861 (microfiche)
  1861–1935 (microfilm)
  (suburbs) 1930–84
    Cincinnati Directory, June 1879. Cincinnati: Williams
    & Co., 1879. F499 .C5A18.

Circleville
  pre 1861 (microfiche)
  (Pickaway Co.) 1947–84

Cleveland
  pre 1861 (microfiche)
  1861–1935 (microfilm)
  1936–74

Cleveland Heights
  (East Cleveland, Shaker Hgts., Lyndhurst, S. Euclid,
    University Hgts.) 1949–63

Clinton
  (Wilmington) 1977, 1979

Collinwood 1899

Columbiana 1863

Columbus
  pre 1861 (microfiche)
  1861–1935 (microfilm)
  (suburbs) 1936–84
    Columbus City Directory, 1884. F499 .C7A18.

Conneaut 1913, 1947, 1950, 1959, 1963–83

Coshocton 1910, 1930–36, 1946, 1958–83

Cuyahoga Falls (suburbs) 1966

Dayton
  pre 1861 (microfiche)
  1886–1935 (microfilm)
  (suburbs) 1936–84

Defiance 1899, 1920, 1936, 1942–55, 1959–64, 1977–80

Delaware
  pre 1861 (microfiche)
  (Delaware Co.) 1899, 1930–37, 1939, 1946, 1950–84

Delphos 1941, 1947, 1957, 1960, 1967, 1969

East Liverpool
  (Calcutta; Glenmoor; Wellsville; Salem; Chester,
    W.Va.; Newell, W.Va.) 1896–1916, 1921–84

East Palestine 1941, 1947, 1949, 1966–70, 1976, 1978

Eaton 1949, 1978

Elyria
  (Lorain) 1896, 1923, 1931, 1936–37, 1943–79

Euclid 1947–63

Findlay
  (Hancock Co.) 1889, 1899, 1904–18, 1923–43, 1946–85

Fostoria
  (Seneca Co.) 1903, 1915, 1919, 1922, 1947, 1951–83

Franklin
  (Carlisle, Chautauqua, Springboro) 1958–60

Freemont 1889, 1897, 1931, 1933, 1941, 1947, 1951,
  1956–78

Galion 1935, 1940–86

Gallipolis 1955, 1959, 1963, 1965, 1972–82

Geneva 1963–84

Girard
  (Avon Park, Church Hill, McDonald, Parkwood,
    Weathersfield) 1933

Greenfield 1958

Hamilton
  pre 1861 (microfiche)
  1886–1984

Hillsboro 1947–49, 1958, 1961, 1968, 1970, 1972

Hudson Village
  (Hudson Township, Twinsburg Township) 1947

Ironton
  (Russell, Ky.) 1899, 1902, 1928, 1930, 1935–83

Jackson 1954, 1964–83

Lakewood 1959, 1977

Lancaster
  (Athens) 1849, 1898, 1928–83

Lebanon 1949–61

Lima 1899, 1903–85

Logan 1947, 1957–68

London 1948, 1962–68

Lorain (suburbs) 1903, 1926, 1929–84

Madison
  (Leroy, Perry) 1970

Mansfield
  pre 1861 (microfiche)

1883, 1899, 1908–41, 1967, 1975, 1984

Marietta
pre 1861 (microfiche)
(Washington Co.) 1898, 1905, 1912–84

Marion
(Marion Co.) 1899, 1909–84

Martin's Ferry 1913, 1957, 1960, 1970, 1974

Maryville
(Alcoa) 1923, 1926, 1941, 1943, 1948, 1959, 1969–74

Massillon 1909–20, 1925–31, 1936, 1940, 1966

Maumee 1941, 1978–83

Medina (see also Medina Co.)
1948, 1952

Miami
(Miami Co.) 1949, 1952, 1957

Miamisburg 1950, 1958, 1961

Middletown 1910, 1912, 1917–84

Montpelier 1940, 1942, 1951, 1953, 1959

Mt. Vernon 1906, 1912, 1952–86

Napoleon 1947–52, 1957, 1959, 1967–74

Nelsonville 1947, 1975

New Lexington 1953, 1957, 1960

New Philadelphia
(Dover, Strasburg) 1907, 1953–84

Newcomerstown 1921–39

Newport
(Toledo) 1967

Niles 1933

Norwalk 1888, 1900, 1904, 1930, 1934, 1946–60, 1969–71, 1979

Norwood 1910–37, 1954

Oberlin 1899, 1961, 1970

Orange 1959, 1978, 1980

Orrville 1958, 1961, 1969, 1973, 1979–82

Painsville
(Fairport, Grand River, Mentor) 1902, 1929, 1930, 1936, 1940, 1942, 1949, 1954, 1957, 1959–84

Parma
(Parma Hgts.) 1941, 1946–63

Perrysburg 1960, 1966, 1978–83

Piqua
(Troy, Miami Co.) 1881, 1898, 1920–85

Poland 1950–72

Pomeroy
(Middleport) 1958

Port Clinton
(Catawba Island) 1956, 1960, 1967

Portsmouth
(North Boston, North Moreland, Scioto Co.) pre 1861 (microfiche)
1899, 1908–84

Ravenna
(Kent) 1955, 1968–74

Rittman 1978–83

Rocky River 1952

Salem 1889, 1902, 1923, 1927, 1930, 1934–84

Sandusky
pre 1861 (microfiche)
1873, 1890–84

Shelby 1908, 1941, 1945–86

Sidney 1931, 1943–85

Springfield
pre 1861 (microfiche)
1900–85

St. Mary's 1946, 1957, 1967, 1969

Steubenville
(Mingo Junction) pre 1861 (microfiche)
1899, 1908–15, 1924–31, 1936–40, 1949, 1983

Sylvania 1962

Tiffin
(Fostoria, Seneca Co.) 1890, 1899, 1903, 1911, 1913, 1920–85

Toledo
pre 1861 (microfiche)
1681–1935 (microfilm)
(suburbs) 1936–85

Toronto 1927, 1933

Trotwood
(Englewood) 1958

Uhrichsville
(Dennison, Gnadenhutten) 1953–85

Union City (see Union City, Ind.)

Urbana 1918, 1948, 1951–84

Van Wert 1895, 1941, 1947, 1950, 1953, 1956, 1958, 1960, 1969

Vermillion
(Berlin Hgts., Huron) 1970

Wadsworth 1946–57, 1964, 1966, 1977

Wapakoneta 1946, 1957, 1966, 1979, 1986

Warren
(Girard, Niles, Newton Falls, Trumball Co.) 1889, 1899, 1910–16, 1919, 1925–40

Washington Courthouse
(Fayette Co.) 1906, 1941, 1946–61, 1979

Waverly 1955, 1958

Wellsville 1908, 1947, 1949, 1953, 1957, 1963–87

Willoughby
(Wickliffe, Willowick) 1949, 1963–83

Wilmington 1947, 1952, 1960, 1962

Wooster 1909, 1930–39, 1946–49, 1954, 1957, 1964, 1973, 1977, 1979

Xenia 1898, 1915, 1918, 1922–30, 1941–81

Youngstown
(Campbell, Girard, McDonald, Struthers) 1880–84, 1889–1941, 1944

Zanesville 1883, 1890, 1900, 1907, 1912–30, 1935, 1937, 1939, 1969

County, Business, and Miscellaneous

Chillicothe 1855, 1918

Clark 1903, 1950

Clinton 1952, 1956, 1978–79

Columbia 1915–20

Coshocton 1954

Crawford 1900, 1963, 1980

Cuyahoga, northeastern
(Ohio Mail) 1905

Darke 1908, 1910, 1916, 1939, 1949, 1955, 1958, 1977–78, 1981, 1985

Defiance 1951

Erie
(Huron, Sandusky) 1905, 1964, 1976

Fairfield 1915, 1952, 1955, 1958, 1964, 1976

Fayette 1940–44, 1951–58, 1964, 1976

Fulton 1948, 1977, 1979

Geauga 1937

Greene 1952

Hamilton 1887–1911, 1939–46

Hancock 1916, 1948–54, 1957, 1963, 1965, 1976–82

Hardin 1916, 1950, 1963, 1966, 1977, 1979

Holmes 1976, 1979

Huron (see also Erie)
1881, 1949, 1953, 1957, 1963, 1965–82

Lake 1951

Licking 1915, 1953, 1964

Logan 1916, 1951–57, 1963, 1965, 1977, 1978

Lorain (see also Cayahoga)
1915, 1948, 1954

Lucas 1947

Madison 1978

Mahoning
(Shenango Valley, Pa.) 1875, 1893

Marion 1950–56, 1964, 1977, 1979

Medina (see also Cuyahoga)
1916, 1949, 1953, 1956, 1976, 1978, 1982

Mercer 1916, 1966, 1977–79

Miami 1965, 1977–81

Montgomery 1911–29

Morrow 1963, 1976, 1978

Muskingum 1956, 1966, 1977–81

Ohio
(region) pre 1861 (microfiche)
Ohio (state) 1852–1902 (see also Eastern, Southern, Western—in Indiana)

Ottawa 1950

Paulding
(Van Wert) 1908

Pickaway 1978

Portage 1903

Preble 1916, 1965, 1978

Putnam (see Henry)

Richland 1915, 1950, 1954, 1957, 1965, 1978

Sandusky (see also Erie)
  1917, 1948, 1951, 1977–79

Seneca 1916–21, 1948–50

Shelby 1916, 1954, 1957, 1964, 1966, 1977–81

Toledo (city) 1891, 1897

Trumbull 1900, 1915, 1951

Tuscarawas 1917, 1949, 1952, 1956, 1965, 1980

Union 1975, 1977–78

Van Wert (see also Paulding) 1951, 1964, 1976–83

Wayne 1950, 1955, 1958, 1964, 1976, 1978, 1982

Wood 1916, 1947, 1951, 1976, 1978

Wyandot 1950, 1965, 1977, 1979, 1980, 1984

Indiana

Historical Highlights

1679	Explored by LaSalle, from France.
1731	Vincennes founded by the French.
1763	Control assumed by England. Initially, French trading posts and small settlements with Catholic churches were established. When the British moved in and successfully fought the French and their Indian allies, they gained control over the area. English settlers arrived in relatively small numbers.
1776	Controlled by England at the start of the American Revolution. George Rogers Clark led a military expedition to Vincennes, claiming the area in 1778 for Virginia. Following the Revolutionary War, Indiana was included in the Northwest Territory, Indiana and Illinois being considered one county.
1800	Indiana Territory established. Included in the territory were the regions later to become the Michigan Territory and the Illinois Territory. Migrants began to come in larger numbers, principally from New England, New York, Kentucky, the Carolinas, and Virginia.
1805	Michigan Territory separated from Indiana Territory.
1809	Illinois Territory separated from Indiana Territory.
1816	Admitted to the Union. The federal government established several land offices, selling land at very reasonable prices. Southerners and Easterners continued to come in, joining with such groups as the Quakers from North Carolina, Virginia, and Ohio. A few German and Dutch settlers also arrived to establish settlements. Other religious groups included Baptists and Mennonites, among others. Settlers travelled by way of the Erie Canal, Ohio River, National Road, and the railroads.
1861	Remained a part of the Union during the Civil War.

Published Record Sources

Guidebooks

Baker, Ronald L., and Marvin Carmony. *Indiana Place Names.* Bloomington, Ind.: Indiana University Press, 1975. F524 .B34.

Carty, Mickey D. *Searching in Indiana: A Reference Guide to Public and Private Records.* Costa Mesa, Calif.: ICE Publishing Co., 1983. F525 .C37.

Franklin, Charles M. *Genealogical Atlas of Indiana.* Indianapolis: Heritage House, 1985. F525 .F725.

Miller, Carollyne L. (Wendel). *Indiana Sources for Genealogical Research in the Indiana State Library.* Indianapolis: Indiana Historical Society, Family History Section, 1984. E1281 .M544.

Reference Guide to Indiana. St. Clair Shores, Mich.: Somerset Publishings, 1977. F524 .R4.

Riker, Dorothy L., comp. *Genealogical Sources. Reprinted from the Genealogical Section, Magazine of History.* Indianapolis: Indiana Historical Society, 1979. F525 .G45.

Census Indexes and Abstracts

Federal

1820   F525 .J317
        Indiana Historical Society. Mary M. Morgan, comp. *The Indiana 1820 Enumeration of Males.* Indianapolis: the society, 1988. F525 .I53.
        Pompey, Sherman L. *Index to the 1820 Census Records of (Several Counties) of Indiana.* Charleston, Oreg.: Pacific Specialties, 1974. F525 .P65.

1830   F525 .J32

1840   F525 .J33
        Indiana State Library, Genealogy Division. *Index, 1840 Federal Population Census, Indiana.* Indianapolis: the library, 1975. F525 .I52.

1850   F525 .J332

1870   Shook, Patricia M. Fox. *1870 Indiana Census Index.* Corona, Calif.: the author, 1986. F525 .S53.

        Includes twelve pamphlets for the counties of Barthomolew, Benton, Delaware, Gibson, Kosciusko, Newton, Noble, Ohio, Putnam, Scott, Tipton, Union. Specify county desired.

All the above publications shown without the name of the compiler or author are by Ronald V. Jackson, Accelerated Indexing Systems.

State

Indiana Historical Society, Family History Section. *Census of Indiana Territory for 1807; Facsimile of the Original Manuscripts of Knox, Dearborn, and Randolph Counties.* Indianapolis: the society, 1980. F525 .C45.

Jackson, Ronald V. *Early Indiana.* Bountiful, Utah: Accelerated Indexing Systems, 1980. F525 .J315.

Biographies

Benesch, Adolph D. *Men of Indiana in 1901.* Indianapolis: Benesch Publishing Co., 1901. F525 .B26.

Boruff, Blanche F., comp. *Women of Indiana.* Indianapolis: Indiana Women's Biographical Association, 1941. F525 .B76.

Hawkins, Hubert H., and Robert A. McClarren. *Indiana Lives, 1967.* Hopkinsville, Ky.: Historical Record Association, 1957. F525 .H3.

Hepburn, William M. *Who's Who in Indiana, 1957.* Hopkinsville, Ky.: Historical Record Association, 1957. F525 .H4.

Memorial Records of Northeastern Indiana. Chicago: Lewis Publications, 1892. F525 .M53.

Pictorial and Biographical Record of LaPort, Porter, Lake, and Starke Counties, Indiana. Chicago: Goodspeed, 1894. F525 .P61.

Portrait and Biographical Record of Montgomery, Parke, and Fountain Counties, Indiana. Chicago: Chapman Brothers, 1893. F525 .P86.

Reed, George I. *Encyclopedia of Biography of Indiana.* 2 vols. Chicago: Century Publishing and Engraving, 1899. F525 .A32.

Woolen, William W. *Biographical and Historical Sketches of Early America.* Indianapolis: Hammond & Co., 1883. F525 .W91.

Land Acquisition

Cowen, Janet C., comp. *Jeffersonville Land Entries, 1808–1818.* Indianapolis: the author, 1984. F525 .C68.

Moudy, Vera Mae (Ginder), comp. *Directory of Land Records Information in the Genealogical Department, Indiana State Library.* Indianapolis: Ye Olde Genealogie Shoppe, 1982. Z1281 .M67.

Waters, Margaret R. *Indiana Land Entries.* Vol. 2, *Vincennes District. Part One—1807–1877.* Indianapolis: the author, 1949. F525 .W33.

Early Settlers

Dorrel, Ruth, comp. *Pioneer Ancestors of Members of the Society of Indiana Pioneers.* Indianapolis. Indiana Historical Society, 1983. F525 .D67.

Family Group Sheets—The Indiana Southern Counties Collection. 4 vols. 1979, 1981. New Albany, Ind.: Southern Indiana Genealogical Society, 1982. F525 .F35.

Franklin, Charles M. *Indiana Territorial Pioneer Records.* 2 vols. 1801, 1820. Indianapolis: Heritage House, 1983. F525 .F73.

Hernandez, Ernie. *Ethnics in Northwestern Indiana.* Gary: Post-Tribune, 1984. F535 .A1H47.

Jones, Gloria B., comp. *Family Album: A Source Book,* Vol. 1. Baltimore: Gateway Press, 1984. F525 .J684.

Society of Mayflower Descendants. *Indiana Mayflower Descendants; Lineages of the Indiana Society.* Indianapolis: the society, 1977. F525 .S63.

Local Records

Franklin, Charles M. *Index to Indiana Wills—Phase 1—Through 1850.* Indianapolis: Heritage House, 1986. F525 .F728.

Harrad, Mildred D., comp. *Hope Star and Hope Star Journal Obituaries 1906–1933.* Flat Rock, Ind.: the author, 1983. F525 .H28.

Historical Records Survey (WPA). *Guide to Public Vital Statistics Records in Indiana.* Indianapolis: Indiana Historical Records Survey, 1941. CD3231 .H5.

Michiana Searcher: Quarterly of Elkhart, Indiana Genealogical Society. Vols. 11–15. F525 .M58.

Covers summer, 1979, through winter, 1983.

Moudy, Vera Mae (Ginder), comp. *Directory of Marriage Information in the Genealogy Department, Indiana State Library.* Indianapolis: Ye Olde Genealogie Shoppe, 1981. Z1281 .M68.

———. *Directory of Wills and Estate Information in the Genealogy Department, Indiana State Library, 1981.* Indianapolis: Ye Olde Genealogie Shoppe, 1981. Z1281 .M683.

Murray, Nicholas R. *Indiana Surname Index. Computer Indexed Marriage Records.* Hammond, La.: Hunting For Bears, Inc., 1984. F525 .I57.

Military Records

American Revolution

Waters, Margaret R. *Revolutionary Soldiers Buried in Indiana: 300 Names Not Listed in the "Roster of Soldiers and Patriots of the American Revolution Buried in Indiana."* Reprint. Baltimore: Genealogical Publishing Co., 1970. E255 .W32.

———. *Revolutionary Soldiers Buried in Indiana; A Supplement. 485 Names Not Listed in the "Roster of Soldiers and Patriots of the American Revolution Buried in Indiana," Nor in "Revolutionary Soldiers Buried in Indiana."* Reprint. Baltimore: Genealogical Publishing Co., 1970. E255 .W3 supplement.

Civil War

Indiana. Adjutant General. *Exhibits and Proof to the Indiana War Claims.* Indianapolis: State of Indiana, ca. 1902. E506 .I39.

Indiana. Adjutant General. *Reports for 1861–1865.* 3 vols. Indianapolis: State of Indiana, 1865. E506.2 .I39.

Trapp, Glenda K. *Index to the Report of the Adjutant General of the State of Indiana. An Everyname Index to Vols. 1, 2, 3.* Evansville, Ind.: Trapp Publications Services, 1985. E506.2 I393T73.

Turner, Ann. *Guide to Indiana Civil War Manuscripts.* Indianapolis: Civil War Centennial Commission, 1965. CD3047 .I5.

Periodicals

Means, Eloise R., and Pearl Brenton. *Hoosier Ancestors Index, 1963–1975.* 4 vols. Indianapolis: the authors, 1969. F525 .M47.

Wolfe, Barbara S. *Index: Hoosier Genealogist, 1861–1983.* Indianapolis: Ye Olde Genealogie Shoppe, 1984. F525 .H63W65.

Directories

City

Alexandria
(Elwood) 1960, 1985

Anderson
(Chesterfield) 1889, 1902–05, 1914–61, 1967–76, 1985

Angola 1931, 1957–84

Attica 1971

Auburn 1925–27, 1931–33, 1940, 1946–52

Bedford
  (Englewood, Lawrence) 1915, 1942–84

Beech Grove 1939–41

Bloomington
  (Monroe Co.) 1913–23, 1927–39, 1945–84

Bluffton 1948–77

Booneville
  (Newburgh) 1974–82

Brazil
  (Clay City, Clay Co.) 1943, 1947, 1950, 1965

Bremen 1958, 1960

Butler (rural routes) 1933

Clinton 1926, 1930, 1943, 1948, 1953, 1958, 1969, 1973

Columbia 1954, 1960, 1962

Columbus 1890, 1898, 1916–34, 1938–42, 1947–83

Connersville 1911–30, 1948–84

Crawfordsville
  (Montgomery Co.) 1917, 1922–84

Crown Point 1978, 1981

Danville
  (Plainfield) 1978

Decatur
  (Adams Co.) 1927, 1947–84

East Chicago 1958

Elkhart 1890, 1899, 1910–83

Elwood 1916, 1929, 1933, 1945–59, 1967–75

Evansville
  pre 1861 (microfiche)
  1861–1935 (microfilm)
  1936–84

Fort Wayne
  pre 1861 (microfiche)
  1861–1881 (microfilm)
  (suburbs) 1866, 1883–1984

Frankfort
  (Clinton Co.) 1913, 1918, 1932, 1937–87

Franklin 1943, 1948, 1952, 1957–83

Garrett
  (Altoona) 1977

Gary 1908–13, 1918–73

Goshen 1929, 1941, 1946–83

Greenfield 1955, 1958, 1961, 1963

Greensburg 1860, 1953, 1957, 1960, 1967, 1977, 1980

Greenwood 1965

Hammond
  (Calumet City, Ill.; Munster; W. Hammond, Ill.)
  1911–19, 1923–80

Hartford 1948, 1958–67

Hobart 1962–83

Huntington
  (Huntington Co.) 1917, 1920–32, 1939, 1941, 1946–85

Indiana (state)
  Indiana Gazetteer and Business Directory. R.L. Polk
  Co. F524.7 .I532.

Indianapolis
  pre 1861 (microfiche)
  1861–1935 (microfilm)
  1936–85

Jeffersonville
  (Charleston, Clarksville, Floyd, New Albany, Clark
  Co.) 1959–68

Kendallville 1926–31, 1936–41, 1947, 1949, 1985

Kokomo
  (Howard Co.) 1889, 1899, 1912–84

Lafayette
  pre 1861 (microfiche)
  (Attica, Crawfordsville, Delphi, Frankfort, Tippecanoe Co.) 1867, 1887, 1899–1983

LaPorte
  (LaPorte Co.) 1897, 1910, 1913, 1923–31, 1938–83

Lawrenceburg
  (Aurora Co.) pre 1861 (microfiche)
  1926, 1965, 1978–82

Lebanon 1963, 1966, 1978, 1980, 1982, 1984

Linton 1954, 1977

Logansport
  pre 1861 (microfiche)
  (Cass Co.) 1887, 1919, 1921, 1926–84
  Logansport Directory, 1899–1900. Indianapolis: R. L.
  Polk Co., 1899. F534 .L83A18.

Madison
   pre 1861 (microfiche)
   1887, 1957–86

Marion
   (Fairmont, Gas City, Jonesboro, Grant Co.) 1899,
   1919–85

Martinsville 1964, 1978, 1982

Michigan City
   (Long Beach, LaPorte Co.) 1913–42, 1947–84

Mishawaka
   (South Bend, suburbs) 1925, 1929–47, 1973–83

Monticello 1958

Mooresville 1964, 1977, 1980

Mt. Vernon 1914, 1972–83

Muncie
   (Delaware Co.) 1889, 1899, 1903, 1909–84

New Albany
   (Jeffersonville) pre 1861 (microfiche)
   (Charlestown, Clarksville, Sellersburg, Clark Co.,
   Floyd Co.) 1865, 1888–1985

New Castle 1889, 1895–1916

Plainfield 1978, 1980

Plymouth
   pre 1861 (microfiche)
   (Kinston) 1887, 1890, 1893, 1896–1924, 1932, 1936

Portland 1897, 1949, 1953, 1960, 1965, 1976, 1982

Princeton 1914, 1916, 1923–35, 1942, 1948, 1965–84

Rensselaer 1958

Richmond
   pre 1861 (microfiche)
   (Wayne Co.) 1890-91, 1897, 1901–84

Rochester
   (Lake Manitou) 1956–61, 1971, 1974

Rushville
   (Rush Co.) 1948, 1962–84

Salem 1979, 1982

Shelbyville
   pre 1861 (microfiche)
   (Shelby Co.) 1936, 1940, 1946–84

South Bend
   (Ardmore, Mishawaka, Osceola, Roseland;
   townships: Centre, Clay, German, Penn, Portage,
   Warren) 1885, 1889, 1903, 1904, 1906, 1919–87

Tell City 1954

Tipton 1942, 1963–86

Union City 1958, 1965–82

Valparaiso
   (Chestertown, South Haven, Porter Co.) 1893, 1902–
   07, 1911, 1921, 1924, 1931, 1939, 1946–85

Vincennes
   (Knox Co.) 1888, 1898, 1900, 1904, 1930, 1935–84

Wabash 1910, 1912, 1918, 1937, 1948, 1963–68, 1978–81

Warsaw
   (Lakeside Addition, Winona Lake) 1941, 1947, 1949,
   1956, 1958, 1961, 1963, 1971, 1974, 1978

Washington 1945–86

Winchester 1947, 1959

County, Business, and Miscellaneous

Adams 1916

Bartholemew 1903, 1965, 1978

Benton
   (Warren) 1919

Boone 1920

Cass 1964, 1978, 1982

Decatur 1963

Eastern, Western, and Southern (includes principal
   cities of Indiana, Kentucky, and Ohio) 1946

Elkhart 1949, 1963, 1965, 1977

Evansville 1906

Fort Wayne 1894

Fountain Park (city)
   (Vermillion) 1920

Greensburg 1895

Hamilton (see Noblesville)

Hendricks 1920

Henry 1979

Howard 1903, 1966, 1979

Huntington 1899

Indiana
  (region) pre 1861 (microfiche)
  (state) 1858–66, 1879–92, 1902, 1910, 1918, 1921

Jasper 1910

Jay 1916, 1927, 1960, 1978, 1979

Jefferson
  pre 1861 (microfiche)

Knox
  1880

Madison 1900, 1916

Monroe 1964

Montgomery 1920, 1963, 1966, 1977, 1981, 1985

Noble 1977

Noblesville (city)
  (Hamilton) 1938, 1948, 1952, 1978–82

St. Joseph (county)
  St. Joseph County Directory and South Bend, Indiana. 1899–1900. South Bend: Charles B. Hibberd Co., 1899. F534 .S7A18.

Shelby 1916

Tama 1885

Tippecanoe 1919, 1965

Vanderburgh 1919

Vermilion (see Fountain Park)

Vigo 1912, 1936

Warren (see Benton)

Wayne 1964, 1978, 1980

Illinois

Historical Highlights

1673   Explored by Marquette and Joliet, from France.

1682   Kaskaskia founded.

1699   Cahokia Catholic mission founded.

French missionaries first settled the Illinois area, and it was governed by the French with its capital in Louisiana.

1763   Control assumed by England following the French and Indian Wars.

1776   Under British control at the time of the American Revolution.

George Rogers Clark led a military expedition into the Illinois region, taking Kaskaskia and Cahokia, and claiming the area for Virginia. In 1784 Virginia gave up its Illinois area claims to the newly created United States of America.

1791   Free land granted by the United States to existing settlers in the area.

As part of the Northwest Territory, southern Illinois began to receive migrants from the Carolinas, Kentucky, Tennessee, and Virginia, coming by way of Kentucky. In 1804 the first federal land office was opened.

1809   Illinois Territory established.

1818   Admitted to the Union.

1832   Black Hawk Indian War.

Lured by free or inexpensive prairie land, settlers from southern states, as well as from New England, began to come into the state, especially after the Indian threat was removed following the Black Hawk War. Joining settlers from other states were Europeans arriving at the Port of New York and using the Erie Canal and the railroads to come to Illinois as their first settlement.

Some years after southern Illinois was populated, Chicago was founded by a group of Norwegians who were soon joined by Hollanders. A decade later, the Irish arrived to help build the railroads. A group of Mormons led by Joseph Smith, forced from Missouri, established a short-lived town of Nauvoo on the Illinois side of the Mississippi River.

1861   Remained in the Union during the Civil War.

Published Record Sources

Guidebooks

Buck, Solon J. *Travel and Descriptions, 1756–1865: Together With a List of County Histories, Atlases, and Biographical Collections, and a List of Territorial State Laws.* Vol. 9, *Illinois State History Library Collection, Biographical Series.* Springfield, Ill.: Illinois State Historical Society, 1914. F535 .I25 V9. (Z1277 .B83).

Irons, Victoria, and Patricia G. Brennan. *Descriptive Inventory of the Archives of the State of Illinois.* Springfield, Illinois State Archives, 1978. CD3204 .I44.

Census Indexes and Abstracts

Federal

1820   F540 .J32
        Norton, Margaret C., ed. *Illinois Census Returns, 1820. Collections of the Illinois State Historical Library.* Vol. 26, *Statistical Series.* Reprint. Baltimore: Genealogical Publishing Co., 1969. F536 .I34543N6.

1830   F540 .J323
        Gill, James V., comp. *Index to the 1830 Federal Census: Illinois Counties of White, Edwards, Wabash, Wayne, Clay, Clinton, St. Clair, Madison, Bond, Fayette, Lawrence.* Danville, Ill.: Illiana Genealogical Publishing Co., 1968. F540 .G49.
        Gill, James V., and Maryan R. Gill, comps. *Index to the 1830 Federal Census: Illinois Counties of Greene, Morgan, Sangamon, Calhoun, Pike, Fulton, Knox, Henry, Adams, Hancock, Warren, Mercer, Peoria, Putnam, Jo Daviess.* Danville, Ill.: Heritage House, 1970. F540 .G48.

1840   F540 .J333
        Wormer, Maxine E. *Illinois 1840 Census Index.* Tompson, Ill.: Heritage House, 1973. F540 .W67.

1850   F540 .J333
        Bloomington-Normal Genealogical Society. *Illinois 1850 Federal Census.* Normal, Ill.: the society, 1978. F540 .U57.

One volume for each county (specify county desired).

1880   Frederick, Nancy G. *The 1880 Illinois Census Index: Soundex Code 200–240; the Code That Was Not Filmed.* Evanston, Ill.: the author, 1981. F540 .F73.

All the above publications shown without the name of the compiler or author are by Ronald V. Jackson, Accelerated Indexing Systems.

State

Jackson, Ronald V. *Early Illinois.* Bountiful, Utah: Accelerated Indexing Systems, 1980. F540 .J297.

Mortality Schedules

Jackson, Ronald V. *Illinois 1850 Mortality Schedule.* Bountiful, Utah: Accelerated Indexing Systems, 1980. F540 .J335.

Biographies

Bateman, Newton. *Biographical and Memorial Editions of the Historical Encyclopedia of Illinois.* 2 vols. Chicago: Munsell, 1915. F539 .B333.

Bench and Bar of Chicago: Biographical Sketches. Chicago: American Biographical Publishing Co., n.d. F548.25 .B45.

Biographical Dictionary and Portrait Gallery of Representative Men of Chicago and the World's Columbian Exposition. Chicago: American Biographical Publishing Co., 1892. F548.25 .B58.

Blenz, Beth, ed. *Encyclopedia of Illinois.* St. Clair Shores, Mich.: Somerset Publishing Co., 1980. F539 .E52.

Book of Chicagoans: Who's Who in Chicago. Chicago: A.N. Marquis, 1905, 1911, 1917, 1926. F548.25 .W63.

Encyclopedia of Biography of Illinois. 3 vols. Chicago: Century Publishing Co., 1902. F540 .E57.

Genealogical and Biographical Records of Cook County, Illinois. Chicago: Lake City Publishing Co., 1894. F540 .C7G3.

Herringshaw, Clark J. *City Blue Book of Current Biography. Edition for 1913–1919.* Chicago: American Publishing Association, 1913–19. F548.25 .H56.

Specify year desired.

Men of Illinois. Chicago: Chicago Historical Society, 1902. F540 .M53.

Miss Livingwell's Criss-Cross Directory of Persons of Polite Society and Old Wealth: Illinois, 1987 Edition. Chicago: Aquarius Rising Press, 1987. F450 .M6.

Moss, John, ed. *Biographical Dictionary and Portrait Gallery of the Representative Men of the United States—Illinois Edition*. 2 vols. Chicago: Lewis Publishing Co., 1896. F540 .M91.

Notable Men of Illinois and Their State. Chicago: Chicago Daily Journal, 1912. F540 .N89.

Portrait and Biographical Record of Clinton, Washington, Marion, and Jefferson Counties (Illinois). Chicago: Chapman Publishing Co., 1894. F540 .P85.

Robson, Charles. *Biographical Encyclopedia of Illinois of the 19th Century*. Philadelphia: Galaxy Publishing Co., 1875. F540 .B57.

Land Acquisition

Felldin, Jeanne R., and Charlotte M. Tucker, comps. *Landowners of Illinois, 1876*. Tomball, Tex.: Genealogical Publications, 1970. F540 .F44.

Ettemo, Ross. *The Dutch Connection in South Cook County Since 1847*. South Holland, Ill.: Park Press, 1984. F547 .C7E88.

Rochefort, Beth, ed. *Prairie Pioneers of Illinois*. Vol. 1. Lincoln, Ill.: Illinois State Genealogical Society, 1986. F540 .R62.

Local Records

Funeral Notices of Southern Illinois, ca. 1891–1931. Owensboro, Ky.: Cook-McDowell, 1980. F540 .F86.

Historical Records Survey (WPA). *Guide to Public Vital Statistics Records in Illinois*. Chicago: Illinois Historical Records Survey, 1941. CD3201 .H48. (Z1277 .G84).

Military Records

General

Illinois. Adjutant General. *Roll of Honor: Record of Burial Places of Soldiers, Sailors, Marines, and Army Nurses of All Wars of the United States Buried in Illinois*. 2 vols. Springfield: 1929. E281 .I29.

United States. General Land Office. Bestor, George C., comp. *Index of the Illinois Military Patent Book*. Peoria: n.p., 1853. E359.4 .U53.

United States. General Land Office. *Index Corrected . . . by Ephraim S. Green and S. P. Kirkbridge*. Bridgeton, Pa.: n.p., 1855. E359.4 .U552.

American Revolution

Illinois State Genealogical Society. Mrs. John S. DeVanney, comp. *Revolutionary Soldiers Buried in Illinois*. Springfield: the society, 1975. E206 .I44.

Walker, Harriet J. *Revolutionary Soldiers Buried in Illinois*. Los Angeles, 1917. Reprint. Baltimore: Genealogical Publishing Co., 1967. F504 .W18. (E255 .W18).

War of 1812

Illinois. Adjutant General. *Roll of Honor . . . .* (See above under "General.")

Volkel, Lowell M. Illinois State Archives. *War of 1812 Bounty Lands in Illinois*. Reprint. Tompson, Ill.: Heritage House, 1977. E359.4 .U55.

Civil War

Illinois. Adjutant General. *Civil War Rosters*. 3 vols. Springfield: State of Illinois. E505.3 .C5. Index to Vol. 1, Joseph A. Huebner. Index to Vols. 2 and 3, Russell L. Knor. Chicago and River Grove, Ill.: n.p., n.d., E505.3 C5 index.

Periodicals

Index to the Yellowjacket: Great River Genealogical Society. Quincy, Ill.: the society, 1975–77. F540 .Y36.

Directories

City

Adrian 1867–68

Alton
  pre 1861 (microfiche)
  1889, 1899, 1923–29, 1961–84

Aurora 1868, 1872, 1895–1904, 1923–82

Beardstown 1926, 1929, 1968

Belleville
  pre 1861 (microfiche)
  (suburbs, E. St. Louis, St. Clair Co.) 1891, 1922–77,
    1981–84

Belvidere 1900–11, 1948–83

Benton
  (West City) 1959, 1964–84

Berwyn 1921

Bloomington
  (Normal, McLean Co.) 1870, 1885–1911, 1917, 1922–
    87

Blue Island 1904, 1921

Cairo
  (Mound City, Alexander Co., Pulaski Co.) 1864, 1887,
    1898, 1915, 1922, 1980

Canton 1893, 1927–85

Carmi 1959–81

Champaign
  (Urbana) 1923–25, 1957–70, 1979

Charleston 1968

Chicago
  pre 1861 (microfiche)
  1861–1935 (microfilm)

Chicago Heights 1914

Chillicothe
  (Livingston Co.) 1926–85

Cicero 1913, 1921–24

Clinton 1922, 1952, 1957

Collinsville 1960–83

Crystal Lake
  (Arca) 1960

Danville (suburbs) 1889, 1910, 1922–85

Decatur 1889, 1899, 1903, 1922–25, 1932, 1938–83

Dekalb
  (Sycamore) 1949–84

Dixon 1902, 1922–28, 1949–71

Downers Grove 1927

East St. Louis
  (Alorton, Fairmont City, National City, Washington
    Pk.) 1924, 1948–70

Edwardsville 1925–83

Effingham 1953, 1959–84

Elgin 1889, 1900, 1903, 1920, 1927–83

Evanston 1887–1963

Freeport 1896–98, 1919, 1921, 1923, 1948–84

Galena
  pre 1861 (microfiche)

Gillespie 1925–29

Grossdale 1907

Harlem 1896

Harrisburg 1927, 1930, 1959, 1964–82

Harvey 1895, 1907, 1914, 1921

Havana 1940

Highland 1962–83

Hillsboro 1926, 1930

Hyde Park
  (Englewood) 1883–89

Irving Park 1899–1901

Jacksonville
  (Morgan Co.) 1890-91, 1899, 1919, 1924–84

Jerseyville 1928

Johnston 1926

Joliet
  1861–1901 (microfilm)
  1902–38, 1966–85

Kankakee
  (Bourbonnais, Bradley) 1896, 1900, 1917, 1922–85

Kewanee
  (Wethersfield) 1911, 1924–83

Keywest 1887–88, 1906, 1911–17, 1923, 1927, 1958–82

Lake 1885, 1889, 1938

Lake Viad 1886–89

LaSalle
(Oglesby, Perry) 1891, 1894, 1898, 1917, 1924–85

Lawrenceville 1977

Lincoln 1889, 1922–85

Litchfield 1952

Lockport 1866, 1874, 1884, 1887–1942, 1947–84

Macomb 1971

Marion 1927–28, 1939, 1959–85

Mattoon 1910, 1927, 1940–84

Maywood 1896, 1917

Mendota 1964–83

Metropolis 1959, 1969, 1972, 1977

Minonk 1908

Moline
pre 1861 (microfiche)
(East Moline, Milan, Rock Island, Silvis) 1899–1905, 1910, 1920–70

Monmouth 1922, 1943, 1952–83

Morgan Park 1910

Morris 1948

Morton
(Westshore, Woodlawn) 1965–83

Mt. Carmel 1912, 1915, 1948, 1968–82

Mt. Vernon 1893, 1912, 1915, 1929, 1939, 1941, 1960–84

Northtown 1940, 1943

Oak Park
(River Forest, Forest Park) 1887–89, 1903, 1922–30

Olney 1953, 1958, 1960, 1969, 1971

Ottawa
(Naplate) 1888, 1924–85

Pana 1925, 1928, 1930, 1935, 1953, 1962–84

Paris 1926, 1930, 1937

Park Ridge
(Des Plaines, Edison Park) 1922

Pekin (Marquette Hgts., N. Pekin, S. Pekin) 1870, 1876, 1887, 1898–1916, 1921–85

Peoria
pre 1861 (microfiche)
(Bartonville) 1861–1935 (microfilm)
(Creve Couer, E. Peoria, Peoria Hgts., W. Peoria) 1936–84

Pontiac 1922–83

Princeton 1929, 1948

Quincy
pre 1861 (microfiche)
1866, 1878–79, 1884, 1898, 1900, 1959–70

Riverdale
(Dolton, South Holland) 1922

Riverside 1903, 1922, 1929

Robinson
(Oblong, Palestine) 1952, 1959, 1964, 1970–83

Rockford
(Harlem Township, Loves Park) pre 1861 (microfiche)
1866, 1874, 1889, 1899, 1903, 1908, 1916–84

Rock Island
pre 1861 (microfiche)
(East Moline, Milan, Moline, Silvis Hgts.) 1899, 1907–83

Rogers Park 1919

Roseland
(Commodore, Interocean, Pullman, West Pullman, Waterfall) 1923, 1963, 1968–71

Salem 1953

Shelbyville 1948, 1952, 1971–82

Springfield
pre 1861 (microfiche)
(Sangamon Co.), 1866–67, 1872, 1874, 1879, 1887, 1891, 1902–16, 1927, 1930, 1934, 1937, 1948–85
Springfield City Directory, 1892–1893. Chicago: U.S. Central Publishing Co., 1893. F549 .S7A18.

St. Charles
(Batavia, Geneva) 1950, 1956–84

Staunton 1926, 1928

Sterling
(Morrison, Rock Falls, Whiteside Co.) 1890, 1895, 1922, 1925, 1930–41, 1946–85

Streator 1898, 1925–83

Summit
(Argo, Clearing, Oak Lawn, Spring Forest) 1922, 1928

Taylorville 1926, 1928, 1932

Tri-Cities
(Batavia, Geneva, St. Charles) 1928, 1932, 1936, 1940, 1943
(Granite City, Madison, Venice) 1925–31, 1937–84

Urbana
(Champaign) 1975

Washington 1968–84

Waterfall (suburbs) 1934–62

Waukegan
(N. Chicago, North Shore, Lake Co.) 1895, 1901–08, 1913, 1916–83

West Frankfort 1926, 1928, 1931, 1965–80

Wheaton
(DuPage Co.) 1915

Wood River
(Cottage Hill, E. Alton, Rosewood Hgts., Roxana, S. Roxana)

Woodlawn 1909

Woodstock 1959

Zion
(Beach Park, Winthrop Harbor) 1962–86

County, Business, and Miscellaneous

Bureau
pre 1861 (microfiche)

Calhoun (see Pike)

Carroll 1917

Champaign 1917, 1950–56, 1975, 1977, 1980

Chicago (city) 1854, 1873, 1884–90, 1900, 1911, 1914, 1928, 1937, 1948–72

Clark (see Crawford)

Coles
(Douglas) 1894, 1918

Cook, northern (see Du Page)

Cook, southern (see Will)

Crawford (see also Robinson, city)
(Clark) 1920

De Kalb 1909, 1917, 1931

Douglas (see Coles)

Du Page
(Cook, northern) 1918, 1925

Edgar 1917

Edwards
(Lawrence, Wabash) 1920

Fulton 1948

Greene
(Jersey) 1919

Grundy
(Kendall) 1917

Henderson (see Warren)

Henry 1910

Illinois
(region) pre 1861 (microfiche)
(state) 1854, 1858, 1860, 1864, 1867, 1878–93
(eastern) (see southeast Missouri)

Iroquois 1908, 1917

Jackson
(Williamson) 1920

Jersey (see Greene)

Jo Daviess 1917

Kane 1911, 1918–19

Kankakee 1908

Kendall (see Grundy)

La Salle 1917

Lake 1917

Lansing 1960

Lawrence (see Edwards)

Lee 1917

Livingston 1898, 1917

Logan 1917

Macon 1922, 1948–75

Macoupin 1919

Marshall
(Putnam, Stark) 1917

McDonough 1917, 1985

McHenry
  (Boone) 1917

McLean 1887, 1910, 1917

Mercer
  (Rock Island) 1918

Monroe (see St. Clair)

Montgomery 1918

Morgan 1915

Ogle 1917

Peoria 1917, 1954

Pike
  (Calhoun) 1919

Putnam (see Marshall)

Randolph
  pre 1861 (microfiche)

Robinson 1928

Rock Island 1939

Sangamon 1915, 1923

Shelby 1918

Southern Illinois (see southeast Missouri)

St. Clair
  (Monroe) 1916, 1919

Stark (see also Marshall)
  1900, 1915, 1949

Stephenson 1917

Steuben 1903

Tazewell 1917, 1932–49

Vermilion 1916, 1918

Wabash (see Edwards)

Warren
  (Henderson) 1918

White 1919

Whiteside 1917

Will
  pre 1861 (microfiche)
  (Cook, southern) 1917–18

Winnebago 1917

Woodford 1917

Missouri

Historical Highlights

1673	Mississippi Valley explored by Marquette and Joliet, from France.
1682	Claimed by LaSalle for France.
1732	St. Genevieve founded by Frenchmen from Illinois.

Prior to the American Revolution the area was populated almost entirely by the French. After the war, Americans from Virginia, Tennessee, and Kentucky, as well as other states, began to arrive, particularly in St. Charles County, site of the state's first capital.

1763	Ceded by France to Spain.
1800	Ceded back to France.
1803	Louisiana Purchase from France.

After the United States negotiated the Louisiana Purchase, the southern portion was designated the District of Orleans, and the northern portion the Louisiana Territory (divided into five districts embracing present day Missouri, Arkansas, and Oklahoma). Eventually, the southernmost district of this Territory became the state of Arkansas.

1812	Missouri Territory organized.
1821	Entered the Union.

The pending statehood for Missouri created a question of whether the federal government could prohibit slavery in that state. The Missouri Compromise of 1820 barred slavery in the Louisiana Territory but permitted it in Missouri as it became a state. The compromise was repealed by Congress in 1854 when it ruled that each state or territory could decide for itself with respect to slavery. Such freedom of choice was upheld by the Supreme Court in 1857 when it declared the original compromise legislation unconstitutional.

Immigrants continued to come into Missouri from eastern states, especially Kentucky and Tennessee, many coming by way of Indiana and Illinois. Beginning about 1830, European immigration began to flow, chiefly from Germany, Ireland, Poland, Bohemia, Switzerland, England, and Italy.

1861   Officially remained a part of the Union during the Civil War.

Loyal state officials elected to remain in the Union, and their decision was supported by the presence of Union military forces stationed in St. Louis. The governor and others, sympathetic to the Southern cause, formed a "rump government" and were accepted into the Confederate States of America. Soldiers from the state fought for both sides.

Published Record Sources

Guidebooks

Campbell, R. A., ed. *Campbell's Gazetteer of Missouri.* St. Louis: the author, 1974. F464 .C13. 2d ed. F464 .C19.

Eaton, David W. *How Missouri Counties, Towns and Streams Were Named. Five articles reprinted from the Missouri Historical Review.* Columbia, Mo.: State Historical Society, 1916. F464 .E14.

Historical Records Survey (WPA). *Early Missouri Archives.* 3 vols. St. Louis: Missouri Historical Society, 1942. CD3331 .M57.

———. *Guide to Public Vital Statistics Records in Missouri.* St. Louis: Missouri Historical Society, 1941. CD3331 .H53.

Missouri. Secretary of State. *Missouri State Archives Bulletin: A Guide to County Records on Microfilm.* Jefferson City: State of Missouri, 1985. CD3337 .A1M57.

Parkins, Robert E. *Guide to Tracing Your Family Tree in Missouri.* St. Louis: Genealogical Research and Products, 1979. F465 .P37.

Census Indexes and Abstracts

Federal

1830   F465 .J3

Glazner, Capitola H. *An Index to the Fifth Census of the United States, 1830. Population Schedules, State of Missouri.* Hot Springs National Park, Ark.: the author, 1966. F466 .G42.

1840   F465 .J32
Nelson, Frances R. and Gwen Brouse, comps. *United States Census, 1840, 6th Census, 1840. Missouri.* 4 vols. Riverside, Calif.: the compilers, 1975. F465 .U57.

Specify county desired.

1850   F465 .J322

All the above publications shown without the name of the compiler or author are by Ronald V. Jackson, Accelerated Indexing Systems.

State

Jackson, Ronald V. *Early Missouri.* Bountiful, Utah: Accelerated Indexing Systems, 1976. F465 .J3778.

Biographies

Cox, James, ed. *Notable St. Louisians in 1900.* St. Louis: Benesch Art Publishing Co., 1900. F474 .S2C85.

Johnson, Anna A. *Notable Women of St. Louis, 1914.* St. Louis: the author, 1914. F474 .S2J67.

Leonard, John W., ed. *The Book of St. Louisians.* St. Louis: St. Louis Republic, 1906. F474 .S2B69.

Shoemaker, Floyd C. *Missouri and Missourians.* 4 vols. Chicago: Lewis Publishing Co., 1943. F466 .S58.

Land Acquisition

Carter, Clarence L. *The Territory of Louisiana—Missouri, 1803–21.* Vol. 13 of *Territorial Papers of the United States.* Reprint. New York: AMS Press, 1973. E173 .C3.

Chadwell, Patricia. *Missouri Land Claims.* New Orleans: Polyanthos, 1976. KFM8255 .M57.

Ericson, Carolyn, and Francis Ingmire. *First Settlers of the Missouri Territory.* Vol. 1, *Grants From the American State Papers—Public Lands.* St. Louis: Ingmire Publications, 1963. F465 .F57.

First Settlers of the Missouri Territory; Containing Grants in the Present States of Missouri, Arkansas, and Oklahoma. St. Louis: Ingmire Publications, 1983. F465 .F57.

Kliethermes, Sharon A. *Missouri School Land Sales.* Loose Creek, Mo.: Dogwood Publications, 1987. LB2827 .K65.

Lowrie, Walter. *Early Settlers of Missouri As Taken From Land Claims in the Missouri Territory.* Easley, S.C.: Southern Historical Press, 1986. F465 .E27.

Ozarks Genealogical Society. *Index of Purchasers. United States Land Sales in Missouri, 1818–1837.* 3 vols. Springfield, Mo.: the society, 1985. F455 .I52.

Ozarks Genealogical Society. *United States Land Sales in Missouri: Springfield Land Office Abstracts, 1835–1846.* 7 vols. Springfield, Mo.: the society, 1982. F455 .V6.

Early Settlers

Billon, Frederic L. *Annals of St. Louis in its Territorial Days From 1804 to 1821.* New York: Arno Press and New York Times, 1971. F474 .S2B58.

Brookes, Linda B. *Pioneer Kentuckians With Missouri Cousins.* 2 vols. St. Louis. Ingmire Publications, 1985. F465 .B763.

Bryan, William S. and Robert Rose. *A History of Pioneer Families of Missouri.* St. Louis: Bryan, Brand & Co., 1935. Reprint. Baltimore: Genealogical Publishing Co., 1977. F465 .B79.

Burgess, Roy. *Early Missourians and Kin.* Venice, Fla.: the author, 1984. F465 .B94.

Coppage, A. Maxim, and Dorothy F. Wulfeck. *Virginia Settlers in Missouri.* Naugatuck, Conn.: the author, n.d. F465 .C6.

Cox, James. *Old and New St. Louis: A Concise History.* St. Louis: Central Biographical Publishing Co., 1894. F474 .S2C87.

Houck, Louis. *Memorial Sketches and Pioneers and Early Residents of Southeast Missouri.* Cape Girardeau, Mo.: Naeder Brothers, 1915. F465 .H83.

Ingmire, Frances. *Citizens of Missouri. 3 vols., 1787–1835.* St. Louis: Ingmire Publications, 1984. F465 .I53.

March, David D.A. *The History of Missouri.* Vol. 3, *Family and Personal History.* New York: Lewis Historical Publishing Co., 1967. Vol. 4, Index. F466 .M35.

Mid-Missouri Genealogical Society. *Mid-Missouri Ancestor Charts.* 3 vols. Jefferson City: the society, 1985. F465 .M59.

Rising, Marsha H. *Genealogical Abstracts From Southwest Missouri Newspapers, 1850–1860.* Springfield, Mo.: the author, 1985. F465 .R57.

Sprague, Stuart S. *Kentuckians in Missouri: Including Many Who Migrated by Way of Ohio, Indiana, and Illinois.* Baltimore: Genealogical Publishing Co., 1983. F465 .S67.

Van Nada, M.L., ed. *The Book of Missourians . . . Opening Decade of the 20th Century.* St. Louis: T. J. Steele & Co., 1906. F465 .V26.

Local Records

Brooks, Linda B. *Missouri Marriages to 1850.* 2 vols. St. Louis: Ingmire Publications, 1983. F465 .B76.

Elsberry, Elizabeth P., comp. *Early Will Records of North Central Counties of Missouri.* Chillicothe, Mo.: the compiler, n.d. F465 .E4.

Heart of America Genealogical Society and Library. *Missouri Cemetery Records Reprinted From the Kansas City Genealogist.* Vol. 1. Kansas City, Mo.: the society, 1981. F465 .M57.

Murray, Nicholas R. *Missouri Surname Index. Computer Indexed Marriage Records.* North Salt Lake, Utah: Hunting For Bears, Inc., 1984. F465 .M58.

Ormesher, Susan, comp. *Missouri Marriages Before 1840.* Baltimore: Genealogical Publishing Co., 1982. F465 .O75.

St. John, Lucretia L. *Book of Obituaries—Missouri No. 2.* Lawson, Mo.: the author, 1980. F465 .B66.

St. Louis Genealogical Society. *St. Louis Genealogical Society Index of St. Louis Marriages, 1804–1876.* 2 vols. St. Louis: the society, 1973. F474 .S2S284.

Stanley, Lois, et al., comps. *Death Records of Pioneer Missouri Women, 1808–1849.* St. Louis: the compiler, 1981. F465 .S749.

———. *Divorces and Separations in Missouri, 1808–1853.* St. Louis: the compilers, 1983. F465 .S75.

————. *Missouri Taxpayers, 1819–1826.* Decorah, Iowa: the compilers, 1979. F465 .S76.

Military Records

American Revolution

Houts, Mrs. Alice K., comp. *Revolutionary Soldiers Buried in Missouri.* Typescript. N.p., 1966. F465 .H85.

War of 1812

Dunaway, Maxinne. *Missouri Military Land Warrants, War of 1812.* Springfield, Mo.: the author, 1985. F465 .D86.

Civil War

Dilts, Bryan L. *1890 Missouri Census Index of Civil War Veterans or Their Widows.* Salt Lake City: Index Publishing Co., 1985. E494 .D5827.

Missouri. Adjutant General. *Official Register of Missouri Troops for 1862 (Officers).* St. Louis: State of Missouri, 1863. E517.3 .M65.

Pompey, Sherman L. *Muster Lists of the Missouri Confederates.* 9 vols. Independence, Calif.: Historical and Genealogical Publishing Co., 1965. E569.3 .P65.

Periodicals

Hodges, Nadine. *Missouri Obituaries, 1880, 1881, 1882. Abstracts from the St. Louis Christian Advocate.* Reprint. Independence, Mo.: Mrs. Howard W. Woodruff, 1975. F465 .H67.

Stanley, Lois, et al., comps. *Early Missouri Marriages in the News, 1820–1853.* St. Louis: Lois Stanley, 1985. F465 .S754.

————. *More Death Records From Missouri Newspapers, 1810–1857.* St. Louis: Lois Stanley, 1985. F465 .S77.

————. *Death Records From the Newspapers: The Civil War Years, 1861–1865.* St. Louis: Lois Stanley, 1983. F465 .S747.

Wilson, George G., et al. *1,300 "Missing" Missouri Marriage Records: from Newspapers, 1812–1853.* St. Louis: Lois Stanley, 1979. F465 .W54.

Directories

City

Aurora
(Mt. Vernon) 1965–81

Blue Springs 1974–82

Bolivar 1967, 1975

Booneville 1968

Branson
(Holister, Forsyth) 1970–76

Brookfield 1929, 1959–80

Butler 1967

Cape Girardeau 1912, 1928–39, 1949–84

Carthage
(Jasper Co.) 1888, 1927, 1937, 1941, 1947–84

Caruthersville 1964, 1966, 1977

Clinton
(Henry Co.) 1964–83

Columbia
(Boone Co.) 1927, 1940, 1947–83

Dexter
(Bloomfield) 1970

Excelsior Springs
(Clay Co.) 1963–81

Farmington
(Flat River) 1968

Festus
(Crystal City, Jefferson Co.) 1963–74

Fulton 1950, 1957, 1959, 1967, 1971

Grandview 1974–76

Hannibal 1911, 1922–39, 1946–84

Harrisonville 1964–66, 1970–83

Independence 1911–12, 1924–82

Jackson 1868

Jefferson City 1925, 1929, 1938, 1943, 1948–71

Joplin 1899, 1904, 1911, 1925–84

Kansas City
pre 1861 (microfiche)
1861–1935 (microfilm)

1936–83

Kennett
  (Dunklin Co.) 1956, 1963–81

Kirksville 1951

Lebanon 1953, 1963–82

Lee's Summit 1967, 1969

Liberty 1962–81

Louisiana 1951

Marshall
  (Saline Co.) 1950, 1959–83

Mexico 1950, 1955, 1960, 1967–71

Moberly 1938, 1948–53

Monett 1964–84

Neosho
  (Neosho Co.) 1976–83

Nevada
  (Vernon Co.) 1928, 1968, 1970

North Kansas City
  (Clay Co.) 1950

Perryville 1968

Poplar Bluff
  (Butler Co.) 1939, 1982–84

Raytown 1960–84

Richmond 1967

Rolla
  (Phelps Co.) 1951, 1960–83

Sedalia
  (Pettis Co.) 1888, 1925–41, 1946–84

Sikeston
  (Miner, Morehouse) 1955, 1958–70

Springfield 1890, 1902–03, 1915, 1926–85

St. Joseph
  (Buchanan Co.) 1867–68, 1890, 1899–1983

St. Louis (City)
  pre 1861 (microfiche)
  1861–1935 (microfilm)
  1936–76

Trenton
  (Grundy Co.) 1951, 1965–81

Warrensburg 1969, 1972

Washington
  (Franklin Co.) 1963–79

Webb City
  (Carterville, Jasper Co.) 1911, 1947

West Plains
  (Mountain View, Willow Springs) 1964–1967, 1969

County, Business, and Miscellaneous

Bates 1884

Cedar (see Greene)

Christian (see Greene)

Dade (see Greene)

Greene
  (Cedar, Christian, Dade, Hickory, Lawrence, Polk)
    1883, 1916, 1920, 1963–65

Hickory (see Greene)

Jasper
  (Newton) 1953, 1956

Lawrence (see Greene)

Macon 1915

Missouri (see also northern Missouri)
  (region) pre 1861 (microfiche)
  (southeast) 1860, 1976, 1879–85, 1889–93, 1898, 1904

Newton (see Jasper)

Nodaway 1894

Northern Missouri
  (Eastern Kansas) 1867

Polk (see Greene)

Southeast Missouri
  (Southern Illinois) 1875

St. Louis
  (Denver) 1870
  (city) 1873, 1918–29
  (county) 1893, 1900, 1909, 1917, 1920–76

Michigan

Historical Highlights

1670s   Explored by Marquette and Joliet, from France.

The first permanent settlement in this area was established by Marquette at Sault Saint Marie in 1668. Detroit was founded in 1701 by a group of fifty French families who received land grants.

1743   King George's War.

1756   French and Indian Wars.

The British fought the French and their Indian allies beginning in 1643 until 1763 at which time the British were victorious and took control of the area from the French.

1776   Under control of England at the time of the American Revolution.

Although the 1783 treaty gave possession of this area to the United States, British troops remained there until 1796 when it officially ceded the lands to the United States. About that time the Indians also began to cede lands to the United States.

1800   As a part of the Northwest Territory, the eastern portion of Michigan was placed in the Ohio Territory; the western portion was placed in the Indiana Territory.

1805   Michigan Territory established.

1837   Admitted to the Union.

After the threat of hostile Indians in the vicinity of Detroit was eliminated, the federal government began to offer public lands for sale in 1818, and migrants began to arrive from New England and New York. The opening of the Erie Canal in 1825 and the coming of the railroads in 1836 increased the flow of people bent on establishing new settlements. In the 1840s, Germans arrived in great numbers, as did Hollanders, Scandinavians, Irish, and other Europeans.

1861   Remained in the Union during the Civil War.

Published Record Sources

Guidebooks

Browne, Valerie G., and David J. Johnson. *A Guide to the State Archives of Michigan: State Records.* N.p.: Michigan Department of State, History Division, 1977. CD3304 .S73.

McGinnis, Carol. *Michigan Genealogy; Sources and Resources.* Baltimore: Genealogical Publishing Co., 1987. Z1297 .M34.

Census Indexes and Abstracts

Federal

1830   F565 .J35
Pompey, Sherman L. *Index to the 1830 Census Records of Berrien, Cass, Crawford, and Van Buren Counties, Michigan Territory.* Charleston, Oreg.: Pacific Specialties, 1974. F565 .P64.

1840   F565 .J332
McGlynn, Estella A., ed. *Index to the 1840 Federal Population Census of Michigan.* Detroit: Detroit Society for Genealogical Research, 1977. F565 .M32.

1850   F565 .J35.

State

Jackson, Ronald V. *Early Michigan Census Records.* Bountiful, Utah: Accelerated Indexing Systems, 1976. F565 .J28.

Russell, Donna V. *Michigan Censuses, 1710–1830, Under the French, British, and Americans.* N.p.: Detroit Society for Genealogical Research, 1982. F565 .M633.

Mortality Schedules

1850   F565 .J35

All the above publications shown without the name of the compiler or author are by Ronald V. Jackson, Accelerated Indexing Systems.

Biographies

American Biographical History of Eminent and Self-made Men—Michigan Volume. Cincinnati: Western Biographical Publishing Co., 1878. F565 .A51.

Cyclopedia of Michigan. New York: Western Publishing Co., 1890. F565 .C98.

Encyclopedia of Michigan: A Volume of Encyclopedia of the United States. St. Clair Shores, Minn.: Somerset Publishing Co., 1981. F566 .E53.

Lanman, Charles. *The Red Book of Michigan. A Civil, Military, and Biographical History.* Detroit: E. B. Smith & Co., 1871. F566 .L28.

Marquis, Albert N., ed. *The Book of Detroiters.* Chicago: A.N. Marquis Co., 1908–14. F574 .D4M3.

Memorial Society of Michigan. *In Memorium: Founders and Makers of Michigan.* Detroit: S.J. Clarke Publishing Co., 1934. F565 .M48.

Men of Michigan: A Collection of Portraits. Detroit: Michigan Art Co., 1904. F565 .M54.

Men of Progress. Detroit: Evening News Association, 1900. F565 .M55.

Michigan Biographies. 2 vols. Lansing: Michigan Historical Commission, 1924. F565 .M62.

Official Michigan Society Register, 1967. Detroit: Michigan Society Register, 1966. F564.6 .M54.

Early Settlers

Denissen, Christian. *Genealogy of the French Families of the Detroit River Region, 1701–1936.* 2 vols. Detroit: Detroit Society for Genealogical Research, 1976, 1987. F572 .D46D46.

Dumbar, Willis F. *Michigan Through the Centuries. Family and Personal History,* Vols. 3 and 4. New York: Lewis Historical Publishing Co., 1955. F566 .D85.

Michigan. State Library. *Family Trails: A Publication of the State Department of Education, Michigan State Library.* Lansing: State of Michigan, 1978. F565 .F35.

Vols. 1 and 2: 1967–69; Vols. 4 and 5: 1977–78.

Prins, Edward. *Dutch and German Ships Passenger Lists, 1846–56.* Holland, Mich.: the author, 1972. F574 .H6P75.

Lists names of many Michigan colonists.

United States Census Office. *1830 Federal Census: Territory of Michigan: With a Guide to Ancestral Trails.* Detroit: Detroit Society for Genealogical Research, 1961. F565 .U6.

Van Koevering, Adrian. *Legends of the Dutch.* Zeeland, Mich.: Zeeland Record Co., 1960. F575 .D9V28.

Local Records

Historical Records Survey (WPA). *Vital Statistics Holdings by Government Agencies—Birth Records.* Detroit: Michigan Historical Records Survey, 1941. CD3301 .H5.

———. *Vital Statistics Holdings by Government Agencies—Inventory of Church and Synagogue Records of Michigan.* Detroit: Michigan Historical Records Survey, 1941. CD3301 .H5.

———. *Vital Statistics Holdings by Government Agencies—Marriage Records.* Detroit: Michigan Historical Records Survey, 1941. CD3301 .H5.

———. *Vital Statistics Holdings by Government Agencies—Death Records.* Detroit: Michigan Historical Records Survey, 1941. CD3301 .H5.

Nar-Al, Inc., comp. *Michigan Cemetery Compendium.* Spring Arbor, Mich.: Nar-Al, 1979. F565 .H37.

Military Records

General

Silliman, Sue I., comp. *Michigan Military Records.* Reprint. Baltimore: Genealogical Publishing Co., 1969. F565 .S58.

Lists Revolutionary War burials in Michigan, territorial Michigan pensions, and Michigan Medal of Honor winners.

Civil War

Ellis, Helen B., comp. *Index to John Robertson's Michigan in the War.* Typescript. Rev. ed. 1882. N.p.: Lansing, n.d. E514 .M62 supplement.

Dilts, Bryan L. *1890 Michigan Census Index of Civil War Veterans or Their Widows—Microforms.* Salt Lake City, Utah: Index Publishing Co., 1985. E494 .D55. (Microfiche 87/2012).

Michigan. Adjutant General. *Records of Service of Michigan Volunteers in the Civil War, 1861–1863.* 46 vols. Lansing: State of Michigan, 1905. E514.3 .M62.

Specify military unit.

———. *Alphabetical General Index to the Public Library Set of 85,271 Names of Michigan Soldiers and Sailors Individual Records.* Lansing: State of Michigan, 1915. E514.3 .M62 Index.

———. *Reports, 1862–66.* 4 vols. Lansing: State of Michigan, 1866. E514.2 .M63.

Periodicals

Chaput, Donald, ed. *Michigan History: Index, Vols. 26–46 (1942–62).* Lansing: Michigan Historical Commission, 1968. F561 .M57. Index.

Detroit Society for Genealogical Research. *Map and Cumulative Index to Vols. 11–15 (1947–52).* Detroit: the society, 1955. F574 .D4D547.

Michigan. Department of State. *Michigan History Index, Vols. 47–57 (1963–73).* Lansing: State of Michigan, 1976. F561 .M57. Index.

Michigan Historical Commission. *Michigan Historical Collections, Vol. 39 (1915). List of Subjects, Authors, and Illustrations, Vols. 1–39.* Lansing: the commission, 1915. F561 .M47.

———. *Index to the Reports and Collections of the Michigan Pioneer and Historical Society, Vols. 1–15 (1874–90).* F561 .M47. Index.

———. *Index to the Reports and Collections of the Michigan Pioneer and Historical Society, Vols. 16–30 (1890–1906).* F561 .M47. Index.

Uhlendorf, B. A., comp. *Analytic Index of the Michigan History Magazine, Vols. 1–25 (1917–1941).* Lansing: Michigan Historical Commission, 1944. F561 .M54.

Directories

City

Adrian 1865, 1890, 1903–84

Albion 1934–37, 1939–51

Allegan 1921–24, 1950, 1953, 1959, 1961–72

Alliance 1911

Alma
(Ithaca, St. Louis, Gratiot Co.) 1836–84

Alpena
(Alpena Co.) 1883–1924, 1927–83

Ann Arbor
(Ypsilanti, Washtenaw Co.) 1888–92, 1895–1901, 1906–20, 1925–82

Battle Creek
(Albion, Bedford, Emmett, Marshall, Pennfield Townships, Springdale, Urbandale) 1884–90, 1896–1983

Bay City
(Essexville, W. Bay City) 1883–1985

Belding 1926, 1950

Benton Harbor
(Miles, St. Joseph) 1907–84

Big Rapids (suburbs) 1884, 1953–63

Birmingham
(Beverly Hills, Bloomfield) 1937–83

Bronson 1950

Cadillac 1930, 1938–84

Calumet
(Hancock, Houghton, Hubbell, Laurium, Lake Linden) 1910, 1912, 1921, 1930

Charlotte
(Eaton Rapids, Olivet, Eaton Co.) 1929, 1940, 1944, 1947, 1951, 1978

Cheboygan
(Indian River, Mackinaw City, Mullett Lake, Topinabec, Cheboygan Co.) 1910–16, 1939, 1958–80

Clarksdale 1904, 1916, 1927–30, 1936, 1946–85

Coldwater
(Quincy) 1905–81

Columbia 1960–67, 1972–84

Dearborn 1926–83

Detroit
pre 1861 (microfiche)
1861–1935 (microfilm)

(suburbs) 1936–70

Dowagiac
(Cassopolis, Cass Co.) 1923, 1938, 1941, 1971, 1973

Down River 1941, 1945–84

East Ann Arbor 1948

East Detroit 1942, 1946, 1951, 1954–58

East Saginaw 1889

Escambia
(Gladstone, Delta Co.) 1902–82

Farmington 1968–77

Fenton
(Holly, Linden) 1929, 1958–84

Ferndale
(Berkley, Hazel Park, Huntington Woods, Oak Park, Pleasant Ridge) 1955–59

Flint
(Genesee Co.) 1888, 1892, 1897, 1903–82

Fordson 1927–28

Gaylord 1977

Grand Haven
(Ferrysburg, Spring Lake) 1928, 1931, 1936–84

Grand Lodge 1972–83

Grand Rapids
pre 1861 (microfiche)
1861–1935 (microfilm)
1936–84

Greenville 1937, 1940, 1950

Hancock
(Houghton, Hurontown, Ripley) 1939, 1973–80

Hastings 1898, 1929, 1936, 1940, 1944, 1947, 1950, 1954, 1956, 1959–82

Highland Park 1916

Hillsdale
(Hillsdale Co.) 1905, 1908, 1911
(Jonesville) 1982

Holland
(Zeeland) 1921, 1929–84

Holly Springs 1975

Houghton 1895–1908, 1916, 1930, 1939

Howell 1956–84

International Falls 1971–80

Ionia
(Ionia Co.) 1903, 1905, 1911, 1936

Iron Mountain
(Dickinson Co.) 1925, 1935, 1959–81

Ironwood 1893, 1901, 1974–82

Ishpeming
(Negaunee) 1929

Jackson
(Jackson Co.) 1869, 1883, 1888–1982

Kalamazoo
(suburbs, Ingham Co.) 1889, 1899–84

Lansing
(suburbs, Ingham Co.) 1873, 1883–92

Lapeer
(Elba, Mayfield, Oregon) 1938, 1961–83

Lincoln Park
(Allen Park, Melvindale) 1929, 1933, 1941–83

Litchfield
(Meeker Co.) 1965-66

Ludington
(Bass Lake, Custer, Epworth Heights, Fountain, Freesoil, Hamlin Lake, Scottville, Walholly) 1940, 1946–85

Manistee
(Manistee Co.) 1874, 1888, 1895–1924, 1929, 1936, 1940, 1945–85

Marquette
(Ishpeming, Negaunee, Marquette Co.) 1894–1984

Marshall 1926–50, 1964–65, 1977–84

Mason 1972–83

Menominee
(Marinette, Wis.) 1887, 1897–1941, 1946–81

Midland 1929, 1935, 1943, 1946, 1949, 1952–69, 1973, 1979

Monroe 1946–84

Mt. Clemens 1907

Muskegon
(suburbs, Muskegon Co.) 1883, 1887–1984

Niles
(Buchanan) 1940, 1945–84

Old Orchard Beach 1933–47

Otsego
  (Plainwell) 1973

Owosso
  (Corunna, Durand, Perry, Shiawassee Co.) 1896–1985

Petoskey
  (Harbor Springs, Emmett Co.) 1903–41, 1946, 1949, 1955, 1958, 1961, 1969–78

Plymouth
  (Northville) 1929–76

Pontiac
  (Auburn Hgts., Keego Harbor, Orchard Lake, Sylvan Lake City) 1898, 1920–62, 1966

Port Huron
  (Marysville, St. Clair Co.) 1885, 1887, 1906, 1909, 1910, 1960–75, 1983

Redford 1925, 1940, 1954, 1956

Rochester
  (Orion, Oxford, Romeo) 1928, 1967–82

Royal Oak
  (Berkley, Clawson, Ferndale, Hazel Park, Huntington Woods, Pleasant Ridge) 1922–60

Saginaw, East 1883, 1885, 1889, 1891–1984

Sault Ste. Marie 1888, 1895–1985

South Haven 1918, 1920, 1937, 1940, 1965

St. Johns
  (Ovid) 1929, 1961, 1967, 1972–83

St. Joseph
  (Benton Harbor, Niles, Berrien Co.) 1904, 1934–40, 1945–56

Sturgis 1915, 1922, 1934, 1940–56, 1976–82

Tecumsee 1965, 1977–84

Traverse City
  (Grand Traverse Co., Leelalnau Co.) 1894, 1900–26, 1930, 1935, 1937, 1940–86

Wayne
  (Garden City, Inkster) 1947, 1951, 1954–60

Wyandotte
  (Ecorse, Ford, Sibley, Trenton, Wyandotte Hgts.) 1907, 1909, 1914, 1921, 1926–40

Ypsilanti 1901, 1903, 1930–85

County, Business, and Miscellaneous

Barry 1917, 1922

Battle Creek (city) 1884

Berrien 1892, 1894

Branch 1965, 1974–79

Calhoun 1869, 1916

Eaton 1916

Gratiot 1964, 1977, 1980

Hamtramck (city) 1938

Hillsdale 1975, 1977, 1985

Ingham 1921

Jackson 1884–85

Kalamazoo 1869

Kent 1917

Lenawee 1897, 1921, 1963, 1965, 1977–83

Livingston 1937

Ludington
  (Mason) 1929, 1935

Macomb 1916

Marquette 1873, 1889

Mason (see Ludington)

Michigan
  pre 1861 (microfiche)
  1856, 1873–1831, 1956–57
    Michigan State Gazetteer and Business Directory For 1863–64. Detroit: Charles F. Clark, 1863. F564.7 .M54.

Monroe 1916

Saginaw 1883

Shiawassee 1917, 1963, 1965

St. Clair 1899, 1912

St. Joseph 1864, 1975–83

Tuscola 1979–80

Van Buren 1916

Wisconsin

Historical Highlights

1673   Explored by Marquette and Joliet, from France.

1763   Control assumed by England.

The French explorers and missionaries established a settlement at Green Bay soon after arriving. Following British victories in 1763, control shifted to England and the area was designated a part of Quebec, Canada.

1776   Part of Canada, under England's control, at the time of the American Revolution.

The treaty with England in 1783 transferred the area to the United States; it was placed in the Northwest territory.

1809   Designated part of the Illinois Territory

1818   Designated part of the Michigan Territory.

1832   Wisconsin Territory established.

Until the close of the Black Hawk Indian War in 1832, and before federal land offices were opened in 1834, there was very little migration into the area—the principal residents being Indians. In the 1830s New Englanders coming by way of Ohio began to arrive to take advantage of the inexpensive lands being offered.

1848   Admitted to the Union.

Following statehood the railroads began to arrive, bringing European immigrants eager for farm land. They came from many countries, especially Norway, Sweden, and Denmark. Others came from Germany, Ireland, Switzerland, Holland, Poland, Russia, and other countries. Indian reservations were established by the federal government to care for those who had been pushed out by the oncoming white settlers.

1861   Remained in the Union at the time of the Civil War.

Published Record Sources

Guidebooks

Gard, Robert E., and L. G. Sorden. *The Romance of Wisconsin Place Names.* New York: October House, 1968. F579 .G3.

Ryan, Carol W. *Searching For Your Wisconsin Ancestors in the Wisconsin Libraries.* N.p.: the author, 1979. Z1351 .R9.

State Historical Society of Wisconsin. James P. Danky, ed. *Genealogical Research: An Introduction to the Resources of the State Historical Society.* Madison: the society, 1979. Reprint. 1986. Z1351 .W82.

Census Indexes and Abstracts

Federal

1840   F580 .J32
Pompey, Sherman L. *Index to the 1840 Census of Dodge, Fond du Lac, Manitowoc, Marquette, Portage, Sauk, Sheboygan, and Winnebago Counties, Wisconsin Territory.* Clovis, Calif.: n.p., 1970. F585 .P6.

1850   F580 .J34

The above publications shown without the name of the author are by Ronald V. Jackson, Accelerated Indexing Systems.

State

Jackson, Ronald V. *Wisconsin 1836 Census Index.* Bountiful, Utah: Accelerated Indexing Systems, 1976. F580 .J317.

Rentmeister, Jean R., comp. *Wisconsin Territorial Census for Fond du Lac County, 1838, 1842, 1847.* Fond du Lac: the compiler, 1979. F587 .F6R46.

Biographies

Aikens, Andrew J., and Lewis A. Proctor, eds. *Men of Progress, Wisconsin.* Milwaukee: The Evening Wisconsin Co., 1897. F580 .A29.

Biographical History of LaCrosse, Trempealeau and Buffalo Counties, Wisconsin. Chicago: Lewis Publishing Co., 1892. F580 .B61.

Commemorative Biographical Records of the Upper Lake Region. Chicago: J. H. Beers & Co., 1905. F580 .C74.

Nelke, D. I. *The Columbian Biographical Dictionary and Portrait Gallery of the Representative Men of the United States—Wisconsin Volume.* Chicago: Lewis Publishing Co., 1895. F580 .N41.

Notable Men of Wisconsin, 1901–02. Milwaukee: Williams Publishing Co., 1902. F580 .N89.

Soldiers and Citizens' Album of Biographical Record of Wisconsin. Chicago: Grand Army Publishing Co., 1890. F580 .S682.

State History, Wisconsin. *Dictionary of Wisconsin Biography.* Milwaukee: North American Press, 1980. F580 .W825.

Early Settlers

Patterson, Betty, ed. *Some Pioneer Families of Wisconsin—An Index.* Madison: Wisconsin State Genealogical Society, 1977. F580 .P36.

Rentmeister, Jeanne. *The Flemish in Wisconsin.* N.p.: the author, n.d. F590 .F57R46.

Rosholt, Malcolm. *From the Indian Lands: Firsthand Account of Central Wisconsin Pioneer Life.* Iola, Wis.: Krause Publishing Co., 1985. F590 .S18R67.

Spominska, Zgodovina. *Historical Memoirs, Willard, Wisconsin.* Willard, Wis.: Slovenski Druzba, 1982. F589 .W66S66.

Military Records

Civil War

Wisconsin. Adjutant General. *Annual Report, 1865.* Madison: State of Wisconsin, 1866. E537 .W81. (Micro 64521.)

Wisconsin Soldiers and Sailors: Reunion Roster. Fond du Lac: the reunion, 1880. E537.3 W83.

Wisconsin. Commission on Civil War Records. *Wisconsin Volunteers.* N.p.: State of Wisconsin, 1915. E537.3 .W822.

Wisconsin. Commission on Civil War Records. *Wisconsin Losses in the Civil War.* N.p.: State of Wisconsin, 1915. E537.3 .W823.

Periodicals

State Historical Society of Wisconsin, Collections. 21 vols. Madison: the society, 1915. F576 .W81.

Volume 21 indexes volumes 1–20.

——. *Wisconsin Magazine of History.* Indexes: vols. 1–15 (1917–31); vols. 16–25 (1932–43); vols. 26–35 (1942–52); vols. 36–45 (1952–62). Madison: the society, 1946; 1955; 1964. F576 .W7 Index.

Directories

City

Appleton
(Combined Locks, Little Chute, Kaukauna, Kimberly, Outagamie Co.) 1919–21, 1925–38

Ashland
(Bayfield, Bessemer, Hurley, Ironwood, Wakefield, Washburn) 1888–1917, 1922–32, 1937–43, 1947–84

Baraboo 1895, 1917

Beaver Dam 1914

Beloite
pre 1861 (microfiche)
(Rockton, S. Beloit) 1889, 1920–83

Brookfield 1963

Chippewa Falls 1907, 1911–29, 1961

Cudahy
(Oak Creek, S. Milwaukee, St. Francis) 1921, 1941, 1962

Eau Claire 1884–1983

Elm Grove 1943–47, 1957, 1975

Fond du Lac
pre 1861 (microfiche)
(suburbs) 1874, 1884, 1901–81
Fond-du-Lac Directory (city and county), 1890–91. Fond du Lac: Bensel-Low Co., 1890. F589 .F64A18.

Green Bay
(Allouez, Ashwaubenon, DePere, Howard) 1894, 1898, 1905–84

Greenfield 1964

Hales Corners 1969

Hudson
  (N. Hudson) 1977

Janesville
  pre 1861 (microfiche)
  (Beloit, Rock Co.) 1899, 1984

Kenosha
  pre 1861 (microfiche)
  1875, 1903–06, 1912–84

La Crosse
  (French Island, Onalaska) 1880, 1888, 1900–84

Madison
  pre 1861 (microfiche)
  1855, 1858, 1866–1984

Manitowoc
  (Manitowoc Co.) 1899, 1915, 1920, 1945

Marinette 1985

Marshfield 1949

Menasha
  (Neenah) 1920, 1924

Merrill
  (Bloomville, Doering, Gleason, Irma) 1921, 1925,
    1930, 1936, 1985

Milwaukee
  pre 1861 (microfiche)
  1861–1935 (microfilm)
  1936–85

Mineral Point
  pre 1861 (microfiche)

Monroe 1922

Neenah
  (Menasha) 1962

Oconomowoc 1925

Oconto
  (Oconto Falls) 1975–82

Oshkosh
  pre 1861 (microfiche)
  1868, 1884, 1889, 1893, 1898, 1903, 1912, 1914–79

Portage 1917

Racine
  pre 1861 (microfiche)
  (Wind Point) 1883–1983

Reedsburg 1985

Rhinelander
  (Lake Tomahawk, Minocqua, Monica, Pelican Lake,
    Three Lakes, Woodruff, Oneida Co.) 1921, 1927,
    1930, 1936–41, 1946–84

River Falls 1977

Sheboygan
  (Kohler, Plymouth, Sheboygan Falls, Sheboygan Co.)
    1895, 1904, 1920–26, 1928–85

South Milwaukee 1921

Stevens Point
  (Park Ridge) 1893, 1901, 1917, 1923, 1927, 1946–84

Sturgeon Bay 1927

Superior 1889–1984

Tomah 1961

Watertown
  (Dodge, Farmas, Jefferson Co.) 1866, 1895–1900,
    1907–19, 1924–86

Waukesha
  pre 1861 (microfiche)
  1899, 1907–85

Wausau
  (Marathon Co.) 1888, 1908–85

West Allis 1904, 1910–85

West Milwaukee 1930, 1935, 1937, 1941, 1945

Whitefish Bay
  (Fox Point, River Hills) 1930–35, 1941, 1946, 1950,
    1956, 1974

County, Business, and Miscellaneous

Brown 1901, 1911, 1916, 1971

Columbia 1910

Dane 1904

Green 1919

Jefferson 1908

Kenosha
  (Racine) 1919

Oneida 1917

Outagamie 1910

Portage 1896

Racine (see Kenosha)

Rock 1867, 1919

Sauk 1905

Sheboygan 1889

Stevens Point 1893, 1901, 1917, 1923, 1927, 1946–84

Trempealeau 1917

Waukesha 1904

Wisconsin (state)
  pre 1861 (microfiche)
  1882–1924
    Wisconsin State Business Directory, 1872–1873.
    Chicago: Evening Journal, 1871. F579.7 .P7.
    *Wisconsin State Gazetteer and Business Directory,
    1879,* Milwaukee: R. L. Polk, 1879. F579.7 .P8.

Minnesota

Historical Highlights

1689   Claimed by France.

For fifty years before France officially claimed the area it was explored by various French traders and missionaries but populated almost exclusively by Indians.

1762   The portion east of the Mississippi River ceded by France to Spain.

1763   The portion west of the Mississippi River given by treaty to England.

1776   Control claimed by both France and England at the time of the American Revolution.

Following the Revolutionary War, England gave control of the lands west of the Mississippi to the United States and designated part of the Indiana Territory. By the Louisiana Purchase from France in 1803, the United States acquired the lands east of the Mississippi River (despite any claims by Spain). Various portions of present day Minnesota were designated as parts of several territories until it became a separate territory. The jurisdictional designations were the following:

In 1809, Lands east of the Mississippi were designated Illinois Territory, and, in 1812, Lands in the southwest were designated Illinois Territory.

1818   Treaty with England officially gave the northwestern lands to the United States; lands east of the Mississippi were given to Michigan Territory.

1818   Lands east of the Mississippi became part of Crawford County, Michigan.

1834   Lands west of the Mississippi became part of Michigan Territory.

1836   All Minnesota lands became part of Wisconsin Territory.

1838   Lands west of the Mississippi became part of Iowa Territory.

During the above listed jurisdictional changes there was little effect on the few settlers who could be found there; the area was still populated almost exclusively by Indians. Beginning in the late 1830s and early 1840s, settlers began to arrive, resulting in the founding of St. Paul and Minneapolis. Migration to surrounding areas resulted in statehood for Iowa and Wisconsin, leaving Minnesota yet to be developed.

1846   Iowa became a state, leaving the lands in Minnesota west of the Mississippi without any government.

1848   Wisconsin became a state, leaving the lands in Minnesota east of the Mississippi without any government.

1849   Minnesota Territory created.

With the creation of the Territory and the opening of federal land offices, as well as the signing of treaties with the Indians, migration of settlers began, using the newly laid railroads. They came primarily from the Scandinavian countries, Germany, Canada, and also from New England and Ireland.

1858   Admitted to the Union.

1861   Remained in the Union during the Civil War.

Following the war, immigration from various countries continued, with the heaviest flow from Scandinavia and Germany.

Published Record Sources

Guidebooks

Lind, Marilyn. *Continuing Your Genealogical Research in Minnesota.* Colquet, Minn.: Linden Tree, 1986. F605 .L66.

Census Indexes and Abstracts

Federal

1850   Harpole, Patricia C., and Mary D. Nagle, eds. *Minnesota Territorial Census, 1850.* St. Paul: Minnesota Historical Society, 1972. F605 .H3.

Pompey, Sherman L. *The 1850 Census Records of Wahnata County, Wisconsin Territory.* Independence, Calif.: Historical Genealogical Publishing Co., 1966. F605 .P64.

1860   F605 .J324

1870   F605 .J3244

The above publications shown without the name of the compiler or author are by Ronald V. Jackson, Accelerated Indexing Systems.

State

Jackson, Ronald V. *Minnesota 1849 Census Index.* Bountiful, Utah: Accelerated Indexing Systems, 1981. F608 .J323.

Pompey, Sherman L. *The 1875 State Census Records of Greenbush, Mille Lacs Counties, Minnesota.* Florence, Oreg.: Western Oregon Genealogical Research Library, 1981. F612 .M38P65.

Mortality Schedules

1860   Finnell, Arthur L., comp. *Index to the 1860 Minnesota Mortality Schedule.* Marshall, Minn.: the compiler, 1978. F605 .F56.

Biographies

Burnquist, Joseph A., ed. *Minnesota and Its People.* Vols. 3 and 4, *Biographical.* Chicago: S.J. Clarke Publishing Co., 1924. F606 .B96.

Compendium of History and Biography of Minneapolis and Hennepin County, Minnesota. Chicago: Henry Taylor & Co., 1914. F614 .M5C77.

Corwall, C. N., comp. *Who's Who in Minnesota.* Minneapolis: Minneapolis Editorial Association, 1941. F605 .W64.

Encyclopedia of Biography of Minnesota. Chicago: Century Publishing and Engraving, 1900. F605 .E56.

Foster, Mary D., comp. *Who's Who Among Minnesota Women.* N.p.: the author, 1924. F605 .W63.

Illustrated Album of Biography of Southwestern Minnesota and Northwestern Iowa. Chicago: Northwest Publishing Co., 1889. F606 .I29.

Little Sketches of Big Folks, Minnesota, 1907. St. Paul: R. L. Polk & Co., 1907. F605 .L77.

Marquis, Albert N., ed. *Book of Minnesotans.* Chicago: A. N. Marquis & Co., 1907. F605 .M3.

Memorial Records of Southwestern Minnesota. Chicago: Lewis Publishing Co., 1897. F605 .M43.

Men of Minnesota. St. Paul: Minnesota History Co., 1902. F605 .M53.

Newson, T. M. *St. Paul Biographical Records.* St. Paul: the author, 1886. F614 .S4N5.

Phelps, Alonzo. *Biographical History of the Northwest.* Vol. 4, *American Biographies and Representative Men.* Boston: Ticknor & Co., 1890. F605 .P53.

Shutter, Marion D., and J.S. McLain, eds. *Progressive Men of Minnesota.* Minneapolis: Minneapolis Journal, 1892. F605 .S56.

United States Biographical Dictionary and Portrait Gallery, Minnesota Volume. New York: American Biographical Publishing Co., 1879. F605 .U58.

Military Records

Civil War

Minnesota. Adjutant General. *Military Forces of the State from 1861 to 1866.* St. Paul: State of Minnesota, 1866. E515.2 .M66.

Periodicals

Katz, Helen T., ed. *Consolidated Index to Minnesota History, Vols. 11–40 (1930–67).* St. Paul and Minneapolis Historical Society, 1983. F601 .M92. Index.

Minnesota History—A Quarterly Magazine. Index, Vols. 1–10. St. Paul and Minneapolis Historical Society, 1931. F601 .M72. Index.

Minnesota Historical Society. *A Complete Guide to the Gopher Historian, 1946–1972.* St. Paul: Minnesota Historical Society Press, 1977. F691 .G6. Index.

Directories

City

Albert Lea
(Freeborn Co.) 1902–09, 1914–16

Alexandria 1974–82

Anoka
(Blaine, Champlin, Coon Rapids) 1957–84

Austin
(Mower Co.) 1901–11, 1922, 1924, 1928, 1931–84

Bemidji 1910, 1927, 1931–46, 1951–84

Biwabik
(Buhl, Chisholm, Eveleth, Gilbert, Hibbing, Virginia) 1922

Brainerd (suburbs) 1901–11, 1922, 1927–32, 1937–83

Burnsville
(Savage) 1967–82

Cloquet
(Carlton, Eska, Scanlon, Carlton Co.) 1927, 1974–83

Crookston 1908, 1930, 1940, 1949–80

Duluth 1883–1985

Edina
(Richfield) 1939

Fairmont
(Martin, Martin Co.) 1940, 1948–84

Faribault
(Northfield, Rice Co.) 1929, 1936, 1939, 1949–83

Fergus Falls 1902–11, 1931–84

Glencoe 1979

Hastings 1962, 1970–79

Hibbing
(Biwabik, Chisholm, Eveleth, Gilbert, Virginia) 1909–17, 1924, 1938–42, 1948–83

Hutchinson 1971–82

Lake Minnetonka 1946–49

Little Falls
(Morrison Co.) 1928, 1949, 1951, 1976, 1980

Mankato
(Blue Earth Co.) 1888, 1892, 1895, 1900–84

Marshall 1962–83

Minneapolis 1861–1901 (microfiche)
(suburbs) 1903, 1908, 1936–81

Minnetonka Lake 1946

Montevideo 1962, 1964

Moorhead
(Fargo, N.D.) 1938–68

Morris 1979

New Ulm
(Brown Co.) 1911, 1961–84

Owatonna
(Steele Co.) 1903–15, 1928, 1940, 1947–84

Pipestone 1961

Plymouth
(Ashland, Holdeness, Meredith, Pemiquewasset Valley) 1919, 1925

Range Towns
(Biwabik, Buhl, Carlton, Cloquet, Ely, Eveleth, Grand Rapids, Hibbing, Knife River, McKinley, Mountain Iron, Scudau, Sparta, Tower, Two Harbours, Virginia, Winton) 1901, 1903, 1907

Redwing 1909, 1911, 1925, 1948

Richfield 1943, 1945

Robindale
(Crystal) 1937

Rochester
  (Olmstead Co.) 1909–84

Spring Lake Park (suburbs) 1948

St. Anthony
  pre 1861 (microfiche)

St. Cloud
  (Sartell, Sauk Rapids, Waite Park) 1894–1912, 1927–
    85

St. Paul
  pre 1861 (microfiche)
  1861–1935 (microfilm)
  (suburbs) 1936–86
    St. Paul City Directory, 1881–82. St. Paul: R. L. Polk,
      1881. F614 .S4A18.

St. Peter
  (Nicolette Co.) 1962–84

Stillwater
  (Bayport, Hudson, Oak Park, Oak Park Heights)
    1890–1919, 1924–30, 1937–84

Thief River Falls 1909, 1911, 1927–40, 1945, 1957–80

Virginia City
  (Eveleth, Gilbert) 1939–43, 1948–84

Wadena 1963

Wilmar
  (Kandiyohi Co.) 1927–32, 1961–82

Winona
  (Winona Co.) 1866, 1898, 1908–84

Worthington
  (Nobles Co.) 1948, 1972–84

County, Business, and Miscellaneous

Clay 1916

Freeborn 1921

Minneapolis
  (St. Paul, cities) 1887

Minnesota (state)
  1878, 1961
  (Montana, North Dakota, South Dakota) 1882–1926
    Minnesota Railroad and River Guide For 1867–68. St.
      Paul: Bailey & Wolfe, 1867. F604.7 .A18.

Rice 1899–1926

St. Paul (city) (see Minneapolis)

Iowa

Historical Highlights

1673	Explored by Marquette and Joliet, from France.
1762	Along with other parts of the Midwest, ceded by France to Spain.
1800	Ceded back to France.
1803	Louisiana Purchase from France.
1808	Part of the Illinois Territory.
1812	Part of the Missouri Territory.
	The area later to become Iowa was sparsely settled until the early 1830s; the chief residents were Indians and a few Frenchmen. Until Indian threats were eliminated and settlement became feasible, the area was designated as part of other territories for purposes of government.
1832	Black Hawk War.
1834	A part of the Michigan Territory.
1836	A part of the Wisconsin Territory.
1838	Iowa Territory established. First federal land offices in the territory opened.
	With the opening of land offices and the designation of lands as bounty for Mexican War veterans, more settlers arrived from eastern states. In the ensuing decade, immigrants arrived in substantial numbers from European countries, primarily from Scandinavia, Holland, Germany, Scotland and Wales.
1846	Admitted to the Union.
1861	Remained in the Union during the Civil War.

Published Record Sources

Guidebooks

Historical Records Survey (WPA). *Guide to Public Vital Statistics in Iowa.* Des Moines: Iowa Historical Records Survey, 1941. CD3231 .H5.

Vogel, Virgil J. *Iowa Place Names of Indian Origin.* Iowa City: University of Iowa Press, 1983. F619 .V63.

Census Indexes and Abstracts

Federal

1850   Jackson, Ronald V. *Iowa 1850 Census Index.* Bountiful, Utah: Accelerated Indexing Systems, 1976. F620 .J34.

State

Jackson, Ronald V. *Iowa 1836 Territorial Census Index.* Bountiful, Utah: Accelerated Indexing Systems, 1976. F620 .J33.

————. *Iowa 1840 Territorial Census Index.* Salt Lake City, Utah: Accelerated Indexing Systems, 1979. F620 .J28.

Shambaugh, Benjamin F., ed. *First Census of the Original Counties of Dubuque and Demore (Iowa Territory).* Des Moines: Historical Department of Iowa, 1897. F622 .W81.

Biographies

Biographies and Portraits of the Progressive Men of Iowa. 2 vols. Des Moines: Conaway & Shae, 1899. F620 .B61.

Petersen, William J. *The Story of Iowa.* Vols. 3 and 4, *Family and Personal History.* New York: Lewis Historical Publishing Co., 1952. F621 .P55.

Reeves, Winona E., ed. *The Blue Book of Iowa Women.* Mexico, Mo.: Missouri Printing and Publishing Co., 1914. F620 .R33.

Stiles, Edward H. *Recollections and Sketches of Notable Lawyers and Public Men of Early Iowa.* Des Moines: Homestead Publishing Co., 1916. F620 .S85.

United States Biographical Dictionary and Portrait Gallery of Eminent and Self-made Men—Iowa Volume. Chicago: American Biographical Publishing Co., 1878. F620 .J58.

Early Settlers

Iowa Genealogical Society. *Surname Index.* Vol. 1. Des Moines: the society, 1972. CS44 .I58a.

Mills, George. *Rogues and Heroes From Iowa's Amazing Past.* Ames: Iowa State University, 1972. F620 .M5.

Local Records

Goranson, Rita, and Jo Ann Burgess, comps. *Miscellaneous Iowa Records.* 4 vols. N.p.: the compilers, 1983. F620 .G67.

Military Records

General

Iowa. Adjutant General. *Roster and Record of Iowa Soldiers in Miscellaneous Organizations of the Mexican War, Indian Campaigns, War of the Rebellion, Spanish-American, and Philippine Wars.* Vol. 6. Des Moines: State of Iowa, 1914. E507.3 .I64.

American Revolution

Iowa Society Daughters of the American Revolution. Abigail Adams Chapter. *Revolutionary Soldiers and Patriots Buried in Iowa.* Marcelline, Mo.: Walsworth Publishing Co., 1978. F620 .D38.

Civil War

Corbin, William E. *A Star for Patriotism.* Monticello, Iowa: the author, 1972. E507 .C67.

Iowa. Adjutant General. *List of Soldiers, Sailors, and Marines Living in Iowa.* Des Moines: State of Iowa, 1888. E494 .I64.

————. *Annual Reports, 1863–64.* 2 vols. Des Moines: State of Iowa, 1867. E507.2 .I64.

Periodicals

Annals of Iowa. Index, Vols. 1–8 (1893–1909); Vols. 9–16 (1909–29). Des Moines: History Department of Iowa, 1912, 1931. F616 .A6. Index.

Dilts, Bryan. *Cumulative Index to the Palimpset, Vols. 1–10 (1920–29); Vols. 11–20 (1930–39)*. Iowa City: State Historical Society of Iowa, 1941, 1942. F606 .P16. Index.

Directories

City

Ames
(Story, Nevada Co.) 1940, 1945, 1949–84

Atlantic 1970–84

Boone
(Boone Co.) 1903–32, 1938, 1941, 1947, 1951–84

Burlington
pre 1861 (microfiche)
1882–1901 (microfilm)
(W. Burlington) 1904, 1908, 1916–83

Carroll 1971–83

Cedar Falls
(Blackhawk Co.) 1948–84

Cedar Rapids 1881, 1888, 1895–1912, 1921–83

Centerville
(Appanoose Co.) 1911

Charles City
(Floyd Co.) 1911–85

Clinton
(Camqucha, Fulton) 1899, 1903, 1921–85

Council Bluffs 1889–1984

Creston
(Union Co.) 1889, 1910–13, 1917, 1927

Davenport
pre 1861 (microfiche)
1861–1881 (microfilm)
(Bettendorf, Scott Co.) 1905, 1909, 1915

Des Moines
1861–1935 (microfilm)
(suburbs) 1936–84

Dubuque
pre 1861 (microfiche)

1867–74, 1877–1903, 1911, 1916–18, 1929, 1937–84

Estherville
(Emmet Co.) 1962–64

Fairfield
(Jefferson Co.) 1927, 1937, 1964–84

Fort Dodge
(Webster Co.) 1902–84

Fort Madison 1925–84

Grinnel
(Poweshiek Co.) 1920, 1940, 1985

Harlan 1973, 1979

Independence 1969

Indianola 1964–84

Iowa City
(Coralville, Johnson Co.) 1901, 1911–85

Jefferson
(Greene Co.) 1963

Knoxville
(Marion Co.) 1951, 1961–83

Manchester 1969

Marion 1958–84

Marshalltown 1891, 1894–1941, 1945–85

Mason
(Clearlake) 1900–85

Newton
(Lamb's Grove, Jasper Co.) 1920, 1929, 1939–84

Oelwein
(Fayette Co.) 1921, 1939, 1941, 1962–82

Oskaloosa
(Beacon, Unia Park) 1947, 1951–84

Ottumwa
(Wapello Co.) 1890, 1899, 1922, 1924, 1929–84

Pella 1971–85

Red Oak 1962–65

Shenandoah
(Clarinda, Page Co., Fremont Co.) 1930–37, 1961, 1969

Sioux City 1884–1985

Spencer 1918, 1921, 1939, 1941, 1945, 1952

Waterloo
  (Elk Run Hgts., Evansdale, Black Hawk Co.) 1888,
    1912, 1921–85

Waverly
  (Bremer Co.) 1901–83

County, Business, and Miscellaneous

Crawford 1947

Greene 1983

Guthrie 1983

Henry
  pre 1861 (microfiche)

Iowa
  (region) pre 1861 (microfiche)
  (state) 1865, 1871, 1882–1922, 1938

*Personal Name Index to the 1856 City Directories of
  Iowa.* Detroit: Gale Research Co., 1980. F620
  .S66.

Linn 1961

Montgomery 1947

Muscatine
  pre 1861 (microfiche)
  1938

Osceola 1912

Polk 1916, 1963, 1965

Shelby 1979, 1983

Webster 1951

Woodbury
  (Dakota, Neb.; Union, Utah) 1884, 1899, 1902–04

CHAPTER 14

Northwestern States

North Dakota • South Dakota • Nebraska
Montana • Wyoming • Idaho
Washington • Oregon • Alaska

Listed below are two works that deal with the Northwest as a whole:

Downs, Winfield S., ed. *Encyclopedia of Northwest Biography.* New York: American Historical Publishing Co., 1941. F852 .E5.

Eminent Men of the Northwest, 1955. Palo Alto, Calif.: C. W. Taylor, 1955. F852 .E48.

North Dakota

Historical Highlights

1803   Part of the Louisiana Purchase from France.

1818   Northeast portion acquired from England.

1861   Dakota Territory established.

Scots and Irish from Canada came in 1812, settling Pembrina; they returned to Canada in 1823. Some Norwegians and other Northern Europeans settled during the mid-1800s, but Indian hostility slowed population growth. The Dakota Territory included the area to become South Dakota and parts of Wyoming and Montana, until 1864 when they were formed into the Montana Territory.

1873   Divided into North Dakota and South Dakota.

1874   Land offices opened in Fargo and Bismarck.

Immigration from Norway, Germany, the Netherlands, Russia, Poland, and other countries increased. Many who had previously settled in Canada and eastern states, such as Michigan, Wisconsin, Iowa, and New York, moved into the new farming communities of the Dakotas. The coming of the railroads facilitated the newcomers' movement.

1889   Admitted to the Union.

Published Record Sources

Guidebooks

Liddle, Janice, comp. *Index to Mary Ann Barnes Williams' Origin of North Dakota Place-names.* Fargo: North Dakota Institute of Regional Studies, 1977. F634 .W552L5.

State Historical Society of North Dakota. *Compiled Table of Contents to the Publications of the State Historical Society of North Dakota, with Authors, Titles, and Subject Indices.* Occasional Publications, No. 3. Bismarck: the society, 1981. F651 .N86. (Micro 38880).

Williams, Mary Ann B. *Origins of North Dakota Place-names.* Washburn, N.D.: the author, 1966. F624 .M29W5.

Census Indexes and Abstracts

Federal

1860	F650 .J29
1970	F650 .J3
1880	F650 .J32
1900	Quiring, Mary Ann, and Lily B. Zwolle, comps. *1900 Federal Census and Index of Turtle Mountain Indian Reservation, Rolette County, North Dakota, 1984.* N.p.: the compilers, n.d. E99 .C6Q47.

All the above publications shown without the name of the compiler are by Ronald V. Jackson, Accelerated Indexing Systems.

Mortality Schedules

1800	Jackson, Ronald V. *Dakota Territorial 1880 Mortality Schedule.* Bountiful, Utah: Accelerated Indexing Systems, 1980. F650 .J325.

Biographies

Memorial and Biographical Records. An Illustrated Compendium of Biography. Chicago: George A. Ogle & Co., 1898. F650 .M54.

Stutenroth, Stella M. *Daughters of Dacotah [sic].* Mitchell, S.D.: Educator Supply Co., 1942. F560 .S75.

White, Hugh L., ed. *Who's Who For North Dakota.* Bismarck: North Dakota State Historical Society, 1954. F635 .W5.

Early Settlers

Berg, Francie M. *Ethnic Heritage in North Dakota.* Washington, D.C.: Attiyel Foundation, 1983. F645 .A1E85.

Dakota Territory. Vols. 1–4. Rapid City, S.D.: The Staff of the *Quarterly,* n.d. F650 .D34.
Covers 1969 to 1973.

Erickson, Marjorie, and Gertrude Olson, eds. *Pioneer Sons and Daughters: History of Adams County.* Hettinger, N.D.: Dakota Buttes Historical Society, 1980. F642 .A2P56.

Pembina Settlement Heritage. A History of the Pembina North Dakota Area. Dallas, Tex.: Taylor Publishing Co., 1976. F642 .P4P45.

Sherman, William C. *Prairie Mosaic: An Ethnic Atlas of Rural North Dakota.* Fargo: North Dakota Institute for Regional Studies, 1982. F645 .A1S54.

Slope Saga. Slope City, N.D.: Slope Sage Commission, 1976. F642 .S6S55.

Directories

City

Bismarck
(Mandan, Burleigh Co.) 1884, 1914–20, 1928, 1932, 1938–83

Devil's Lake 1909, 1971–80

Dickinson
(Billings, Dunn, Stark Co.) 1910–19, 1967–81

Fargo
(Dilworth, Moorehead, Riverside, W. Fargo) 1883, 1891–1984

Grafton 1964–82

Grand Forks
(E. Grand Forks) 1889–1984

Jamestown
(Stutsman Co.) 1912–20, 1930, 1932, 1937–83

Mandan
(Bismarck, Grant Co., Morton Co.) 1912, 1915, 1917, 1938–66

Minot
(Ward Co.) 1922, 1924, 1930, 1933, 1938, 1940, 1945, 1949–84

Valley City
(Barnes Co.) 1906, 1908, 1914, 1916, 1927, 1937, 1947, 1952, 1955–67, 1971–84

Wahpeton 1905, 1910, 1972–82

Williston
(Williams Co.) 1911, 1916, 1918, 1959–81

County, Business, and Miscellaneous

North Dakota (see also Minnesota)
  (state) 1955, 1958
   North Dakota State Gazetteer, 1921–22. F634.7 .N87.

Richland 1891

Sheridan 1913

Ward 1905–17

South Dakota

Historical Highlights

1803	Part of the Louisiana Purchase from France.
1861	Dakota Territory established.

South Dakota was originally designated part of the Missouri Territory. Subsequent designations put eastern parts in the territories of Minnesota, Iowa, Wisconsin, and Michigan; western parts were designated part of the Nebraska Territory until the Dakota Territory was established. Until 1864, parts of Montana and Wyoming were also designated part of the Dakota Territory.

1887	South Dakota Territory established.
1889	Admitted to the Union.

Enactment of the Homestead Laws of 1862, discovery of gold in the Black Hills in 1874, and expanded rail service from eastern states led to growth of immigration. Settlers primarily came from Minnesota, Iowa, Wisconsin, and Illinois, with a heavy influx of Scandinavians, as well as Czechs, Poles, Germans, and German-Russians, most of whom had previously immigrated to nearby states.

Published Record Sources

Guidebooks

Laubersheimer, Sue, ed. *A Selected Annotated Bibliography: South Dakota. Changing, Changeless, 1889–1989.* Pierre: South Dakota Library Association, 1985. Z1335 .S66.

Parker, Watson, and Hugh Lambert. *Black Hills Ghost Towns.* Chicago: Swallow Press, 1974. F657 .B6P29.

Sneve, Virginia Driving Hawk, ed. *South Dakota Geographic Names.* Sioux Falls: Brevet Press, 1973. F649 .S58.

Turchen, Lesta V., and James D. McLaird. *County and Community: A Bibliography of South Dakota Local Histories.* Mitchell, S.D.: the author, 1979. Z1335 .T87.

Writer's Program, South Dakota. *South Dakota Place-names.* Vermillion, S.D.: University of South Dakota, 1940. F649 .W75.

Census Indexes and Abstracts

Federal

1860	F650 .J29
1870	F650 .J3

Both of the above publications are by Ronald V. Jackson, Accelerated Indexing Systems.

1895	South Dakota. Commissioner of Labor Statistics and Census. *Census Report of South Dakota for 1895.* Pierre: State of South Dakota, 1895. HA631.5.

Mortality Schedules

1880	Jackson, Ronald V. *Dakota Territorial 1880 Mortality Schedule.* Bountiful, Utah: Accelerated Indexing Systems, 1980. F650 .J325.

Biographies

Coursey, Oscar W. *Who's Who in South Dakota.* 5 vols. Mitchell, S.D.: University of South Dakota, 1940. F649 .W75. 1914 ed., F650 .C86.

Dvorak, Joseph A., comp. *Memorial Book. History of the Czechs in the State of South Dakota.* Tabor, S.D.: The Czech Heritage Research Society, 1980. F660 .B67D8813.

Graber, Arthur, comp. *Swiss Mennonite Ancestors and Their Relationship From 1775.* Freeman, S.D.: Pine Hill Press, 1980. F660 .M45G7.

Swiss-Germans in South Dakota (From Volhnia to Dakota Territory), 1874–1924. Freeman, S.D.: Pine Hill Press, 1974. F660 .S9S94.

Local Records

Some Black Hills Area Cemeteries. 3 vols. in 1. Rapid City: Rapid City Society for Genealogical Research, 1973. Reprint. N.p.: n.p., 1979. F657 .B6S66.

Directories

City

Deadwood
(Lead, Spearfish, Lawrence Co.) 1962–72

Huron 1908–83

Lead
(Deadwood, Spearfish, Lawrence Co.) 1974–81

Mitchel
(Davison Co.) 1903–15, 1928, 1930, 1937–85

Pierre
(Fort Pierre, Hughes Co., Sully Co.) 1884, 1890, 1910, 1913, 1961–83

Rapid City
(Rapid Valley, Pennington Co.) 1918, 1928–83

Watertown
(Lake Kampeska, Codington Co.) 1909, 1916, 1919, 1926, 1929, 1939, 1942, 1948–82

Yankton
(Yankton Co.) 1892, 1925, 1940, 1949–83

County, Business, and Miscellaneous

Lincoln 1942, 1947

Meade 1939

Minnehaha 1939, 1941

South Dakota (see also Minnesota)
(state) 1913

Nebraska

Historical Highlights

1803   Part of the Louisiana Purchase from France.

1812   Designated part of Missouri Territory.

1834   Divided into three sections, each placed in different territories: Arkansas, Michigan, Missouri.

Populated only by Indians until the first white settlement at Bellevue in 1810. Migration increased with the use of the Oregon Trail along the Platte River when people headed to the California gold mines and the west in general. Most settlers were from the eastern states, but large numbers of Germans arrived after the Homestead laws were enacted in 1862 and the railroad arrived. As settlers came during the 1850s, Indians began to cede many of their lands to the United States.

1867   Admitted to the Union.

Published Record Sources

Guidebooks

Fitzpatrick, Lilian L. *Nebraska Place-names.* University of Nebraska Press, 1960. F664 .F55.

Perkey, Elton A. *Nebraska Place-names.* Lincoln: Nebraska State Historical Society, 1982. F661 .N3.

Census Indexes and Abstracts

Federal

1860   F665 .J33

Mortality Schedules

1860   F665 .J328
1870   F665 .J3285
1880   F665 .J329

All the above publications are by Ronald V. Jackson, Accelerated Indexing Systems, Bountiful, Utah.

Biographies

Biographical and Genealogical History of South-eastern Nebraska. 2 vols. New York: Lewis Publishing Co., 1904. F666 .B6.

Biographical Souvenir of the Counties of Buffalo, Kearney, Phelps, Harlan, and Franklin, Nebraska. Chicago: F.A. Batty & Co., 1890. Reprint. Omaha: Nebraska State Genealogy Society, 1983. CT246 .B56.

Compendium of History: Reminiscences and Biography of Western Nebraska. Chicago: Alden Publishing Co., 1909. F665 .C73.

Illustrated Biographical Album of Northwestern Nebraska. Omaha: National Publishing Co., 1893. F665 .I29.

Memorial and Biographical Records and Illustrations. Compendium of Biography of Butler, Polk, Seward, York and Fillmore Counties, Nebraska. Chicago: Charles A. Ogle & Co., 1899. F665 .M53.

Morton, Julius S. *Illustrated History of Nebraska*. 3 vols. Lincoln: Jacob North & Co., 1905. F666 .M89.

Omaha Bee. *Nebraskans, 1854–1904*. Omaha: Bee Publishing Co., 1904. F665 .05.

Portrait and Biographical Album of Otoe and Cass Counties, Nebraska. Chicago: Chapman Press, 1889. F665 .P6.

Who's Who in Nebraska. Lincoln: Nebraska Press Association, 1940. F665 .W56.

Early Settlers

Sobotka, Margie, comp. *Czech Immigrant Passenger List (for Nebraska), 1879*. N.p.: the compiler, 1982. F675 .B67S63.

Periodicals

Loudon, Betty L., comp. *Index-Guide. Nebraska History Magazine, Vols. 40–60 (1959–79)*. Vol. 29. Lincoln: Nebraska Historical Society, 1984. F661 .N3.

Sittler, Melvin. *Sittler Index of Surnames for Which Information Has Been Extracted from the Lincoln Nebraska State Journal, 1873–99*. 4 vols. Lincoln: Lincoln-Lancaster Genealogical Society, 1984. F672 .L4S57.

Directories

City

Alliance 1986

Beatrice
(Cage Co.) 1893, 1904, 1925–83

Bellevue
(suburbs, Papillion) 1966–68

Crete
(Saline Co.) 1964

Fairbury
(Jefferson Co.) 1960–80

Falls City
(Richardson Co.) 1960–82

Freemont 1885, 1893, 1903–31, 1935–43, 1947–84

Grand Island
(Hall Co.) 1908, 1912, 1964, 1969–84

Hastings
(Adams Co.) 1893, 1903–84

Kearney
(Buffalo Co.) 1909–17, 1922–26, 1931, 1933, 1937–41, 1947–83

Lincoln 1878, 1883, 1889, 1899, 1983

McCook 1931, 1948, 1953–83

Nebraska City
(Otoe Co.) 1891, 1893, 1960–81

New York 1907, 1909, 1912, 1973

Norfolk
(Madison Co., Buffalo Co. 1950) 1896, 1911–84

North Platte
(Lincoln Co.) 1947–83

Oakland
(Uehling) 1951

Omaha 1861–1935, 1936–84 (microfilm)

Scottsbluff
  (Gering, N. Platte Valley, Scotts Bluff Co.) 1918, 1920,
    1926–34, 1941, 1945, 1948–84

South Omaha 1892, 1894, 1899

South Sioux City
  (Dakota Co.) 1957, 1960–85

Valentine 1963

County, Business, and Miscellaneous

Butler 1918

Dakota (see Woodbury, Iowa)

Douglas
  (Sarpy) 1963–83

Hall 1956

Jefferson 1924

Lancaster 1946

Nebraska (state) 1879, 1882–93, 1907–17

Polk 1916–24

Sarpy 1963–83

Sarpy (see Douglas)

Thayer 1924

Montana

Historical Highlights

1803　　Part of Louisiana Purchase from France.

1805　　Explored by Lewis and Clark.

1846　　Ceded by England to the United States, in
　　　　accordance with the Oregon Treaty.

　　　　Prior to obtaining the area from France, the
　　　　white men in the area were mainly French,
　　　　Scotch, and a few English fur traders. Set-
　　　　tlement was very limited and continued to
　　　　be slow for many decades.

1862　　Gold discovered.

1863　　Designated part of the Oregon Territory.

1864　　Montana Territory established; Virginia
　　　　City named its capital.

1866–76　Indian wars.

　　　　The presence of Indians continued to slow
　　　　settlement. The coming of the railroad and
　　　　discovery of gold (and copper and silver
　　　　twenty years later) attracted European set-
　　　　tlers who worked the mines. They came
　　　　from Ireland, Germany, Austria, Poland,
　　　　Czechoslovakia, and other countries.

1867　　First federal land office in the territory.

1889　　Admitted to the Union.

Published Record Sources

Guidebooks

Cheney, Roberta C. *Names on the Face of Montana.
  The Story of Montana's Place Names.* Missoula:
  University of Montana, 1971. F729 .C5.

Davis, Jean W., comp. *Shallow Diggin's: Tales From
  Montana Ghost Towns.* Caldwell, Idaho: Caxton
  Printers, 1962. F731 .D25.

Miller, Don C. *Ghost Towns of Montana.* Boulder,
  Colo.: Pruett Publishing Co., 1974. F731 .M62.

Census Indexes and Abstracts

1870　　Jackson, Ronald V. *Montana Territory
　　　　1870 Census Index.* Bountiful, Utah:
　　　　Accelerated Indexing Systems, n.d.
　　　　F730 .J32.
　　　　Marshall, Thelma L., comp. *Montana Ter-
　　　　ritory 1870 Census Index.* Great Falls:
　　　　Licini's Print Shop, 1979. F730 .M18.

Biographies

Burlingame, Merrill G. *A History of Montana.* Vol.
  3, *Family and Personal History.* New York: Lewis
  Historical Publishing Co., 1957. F731 .B95.

Progressive Men of the State of Montana. Chicago:
  A. M. Bowen & Co., ca. 1905. F730 .P7.

Progressive Years. Madison County. Vol. 2, *1920–50.* Great Falls: Madison County History Association, 1983. F731 .M2M33.

Stout, Tom. *Montana: Its Story and Biography.* 3 vols. Chicago: American Historical Society, 1921. F737 .S875.

Early Settlers

Pioneer Trails and Trials: Madison County, 1863–1920. Vol. 1. Great Falls: Madison County Historical Association, 1976. F737 .M2M33.

Raymer, Robert G. *Montana. The Land and the People.* 3 vols. Chicago: Lewis Publishing Co., 1930. F731 .R26.

Sanders, James U., ed. *Society of Montana Pioneers: Constitution, Members, and Officers.* Vol. 1, *Register.* Akron, Ohio: the society, 1899. F726 .S6.

Local Records

Moog Una. *Cemetery Inscriptions and Church Records . . . .* Chester, Mont.: Broken Mountains Genealogical Society, 1986. F730 .M66.

Directories

City

Anaconda 1956–65

Billings
(Laurel, Red Lodge, Carbon Co., Yellowstone Co.) 1901–82

Bozeman
(Gallatin Co.) 1892, 1900–82

Butte 1890–1983

Dillon City
(Beaverhead Co.) 1906–17

Glasgow
(Valley Co.) 1962, 1964

Glendive
(W. Glendive) 1964-65, 1970–74

Great Falls
(Black Eagle, Cascade Co.) 1901–80

Hardin 1965–66

Havre 1929–33, 1938, 1941, 1947, 1954–80

Helena 1887–1985

Kalispell
(Columbia Falls, Flathead, Whitefish, Lincoln Co.) 1966–75

Lewiston
(Judith Basin, Fergus Co., Petroleum Co.) 1904–83

Livingston
(Big Timber, Park, Sweet Grass Co.) 1904–82

Miles City
(Ekalaka, Forsythe, Glendive, Custer Co., Rosebud Co.) 1948, 1952–83

Missoula
(Hamilton, Stevensville, Ravalli Co.) 1891, 1901–17, 1922–83

Sidney
(Fairview) 1964-65, 1971, 1977, 1980

County, Business, and Miscellaneous

Blaine (see Hill)

Cascade 1915

Fergus 1916

Hill
(Blaine, Chouteau) 1913

Jefferson (see Madison)

Madison
(Jefferson) 1915

Missoula 1915

Montana (see also Minnesota)
(state) 1884

Montana Territory
1861–81 (microfilm)

Park 1915

Wyoming

Historical Highlights

1805   Explored by Lewis and Clark.

1807   Yellowstone area explored by John Coulter.

1834   Fort Laramie established.

1843   Fort Bridger established.

1868   Territory of Wyoming established.

Very few who traveled through Wyoming en route to California chose to stay. Forts at Laramie and Bridger served as way stations for the western bound travellers and for protection from hostile Indians. Even with land available in the public domain (Homestead Law of 1862 and Desert Land Act of 1877), few settled there. Eventually, the area became a huge cattle pasture and settlers from midwestern and southern states arrived to engage in cattle ranching. Joining them were European immigrants from England, Germany, and several other countries. Immigration was only somewhat increased as a result of the coming of the railroad in 1869.

1890   Admitted to the Union.

Published Record Sources

Guidebooks

Historical Encyclopedia of Wyoming. 2 vols. Cheyenne: Wyoming Historical Society, 1970. F761 .H5.

Pence, Mary Lou, and Lola M. Hamsher. *The Ghost Towns of Wyoming.* New York: Hastings House, 1956. F761 .P4.

Census Indexes and Abstracts

1870   F760 .J29

1880   F760 .J3

1910   Dilts, Bryan L., comp. *1910 Wyoming Census Index Microforms.* Salt Lake City: Index Publishing Co., 1985.

The above publications shown without the name of the compiler are by Ronald V. Jackson, Accelerated Indexing Systems.

Biographies

Bartlett, Ichabod S., ed. *History of Wyoming.* 3 vols. Chicago: S. J. Clarke Publishing Co., 1918. F761 .B28.

Beach, Cora M. *Women of Wyoming.* 2 vols. Casper: the author, 1927. F760 .B36.

Beard, Frances B., ed. *Wyoming From Territorial Days to the Present.* 3 vols. Chicago: American Historical Society, 1933. F761 .B36.

Progressive Men of the State of Wyoming. Chicago: A.W. Bowen & Co., 1903. F760 .P9.

Early Settlers

Burns, Robert H., Andrew S. Gillespie, and William C. Richardson. *Wyoming's Pioneer Families.* Laramie: Top-of-the-World Press, 1955. F761 .B88.

Directories

City

Casper
(Natrona Co.) 1917–82

Cheyenne 1905–26, 1931–85

Gillette 1963

Giowanda
(Cattarangus, E. Otto, Otto, S. Dayton) 1964

Laramie
(Albany Co.) 1911–83

Rawlins 1976

Riverton 1985

Rock Springs
(Green River, Sweetwater Co.) 1931, 1934, 1939, 1944, 1950, 1954–81

Tarrington 1963

Thermopolis 1963

County, Business, and Miscellaneous

Wyoming (state) 1904, 1912, 1919, 1932

Idaho

Historical Highlights

1805   Explored by Lewis and Clark.

1846   In accordance with the Webster-Ashburton Treaty, ceded by England to the United States.

1853   Northern part designated part of Washington Territory; southern part remained as part of Oregon Territory but was later also designated part of Washington Territory.

1860   Believing it was within Utah, Mormons from England established Franklin.

1863   Idaho Territory established.

Among the first settlers were miners, missionaries, and farmers from other states. Discovery of gold spurred many to come seeking wealth; others came to provide commercial support. Farmers and cattle raisers settled in southeast Idaho, and the population grew throughout the balance of the nineteenth century.

1890   Admitted to the Union.

Published Record Sources

Guidebooks

Federal Writers Program. *The Idaho Encyclopedia.* Caldwell, Idaho: State of Idaho, 1938. F746 .F46.

Miller, Don C. *Ghost Towns of Idaho.* Boulder, Colo.: Pruett Publishing Co., 1976. F746 .M5.

Sparling, Wayne. *Southern Idaho Ghost Towns.* Caldwell, Idaho: Caxton Printers, 1974. F746 .S64.

Census Indexes and Abstracts

Federal

1870   Idaho Genealogical Society. *Idaho Territory Federal Population Schedules and Mortality Schedules 1870.* Boise: the society, n.d. F745 .I27.
Jackson, Ronald V. *Idaho Territory 1870 Census Index.* Bountiful, Utah: Accelerated Indexing Systems. F745 .J284.

1880   Idaho Genealogical Society. *Idaho Territory Federal Population Schedules and Mortality Schedules, 1880.* Boise: the society, 1976. F745 .I27.
Jackson, Ronald V. *Idaho Territory 1880 Census Index.* Bountiful, Utah: Accelerated Indexing Systems, n.d. F745 .J285.

Mortality Schedules

1870   (See Federal 1870 above.)

1880   (See Federal 1880 above.)

Biographies

Beal, Merrill D. *History of Idaho.* Vol. 2, *Personal and Family History.* New York: Lewis Historical Publishing Co., 1959. F746 .B335.

French, Hiram T. *History of Idaho.* 3 vols. Chicago: Lewis Publishing Co., 1914. F746 .F87.

Hawley, James H., ed. *History of Idaho the Gem of the Mountains.* 4 vols. Chicago: S. J. Clarke Publishing Co., 1920. F746 .H39.

Illustrated History of North Idaho; Embracing Nez Perce, Idaho, Latah, Kootenai and Shoshone Counties. N.p.: Western Historical Publishing Co., 1903. F746 .I28.

Progressive Men of Bannock, Bear Lake, Bingham, Fremont, and Oneida Counties, Idaho. Chicago: A.W. Bowen & Co., 1904. F745 .P96.

Land Acquisition

Thousands of Idaho Surnames: Abstracted From Rejected Federal Land Applications. 5 vols. Portland, Oreg.: Genealogical Forum of Portland, Oregon, 1980. F745 .T47.

Local Records

Powell, Barbara V. *Citizens of North Idaho. Nez Perce County Vital Statistics: Probate Courts, Births, Deaths.* Medical Lake, Wash.: the author, 1986. F745 .P68.

Periodicals

Powell, Barbara V. *Citizens of North Idaho: Newspaper Abstracts, 1862–1875.* Medical Lake, Wash.: the author, 1986. F745 .P68.

Directories

City

Blackfoot
(Aberdeen, Firth, Shelley, Bingham Co.) 1960–84

Boise
(suburbs, Ada Co.) 1901–83

Burley 1959–80

Caldwell
(Nampa, Canyon Co.) 1948–82

Coeur D'Alene
(Kootenai Co.) 1910, 1923–40, 1947–83

Idaho Falls
(Bingham, Bonneville, Butte, Clark, Fremont, Jefferson, Madison) 1911–30, 1939, 1941, 1946–84

Jasper 1954, 1968–84

Jerome 1938

Kootenai
(Bonner, Shoshone) 1912–16

Lewiston
(Clarkston City, Wa.; Asotin Co., Wa.; Nez Perce Co.) 1903, 1931, 1948

Montpelier
(Bancroft, Georgetown, Grace, Paris, Soda Springs, Bear Lake Co., Caribou Co.) 1961

Moscow
(Clearwater; Latah; Nez Perce Co.; Pullman, Wa.; Asotin Co., Wa.) 1909, 1912, 1914, 1916, 1957–80

Muscatine 1889–99, 1929–84

Nampa
(Caldwell, Parma, Canyon Co.) 1945–82

Payette
(Weiser; Ontario, Oreg.) 1945, 1951, 1955, 1962, 1964

Pocatello
(American Falls, Chubbeck, Alameda Co., Bannock Co.) 1902–27, 1934–42, 1946–83

Rexburg
(Rigby, Sugar City) 1960

Rupert
(Minidoka Co.) 1959–77

Sandpoint
(Bonner Co.) 1910

Twin Falls
(Buhl City, Cassia Co., Gooding Co., Jerome Co., Minidoka Co.) 1923, 1925, 1928, 1930, 1936–83

Wallace
(Shoshone Co.) 1908, 1910, 1924

Weiser City
(Adams Co., Washington Co.) 1913, 1915

County, Business, and Miscellaneous

Blaine (see Twin Falls)

Camus (see Twin Falls)

Canyon
1913, 1915
(Gem, Fayette, Washington) 1916–26, 1930, 1936

Cassia (see also Twin Falls)
1917

Gem (see Canyon)

Gooding (see Twin Falls)

Idaho (see also Oregon and Washington)
(state) 1901–18

Jerome (see Twin Falls)

Latah
(Nez Perce) 1905, 1907

Lincoln (see Twin Falls)

Minidoka (see Twin Falls)

Nez Perce (see also Latah)
1908, 1910, 1919

Payette (see Canyon)

Twin Falls
(Blaine, Cassia, Gooding, Lincoln, Minidoka) 1914, 1916, 1918

(Cassia, Lincoln) 1912

Washington (see Canyon)

Washington

Historical Highlights

1778   Explored by English captains James Cook and George Vancouver. Although previously explored by the Spanish, after Cook and Vancouver arrived, England claimed the area.

1806   Explored by Lewis and Clark.

1810   Fur trading post at Spokane built by a British-Canadian firm.

1811   Fur company built near Spokane (Astoria) by John Jacob Astor, an American.

1814   Astoria captured by the British during the War of 1812; it was returned to the United States following the war.

1818   Oregon region (including Washington region) jointly controlled by England and the United States.

         Few settlers came to the region and both England and the United States claimed jurisdiction based on their respective fur businesses. Commercial groups came to set up business in the area, and forts and missions were established to protect and support them.

1846   Northern boundary between Canada agreed to by England and the United States.

1848   Oregon Territory established and included Washington.

1852   Washington Territory created.

         The population being heavily male, consisting of miners and fur traders plus a few farmers, a project to bring young women (the Mercer girls) from New England to become school teachers and wives was im-

plemented in 1864 and 1866. The completion of railroad lines in 1883 and 1893 spurred immigration, although some Washington residents moved on to Idaho and Alaska when gold was discovered there. Those who remained turned to fishing, farming, and apple raising.

1889   Admitted to the Union.

Published Record Sources

Guidebooks

Abbott, Newton C., and Fred E. Carva. *The Evolution of Washington Counties.* Yakima: Yakima Valley Genealogical Society and the Klickitat County Historical Society, 1978. F891 .A23.

Hitchman, Robert. *Place Names of Washington.* N.p.: Washington State Historical Society, 1985. F889 .H57.

Miller, Don C. *Ghost Towns of Washington and Oregon.* Boulder, Colo.: Pruett Publishing Co., 1977. F891 .M54.

Phillips, James W. *Washington State Place Names.* Seattle: University of Washington Press, 1971. F889 .P47.

Census Indexes and Abstracts

Federal

1860   F870 .W315
        Stucki, J. U., comp. *Index to the First Federal Census, Territory of Washington, 1860.* Huntsville, Ark.: Century Enterprises, Genealogical Services, 1972. F890 .S8.

1870   F890 .J29

1880   F890 .J3

All the above publications shown without the name of the compiler are by Ronald V. Jackson, Accelerated Indexing Systems.

State

Lines, Jack M. *Klickitat County Territorial Census, 1871, 1883, 1885, 1887, 1889.* Yakima, Wash.:

Yakima Valley Genealogical Society, 1983. F897 .K6L56.

Biographies

Bagley, Clarence B. *History of King County, Washington*. Vols. 2 and 3, *Biographical*. Chicago: S. J. Clarke Publishing Co., 1929. F897 .K4B14.

Hawthorne, Julian, ed. *History of Washington*. 2 vols. New York: American History Publishing Co., 1893. F891 .H3.

Hines, Harvey K. *An Illustrated History of the State of Washington*. Chicago: Lewis Publishing Co., 1893. F891 .H66.

Illustrated History of Big Bend Country: Embracing Lincoln, Douglas, Adams, and Franklin Counties. Spokane: Western Historical Publishing Co., 1904. F897 .C7I29.

Illustrated History of Klickitat, Yakima, and Killitas Counties, With an Outline of the Early History of Washington. N.p.: Interstate Publishing Co., 1904. F897 .K613.

Illustrated History of Southeastern Washington, Including Walla Walla, Columbia, Garfield and Asotin Counties. Spokane: Western Historical Publishing Co., 1906. F897 .A18I29.

Stewart, Edgar I. *Washington: Northwest Frontier*. Vols. 3 and 4, *Family and Personal History*. New York: Lewis Publishing Co., 1957. F891 .S87.

Land Acquisition

Washington Territory Donation Land Claims. An Abstract of Information in the Land Claim Papers of Persons Who Settled in Washington Territory Before 1856. Seattle: Seattle Genealogical Society, 1980. F890 .W328.

Local Records

Buckley-King Mortuary Records, 1833–1903. Tacoma: Tacoma-Pierce County Genealogical Society, 1984. F890 .B83.

Catholic Church Records of the Pacific Northwest: Vancouver. Vols. 1 and 2, *Stellamarie Mission*. St. Paul, Oreg.: French Prairie Press, 1972. F880 .C3713.

Winters, Jean. *Early Military Tombstone Inscriptions in Washington State*. Pasco, Wash.: the author, 1982. F890 .W5.

Directories

City

Aberdeen
(Hoquiam) 1939–82

Anacortes 1966

Auburn
(Algona, Pacific) 1968–75

Bellevue
(suburbs, Kirkland) 1959–84

Bellingham
(Whatcom Co.) 1904–82

Bremerton
(Port Orchard, Kitsap Co.) 1909–84

Burien
(White Center) 1960–74

Camus
(Washougal) 1938

Centralia
(Chehalis, Lewis Co.) 1939–83

Ellensburg
(Kittitas Co.) 1904–80

Enumclaw
(Buckley) 1967–74

Ephrata
(Soap Lake) 1953–80

Everett
(Snohomish Co.) 1893, 1901–84

Grays Harbor
(Aberdeen, Elma, Hoquiam, Montesano, Chehalis Co.) 1907–13

Kelso
(Longview) 1940–84

Longview 1925, 1929

Lynwood 1967–73

Marysville 1936, 1958

Moses Lake 1953–83

Mountlake Terrace 1968–73

Mt. Vernon
(Burlington, Sedro Woolley) 1962, 1965, 1973–81

Oak Harbor 1965

Olympia
(Lacey, Tumwater, Mason Co., Thurston Co.) 1902,
1909–85

Omak
(Okanogan) 1955

Pasco
(Kennewick, Richland) 1952–83

Port Angeles
(Forks, Jefferson, Port Townsend, Sequim, Clallam
Co.) 1907–80

Port Townsend 1962

Puyallup
(Graham, Orting, N. Puyallup, Sumner) 1947–84

Quincy 1967–83

Renton
(Bryn Mawr, Kennydale) 1947–74

Seattle
pre 1861 (microfiche)
1861–1901, 1902–85 (microfilm)

Sedro Woolley
(E. Skagit Co.) 1959, 1963

Shelton 1960–68

Snohomish
(Monroe) 1954, 1957, 1959

Spokane
(suburbs, Greenacres, Liberty Lake, Veradale) 1892–
1984

Spokane Falls 1889-90

Spokane Valley
(Dishman, Green Acres, Millwood, Opportunity, Orchard Ave., Otis Orchards) 1936

Sunnyside
(Grandview, Prosser) 1964, 1966, 1968

Tacoma
(suburbs) 1889–1985
(Seattle) 1907–09

Vancouver
(Camas, Washougal) 1907–21, 1928–40, 1946–83

Walla Walla 1893, 1902–67

Weirton 1964–85

Wenatchee
(Cashmere, Chelan, E. Wenatchee, Douglas Co.)
1907, 1909, 1922–42, 1946–84

Whatcom
(Whatcom Co.) 1902-03

Yakima
(N. Yakima, Yakima Co.) 1913–85

County, Business, and Miscellaneous

Adams
(Franklin) 1908–10
(Lincoln) 1912–18

Benton
(Franklin, Klickitat) 1911–16

Chehalis (see Grays Harbor)

Chelan
(Douglas, Grant, Okanogan) 1910–21

Douglas (see Chelan)

Ferry (see Stevens)

Franklin (see Adams and Benton)

Garfield (see Whitman)

Grant (see Chelan)

Grays Harbor (city)
(Chehalis) 1903, 1905, 1915–24

King (see North King)

Latah (see Whitman)

Lewis 1904, 1908–37

Lincoln (see also Adams) 1908–10

North King
(Snohomish, southern) 1974

Okanogan (see Chelan)

Pacific (see Lewis)

Pend Oreille (see Stevens)

Pierce 1911, 1915

Shilauguamish Valley 1955

Skagit 1902, 1907–17, 1923, 1929, 1937, 1941, 1948, 1959,
1962

Snohomish (see North King)

Snohomish, southwest 1962

South King 1976–83

Spokane 1909–19

Stevens
(Ferry, Pend Oreille) 1909, 1911–16

Washington (state) (see Oregon and Pacific Coast)

Whitman
(Garfield, Latah) 1904, 1908–17, 1921, 1930

Yakima 1903–11, 1971

Oregon

Historical Highlights

1778	Following explorations by the Spanish, the coastal area was explored by Captain James Cook from England.
1805	Explored by Lewis and Clark. Fort Clatsop built on the Columbia River.
1811	Fur trading company established by John Jacob Astor, an American; later transferred to the Northwest Company and then to the Hudson Bay Company.
1819	Southern border agreed to by treaty between Spain and the United States.
1946	Wagon trains brought farmers from eastern states. Farmers from eastern states and immigrants from Europe came over the Oregon Trail in covered wagons. Northern border agreed to by treaty between England and the United States.
1850	Oregon Donation Land Law enacted. With free land offered to settlers willing to remain and improve the property, population increased due to an influx of settlers from eastern states and Europe.
1853	Washington Territory separated from Oregon Territory.
1863	Gold seekers joined farmers and other migrant settlers. After statehood, a project was implemented to bring young women (Mercer girls) to the area to teach school and to marry.

Published Record Sources

Guidebooks

McArthur, Louis A., ed. *Oregon Geographic Names.* 5th ed. N.p.: Press of Oregon Historical Society and the editor, 1982. F874 .M16.

Census Indexes and Abstracts

1850	F875 .J3 Pompey, Sherman L., comp. *The 1850 Census Records of Oregon Territory.* Albany, Oreg.: the compiler, 1985–86. F875 .P2.
1860	F875 .J33 Dilts, Bryan L., comp. *1860 Oregon Census Index Microforms.* Salt Lake City: Index Publishing Co., 1983. (Micro 87/2009).
1870	F875 .J34 Dilts, Bryan L., comp. *1870 Oregon Census Index Microforms.* Salt Lake City: Index Publishing Co., 1985. (Micro 87/2000).

Biographies

Brandt, Patricia, and Nancy Guildford, eds. *Oregon Biography Index.* Corvallis, Oreg.: Oregon State University, 1976. Z5305 .U5B7.

Capitol's Who's Who For Oregon, 1936–37. Portland: Capitol Publishing Co., 1936. F875 .C35.

Cogswell, Philip, Jr. *Capitol Names. Individuals Woven in Oregon's History.* Portland: Oregon Historical Society, 1977. CT256 .C63.

Corning, Howard M. *Dictionary of Oregon History.* Portland: Binford & Mort, 1956. F874 .C6.

Gaston, Joseph. *The Centennial History of Oregon, 1811–1912.* 4 vols. Chicago: S. J. Clarke Publishing Co., 1912. F876 .G25.

Illustrated History of Baker, Grant, Malheur, and Harney Counties; With a Brief Outline of Early History of the State of Oregon. Spokane: Western History Publishing Co., 1902. F876 .I29.

Illustrated History of Central Oregon; Embracing Wasco, Sherman, Gilliam, Wheeler, Crook, Lake, and Klamath Counties. Spokane: Western History Publishing Co., 1905. F876 .I3.

Portrait and Biographical Records of Western Oregon. Chicago: Chapman Publishing Co., n.d. F875 .P85.

Portrait and Biographical Record of the Willamette Valley, Oregon. Chicago: Chapman Publishing Co., 1903. F882 .W6P8.

Land Acquisition

Genealogical Material in Oregon Donation Land Claims. 5 vols. Portland, Oreg.: n.p., 1957. F875 .G4.

> Abstracted from Applications by the Genealogical Forum of Portland, Oregon.

Gurley, Lottie L. *Genealogical Material in Oregon Provisional Land Claims, Abstracted. 1845–1859.* 8 vols. Portland: Genealogical Forum of Portland, Oregon, 1982. F875 .G8.

Early Settlers

Bond, Rowland. *Early Birds in the Northwest.* Nine Mile Falls, Wash.: Spokane House Enterprises, 1983. F880 .B69.

Local Records

Munnick, Harriette E., comp. *Catholic Church Records of the Pacific Northwest: Oregon City Register (1842–1890); Salem Register (1864–1885); Jacksonville Register (1854–1885).* Portland: Binford & Mort, 1984. F875 .M86.

———. *Catholic Church Records of the Pacific Northwest: Roseburg Register and Missions (1853–1911); Portland Register (1852–1871).* Portland: Binford & Mort, 1986. F885 .C3M86.

———. *Catholic Church Records of the Pacific Northwest: St. Louis Register, Vol. 1 (1845–1968); St. Louis Register, Vol. 2 (1869–1900); Gervais Register (1875–1893); Brooks Register (1893–1909).* Portland: Binford & Mort, 1982. F875 .C365.

———. *Catholic Church Records of the Pacific Northwest: St. Paul. Vols. 1, 2, 3 (1839–1898).* Portland: Binford & Mort, 1979. F875 .C37.

Oregon. Department of Transportation. *Oregon Cemetery Survey.* Salem: State of Oregon, 1978. F877 .O63.

> Contains names of cemeteries, not people.

Periodicals

Beaver Briefs, Index to Vols. 1–10 (1969–1978). Supplement. Salem: Willamette Valley Genealogical Society, 1968. F882 .W6B4 supplement.

Connette, Earle, comp. *Pacific Northwest Quarterly Index.* Hamden, Conn.: Shoe String Press, 1964. F886 .W28.

Directories

City

Albany
(Lebanon, Sweet Home, Linn Co.) 1905, 1946–47

Ashland
(Central Pt., Drain, Gold Hill, Grants Pass, Hopkinton, Jacksonville, Medford, Oakland, Phoenix, Roseburg, Talent, Upton, Yoncalla) 1906–07, 1912, 1964

Astoria
(Gearhart, Hammond, Seaside, Warrenton, Westport, Clatsop Co.) 1890, 1904–25, 1931–81

Baker City
(Haines, Huntington, La Grande, Union, Umatilla, Baker Co.) 1893, 1908–10, 1925–39, 1941–56, 1966–80

Beaverton
(Aloha, Cedar Hills, Fairvale, Huber, Portland Hgts., W. Slope) 1959–84

Bend
(Pineville, Redmond, Deschute Co., Crook Co.) 1936–80

Coos Bay
(North Bend) 1954

Corvallis
(Philomath) 1951–84

Dallas
  (Wasco, Sherman Co.) 1883, 1905, 1917–30, 1936, 1946–84

Eugene
  (Lane Co.) 1905–1947

Grants Pass
  (Josephine Co.) 1946

Gresham 1962

Hillsboro
  (Forest Grove, Western, Washington Co.) 1952

Hood River
  (Antelope, Dalles, Dufur, Shaniko) 1908, 1948

Klamath Falls
  (Klamath Co.) 1933–84

LaGrande
  (Alicel, Cove, Elgin, Imblen, Island City, Union, Union Co.) 1939–84

Lebanon
  (Sweet Home, East Line Co.) 1950, 1953

McMinnville
  (Newburg, Yamhill Co.) 1947, 1949, 1952

Medford
  (Jackson Co.) 1933–85

Ontario
  (Payette; Weiser, Idaho) 1957, 1959

Oregon City
  (Bolton, Canewah, Gladstone, Park Place, West Linn, Willamette) 1941, 1953, 1960–84

Pendleton
  (Hermiston, Pilot Rock, Stanfield, Weston, Pendleton Co., Umatilla Co.) 1941, 1946–83

Portland
  1861–1901 (microfilm)

Puget Sound (suburbs) 1887-88

Roseburg
  (Douglas Co.) 1946–56

Salem
  (Marion Co.) 1889, 1891, 1893, 1905–17, 1921, 1924–85

Scappoose 1953

Seaside
  (Cannon Beach, Gearhart) 1949, 1952

St. Helens 1968

Tillamook 1968

Wasco
  (Hood River, Sherman Co.) 1910, 1913

County, Business, and Miscellaneous

Benton (see Linn)

Clakamas (see also Multnomah)
  1942, 1947

Coos 1907, 1909, 1913–48

Crook (see Deschutes)

Deschutes
  (Crook, Jefferson) 1921, 1924

Douglas (see Jackson)

Garvin 1935

Gilliam
  (Grant, Morrow, Umatilla) 1959

Grant (see Gilliam)

Harney (see Malheur)

Jackson
  (Josephine, Douglas) 1910, 1911–14, 1921

Jefferson (see Deschutes)

Josephine (see Jackson)

Knox 1915, 1950, 1964, 1976–81

Lincoln 1938, 1950

Linn 1913

Malheur
  (Harney) 1911, 1970, 1972

Multnomah
  (Clackamas, Washington) 1906

Oregon
  (state) 1873, 1881, 1883
  (Idaho, Washington) 1886
  (Alaska, Washington) 1901–26, 1931
  (eastern) 1899

Pendleton (city)
  (Umatilla) 1925–39

Puget Sound (city) 1972

Umatilla (see also Pendleton)
  1912–21

Union
  (Wallowa) 1914, 1917

Wallowa (see Union)

Washington (see Multnomah and Yamhill)

Yamhill
  (Washington) 1909, 1912, 1956

Youngstown (city) 1893

Alaska

Historical Highlights

1728   The northern strait explored by Captain Vitus Bering, a Dane in the service of the Russian navy.

1749   Orthodox Russians colonize Fox Island.

1778   Explored by Captain James Cook.

1791   Explored by Captain George Vancouver.
        Following the establishment at Fox Island, other Russians settled at other Alaska locations, including Kodiak Island. Explorers, fur traders, and fishermen also came, mainly from France, Holland, Portugal, and England, as well as Americans (mostly from Boston). The Hudson Bay Company was established to deal in furs brought in by the native Eskimo hunters.

1824   Location of southern border agreed to by Russia and the United States.

1867   Purchased by the United States from Russia.

1897   Klondike Gold Rush.

1903   Location of boundary between Alaska and Canada agreed to.
        After Russia granted equal trading rights to England and the United States in 1824 and 1825, it began to lose money and decided to sell the region to the United States. Gold discovered in the Klondike and other gold discoveries around the turn of the century attracted miners and settlers.

1912   Alaska Territory established.

1942   Alaska Highway built; following this, American military personnel assigned to Alaska.

1959   Admitted to the Union.

Published Record Sources

Guidebooks

Alaska. Department of Administration. *State of Alaska Geographic Location Codes.* State of Alaska, 1979. F902. A24.

Alaska-Yukon Gazetteer, 1923. Seattle, Wash.: R. L. Polk & Co., 1923. F902.7 .A.

Orth, Donald, Jr. *Dictionary of Alaska Place Names and Geological Survey.* Professional Paper 567. Washington, D.C.: Government Printing Office, 1967. QE75 .P9 No. 567 (F902 .07).

Census Indexes and Abstracts

1870–1907 Jackson, Ronald V. *Alaska Census Records, 1870–1907.* Bountiful, Utah: Accelerated Indexing Systems, 1976. F903 .J32.

1900   Ducker, James H. *Carmack's Alaskans: A Census Study of Alaskans in 1900.* Alaska: n.p., n.d. HA235 .D83.

Biographies

Chase, William H. *Pioneers of Alaska. The Trail Blazers of Bygone Days.* Kansas City, Mo.: Burton Publishing Co., 1951. F901 .C47.

Tewkesbury's Who's Who in Alaska and Alaska Business Index, 1947. Seattle: Tewkesbury Publishing Co., 1947. F903 .T4.

Local Records

Alaska's Kenai Peninsula Death Records and Cemetery Inscriptions. Kenai, Alaska: Kenai Totem Tracers, 1983. F912 .K4A43.

Bradbury, Connie, et al. *Alaska People Index.* 2 vols. Fairbanks: Alaska Historical Commission Studies in History No. 203, 1986. F903 .B7.

Periodicals

Chang, Tohsook P., and Alden M. Rollins, eds. *The Anchorage Times Index, 1915–1965.* Anchorage: University of Alaska, 1979. F903 .A5.

Chang, Tohsook P., ed. *The Anchorage Times Obituaries Index, 1966–1980.* Anchorage: University of Alaska, 1981. F903 .A5.

Directories

City

Anchorage (suburbs) 1960–84

Juneau
(Aulse Bay, Douglas) 1961–81

Ketchikan 1962–82

County, Business, and Miscellaneous

Alaska (territory) (see also Oregon, Washington)
(Yukon state) 1903–18, 1932

CHAPTER 15

Southwestern States

Kansas • Oklahoma • Texas • Colorado
New Mexico • Utah • Arizona • Nevada
California • Hawaii

Holdings that deal with the southwestern states in general include the following:

Dugard, Rene G. *Dictionary of Spanish Place Names.* 4 vols. France: Editions des Deux Mondes, 1983. F851 .C68.

Vol. 1, California; Vol. 2, Oregon, Washington, British Columbia, Alaska; Vol. 3, New Mexico; Vol. 4, Texas, Arizona.

Encyclopedia of the New West . . . Texas, Arkansas, Colorado, New Mexico, Indian Territory. Marshall, Tex.: United States Biographical Publishing, 1881. F385 .S74.

Notable Women of the Southwest. A Pictorial Biographical Encyclopedia of the Leading Women of Texas, New Mexico, Oklahoma, and Arizona. Dallas: William T. Hardy, 1938. F786 .N67.

Southwest Historical Series. 12 vols. Glendale, Calif.: Arthur M. Clark, 1943. F786 .S752.

Volume 12 is an index.

Births, Deaths and Marriages from El Paso Newspapers Through 1885 for Arizona, Texas, New Mexico, Oklahoma, and Indian Territory. Easley, S.C.: Southern Historical Press, 1982. F786 .B63.

Kansas

Historical Highlights

1803   Part of the Louisiana Purchase from France.

1854   Kansas Territory established.

The first significant movement of settlers into Kansas took place in 1821 when the Santa Fe Trail opened a path to the West. Until they were removed to the Indian Territory established by the federal government, hostile Indians prohibited any appreciable population increase. With personal safety more assured, settlers from New England, the Midwest, and the south-central states arrived to form colonies and engage in farming. Immigrants from Germany, Ireland, and other European countries also came, brought in by land companies operating in conjunction with the expanding railroad system. Lured by the hope of religious freedom, they included Quakers, Mennonites, and Baptists, among others.

1861   Admitted to the Union.

Published Record Sources

Guidebooks

Fitzgerald, Daniel. *Ghost Towns of Kansas.* Vol. 3. Holton, Kans.: Bell Graphics, 1982. F681 .F57.

Rydjord, John. *Kansas Place-names.* Norman: University of Oklahoma Press, 1972. F679 .R9.

Census Indexes and Abstracts

Federal

1855   F680 .J35

1860   F680 .J348

Mortality Schedules

1860   F680 .J349
         Franklin, Helen H. *The Mortality Schedule of the Territory of Kansas, 1860.* N.p.: n.d. F680 .F7.

1870   F680 .M65
         Franklin, Helen H. *1870 Mortality Schedule of Kansas.* N.p.: n.d. F680 .F69.

1880   Carpenter, Thelma. *Index to 1880 Mortality Schedule of Kansas.* N.p.: n.d. F680 .C37.

All the above publications shown without the name of the compiler or author are by Ronald V. Jackson, Accelerated Indexing Systems.

Biographies

Biographical History of Central Kansas. 2 vols. New York: Lewis Publishing Co., 1902. F680 .B61.

Connelley, William E. *History of Kansas People.* Chicago: American Historical Society, 1928. F681 .C74.

Genealogical and Biographical Record of Northeast Kansas. Chicago: Lewis Publishing Co., 1900. F680 .G32.

Illustriana: Kansas Biographical Sketches. Hebron, Kans.: Illustriana, Inc., 1933. F680 .B24.

Kansas the First Century. Family and Personal History. Vols. 3 and 4. New York: Lewis Historical Publishing Co., 1956. F681 .K193.

Kansas. Supplementary Volume of Personal History. 2 parts. Chicago: Standard Publishing Co., 1912. F679 .K16.

Lowry, Mildred L. *Who When Where in Kansas.* 3 vols. Pittsburg, Kans.: the author, 1973. F680 .L68.

Early Settlers

Forgotten Men. Settlers of Kansas. 2 vols. Topeka: Kansas Council of Genealogical Societies, 1982. F680 .F67.

Kansas Pioneers. Topeka: Topeka Genealogical Society, 1976. F680 .K33.

Robertson, Clara H. *Kansas Territorial Settlers of 1860 Who Were Born in Tennessee, Virginia, North Carolina, and South Carolina.* Baltimore: Genealogical Publishing Co., 1976. F680 .R6.

Local Records

Ford, Don L. *Abandoned and Semi-active Cemeteries of Kansas.* 2 vols. Salem, Mass.: Higginson Books, 1985. F680 .F66.

Gardiner, Allen. *Monumental Inscriptions From Jackson County, Kansas Cemeteries.* Topeka: the author, 1981. F687 .J2G37.

Historical Records Survey (WPA). *Guide to Public Vital Statistics in Kansas.* Topeka: Kansas Historical Records Survey, 1942. CD3241 .H5.

Military Records

Cornish, Dudley T. *Kansas Negro Regiments in the Civil War.* N.p.: State of Kansas. Commission on Civil Rights, 1969. E508.4 .C6.

Kansas. Adjutant General. *Annual Reports of the State of Kansas, 1862, 1865, 1866, 1868.* Topeka: State of Kansas, 1902. E508.2 .K164.

National Society Daughters of the American Revolution—Kansas. John Haupt Chapter, comp. *Index to the Kansas Militia in the Civil War.* Topeka: the society, 1979. E508.3 .D38.

Periodicals

Barry, Louise, comp. *Subject and Author Guide-Index, the Kansas Historical Quarterly, Vols. 1–33 (1931–1967)*. Topeka: Kansas State Historical Society, 1967. F676 .K332.

Comprehensive Index, 1875–1930, To Collections, Biennial Reports, and Publications of the Kansas State Historical Society. Topeka: Kansas State Historical Society, 1959. F676 .K3305.

Directories

City

Abilene
(Dickinson, Dickinson Co.) 1928

Arkansas
(Cowley Co.) 1925–38, 1964

Atchison
pre 1861 (microfiche)
(Atchison Co.) 1865, 1876, 1880, 1891, 1899, 1903–26, 1928, 1941–50, 1972–82

Baxter Springs
(Columbus, Galena) 1970–82

Beloit
(Mitchell Co.) 1964–80

Chanute
(Neosha Co.) 1905–16, 1927–31, 1936, 1938, 1946–83

Cherryvale 1925

Coffeyville 1925–41, 1947–82

Colby
(Thomas Co.) 1962–65, 1970–82

Concordia 1948

Culver City
(Palms) 1927, 1931, 1937, 1949, 1964

Dodge City
(Ford Co.) 1953–84

El Dorado 1926–84

Emporia 1900–84

Fort Scott 1870, 1888, 1891

Fredonia 1925, 1942, 1963–74, 1980–82

Garden City
(Lakin, Finney, Kearney Co.) 1907, 1926

Great Bend
(Barton Co.) 1952–84

Hays
(Ellis Co.) 1963–84

Haysville 1957

Hutchinson 1904–24, 1933–41

Independence 1926–41, 1947–82

Iola
(Elsmore, Humboldt, La Harpe, Moran, Allen Co.) 1903–12, 1916, 1927, 1929, 1965–76

Junction City
(Geary Co.) 1905, 1948, 1959–82

Kansas City 1889, 1899, 1904, 1909–16, 1924–82

Lawrence
(Douglas Co.) 1879, 1883, 1888, 1900–19, 1925, 1927, 1961–83

Leavenworth
pre 1861 (microfiche)
(Lansing, Leavenworth Co.) 1866, 1874–1903, 1911–15, 1925–40, 1947–82

Liberal 1964–84

Manhattan
(Pottowatomie Co., Riley Co.) 1939–82

Marysville
(Marshall Co.) 1964–65

McPherson 1948

Mission (suburbs) 1962–64

North Topeka 1923

Olathe
(Gardner) 1961–83

Ottawa
(Franklin Co.) 1900–41, 1946–84

Paola
(Osawatomie) 1965–78

Parsons
(Labette Co.) 1900–20, 1928, 1930, 1938, 1943, 1963–84

Pittsburg 1947–84

Pratt 1926

Russell 1985

Salina
  (Saline Co.) 1901–85

Shawnee Mission Area
  (countryside, Fairway, Indian Hills, Leawood,
  Lenexa, Merriam, Mission, Mission Hills, Mis-
  sion Woods, Overland Park, Prairie Village,
  Roeland Park, Shawnee, Westwood, Westwood
  Hills) 1965–86

Topeka
  1861–81 (microfilm)
  (Shawnee Co.) 1887, 1899, 1902, 1907–16, 1921–82

Valley Center 1958

Wellington 1927, 1929, 1943, 1948, 1953, 1959–84

Wichita
  (suburbs, Sedgewick Co.) 1958–83
  1888–1984

Winfield
  (Cowley Co.) 1927–84

County, Business, and Miscellaneous

Allen 1901

Chanute
  (Neosho) 1903

Crawford 1901, 1959

Franklin-Douglas 1920

Gallatin (see Saline)

Johnson (see Leavenworth)

Kansas (state) 1866, 1878–1912

Kansas, eastern (see Northern Missouri)

Leavenworth
  (Johnson, Wyandotte) 1921

Neosho (see Chanute)

Northeast Johnson 1953–61

Saline 1913

Sedgwick 1920, 1953, 1957

Wyandotte (see also Leavenworth)
  1935, 1982

Oklahoma

Historical Highlights

1803   Louisiana Purchase from France.

1812   Designated part of Missouri Territory.

1819   Designated part of Arkansas Territory.

1830   Indians from the East removed to reserva-
        tions west of the Mississippi River.

1854   Indian Territory established.

        Native Indians of this region include the
        Arapahoe, Caddo, Cheyenne, Comanche,
        Kiowa, Osage, Pawnee, and Wichita. Added
        to these tribes were the Seminole, Creek,
        Chickasaw, and Cherokee who were
        removed from Georgia, North Carolina, and
        Florida. The Indian Territory was divided
        into the Cherokee Nation, Choctaw Nation,
        and Chickasaw Nation. Because the land
        was owned almost exclusively by Indians, the
        few white settlers in the region leased lands
        from them until such time as the federal
        government opened up new areas to white
        settlement or moved Indians from their
        lands (by force, purchase, or negotiation).

1889   Homestead land rush.

        When the government opened areas to
        homesteading, farmers from Illinois, Iowa,
        and Kansas rushed to the western and
        northwestern portions of the region, and
        farmers from Arkansas, Missouri, and
        Texas rushed to the southern portions.

1890   Separated into Oklahoma Territory and In-
        dian Territory.

1893   Cherokee Strip land rush.

        The Dawes Commission negotiated to pur-
        chase additional Indian lands, and a strip of
        land in the center of the region was opened
        to claims on a first-come, first-served basis.

1896   Boundary dispute between Texas and Ok-
        lahoma resulted in Greer County being
        placed in Oklahoma.

1907	Indian Territory and Oklahoma Territory reunited and admitted to the Union as Oklahoma.

Published Record Sources

Guidebooks

Morris, John W. *Ghost Towns of Oklahoma.* Norman: University of Oklahoma Press, 1977. F694 .M8195.

Ruth, Kent. *Oklahoma Travel Handbook.* Norman: University of Oklahoma Press, 1977. F692.3 .R87.

Shirk, George H. *Oklahoma Place Names.* Norman: University of Oklahoma Press, 1965, 1974. F692 .S5.

Vivens, Willie (Hardin), ed. *SW Oklahoma Keys.* Oklahoma City: SW Oklahoma Historical Society, 1982. F693 .S95.

Census Indexes and Abstracts

1860	Woods, Frances J. *Indian Lands West of Arkansas (Oklahoma): Population Schedules of the United States Census of 1860.* N.p.: Arrow Print Co., 1964. F693 .W68.
1910	Lawson, Rowena, comp. *1910 Indian Population, Oklahoma, Craig County.* Honolulu, Hawaii: the compiler, 1983. E78 .O45L38.

Biographies

Barrett, Charles F. *Oklahoma After Fifty Years: A History of the Sooner State and its People, 1889–1939.* Oklahoma City: Historical Record Association, 1941. F694 .B35.

Boren, Lyle H. *Who is Who in Oklahoma.* Guthrie, Okla.: Co-operative Publishing Co., 1935. F693 .W54.

DeWitz, Paul W. H., ed. *Notable Men of Indian Territory at the Beginning of the Twentieth Century, 1904–1905.* Muskogee: Southwestern Historical Publishing Co., 1905. F693 .D48.

Fulkerson, Mary Jane, and Jack Hoopes, eds. *Who's Who in Oklahoma, 1964. Leadership Index.* Muskogee: Leadership Index, Inc., 1964. F693 .W55.

Harlow, Rex F., comp. *Makers of Government in Oklahoma.* Oklahoma City: Harlow Publishing Co., 1930. F693 .H237.

———. *Oklahoma Leaders: Biographical Sketches of the Foremost Living Men of Oklahoma.* Oklahoma City: Harlow Publishing Co., 1928. F693 .H24.

———. *Successful Oklahomans: A Compilation of Biographical Sketches.* Oklahoma City: Harlow Publishing Co., 1927. F693 .H25.

Hoffman, Gene R., et al., eds. *Oklahomans and Their State: A Newspaper Reference Work.* Oklahoma City: Oklahoma Biographical Association, 1919. F693 .O41.

O'Beirne, Harry F., and Edward S. O'Beirne. *The Indian Territory. Its Chiefs, Legislators and Leading Men.* St. Louis: C. B. Woodward Co., 1892. F693 .O13.

Land Acquisition

Cook, Fredra M. *Forgotten Oklahoma Records.* "Cherokee Land Allotment Book." Cullman, Ala.: Gregath Co., 1981. F693 .C66.

Early Settlers

Hall, Ted B. *Oklahoma Indian Territory.* Fort Worth, Tex.: American Reference Publishers, 1971. F693 .H233.

Our Ellis County Heritage, 1885–1974, Vol. 1. Gage, Okla.: Ellis County Historical Society, 1974. F693 .O97.

Local Records

Bode, Frances M. *Oklahoma Territory Weddings.* Greary, Okla.: Pioneer Book Committee, 1983. F693 .B63.

Massey, Lynda S., and Clara M. Nash, comps. *Index to Marriages of Oklahoma Indian Territory; Compiled From Book I, Atoka, Oklahoma, 1897–1901.* Cartwright, Okla.: the compilers, 1980. F693 .M4.

Tiffee, Ellen. *Oklahoma Marriage Records.* 6 vols. Vol. 1, *Choctaw Nation, 1890–1892;* Vol. 2, *Choctaw Nation, 1892–1894;* Vol. 3, *Indian Territory,*

1894–1895, Credentials 1890, 1894; Vol. 4, *Indian Territory, 1895–1896;* Vol. 5, *Indian Territory, 1896–1897;* Vol. 6, *Indian Territory, 1897–1900.* McAlester, Okla.: the author, 1970. F693 .T53.

Wever, Orpha J. *Probate Records, 1892–1904. Northern District Cherokee Nation.* 2 vols. Vinita: Northeast Oklahoma Genealogical Society, 1982. F693 .W48.

Periodicals

Blackburn, Bob L., ed. *Chronicles of Oklahoma Cumulative Index, Vols. 38–57 (1960–1979).* N.p.: Oklahoma Historical Society, 1983. F691 .C55.

Looney, Rella W., comp. *Chronicles of Oklahoma, Cumulative Index, Vols. 1–37 (1921–1959).* Oklahoma City: Oklahoma Historical Society, 1961. F691 .C55.

Directories

City

Ada 1930, 1936–41

Altus
(Johnson Co.) 1929, 1962, 1971–79

Alva 1956

Anadarko 1966

Ardmore
(Carter Co.) 1907–26, 1928–84

Bartlesville
(Washington Co.) 1925–85

Blackwell
(Kay Co.) 1930–41, 1946, 1950

Broken Arrow 1973–84

Chickasha
(Grady Co.) 1927–40, 1947–83

Clinton 1962–81

Cushing
(Stillwater) 1926, 1930, 1938, 1964

Drumright 1926

Duncan 1928

Durant 1908, 1910, 1915, 1963

El Reno
(Canadian Co.) 1909, 1928, 1930, 1958, 1962–82

Elk City 1962, 1968–77

Enid 1905–83

Frederick
(Tillman Co.) 1919

Guthrie 1898, 1905–15, 1926, 1930

Guymon 1959, 1961, 1963, 1968, 1970, 1974–80

Idabel
(suburbs, Broken Arrow) 1963

Lawton
(Comanche Co.) 1903–17, 1926–84

McAlester
(Aldersen, Krebs, Pittsburg Co.) 1907–30, 1937, 1942, 1946, 1951, 1956–84

Miami
(Commerce, North Miami, Picher, Ottawa Co.) 1927–31, 1938, 1941, 1946, 1948, 1960–82

Muskogee
(Muskogee) 1903–84

Oklahoma City 1899–1983

Okmulgee 1946, 1951, 1958–83

Pawhuska
(Osage Co.) 1925, 1928

Ponca City
(Kay Co.) 1930–42, 1946–83

Sapulpa 1946, 1951, 1958–84

Seminole 1930

Shawnee
(Tecumseh) 1906–41, 1946, 1949–84

South McAlester
(Alderson, Bushy, Krebs, McAlester) 1905

Tulsa 1909, 1912–83

Wewoka 1937

Woodward 1977, 1979, 1982

County, Business, and Miscellaneous

Grant 1897

Muskogee 1909, 1913

Stephens 1924

Texas

Historical Highlights

1718   Seat of government established at San Antonio mission and military post.

1727   Mexican province of Texas established. Part of area claimed by France.

1803   Louisiana Purchase from France.

1812   Mexico, including the Texas region, declared its independence from Spain.

1819   United States and Mexico agreed to location of border between Texas and Louisiana.

During the late seventeenth and early eighteenth centuries, missions and forts were built by the Spanish in present day Texas. Spain sent colonists to the San Antonio area, and some Roman Catholics from Louisiana also migrated to Texas.

1821   San Felipe de Austin settled by Americans under the leadership of Stephen Austin.

1836   Texas declared its independence from Mexico—Battle of the Alamo. Independent Republic of Texas established.

Refusing to acknowledge Mexico's dictator, Santa Anna, and eventually winning its independence, Texas was settled by migrants from Alabama, Mississippi, and several other southern and midwestern states, coming down the Natchez Trace. Catholics were encouraged; Protestants were allowed by special permission. Some Germans came by way of New Orleans and Galveston.

1845   Admitted to the Union.

1845–48 Mexican War. Officially ceded to the United States.

1861   Seceded from the Union and joined the Confederate States of America.

Published Record Sources

Guidebooks

Baker, T. Lindsay. *Ghost Towns of Texas*. Norman: University of Oklahoma Press, 1986. F387 .B35.

Coursey, Clark. *Courthouses of Texas*. Brownwood, Tex.: Banner Printing Co., 1962. F387 .C6.

Davis, Ellis A., and Edwin H. Grobe. *New Encyclopedia of Texas*. 4 vols. Dallas: Texas Development Bureau, n.d. F385 .D27.

Encyclopedia of Texas. St. Clair Shores, Mich.: Somerst Publishing, 1982. F384 .E52.

Gennett, Henry. *A Gazetteer of Texas*. Washington, D.C.: Department of the Interior. United States Geological Survey, 1904. F384 .G20.

Kennedy, Imogene K., and J. Leon Kennedy. *Genealogical Records in Texas*. Baltimore: Genealogical Publishing Co., 1987. F386 .K46.

King, Dick. *Ghost Towns of Texas*. San Antonio: Naylor Co., 1953. F385 .K55.

Tarpley, Fred. *1001 Texas Place Names*. Austin: University of Texas Press, 1980. F384 .T28.

Texas Gazetteer. Wilmington, Del.: American Historical Publications, 1985. F384 .T39.

Texas. State Library, Archives Division. Jean Careford, ed. *Guide to Genealogical Sources in the Texas State Archives*. Austin: State of Texas, 1984. Z1339 .T352.

Williams, J. W. *Old Texas Trails*. Burnet, Tex.: Eakin Press, 1979. F386 .W66.

Census Indexes and Abstracts

Federal

1840   White, Gifford E., ed. *The 1840 Census of the Republic of Texas*. Austin: Pemberton Press, 1966. F390 .W59.

1850   Carpenter, Mrs. V. K. *The State of Texas Federal Population Schedules; Seventh Census of the United States, 1850*. 5 vols. Huntsville, Ark.: Century Enterprises, 1969. F385 .U54.

Jackson, Ronald V. *Texas 1850 Census Index.* Bountiful, Utah: Accelerated Indexing Systems, 1976. F385 .J16.

1860   Felldin, Jeanne R. *1860 United States Census Surname Index; The Texas Counties of Bosque, Bowie, Brazoria, Brazos, Brown, Burnet, Calhoun, and Comanche.* Tomball, Tex.: Genealogical Publications, 1976. F386 .F44.

Republic of Texas

Mullins, Marion D. *The First Census of Texas, 1829–1836, to Which are Added Texas Citizenship Lists, 1821–1845, and Other Early Records of the Republic of Texas.* Washington, D.C.: National Genealogical Society, 1976. CD42 .N43 No. 22 (F385).

Schluter, Helen G. *1835 Sabine District, Texas Census.* Fort Worth: the author; Nacogdoches: Ericson Books, 1983. F392 .S11S37.

Biographies

Biographical Souvenir of the State of Texas. Chicago: F. A. Battey & Co., 1889. Reprint. Easley, S.C.: Southern Historical Press, 1978. CT262 .B56.

Brooks, Elizabeth. *Prominent Women of Texas.* Akron, Ohio: The Werner Co., 1896. F385 .B86.

Connor, Seymour V. *The Peters Colony of Texas: A History and Biographical Sketches of the Early Settlers.* Austin: Texas State Historical Association, 1957. F390 .C73.

Crowell, Evelyn M., ed. *Texas Edition: Men of Achievement.* Dallas: John Morane, 1948. F385 .C76.

Dixon, Samuel H., and Louis W. Kemp. *The Heroes of San Jacinto.* Houston: Anson Jones Press, 1932. F390 .D57.

History of Texas: Supplemented with Biographical Mention of Many Prominent Persons and Families of the State. Chicago: Lewis Publishing Co., 1896. Reprint. N.p.: Ericson-Ingmire-Hudson Heritage, 1983. F386 .H67.

History of Texas; Together with a Biographical History of Tarrant and Parker Counties. Chicago: Lewis Publishing Co., 1895. F386 .H69.

Johnson, Francis W. *A History of Texas and Texans.* 5 vols. Chicago: American Historical Society, 1914. F386 .J66.

Volumes 4 and 5 are biographical.

Kemp, Louis W. *The Signers of the Texas Declaration of Independence.* Salado, Tex.: Anson Jones Press, 1944. F390 .K28.

Lynch, James D. *The Bench and Bar of Texas.* St. Louis: Nixon-Jones Printing Co., 1885. F385 .L96.

McAdams, Ira May. *Texas Women of Distinction.* Austin: McAdams Publications, 1962. F385 .M19.

Moreland, Sinclair. *The Texas Women's Hall of Fame.* Austin: Biographical Press, 1917. F385 .M83.

Morris, Harry J., comp. *Citizens of the Republic of Texas.* Dallas: Texas State Genealogical Society, 1977. F385 .C57.

Pickrell, Annie D. *Pioneer Women in Texas.* Austin: E. L. Steck, 1929. F385 .P59.

Samuels, Nancy T., and Barbara R. Knox, comps. *Old Northwest Texas: Historical—Statistical—Biographical.* 2 vols. Fort Worth: Fort Worth Genealogical Society, 1980. F386 .S17.

Texian Who's Who: A Biographical Dictionary of the State of Texas. Dallas: The Texian Co., 1937. F385 .T49.

Land Acquisition

Abstract of the Original Titles of Record in the General Land Office. Austin: Pemberton Press, 1964. F385 .T485.

Burr, Betty F., comp. *Nacogdoches Archives 1835 Entrance Certificates.* St. Louis: Ingmire Publications, 1982. F385 .B94.

Ericson, Carolyn R. *Nacogdoches Headrights; A Record of the Disposition of Land in East Texas and in Other Parts of that State, 1838–1848.* New Orleans: Polyanthos, 1977. F392 .N2E746.

Harris County Genealogical Society. *Original Land Holders of Some Texas Counties.* 2 vols. Pasadena, Tex.: the society, 1976. F385 .H34.

Miller, Thomas L. *Bounty and Donation Land Grants of Texas, 1835–1888.* Austin: University of Texas Press, 1967. UB374 .T4M5.

Texas. Department of Agriculture. *Texas Family Land Heritage Registry*. 4 vols. Austin: State of Texas, 1974. F386 .T334a. (HD1775 .T4T43).

White, Gifford. *1840 Citizens of Texas*. 2 vols. St. Louis: Ingmire Publications; Nacogdoches: Ericson Books, 1983. F385 .W53.

Volume 1, Land Grants; Volume 2, Tax Rolls.

———. *Character Certificates in the General Land Office of Texas*. St. Louis: Ingmire Publications, 1985. F385 .W533.

Early Settlers

Ancestor Charts. 3 vols. Waxahachie, Tex.: Ellis County Genealogical Society, 1981. F385 .A77.

Austin, Stephen F. *Register of Families*. Nacogdoches: Ericson Books, 1984. F385 .A895.

Best, Hugh. *Debrett's Texas Peerage*. New York: Coward-McCann, 1983. F385 .B46.

Castaneda, Carlos E. *A Report on the Spanish Archives in San Antonio, Texas*. San Antonio: Yanaguana Society, 1937. F381 .Y36.

Daughters of the Republic of Texas Lineage Book Commission. Founders and Patriots of the Republic of Texas. *The Lineages of the Members of the Republic of Texas*. Austin: the society, 1963. F385 .D25.

Dworaczyk, Edward J., comp. *The First Polish Colonies of America in Texas: Containing also the General History of the Polish People in Texas*. San Antonio: Nayor Co., 1969. F395 .P709.

Ericson, Carolyn R. *Nacogdoches, Gateway to Texas, A Biographical Directory*. 2 vols. Nacogdoches: Ericson Books, 1967. F392 .N24E74.

Vol. 1, 1773–1849; Vol. 2, 1850–80.

Ericson, Carolyn, and Francis T. Ingmire. *First Settlers of the Republic of Texas*. 2 vols. Vol. 1, *Austin—Jasper;* Vol. 2, *Jefferson—Washington*. Nacogdoches: Ericson Books, 1982. F385 .E74.

Flannery, John B. *The Irish Texans*. San Antonio: University of Texas, 1980. F395 .I6F55.

Geue, Chester, and Ethel H. Geue. *A New Land Beckoned: German Immigration to Texas, 1844–1847*. Baltimore: Genealogical Publishing Co., 1982. F395 .G3G38.

Geue, Ethel H. *New Homes in a New Land: German Immigration to Texas, 1847–1861*. Waco: Texian Press, 1970. F395 .G3G39.

Huguenot Society of the Founders of Manakin in the Colony of Virginia, Texas Branch, Texas. *Charter Members of the Huguenot Society . . . .* Dallas: the society, 1952. F385 .H84.

Galveston County Genealogical Society. *Ships Passenger Lists. Ports of Galveston, Texas*. Easley, S.C.: Southern Historical Press, 1984. F385 .S53.

Marsh, Helen C., and Timothy Marsh. *Tennesseans in Texas*. Easley, S.C.: Southern Historical Press, 1986. F385 .M264.

Morris, Mrs. H. J., ed. *Citizens of the Republic of Texas*. Dallas: Texas State Genealogical Society, 1977. F385 .C57.

North Texas Genealogical Association. *Family Roots. Lineage Charts*. Wichita Falls, Tex.: the association, 1983. F385 .F34.

Purl, Benjamin T., and Alma N. Barnes. *Republic of Texas. Second Class Headrights, March 2, 1836–October 2, 1837*. San Jacinto Chapter, Daughters of the Republic of Texas, 1974. F385 .P87.

Ray, Worth S. *Austin County Pioneers*. Austin: the author, 1949. F385 .R38.

Sowell, Andres J. *Early Settlers and Indian Fighters of Southwest Texas*. 2 vols. New York: Argosy-Antiquarian Ltd., 1964. F385 .S7.

Steele, James L. *Early Settlers of Texas*. Sun City Center, Fla.: the author, 1981. F385 .S84.

United States. House. *Claim of the State of Texas. Report on Claim, 1855–1860*. N.p., n.d. F391 .U62.

White, Gifford. *Mercer Colonists: Fenton Mercer and His Texas Colony*. N.p.: the author, 1984. F385 .W535.

Young, Louise M. *Peters Colonists: Their Descendants and Others Who Settled North Texas*. Chicago: Adams Press, 1972. F385 .Y6.

Local Records

Bender, Lucy, comp. *Marriage, Birth, and Death Records of Families . . . Who Emigrated from Virginia to Kentucky and from There to Texas, 1850 to 1895*. N.p.: the compiler, 1937. F385 .B456.

Biggerstaff, Inez. *4000 Tombstone Inscriptions From Texas, 1745–1870. Along the Old San Antonio Road and the Trail of Austin's Colonists.* N.p.: the author, 1952. F385 .B5.

Diamond-Collier, Dorothy R. *Concordia Cemetery Records.* 6 vols. Vol. 1, *Confederate and Spanish War Veterans (A—M);* Vol. 2 *(M—Z);* Vol. 3, *Masonic Section;* Vol. 4, *Catholic Section;* Vol. 5, *Catholic Section, No. 2, 1915–1920;* Vol. 6, *Catholic Section, 1918–1929.* El Paso: the author, 1987. F394 .E4D5.

——. *McGills Pauper Cemetery Records, 1939–1951.* El Paso: the author, 1984. F394 .E4D53.

——. *Old Mount Carmel Cemetery Records, 1939–1942.* El Paso: the author, 1984. F394 .E4D535.

East Texas Family Records. 9 vols. Tyler: East Texas Genealogical Society Quarterly, 1977–85. F385 .E22.

Volumes 1–4, 1977–80; volumes 4–6, 1981–82; volumes 7–8, 1983–84; volume 9, 1985.

Frazier, John P., comp. *Northwest Texas Cemeteries.* 2 vols. Pittsburg, Tex.: the compiler, 1976. F385 .F64.

Grammer, Norma R., comp. *Marriage Records of Early Texas, 1824–1898.* Ft. Worth: Fort Worth Genealogical Society, 1971. F385 .M263.

Gracy, Alice D., et al., comps. *Early Texas Birth Records, 1838–1878.* Easley, S.C.: Southern Historical Press, 1978. F385 .G7.

Index to Probate Cases of Texas. San Antonio: Statewide Records Project, 1940. F385 .A25.

State county desired.

Ingmire, Frances T. *Texas Ranger Service Records, 1830–1846.* St. Louis: Ingmire Publications, 1982. F385 .I538.

——. *Texas Ranger Service Records, 1847–1900.* 6 vols. St. Louis: Ingmire Publications, 1982. F385 .I538.

Marked Gravesites of Citizens of the Republic of Texas: An Indexed Guide to 436 Early Citizens Burial Places. Austin: Daughters of the Republic of Texas, 1987. F385 .M25.

Marriage Records From Sixteen Texas Counties. Tomball, Tex.: Chaparral Genealogical Society, 1980. F385 .M26.

McLean, Malcolm D., comp. *Papers Concerning Robertson's Colony in Texas.* 13 vols. Arlington, Tex.: UTA Press, 1986. F389 .M17.

Mulling, Marion D., comp. *Republic of Texas Poll Lists for 1846.* Baltimore: Genealogical Publishing Co., 1974. F385 .M84.

Crabtree, Oradell, comp. *Republic of Texas Marriage Records.* 3 vols. St. Louis: Ingmire Publications, 1985. F385 .R46.

Volume 1, 1824–35; volume 2, 1829–44, Brazoria County; volume 3, 1837–45, Colorado County.

Pompey, Sherman L. *The 1840 Tax Lists of Austin, Bastrop, Montgomery, and Washington Counties, Republic of Texas.* Charleston, Oreg.: Pacific Specialties, 1974. F385 .P65.

Swenson, Helen. *8800 Texas Marriages, 1824–1850.* 2 vols. St. Louis. Frances Ingmire, 1981. F385 .S93.

Wallace, Ernest, and David M. Vigness, eds. *Documents of Texas History.* Lubbock: Texas Tech. College, 1962. F386 .W32.

Military Records

General

Brown, John H. *Indian Wars and Pioneers of Texas.* Austin: L. E. Daniell, Publishers, 1880. Reprint. Easley, S.C.: Southern Historical Press, 1978. F385 .B87.

Devereaux, Linda E. *The Texas Navy.* Nacogdoches: Ericson Books, 1983. F385 .D48.

Ingmire, Frances T., comp. *Texas Frontiersmen, 1839–1860: Minute Men, Militia, Home Guards, Indian Fighters.* St. Louis: Ingmire Publications, 1982. F385 .I53.

Republic of Texas

Barron, John C., et al. *Republic of Texas Pension Application Abstracts.* Austin: Austin Genealogical Society, 1987. F385 .R465.

Civil War

Dilts, Bryan L., comp. *1890 Texas Census Index of Civil War Veterans or Their Widows.* Salt Lake City: Index Publishing Co., 1984. E494 .D585.

Miller, Thomas L. *Texas Confederate Scrip Grantees, Confederate States of America.* Texas: the author, 1985. F385 .M55.

Sistler, Byron. *1890 Civil War Veterans Census, Tennesseans in Texas.* Nashville: Sistler & Associates, 1978. E494 .S593.

Periodicals

Central Texas Genealogical Society Quarterly, Index 1958–1975. Waco: the society, 1975. F385 .H35.

Southwestern Historical Quarterly. Austin: Texas State Historical Association, 1950, 1960, 1980, 1984. F381 .T45. Index.

Indexes: volumes 1–40, 1897–1937; volumes 48–46, 1937–57; volumes 61–70, 1957–67; volumes 71–80, 1967–77.

Directories

City

Abilene
  (Impact) 1963–82

Alice 1942–49, 1957–84

Alvin
  (Friendswood, Pearland) 1962–67, 1973–80

Amarillo 1908–84

Andrews 1957, 1959, 1986

Angleton
  (Danbury) 1962–81

Arlington 1960–84

Athens
  (Henderson Co.) 1963–79

Atlanta 1969–73

Austin
  pre 1861 (microfiche)
  (Rollingwood Village, W. Lake Hills) 1958–84

Ballinger 1902, 1909

Baytown
  (Crosby, Highlands) 1967–74

Beaumont
  (Nederland, Port Neches) 1903–83

Beeville 1948, 1957–80

Bellaire 1963

Big Spring
  (Howard Co.) 1928, 1984

Bonham 1961–80

Brady
  (McCulloch Co.) 1962, 1970–73

Brazosport (suburbs) 1962–83

Brownsville 1927, 1938–56

Brownwood 1909, 1911, 1919–31, 1947, 1949, 1955–59

Bryan College Station 1965–83

Carthage 1963, 1970, 1973

Childress 1927–30

Cisco City 1929

Clear Lake area 1964–77

Cleburne 1907–49, 1957–73

Cleveland 1961, 1965

Coleman 1929, 1962

Commerce 1971–79

Conroe 1960–85

Corpus Christi 1927, 1940–84

Corsicana 1895, 1902, 1908–15, 1922–31, 1936–84

Crockett
  (Grapeland, Lovelady, Houston Co.) 1964, 1967

Dallas 1861–1935, 1936–83 (microfilm)

Del Rio 1940, 1959–84

Denison
  (Sherman) 1887, 1891, 1896–1985

Denton 1913, 1939, 1947, 1951, 1961, 1966, 1977–83

Dickinson
  (suburbs, League City) 1963

Dimmit 1960–68

Dumas 1957–83

Eastland 1926, 1928

Edinburg 1941–57

El Campo
  (suburbs, Wharton) 1963–77

El Paso 1896, 1901–84

Electra 1926

Fort Stockton 1862–83

Fort Worth
  1861–1935 (microfilm)
  (suburbs), 1936–81

Fredericksburg 1965, 1972, 1975, 1978

Friona 1960–68

Gainesville 1888, 1898, 1907–15, 1949

Galveston
  pre 1861 (microfiche)
  1861–1935, 1936–82 (microfilm)

Garland 1949, 1961–79

Gladewater 1957, 1961, 1971–79

Graham
  (Eliasville, New Castle) 1961–75

Grand Prairie 1948, 1950, 1956–80

Grapevine 1972

Greenville 1911–16, 1939, 1941, 1946, 1949, 1956

Harlingen
  (Texas City) 1935, 1939–61

Hearne 1967

Henderson 1935–41, 1947, 1957–85

Hereford
  (Dimmitt, Friona) 1960–84

Hillsboro
  (Hills Co.) 1912–13

Houston 1882–1984

Irving 1961–79

Jacksonville 1930, 1958–83

Jasper 1960, 1965, 1970–74

Kermit
  (Jal, N.M.; Wink) 1964–77

Kerrville 1947, 1958–84

Kilgore 1936, 1938, 1947, 1957–83

Killeen
  (Harken Heights) 1961–82

Kingsville 1957–81

Lamesa 1948

LaPorte
  (Seabrook) 1964

Laredo 1930

Lewisville 1966

Liberty
  (Dayton) 1963–81

Livingston 1972

Lockhart 1972

Longview
  (Gladewater, Goldwater Road, Greggton) 1914,
    1934–47, 1957–85

Loveland 1985

Lubbock 1910, 1926–83

Lufkin
  (Herty, Keltys) 1922, 1925, 1928, 1940, 1946, 1957–83

Marlin
  (Falls Co.) 1914

Marshall
  (Longview, Tyler) 1900, 1912, 1914, 1937–41, 1946–59,
    1968, 1973

McAllen 1936–60

McKinney 1940, 1949, 1956, 1960, 1964, 1971, 1975

Memphis
  (Hall Co.) 1930

Mexia 1947, 1961, 1976

Midland 1928, 1930, 1937–84

Mineral Wells
  (Palo Pinto Co.) 1907, 1909, 1914, 1920, 1924, 1927,
    1949, 1960–75

Mission 1942, 1945, 1949, 1955, 1959

Nacogdoches 1960–68, 1975–80

New Braunfels 1986

Odessa 1961

Olney
  (Newcastle) 1965

Orange
  (Blanel, Bruner, Cove Additions, Pinehurst, W.
    Orange) 1951–84

Overton
  (suburbs, Arp, Troup) 1939

Palestine 1911, 1914, 1935–41

Pampa 1929–82

Paris
(Lamar Co.) 1891, 1896, 1908–24, 1929, 1956, 1984

Perrytown 1973–80

Plainview
(Hale Co.) 1909, 1912, 1939, 1960–80

Plano 1980

Port Arthur
(Griffing, Lakeveiw, Nederland, Pear Ridge, Port Neches, Sabine, Sabine Pass) 1911–84

Port Lavaca
(Port Comfort) 1962–82

Ranger City 1926

Raymondville 1957, 1960, 1963

Richardson
(Buckingham) 1976, 1980

Rosenberg
(Richmond) 1950, 1962–82

Rusk
(Alto, Cherokee Co.) 1964, 1973

San Angelo 1908–85

San Antonio
1861–1901 (microfilm)
(Alamo Heights, Balcones Heights, Castle Hills, Olmos Park, Terrell Hills) 1902–42, 1946–83

San Benito 1929, 1937–41, 1950

San Marcos
(Kyle) 1963, 1972–82

Seguin
(Marion, McQueeney, Kingsbury) 1963–80

Sherman
(Denison) 1887, 1891, 1896, 1899, 1901, 1910–84

Silsbee 1967, 1972

Silver City 1913

Snyder 1960–83

Spearman
(Grover Co., Harford Co.) 1963–83

Stephenville 1940

Sulphur Springs
(Hopkins Co.) 1914, 1956, 1963–84

Sweetwater 1911, 1927, 1929, 1970–81

Taylor 1940, 1986

Temple 1909–17, 1939, 1946, 1957–84

Terrell 1912, 1941, 1947, 1976, 1978

Texarkana (see Texarkana, Arkansas)

Texas City 1963–84

Tulia
(Cress, Happy) 1964, 1967, 1970–80

Tyler 1913, 1923–85

Uvalde 1960–82

Vernon
(Wilbarger Co.) 1946–82

Victoria 1913, 1943–48, 1957–83

Vidor
(Rose City, Orange Co.) 1955, 1964–82

Waco
(Bellmead, Beverly Hills, Woodway) 1886–1931, 1936–84

Waxahachie 1913, 1948, 1952

Weatherford
(Parker Co.) 1961–80

Wichita Falls 1909–85

Willacy 1937

Windcrest 1969

County, Business, and Miscellaneous

Garza 1878, 1884, 1896

Lower Rio Grande Valley 1929–36

Matagorda 1964, 1967, 1972–75

Park Cities 1946

Smith 1955

Tarrant 1954

Texas (state) 1878, 1884, 1896

Travis 1954

Waco 1894

Colorado

Historical Highlights

1803   Louisiana Purchase from France.

1806   Explored by United States Army officer, Zebulon M. Pike.

1846–48 Mexican War.

During the eighteenth century the region was explored and controlled by Spain and then by France, but there was little or no settlement. American explorers came in the early 1800s, and fur traders arrived to collect pelts for eastern and Canadian fur companies. The Louisiana Purchase transferred the eastern and central part to the United States. After the Mexican War the western part also became a part of the United States.

1850   Designated part of New Mexico Territory.

1858   Gold discovered near Denver.

A rush of prospectors arrived to seek gold; the population was almost exclusively male. When the dream of wealth from gold dissolved because of small yields and the continuing Indian Wars, the population increased little until the next decade.

1861   Colorado Territory established.

1870   Railroads arrived.

With the coming of the railroads and another gold discovery in the San Juan Mountains, permanent settlers began to arrive; many became farmers and established families.

1876   Admitted to the Union.

Published Record Sources

Guidebooks

Brown, Robert L. *Colorado Ghost Towns—Past and Present.* Caldwell, Idaho: Caxton Printers, 1972. F776 .B66.

———. *Ghost Towns of the Colorado Rockies.* Caldwell, Idaho: Caxton Printers, 1968. F776 .B67.

———. *Jeep Trails to Colorado Ghost Towns.* Caldwell, Idaho: Caxton Printers, 1963. F776 .B7.

Dallas, Sandra. *Colorado Ghost Towns and Mining Camps.* Norman: University of Oklahoma Press, 1985. F778 .D35.

Eberhart, Perry. *Ghosts of the Colorado Plains.* Athens, Ohio: Ohio University Press/Swallow Press, 1986. F777 .E238.

———. *Guide to the Colorado Ghost Towns and Mining Camps.* Denver: Sage Books, 1959. F776 .E2.

———. *Guide to the Colorado Ghost Towns and Mining Camps.* Athens, Ohio: Ohio University Press/Swallow Press, 1981. F777 .E24.

Shaffer, Ray. *A Guide to Places on the Colorado Prairie, 1540–1975.* Boulder, Colo.: Pruett Publishing Co., 1978. F776 .S5.

Census Indexes and Abstracts

Federal

1870   Weld County Genealogical Society. *1870 Colorado Territory Census Index.* Greeley, Colo.: the society, 1977. F775 .W52.

1880   Jackson, Ronald V. *Colorado 1880 Census Index.* Bountiful, Utah: Accelerated Indexing Systems, 1980. F775 .J3.

Mortality Schedules

1870   Jackson, Ronald V. *1870 Mortality Schedule.* Bountiful, Utah: Accelerated Indexing System, 1980. F775 .J32.

1880   Jackson, Ronald V. *1880 Mortality Schedule.* Bountiful, Utah: Accelerated Indexing Systems, 1980. F775 .J33.

Biographies

Byers, William N. *Encyclopedia of Biography of Colorado.* Chicago: Century Publishing, 1901. F775 .B98.

Capitol's Who's Who for Colorado. Denver: Capitol Publishing, 1941. F775 .C3.

Colorado Families: A Territorial Heritage. Denver: The Colorado Genealogical Society, 1981. F775 .C64.

Hafen, Leroy R., ed. *Colorado and Its People.* Vols. 3 and 4, *Personal and Family History.* New York: Lewis Historical Publishing Co., 1948. F776 .H1293.

Portrait and Biographical Record of Denver and Vicinity, Colorado. Chicago: Chapman Publishing Co., 1898. F784 .D4P8.

Progressive Men of Western Colorado. Chicago: A.W. Bowen & Co., 1905. F775 .R41.

Representative Men of Colorado in the Nineteenth Century. Denver: Rowell Art Publishing Co., 1902. F775 .R42.

Smiley, Jerome C. *Semi-Centennial History of the State of Colorado.* 2 vols. Chicago: Lewis Publishing Co., 1913. F776 .S47.

Stone, Wilbur F. *History of Colorado.* 4 vols. Chicago: S. J. Clarke Publishing Co., 1918. F776 .S88.

Who's Who in Colorado. Boulder, Colo.: Colorado Press Association, 1938. F775 .W56.

Early Settlers

Bromwell, Henrietta, comp. *Fifty-Niners' Directory. Colorado Argonauts of 1859.* 2 vols. Denver: the compiler, 1926. F780 .B86.

Local Records

Merrill, Kay R. *Colorado Cemetery Directory.* Denver: Colorado Council of Genealogical Societies, 1985. F775 .C63.

Periodicals

Colorado Genealogical Index. Vols. 1–10, 1939–49. 2 parts. Denver: the society, 1969. F771 .C4 supplement. Index.

Colorado Genealogical Index. Vols. 11–20, 1950–59. 2 parts. Denver: the society, 1974. F771 .C4 supplement. Index.

Colorado Genealogist Index. Vols. 21–40, 1960–79. Denver: the society, 1979. F771 .C4 Index.

Merrill, Kay R., comp. *Subject Index to the Colorado Genealogist. Vols. 1–42, 1939–81.* Denver: the society, 1982. F771 .C4 Index.

Directories

City

Alamosa
(Conejos, Saguache Co.) 1911–60

Boulder
(Broomfield, Longmont, Boulder Co.) 1903, 1913, 1938–84

Canon City
(Florence) 1985

Clear Creek 1898

Colorado Springs
(Colorado City, Cragmoor, Manitou Sprgs., Security Village, Streiton Meadows) 1879–88, 1898, 1903–82

Delta
(Delta Co.) 1912, 1970–77

Denver
pre 1861 (microfiche)
1861–1935 (microfilm)
(suburbs) 1945–84

Durango
(San Juan Basin) 1911, 1915

Fort Collins
(Loveland, Larimer Co.) 1906, 1917, 1922–38, 1948, 1979

Golden City 1947

Grand Junction
(Mesa Co.) 1903–31, 1935–84

Greeley 1986

LaJunta 1911, 1932, 1962–84

Leadville
   (Lake Co.) 1881–1909, 1963–79

Longmont
   (Boulder, Lafayette, Louisville, Boulder Co.) 1959–84

Monte Vista 1961

Montrose
   (Montrose Co.) 1912, 1969–77

Pueblo 1899–1985

Salida
   (Chaffee Co.) 1904, 1906, 1908, 1913, 1916, 1922, 1927

Trinidad
   (Las Animas Co.) 1904–35, 1960–85

Walsenburg
   (Huerfano Co.) 1963–83

County, Business, and Miscellaneous

Arapahoe 1932

Boulder 1896, 1916–36

Crowley (see Otero)

Denver (city) 1936

Jefferson 1933, 1961

Otero
   (Crowley) 1914

New Mexico

Historical Highlights

1610   Santa Fe established by Spain.

1680   Pueblo Indians successfully rebelled against Spain.

1692   Pueblo Indians submitted to Spanish army control.

1821   Mexico declared its independence from Spain.

        Until Mexico became independent, nearly all the inhabitants of the New Mexico area were the Spanish and native Indians, governed by Mexican officials. Americans began to arrive in the 1820s.

1822   Santa Fe Trail opened linking Independence, Missouri, and Santa Fe.

1846–48 Mexican War. New Mexico ceded to the United States.

1850   New Mexico Territory established, included Colorado and Arizona.

1854   Gadsden Purchase added new land to New Mexico Territory.

1861   Colorado Territory separated from New Mexico Territory.

1863   Arizona Territory separated from New Mexico Territory.

        During the Civil War, Confederates attempting to organize the inhabitants for the South were defeated by Union troops who then controlled the territory.

1866   Gold discovered at Pinos Altos.

1869   Silver discovered at Silver City.

        In addition to miners who came seeking gold and silver, sheep and cattle farmers also settled on the public domain lands. Irrigation projects and cheap land beckoned farmers from eastern and midwestern states, but speculation and fraud required many land claims to be settled by the courts after years of litigation. In addition, earlier grants by Spain and Mexico had to be adjudicated.

1912   Admitted to the Union.

Published Record Sources

Guidebooks

New Mexico—A County Guide Series. 5 vols. Truth or Consequences, N.M.: The Talking Box, 1986. F696 .N57.

   Vol. 1, Santa Fe; Vol. 2, Barnalillo; Vol. 3, Dona Ana; Vol. 4, San Juan; Vol. 5, Lea.

Census Indexes and Abstracts

Federal

1850   F795 .J33
        Windham, Margaret L., ed. *New Mexico 1850 Territorial Census*. Albuquerque: New Mexico Genealogical Society, 1976. F795 .W5.

1860   F795 .J33

The above publication shown without the name of the compiler or author are by Ronald V. Jackson, Accelerated Indexing Systems.

State

Olmstead, Virginia L., comp. *Spanish and Mexican Colonial Censuses of New Mexico, 1790, 1827, 1828, 1845*. Albuquerque: New Mexico Genealogical Society, 1975. F795 .S67.

————. *Spanish and Mexican Censuses of New Mexico, 1750–1830*. Albuquerque: New Mexico Genealogical Society, 1981. F795 .045.

Twitchell, Ralph E. *Spanish Archives of New Mexico*. Reprint. New York: Arno Press, 1976. F791 .T85.

Biographies

Abousleman, Michel D., ed. *Who's Who in New Mexico, 1957*. Albuquerque: Abousleman Co., 1937. F795 .W56.

Land Acquisition

Pearson, Jim B. *The Maxwell Land Grant*. Norman: University of Oklahoma Press, 1961. F802 .M38P4.

Early Settlers

Chavez, Fray A. *Origins of New Mexico Families in the Spanish Colonial Period*. Santa Fe: William Gannon, 1854–75. F795 .C5.

Local Records

Albuquerque Baptisms, 1706–1850. Albuquerque: New Mexico Genealogical Society, 1983. F804 .A3A52.

Brewer, Mary, comp. *New Mexico Cemeteries*. 2 vols. Vol. 1, *Bernalillo Co., Mount Calvary;* Vol. 2, *Some Valencia Co. Cemeteries*. Albuquerque: New Mexico Genealogical Society, 1979. F795 .B73.

Directories

City

Albuquerque 1908–20, 1927–84

Artesia (rural routes) 1953–81

Carlsbad
(Happy Valley) 1946–83

Clovis 1939, 1946, 1948, 1957–64

Farmington
(Aztec, Bloomfield, San Juan, San Juan Co.) 1961–83

Gallup
(McKinley Co.) 1947, 1951–83

Grants
(Milan) 1958–79

Hobbs 1946–83

Jal
(Eunice, Livingston, Tatum) 1960

Las Cruces
(Mesilla Park) 1940, 1948, 1951, 1960, 1964–84

Las Vegas 1895

Littleton 1903

Lovington
(Eunice, Jal, Tatum, Lea Co.) 1960–62, 1985

Manchester (suburbs) 1965–82

Portales 1947, 1956, 1963–78

Raton 1917

Roswell 1912–22, 1930–34

Santa Fe 1928–84

Truth or Consequences
(Williamsburg) 1965, 1970, 1973

Tumcumcari 1909, 1948, 1951, 1957–67, 1972–76

County, Business, and Miscellaneous

New Mexico
(including El Paso, Texas) 1902, 1913, 1946

A Complete Business Directory of New Mexico and Gazetteer of the Territory For 1882. Santa Fe: New Mexico Publishing Co., 1882. F794.7 .C73.

Utah

Historical Highlights

1824   Great Salt Lake discovered by Jim Bridger.

1847   First Mormons arrive, led by Brigham Young.

The Church of Jesus Christ of Latter-day Saints (Mormons) was founded in 1830 in New York by Joseph Smith. The movement grew and expanded westward through the Midwest as far as Nauvoo, Illinois, where Smith and his followers established a settlement. Smith and his brother were killed nearby in 1844. The group then split, and one faction led by Brigham Young left in 1846 to travel through Wyoming, arriving in the Great Salt Lake area in 1847. Immigrants who converted to Mormonism in England, Scandinavia, and other European countries also came to the Utah area.

1848   Mexican War. Utah ceded to the United States.

1849   Governed by Brigham Young, the State of Deseret was founded, which included present-day Utah, Arizona, Nevada, and parts of New Mexico, Colorado, Wyoming, and California.

1850   Territory of Utah established.

1856   Thousands of Mormon immigrants arrived from the Midwest—many pulling their belongings in handcarts.

1890   Polygamy prohibited by the Mormon church.

1896   Admitted to the Union.

Published Record Sources

Guidebooks

Carr, Stephen L. *The Historical Guide to Utah Ghost Towns.* Salt Lake City: Western Epics, 1972. F826 .C27.

Utah. State Department of Education. *Origins of Utah Place Names.* Salt Lake City: Writers' Project, 1940. F824 .W75.

Census Indexes and Abstracts

Federal

1850   F825 .J33
        Kearl, J.R., et al., comps. *Index to the 1850, 1860, and 1870 Censuses of Utah: Heads of Households.* Baltimore: Genealogical Publishing Co., 1981. F825 .K4.

1860   F825 .J34
        Kearl, J.R. (see 1850)

1870
        Kearl, J.R. (see 1850)

State

Dilts, Bryan L. *1856 Utah Census Index: An Every Name Index.* Salt Lake City: Index Publishing Co., 1983. F825 .D54.

Mortality Schedules

1850   F825 .J335

1860   F825 .J336

All the above publications shown without the name of the compiler or author are by Ronald V. Jackson, Accelerated Indexing Systems.

Biographies

Biographical Record of Salt Lake City and Vicinity. Chicago: National Historical Record Co., 1902. F824 .S17B6.

Simmons, Ralph B., ed. *Utah's Distinguished Personalities.* Salt Lake City: Personality Publishing Co., 1933. F825 .S56.

Sutton, Wain. *Utah. A Centennial History*. Vol. 3, *Personal and Family Records*. New York: Lewis Historical Publishing Co., 1949. F826 .S8.

Warrum, Noble, ed. *Utah Since Statehood: Historical and Biographical*. 4 vols. Chicago: S. J. Clarke Publishing Co., 1920. F826 .W3.

Early Settlers

Alter, J. Cecil. *Utah: The Storied Domain*. 3 vols. Chicago: American Historical Society, 1932. F826 .A47.

Greer, Leland H. *The Founding of an Empire. The Exploration and Colonization of Utah, 1796–1856*. Salt Lake City: Bookcraft, 1947. F826 .C9.

Knecht, William L., and Peter L. Crowley. *History of Brigham Young, 1847–1867*. Berkeley, Calif.: MassCal Association, 1964. F826 .H69.

Military Records

Utah State Archives. *Veterans With Federal Service Buried in the State of Utah; Territorial Period to 1965; Duchesne Co., Uintah Co.* Salt Lake City: The State Archives, 1965. F825 .U85A5.

Directories

City

Cedar City 1971–81

Kearns 1956

Logan
(Cache Co.) 1904–29, 1935–36, 1946–84

Ogden 1890–1984

Provo
(Orem, Springfield, Utah Co.) 1901–05, 1911–83

St. George
(Bloomington, Bloomington Mills, Santa Clara, Washington Co.) 1971–80

Salt Lake City 1861–1901
(suburbs, Garfield, Magna, Midvale, Murray, Sandy) 1902–83

Tooele
(Grantsville) 1970–84

Utah (state)
(Salt Lake City) 1874, 1879

County, Business, and Miscellaneous

Union (see Woodbury, Iowa)

Utah (county) 1907

Utah (state) (see also Salt Lake City)
1900, 1903, 1908, 1912, 1916, 1918–27

Arizona

Historical Highlights

1651	Known as Pimeria Alta; region controlled by Spain.
	Under Spain's rule, Catholic missionaries arrived to convert and teach the native Indians. Self governing missions established.
1821	Controlled by Mexico.
1846–48	Mexican War. Boundary between Mexico and United States established.
1848	California gold rush depleted Arizona population as men left to prospect in California.
1850	Mormons began establishing settlements in rural areas.
1851	Designated part of New Mexico Territory.
1863	Arizona Territory established.
1912	Admitted to the Union.

Published Record Sources

Guidebooks

Sherman, James E., and Barbara H. Sherman. *Ghost Towns of Arizona*. Norman: University of Oklahoma Press, 1969. F811 .S47.

Census Indexes and Abstracts

Federal

1860	F810 .J32

Underhill, Lonnie E., comp. *Index to the Federal Census of Arizona for 1860, 1864, and 1870.* Tucson: Roan Horse Press, 1981. F810 .F4 supplement.

United States Congress. *Federal Census, Territory of New Mexico and Territory of Arizona.* Washington, D.C. Government Printing Office, 1965. F810 .F4.

1864	F810 .J323

Underhill (see 1860)

United States Congress (see 1860)

Schreier, Jim, and Mary Schreier, comps. *An Index to the Territorial Manuscript of the 1864 Census of Arizona; Correlated to the Historical Records Survey of 1938 and the United States Document No. 13, 1965.* Phoenix: the compilers, 1975. F810 .S37.

1866	Schreier, Jim, and Mary Schreier. *An Index to the 1866 Census of the Arizona Territory.* Phoenix: Arizona Territorial Genealogy, 1975. F810 .S36.
1870	F810 .J325

Underhill (see 1860)

United States Congress (see 1860)

1880	F810 .J327

Mortality Schedules

1870	F810 .J324
1880	F810 .J322

All the above publications shown without the name of the compiler or author are by Ronald V. Jackson, Accelerated Indexing Systems.

Biographies

Goff, John S. *Arizona Biographical Dictionary.* Cave Creek, Ariz.: Black Mountain Press, 1983. CT223 .G64.

————. *Arizona Territorial Officials.* 3 vols. Vol. 1, *Supreme Court Justices, 1863–1912;* Vol. 2, *The Governors, 1863–1912;* Vol. 3, *The Delegates to Congress, 1863–1912.* Cave Creek, Ariz.: Black Mountain Press, 1975. F810 .G63.

Lockwood, Frank C. *Pioneer Portraits.* Tucson: University of Arizona Press, 1968. F810 .L845.

————. *Thumbnail Sketches of Famous Arizona Desert Riders, 1538–1946.* Freeport, N.Y.: Books for Librarians Press, 1946, 1971. F810 .L85.

McClintock, James H. *Arizona.* Vol. 3, *Biographical.* Chicago: S. J. Clarke Publishing Co., 1916. F811 .M12.

Men and Woman of Arizona, Past and Present. Phoenix: Pioneer Publishing Co., 1940. F810 .M4.

Peplow, Edward H. *History of Arizona.* Vol. 3, *Family and Personal History.* New York: Lewis Historical Publishing Co., 1958. F811 .P4.

Sloan, Richard E. *History of Arizona.* Vol. 3, Biographical. Phoenix: Record Publishing Co., 1936. F811 .S63.

Who's Who in Arizona in Business Professions and Arts. Vol. 1, *1938–40.* Phoenix: Arizona Survey Publishing Co., 1958. F810 .W56.

Local Records

Arizona Death Records. An Index Compiled from Mortuary, Cemetery, and Church Records. 3 vols. Tucson: Arizona Genealogical Society, 1976. F810 .A73.

Directories

City

Ajo
 (Gila Bend) 1980

Bisbee (suburbs) 1914–18, 1924–26, 1940–52, 1957

Casa Grande
 (Coolidge, Eloy, Florence, Pinal Co.) 1960–81

Chandler
 (Gilbert) 1980

Douglas
 (Bisbee) 1915, 1921–29, 1940, 1942, 1961–79

Flagstaff 1950, 1958, 1961

Glendale (suburbs) 1957–67

Globe
 (Central Hgts., Claypool, Inspiration, Miami) 1916, 1921, 1923, 1930, 1965, 1970, 1973

Kingman
   (Mohave Co.) 1959–76

Lake Havasu 1973–77

Mesa
   (Apache Junction, Chandler, Chandler Heights, Gilbert, Higly, Queen Creek, Tempe) 1940, 1952, 1958–66, 1970, 1976–81

Miami
   (Globe) 1928

Phoenix
   (Salt River Valley) 1912–32, 1936–80

Prescott
   (Yavapai Co.) 1923, 1928, 1929

Safford
   (Central, Clifton, Moronel, Pina, Solomon, Thatcher) 1950, 1958–79

Scottsdale
   (Paradise Valley) 1956–67

Sierra Vista 1980

Sun City 1978–79

Tucson 1899–1900, 1912–23, 1928–41, 1944–83

Yuma
   (Somerton) 1949, 1956

County, Business, and Miscellaneous

Arizona
   (state) 1912, 1916, 1921, 1936–39
   (New Mexico) 1897, 1912

Phoenix (city) 1978

Tucson 1911

Nevada

Historical Highlights

1775   Visited by Spanish explorers and missionaries en route to California.

1825   Explored by fur trappers from Hudson Bay Company.

Later explorers included Americans Kit Carson, John C. Fremont.

1830   Spanish Trail to California established.

1833   California Trail established.

The region to become Nevada was merely a pathway to California for most settlers, both before and after the California gold rush. Up to this time population was very small.

1848   Mexican War. Acquired as a part of California by the United States.

1850   Designated part of Utah Territory.

Organized by Mormons sent from Salt Lake City, the first permanent settlement was Mormon Station (renamed Genoa). Many settlers became dissatisfied with Mormon control and petitioned to be annexed by California. This movement was cancelled when Mormons withdrew in 1857.

1859   Silver discovered at the Comstock Mine near Virginia City.

Speculators, miners, businessmen, and others rushed to the region to prospect and support the greatly increased population.

1861   Nevada Territory established.

1864   Admitted to the Union.

1873   Silver discovered once more (Big Bonanza Mine) at Davidson Mountain. Boom lasted until about 1880.

Published Record Sources

Guidebooks

Abbott, Allan L. *Nevada Ghost Towns and Trails.* Anaheim, Calif.: Abbott & Abbott, 1969. F841 .A36.

Averett, Walter R. *Directory of Southern Nevada Place Names.* Las Vegas: the author, 1962. F839 .A8.

Carlson, Helen S. *Nevada Place Names: A Geographical Dictionary.* Reno: University of Nevada Press, 1974. F839. C37.

Leigh, Rufus W. *Nevada Place Names: Their Origin and Significance.* Salt Lake City: the author, 1964. F839 .L4.

Miller, Donald C. *Ghost Towns of Nevada.* Boulder, Colo.: Pruett Publishing Co., 1979. F841 .M52.

Nevada Historical Society. L. James Higgins, ed. *A Guide to the Collections at the Nevada Historical Society.* Reno: the society, 1975. Z1309 .N35.

Nevada Historical Society. Eric Moody, comp. *An Index to the Publications of the Nevada Historical Society, 1907–1971.* Reno: the society, 1977. Z1309 .M66.

Nevada State Library. Joyce C. Lee, comp. *Genealogical Prospecting in Nevada: A Guide to Nevada Directories.* Reno: State of Nevada, 1984. Z1309 .L43.

Paher, Stanley W. *Nevada Ghost Towns and Mining Camps.* Berkeley, Calif.: Howell-North Books, 1970. F842 .P3.

Census Indexes and Abstracts

Federal

1870   F840 .J3

1910   Dilts, Bryan L. *1910 Nevada Census Index; Heads of Households and Other Surnames in Household Index.* Salt Lake City: Index Publishing Co., 1983. F840 .A17.

Mortality Schedules

1870   F840 .J29

The above publication, shown without the name of the author, is by Ronald V. Jackson, Accelerated Indexing Systems.

Biographies

Moore, Boyd. *Nevadans and Nevada.* San Francisco: the author, 1950. F840 .M6.

Parker, J. Carlyle, and Janet G. Parker. *Nevada Biographical and Genealogical Index.* Turlock, Calif.: Marietta Publishing Co., 1986. Z1309 .P37.

Poulton, Helen J. *Index to History of Nevada, 1881.* Reno: University of Nevada Press, 1966. F841 .P6.

Who's Who in Nevada. Los Angeles: Bessie Beatty, 1907. F840 .W6.

Early Settlers

Collins, Charles, comp. *Mercantile Guide and Directory of Virginia City, Gold Hill, Silver City, and American Cities of Nevada, 1864–65.* San Francisco: Agnew & Deffbaugh, 1864. F849 .V8A18.

Ratay, Myra S. *Pioneers of the Ponderosa: How Washoe Valley Rescued the Comstock.* Sparks, Nev.: Western Products and Publishing Co., 1973. F847 .W3R37.

Scrugham, James G., ed. *Nevada. A Narrative of the Conquest of a Frontier Land.* 3 vols. Chicago: American Historical Society, 1935. F841 .S35.

Volume 1, index.

Local Records

Ellison, Marion. *An Inventory and Index to the Records of Carson County, Utah and Nevada Territories, 1855–1861.* Reno: Grace Dangberg Foundation, 1984. F847 .C37E45.

Taylor, Richard B., comp. *The Nevada Tombstone Record Book.* Las Vegas: Nevada Families Project, 1986. F840 .T4.

Directories

City

Carson City
  (Virginia City) 1964–85

Elko 1965–79

Ely
  (White Pine Co.) 1958, 1964–77

Henderson
  (Boulder City) 1959

Las Vegas
  (Boulder City, Henderson, N. Las Vegas, Clark Co.) 1930, 1970–75

Reno
  (Carson City, Sparks, Washoe Co.) 1913, 1917–85

Virginia City
  (Carson City, Gold Hill, Reno, Silver City) 1873, 1878

County, Business, and Miscellaneous

Nevada
  (territory) pre 1861 (microfiche)
  (state) 1862, 1907, 1912, 1914
    First Directory of Nevada Territory, 1862. San Francisco: Valentine & Co., 1862. F839.5 .K4.

California

Historical Highlights

1769   Spain established San Diego.

1770–1823 Spanish missions established at regular intervals along the Pacific Coast.

1774   Anza Trail opened from Sonora, Mexico, to California.

1782   San Jose founded.

1796   First Americans arrived by ship.

1804   Upper California became an independent province.

1822   Mexico takes control from Spain. Upper California and Lower California joined; re-separated in 1830.

1839   John Sutter, from Switzerland, organized the Sacramento River Valley as "New Helvetia."

1841   First wagon trains arrived, departing from Missouri.

1846–48 Mexican War. California ceded to United States.

1848   Gold discovered at Sutter's Mill.

1850   Admitted to the Union.
    Following statehood, the Chinese came to northern California, with Japanese following in the early 1900s.

Published Record Sources

Guidebooks

California Historical Survey Commission. Owen C. Coy, ed. *Guide to the County Archives in California.* Sacramento: State of California, 1919. CD3111 .A5.

Florin, Lambert. *California Ghost Towns.* Seattle: Superior Publishing Co., 1971. F868 .F56.

Gudde, Erwin G. *California Place Names: A Geographical Dictionary.* Berkeley, Calif.: University of California Press, 1949. F859 .G79.

Marinacci, Barbara, and Rudy Marinacci. *California Spanish Place Names: What They Are and How They Got There.* San Rafael, Calif.: Presidio Press, 1980. F861 .M32.

Palmer, Theodore S. *Place Names of the Death Valley Region in California and Nevada.* N.p.: the author, 1948. F868 .D2P28.

Sanders, Patricia. *Searching in California: A Reference Guide to Public and Private Records.* Costa Mesa: ISC Publications, 1982. F860 .S36.

Sanchez, Nellie V. *Spanish and Indian Place Names of California.* San Francisco: A. M. Robertson, 1900. F862 .S22.

Census Indexes and Abstracts

Federal

1850   Jackson, Ronald V. *California 1850 Census Index.* Bountiful, Utah: Accelerated Indexing Systems, 1978. F860 .J24.
    Bowman, Alan P., comp. *Index to the 1850 Census of the State of California.* Baltimore: Genealogical Publishing Co., 1972. F860 .B6.

1860   Dilts, Bryan L., comp. *1860 California Census Index: Heads of Households and Other Surnames in Households Index.* Salt Lake City: Index Publishing Co., 1984. F860 .D54.

State

Jackson, Ronald V. *Early California.* Bountiful, Utah: Accelerated Indexing Systems, 1980. F860 .J238.

Biographies

Armstrong, Alice C. *Who's Who in California, 1955–1978.* 12 eds. San Clemente: Who's Who History Society, 1978. F860 .W628.

Eminent Californians, 1953–1956. Palo Alto, Calif.: C.W. Taylor, Jr., 1953, 1956. F860 .E53.

Fletcher, Russell H. *Who's Who in California.* Vol. 1, *1942–43.* Los Angeles: Who's Who Publishing Co., 1941. F860 .W634.

Guinn, J. M. *History of the State of California and Biographical Record of the Sierras.* Chicago: Chapman Publishing Co., 1906. F861 .G95.

Historical Volume and Reference Works: Including Biographical Sketches of Leading Citizens. 5 vols. Los Angeles: Historical Publishers, 1962. F869 .A15H55.

Hunt, Rockwell D. *California and Californians.* 5 vols. San Francisco: Lewis Publishing Co., 1926. F861 .H93.

McCroarty, John S. *California of the South: A History.* Vols. 2–5, *Biographical.* Chicago: S. J. Clarke, 1933. F867 .M22.

———. *Los Angeles From the Mountains to the Sea.* 3 vols. American History Society, 1921. F869 .L8M14.

Men of California, 1900–1902. San Francisco: Pacific Art Co., 1901. F860 .M543.

Men of California. Western Personalities and Their Affiliations. San Francisco: Western Press Report, 1925. F860 .M535.

Press Reference Library. Notables of the Southwest. Los Angeles: The Los Angeles Examiner, 1912. F860 .P93.

Rodman, Willoughby. *History of the Bench and Bar of Southern California.* Los Angeles: W. J. Porter, 1909. F860 .R69.

Shuck, Oscar T. *Bench and Bar in California: History, Anecdotes and Reminiscences.* San Francisco: Occident Printing House, 1889. F860 .S56.

Who's Who Among the Women of California. San Francisco: Security Publishing Co., 1922. F860 .W62.

Land Acquisition

Avino, Rose H. *Spanish and Mexican Land Grants in California.* New York: Arno Press, 1976. HD211 .C2A93.

Ross, Ivy B. *The Confirmation of Spanish and Mexican Land Grants in California.* San Francisco: R. and E. Research Association, 1974. KFC808 .R6.

Scott, Florence. *Royal Land Grants North of the Rio Grande, 1777–1821.* Rio Grande, Tex.: LaRetama Press, 1969. F392 .R5S44.

Early Settlers

Bancroft, Hubert H. *California Pioneer Register and Index, 1542–1848; Including Inhabitants of California, 1769–1800; and List of Pioneers.* Baltimore: Regional Publishing Co., 1964. F860 .B27.

California Society, Daughters of the American Revolution. *Records of the Families of California Pioneers.* 2 vols. N.p.: the society, 1927. F860 .D37.

Haskins, Charles W. *Index to the Argonauts of California.* New Orleans: Polyanthos, 1975. F865 .H352S63.

Ship passenger lists of 1849.

Mutnick, Dorothy G. *Some Alta California Pioneers and Descendants.* Lafayette, Calif.: Past Time Publishers, 1982. F860 .M87 folio.

Northrup, Marie E. *Spanish-Mexican Families of Early California, 1769–1850.* 2 vols. Burbank: Southern California Genealogical Society, 1984. F870 .M5N67.

Parker, Nathan C. *Personal Name Index to the 1856 City Directories of California.* Detroit: Gale Research Co., 1980. F860 .P37.

Quigley, Hugh. *The Irish Race in California and on the Pacific Coast.* San Francisco: A. Roman & Co., 1878. F870 .I6Q6.

Allen, Walter C., ed. *Society of California Pioneers—Centennial Roster.* San Francisco: the society, 1948. F856 .S65.

Local Records

Alsworth, Mary D., comp. *Gleanings From Alta California Marriages and Deaths Reported in the First Newspapers Published in California, 1846–*

1850. Rancho Cordova, Calif.: Dean Publications, 1980. F860 .A44.

Pompey, Sherman L. *Genealogy Records of California*. Fresno: the author, 1968. F861 .P6.

Periodicals

Hager, Eva Marie, and Everett G. Hager, eds. *Index to California Historical Quarterly, Vols. 41–54 (1962–1875)*. San Francisco: California Historical Society, 1977. F856 .C24.

Hager, Anna Marie, and Everett G. Hager, comps. *Pacific Historical Review: A Cumulative Index to Vols. 1–43 (1932–1974)*. Berkeley: University of California Press, 1976. F851 .P18 index.

Index: Pony Express Courier (June 1934–May 1944); The Pony Express (June 1944–May 1954). Sonora, Calif.: Pony Express Publications, 1955. F856 .P7.

Directories

City

Alhambra
(El Monte, Garvey, Monterey Park, Rosemead, San Gabriel, Temple City, Wilmar) 1910–11, 1920–31, 1935, 1937, 1940–43, 1946, 1949, 1952–56, 1962–64

Anaheim
(Fullerton, N. Orange Co.) 1919

Arcadia 1959–65

Auburn 1961, 1967–69

Azusa
(Baldwin Park, Covina, Glendora, Puente) 1923, 1952

Bakersfield
(Kern City) 1906–85

Baldwin Park
(Covina, W. Covina) 1931, 1947–52

Banning
(Beaumont) 1949

Barstow 1971

Bell
(Maywood) 1949

Bellflower 1940, 1946–50

Beverly Hills 1930, 1944

Burbank
(Roscoe, Paroima) 1936–54, 1970

Burlingame
(Hillsborough, Milbrae, San Mateo) 1958–67

Chico
(Oroville, Paradise) 1911–85

Coalinga 1962–66

Compton
(Clearwater, Hynes, Lynwood, Willowbrook) 1940, 1946–51

Concord 1961–64

Crescent City 1967–82

Crescenta
(Canada Valley) 1974

Davis 1970

Delano
(Earlimart, McFarland) 1951, 1958–81

Downey 1948–50

El Monte 1946–50

Eureka 1902–81

Fairfield
(Suisun City) 1961–82

Fontana 1973

Fresno
(Fresno Co.) 1887, 1898, 1900–82

Gilroy
(Morgan Hill, San Martin) 1962–83

Glendale
(Casa Verdago, Tropico) 1913, 1915, 1923, 1931, 1936, 1943, 1949–73

Grass Valley
(Nevada City) 1865, 1965–79

Hanford
(Corcoran, Lemoore) 1959–83

Hayward
(San Leandro) 1925–40, 1946–73

Hollister 1961–82

Hollywood 1906

Huntington Beach 1941

Huntington Park
  (Walnut Park) 1930–40, 1948

Imperial Beach
  (S. San Diego) 1971

Imperial Valley 1910, 1918–42, 1947–52, 1957–84

Indio 1971

Inglewood
  (Hawthorne, Lennox) 1927–42, 1947, 1950

Laguna Beach
  (Aliso Vista, Bluebird Canyon Park, Coast Royal, Emerald Bay, Laguna Canyon, S. Laguna, Three Arch Bay) 1937

LaJolla 1945–66

Lake Tahoe area 1961

Lakewood
  (Bellflower, Lakewood Plaza) 1952

Lamar
  (Las Animas, Bent Co., Prowers Co.) 1912, 1963–83

Lodi
  (Acampo, Galt, Lockeford, Victor, Woodbridge) 1957–84

Lompoc
  (Mission Hills, Vandenberg Village) 1970–77

Long Beach
  (Signal Hill) 1907, 1910–68

Los Angeles
  1861–1935 (microfilm)
  1936–42

Los Banos
  (Dos Palos) 1961, 1964–65

Los Gatos
  (Campbell, Monte Sereno, Saratoga) 1956–67

Lynwood 1948, 1952

Madera
  (Chowchilla) 1924, 1958, 1962, 1964, 1971–81

Malibu 1954–55, 1958

Manteca
  (Lathrop, Ripon) 1961, 1968–82

Martinez 1961

Marysville
  pre 1861 (microfiche)

(Linda, Live Oak, Olivehurst, Wheatland, Sutter Co., Yuba Co.) 1934–85

Menlo Park
  (Atherton, Portola Valley, Redwood City, Woodside) 1957–78

Merced
  (Atwater, Atwota, Chowchilla, Livingston, Madera) 1914–41, 1946, 1955, 1960–84

Modesto
  (Crows Landing, Denair, Hughson, Keyes, Newman, Oakdale, Patterson, Salina, Turlock, Stanislaus Co.) 1910–42, 1946–83

Monrovia
  (Arcadia, Duarte) 1923–39, 1944–71

Montebello 1948–52

Monterey
  (Carmel, Del Ray Oaks, Pacific Grove, Sand City, Seaside) 1947–86

Monterey Park 1963, 1965, 1970

Mountain View 1962–73

Napa
  (Calistoga, Oakville, Rutherford, Sanitarium, St. Helena, Yountville, Napa Co.) 1908–42, 1947–79

Nevada City
  pre 1861 (microfiche)

Oakland
  (Alameda, Berkeley, Emeryville, Piedmont) 1869, 1872, 1881–84, 1899–1918, 1922–43, 1967
  Oakland City Directory, 1921. F869 .02A18.

Ontario
  (Alta Loma, Chino, Cucamonga, Etiwanda, Upland) 1945–51

Oroville
  (Palermo, Paradise, Thermalite) 1960–84

Oxnard
  (El Rio, Port Huenemo) 1962–78

Palm Springs 1939, 1946–58

Palo Alto
  (E. Palo Alto, Menlo Park, Ravenswood, Stanford) 1914, 1926–76

Palos Verdes 1969–76

Paradise 1962–84

Pasadena
(Altadena, Lamanda Park, San Marino) 1895, 1907–76

Paso Robles
(Atoscadero, Morro Bay) 1963, 1965

Petaluma
(Cotati, Penn Grove) 1895, 1947–81

Pittsburg
(Antioch, W. Pittsburg, Shore Acres) 1931, 1937, 1947–84

Placerville 1961

Pomona
(Chino, Claremont, Ontario, San Dimas, Upland) 1911–40, 1945–51

Porterville
(Lindsay, Poplar, Terra Bella, Strathmore, Village Gardens, Woodville) 1959–82

Red Bluff
(Antelope Valley) 1960, 1967

Redding
(Anderson, Central Valley, Cottonwood, Project City) 1935, 1949–84

Redlands 1900, 1902, 1914–39

Redondo
(Hermosa, Manhattan Beaches) 1915, 1921, 1925, 1927, 1931, 1936, 1947, 1952

Redwood City
(Atherton, Belmont, Fair Oaks, Menlo Park, San Carlos) 1911, 1927–33, 1937–41, 1946–64

Richmond
(Martinez, San Pablo, Stege) 1912–42, 1950–64

Riverside 1905–49

Roseville
(Citrus Hgts.) 1960–83

Sacramento
pre 1861 (microfiche)
1861–1881 (microfilm)
(suburbs) 1874, 1899–1978

Salinas
(Monterey, Pacific Grove) 1926, 1928, 1933, 1937–41, 1946–81

San Bernardino
(Altahoma, Colton, Cucamonga, Etiwando, Ontario, Redlands, Rialto, Uplands) 1904–49

San Bruno 1950–59

San Carlos 1958–63

San Diego
(Chula Vista, Coronado, El Cajon, Imperial Beach, LeMesa, Lemon Grove, National City, San Diego Co.) 1899, 1903–80

San Dieguito 1975, 1978, 1952–60

San Fernando Valley 1921–30, 1937, 1945–49

San Francisco
pre 1861 (microfiche)
1861–1935 (microfilm)
1936–81

San Gabriel 1962–71

San Joaquin
(Merced, Stanislaus, Tuolumne) 1881

San Jose
(Santa Clara Co.) 1870, 1887–1977

San Leandro 1953–65

San Luis Obispo
(Arroyo Grande, Grover City, Pismo Beach, Shell Beach, San Luis Obispo Co.) 1908, 1912, 1914, 1942, 1946, 1950–82

San Marino 1936, 1949–76

San Mateo
(Burlingham, Hillsborough) 1910, 1935–36, 1943–45, 1950–76

San Pedro
(Wilmington) 1908, 1920–59

San Rafael
(Fairfax, San Anselmo, Sausalito, Marin Co.) 1905, 1911, 1925, 1960–70

Sanger 1965, 1972–76

Santa Ana
(Garden Grove, Orange, Tustin) 1910, 1921, 1923, 1948

Santa Barbara
(Carpenteria, Coleta, Gioleta, Hope Ranch Park, Montecito, Santa Maria, Summerland, Santa Barbara Co.) 1886, 1888, 1904–83

Santa Cruz
(Aptos, Boulder Creek, Capitola, Watsonville, Santa Cruz Co.) 1907, 1910, 1925–41, 1948–81

Santa Maria
(Guadalupe, Lompoc, Orcutt, N. Santa Barbara Co.)
1914, 1938, 1958–83

Santa Monica
(Brentwood Heights, Ocean Park, Sawtelle,
Westgate, Venice, W. Los Angeles) 1911–40,
1947, 1952, 1954, 1963–80

Santa Rosa
(Cloverdale, Healdsburg, Sebastopol, Sonoma Co.)
1903–18, 1926, 1929, 1935, 1963–80

Selma
(Fowler, Kingsburg) 1962–76

South Gate
(Walnut Park) 1938, 1940

South Pasadena
(San Marino) 1926–81

Sterling 1947

Stockton
pre 1861 (microfiche)
(San Joaquin Co.) 1888, 1898, 1902–84
Bishop's Stockton Directory For 1876–76. F869
.S8A18.
*Valley Directory Company's Stockton City Directory
For 1896–97.* F869 .S8A18.

Sunland 1949, 1974

Temple City 1948–59

Toft
(Fellow, Ford City, Maricopa) 1926, 1949–84

Torrance 1946, 1949

Tracy 1956–84

Tujunga
(Sunland) 1949

Tulare
(Pixley, Tipton, Woodville) 1959–82

Turlock
(Denair, Hilmar, Keyes, Patterson) 1962–82

Ukiah
(Calpella, Talmage, Redwood Valley) 1961

Vallejo City
(Benicia, Fairfield, Suisun, Solano Co.) 1904, 1911–
42, 1947–84

Van Nuys
(Canoga Park, Reseda, San Fernando) 1936

Ventura
(Fillmore, Ojai, Oxnard, Port Hueneme, Santa Paula,
Ventura Co.) 1908, 1931–79.

Visalia
(Dinuba, Exeter, Farmersville, Ivanhoe, Lindsay,
Portersville, Tulare City, Woodlake, Tulare Co.)
1910–18, 1959–84

Vista City 1956, 1974

Walnut Creek 1961–68

Watsonville
(Aptos, Capitola, Freedom, Santa Cruz, Soquel,
Santa Cruz Co.) 1873, 1937, 1946, 1958–83

Watts
(Compton) 1913–14, 1916, 1921–27

Westwood Hills
(Bel-Air, Brentwood, Chevoit Hills, Holmby) 1933–
37, 1940

Whittier
(Rivera) 1920, 1922, 1928–76

Woodland 1939, 1948–82

Yucca Valley 1959

County, Business, and Miscellaneous

California (state)
1888, 1906, 1931
(Pacific Coast) 1883
*California State Gazetteer and Business Directory,
1904–15.* San Francisco: Suits-Shuman Co., 1904.
F859.7 .C2.

Goleta 1951

Inglewood 1953, 1955

Los Angeles 1898, 1959–63, 1965–66, 1971;
(New York State people in) 1909

Marin 1939, 1942, 1946, 1949, 1958

Monterey (see Santa Clara)

North Hollywood (city) 1951

North Orange 1945

Oakland (city) 1881, 1906

Orange (see South Orange)

Orange, north 1903, 1911, 1924–31, 1937, 1940–41, 1948

Pacific Coast
(Oregon, Washington) 1867, 1871, 1878–99

Sacramento 1939, 1941

San Benito (see Santa Clara)

San Diego 1947–48

San Francisco (city) 1856, 1863, 1877, 1884, 1887, 1891, 1904, 1906

San Joaquin 1878, 1900

San Mateo (see Santa Clara)

Santa Clara
  (Monterey, San Benito, San Mateo, Santa Cruz) 1945, 1947

South Orange 1945, 1947

Ventura 1908–21, 1926–30

Hawaii

Historical Highlights

1200	Tahitians arrive and overthrow Polynesians who had come many centuries before.
1778	Discovered by Captain James Cook, from England.
1786	Visited by American ships from Oregon en route to China.
1790–1810	Ruled by King Kamehameha.
1820	Protestant missionaries from New England arrive.

The arrival of American missionaries prompted interest by other religious missionary groups. Roman Catholics arrived in 1827, but were forced to depart by the Protestants in 1831; in 1839 they were permitted to return after France blockaded Honolulu until religious freedom was guaranteed. In succeeding years, other denominations followed: Quakers in 1835, Mormons in 1850, Church of England (Anglicans) in 1862, and Episcopalians in 1866. Other settlers came from Asia and Europe during the last half of the 1800s. Pineapple and sugar plantations established.

1885	Japanese arrive.
1887	Pearl Harbor designated a United States Naval Station.
1894	Republic of Hawaii established.
1898	Annexed to United States.
1900	Hawaii Territory established.
1959	Admitted to the Union.

Published Record Sources

Guidebooks

Pukui, Mary W. *Place Names in Hawaii.* Rev. and enlarged ed. Honolulu: University Press of Hawaii, 1974. DU622 .P79.

Land Acquisition

Hindman, Dennis M. *Crown Land Compensation Claim, Presented to 95th Congress, 1st Session.* N.p., 1977. KFH451 .H5.

Early Settlers

Chun, James M. *The Early Chinese in Funaluu.* Pulaluu, Honolulu, Hawaii: Hawaii Chinese History Center, 1983. DU628 .P86C47.

McKinzie, Edith K. *Hawaiian Genealogies: Extracted from Hawaiian Language Newspapers.* Laie, Hawaii: Institute for Polynesian Studies, Brigham Young University, 1986. CS2209 .A2M34.

Sandwich Island Mission, Maternal Association. *Names of the Members and Children Belonging to the Maternal Association of the Sandwich Islands Mission, September, 1854.* Honolulu: Mission Press, 1854. BU3680 .H2543.

Schmitt, Robert C. *The Missionary Censuses of Hawaii.* Honolulu: Department of Anthropology, Bernice Pauahi Bishop Museum, 1973. HB3525 .H5S32.

Directories

City

Honolulu 1884, 1888–1985

County, Business, and Miscellaneous

Hawaii
  (Kauai, Maui) 1880, 1890, 1954, 1957, 1960–85

Index

E

F

G

L

Land acquisition
Alabama, 277; California, 366; Delaware, 227; Florida, 258; Georgia, 253; Hawaii, 371; Idaho, 333; Illinois, 301; Indiana, 295; Kentucky, 265; Louisiana, 283; Maryland, 223; Massachusetts, 185-86; Mississippi, 280; Missouri, 306-07; New Mexico, 359; New York, 201; North Carolina, 243; Ohio, 289; Oklahoma, 347; Oregon, 339; Pennsylvania, 215; Tennessee, 270; Texas, 350-51; Vermont, 182-83; Virginia, 233-34; Washington, 336

Land records, 61-65

LCCC (Library of Congress Computerized Catalog), 12-13

Library of Congress Computerized Catalog. *See* LCCC

Library of Congress Information System. *See* LOCIS

Library of Congress Quarterly Reports, 22

Library of Congress
catalog card number, 10; Cataloging Distribution Service, 9; cataloging system, 9-10; Computer Catalog Center, 12; facilities available at, 9; how to locate a publication at, 13-14; how to obtain a publication at, 10-12; locations of buildings (map), 4; personal visits to, 9; Research Guidance Office, 9; rules of procedure, 9; staff assistance at, 8; subject headings of, 9; use of cameras at, 9; use of databases outside the, 13; written queries to, 8

Lineage societies. *See* patriotic and lineage societies

Local histories, 46-47

Local History and Genealogy Reading Room, 15-21
microform collections in the, 30; periodicals in the, 95-98

Local records
Alabama, 277; Alaska, 341-42; Arizona, 362; Arkansas, 274-75; California, 366-67; Colorado, 357; Connecticut, 196; Delaware, 227-28; District of Columbia, 229; Florida, 259; Georgia, 253-54; Idaho, 334; Illinois, 301; Indiana, 296; Iowa, 322; Kansas, 344; Kentucky, 265-66; Louisiana, 283-84; Maine, 177; Maryland, 223-24; Michigan, 311; Mississippi, 280; Missouri, 307-08; Montana, 331; Nevada, 364; New Hampshire, 180; New Jersey, 210; New York, 201-02; North Carolina, 243-44; Ohio, 289-90; Oklahoma, 347-48; Oregon, 339; Pennsylvania, 216; Rhode Island, 193; South Carolina, 248-49; South Dakota, 328; Tennessee, 270-71; Texas, 351-52; Vermont, 183; Virginia, 235-36; Washington, 336; West Virginia, 240

LOCIS (Library of Congress Information System), 12, 18, 28

Lot number, 32

Louisiana
biographies, 283; census, 282-83; directories, 285-86; early settlers, 283; guidebooks, 282; historical highlights, 282; land acquisition, 283; local records, 283-84; military records, 284; newspaper indexes, 88; periodicals, 285; social registers, 56

Lutheran, 80

M

Maine
biographies, 176-77; census, 176; directories, 177-78; early settlers, 177; historical highlights, 176; local records, 177; military records, 177; newspaper indexes, 88; periodicals; social registers, 57

Manuscript Division Reading Room, 22-27

Manuscript Division—Dictionary Catalog of Collections, 24

Manuscript Division—Reference Index for the Dictionary Catalog of Collections, 24
surnames listed in, 23

Maps, 65-72
Civil War, 72; explorers' trails, 71; fire insurance, *see* urban building; land ownership, 68; panoramic, 71; railroad, 72; treasure, 72; urban building, 69; ward, 68-69

Marriage notices, 37. *See also* newspaper indexes

Marriage records. *See* local records

Maryland
biographies, 223; census, 222-23; directories, 225-26; early settlers, 223; guidebooks, 222; historical highlights, 221-22; land acquisition, 223; local records, 223-24; military records, 224-25; newspaper indexes, 88; social registers, 57

Massachusetts
biographies, 184-85; census, 184; directories, 188-92; early settlers, 185; guidebooks, 184; historical highlights, 184; local records, 185-86; military records, 186-87; newspaper indexes, 88; periodicals, 187-88; social registers, 56

Mennonite, 80

Methodist, 80

Mexican War, 106

Mexico
directories, 134; social registers, 57

Michigan
biographies, 311; census, 310; directories, 312-14; early settlers, 311; guidebooks, 310; historical highlights, 310; local records, 311; military records, 311-12; newspaper indexes, 88; periodicals, 312; social registers, 57

Microfiche, telephone directories on, 29-30

O

P

Q

R